Regional Schools in Hellenistic Sculpture

Regional Schools in Hellenistic Sculpture

Proceedings of an International Conference held at the American School of Classical Studies at Athens, March 15–17, 1996

Edited by
Olga Palagia and William Coulson

Oxbow Monograph 90
1998

Published by
Oxbow Books, Park End Place, Oxford OX1 1HN

ISBN 1 900188 45 7

This book is available direct from
Oxbow Books, Park End Place, Oxford OX1 1HN
(Phone: 01865-241249; Fax: 01865-794449)

and

The David Brown Book Company
PO Box 5111, Oakville, CT 06779, USA
(Phone: 860-945-9329; Fax: 860-945-9468)

Printed in Great Britain by
The Short Run Press
Exeter

Foreword

The papers in this volume are based on an international conference sponsored and hosted by the American School of Classical Studies at Athens in March 15–17, 1996. It was the second conference on Greek sculpture organized by the School. The success of the first, held in 1992, focusing on sculpture from Arcadia and Laconia, showed that sculpture is still a major concern in a changing world. Traditional archaeology is suddenly at a turning point, having to justify its methods to a new brew of theoretical archaeologists who are increasinly out of touch with the object of their study. Greek sculpture still lies at the core of the study of Classical archaeology, which can only be renewed through the painstaking investigation of details. It can still be full of surprises, rewarding and exhilarating, ever fresh and unpredictable.

During the course of the Arcadian and Laconian conference, local characteristics became particularly highlighted, and this raised the question whether regional schools can be as easily detected in other areas of the Greek world. We selected the Hellenistic period because it presents particularly complex problems of cultural interaction, which can only be tackled by a collaborative effort. The old, broad characterizations of Asianism for Hellenistic sculpture in East Greece and Classicism for the Athenian production are in urgent need of revision in the light of new discoveries.

Are there any means of defining regionalism more closely? Was there interaction between local schools? What was the impact, for example, of itinerant sculptors who roamed from Athens to central Greece, to Rome, to Delos? Were regional schools really distinct in the Hellenistic period and what are the means of distinguishing them?

The presentation of many unpublished sculptures in this volume sheds light on previously grey areas like the third century, itinerant Athenian sculptors in Greece proper, and the interaction of Rhodes and the islands of the Aegean and Caria in the aftermath of the Mausoleum.

The conference could not have taken place without the help of a number of people. First and foremost, the School's administrator, Mrs. Maria Pilali, handled administrative details and later typed several papers for publication. The School's Secretary, Dr. Robert Bridges, also took care of administrative details and organized the audio-visual equipment. Both bore the administrative brunt with cheerfulness beyond the call of duty.

The two days of papers were followed by a trip to the Archaeological Museums of Eretria, Chalkis, and Thebes. We are grateful to Dr. Effie Sapouna-Sakellaraki and the staff of the Ephoreia of Prehistoric and Classical Antiquities at Chalkis, as well as to Dr. Vasilis Aravantinos and the staff of the Ephoreia at Thebes for facilitating our museum visits.

Olga Palagia
William Coulson

Bibliographical abbreviations follow the guidelines of the German Archaeological Institute as published in *AA* 107, 1992, 743–749.

Contents

Foreword by Olga Palagia and William Coulson v

Program of the Conference ix

Mary C. Sturgeon
Hellenistic Sculpture at Corinth. The State of the Question 1

Olga Palagia
The Enemy Within: A Macedonian in Piraeus 15

Katherine A. Schwab
The Lysippan Herakles as Vajrapani in Hadda 27

Μέλπω Ι.Πωλογιώργη
Το γυναικείο άγαλμα του Αρχαιολογικού Μουσείου Πειραιώς αρ. ευρ. 5935 35

Petros Themelis
Attic Sculpture at Kallipolis (Aitolia). A Cult Group of Demeter and Kore 47

Wilfred Geominy
The So-called Delphi Philosopher and his Context 61

Hoyer von Prittwitz
The Divine Circle: The Roundels of Mahdia 69

Janet B.Grossman
Hellenistic Sculpted Funerary Monuments from the Athenian Agora 75

Andrew Stewart
Goddess or Queen? A Colossal Marble Head in the Athenian Agora 83

Mark D. Fullerton
Atticism, Classicism, and the Origins of Neo-Attic Sculpture 93

Ιφιγένεια Κ. Λεβέντη
Η Υγεία του Νικηράτου του Αθηναίου. Συμβολή στη μελέτη της πρώιμης γλυπτικής της Περγάμου . 101

John R.Marszal
Tradition and Innovation in Early Pergamene Sculpture 117

Δημήτρης Δαμάσκος
Ενα κολοσσικό κεφάλι Ηρακλή από το Πέργαμο 129

Βασιλική Μαχαίρα
Παρατηρήσεις σχετικά με την θεματική παραγωγή της "Σχολής" της Ρόδου 137

Carol C. Mattusch
Rhodian Sculpture: A School, a Style, or Many Workshops? 149

Ira S. Mark
The Victory of Samothrace 157

Ισμήνη Τριάντη
Ελληνιστικά αγάλματα της Μήλου 167

Philippe Jockey
Neither School nor *Koine*: The Local Workshops of Delos and their Unfinished Sculpture 177

Beryl Barr-Sharrar
Some Observations Concerning Late Hellenistic Bronze Production on Delos 185

John Pedley
Problems in Provenance and Patronage: A Group of Late Hellenistic Statuettes from Paestum 199

Αλέξανδρος Μάντης
Τα ανάγλυφα φατνώματα του Ιερού της Σαμοθράκης 209

Θεοδοσία Στεφανίδου-Τιβερίου
Ο πώρινος Ατλας από την αρχαία Αγορά της Θεσσαλονίκης 227

Geoffrey B.Waywell
The Lion from the Lion Tomb at Cnidus 235

Peter Higgs
After the Mausoleum: Hellenistic Sculptures from Bodrum in the British Museum 243

R.R.R. Smith
Hellenistic Sculpture under the Roman Empire: Fishermen and Satyrs at Aphrodisias 253

Linda Jones Roccos
Votive Reliefs to Apollo Kitharoidos from Asia Minor: External and Regional Influence 261

Elena Walter-Karydi
Dangerous is Beautiful. The Elemental Quality of a Hellenistic Scylla 271

Caroline Houser
The "Alexander Sarcophagus" of Abdalonymos: A Hellenistic Monument from Sidon 281

Program

Day I. Friday, March 15, 1996

9:15-9:50	REGISTRATION
9:50-10:00	*Opening Remarks by the organizers, William D.E. Coulson and Olga Palagia*

Session I: CORINTH, LYSIPPOS AND BEYOND

Chairman:	William D.E. Coulson
10:00-10:20	Mary C. Sturgeon, *"Hellenistic Sculpture at Corinth. The State of the Question."*
10:20-10:40	Olga Palagia, *"The Enemy Within: A Macedonian in Piraeus."*
10:40-11:00	Katherine A. Schwab, *"The Lysippan Herakles as Vajrapani in Hadda."*
11:00-11:30	Coffee

Session II: ATHENS

Chairman:	Nikolaus Himmelmann
11:30-11:50	Μέλπω Πωλογιώργη, *"Το άγαλμα του Μουσείου Πειραιώς αρ. ευρ. 5935."*
11:50-12:10	Petros Themelis, *"Attic Sculpture from Kallipolis in Aitolia."*
12:10-12:30	Andrew Stewart, *"Queen or Goddess? A Colossal Female Head in the Athenian Agora."*
12:30-12:50	Janet B.Grossman, *"Funerary Monuments from the Athenian Agora."*
12:50-13:10	Mark D. Fullerton, *"Atticism versus Classicism in Neo-Attic Sculpture."*

Session III: PERGAMON

Chairman:	Petros Kalligas
16:00-16:20	John Marszal, *"Conservatism in Early Pergamene Sculpture."*
16:20-16:40	Ιφιγένεια Λεβέντη, *"Η Υγεία του Νικήρατου του Αθηναίου: συμβολή στη μελέτη της πρώιμης γλυπτικής της Περγάμου."*
16:40-17:00	Δημήτρης Δαμάσκος, *"Μία κολοσσική κεφαλή του Ηρακλή από το Πέργαμο."*
17:00-17:40	Coffee

Session IV: SAMOTHRACE, THASOS AND THE NORTH

Chairman:	Evelyn B. Harrison
17:40-18:00	Αλέκος Μάντης, *"Τα ανάγλυφα φατνώματα του Ιερού της Σαμοθράκης."*
18:00-18:20	Ira S. Mark, *"The Victory of Samothrace."*
18:20-18:40	Catherine Vanderpool, *"Defining a Style: A Female Group from Thasos."*
18:40-19:00	Θεοδοσία Στεφανίδου-Τιβερίου, *"Ο πώρινος Ατλας από την Αρχαία Αγορά της Θεσσαλονίκης."*
19:15	Preview of an exhibition of books and paintings in the Gennadius Library on the 175th anniversary of the Greek War of Independence.
20:00	Reception for participants in Loring Hall of the American School of Classical Studies.

Day II. Saturday, March 16, 1996

Session V : *Rhodes and Caria*

Chairman:	Olga Palagia
9:00-9:20	Βάνα Μαχαίρα, *"Παρατηρήσεις σχετικά με την θεματική παραγωγή της "Σχολής" της Ρόδου."*
9:20-9:40	Carol C. Mattusch, *"Rhodian Sculpture: A Regional School or a Universal Style?"*
9:40-10:00	Geoffrey Waywell, *"The Lion from the Lion Monument at Knidos."*
10:00-10:20	Peter Higgs, *"Some Fragments of Draped Female Figures from Halikarnassos."*
10:20-10:40	R.R.R. Smith, *"Hellenistic Sculpture Under the Roman Empire: Fishermen and Satyrs at Aphrodisias."*
10:40-11:20	Coffee

Session VI *Varia*

Chairman:	John H. Oakley
11:20-11:40	John Griffiths Pedley, *"Problems in Provenance and Patronage: A Group of Late Hellenistic Marble Statuettes from Paestum."*
11:40-12:00	Caroline Houser, *"The Alexander Sarcophagus in Light of Recent Discoveries in Athens and Macedonia."*
12:00-12:20	Wilfred Geominy, *"The Delphi Philosopher and his Context."*
12:20 12:40	Hoyer von Prittwitz, *"The Divine Circle: The Roundels of Mahdia."*
12:40-13:00	Δημήτρης Καζιάνης, *"Χάλκινο άγαλμα από την Κάλυμνο."*

Session VII: East Greece and the Cyclades

Chairman:	Sir John Boardman
16:00-16:20	Linda Jones Roccos, *"Votive Reliefs to Apollo from Asia Minor: Regional or External Influence?"*
16:20-16:40	Elena Walter-Karydi, *"Dangerous is Beautiful: The Elemental Quality of a Hellenistic Scylla."*
16:40-17:00	Beryl Barr-Sharrar, *"Some Observations Concerning Late Hellenistic Bronze Production on Delos."*
17:00-17:20	Philippe Jockey, *"Neither School nor Koine: The Local Workshops of Delos and their Unfinished Sculptures."*
17:20-17:40	Ισμήνη Τριάντη, *"Ελληνιστικά γλυπτά της Μήλου."*
20:00	Dinner for speakers and chairmen in Loring Hall of the American School of Classical Studies.

Day III. Sunday, March 17, 1996

Day trip to the Museums of Eretria, Chalkis and Thebes.

Hellenistic Sculpture at Corinth. The State of the Question

Mary C. Sturgeon

It has long been assumed that most of the surviving sculpture at Corinth is Roman because of Mummius' destruction of Corinth in 146 B.C. and the subsequent growth of the large Roman city in place of the Greek.[1] A survey of the holdings of the Corinth Museum shows, however, that this is not the case. In fact, recent examination reveals a number of sculptures of possible Hellenistic date. Here, I will first survey representative types and then focus on some heads, drawing from collections of the museums at both Corinth and Isthmia.

Corinth was famous for its bronzes in antiquity, as we hear from many literary sources. Two small bronzes from Hellenistic contexts provide a tantalizing glimpse. A bronze mirror cover, dated ca. 250 B.C., was found in a grave in the northwest quarter of the city (Fig. 1). Here, three women appear in a landscape setting against a background of rocks and a column or tree. The central, seated figure leans against the knees of a woman who is braiding her hair, recalling vases illustrating preparations for marriage, although the motif of braiding the hair is unusual. The subject, possibly a depiction of the Horai at a rural shrine, and the fact that bronze mirrors are noted in the Greek Anthology as dedications to Cyprian Aphrodite suggest a connection with Aphrodite, the city goddess of Corinth.[2]

A second piece, a bronze votive plaque with traces of silver plating, contains an incised, seated Hermes, a branch suggesting a worshipper approaching from right.[3] The plaque appears to be a smaller version of a votive relief in marble from the fourth century B.C. In addition, Hellenistic terracotta figurines of Corinthian manufacture, such as groups of girls in St. Petersburg and Boston, have long been recognized for their artistic quality.[4] These bronzes and terracottas give some idea of the varied materials used for Hellenistic sculptures at Corinth.

Context establishes a Hellenistic date for a number of small sculptures in marble, such as a head of a girl

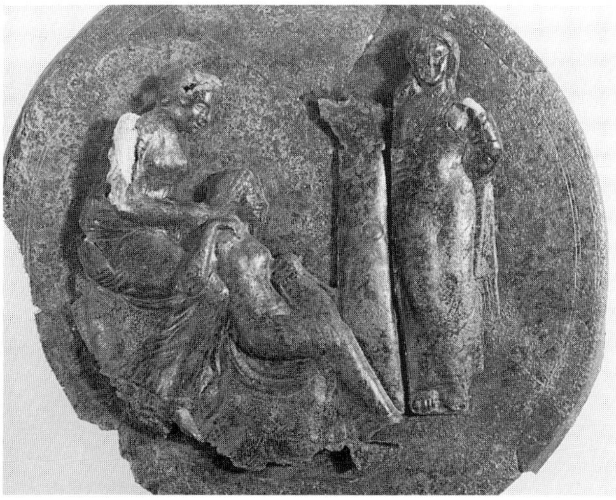

Fig. 1. Bronze mirror.
Corinth, Archaeological Museum MF 11562.

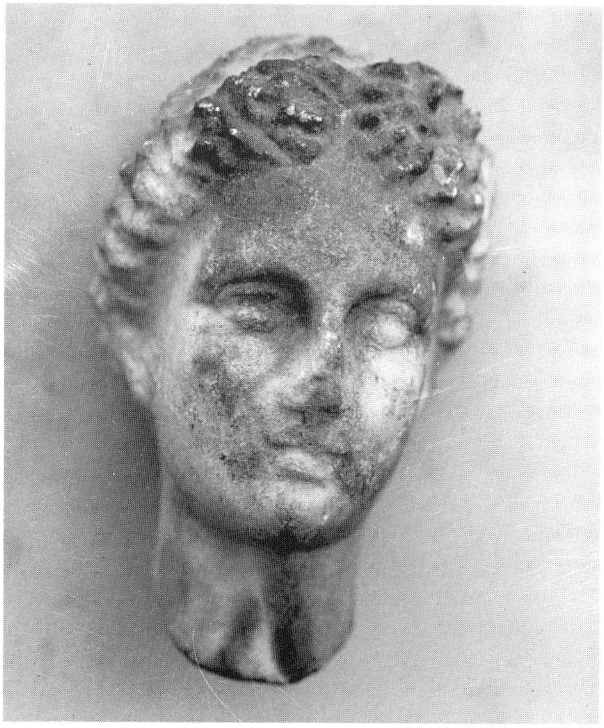

Fig. 2. Head of a girl.
Corinth, Archaeological Museum S 2556.

discovered in Well XX of the South Stoa, in Shop 20 (Fig. 2). Unfortunately, the head was stolen in 1990. Found with Mummian destruction debris and with coins of Sikyon dated 323–251 B.C., the head can be dated to the first half of the third century B.C.[5] The style is soft and delicate, the wavy hair almost impressionistic in treatment, not unlike some Corinthian counterparts in terracotta from the third century.[6] It has been suggested that the flat break at the back indicates that it derives from a relief, but the rendering appears more fully rounded than is usual for relief sculptures of this size, so a figurine seems more likely.

Not surprisingly, Aphrodite is well represented. For example, a fragmentary statuette depicting Aphrodite practically nude, her mantle falling from her shoulder, was found in a well of the Southwest Forum in a Hellenistic context (Fig. 3). Similarly, nude figures with mantles hanging from one shoulder are seen in many small marbles and terracottas.[7]

A larger relief represents Aphrodite or a nymph disrobing, shown frontally (Fig. 4). The elongated proportions, rendering, and drapery arrangement, which recall the Rhodian "Aphrodite on a rock," suggest a Hellenistic date. The leg of a horse survives behind her, possibly a symbol of Aphrodite Ephippos.[8] Context also establishes Hellenistic dates for some aniconic heads. The first was found in the access shaft to a Hellenistic cistern east of the theater (Fig. 5). Here a life-size head wears short, unparted hair, arranged as if it was pulled down over the face like a knitted cap. The loose, wavy hair recalls that of some fourth-century male types, like the Fogg Meleager. The band crossing the front is painted red as are the ears, the paint applied directly onto the limestone, without a layer of stucco. The coiffure suggests a male subject and the omission of facial features indicates non-human or religious significance, so the head may be associated with Hermes, perhaps as Psychopompos.[9]

Aniconic heads are well-known from Cyrene where, however, they take the form of busts extending to the shoulders or mid-torso.[10] The Corinth examples, in contrast, show no signs of a bust, but are formed as cylindrical shafts. The lowered hairline and absence of facial features creates an enigmatic impression. This is also the case with a second head which has been called a phallic marker

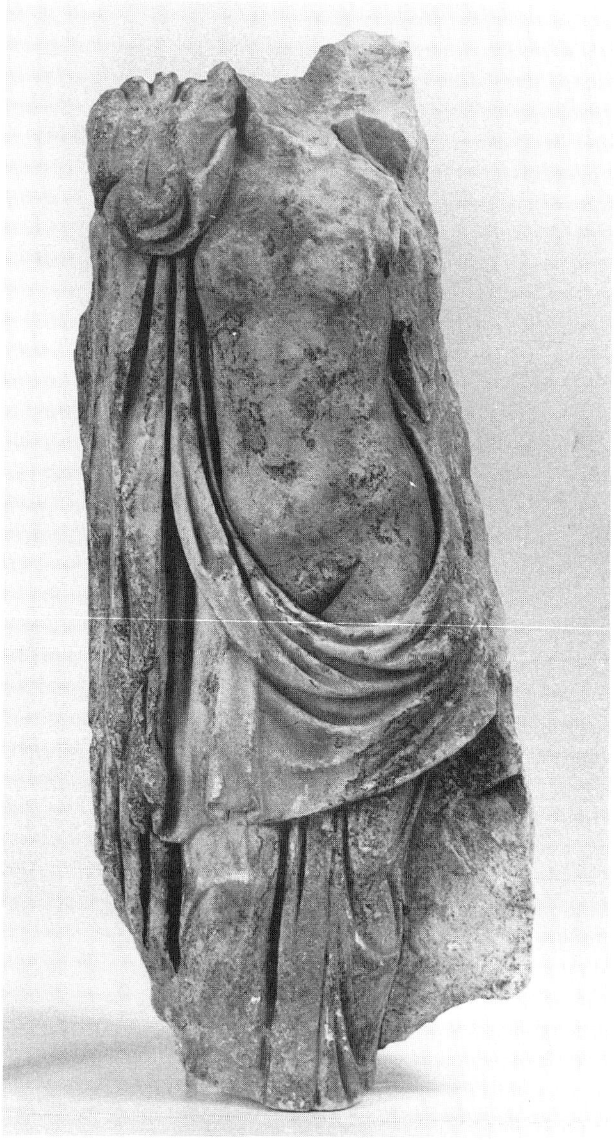

Fig. 4. Relief of Aphrodite or nymph. Corinth, Archaeological Museum S 2722.

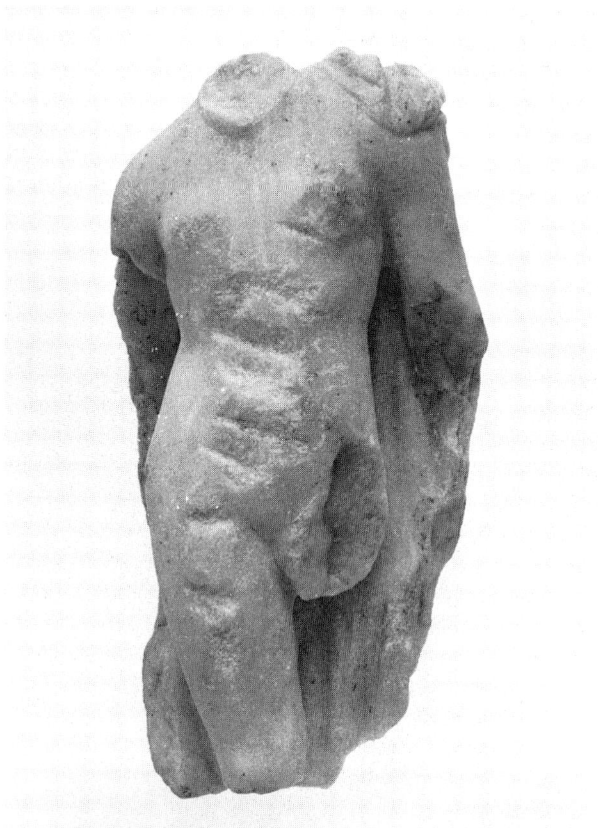

Fig. 3. Aphrodite statuette. Corinth, Archaeological Museum S-89–6.

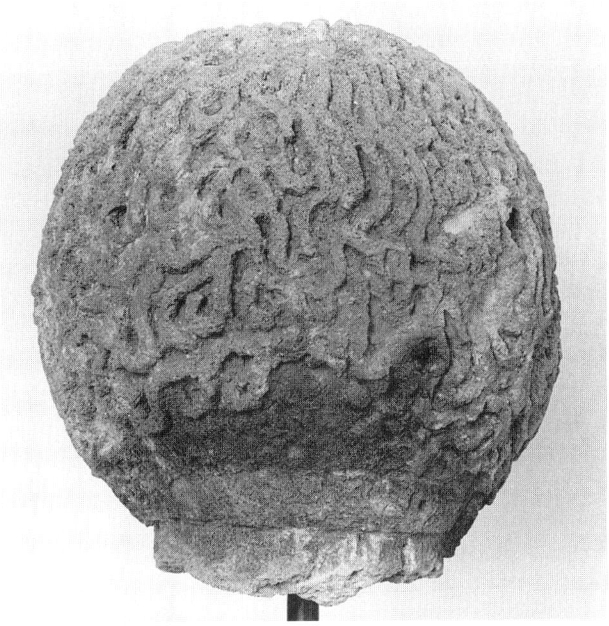

Fig. 5. Aniconic head of Hermes (?). Corinth, Archaeological Museum S-81–6.

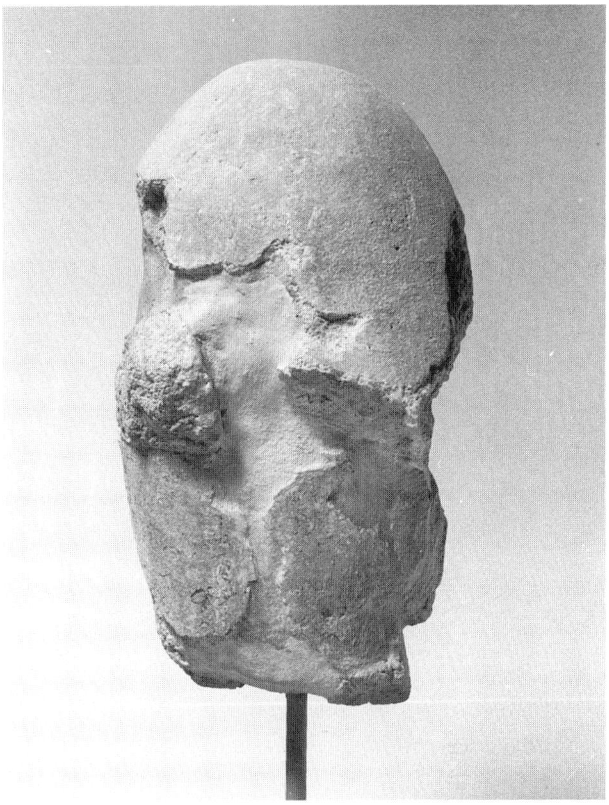

Fig. 6. Aniconic head of Athena (?). Corinth, Archaeological Museum A 415.

(Fig. 6). Given the presence of aniconic heads at Corinth, however, and the absence of other phallic markers, the possibility that it represents a helmeted figure in aniconic format, such as Athena, should be considered. This and the next example were found together in a cistern complex in the western part of the city.[14]

The third aniconic image has been dated to the third or first half of the second century B.C. Here, the hair is pulled in rope-like strands into a knot at the top of the crown, a style worn by young girls, so a deity such as Kore may be intended (Fig. 7). The findspot, within the city walls, is near a cemetery area. This piece and the previous each have one coat of relatively unweathered plaster, so they probably were not displayed for long.[12]

The fourth, which comes from Korakou, is one of a pair, each with the hair pulled into a knot at back (Fig. 8). The shaft continues above the hair, resembling a polos. Aphrodite and Artemis wear this hairstyle, but Aphrodite is the more appealing suggestion, as we could then visualize this pair of aniconic heads alluding to Aphrodite's maritime aspect, used as grave markers on the bluff that overlooks the Lechaion harbor. Their probable funerary use recalls Aphrodite Melainis whom Pausanias (2.2.4) locates at the northeastern edge of the city, and a sanctuary of Aphrodite is also mentioned at Lechaion.[13]

Because of their secondary findspots, the Corinth busts' original context, function and significance are not immediately clear. The aniconic busts in Cyrene were found in cemeteries and have been interpreted as symbolic depictions of underworld deities ascending to take the soul of the deceased to the underworld. As the worship of Demeter and Persephone is strong in Cyrene, the busts are usually connected with these deities, especially Persephone. Other examples are found in sanctuaries of the

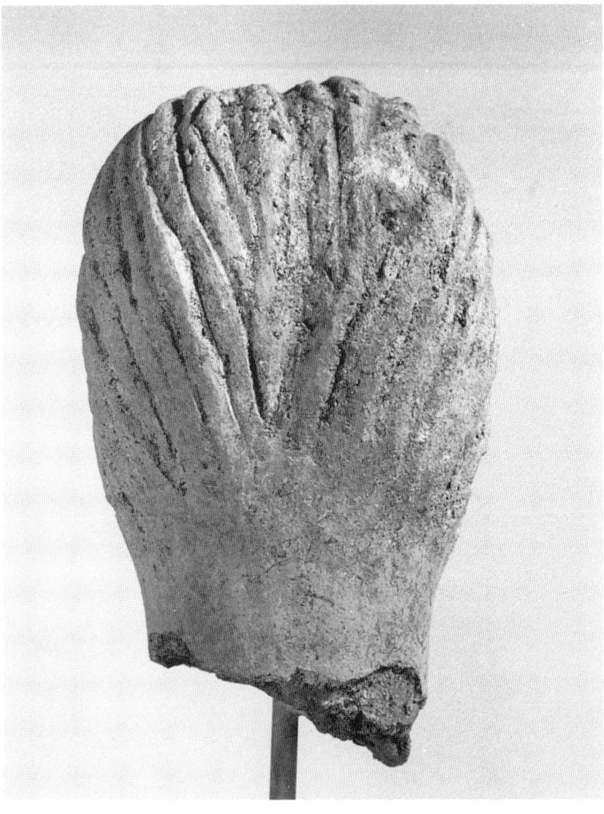

Fig. 7. Aniconic head of Kore (?). Corinth, Archaeological Museum S 2714.

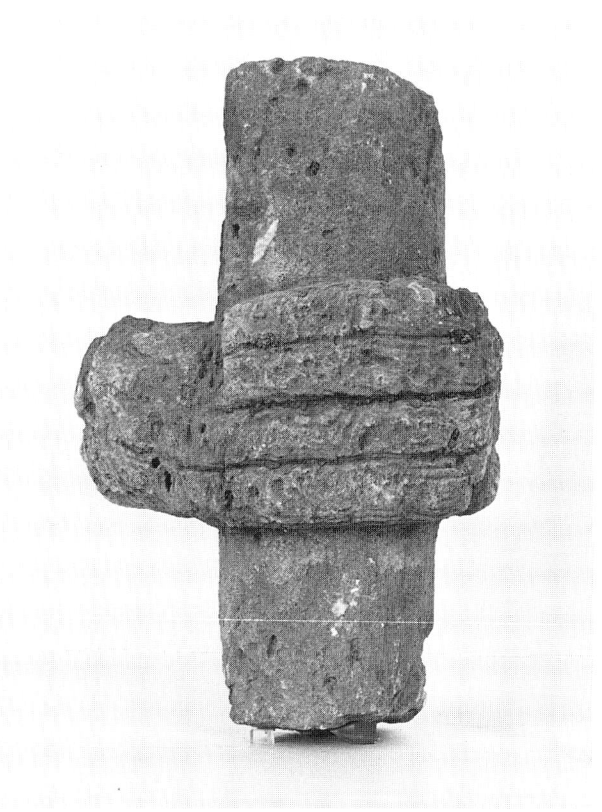

Fig. 8. Aniconic head of Aphrodite (?). Corinth, Archaeological Museum S-85–4.

same deities in Sicily. The closest comparison to the shaft form of the Corinth figures is provided by a terracotta tube from Agrigento embellished only with a fringe of hair and ears. Since the Agrigento piece is a hollow tube, it could facilitate pouring libations to the underworld deities.[14] Plain shaft monuments of similar shape, size and material to the busts from Korakou, but without hair, have been found in various parts of Corinth, but none of these contains a horos inscription, establishing it as a property marker. As funerary monuments, the aniconic heads may perpetuate indigenous religious images which represented divine beings in enigmatic, mystical ways, their hairdos updated to correspond with current styles.[15]

Notably, all of Corinth's aniconic heads are of limestone, some coated with stucco. Previously, limestone had been considered a material used for sculpture in the Corinthia in the Archaic period: witness, for instance, the lions from Loutraki and the Isthmia kouros.[16] The aniconic heads, dated by context, indicate the continued use of limestone for sculpture into the Hellenistic period.

Two further examples of limestone sculpture can be added. The first is a female head in the round, found in 1901 (Fig. 9). Here, we should observe the way stucco is used, for it is not applied with even thickness, as if to cover the rough material and give the appearance of marble. Rather, its varied thickness shows that, as the stucco was applied, the shape of the piece could be altered and modeling achieved, in a manner analogous to work done in wax during bronze-making. This seems important, since the northeastern Peloponnesos was a major center for bronze sculpture. Local artisans would have made less expensive figures in limestone and stucco as well as in terracotta, these materials being available locally, although marble, and therefore marble-workers, would have been imported.[17]

Another limestone piece is a draped male bust which comes from a bust in the round rather than a relief (Fig 10).[18] The bust form, which is cut out at back, may indicate a Roman rather than a Hellenistic date, but it recalls the terracotta medallion bust from Corinth, dated to the late fourth or early third century B.C. (Fig. 11).[19] The terracotta bust, in particular, suggests that Corinth may have figured prominently in the formation of the portrait bust.

That portrait sculpture was no stranger to Hellenistic Corinth is confirmed by the statue of a general (Fig. 12), found in the southwestern Forum north of the Colonnaded Hall, a statue which Cathy Vanderpool has dated to the first half of the second century B.C. through comparison with works from Pergamon.[20] Wearing a modeled cuirass with fleshy belly, the right arm probably raised to support a spear, this vigorous-looking figure would have presented the triumphant image of a victorious military leader. As the figure was recut in Roman times, probably for use as a trophy, the statue likely depicted a Greek general, one associated with the levying of taxes for the defense of Corinth, such as the second century general Kritolaos or Diaios.[21]

There is little evidence for marble working at Corinth. Isthmia, however, provides two unfinished works which

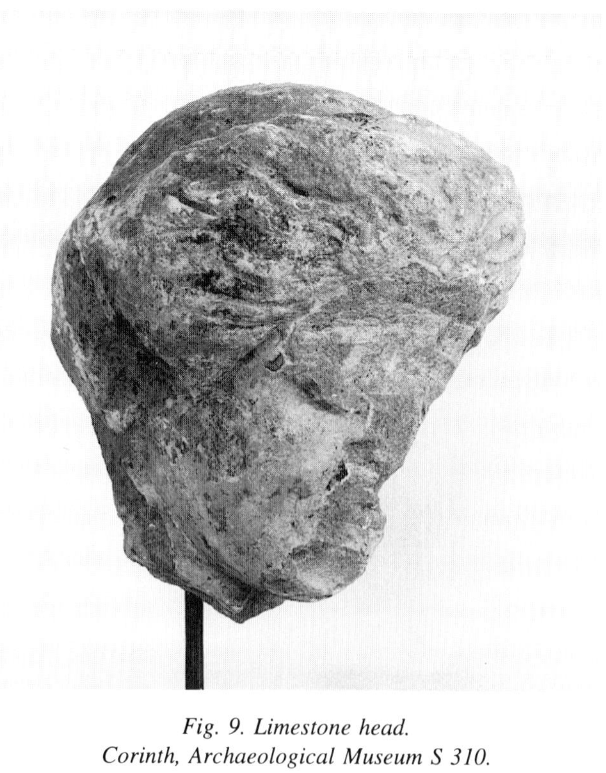

Fig. 9. Limestone head. Corinth, Archaeological Museum S 310.

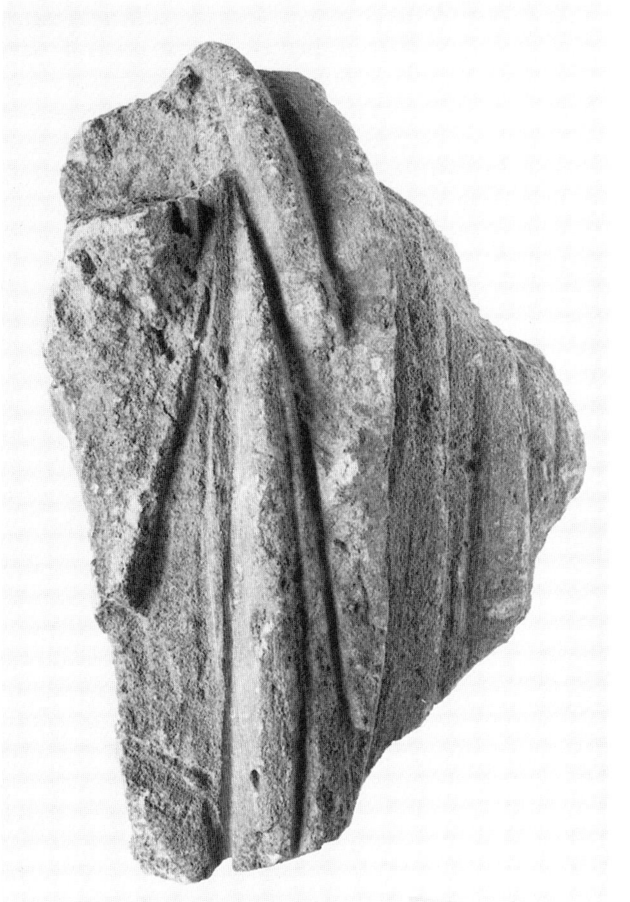

Fig. 10. Limestone bust. Corinth, Archaeological Museum S1663.

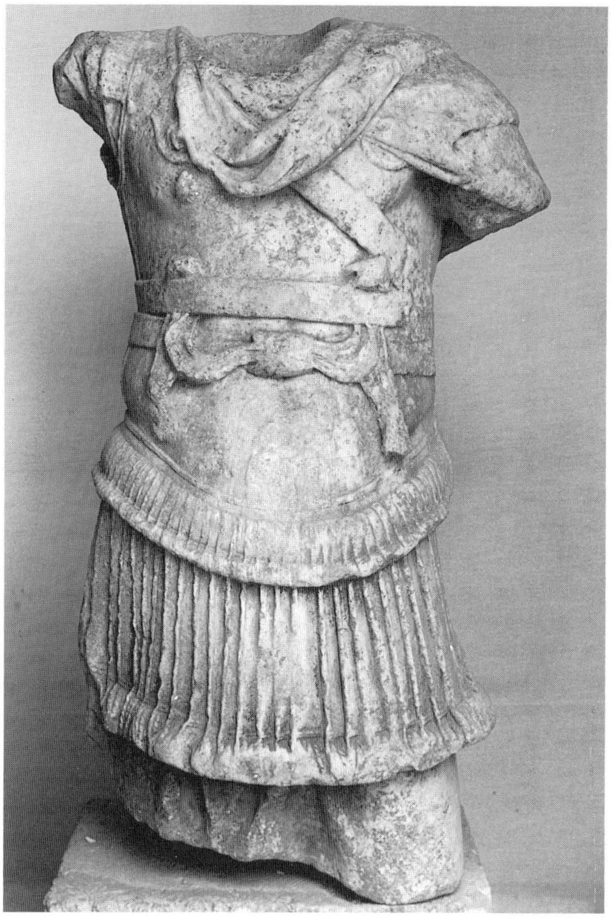

Fig. 12. Cuirassed Statue. Corinth, Archaeological Museum S3356.

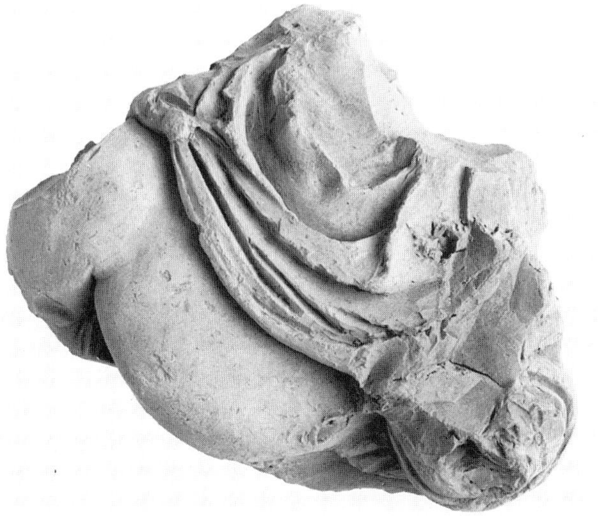

Fig. 11. Terracotta bust. Corinth, Archaeological Museum SF-5.

show that the production of small pieces, at least, occurred near the Poseidon Sanctuary in Hellenistic times. The lower half of an Aphrodite statuette was discarded before it was finished and attached to the upper half. Isotopic analysis by Norman Herz shows it is calcitic and likely to be Thasian marble from Cape Phanari.[22] In another example, a right hand holding a patera, the inner side of the bowl is only half cut-out, the pinprick remaining from the measuring device. Found on the Rachi, it comes from a late fourth to third century B.C. context and is probably Pentelic marble.[23]

As elsewhere, popular late fourth-century-to-Hellenistic types, such as the Large and Small Herculaneum women, are frequently reproduced at Corinth in the Roman period. Rarer types also exist, which may give some idea of what stood here in Hellenistic times. One example is a figure which Hans Lauter has interpreted as a Trajanic version of a model from ca. 280 B.C. on which the Antium Girl is based (Fig. 13). His reconstruction suggests that this figure, possibly a votary, once held a tablet or serving tray. A fifth-century bronze statuette in Boston said to be from Corinth presents the same motif, but it would be unusual for a young girl to be depicted on the scale of the Corinth statue. Similarity to the body herm of Dionysos in the Museo Nazionale in Rome, as well as the sleeved chiton and closed shoes, makes interpretation as Dionysos more likely.[24]

In addition, draped figures of probable Hellenistic date survive, like the lower half of a large female figure (Fig.

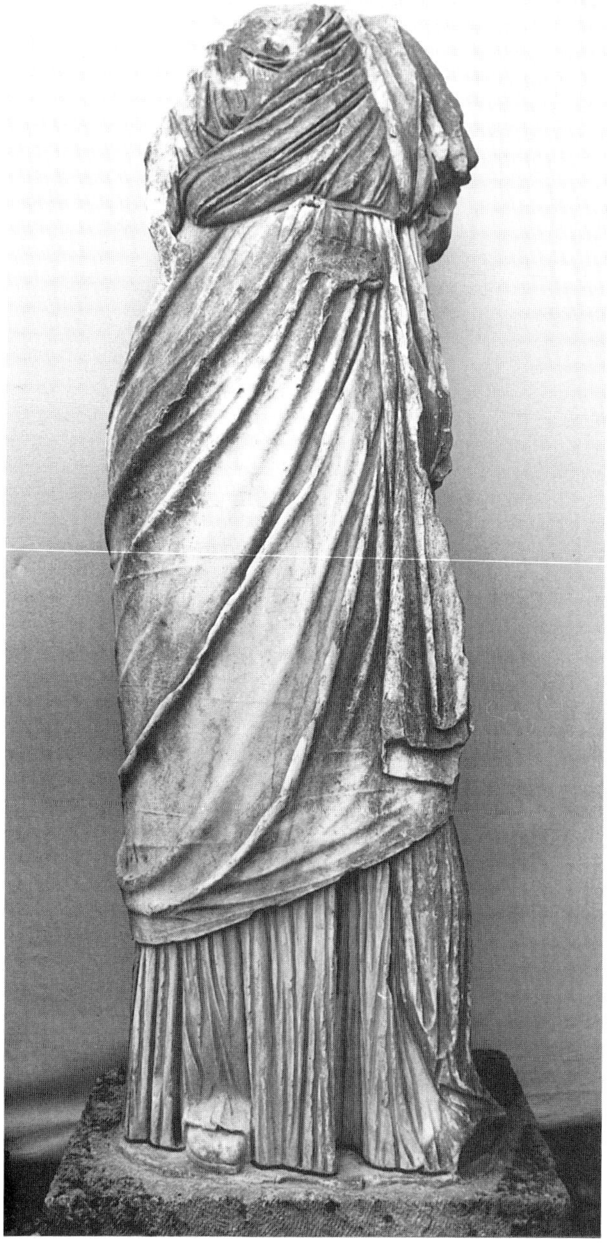

Fig. 13. Statue of Dionysos.
Corinth, Archaeological Museum S 1294.

modeled on the large statue from the Athenian Agora which Evelyn Harrison has interpreted as Aphrodite Hegemone.[27]

Hellenistic statues of children survive from both Corinth and Isthmia. At Isthmia, for example, the girl Klio, sitting with her duck, is dedicated to Demeter, as the inscription reveals.[28] A hare is an equally common pet, as seen in a boy from Corinth.[29] Also from Corinth, the head from a Herakliskos of Parian marble (Fig. 15), found in a well of the house with pebble mosaic east of the theater, probably stems from a standing figure and forms an early example of the type. And seated figures of African boys, in black steatite and terracotta, functioned as boxes and rattles.[30]

The six remaining pieces, dated Hellenistic by style, pose interesting questions. A running Artemis was probably found near the Sacred Spring in 1902 (Fig. 16).[31] It wears a double-belted chiton and deerskin, the head of which is tied above the soft, fleshy stomach. This figure is close to a statue in the Ny Carlsberg Glyptotek in

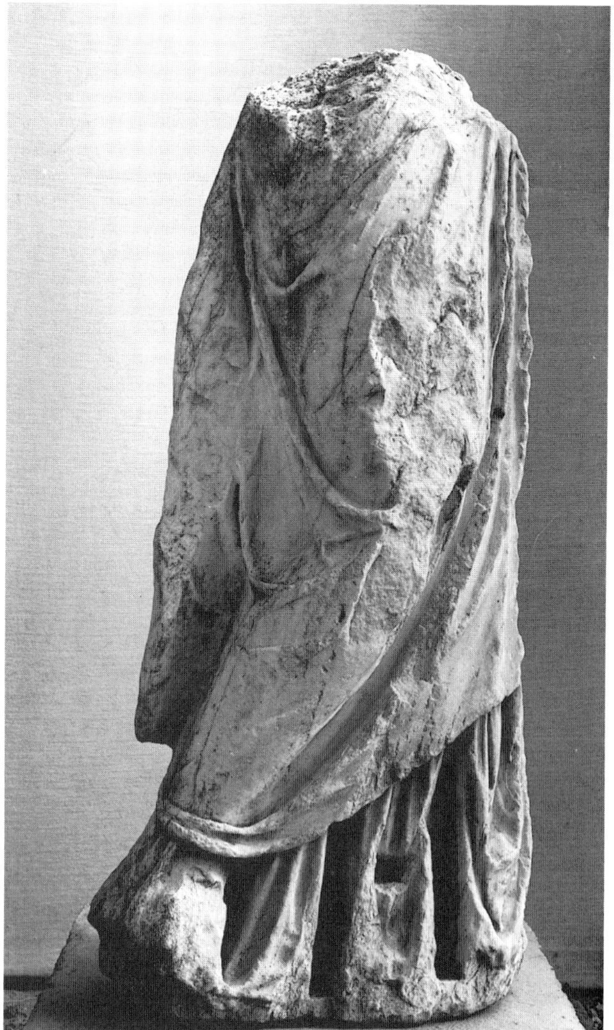

Fig. 14. Lower torso of draped female figure.
Corinth, Archaeological Museum S 63.

14). This torso, with its deep-cut, wide furrows and irregular surfaces, can be compared in pose and style with Hellenistic figures from Kos and elsewhere, though it eschews press folds and chiton folds seen through the mantle in favor of a simpler, perhaps mainland style.[25]

The Archaistic style is exemplified by a large statuette of late Hellenistic or early Roman date, probably a votive, which may represent a depiction of an Archaic statue, like the idol on which the Dionysos of Corinth/Copenhagen type is leaning.[26]

Smaller figures include a late Hellenistic Aphrodite statuette with part of Eros on her shoulder, a type well-known from Rhodes. The Corinthian figure seems

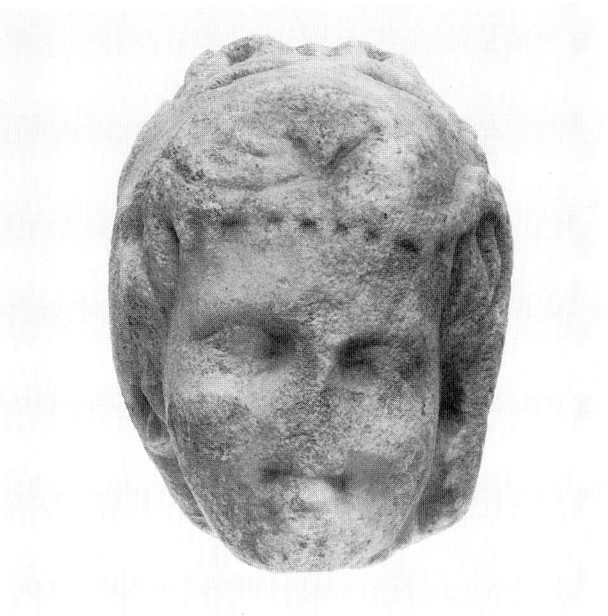

Fig. 15. Head of Herakliskos.
Corinth, Archaeological Museum T 98.

Copenhagen, said to come from near Corinth, which stands about 0.50 meter tall. As autopsy of the Copenhagen figure, with its soft facial features and hair, indicates, it is of Hellenistic style; it suggests a Hellenistic date for the figure in Corinth.[32]

A third figure with torso of similar configuration, found on the Loryma Peninsula opposite Rhodes, is of late Hellenistic date. But the Loryma statue, which is from a cemetery, supports a different head type and bears an inscribed dedication to Artemis Soteira. Related examples of different dates are known from Attica and elsewhere.[33]

The Athens and Copenhagen figures suggest an Early Hellenistic workshop, probably Attic, that specialized in making 0.50 meter tall statuettes for Corinth and producing marble figures in repetitive series. These three figures show that the practice of combining one body type with different head types to represent related deities was well established by the Hellenistic period.[34]

A life-size head of a girl wearing a scarf, her hair in a knot at the nape, was found east of the South Basilica (Fig. 17). Probably of Parian marble and dating stylistically from the late fourth century, the top of the head was pieced at an angle, the joining surface carefully smoothed, with no dowel cuttings or tooling to facilitate attachment. The added segment would not have been noticeable from the primary viewing side, the three-quarter right view.[35] The depiction of a girl wearing a scarf is unusual in marble sculpture, though many examples exist in terracotta, like a head found on the Rachi at Isthmia. The specific findspot, in the South Slope cistern with destruction debris of ca. 198 B.C., provides a clear date for the terracotta. As this cistern is located just below the shrine probably to Demeter and Kore, a connection to those deities has been posited.[36]

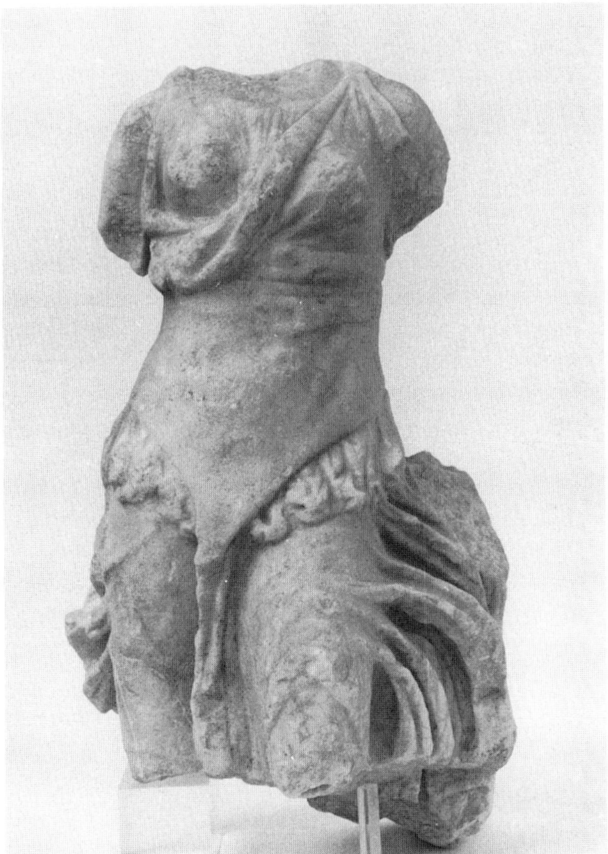

Fig. 16. Statuette of running Artemis.
Corinth, Archaeological Museum S 312.

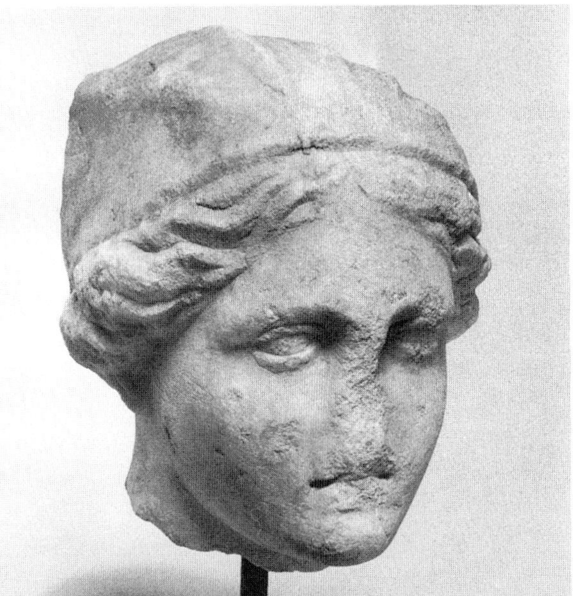

Fig. 17. Head of girl with a scarf.
Corinth, Archaeological Museum S 1820.

Scarves worn by other terracotta figures are connected with the term "tagidion" or "little roof" which they resemble. These include many dancers, such as a fine example from Athens in Berlin of the late fourth century for which religious interpretations are advanced.[37] The two marble examples with similar scarves which are the most familiar present quite different subjects. One is the Delian group of Aphrodite, Eros and Pan in Athens which Meyer has dated ca. 110 B.C.,[38] the other the Hellenistic type known as the Drunken Old Woman through versions in Munich and Rome. What might these figures have in common? A religious context is clear for the Delos group, because it was found in the shrine of the House of the Poseidoniasts of Berytos. Zanker, Wrede and others have interpreted the Drunken Old Woman as a devotee of Dionysos, based on the costume, the ivy wreath on the vase and the vase shape.[39] The scarf likely indicates that the Corinth figure depicted an initiate or participant in religious rites, perhaps for Artemis or Demeter and Kore. Moreover, the coiffure shows that the subject was probably unwed, like representations of Artemis and of numerous girls on Attic grave stelai, and the deep drilling in the knot finds parallels with girls' hairdos from the late fourth and early third centuries.[40] Our head was probably made ca. 340–330 B.C.[41]

A second head wearing a "little roof"-like scarf is from a statue of an old woman (Fig. 18). This badly-worn figure wears a scarf or veil across the forehead under a thicker scarf.[42] She recalls the old woman wearing a scarf who officiates as priestess in the sacrifice to Magna Mater/Kybele on the relief in the Villa Albani, a parallel which suggests interpretation of the Corinth woman as a priestess.[43] Further, the corkscrew curls beside the face recall

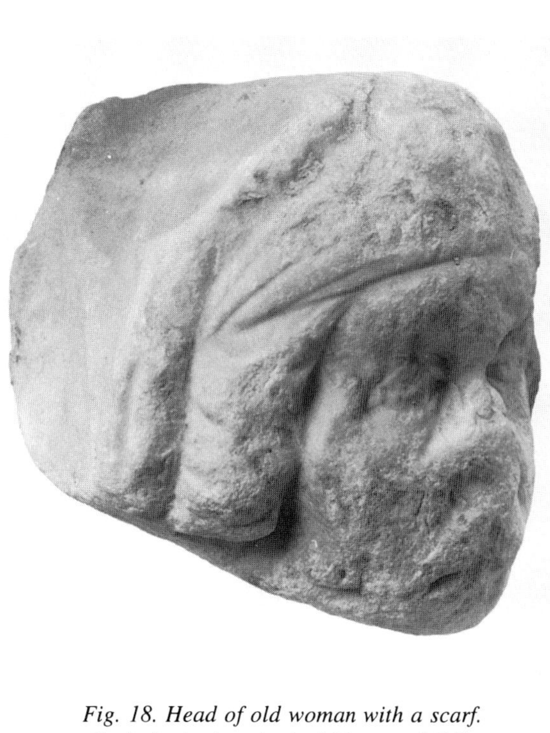

Fig. 18. Head of old woman with a scarf. Corinth, Archaeological Museum S 743.

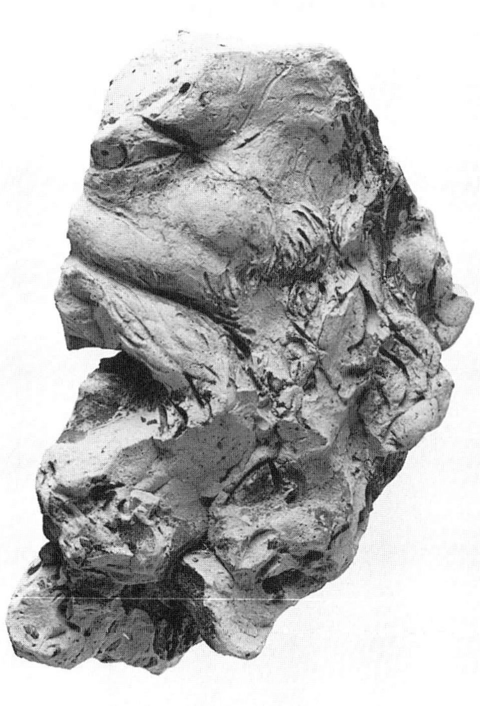

Fig. 19. Terracotta head of a satyr. Corinth, Archaeological Museum SF-81-1.

a head from Alexandria interpreted as a priestess of Isis.[44] If the connection can be made here, this would be one of several sculptures associated with the Isis cult at Corinth.[45] A notable feature in the old woman are the incised pupils and irises, which are similar to the incision on some Hellenistic terracottas from Corinth. A fragmentary satyr head provides the best example of this technique, which was clearly used in some Hellenistic sculptures at Corinth in both marble and terracotta (Fig. 19).[46]

A head of a girl with her hair in a knot high on the crown, of Pentelic marble, was found west of the Forum (Fig. 20). This head, tilted and turned to its right, is characterized by soft facial features and hair. The hair rendering is somewhat indistinct on the sides, but the knot, arranged to be visible in frontal view, contains individual locks twisted, pulled forward and accentuated with the drill.[47] The figure may represent a Muse, as Waywell has proposed for the so-called Hygieia head from Tegea, a girl as a muse, an association possible for a funerary statue, or a nymph – a companion of Aphrodite and a subject most suitable for Corinth. The high bunch with curls pulled forward is similar to that of the figure at right in the best preserved slab of the Mantineia Base.[48] Our figure derives from the late fourth to early third century B.C.

A larger, more battered head of a young girl wears her hair in a simplified melon-coiffure, pulled to a bunch at the upper crown (Fig. 21). The high, rounded cranium, large eyes, and rounded cheeks denote her youth. Finish of the sides is sketchy, and the back was pieced. The

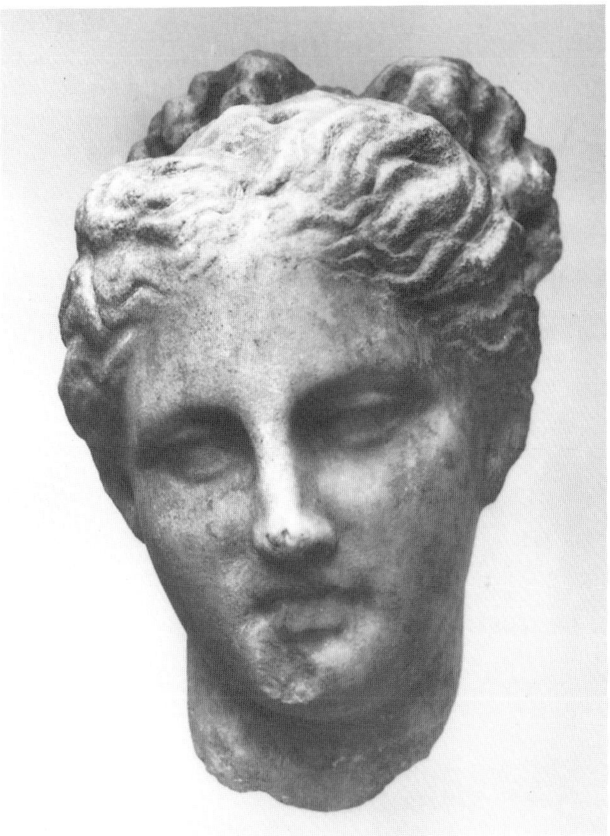

Fig. 20. Head of a girl with topknot hairdo.
Corinth, Archaeological Museum S 2389.

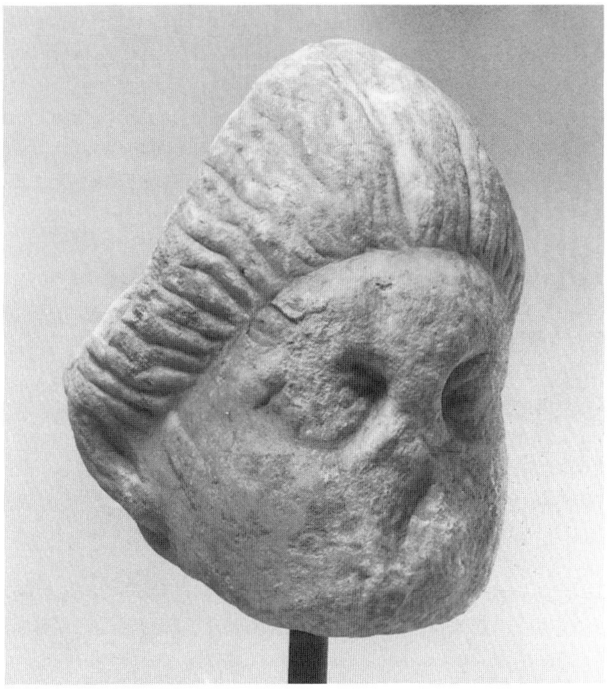

Fig. 21. Head of a girl.
Corinth, Archaeological Museum S 2732.

large rectangular cutting in the top suggests a large addition or the means of attachment to a naiskos or pediment, of the first half of the third century.[49]

A head of a girl of Parian marble was found in 1897, probably in the Peribolos of Apollo near the fourth to third century B.C. naiskos, Temple A (Fig. 22). This head is under life-size, and, judging from the late fourth-century acroteria from the Artemis Temple at Epidauros which it resembles, it may have stood about one meter tall. The top of the head, which was added separately, rested on two planes secured by two dowels on one side. Heavy weathering, dowels, and comparison with the Epidauros acroteria, suggest that this sculpture stood out of doors for a long time.[50]

Our head, in its rather simple, austere style, resembles the Epidauros heads of ca. 320 B.C. Moreover, it looks like a somewhat drier, younger version of the Tegea head of ca. 340 B.C., with its shallow eyes and straight cheeks, but the hair of our head is thicker, with locks appearing to dribble down the side, like locks on some Early Hellenistic Corinthian terracottas.[51]

The subject is a teenage girl, her hair once pulled into two knots, one on the crown, the second at the nape. The open mouth suggests an emotional state, the head's position, turned to its left and pulled back on the neck, that the figure is pulling away from someone. In addition, the size of the dowels and the likely shape of the attachment,

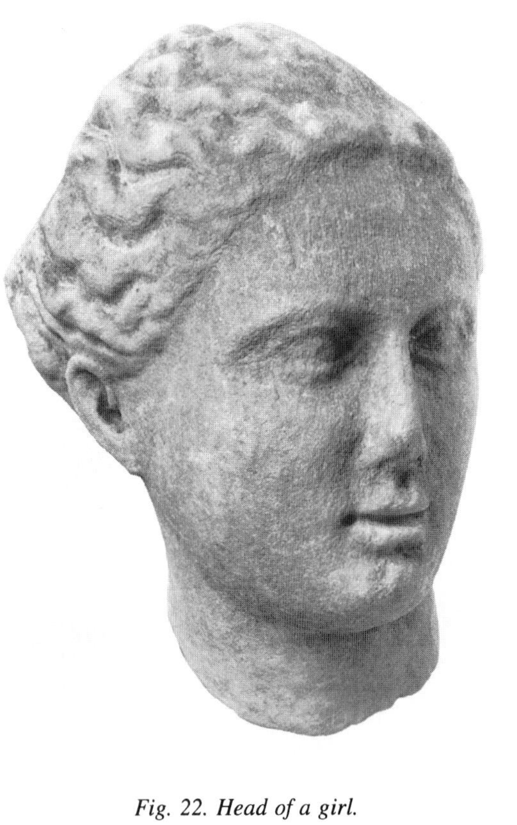

Fig. 22. Head of a girl.
Corinth, Archaeological Museum S 19.

with a right angle for the resting surface, suggests that the object added was larger than just the top of the head, as if containing the hand of an attacker pursuing the girl from left. So, the head may survive from an abduction scene, as in some central acroteria of the classical period.[52]

In summary, this overview, though incomplete, presents a complex picture of Hellenistic sculpture from Corinth. I have not included funerary or votive reliefs, of which a number survive, and a review of the inscriptions produces more, but the fragmentary state of inscriptions from Corinth precludes connecting inscriptions with statues.[53] While the evidence does not indicate the existence of a Corinthian School of sculpture in Hellenistic times, we can characterize the kinds of sculptural activities and preferences indicated by the finds. Not surprisingly, the best represented period is Early Hellenistic, and sizes include figurines, statuettes one-half and one meter tall, and statues life-size and over.

Greatest emphasis in subject matter is given to Aphrodite, the city's patron goddess, with major deities at Corinth also included: Athena, Artemis, Herakles and Hermes. The statue of a General represents a significant public figure. Questions of context, patron, or public versus private dedication cannot be answered definitively, but general findspots are helpful for some. An important aspect is Corinth's preference for varied materials in its sculpture: bronze, terracotta, and limestone – with or without stucco overlay – and marble from Penteli, Paros and Thasos. Older forms, such as aniconic heads, adopt contemporary hairstyles. Architectural sculpture is represented as well as votive statues, the most interesting of which are the depictions of women, young and old, who played an important role in perpetuating the religious cults of the city.[54]

Corinth was a city of considerable size in the Hellenistic period, marked by diversity in occupation, levels of wealth, and religious cults. It would be a mistake to expect a single sculptural style to characterize the art of this Hellenistic city, as the varied material in this survey reminds us. Rather, we should envision a combination of ready-made imports and workshops from various areas catering to the varied needs and interests of Corinth's heterogeneous populus.[55]

Acknowledgements

I would like to thank the organizers of this conference, Olga Palagia and William D.E. Coulson, who provided the impetus for this study, the Greek Archaeological Service for permission to work at Corinth, Dr. Charles K. Williams, II, for permission to study this material and Dr. Nancy Bookidis for help with photographs, most of which are the fine work of Lenio Bartzioti and Ino Ioannidou. Stella Bouzaki acted as conservator. I am grateful to the University Research Council of the University of North Carolina at Chapel Hill for their support. Appreciation is due also to my research assistant, Mary Fournier, for help with various aspects of the project. All photographs are courtesy of the Corinth Excavations, American School of Classical Studies at Athens. I also thank John Camp, Director of the Agora Excavations, for permission to mention sculptures in the Agora collection.

Abbreviations

Clairmont	Ch. Clairmont, *Classical Attic Tombstones* (1993)
Comstock – Vermeule	M.B. Comstock and C.C. Vermeule, *Sculpture in Stone. The Greek, Roman and Etruscan Collections of the Museum of Fine Arts, Boston* (1976)
Gualandi	G. Gualandi, *ASAtene* N.S. 38, 1976, 56ff.
Johnson	F.P. Johnson, *Corinth* IX.1, *Sculpture 1896–1923* (1931)
Marcadé	J. Marcadé, *Au Musée de Délos* (1969)
Merker	G.S. Merker, *The Hellenistic Sculpture of Rhodes* (1973)
Ridgway 1981	B.S. Ridgway, *Hesperia* 50, 1981, 426ff.
Robinson	H.S. Robinson, *Hesperia* 38, 1969, 20ff.
Sturgeon	M.C. Sturgeon, *Isthmia* IV, *Sculpture* I. *1952–1967* (1987)
Thompson	D.B. Thompson, *Troy* Suppl. 3, *The Terracotta Figurines of the Hellenistic Period* (1963)

Notes

1. Cf. Ridgway 1981; although Johnson gave Hellenistic dates for some sculptures from the early excavations, these received relatively brief treatment.
2. MF 11562, Grave 1963–10; E.G. Pemberton, *Hesperia* 54, 1985, 292 ff., no. 45, pl. 85. The shape of the top of the "column" suggests a Corinthian capital. *Greek Anthology*, W.R. Paton transl., Loeb ed. I (1927) 6,1; 18–20; 210–211.
3. MF 8968: O. Broneer, *Hesperia* 16, 1947, 242, pl. 63, fig. 25.
4. Two women, St. Petersburg, Hermitage 578: ca. 350–300 B.C. F. Winter, *Die Typen der figürlichen Terrakotten* III.2 (1903) 3, no. 8; X. Gorbunova and I. Saverkina, *Greek and Roman Antiquities in the Hermitage* (1975) no. 92, second half of the fourth century. Boston, Ephedrismos Group, MFA 03.894, H. 0.248 m: J.P. Uhlenbrock (ed.), *The Coroplast's Art: Greek Terracottas of the Hellenistic World* (1990) 128 ff., cat. 20 (Merker), late fourth to early third century, retouching noted; another Corinthian-made version of this subject stands over 0.40 m tall, cf. R. Kekulé von Stradonitz, *Ausgewählte griechische Terrakotten im Antiquarium der königlichen Museen zu Berlin* (1903) 16, pls. xvii–xviii.
5. S 2556, p.H. 0.093 m; O. Broneer, *Hesperia* 16, 1947, 242, pl. 63, fig. 24. Ridgway 1981, 427 n. 19, late fourth century date. A small arm from a figurine [S 2549] was also found in South Stoa Well XX in a Hellenistic context.
6. Cf., e.g., MF 1417, G.R. Davidson, *Corinth* XII, *The Minor Objects* (1952) 45, no. 264, pl. 22, third century B.C.
7. S-89-6, p.H. 0.154 m, well 1976–1. Cf. *LIMC* II (1984)

s.v. Aphrodite, no. 774 (A. Delivorrias); marble statuette from near Smyrna in Boston, in reversed pose, with dolphin support, MFA 03.760, Comstock – Vermeule, no. 177; cf., e.g., a similar ivory statuette from Pompeii and terracottas from Hierapytna, Priene and Myrina: *LIMC* II s.v. Aphrodite, under no. 774 and nos. 775–781.

8. S 2722, p.H. 0.58 m. Cf. L.R. Farnell, *The Cults of the Greek States* 2 (1896) 641 ff.; 676; for a torso similarly exposed from the front, Merker no. 8; Gualandi 56 ff.; *LIMC* II s.v. Aphrodite, no. 879; or from the back, being disrobed, Delos A 4156: Marcadé, 390 ff., pl. 25.

9. S-81–6, p.H. 0.234 m. C.K. Williams, II, *Hesperia* 51, 1982, 124 ff., pl. 39, found in Manhole 1981–6 in Hellenistic fill. Ridgway 1981, 428 n. 25.

10. M. Sturgeon, *Archaeology* 28, 1975, 230–237; L. Beschi, *ASAtene* N.S. 31–32, 1969–70, 133–341, on aniconism 326 ff.; cf. also, e.g., A. Donohue, *'Xoana' and the Origins of Greek Sculpture* (1988) 195ff., 219ff. n. 113; U. Kron in H. Froning, T. Hölscher and H. Mielsch (edd.), *Kotinos, Festschrift für Erika Simon* (1992) 56 ff. with references, and M.H. Jameson, D. Jordan and R. Kotansky, *A 'Lex Sacra' from Selinous* (1993) 98ff.

11. A 415, p. H. 0.268 m. Robinson 20 ff., no. 39, pl. 8. G. Daux, *BCH* 88, 1964, 705, called it a phallic marker.

12. S 2714, p.H. 0.232 m, from Manhole 63–5; Robinson 20, no. 38, pl. 8; Williams (supra n. 9) 125 ff. : third or first half of second century B.C., comparing the Knidian Aphrodite type's coiffure. S 2714, A 415 and an undecorated cippus appear in D. Kurtz – J. Boardman, *Greek Burial Customs* (1971) 242 ff., fig. 52, "phallos" monuments from Asia Minor : figs. 50–51. Ridgway 1981, 428 n. 25.

13. S-85–4, p.H. 0.308 m; the bluff called Korakou has produced a number of graves. The second is in the Restaurant, the Arkhontikon, near Lechaion Harbor. Cf. a similar aniconic head in Athens, NM 4816, total H. 0.43, Diam. 0.14, H. base 0.075 m, Beschi (supra n. 10) 332 ff. n. 5, figs. 120a–b, a hole ca. 2 cm. wide in the back of the base and plaster only on the upper half of the base indicate it was set into another block, possibly from Corinth; so also Williams (supra n. 9) 125 ff. n. 10; the short hairdo recalls the hair of some women on fourth-century grave stelai and of some Apollo types. Although the findspot is unknown, close correspondence between the objects in Corinth and Athens exists regarding the oolitic limestone, fine stucco coating, and reddish earth stains. On Lechaion see, e.g., J. Wiseman, *The Land of the Ancient Corinthians, SIMA* 50 (1978) 87f.; Aphrodite sanctuary, Pseudo-Plutarch, *Sept. Sap. Conviv.* 2: F. Babbitt, *Plutarch's Moralia* II, Loeb ed. (1928) 349.

14. P. Marconi, *Agrigento* (1929) 46 ff., pl. 15; S. Ferri, *Divinità ignote* (1929) 15 ff.; 36 ff., figs. 5 ff.; 22ff.; D. White, *AJA* 71, 1967, 342 ff., who dates those from Selinus ca. 409–250 B.C. Flat, aniconic stelai are known from Pompeii, Beschi (supra n. 10) 331 ff., fig. 119, as well as the Kertch/ Chersonessos region, references in Robinson 20.

15. Robinson 7, nos. 26–28, A 418; A 416; A 417, plan fig. 1, found in Manhole 8 of the Anaploga water tunnel system in a fill dated late fourth to early third century B.C., were interpreted as markers for property or sacred areas, their obsolescence associated with changes in the control of Corinth in the post-Alexander period. C.K. Williams, II, *Hesperia* 44, 1975, 9, no. 2, pl. 2, A-74–19, limestone cippus on a square base (H. 0.262, Diam. shaft 0.142 m, covered with coarse stucco with a fine surface) found in the Southwest Forum, which he considers probably a property or temenos marker. Cf. also the iconic marble heads set into a limestone base which may have crowned an altar, Larissa Museum, S.G. Miller, *Calif St Cl Ant* 7, 1974, 231ff., pl. 3,2, fig. 4, the multiple herms in Tegea and the veiled woman, possibly Demeter or an initiate, on the votive relief from Livadia, Boiotia, Athens NM 3942, C.R. Long, *The Twelve Gods of Greece and Rome* (1987) 24; 30; 40, figs. 62; 75; 106; *LIMC* II (1984) s.v. Artemis, no. 1186 (L. Kahil).

16. Loutraki lions: F. Johansen, *Ny Carlsberg Glyptotek, Catalogue, Greece in the Archaic Period* (1994) 36 ff., nos. 2–3; Sturgeon no. 3. On sphinxes: J.C. Wright, *Hesperia* 46, 1977, 245 ff. Siren: A.N. Stillwell, *Corinth* XV i, *The Potters' Quarter* (1948) 70 ff., pls. 26–27; B.S. Ridgway, *The Archaic Style in Greek Sculpture*[2] (1993) 228, fig. 100. Lion from Perachora: Comstock-Vermeule no. 15, ca. 550 B.C.; Ridgway op.cit., 221 ff., fig. 92. Boston head allegedly from Sikyon, now thought Cypriot: Ridgway, op.cit., 128; 157 nn. 4 and 13; 364 nn. 8 and 22, fig. 43; Comstock – Vermeule no. 14; N. Bookidis, *Hesperia* 39, 1970, 313–325. Limestone lion head, S 3539, Ridgway 1981, 424. Limestone fragments found near the Apollo Temple: K. Hartswick, forthcoming. Notably, different types of limestone are represented here. Corinthian limestone quarries are being studied by Dr. Chris Hayward: *Newsletter*, American School of Classical Studies at Athens, Spring 1995, 3.

17. S 310, p.H. 0.165 m; Johnson no. 131; found in a hole between the Propylaia and an apse of Peirene. Cf. J. Marcadé, *BCH* 76, 1952, 128 ff., who calls Hellenistic stuccoed poros on Delos an imported Alexandrian technique.

18. S 1663, p.H. 0.27 m.

19. SF-5, p.H. 0.132 m; N. Bookidis, *Hesperia* 51, 1982, 246, pls. 67 ff. Limestone architectural sculptures of post-classical date are less surprising from Italy; cf., e.g., in the second century B.C. figured capitals from Pompeii, Casa dei Capitelli Figurati (VII.4.57), P. Zanker, *Pompeji* (1995) 43 ff., figs. 6–7; M. Moltesen in P. Bilde et al. (edd.), *Aspects of Hellenism in Italy: Towards a Cultural Unity?* (1993) 229 ff. A few limestone sculptures are cited from Delos, with possible Egyptian influence: Marcadé 102; 454 ff., A 1813; A 2148.

20. S 3356, p.H. 1.10 m. C. de Grazia (Vanderpool), *Hesperia* 46, 1977, 73 ff., no. 30, pl. 27; C.K. Williams, II, *Hesperia* 46, 1977, 58.

21. See Polybios 38.10–18; Pausanias 2.1.2.

22. IS 250, p.H. 0.267 m; Sturgeon no. 22.

23. IS 127, p.L. 0.07 m; Sturgeon no. 101.

24. S 1294, p.H. 1.665 m neck to top of plinth; H. Lauter, *AM* 86, 1971, 147–161, reconstruction drawing p. 148, fig. 1. Antium Girl: Helbig[4] III, no. 2270 (von Steuben). Boston: R. Tölle-Kastenbein, *Frühklassische Peplosfiguren, Originale* (1980) no. 10a., pl. 46; for a Delian statuette with tray, see Marcadé, A 1852. 194 pl. 64, Venice relief, W. Fuchs, *Die Skulptur der Griechen* (1983) fig. 627. As Dionysos: A.H. Borbein, *JdI* 88, 1973,

141 ff. n. 421; E. Simon, *Gymnasium* 84, 1977, 359 n. 35; H.-U. Cain in M. Wörrle – P. Zanker (edd.), *Vestigia* 47, *Stadtbild und Burgerbild im Hellenismus* (1995) 115 ff.; Dionysos herm, A. Giuliano (ed.), *Museo Nazionale Romano* I, 5 (1983) no. 68.

25. S 63, p.H. 1.25 m; Johnson no. 112. A. Linfert, *Kunstzentren hellenistischer Zeit* (1976) 78, figs. 165–166, Kos 74; Gualandi 78 ff.

26. S 2411, p.H. 0.37 m. M. Fullerton, *The Archaistic Style in Roman Statuary* (1990) 172 ff.; 179, no. 8IA6, fig. 82. Merker 33, no. 133, figs. 77–79. S 2503, p.H. 0.77 m; *LIMC* III (1986) s.v. Dionysos, no. 126c. (Jacobsen type) (C. Gasparri); E. Pochmarski, *Das Bild des Dionysos in der Rundplastik der klassischen Zeit Griechenlands* (1974) 73; 77. Cf. also the related Apollo type, *LIMC* II (1984) s.v. Apollon, no. 233 (O. Palagia).

27. S 429, p.H. 0.35 m; Johnson no. 53, called "late work;" M.E.C. Soles, *Aphrodite at Corinth: A Study of the Sculptural Types* (diss. Yale University 1976) no. 45; *LIMC* II (1984) s.v. Aphrodite, no. 303 (A.Delivorrias), late Hellenistic; B.S. Ridgway, *Hellenistic Sculpture* I (1990) 217, pl. 100: Roman. Agora statue: E.B. Harrison, *Akten des XIII. internationalen Kongresses für klassische Archäologie, Berlin 1988* (1990) 346, probably set up soon after the altar of 197/6 B.C. outside the northwest corner of the Agora. On Rhodes, see Merker 27 ff., figs. 19–25; Gualandi 7 ff.

28. IS 254, p.L. 0.404 m; Sturgeon 115, no. 25, early Hellenistic.

29. S 858, p.H. 0.23 m; Johnson no. 102, dog or hare. For the soft anatomy and motif of a boy clutching an animal against his body, cf., e.g., Marcadé pls. 51–52.

30. T 98, p.H. 0.125 m; see forthcoming volume on freestanding and large architectural sculpture from the Corinth Theater by M. Sturgeon. On Herakliskos, cf. *LIMC* IV (1988) s.v. Herakles, nos. 1221–1256 (O. Palagia); for similar rendering of eyes and cheeks, cf. the statue of a young girl in Delphi: H. Ruhfel, *Das Kind in der griechischen Kunst* (1984) 218, fig. 88, ca. 300–280 B.C. Boys: F. Snowden, *Blacks in Antiquity* (1970) 28; 72, fig. 42; Boston, Comstock – Vermeule no. 112; Corinth, T 2001, T.L. Shear, *AJA* 34, 1930, 429, fig. 19; G. Karo, *AA* 1931, col. 248, fig. 23 (stolen).

31. S 312, p.H. 0.351 m; Johnson no. 34; *LIMC* II (1984) s.v. Artemis, no. 348 : Roman copy, the right breast erroneously described as uncovered.

32. NCG inv. no. 1653, H. 0.51 m; *LIMC* II (1984) s.v. Artemis/Diana, no. 34b (E.Simon): Early Imperial; *EA* 3829.

33. London, B.M., sculpture no. 1559; Reinach, *RSt* II.i, 316.10; Farnell (supra n. 8) pl. 32a, dated ca. 125–75 B.C. in Museum label. Cf. multiple variations of this type, e.g., Athenian Agora, S 624, T.L. Shear, *AJA* 40, 1936, 198, fig. 16, who notes red paint on the deerskin; *LIMC* II, s.v. Artemis/ Diana, no. 34; the Agora Excavations has four additional examples of different sizes and details (S 911, S 912, S 1394, S 1399). See also G. Riemann, *Kerameikos* II (1940) 128, no. 182, pl. 39; Volos Museum, nos. 504, 554; Athens, NM 2132 and 2875; Berlin, no. 65; *LIMC* II 652 s.v. Artemis/Diana; Marcadé, 220, pl. 37, A 5178, the "Thracian" Artemis (?). Fragments of an analogous life-size figure, dated late fourth to early third century B.C., found around the temple of Artemis Orthia at Messene, are interpreted as the cult statue: P. Themelis, in R. Hägg (ed.), *Ancient Greek Cult Practice from the Epigraphical Evidence* (1994) 105 ff., fig. 8. The documentary relief of Bendis from Piraeus in Copenhagen, dated by inscription to 329/28 B.C., shows Bendis in the same format as the Corinth and Copenhagen statuettes, with the addition of the Phrygian cap with soft flaps reaching the shoulders, NCG 231, M. Moltesen, *Ny Carlsberg Glyptotek, Catalogue, Greece in the Classical Period* (1995) 138 ff.; C.L. Lawton, *Attic Document Reliefs. Art and Politics in Ancient Athens* (1995) no. 47; *LIMC* III (1986) s.v. Bendis, no. 4 (Goceva-Popov) = *LIMC* s.v. Asklepios, no. 211. See also the votive relief from Piraeus in London, B.M. 2155, *LIMC* III s.v. Bendis, no. 3; the Bendis format, probably established after the introduction of the cult to Attica just before 429/28 B.C., was later used for Dionysos, Moltesen, op.cit., 140; cf., e.g., the Eleusinian relief from Karystos in Chalkis, Archaeological Museum 337, E.S. Sakellaraki, *Chalkis* (1995) 89; 92, fig. 54, mid-fourth century.

34. For earlier examples of similar body types combined with different head types, see V.M. Strocka, *JdI* 94, 1979, 143 ff.

35. S 1820, p.H. 0.204 m. For other female heads from Corinth with full features and nearly straight cheeks, cf., e.g., S 58, Johnson no. 126 : Hellenistic; possibly late fourth century. On the angled piecing of heads in the Hellenistic period and gravity-assisted joins, see, e.g., P.C. Bol, *Die Skulpturen des Schiffsfundes von Antikythera* (1972) 93 ff., nos. 25; 37; Marcadé 109 ff., A 4136; 318, pl. 69; Marcadé (supra n. 17) 96 ff.; 103; on the Kneeling Gaul/Mykonos Head, P. Moreno, *Scultura ellenistica* (1994) 302 ff., figs. 376; 386, n. 579; Ridgway, *Hellenistic Sculpture* I, 297 ff., pl. 154; Marcadé in *Akten XIII. Kongresses, Berlin* 148 ff.; E. Dygve – F. Poulsen, *Das Heroon von Kalydon* (1934) 73 ff.; R. Kabus-Preisshofen, *Die hellenistische Plastik der Insel Kos*, 14. Ergh. *AM* (1989) nos. 85; 92; H.-H. von Prittwitz und Gaffron in G. Hellenkempier Salies (ed.), *Das Wrack* (1994) 303 ff. On piecing in various periods: A. Claridge in M. True and J. Podany (edd.), *Marble. Art Historical and Scientific Perspectives on Ancient Sculpture* (1990) 135 ff.

36. Isthmia, inv. IM 116; O. Broneer, *Hesperia* 24, 1955, 139, pl. 56b, upper right; V.R. Anderson-Stojanovic in *Hellenistic Pottery Conference* 1994, Abstracts, 5, and *AJA* 92, 1988, 268 ff., where the sanctuary is identified as that of Demeter Malophoros; *Hesperia* 62, 1993, 270 n. 73; *Hesperia* 65, 1996, 63; 93 ff., plan fig. 3.

37. On kerchief, "tagidion" see Thompson 50–52 and *Hesperia* 32, 1963, 360, pl. 75. Berlin, Staatliche Museen, T.C. 6822, V. Zinserling, *Die Frau in Hellas und Rom* (1972) fig. 56; Thompson 50, cites this as one of the earliest examples of such a kerchief, and dates it to the late fourth century.

38. NM 3335; *LIMC* II s.v. Aphrodite, no. 514; H. Meyer, *AM* 103, 1988, 203–220. Marcadé 437; 439, pl. 50 calls this a "bathing cap," worn to protect Aphrodite's head while she bathes. Cf. also the head of a woman wearing a similar scarf in Athens, Agora S 491.

39. P. Zanker, *Die trunkene Alte* (1989) 35 ff., figs. 4–5; 23;

25–26; cf. *Greek Anthology* 7,423, W.R. Paton transl., Loeb ed. II (1919) 231; H. Wrede, *RM* 95, 1988, 97 ff. and *RM* 98, 1991, 168 ff., pl. 40; R. Thomas, *RM* 101, 1995, 149 ff. Cf. also, e.g., short scarves worn by the bronze krotalist from the Mahdia wreck and by Alexandrian terracottas, Wrede, op.cit. 1988, pls. 40,3; 43,3–4; S. Pfisterer-Haas in Hellenkempier Salies, *Das Wrack* 483 ff.; bronze statuette in Vienna, E. Reisch, *ÖJh* 19/20, 1919, 311f., J. Bankó, *ÖJh* 19/20, 1919, 296ff., fig. 191, pl. 6.

40. On feminine priesthoods: A. Mantis, Προβλήματα της εικονογραφίας των ιερειών και των ιερέων στην αρχαία ελληνική τέχνη (1990); U. Kron in P. Hellström – B. Alroth (edd.), *Religion and Power in the Ancient Greek World, Boreas* 24 (1996) 139 ff. with references. Artemis: cf., e.g. the metope from Temple E at Selinus, *LIMC* II s.v. Artemis, no. 1407; C. Marconi, *Selinunte. Le metope dell' Heraion* (1994) 186, fig. 43; Clairmont, 1.327; 1.148; 1.187; 1.188; 1.797; 1.971; 2.307a; 2.319a; 2.424; 2.426b; 2.487; 2.488. On drilled hairknots, cf., e.g., G.M.A. Richter, *AJA* 48, 1944, 229 ff., figs. 1–3; 6; 11; E. Reeder, *Hellenistic Art in the Walters Art Gallery* (1988) no. 16.

41. It falls somewhere between the Attic grave relief of Melite of ca. 350 (NM 720), Clairmont, no. 1.315, and the stele with two girls in New York of ca. 320, Richter (supra n. 40). In comparison with Melite's stele the Corinth head is shorter, more oval, and the cheeks slope inward more quickly, suggesting a later date, though differences of the subjects' ages, marble type, and regional origin doubtless also play a role.

42. S 743, p.H. 0.143 m; Johnson no. 130: probably a copy of a Hellenistic realistic statue, not a portrait. Villa Albani, T. Schreiber, *Die hellenistischen Reliefbilder* (1894) pl. 66; Helbig[4] IV, no. 3301; P.C. Bol (ed.), *Forschungen zur Villa Albani* III (1992) no. 292; Zinserling (supra n. 37) fig. 97; Wrede (1991, supra n. 39) 184, pl. 48,3. See also the fragmentary silver relief from a kalathos which shows a woman making offerings to an idol of Artemis, Bologna, Museo Civico, Hellenistic, *LIMC* II s.v. Artemis, no. 1037. For Roman examples of priestess dress, cf., e.g., E. Rosenbaum, *Cyrenaican Portrait Sculpture* (1960) nos. 39. 43; Comstock – Vermeule no. 355.

44. Alexandria, Museo greco-romano, inv. 25449. A. Adriani, *Testimonianze e monumenti di scultura alessandrina* (1948) pls. 1–2 (cf. figures in Ince, Florence, pl. 13); M. Bieber, *The Sculpture of the Hellenistic Age* (1961) 89–90, figs. 328–329; Moreno (supra n. 35) 321, fig. 403.

45. Cf. S 720, Johnson no. 123; S 3609, S 3634 (identified by C.M. Edwards), and see E. Milleker, *Hesperia* 54, 1985, 121 ff.

46. SF-81-1, p.H. 0.137 m; Bookidis (1982, supra n. 19) 241 ff.; 244, pl. 68, on incised pupils and irises in the Hellenistic period. Ridgway, *Hellenistic Sculpture* I, 326, calls it a centaur.

47. S 2389, p.H. 0.12 m. Cf., e.g., grave stele of Mnesagora and Nikochares, Athens, NM 3845, Ruhfel (supra n. 30) 130, fig. 53; Clairmont 1.610.

48. Athens, NM 3602, R. Lullies and M. Hirmer, *Greek Sculpture* (1960) 88, pl. 205; A.F. Stewart, *Skopas of Paros* (1977) 83f.; G.B. Waywell in O. Palagia – W. Coulson (edd.), *Sculpture from Arcadia and Laconia* (1993) 83, fig. 6, ca. 340–30 B.C. For other examples of this hairstyle in marble statuary from Corinth, cf. Corinth S 2124, S 2523, cited by Merker in Uhlenbrock (supra n. 4) 60. On various types of hair knots cf., e.g., Ridgway, *Hellenistic Sculpture* I, 56; 107 n. 43; 232; 253, in terracottas: Thompson 36 ff.; 42 ff. Mantineia base, NM 216, Thompson pl. 59, details of heads. On nymphs, cf. C.M. Edwards, *Greek Votive Reliefs to Pan and the Nymphs* (diss. New York Univ. 1985) 11–19; 41–49.

49. S 2732, p.H. 0.15 m, fine-grain marble, cutting: 0.017 × 0.017 × D. 0.02 m. Cf. Thompson 38 ff. for coiffure. The summary rendering may be attributed to architectural use rather than to a lesser artist. A Classical head of Aphrodite, Corinth S 1203, Johnson no. 167, has a similarly large rectangular cutting on top with no trace of an attached object.

50. S-19, p.H. 0.164 m; Johnson no. 42, no date. Soles (supra n. 27) no. 50, labelled Aphrodite, no date. On Temple A, H.E. Askew in R. Stillwell et al., *Corinth* I, ii, *Architecture* (1941) 4–16. Epidauros: N. Yalouris, *ADelt* 22, 1967, A, Meletai, 25–37, pls. 22; 32–33, dated toward the beginning of the fourth quarter of the fourth century;

51. MF 13,748, found in the Demeter Sanctuary at Corinth, publication by G. Merker forthcoming. Uhlenbrock (supra n. 4) 1, color pl. 1, and Merker in Uhlenbrock (supra n. 4) 54 ff.; 59 for comments on archaeological confirmation of reported proveniences of terracottas from Corinth; 60.

52. See, e.g., E.B. Harrison, in H. Froning, T. Hölscher, H. Mielsch (edd.), *Kotinos, Festschrift für Erika Simon* (1992) 204 ff.

53. On funerary and votive reliefs, see Johnson nos. 253–271. 287. 298; B.D. Meritt, *Corinth* VIII, i, *Greek Inscriptions 1896–1927* (1931) 86 ff.; J.H. Kent, *Corinth* VIII, iii, *The Inscriptions 1926–1950* (1966) nos. 24; 34 (relief to Zeuxippos); 36; C.K. Williams, II, *Pre-Roman Cults in the Area of the Forum of Ancient Corinth* (diss. Univ. of Pennsylvania, 1978) 28 ff.; Ridgway 1981, 427 ff.

54. For work on the religious cults of Corinth, see, e.g., R. Lisle, *The Cults of Corinth* (diss. Johns Hopkins, 1955); D.E. Smith, *Harvard Theological Review* 70, 1977, 200–231; Williams (supra n. 53) ; id., *Hesperia* 50, 1981, 412–418; id. in M.A. Del Chiaro (ed.), *Corinthiaca. Studies in Honor of Darrell A. Amyx* (1986) 12–24, with references.

55. Even large-scale terracotta sculpture could be imported. See, e.g., the third-century head of Aphrodite (?) possibly from South Italy: I.B. Romano, *Hesperia* 63, 1994, 93, no. 91, pl. 29, its hair, stephane and earring once gilded, MF 9249. *LIMC* II s.v. Aphrodite, no. 1071.

The Enemy Within: A Macedonian in Piraeus

Olga Palagia

τὴν Μακεδόνων ὑπερηφανίαν καὶ μὴ
τὴν τοῦ δικαίου δύναμιν ἰσχύειν παρ' ἑκάστοις

Hypereides, *Funeral Speeech*, 20

The torso Piraeus Museum 3776 (Figs. 1; 4; 7; 9; 10; 11; 15) was rescued by the Antiquities Service from a garbage dump in Moschato, near Piraeus, in 1977. Its original location is unknown. Traces of mortar on the surface indicate that it was reused as building material. The torso belonged to a slightly over life-size statue of a man in a voluminous chlamys and a thick, woollen chiton.[1] It is made of Pentelic marble, a micaceous streak running across the front from top to bottom. There is evidence of piecing at three points. The head with the neck were carved separately and inserted into a cavity of which only the bottom remains, carrying tool marks.[2] The right forearm, extended sideways, was made separately to save marble, and attached by means of two dowels (Fig. 9).[3] The join was smoothed with a claw chisel and a rasp on top. Finally, the bottom edge of the chlamys in front was carved separately and attached to the smooth join by means of three nails (Figs. 10–11). This seems more like a repair, contemporary with the carving of the statue and probably due to a flaw in the marble. A similar repair may be observed on the lower abdomen and upper right thigh of a statue of Aphrodite, Athenian Agora S 37, also of Pentelic marble.[4]

The short chiton is belted at the waist, though the belt is not modelled, and has longish sleeves slit at the bottom and stopping short of the elbows, the right sleeve being ampler. Loose material over the belt forms kolpoi, the left one being longer, even though the left arm was not raised but attached to two struts on the thigh. As the left leg is slightly advanced, the lower left side of the statue sags. This movement is counterbalanced by the left shoulder which looks higher because the end of the chlamys is folded back over the arm. The chiton is heavily undercut between the legs and its thick texture enlivened by press folds, forming criss-cross patterns on the skirt (Fig. 11). Rasp marks are evident all over the drapery.

The ample woollen chlamys is fastened on the right

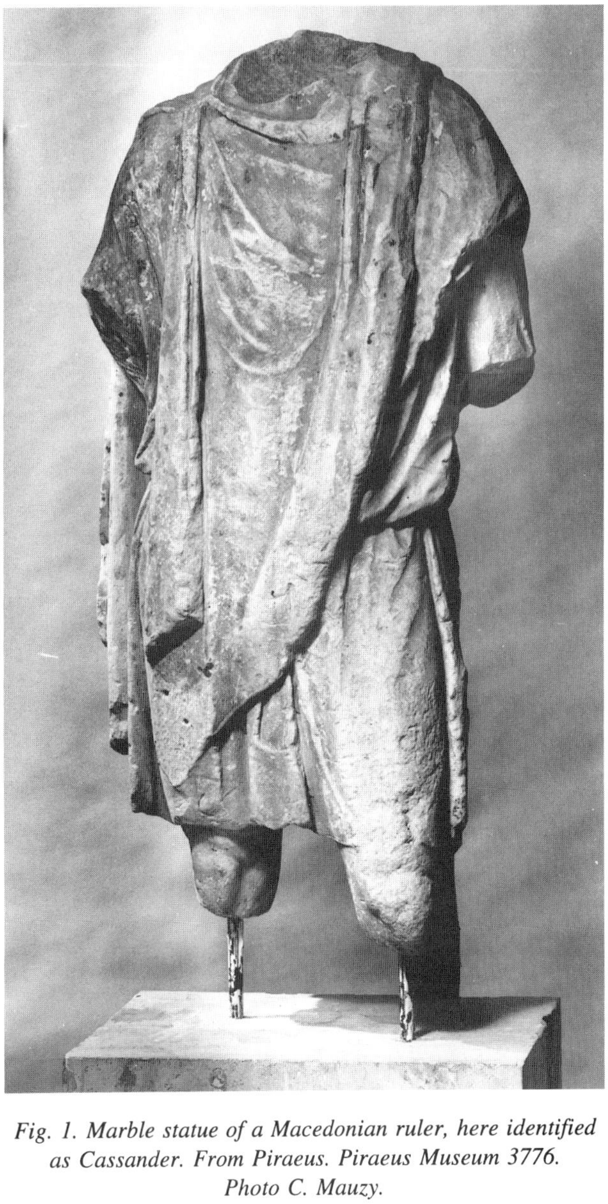

Fig. 1. Marble statue of a Macedonian ruler, here identified as Cassander. From Piraeus. Piraeus Museum 3776. Photo C. Mauzy.

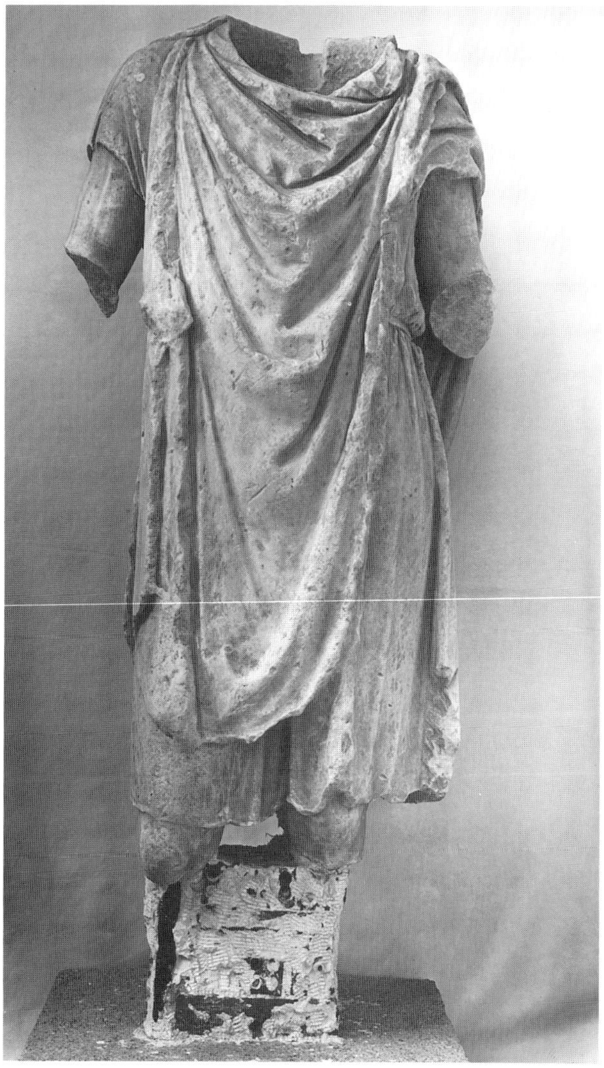

Fig. 2. Marble statue of a Macedonian ruler, here identified as Cassander. From Chalkis. Chalkis Museum 10. Photo DAI Athens, Chalkis 146.

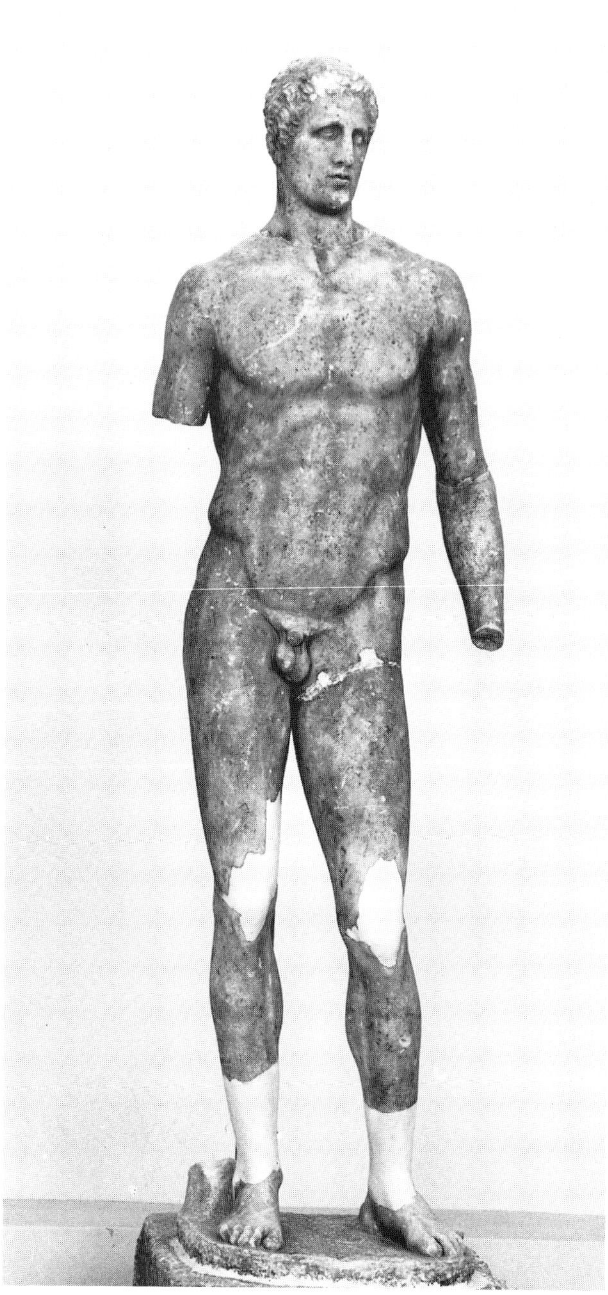

Fig. 3. Agias. Delphi Museum 1875. Photo École Française d' Athènes.

shoulder, falling in heavy pleats. The clasp is not indicated. The cloak was meant to envelop the body but has been folded back, not only over the left shoulder but also over the right side. The vertical folds behind the right arm were undercut with a running drill. Even though the rear was probably not meant to be seen, it is meticulously finished by a few bold strokes (Fig. 15). The drapery style avoids contrasts of light and shade but is very good at suggesting volume; the thick, heavy texture of the clothes is rendered realistically.

All the drama is reserved for the stance. The statue must have been placed at an angle since it is at its best when seen at a three quarter view from its proper left. This side is more carefully finished with the head also turning left (Fig. 7). The left side is, in fact, expanded while the right is contracted. Under the heavy garments the figure is full of nervous energy, highlighted by the restless stance which gives the impression of walking when viewed from his proper right. He seems, in fact, in the process of shifting his weight from one leg to the other in the manner of an athlete relaxing after his exertions (Fig. 4).

The thick, woollen fabric of the clothes, appropriate to a northern climate, and particularly the semi-circular shape of the chlamys, betray a Macedonian.[5] This costume first appears in Macedonian art in the last quarter of the fifth century. Good parallels are offered by a) the warrior on a grave relief of ca. 425 from Vergina in the Thessaloniki Museum,[6] b) Hermes in purple chiton and blue chlamys with purple border from the façade of the "Judgment Tomb" at Leukadia[7] and c) the Macedonians on the façade of the Macedonian tomb at Agios Athanasios which

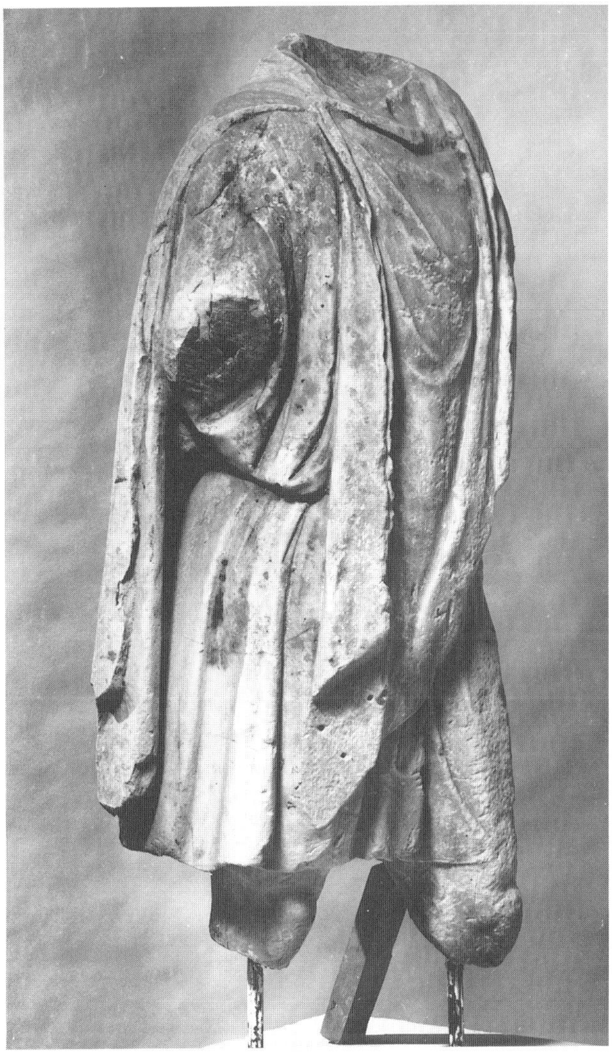

Fig. 4. Piraeus Museum 3776. Photo C. Mauzy.

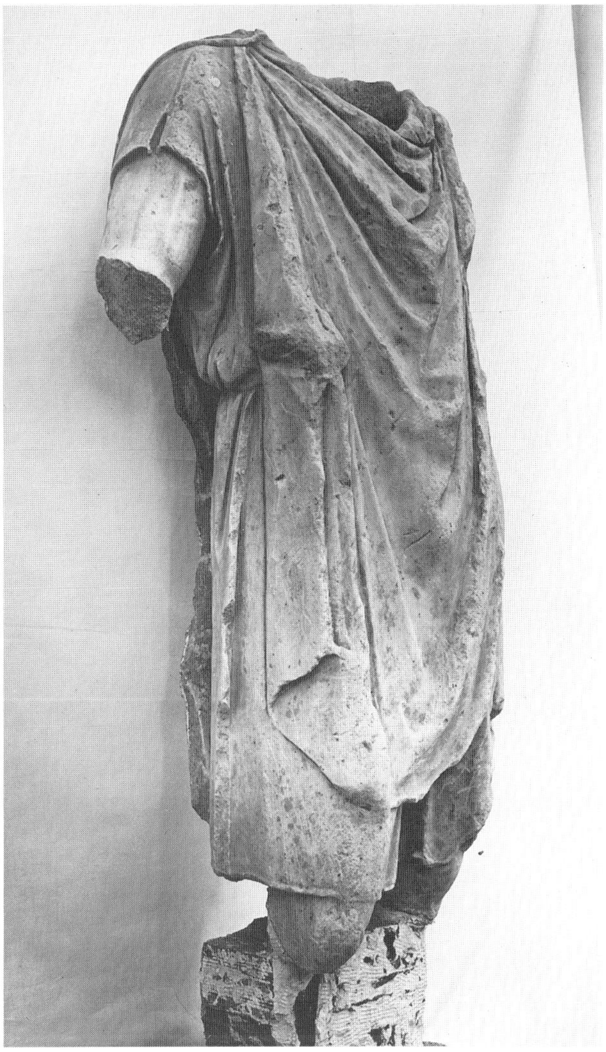

Fig. 5. Chalkis Museum 10. Photo DAI Athens, Chalkis 147.

came to light in 1994.[8] Both frescoes may be dated to the late fourth century. The chlamys and chiton were customary not only to the Macedonian military but also to their rulers as attested by Alexander's daily garb described by Athenaios,[9] "purple chlamys and purple chiton with a white central stripe" and by the identical costume of Lysias, a dynast of Tarsos, who flourished possibly under Seleukos II and/or III.[10]

The Macedonian chlamys is also prominent in the portraiture of Alexander's Successors. Because these portraits have come down to us in the form of busts, we lack the evidence of the body types. For our purposes, we need cite only three marble herms from the Villa dei Papiri in Herculaneum, reproducing the features of Demetrios Poliorketes,[11] Philetairos of Pergamon[12] and an unidentified Macedonian ruler.[13] The chlamys was also adopted for the coin portraits of the Ptolemies, Ptolemy IV and V in particular.[14]

Closest to our Macedonian in date, type and scale are two statues from southern Greece, also headless. We begin with the so-called Chalkis Ruler (Figs. 2; 5; 13).[15] It is of Pentelic marble, of the same size as the Piraeus statue, and came to light east of Chalkis. The head and neck were made separately and inserted into a cavity, being additionally fastened with a dowel at the back. A support running along the length of the left lower leg may betray a bronze prototype (Fig. 13). The Chalkis torso can be properly described as a version of the Piraeus one. The position of the legs is reversed, both arms are bent at the elbow, the right shoulder is slightly raised and the girdle plastically rendered. The chiton sleeves are shorter. Since the legs are placed closer together, the walking impression disappears. As a result of a higher placement of the girdle, the figure looks slightly elongated. On the other hand, the pointed end of the chlamys is pendent over the right leg as in the Piraeus statue, the head is turned in the same direction and the oblique setting is retained. The statue rotates slightly around its axis. The chlamys is covered with rasp marks and is literally scarred by drill channels but looks lighter; the remains

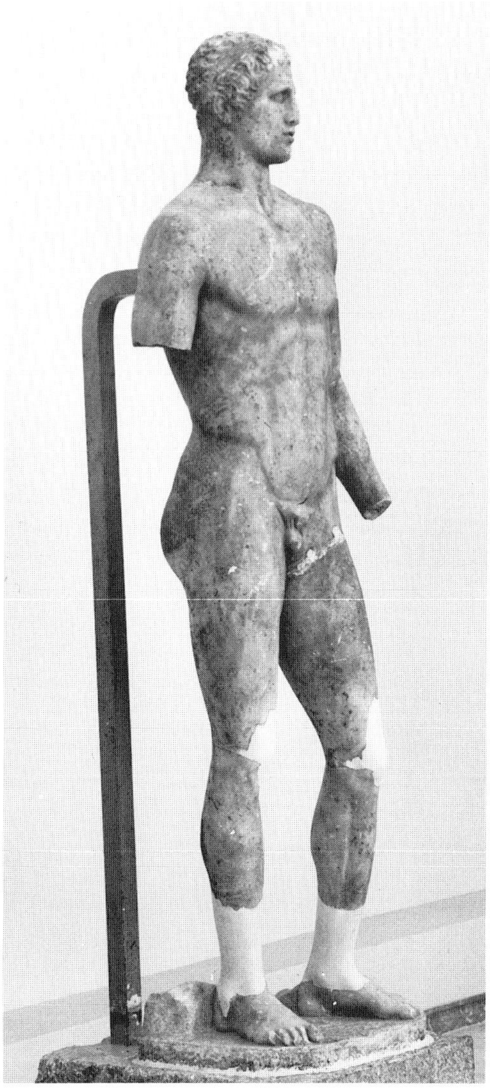

Fig. 6. Agias. Delphi Museum 1875. Photo École Française d' Athènes.

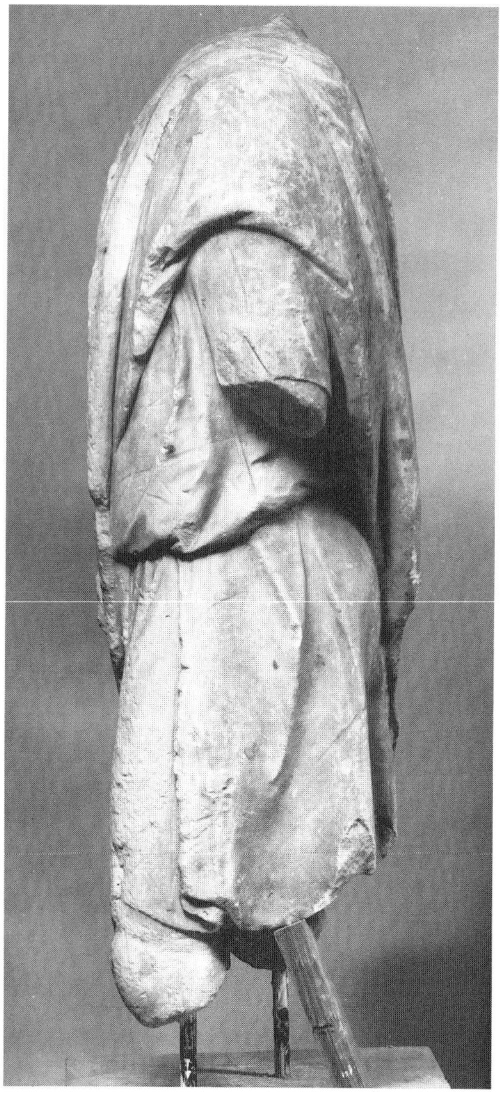

Fig. 7. Piraeus Museum 3776. Photo C. Mauzy.

of an attribute, perhaps a sword held across his right side, are visible over the edge of the chlamys at waist height. Even though he lacks the quality of the Piraeus torso, the Chalkis Ruler is obviously indebted to it or to its prototype. Although we are evidently dealing with the portrait statue of a Macedonian dignitary, the historical implications of its presence in Chalkis have never been properly explained.

Third in our series comes Aknonios, tetrarch of the Thessalians (Figs. 12; 14; 16).[16] He belonged to a gallery of dynastic portraits, dedicated to Apollo at Delphi.[17] The group is credited to the piety of Daochos II, tetrarch of the Thessalians, while he served as *hieromnemon* at Delphi between 336 and 332.[18] Of the three portraits depicting rulers, Aknonios (named "tetrarch of the Thessalians" on the base) wears the Thessalian chlamys, Daochos I[19] ("ruler of all Thessalians") wears the Macedonian, semi-circular variety, while the missing Daochos II,[20] also named tetrarch, may have worn either one judging by his shoes and leg support which echo those of the other two. The fact that the Macedonian chlamys is worn by a Thessalian (Daochos I) is readily explained by Daochos II's close alliance with Philip II of Macedon and reflects his own Macedonian sympathies rather than a family tradition about which nothing is known.[21] The Aknonios is not a true portrait since it depicts a long dead ancestor of the early fifth century. And it is no match for the quality of the Piraeus statue. It is more extensively pieced[22] and, like the Chalkis Ruler, needs a support behind the left leg. In addition, only Aknonios' front was meant to be seen as he looks flat from the sides (Fig. 14). Besides, the pointed end of the Thessalian chlamys falls over the left leg and both arms were raised. The walking impression has again vanished. Compared to the life-like Piraeus torso, Aknonios' body appears more like a mass of drapery hanging over a shapeless trunk. Only the rear of his chlamys (Fig. 16) approaches the quality of the Piraeus statue (Fig. 15).

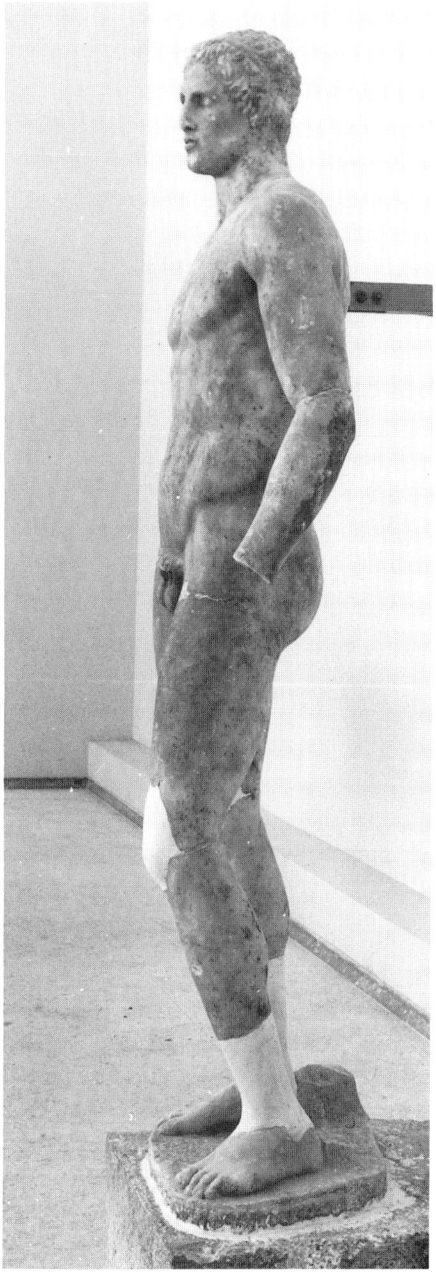

Fig. 8. Agias. Delphi Museum 1875. Photo École Française d' Athènes.

It has often been suggested that the Daochos group consists of workshop copies in marble after bronzes set up at Pharsalos.[23] This suggestion was based on the existence of another statue base for Agias at Pharsalos; its inscription, copied from two separate fragments in 1811 and 1895 and since lost, contained a more or less identical epigram (with an additional stanza) as well as Lysippos' signature.[24] The extraneous supports of Daochos' statues were seen as evidence that they copied bronzes until the discovery of the funerary Kallithea Monument of the late fourth century which includes a statue with struts behind the ankles.[25] It should be pointed out, however, that this is in fact a version of the Agias, and may well copy the struts along with everything else.

The possibility that the Daochos group consists of copies of bronzes and the connection with the workshop of Lysippos are still hotly debated.[26] It can be nevertheless argued that at least the Aknonios is, by reason of its quality, a botched copy of a bronze prototype.

The affinities of the Piraeus torso with the Daochos dedication go beyond the Aknonios. Not only does his oblique placement recall Sisyphos I,[27] but his ponderation and "pendulum" stance are directly related to the Agias (Figs. 3; 6; 8).[28] The positions of their arms and legs and the turn of their heads are identical. They are both meant to be viewed from their proper left, both imbued with a nervous energy due to their restless stance. The Piraeus statue, however, lacks Agias' light touch, being weighed down by his heavy drapery which exudes an air of authority. His close relation to the Daochos group may betray a workshop affinity. The opaque drapery with press folds forming patterns familiar from grave reliefs of the later part of the fourth century, such as the Stele of the Farewell,[29] point to a date somewhat more advanced than the Daochos group. But what is an over life-size statue of a Macedonian doing in Piraeus? And could its presence there have served the same function as the Ruler in Chalkis?

As a result of the disastrous conclusion of the Lamian War against Antipater and Krateros, the Athenians suffered a Macedonian garrison to be installed at the port of Mounychia in Piraeus in August 322.[30] After a brief interval of renewed struggle for independence and a temporary restoration of the democracy in 318, Athens came to terms with Antipater's son, Cassander, in 317. Cassander not only installed his own garrison in Piraeus but also imposed a regime of his choice, headed by Demetrios of Phaleron.[31] Demetrios' rule was abolished in 307, when Athens fell into the hands of his namesake, Demetrios Poliorketes.[32] Meanwhile, Chalkis had been a Macedonian stronghold since the early years of Alexander the Great[33] and was under Cassander's control at least between 317 and 313.[34]

Demetrios of Phaleron's sumptuary laws which restricted the use of expensive grave monuments are generally agreed to date from the beginning of his rule.[35] These restrictions render unlikely the erection of over life-size grave statues, even of Macedonians, in this period, and no funerary statues of Macedonians are conceivable earlier. The Piraeus torso is better explained as the honourary portrait of a Macedonian. Honours to Macedonians in this troubled period were politically expedient and are in fact documented by *IG* II[2] 450 of 313 from the Acropolis honouring Cassander's ally, the Macedonian Asander, satrap of Caria.[36] Among other extravagant honours, he was allowed to set up a bronze equestrian portrait of himself (at his own expense) anywhere in the Agora but near the Tyrannicides. Honours to a Macedonian in this period are illustrated by the record relief Acropolis Museum 3006 (Fig. 17), where Athena crowns a man in Macedonian chlamys in the presence of a personification.[37]

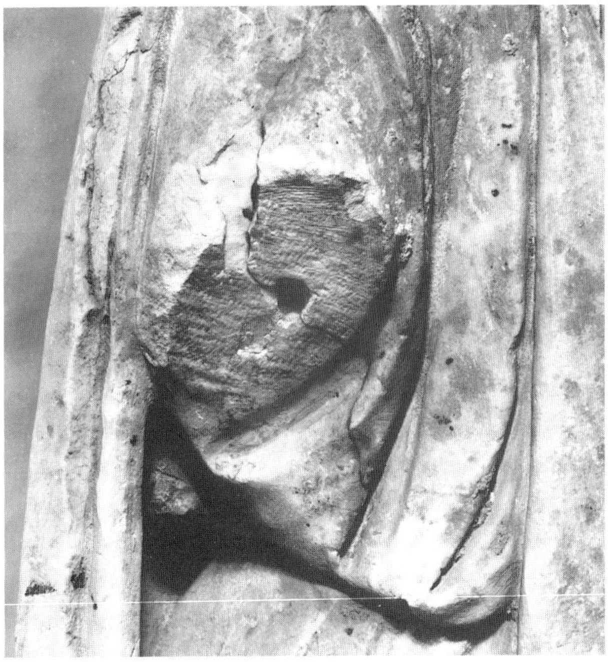

Fig. 9. Piraeus Museum 3776. Detail of right arm. Photo C. Mauzy.

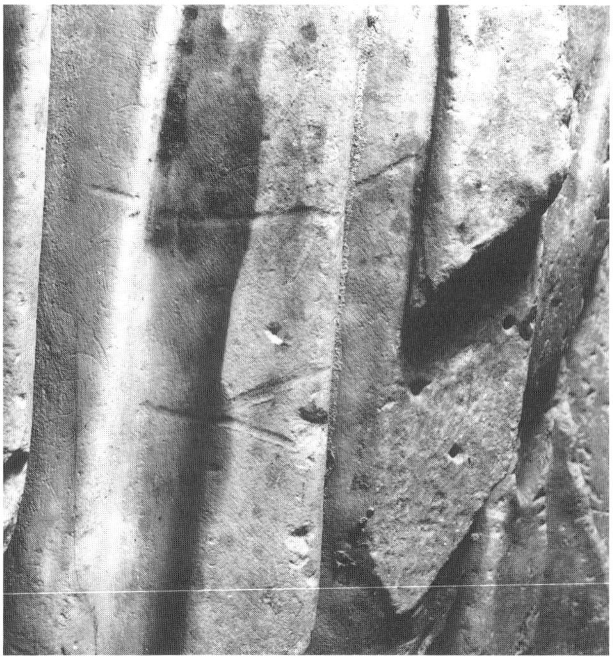

Fig. 11. Piraeus Museum 3776. Detail. Photo C. Mauzy.

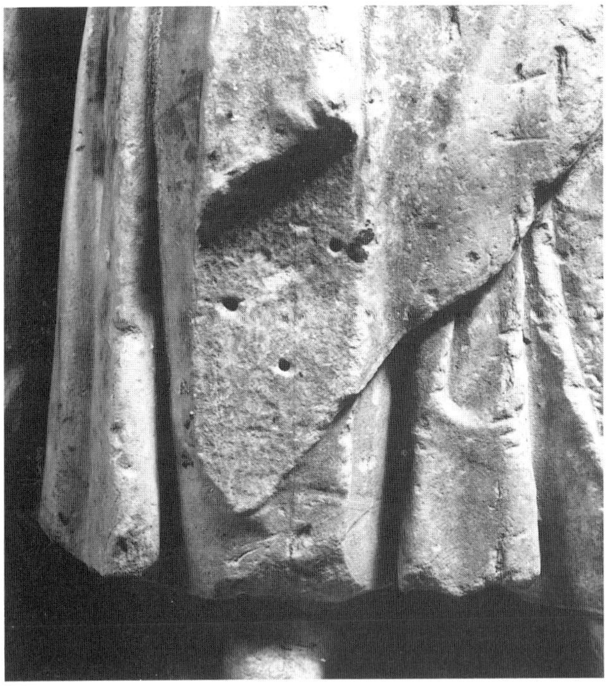

Fig. 10. Piraeus Museum 3776. Detail of chlamys join. Photo C. Mauzy.

The fact that the honorand sports a long beard whereas Macedonians tended to be clean shaven from Alexander onward,[38] may point either to someone of Philip II's generation, who had not joined Alexander's expedition, or to someone of rather advanced age.

Antipater is a possible candidate : he was sent to Athens, along with Alexander, by Philip II to negotiate the peace after the battle of Chaironeia in 338 and was awarded a *proxeny* as well as Athenian citizenship.[39] A second possibility is that the honorand on the relief Fig. 17 is none other than Asander himself, in which case the Acropolis relief once decorated the top of *IG* II^2 450. Both are of Pentelic marble, of identical width and thickness. Unfortunately, not only is the bottom of the relief broken off but the decree itself survives in two non-joining fragments. The bottom fragment is now in the British School at Athens, while the top is in the British Museum, being part of the Elgin collection. The rear of the British Museum fragment was sawn off to reduce its weight and less than half the thickness survives (0.06 m). What remains of the top shows that it was smoothed with a claw chisel in preparation for a join (Fig. 18). If a relief was added here, it would have been secured in place with dowels or a tenon but since most of the rear of the stele was removed, the cuttings presumably disappeared. The composite stele would thus have been about two meters high. The fact that the direction of the point marks on the rear of Acropolis Museum 3006 does not match that on the rear of the British School fragment is no obstacle since the relief was carved separately. More problematic is the fact that the extant inscription is complete at the top: composite stelai tended to include the preamble and indeed part of the inscription in the upper half, along with the relief. Record reliefs and their decrees were of course normally carved in one piece except in cases of very high monuments. A good case in point is another stele from the Acropolis, originally over two meters high. It also dates from the period of Macedonian domination, in 294, and honours Herodoros, a friend of Poliorketes, with favours similar to those offered to Asander, including a bronze statue in the Agora.[40]

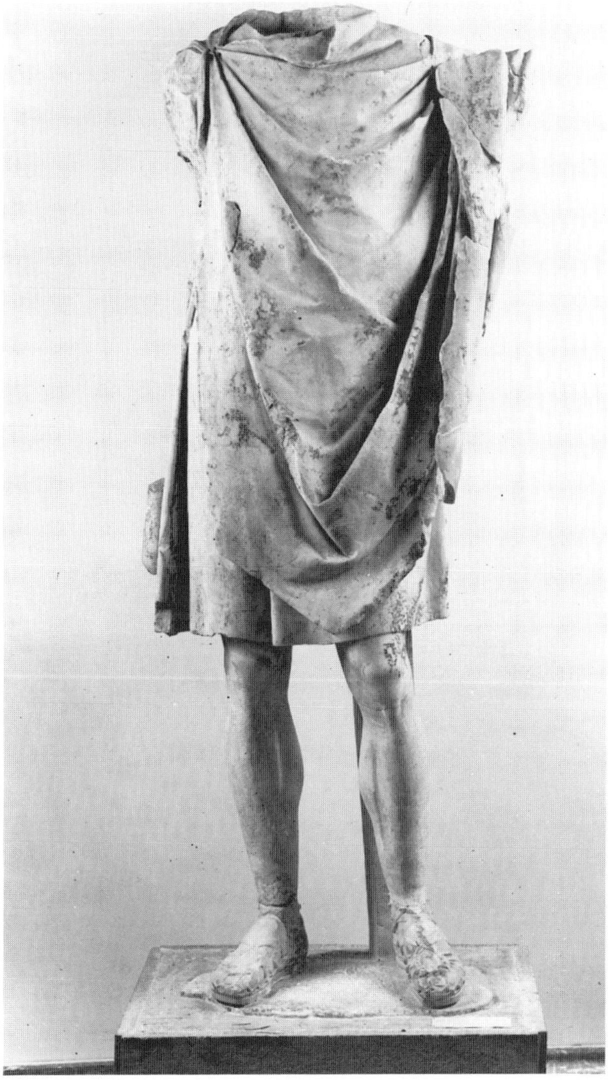

Fig. 12. Aknonios. Delphi Museum 1827+1922γ. Photo École Française d' Athènes.

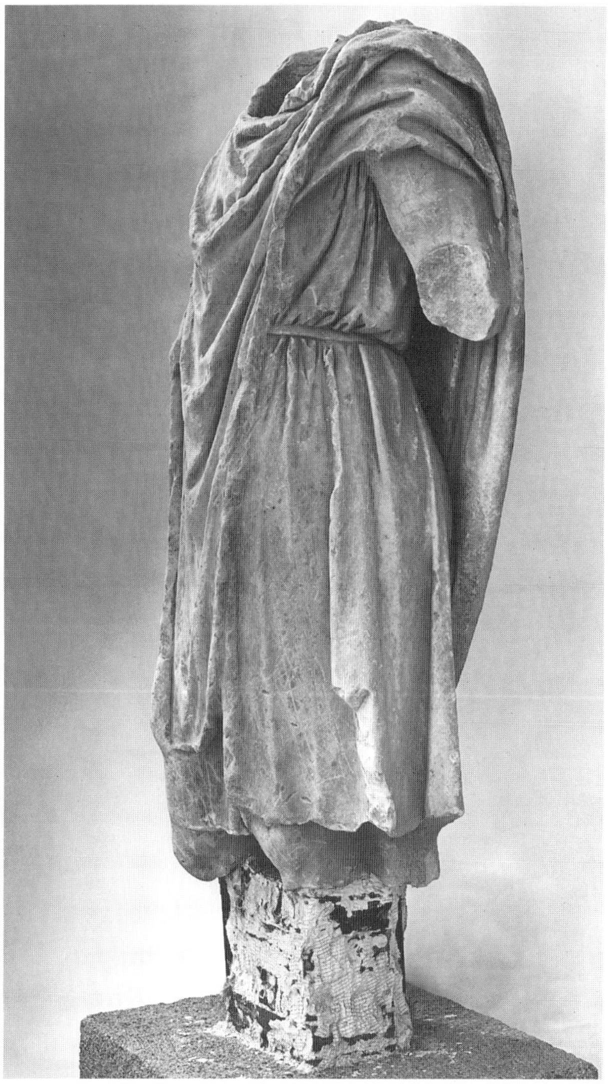

Fig. 13. Chalkis Museum 10. Photo DAI Athens, Chalkis 149.

Even more extravagant were the honours voted to Antigonos the One-Eyed and his son Demetrios Poliorketes after their "liberation" of Athens in 307; amongst other things, their golden statues in a chariot were to be set up next to the Tyrannicides acknowledging that they too were saviours of the city.[41] In addition, the fragments of a gilded bronze horseman recovered from a well in the Athenian Agora are associated with Demetrios' equestrian statue erected next to the statue of Democracy between 305 and 301.[42]

We are still left in the dark about the marble statue of a Macedonian in Piraeus which seems moreover to have a "double" in Chalkis. This is hardly surprising in view of the function of both Piraeus and Chalkis as Macedonian strongholds. The existence of two very similar marble portrait statues in a sea of bronzes may indicate that they were echoes of a bronze prototype or two related ones, presumably standing in Macedonia. They must have portrayed a king or an individual with kingly aspirations who advertised them in Athens. The earliest candidate that comes to mind is Cassander, who controlled Athens between 317 and 307. According to Diodoros (19.52.1–2), in 316 Cassander was sufficiently in control of Macedonia to aspire after its crown. He married Alexander's half-sister, Thessaloniki, to establish a claim to the throne, and founded a city naming it Cassandreia after himself, being moreover the first Successor to emulate Alexander in this. In the same year he hired Lysippos to design an amphora for the wine produced in the area of his new city.[43] After his successful portrayal of Alexander which turned him into something approaching a court sculptor of Macedon,[44] Lysippos seems to have been employed by aspirants to the Macedonian throne, beginning with Cassander's brother-in-law, Krateros.[45] In 322 Krateros commissioned from him the bronze group of Alexander's hunt at Delphi to advertise his dynastic claim.[46] Cassander may have met Lysippos through Krateros or during his Peloponnesian campaign in 317 when he may have held Sikyon briefly, though nothing is attested in the sources.[47] One would expect Lysippos' services to Cassander to

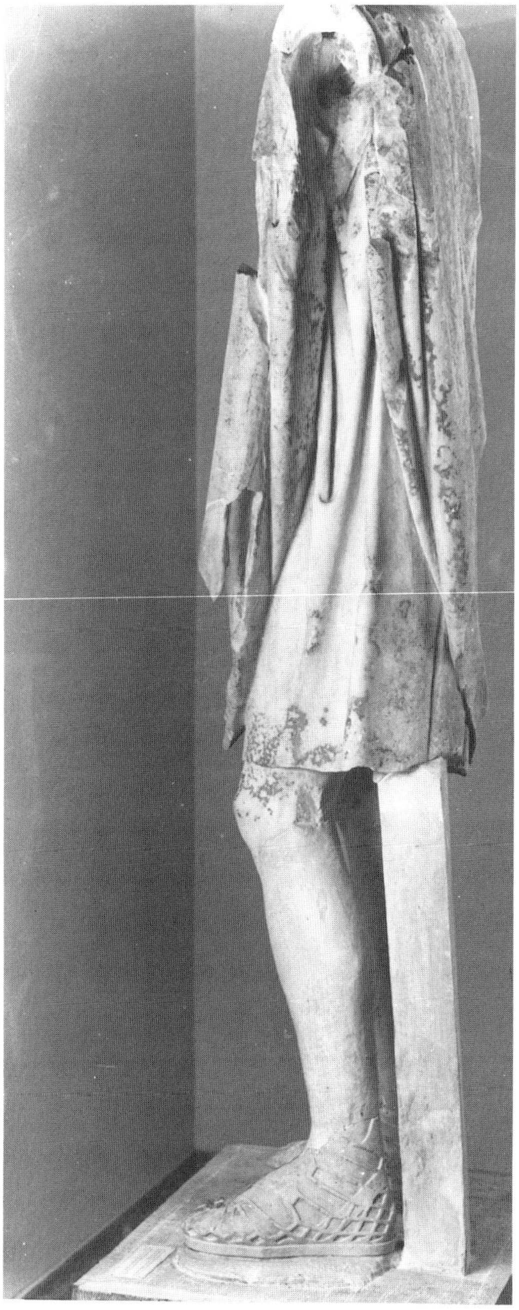

Fig. 14. Aknonios. Delphi Museum 1827+1922γ. Photo École Française d' Athènes.

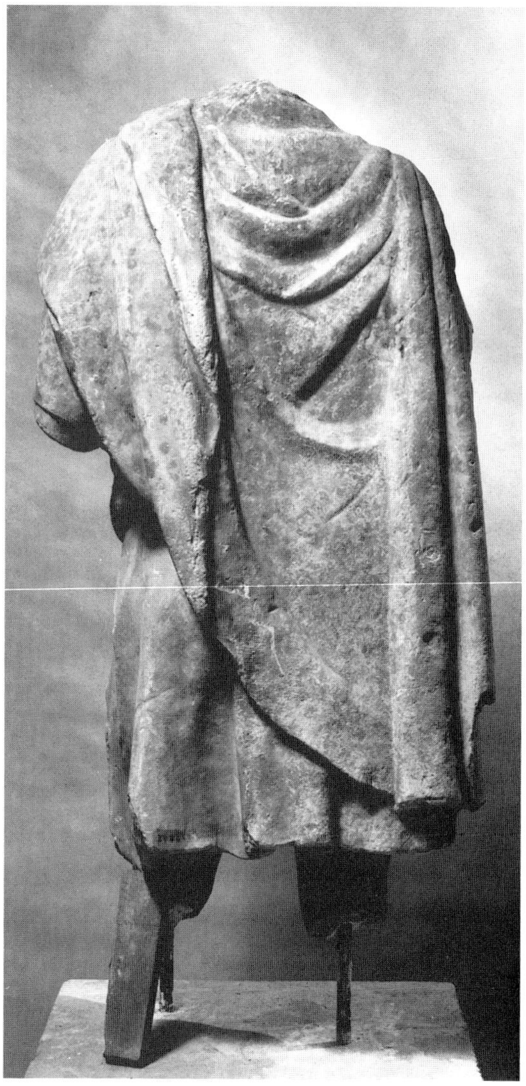

Fig. 15. Piraeus Museum 3776. Photo C. Mauzy.

have extended beyond a mere amphora design. A royal portrait seems quite in order here, and Lysippos could easily have invented one of the earliest body types of a Macedonian royal portrait donning the purple Macedonian chiton and chlamys.

Two possible royal portraits of Cassander are attested. The first is known from a statue base dedicated by Cassander himself as king of the Macedonians in the sanctuary of Olympian Zeus at Dion.[48] The statue was probably of bronze and could have represented either Cassander himself or Zeus. Cassander did not assume the title "King of the Macedonians" until 305/4, which gives a *terminus post quem* for the statue.[49] The second possible portrait stood beyond the Macedonian borders and was part of a group in Larissa viewed by Pyrrhos, king of Epirus.[50] Cassander was placed next to statues of Philip, Alexander, Perdikkas[51] and "other kings". Regardless of which Perdikkas is meant here or even which Philip (II or III), Cassander is clearly portrayed in the midst of an Argead group portrait.[52] We are entering the realm of speculation, but let us assume for the moment a single dedicant for the group. Unless it was set up by one of Cassander's sons immediately upon his death, it is not easy to find a historical explanation for its commission other than an attempt at gaining legitimacy by Cassander himself. Despite Cassander's well-known aversion to Alexander,[53] he is said to have commissioned Philoxenos of Eretria to paint a battle piece of Alexander and Dareios, and this too could have formed part of his dynastic propaganda after he assumed control of Macedonia.[54]

The close relation of the Piraeus statue to the Agias

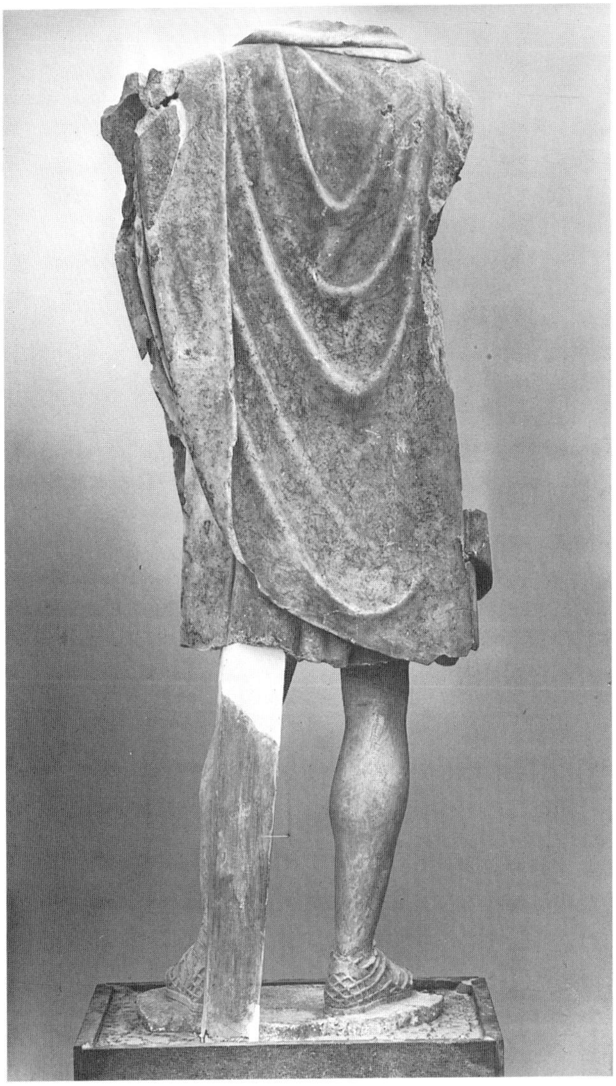

Fig. 16. Aknonios. Delphi Museum. Photo École Française d' Athènes.

has already raised the question of its pertinence to the workshop of Lysippos. The contrast between an "open" and a "closed" side are also signs of a Peloponnesian workshop in the Polykleitan tradition. But what would Lysippos' work be doing in Athens, a city with a strong sculptural tradition of its own? His presence there could be readily explained by his association with the Macedonians. His bronze statue of Sokrates in the Pompeion[55] has been ingeniously ascribed to the patronage of Demetrios of Phaleron who was an admirer of Sokrates.[56] The political climate of his oligarchic regime would certainly be better suited for such a commission. Lysippos is also credited with a bronze Satyr in Athens, possibly a choregic monument, which should be dated after Demetrios' abolition of festival liturgies ca. 316.[57] Perhaps a date ca. 316 would be convenient for Lysippos' activity in Athens. There is a dearth of Athenian sculpture from that period. The years of crisis must have taken their toll on public monuments. We have already mentioned the bronze portrait of Asander set up by himself in 313.[58] Two record reliefs from the archonship of Theophrastos which were tentatively ascribed to 313/2, have recently been shown to belong to 340/39.[59] The only securely dated record relief of this period honours Euphron of Sikyon during the brief democratic interval of 318.[60] Although Euphron's unstable stance is somewhat comparable to the Piraeus torso, the linear draperies of Athena and Demos are a far cry from the realism of our statue. One need only look at the early third-century portrait of Menander by the sons of Praxiteles as reconstructed by Klaus Fittschen to realise that the course of Athenian sculpture was set in quite a different direction.[61] Even though Menander's Macedonian sympathies are flaunted in public by his clean shaven face, the affected elegance of his pose and the subordination of the drapery to his body belong to the Classical tradition of the Attic School.

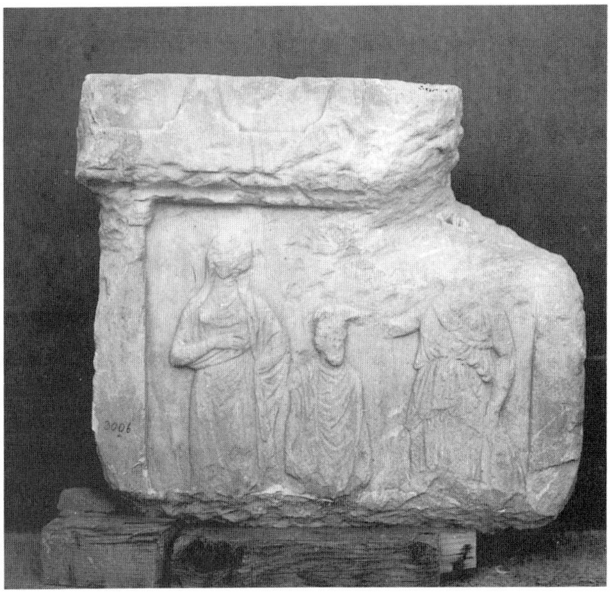

Fig. 17. Document relief. From the Acropolis. Acropolis Museum 3006. Photo Acropolis Museum.

Acknowledgements

I am most grateful to Eleni Konsolaki for granting the publication rights to Piraeus Museum 3776; to Giorgos Steinhauer and Melpo Axioti of the Second Ephoreia of Antiquities for providing every facility for its study; to Ismene Trianti for facilitating access to the relief Acropolis Museum 3006; and to Dyfri Williams and Richard Tomlinson for facilitating access to the two fragments of IG *II² 450 in the British Museum and the British School at Athens respectively. I am also indebted to Peter Green for historical information. My warmest thanks to Brian Bosworth for answering endless questions about Cassander and his fellows, as well as reading a draft of this paper and making useful comments. All mistakes are my own.*

All dates are B.C.

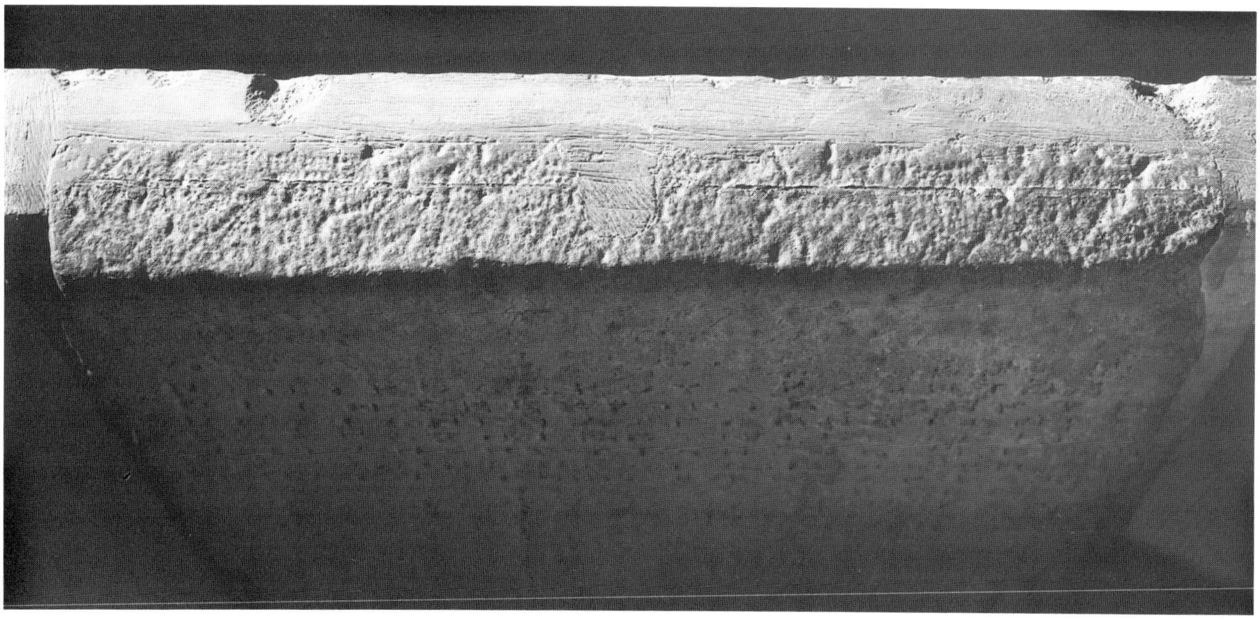

Fig. 18. IG *II^2 450 (top). British Museum 1816.6–10.187. Photo courtesy of the Trustees of the British Museum.*

Notes

1. Missing: head and neck, forearms and hands, lower legs and feet. Extant height, 1.21 m. Height from right shoulder to knee, 1.12 m. Height of left thigh, 0.45 m. Estimated original height, ca. 1.97–2.00 m.
2. The cavity was hollowed out with a point. Its bottom now measures 0.16 x 0.185 m.
3. Each dowel hole measures 0.28 x 0.2 m. The bottom dowel is now filled with dirt. The join measures 0.15 x 0.115 m.
4. O. Palagia, in *Marbres helléniques, de la carrière au chef-d'oeuvre* (exhib. cat. 1987) 82, fig. 6.
5. Compare Plut. *Al.* 26.5, on the city plan of Alexandria: "κυκλοτερῆ κόλπον ἦγον, οὗ τὴν ἐντὸς περιφέρειαν εὐθεῖαι βάσεις ὥσπερ ἀπὸ κρασπέδων το σχῆμα χλαμύδος ὑπελάμβανον..." Cf. also Pliny *NH* 5.62; Arr. *Anab.* 7.9.2. The Macedonian costume in general is discussed, with further examples, by C.Saatsoglou-Paliadeli, *JHS* 113, 1993, 143–146. The Thessalian chlamys is of similar thick fabric but lacks the semi-circular shape : ead. in *Alessandro Magno. Storia e mito* (exhib. cat. 1995) 113–114.
6. Saatsoglou-Paliadeli (1993, supra n. 5) 144, pl. 2a.
7. Ph.M. Petsas, *'Ο τάφος τῶν Λευκαδίων* (1966) 124–129, pls. 6 and Z.
8. Reported in the Athens press: *Kathimerini*, February 5 and July 23, 1995.
9. Athen. 12.537, "τὰ μὲν ἄλλα σχεδὸν καὶ καθ' ἑκάστην ἡμέραν χλαμύδα τε πορφυρᾶν καὶ χιτῶνα μεσόλευκον καὶ καυσίαν ἔχουσαν τὸ διάδημα τὸ βασιλικόν..."
10. Athen. 5.215, "τύραννος ἦν, πορφυροῦν μὲν μεσόλευκον χιτῶνα ἐνδεδυκώς, χλαμύδα δὲ ἐφεστρίδα περιβεβλημένος πολυτελῆ ..." This Lysias may be identical with the personage in *OGIS* 272 and 277, *RE* 13b (1927) s.v. Lysias (8).
11. Naples, National Museum 6149. M.R. Wojcik, *La villa dei papiri ad Ercolano* (1986) 52–53, B 1, pl. 30; R.R.R. Smith, *Hellenistic Royal Portraits* (1988) cat. no. 4, pls. 4–5.
12. Naples, National Museum 6148. Wojcik (supra n. 11) 60–61, B 7, pl. 36; Smith (supra n. 11) cat. no. 22, pl. 17.
13. Naples, National Museum 6151. Wojcik (supra n. 11) 54–55, B 3, pl. 32; Smith (supra n. 11) cat. no. 7, pl. 8.
14. H. Kyrieleis, *Bildnisse der Ptolemäer* (1975) 42–43, pl. 30,1 (Ptolemy IV); 52, pl. 40,1 (Ptolemy V).
15. Chalkis Museum 10. Extant height, 1.23 m. T. Dohrn, *AntPl* 8, 1968, 46, pls. 36a–b; 37a–b.
16. Delphi Museum 1827+1922γ. Pentelic marble. Extant height, 1.80 m; estimated original height, 2.05–2.10 m. Dohrn (supra n. 15) 36–38, figs. 6–7, pls. 26–28; *Guide de Delphes. Le musée* (1991) 93, fig. 56.
17. Delphi Museum. For the Monument see Dohrn (supra n. 15) 33–53, pls. 10–35; J.Pouilloux, *FdD* II, *La Région nord du sanctuaire* (1960) 67–78; id., *FdD* III,4, *Les Inscriptions de la terrasse du temple et de la région nord du sanctuaire* (1976) 134–138, no. 460; P. Moreno, *Vita e arte di Lisippo* (1987) 34–43; B.S. Ridgway, *Hellenistic Sculpture* I (1990) 46–50; *Guide de Delphes. Le musée* 91–98 (with further bibliography); Moreno (ed.), *Lisippo, l'arte e la fortuna* (1995) 81–85. See also here, p. 64.
18. The dedicatory inscription names Daochos II both tetrarch of the Thessalians and *hieromnemon* at Delphi. Daochos owed his appointment at Delphi to Philip II. For the date of the Monument, see Pouilloux, *FdD* III,4 (supra n. 17) 136. A discordant note was struck by S.Lattimore, *AJA* 79, 1975, 87–88, lowering the date to ca. 300.
19. Delphi Museum 1828+1922α. Pentelic marble. Dohrn (supra n. 15) 38–39, figs. 8–9, pl. 29.
20. Delphi Museum 1828+1922β. Pentelic marble. Dohrn (supra n. 15) figs. 10–11.
21. On Daochos II's close relations with Philip II see now B. Helly, *L'état thessalien* (1995) 63.
22. Both arms were made separately, and so were the head and neck.
23. E. Preuner, *Ein delphisches Weihgeschenk* (1900) 39–47; J. Marcadé, *Recueil des signatures de sculpteurs grecs*

I (1953) 68; Moreno, *Vita e arte di Lisippo* 34–43; id. (ed.), *Lisippo, l'arte e la fortuna* 81–82; *Guide de Delphes. Le musée* (supra n. 17).

24. Not much can be made of the fact that the number of Agias' Pythian victories, erroneously given as five on the Pharsalos base, was corrected to three on the Delphi base. *IG* IX,2 249; L. Moretti, *Iscrizioni agonistiche greche* (1957) no. 29; Marcadé (supra n. 23); W. Spoerri, in D. Knoepfler (ed.), *Comptes et inventaires dans la cité grecque* (1988) 139–140.

25. Ridgway (supra n. 17) 32; Ch.W. Clairmont, *Classical Attic Tombstones* (Kilchberg 1993) Intr. vol. 59, fig. 25.

26. Disputed by S. Adam, *The Technique of Greek Sculpture* (1966) 99, who thought that the competent carving should exclude the possibility of workshop copies. This by no means follows. See also Ridgway (supra n. 17). Sisyphos II (Delphi Museum 1551+1435+11785), bearing no relation to Lysippos' style and evidently not copying a bronze, is often used against the idea that the Daochos statues are copies. I hope to be able to demonstrate elsewhere (O. Palagia and N. Herz , "Investigation of Marbles at Delphi," forthcoming in the Acts of ASMOSIA V) that this statue was wrongly attributed to the Daochos Monument. The fact that it is of Parian marble while the rest of the statues are Pentelic also militates against the association. Its pertinence is also questioned by Ridgway (supra n. 17).

27. Delphi Museum 1921+1953. Pentelic marble. Dohrn (supra n. 15) 39–40, pl. 30.

28. Delphi Museum 1875. Pentelic marble. Height, 1.97 m. Dohrn (supra n. 15) 34–35, pls. 10–20; C.M. Edwards, in O. Palagia and J.J. Pollitt (edd.), *Personal Styles in Greek Sculpture*, *YaleClSt* 30 (1996) 135–137, fig. 72.

29. Athens National Museum 870. Adam (supra n. 26) 117–120, pls. 64a and 66c; Clairmont (supra n. 25) III, 397–398, no. 3.461.

30. Diod. 18.18.6 and 18.48.1; Plut. *Phok.* 28. W.S. Ferguson, *Hellenistic Athens* (1911) 20–21; L.A. Tritle, *Phocion the Good* (1988) 130; C. Habicht, *Athen. Die geschichte der Stadt in hellenistischer Zeit* (1995) 51.

31. Diod. 18.74.3. Ferguson (supra n. 30) 36–37; A.B. Bosworth, *Chiron* 22, 1992, 71; id., *CQ* 44, 1994, 63 and n. 48; Habicht (supra n. 30) 61–62.

32. Diod. 20.45; Ferguson (supra n. 30) 63–64; Habicht (supra n. 30) 74–75.

33. In 335, after the Theban revolt: Arr. *Anab.* 2.2.4.

34. Diod. 19.35.3–4 and 77.4–6. See also Plut. *Demetr.* 23-27.

35. Cic. *Leg.* 2.26.66. Ferguson (supra n. 30) 43 suggested 316/5. See also R.H.W. Stichel, *AA* 107, 1992, 433; Habicht (supra n. 30) 65. See also Grosman in this volume, pp. 75; 80 nn. 4–5.

36. Width, 0.52 m; thickness, 0.15 m. Height of top fragment, 0.648 m, of bottom fragment, 0.525 m. A substantial part of the document is missing. *IG* II^2 450. *SEG* XXXI 271. A. Wilhelm, *BSA* 7, 1900/01, 156–162, fig. 53; J.R. Ellis, *BSA* 63, 1968, 229. Asander's identity is a vexed question. See A.B. Bosworth, *A Historical Commentary on Arrian's History of Alexander* 1 (1980) 130; M.J. Osborne, *Naturalization in Athens* 2 (1982) 113–115, D 42; W. Heckel, *The Marshals of Alexander's Empire* (1992) 385; Bosworth, *ClQ* 43, 1993, 421–422; Habicht (supra n. 30) 71–72.

37. Width, 0.52; thickness, 0.15 m; height, 0.53 m. O. Walter, *Beschreibung der Reliefs im kleinen Akropolismuseum in Athen* (1923) 12–13, no. 12; *LIMC* III (1986) s.v. Boule no. 13 (V. Komninos); M. Meyer, *Die griechischen Urkundenreliefs* (1989) 281, cat. A 55, pl. 18,2; C.L. Lawton, *Attic Document Reliefs* (1995) cat. no. 140.

38. Alexander is said to have ordered his army to shave so as not to give the enemy a beard to pull: Athen. 13.564. For the other sources see Jacoby, *FGrHist* IID 504

39. Hyp. frg. 19.2. Heckel (supra n. 36) 40.

40. Acropolis Museum 4063+2307. Restored height, 2.22 m. *IG* II^2 646. *SEG* XXXI.88 and 271. Walter (supra n. 37) 8–9, no. 9; Meyer (supra n.37) 312, A 169, pl. 45,2; Lawton, *Hesperia* 61, 1992, 241, pl. 62b–d; Lawton (supra n. 37) 109–110, no. 59, pl. 31. Lawton, *Hesperia* 61, 1992, 239–251 discusses all extant examples of composite stelai.

41. Diod. 20.46.2. R.E. Wycherley, *Literary and Epigraphical Testimonia*, *Agora* III (1957) no. 264.

42. Demetrios decree, Epigraphical Museum 12749, Wycherley (supra n. 41) no. 696; O. Palagia, *Hesperia* 51, 1982, 112 and n. 82. Gilded statue of horseman in the Agora : T.L. Shear, Jr., *Hesperia* 42, 1973, 165–168, pl. 36; C. Houser in B. Barr-Sharrar and E.N. Borza (edd.), *Macedonia and Greece in Late Classical and Early Hellenistic Times*, National Gallery of Art, Washington, DC, *Studies in the History of Art* 10 (1982) 230–238, figs. 3–7;9; J.M. Camp, *The Athenian Agora* (1986) 164, fig. 138; C.C. Mattusch, *Classical Bronzes. The Art and Craft of Greek and Roman Statuary* (1996) 125–129, fig. 4,11.

43. Athen. 11.784.

44. A. Stewart, *Faces of Power* (1993) 72–78 and *passim*; Moreno (ed.), *Lisippo, l'arte e la fortuna* 63–67; 148–171; 331–346.

45. Krateros married Phila, Antipater's daughter, in 322: Diod. 18.18.7.

46. *FdD* III,4.2 no. 137; L. Moretti, *Iscrizioni storiche ellenistiche* 2 (1975) no. 73; Stewart (supra n. 44) 270–277; 390–392 T 108–111; Moreno (supra n. 44) 172–175. See also Marszal in this volume, p. 124 n. 15.

47. For Cassander's siege of Tegea see Diod. 19.35.1. On Cassander's Peloponnesian campaign of 317 : Bosworth, *Chiron* 22, 1992, 71–72.

48. Dion Museum 5443. Βασιλεὺς Μακεδό[νων]/ Κάσσανδρος Ἀντιπ[άτρου] / Δὶι Ὀλυμπίῳ. Height, 0.48 m, width, 0.74 m, depth, 0.85 m. *SEG* XXXIV 620. D.Pantermalis, in *Πρακτικά Η΄ διεθνούς συνεδρίου ελληνικής και λατινικής επιγραφικής* 1 (1984) 271–272, fig. 1.

49. Diod. 20.53.4; Plut. *Demetr.* 18.2. *CAH*^{2} VII,1, 58.

50. Lucian, *Adversus indoctum* 21.

51. Stewart (supra n. 44) 411 suggests that he was the founder of the Argead line.

52. In a paper entitled "Hephaestion's Pyre and the Royal Hunt of Alexander" to be published in the Acts of the conference *Alexander the Great: History and Romance*, edited by A.B. Bosworth, I argue that the Larissa statues formed a hunting group comprising Alexander the Great, Philip III Arrhidaios, Perdikkas the Bodyguard, Cassander and other Successors.

53. *Cf.* Plut. *Al.* 74 and *Demetr.* 37. R.M. Errington, in *Alexandre le Grand, Entretiens Hardt* 22 (1975), 151–152; 164; A.B. Bosworth, *Commentary on Arrian's History of Alexander* 2 (1995) 87.
54. Pliny, *NH* 35.100. Stewart (supra n. 44) 130–150 and 431, col. pls. 4–6 discusses the possible relation of this painting to the Alexander Mosaic from Pompeii, Naples 10020. He also offers an alternative dating of Philoxenos' picture to 334–324, soon after the battle and before Cassander's traumatic encounter with Alexander in Babylon in 323.
55. Diog. Laert. 2.43. Edwards (supra n. 28) 143–145. *Contra* the attribution to Lysippos : E.Voutiras, *AM* 109, 1994, 134–161.
56. Diog. Laert. 5.81. Suggested by Moreno, *Vita e arte di Lisippo* 192–198; id., *Scultura ellenistica* (1994) 31–35; id. (ed.), *Lisippo, l'arte e la fortuna* 256–265. Since Sokrates was perceived as an enemy of the Athenian democracy, it is reasonable to suppose that his statue was erected after its fall. Zanker's suggestion that it was part of the Lykourgan programme of civic renewal of the 330s is not supported by the evidence : P. Zanker, *The Mask of Socrates* (transl. A. Shapiro, 1995) 58 and n. 30.
57. Pliny *NH* 34.64. See also Moreno (ed.), *Lisippo, l'arte e la fortuna* 251–255. Demetrios of Phaleron's replacement of state festival liturgies with the *agonothesia* stopped the dedication of choregic monuments after 316/315: Ferguson (supra n. 30) 55; A.W. Pickard-Cambridge, *The Dramatic Festivals of Athens*[2] (1968) 91–92; Habicht (supra n. 30) 66. *Agonothetai* were known to dedicate monuments but the earliest documented one dates from 307, presumably after Demetrios' departure : *IG* II[2] 3073; Pickard-Cambridge, *The Dramatic Festivals of Athens*[2] 92 and 120.
58. Supra n. 36.
59. Athens, Epigraphical Museum 13262. *SEG* XXXVI 186; Meyer (supra n. 37) 305, cat. A 141, pl. 44,2; Lawton (supra n. 37) 148, cat. no. 154, pl. 81. St. Petersburg, Hermitage A 1105. *IG* II[2] 1202; *SEG* XXXVI 186; Meyer (supra n. 37) 306, cat. A 140, pl. 44,1; Lawton (supra n. 37) 148–149, cat. no. 155, pl. 82. That the two reliefs are more likely to belong to the archonship of Theophrastos in 340/39 was demonstrated by S.V. Tracy, *Athenian Democracy in Transition: Attic Letter-Cutters of 340 to 290 B.C.* (1995) 96–100, who identified the cutter of *IG* II[2] 1202 with the mason of *IG* II[2] 244 (dated to 338–320). (I am grateful to Kevin Clinton for this reference.)
60. Athens National Museum 1482. *IG* II[2] 448. Meyer (supra n. 37) 303, A 134, pl. 39,1; Lawton (supra n. 37) 107, no. 54, pl. 28.
61. K. Fittschen, *AM* 106, 1991, 243–279, pls. 74–77; Zanker (supra n. 56) 78–83.

The Lysippan Herakles as Vajrapani in Hadda

Katherine A. Schwab

When the discovery of a clay statue of Herakles from Tepe Shutur was reported in 1974, specialists in Buddhist archaeology began to debate its date and representation in a niche within one of several Buddhist shrines and monastic sites at Hadda in Afghanistan.[1] Recent publications by J. Boardman have brought the statue to an audience specializing in Greek art.[2] The statue's resemblance to the Herakles Epitrapezios by Lysippos serves as testimony to the enduring Hellenistic legacy which flourished in Greek Bactria and later south of the Hindu Kush, especially in the region from Begram to Hadda. Coins and the probability of a workshop model may explain how images from the Hellenistic world were reproduced in this fringe area of the Greek East even after the West had become part of the Roman Empire. The choice of representing Vajrapani, the guardian figure of the Buddha, as specifically Herakles Epitrapezios points to an aristocratic patron of Greek descent, probably from Begram, who wished to dedicate an exceptionally lavish assemblage of sculpture during the second century A.D. at one of the most important Buddhist sites for the veneration of relics in the Indian northwest.

A close examination of the head of Herakles not only underscores its Mediterranean origins but the connection to Lysippan representations of the Greek hero (Fig. 1). The thick curly hair and beard, and the deep-set eyes in a face turned to the left are features familiar to all of us. Herakles wears a lionskin, but the placement of the lion's head resting on Herakles' left shoulder is unusual.[3] Where we would expect to find the club, however, we instead see a *vajra*, or adamantine thunderbolt, balanced on his sharply bent right leg. Additionally, Herakles is dwarfed by the large robed arm of a seated figure.

In a view of the niche prior to restoration it is quite apparent that the other figures are Buddhist monks and Bodhisattvas surrounding the large central figure of the Buddha seated in a pose of meditation (Fig. 2). I know of no other example from Central Asia in which such a distinctly Greek-looking image is placed explicitly next to the Buddha to function in a dual role. Herakles is both the Greek hero and Vajrapani, a tree spirit that evolved into a guardian figure for the Buddha. Early images of Vajrapani show a pot-bellied man wearing a turban and jewelry. Only at Tepe Shutur do we see the Buddhist Vajrapani virtually transformed into the purely Greek Herakles. Much has been written about Vajrapani and his fusion with Herakles in Central Asia, especially by E. Lamotte, F. Flood and M. Carter, and the two figures reflect an assimilation that was particularly successful in Gandharan Buddhist art during the Kushana period.[4] In Gandharan art Greco-Roman visual language and iconography were adopted by the Kushan Dynasty in the northwest region of their empire as a vehicle to express their dynastic origins. Classical Mediterranean imagery had previously flourished in this region; thus, such usage was all the more effective to legitimate the Kushan dynasty.[5]

Portraiture is one of the features that the Kushan Dynasty, the rulers of Gandhara in northwest India, adapted from Greek Hellenistic and Roman Imperial art for their own needs.[6] The Kushans, a semi-nomadic people, had not developed an artistic legacy of their own; thus the prevailing styles in Central Asia – Indo-Greek, Indo-Afghan, Parthian and Indian – were fused together for Buddhism, the religion they had adopted and promoted. Oddly enough, the preference for the Indian tradition remains the dominant style in the southeast region of the Kushan Empire, especially around Mathura.[7] It is all the more curious since the east coast of India had extensive trade contact with Roman ship merchants. In other words, contact with the west did not substantially influence or alter the Mathura tradition.

In the northwest region of the Kushan Empire, however, in Gandhara and west of the Khyber Pass, the visual languages of Greece, especially from the Hellenistic period, and also of Rome are widely used.[8] Characteristically, the relaxed stance, the more fully developed anatomy, the drapery that falls in a rich array of folds, and an emphasis on physical beauty are all features that reveal a decided taste and preference for the Greco-Roman tradition.

Gandharan art strongly reflects Hellenistic as well as Roman sculpture of the first and second centuries. Among

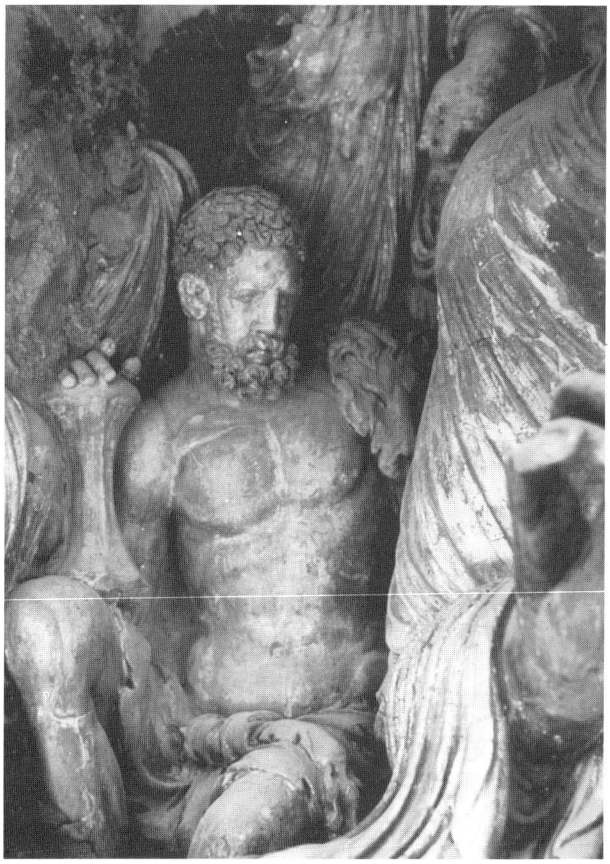

Fig. 1. Herakles Vajrapani in niche V 2, Tepe Shutur, Hadda. Photo courtesy F. Tissot.

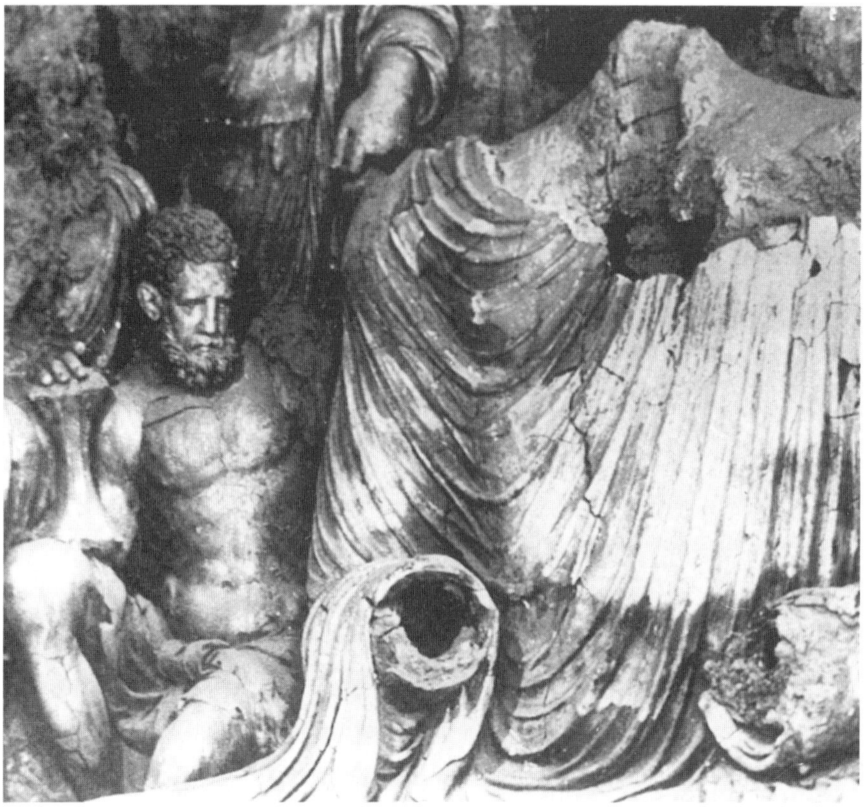

Fig. 2. Herakles Vajrapani, Hadda, before restoration. Photo after M.L. Carter, Proceedings of the Second European Conference of Iranian Studies *(1995) pl. 19,2.*

the best examples is the well known marble head of a Bodhisattva of the second or third century, in the Ortiz Collection, featured on the cover of Boardman's *The Diffusion of Classical Antiquity*.[9] The excellent carving and stone material may point to a western artist working for an eastern buyer.[10]

The Kushan Empire in India included two large clusters of cities – the southeast region with Mathura as the center, and the northwest region of Gandhara with Peshawar and later Taxila as the center. Equally important are the two river systems, the Indus and the Ganges, which linked the interior regions with trade routes to the east and to the west. The mountainous terrain further defined the region – Hadda is located approximately 9 km. south of Jalalabad, which is south of the Hindu Kush (and therefore Bactria) and it is to the west of the Khyber Pass, the Peshawar Valley and Taxila in Gandhara (Fig. 3).

Hadda, which means 'market,' centered around the purported relic of the ushnisha, or bony protuberance on top of the Buddha's head.[11] The presence of the ushnisha relic, which was kept in a large stupa or dome-like structure, brought large numbers of monks and pilgrims to Hadda, thus prompting the establishment of over thirty sacred sites – shrines and monasteries. Located approximately halfway between Peshawar in Gandhara and Begram in Kapisa on the Silk Road to the West, Hadda was well situated for both trade and travelers.

Tepe Shutur, where the figure of Herakles was found, is one of the northern monastic centers at Hadda. Initially, it began as a meditation cave in a hillside facing southwest toward the Great Stupa. The monastery developed above the cave, up on the hill. Excavations reveal a large monastic complex adjacent to a sanctuary containing a stupa, surrounded by 64 niches each with individual altars filled with sculptures of the Buddha and attending figures. The Herakles Vajrapani is located in niche V 2, the only niche with Greek figures adapted for the Buddhist monastic complex. The other niches were filled exclusively with Buddhist figures including a meditating Buddha flanked by monks, donors and Bodhisattvas – saints well advanced on the Path to Nirvana.

Representations of Herakles in Central Asia are well documented.[12] While some examples were locally made, others were imported from the west especially from Alexandria, such as the statuette of Serapis-Herakles from Begram, northwest of Hadda.[13] Greek traders had preceded Alexander the Great in Central Asia, but the greatest cultural impact was precipitated by his campaigns and penetration into the Punjab region. Alexander as Herakles, well known from coins, remained a popular image in the east, thus the link between ruler and hero flourished in the northwest of Central Asia long after Alexander's death.

In 1962 D. Ingalls suggested that the form and name of Lakuliśa – the mythic founder of a sect of Shivism whose name in Sanskrit means "Lord who has a club" – were taken from Herakles. The name is linguistically

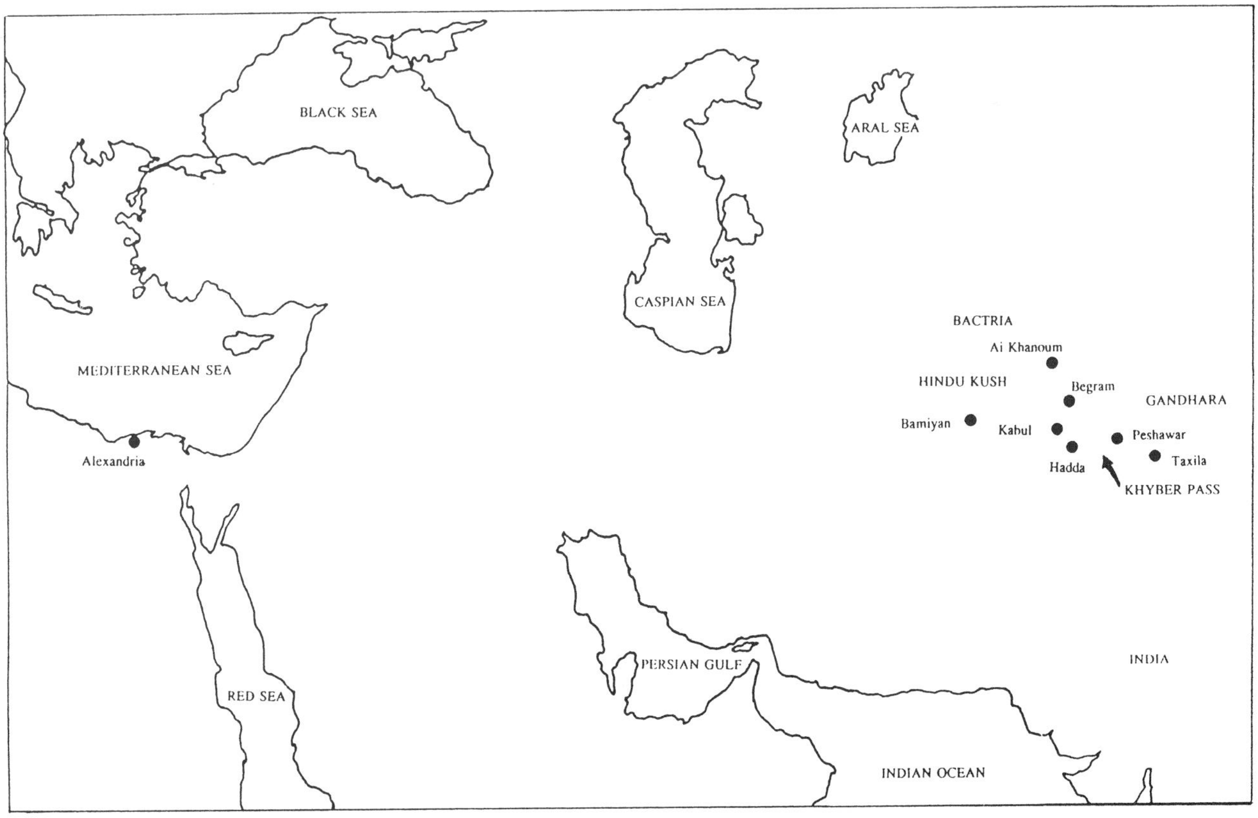

Fig. 3. Map of western and central Asia. Adapted from Errington and Cribbs, Crossroads, *3,5.*

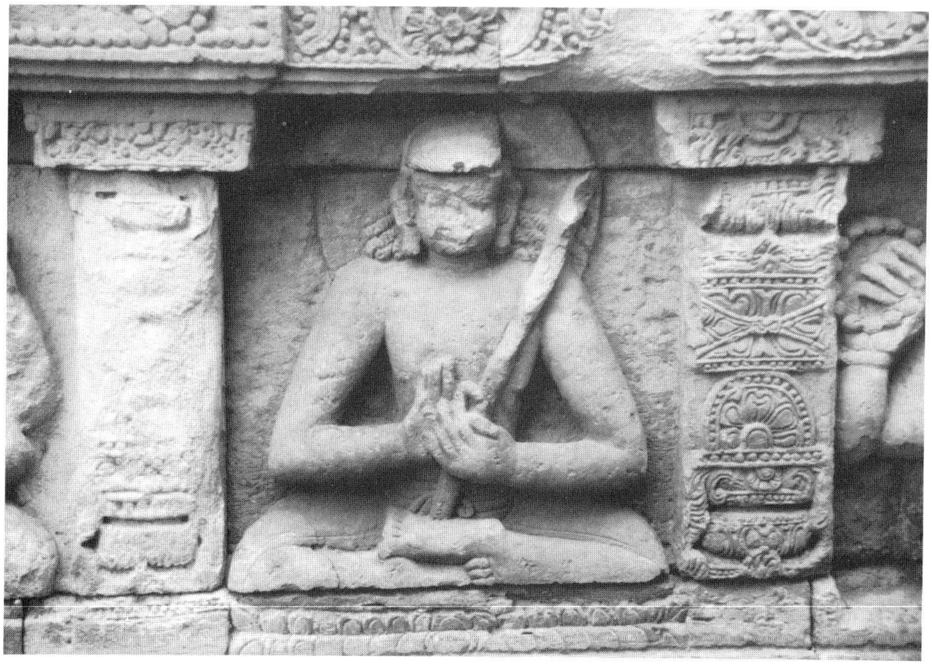

Fig. 4. Relief of Lakuliśa, seventh century A.D., north wall of the Parasuramesvara Temple, Bhubaneswar, Orissa. Photo source: R.M. Davidson.

almost identical with Herakles, and Ingalls' proposal is highly suggestive and perhaps merits renewed study.[14] If his analysis is correct, the popularity and exceptionally enduring quality of Herakles are reflected in a seventh-century stone relief of Lakuliśa from the capital of Orissa, in southeastern India (Fig. 4).

In Greek Bactria, north of the Hindu Kush, King Euthydemos I, who ruled from 230–200 B.C., included a representation of Herakles Epitrapezios on the reverse of his silver tetradrachm.[15] Herakles balances the club on his right knee while sitting on his lionskin which covers a rock. The choice of this particular image of Herakles which reflects a statue by Lysippos, suggests that the image had achieved a level of fame which would be recognized in Greek Bactria during the Hellenistic period.[16] Even prior to Lysippos, the image of a bearded Herakles seated on a lionskin, propping his club up on his right leg, was known by the late fifth century B.C., as on an Attic red-figured pelike from Athens, attributed to the Herakles Painter, formerly in Berlin but now lost (Fig. 5).[17]

According to E. Bartman, the Lysippan sculpture was invented on a small scale from which small and large replicas were made and enjoyed popularity in both Hellenistic and Roman society.[18] Where these replicas were produced, to meet the demands of the market, remains a difficult question. Martial's description of the statue includes the association of Alexander the Great as owner. Whether or not this is true, the embellished connection to Alexander would not have been lost on later owners. Surely this association was understood and desired by the Bactrian king. The Epitrapezios type appears as well on coins of Nabis in Sparta, 206–197 B.C.[19] Furthermore, a colossal head of Herakles found in Sparta has prompted H.G. Martin to ask if it belongs to a cult statue of Herakles Epitrapezios.[20]

Roman examples of heads of the Epitrapezios type, such as those now in Basel, London and Boston, are mostly large in scale.[21] Unlike the Hadda Herakles, these heads exhibit a broader face – in fact, they exude strength and power. Closer in pose to the Herakles at Hadda is a clay figurine of the first century B.C., from Sinalunga, now in Florence, which shows a wreathed Herakles who positions the club on his right leg, similar to the *vajra*.[22] Equally obvious are the distinctive characteristics of the Hadda example – his longer and more narrow face, the sharper turn of his head toward the meditating Buddha at center, the slender torso, and his compact seated position on a rock in order to fit into the corner of the niche.

Although the Herakles at Hadda reveals a fusion of the familiar and unfamiliar, a comparison with another Herakles-Vajrapani, a Gandharan relief in London, from the second to third century A.D., highlights the standard representation of Vajrapani in Central Asia.[23] Immediately identifiable by his *vajra* or adamantine thunderbolt, he is a partly nude figure, wearing the lionskin tied in front with the lion's head worn as a helmet. Furthermore, this figure sports a moustache, but lacks the luxuriant curls of hair and beard of the Hadda example. The Gandharan relief, with the accompanying Bodhisattvas and monks, emphasizes the Vajrapani aspect, with only the lionskin for evidence of the Greek hero.

In the same niche at Hadda, the excavators found a kneeling female figure, resembling Tyche, holding a large

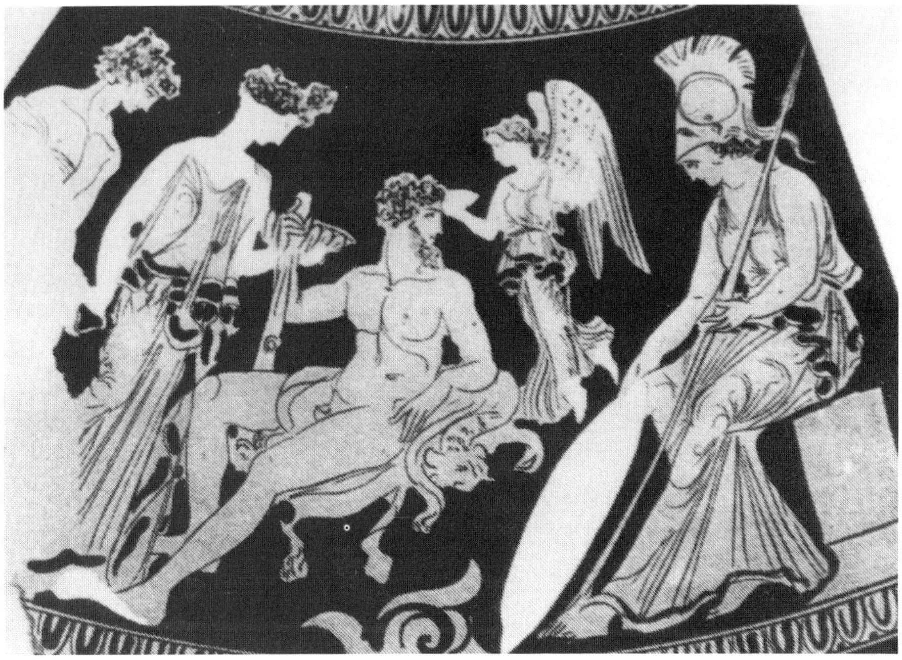

Fig. 5. Attic red-figure pelike, attributed to the Herakles Painter, late fifth century B.C., once Berlin. Photo after LIMC *V (1990) s.v. Herakles, no. 3324.*

cornucopia filled with fruits and grains.[24] The full view of the Tyche shows an unusual fusion of features including the hair of Hellenistic Aphrodites and a pose that is a mirror image of Herakles and which perhaps coincidentally recalls the Crouching Aphrodite from Rhodes.

Tyche was also popular in Central Asia, as attested by a silver cup found in Gandhara and made in the first century B.C. in either Alexandria or Asia Minor, perhaps for an eastern owner.[25] She supports a large horn filled with grapes, pomegranates and ears of corn as she stands in a rustic setting. Tyche is adapted for the Buddhist Hariti, an ogress with a reputation for eating children who was transformed by the Buddha into a guardian of children and as an image of fruitfulness. A third-century Gandharan relief in London shows Hariti, wearing her hair tied up in a bow, and dressed in a long sheer garment with her right shoulder bare.[26] Good fortune has merged with the potential of her fecundity and the protection of children – characteristics we associate with Aphrodite and Artemis.

In niche V 2 at Tepe Shutur, Herakles embodies strength, heroic status and ultimate immortality. Vajrapani represents perpetual protection of the Buddha, by using his *vajra* or diamond thunderbolt which is symbolic of adamantine truth and necessary for conversion. The combined strength and guardianship of Herakles and Vajrapani is especially apt while protecting the Buddha who is vulnerable while in a meditative state. Moreover, Herakles, in his Greek representation, is a supporter of Buddhism and, like Vajrapani who was originally a tree spirit, he is now part of the Buddhist pantheon. From the perspective of the abbot of the monastery, whose permission was essential for this dedication, Herakles as a non-mainstream Indian has been appropriated to represent Vajrapani. In other words, the Greek hero has converted to Buddhism to work for the welfare of all human beings.

The choice to emphasize the Greek Lysippan image of Herakles as the flanking figure over that of the prevailing Gandharan Vajrapani is unique, and it suggests that the donors or patrons of this niche were especially interested in perpetuating the Greek legacy, one which had endured for centuries in that region, first in Bactria, especially at Aï Khanoum, and later south of the Hindu Kush between Begram and Hadda. Although the Greek political power was eventually replaced by the Śakas and Kushans, the Greek artistic legacy, cultural ancestry, economy and language continued to serve those in power.

Stucco was an inexpensive medium, widely used throughout the region due to the scarcity of good carving stone. Faces of figures were made from molds, such as the outstanding fourth century head of a Buddha probably from Hadda and now in London.[27] The back of the head and the hair were shaped separately, and then the entire surface was coated in fine plaster and painted. Heads were usually made separately and inserted with a dowel into the body made of a lesser grade of clay core and plastered surface.[28]

If molds facilitated mass production, then we can assume that a prototype existed. Although rare, M. Taddei has reported on a Hellenistic prototype excavated in a workshop in Swat, north of Gandhara.[29] Tarzi did not find a workshop during his excavation at Hadda; however, he concluded that it must have been an important cultural center following the earlier Greek period.[30] The high quality of the statue of Herakles strongly points to a prototype that must have been in the region, possibly in the Begram vicinity. It may very well have been conveyed as part of the cargo from the Eastern Mediterranean which was sent by ship to both the west and east coasts of India and thus provided a continuous supply of objects and goods for a ready market.[31]

The dates proposed for the figures in this niche range from the early second century to the fourth century, although the early second century date seems increasingly plausible on stylistic grounds. Much more so than in the Mediterranean region, chronology remains a difficult problem in Central Asia at this time due to an absence of indigenous histories or record-keeping outside of a few inscriptions.[32]

Tarzi reported that the fragmentary lower bodies of two donors or patrons and two Bodhisattvas that belonged to niche V 2 were of high quality similar to the representations of Herakles and Tyche. Additionally, he describes an exceptionally fine clay head with ruby eyes as belonging to one of the two Bodhisattvas.[33] Sadly, the current civil war between the mujahideen factions in Afghanistan has resulted in the destruction of Tepe Shutur and its museum. According to reports, the figures in niche V 2 have been destroyed.[34] A fine clay head with garnet eyes from Hadda and now in the South Asian Galleries of the Metropolitan Museum of Art in New York, reflects the quality of the head described by Tarzi. The sculpture serves as a reminder of the exceptional artistic levels achieved at Hadda as a response to the Hellenistic period and a perpetuation of it as sculpture created to honor sacred Buddhist shrines. Equally, it reminds us of what is now lost.

The patrons were surely expecting to receive extraordinary merit for the lavish and unusual clay and stucco figures of Herakles-Vajrapani and Tyche-Hariti in addition to the strictly Buddhist figures in the assemblage, including a Bodhisattva head with ruby eyes. The placement of niche V 2, with these exceptional sculptures, is conspicuous for it was the first one seen by the monks as they entered the shrine area of the central stupa.[35] The entrance on the northern perimeter of the shrine is a possible later alteration to an earlier straight axis approach to the shrine. Upon leaving the adjacent vihara where they resided, the monks would have first seen the Great Stupa to the south of Tepe Shutur, before entering the shrine area and seeing niche V 2. Such an important location could only have been made possible through an agreement among the patron, artist, monastery abbot and the leader of the lay association that controlled the monastery.[36]

The artist, of superior ability, was not only thoroughly familiar with the technique of mold-made clay and stucco sculpture, but he had a convincing understanding of Greek sculpture and was capable of creating images desired by the patrons.[37] The lay association and abbot of the monastery would have benefited from this remarkable assemblage, since Herakles and Tyche are now shown as part of the Buddhist pantheon. This visual claim of Herakles and Tyche as among the newly converted reflects the practice of Greeks in this region converting to Buddhism, and therefore underscores the influence of the patrons and their Greek descent, for the choice of two conspicuously Greek figures would serve no purpose for a patron of Kushan or Gandharan descent. Equally compelling is the selection of Herakles Epitrapezios, an image linked to Greek Bactria, Hellenistic rulers in the eastern regions and ultimately to Alexander the Great.

Acknowledgements

I wish to thank the organizers, Professors Olga Palagia and William Coulson for the opportunity to discuss a sculpture of Herakles Epitrapezios from Hadda in Afghanistan, a location which is often considered "beyond" the usual understanding of the Hellenistic world and its regional schools of sculpture. Equally, I wish to thank Sir John Boardman, Dr. Martha Carter, Dr. Ronald Davidson and Dr. Elizabeth Bartman for sharing their expertise during the preparation of this paper. I am grateful to have had the good fortune to study with the late Prof. Alexander Soper who introduced me to Gandharan art. Particular thanks are due to the Department of Greek and Roman Art and the Thomas J. Watson Library at the Metropolitan Museum of Art for their support and assistance, and to Dean Orin Grossman of Fairfield University for his generous support.

Abbreviations

Boardman, *Diffusion*	J. Boardman, *The Diffusion of Classical Art in Antiquity* (1994)
Errington and Cribb, *Crossroads*	E. Errington and J. Cribb (edd.), *The Crossroads of Asia: Transformation in Image and Symbol in The Art of Ancient Afghanistan and Pakistan* (1992)
Rosenfield, *Dynastic Arts*	J. Rosenfield, *The Dynastic Arts of the Kushans* (1967)
Tarzi, *Hadda*	M. Tarzi, *CRAI* 1976, 381–410.

Notes

1. W. Ball, *Archaeological Gazetteer of Afghanistan* 1, 1982, 116–118, no. 404: Hadda. C. Mustamandi, *Afghanistan* 26, 1974, 75–77; Tarzi, *Hadda*, 393–397. For the best color illustration see F. Tissot, *Les arts anciens du Pakistan et de l'Afghanistan* (1987) fig. 16.
2. J. Boardman, *The Oxford Dictionary of Classical Art* (1993); Boardman, *Diffusion*; Errington and Cribb, *Crossroads*, an exhibition at the Fitzwilliam Museum on the use and adaptation of images from Greece and Rome in Central Asia. See also J. Boardman, *Classical Art in Eastern Translation, The Seventeenth J.L. Myres Memorial Lecture*, 1993.
3. Boardman, *Diffusion*, 141. For Roman copies of the type

see E. Bartman, *Ancient Sculptural Copies in Miniature* (1992) 147–186, esp. 171 and fig. 74.

4. E. Lamotte, *Mélanges de Sinologie offerts à Monsieur Paul Demiéville* (1966) 113–159; F.B. Flood, *South Asian Studies* 5, 1989, 17–27; M.L. Carter, *Proceedings of the Second Conference of Iranian Studies* (1995) 119–140.
5. A. Soper, *Artibus Asiae* 12, 1949, 252–283; id., *AJA* 55, 1951, 301–319. For the most thorough study of Kushana art, see Rosenfield, *Dynastic Arts*.
6. Rosenfield, *Dynastic Arts*, 12–13.
7. For example, New York, MMA 1979.6: Standing Buddha, Gupta period, fifth century, *MetrMusB*, Spring 1994, 26, fig. 15.
8. For example, New York, MMA 1991.75: Standing Bodhisattva Maitreya, Gandhara, late second – early third century, *MetrMusB* Spring 1994, 21, fig. 5.
9. Boardman, *Diffusion*, 145; G. Ortiz, *The George Ortiz Collection* (1994) no. 173.
10. As suggested by M.L. Carter, personal communication, February 1996.
11. Hadda originally meant market, according to R.M. Davidson, personal communication, January 1996.
12. Errington and Cribb, *Crossroads*, 99–102, bronze figurines nos. 102–104; S. Downey, *The Heracles Sculpture, Dura-Europos* (1969) esp. 5; 78. A Herakles cult flourished from the fourth through the second century B.C. at Aï Khanoum, a Greek site, cf. S. Sherwin-White and A. Kuhrt, *From Samarkand to Sardis* (1993) 178; Ball (supra n. 1) 30–32.
13. Downey (supra n. 12) 14, probably made in Alexandria or elsewhere in the Roman world, then imported.
14. Herakles >**he la kileśa* >*ḣelakuliśa*: the Gandhari vernacular preserved the sibilants necessary for this linguistic transformation: I thank R.M. Davidson for completing the translation and for bringing this to my attention. D. Ingalls, *Harvard Theological Review* 1962, 281–298, esp. 293.
15. Errington and Cribb, *Crossroads*, 79, no. 70.
16. Downey (supra n. 12) 4–5: first used by Antiochos II at Kyme, copied by Euthydemos of Bactria, and later by Hyspaosines of Charax. The type appeared in sculpture at Hatra and Palmyra, and on a plaque at Old Nysa, northwest of Begram.
17. Once Berlin, Staatliche Museum, F 2626. *LIMC* V (1990) s.v. Herakles, no. 3324 (Laurens); Beazley, *ARV*^{2} 1472.1; *Addenda*^{2} 381.
18. Bartman (supra n. 3) 171.
19. H.G. Martin, *Römische Tempelkultbilder* (1987) 169, fig. 40.
20. Sparta Museum 52. Martin (supra n. 19) 170, fig. 41. For the head see also *LIMV* IV (1988) s.v. Herakles, no. 1312 (Palagia).
21. Basel, Antikenmuseum, BS 204: *LIMC* IV s.v. Herakles, no. 714 (Palagia); London BM 1824.2–1.5: *LIMC* IV s.v. Herakles, no. 715 (Palagia); Boston, MFA 1976.6: *LIMC* IV s.v. Herakles, no. 716 (Palagia). Dates range from the late first to the early second centuries A.D.
22. Florence, Mus. Arch. TC 87.937: *LIMC* IV s.v. Herakles, no. 990 (Palagia).
23. London, BM 1970.7–18.1: Errington and Cribb, *Crossroads*, 26; 132, no. 134; Flood (supra n. 4) 18, fig. 1.
24. Boardman, *Diffusion*, 142, fig. 4.88; Tarzi, *Hadda*, 398–399, figs. 12–13.
25. Coll. A.I.C.: Errington and Cribb, *Crossroads*, x–xi, 91–94, no. 97. For a recent discussion of Tyche, see S.B. Matheson et al., *An Obsession with Fortune, Yale University Art Gallery Bulletin* 1994.
26. London, BM OA 1950.7–26.2: Errington and Cribb, *Crossroads*, 25; 134–135, no. 136.
27. London, Victoria and Albert Museum, IS 3–1931: Rosenfield, *Dynastic Arts*, 215, no. 120.
28. J. Marshall, *Taxila* 1, 1975, 513–517; 523; A.v. Le Coq, *Buried Treasures of Chinese Turkestan* (1928) 80–81; K.M. Varma, *Technique of Gandharan and Indo-Afghan Stucco Images* (1987).
29. M. Taddei, *East and West*, N.S. 15, 1965, 174–178.
30. F. Holt in P. Green (ed.), *Hellenistic History and Culture* (1993) 54–64, where he discusses the Greek exploitation of a fringe region of the Hellenistic world, and the intensification of cultural interaction following the demise of the Mauryan empire after the third century B.C. Such interaction resulted in the Herakles at Hadda and an Indian ivory excavated in Pompeii, cf. E.C.L. During Caspers, *South Asian Archaeology* 1979, 341–353.
31. L. Casson, *The Periplus Maris Erythraei* (1989) esp. lines 37–60.
32. Rosenfield, *Dynastic Arts*, 3; 5; K. Khandalavala, in F.M. Asher and G.S. Gai (edd.), *Indian Epigraphy: Its Bearing on the History of Art* (1985) 61–71. See also, F. Tissot, *Investigating Indian Art* (1987) 363–368; R.M. Davidson, in A. Hirakawa, *History of Indian Buddhism* 2, trans. P. Groner (forthcoming).
33. Tarzi, *Hadda*, 393.
34. Ball (supra n. 1) 116, no. 404. See also, N.H. Duprée, *Archaeology*, March/April, 1996, 42–51, who reports that the museum in Kabul has lost 70% of its objects, mostly from bombing between rival factions trying to control the capital. Much of what remains in the museum is damaged. Some of the objects have intermittently appeared on the art market; a dilemma due to the lack of a secure place within Afghanistan.
35. Tarzi, *Hadda*, 383, fig. 1.
36. For the most recent discussion see G. Schopen, *Journal of the International Association of Buddhist Studies* 19, 1996, 81–126.
37. See also Boardman, *Diffusion*, 142.

Το γυναικείο άγαλμα του Αρχαιολογικού Μουσείου Πειραιώς αρ. ευρ. 5935

Μέλπω Ι. Πωλογιώργη

Το μαρμάρινο άγαλμα μιας όρθιας ενδεδυμένης γυναικείας μορφής (εικ. 1–4), μεγέθους λίγο μεγαλύτερου από το φυσικό, το οποίο ήλθε στο φως σχετικά πρόσφατα κάτω από ανεξακρίβωτες συνθήκες, στολίζει σήμερα την έκθεση γλυπτών στο Αρχαιολογικό Μουσείο Πειραιώς (αρ. ευρ. 5935).[1] Το άγαλμα εντοπίστηκε στη χωματερή των Άνω Λιοσίων, βόρεια των Αθηνών, από συνεργείο υπαλλήλων του Οργανισμού Τοπικής Αυτοδιοίκησης στις 23 Δεκεμβρίου 1991.[2] 'Ισως δεν μάθουμε ποτέ τον πρωταρχικό τόπο εύρεσης του αγάλματος, καθόσον παρά τις έρευνες οι συνθήκες μεταφοράς του στη χωματερή παραμένουν έως σήμερα άγνωστες και οι δράστες, οι οποίοι πιθανώς ενέχονται σε απόπειρα αρχαιοκαπηλίας, ασύλληπτοι. Εντούτοις η υπόθεση ότι προέρχεται από κάποια θέση στην Αττική φαίνεται λογική.

Το άγαλμα, από λευκό πεντελικό μάρμαρο πολύ καλής ποιότητας, σώζεται ακέφαλο (εικ. 1). Το μέγιστο ύψος του μαζί με τη σύμφυτη πλίνθο ανέρχεται σε 1.635 μ. και χωρίς αυτήν σε 1.58 μ.[3] Η κεφαλή

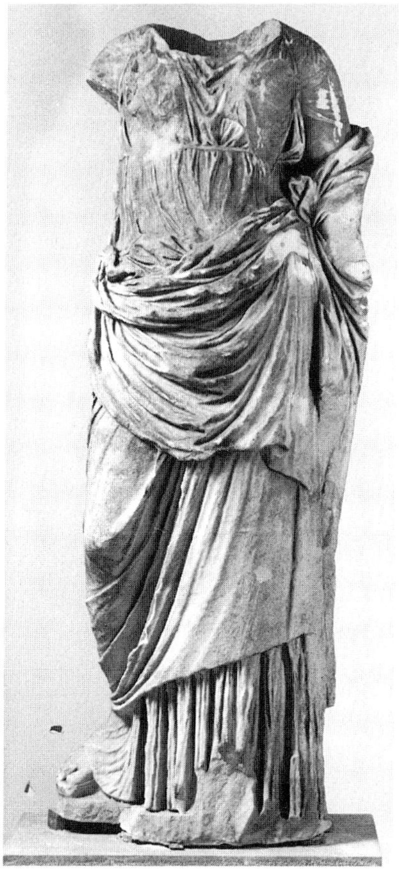

Εικ. 1 Άγαλμα Μουσείου Πειραιώς αρ. ευρ. 5935. Κύρια όψη.

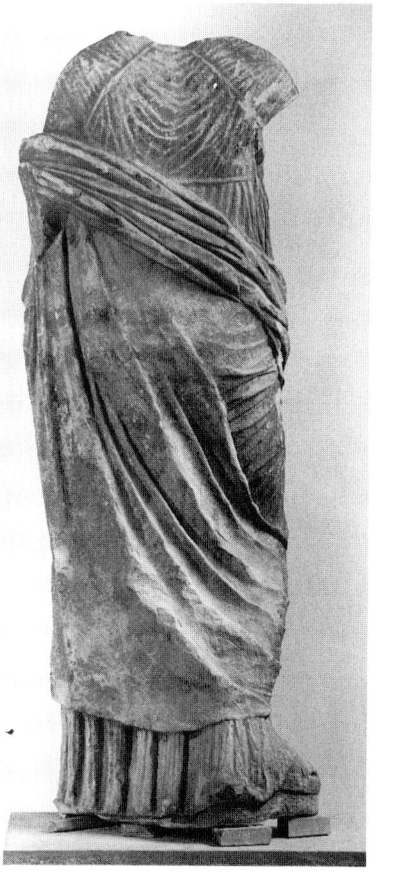

Εικ. 2. Άγαλμα Μουσείου Πειραιώς αρ. ευρ. 5935. Πίσω όψη.

ήταν χωριστά δουλεμένη και έμπαινε ένθετη στον ευρύ και βαθύ τόρμο που ανοίγεται στο επάνω μέρος του κορμού. Κατασκευασμένα σε ιδιαίτερα τεμάχια μαρμάρου ήταν και τα τμήματα των χεριών που λείπουν, δηλαδή όλο το δεξί χέρι αρκετά ψηλότερα από το μέσον του βραχίονα, και το αριστερό άκρο χέρι με μικρό τμήμα του πήχυ.

Η κατεργασία με την αναθύρωση στην κάτω επιφάνεια του δεξιού βραχίονα, η σχεδόν ημικυκλική κοίλανση στο πλευρό του κορμού και στη συνέχεια ο ορθογώνιος και με ελαφρά λοξή κλίση τόρμος που ανοίγεται λίγο ψηλότερα από το ζώσιμο του χιτώνα (εικ. 5–7) φανερώνουν την προετοιμασία για την προσαρμογή του χεριού και την στερέωσή του στον κορμό με γόμφο. Με ανάλογο τρόπο – που δεν θεωρείται πολύ συνηθισμένος – προσαρμοζόταν και στερεωνόταν στον κορμό το δεξί χέρι του γυναικείου αγάλματος στο Μουσείο Δελφών αρ. ευρ. 1817 (σελ. 62, εικ. 3) και του ανδρικού ενδεδυμένου αγάλματος στο ίδιο Μουσείο αρ. ευρ. 1820 (σελ. 63, εικ. 4), πιθανώς Διονύσου, για τα οποία υποστηρίχθηκε τελευταία η χρονολόγηση στην καμπή του 4ου προς τον 3ο αι. π.Χ., η ερμηνεία τους μαζί με τον λεγόμενο φιλόσοφο των Δελφών (σελ. 62, εικ. 2) ως τριών μορφών αναθήματος στο βόρειο τμήμα του ιερού του Απόλλωνος στους Δελφούς και η απόδοσή τους στο ίδιο εργαστήριο.[4] Με παραπλήσιο τρόπο φαίνεται ότι γινόταν η προσαρμογή του δεξιού χεριού και στο άγνωστης προέλευσης μαρμάρινο γυναικείο άγαλμα στο Μουσείο Πειραιώς αρ. ευρ. 3637 (εικ. 8–9), μεγίστου σωζόμενου ύψους μαζί με την πλίνθο 1.47 μ., ένα αττικό έργο, ομοίως από την καμπή του 4ου προς τον 3ο αι. π.Χ.[5] Δυστυχώς ο δεξιός βραχίονας είναι αποκρουσμένος από τον ώμο, αλλά στο πλευρό, πάνω από το ζώσιμο του χιτώνα και σε κατάλληλα προετοιμασμένη επιφάνεια, σώζονται δύο ορθογώνιοι τόρμοι γόμφωσης. Στο άκρο του αριστερού πήχυ (εικ. 1, 4 και 10), ο οποίος είναι ισχυρότατα αποκρουσμένος στο πλάι, διακρίνεται κατεργασία με θραπινάκι και διατηρούνται υπολείμματα του ορθογώνιου τόρμου για την γόμφωση του υπολοίπου χεριού.

Ορισμένες από τις κρεμαστές πτυχές του ιματίου στην αριστερή πλευρά του κορμού (εικ. 4), τμήμα των πτυχών του χιτώνα στο κάτω άκρο της κύριας όψης, το αριστερό άκρο πόδι που θα πρόβαλλε από το ένδυμα και μικρά κομμάτια από την πλίνθο έχουν αποκοπεί (εικ. 1). Και οι δύο μαστοί είναι αποκρουσμένοι. Σημαντικές κακώσεις διαπιστώνονται στην

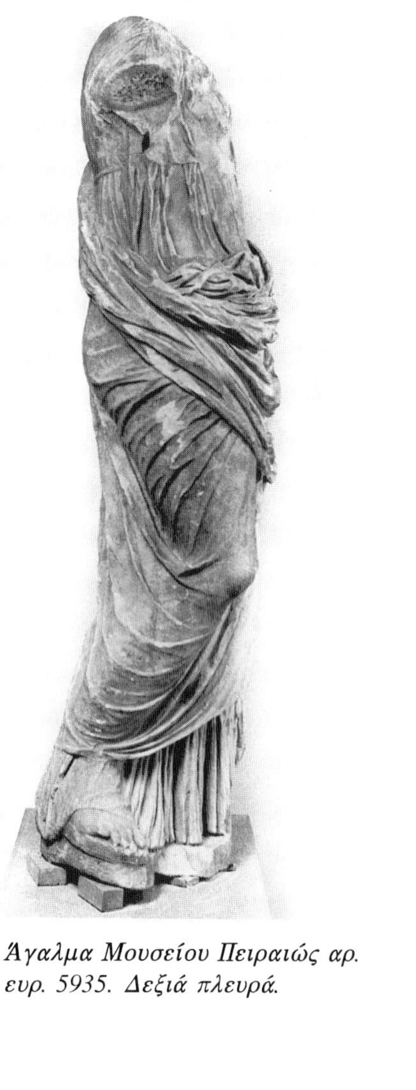

Εικ. 3. Άγαλμα Μουσείου Πειραιώς αρ. ευρ. 5935. Δεξιά πλευρά.

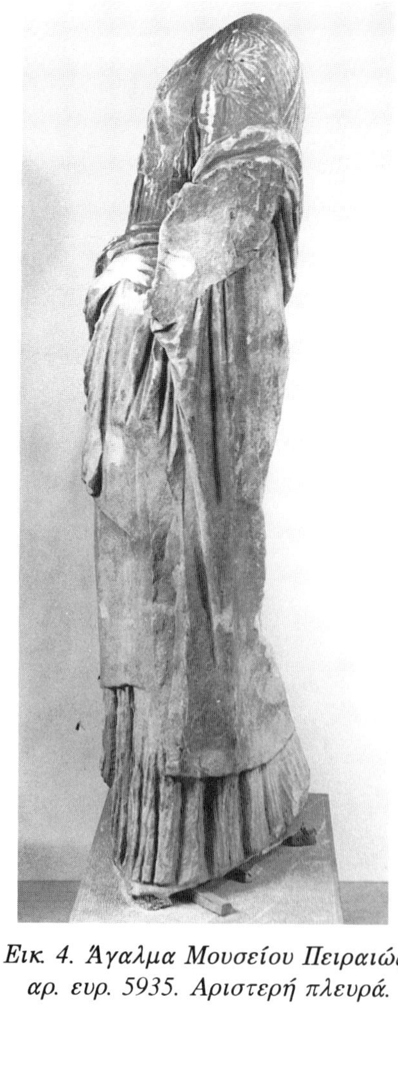

Εικ. 4. Άγαλμα Μουσείου Πειραιώς αρ. ευρ. 5935. Αριστερή πλευρά.

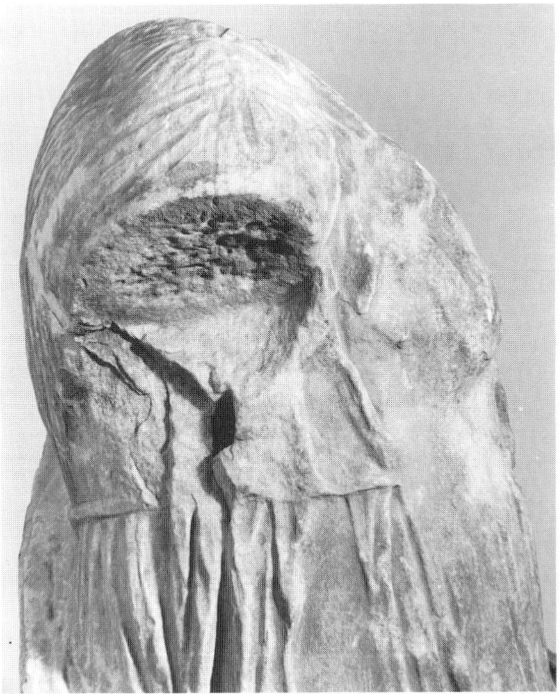

Εικ. 5. Άγαλμα Μουσείου Πειραιώς αρ. ευρ. 5935. Λεπτομέρεια δεξιάς πλευράς.

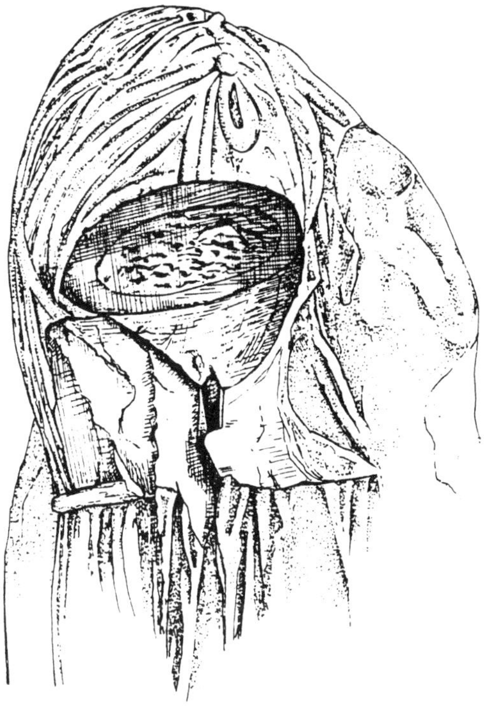

Εικ. 6. Άγαλμα Μουσείου Πειραιώς αρ. ευρ. 5935. Λεπτομέρεια δεξιάς πλευράς.

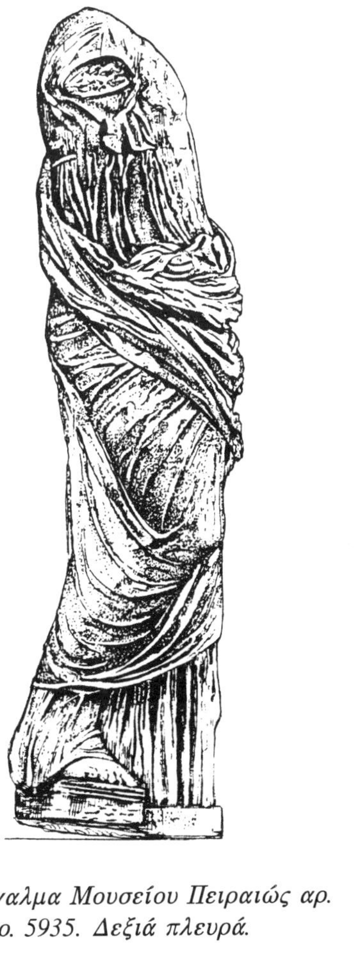

Εικ. 7. Άγαλμα Μουσείου Πειραιώς αρ. ευρ. 5935. Δεξιά πλευρά.

περιοχή γύρω από τον ορθογώνιο τόρμο στην δεξιά πλευρά του κορμού (εικ. 3) και ελαφρότερες αποκρούσεις και εκδορές υπάρχουν σε διάφορα σημεία. Η επιδερμίδα του μαρμάρου είναι φθαρμένη.

Η πλίνθος, η οποία προσαρμόζεται στο γενικό σχήμα του αγάλματος, έμπαινε ένθετη σε βάση. Το ύψος της ανέρχεται στην κύρια όψη σε 0.06 μ. περίπου, ενώ στην πίσω πλευρά είναι αισθητά μειωμένο. Στην κάτω επιφάνεια της πλίνθου, όχι ακριβώς στο μέσον της αποστάσεως από τις πλάγιες πλευρές, υπάρχει ένας μεγάλος ορθογώνιος τόρμος γόμφωσης (εικ. 11). Γύρω από αυτόν είναι εμφανής η πρωταρχική κατεργασία με το βελόνι. Η υπόλοιπη επιφάνεια δουλεύτηκε με την οδοντωτή ξοΐδα στη σημερινή εποχή, πιθανώς από τους αρχαιοκάπηλους, για να στηθεί το άγαλμα όρθιο.

Η γυναικεία μορφή στηρίζει το βάρος του σώματος στο αριστερό πόδι. Ο αντίστοιχος γοφός είναι προτεταμένος. Το άνετο δεξιό σκέλος λυγίζει έντονα στο γόνατο και φέρεται στο πλάι και ελαφρά προς τα πίσω. Ο αριστερός ώμος δείχνει μια σχεδόν ανεπαίσθητη υπερύψωση σε σχέση με τον δεξιό. Το αριστερό χέρι κάμπτεται προς τα εμπρός, πιέζοντας με τον αγκώνα το ένδυμα στο πλευρό. Ο πήχυς παρουσιάζει ελαφριά κλίση προς τα έξω. Το δεξί χέρι ίσως ήταν χαμηλωμένο, αλλά δεν αποκλείεται και η περίπτωση να ήταν λυγισμένο στον αγκώνα και προτεταμένο. Στους ώμους δεν υπάρχουν ίχνη βοστρύχων. Οποιεσδήποτε ενδείξεις για τα χαρακτηριστικά προσδιοριστικά σύμβολα που θα κρατούσε η μορφή και που θα βοηθούσαν σε μιαν αναντίρρητη αναγνώριση της ταυτότητάς της λείπουν εντελώς.

Η στάση της μορφής με το τέντωμα της δεξιάς πλευράς, το λύγισμα της μέσης στην αριστερή πλευρά και τον τονισμό του γοφού σε αντιστάθμισμα της φοράς και της προβολής του άνετου σκέλους μπορεί να παραβληθεί με του χάλκινου παιδός από τη θάλασσα του Μαραθώνα, γύρω στα 330 π.Χ., όπου αντικατοπτρίζεται το Πραξιτελικό πνεύμα.[6] Ως προς τις γυναικείες μορφές, ίδια σύγκριση μπορεί να γίνει και με το ρωμαϊκό αντίγραφο της ημίγυμνης Αφροδίτης από την Arles, το πρωτότυπο του οποίου αποδίδεται στον ίδιο καλλιτέχνη.[7]

Η μορφή φοράει ποδήρη και πλούσιο σε πτυχές ιωνικό χιτώνα και φαρδύ ιμάτιο. Ο χιτώνας έχει κοντές, κουμπωμένες στο πλάι χειρίδες και είναι ζωσμένος κάτω από το στήθος και γύρω από τις μασχάλες και τους ώμους με στρογγυλά κορδόνια που διασταυρώνονται ψηλά στην πλάτη (εικ. 1–2), το αρχαίο όνομα των οποίων ήταν πιθανώς *στρόφιον*.[8] Το ψηλό ζώσιμο του χιτώνα είναι ένα χαρακτηριστικό γνώρισμα του ενδύματος που απαντάται από το τελευταίο τρίτο του 4ου αι. π.Χ.[9] Το ζώσιμο με τα κορδόνια γύρω από τους ώμους φοράνε συνήθως κορίτσια, νεαρές θεότητες και μορφές σε δράση, όπως η Άρτεμις, η Κόρη, η Υγιεία, Μούσες, προσωποποιήσεις, ηνίοχοι, θεραπαινίδες σε επιτύμβια μνημεία, κ.ά.[10]

Η διαφορετική υφή του υφάσματος των δύο ενδυμάτων στο άγαλμα του Μουσείου Πειραιώς είναι ευκρινής και δημιουργεί έντονη αντίθεση. Ο χιτώνας είναι λεπτός και διαφανής, το ιμάτιο κρουστό και βαρύ. Η διάθεση των πτυχών δημιουργεί μια συνεχή εναλλαγή φωτισμένων και σκιασμένων επιφανειών. Το σώμα κάτω από τα ενδύματα, τα οποία παρακολουθούν με συνέπεια τους όγκους του, πάλλεται από ζωή.

Η απόδοση της πτύχωσης του χιτώνα επάνω και κάτω από το ζώσιμο (εικ. 1 και 3) τονίζει την διαφάνεια του ενδύματος και εξαίρει την πλαστικότητα του σφριγηλού σώματος. Ανάμεσα στους μαστούς οι πτυχές πέφτουν χαλαρά, σχηματίζοντας ελαφρούς κυματισμούς. Τα κορδόνια γύρω από τους ώμους συντελούν στην τέλεια εφαρμογή του ενδύματος στους βραχίονες, ενώ η δέσμη των πτυχών που ξεφεύγει πάνω από το ζώσιμο στην αριστερή πλευρά του στήθους υπογραμμίζει την αφθονία του υφάσματος. Αραιές δέσμες λεπτών και ανήσυχων πτυχών που τρεμοπαίζουν σχηματίζουν κάτω από το ζώσιμο μεγάλες ανοιχτές καμπύλες που σβήνουν μαλακά, ώστε να προβάλλεται η εύχυμη γυναικεία σάρκα γύρω από τον αφαλό. Ακριβώς το ίδιο πνεύμα χαρακτηρίζει την διατύπωση της πτύχωσης του χιτώνα στον κολοσσικό κορμό της αθηναϊκής Αγοράς S 2370, που βρέθηκε μπροστά στη Βασίλειο Στοά.[11] Το έργο αυτό χρονολογήθηκε από την Ο.Παλαγγιά στα 330–320 π.Χ.,[12] ενώ άλλοι μελετητές υποστήριξαν τη χρονολόγηση γύρω στα 310 π.Χ.[13] Οι ίδιες καλλιτεχνικές τάσεις αναγνωρίζονται και στο θραύσμα του Μουσείου Ακροπόλεως αρ. ευρ. 930,[14] από την δεξιά

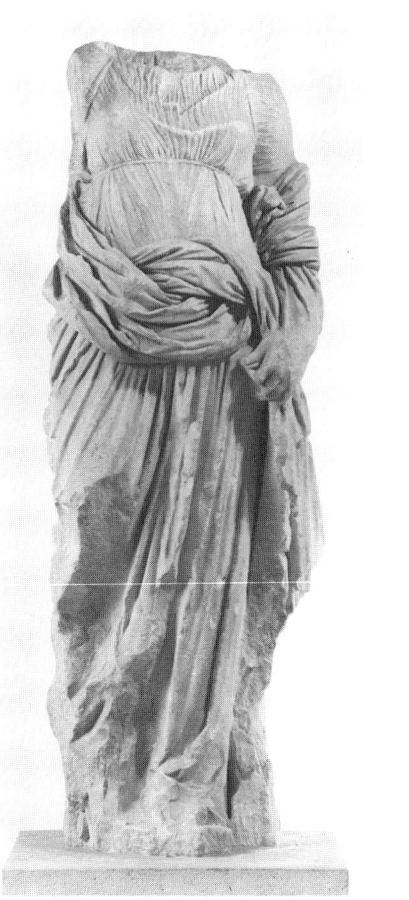

Εικ. 8. Άγαλμα Μουσείου Πειραιώς αρ. ευρ. 3637. Κύρια όψη.

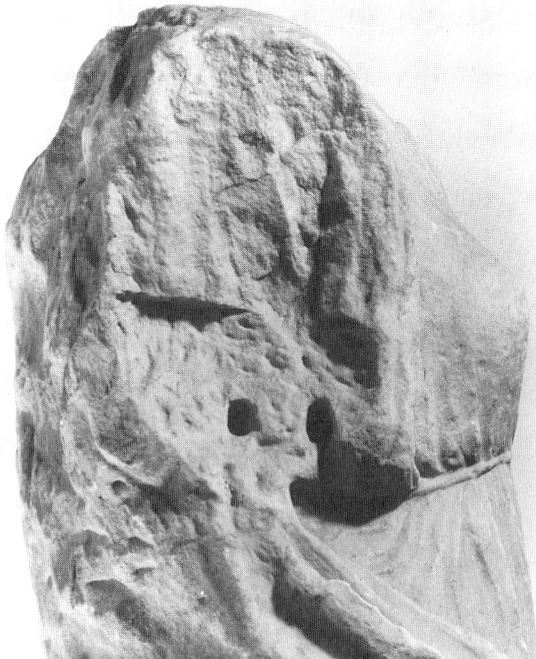

Εικ. 9. Άγαλμα Μουσείου Πειραιώς αρ. ευρ. 3637. Λεπτομέρεια δεξιάς πλευράς.

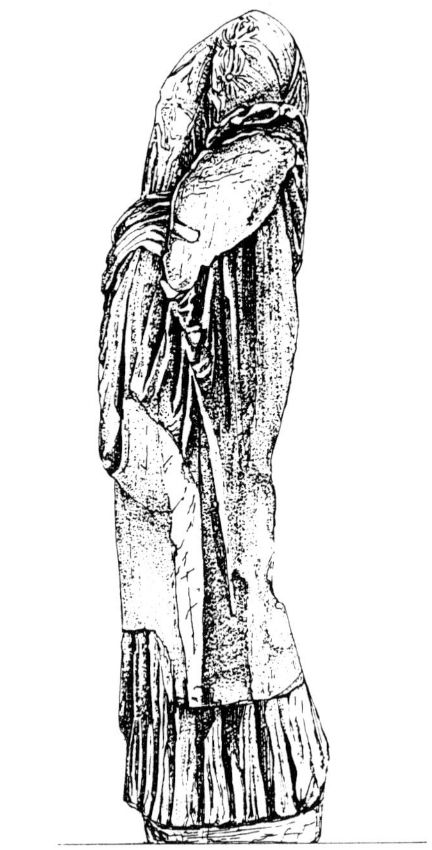

Εικ. 10. Άγαλμα Μουσείου Πειραιώς αρ. ευρ. 5935. Αριστερή πλευρά.

πλευρά του κορμού γυναικείου αγάλματος, το οποίο παλιότερα είχε θεωρηθεί παρθενώνειο και μάλιστα είχε συνδεθεί με μορφές των αετωμάτων. Η Ο. Παλαγγιά παρατήρησε τη στενή σχέση του θραύσματος με τον κορμό της Αγοράς.[15] Ο Γ. Δεσπίνης αποσυσχέτισε το θραύσμα οριστικά από τα παρθενώνεια γλυπτά και υπέδειξε τη χρονολόγησή του στην ελληνιστική εποχή.[16]

Στο κάτω τμήμα του χιτώνα (εικ. 1) βαθιές αύλακες ξεχωρίζουν δέσμες λεπτών και πυκνών πτυχών που δεν πέφτουν ολόισιες, αλλά δημιουργούν ελαφρούς κυματισμούς. Με ανάλογο τρόπο αποδίδεται η πτύχωση του χιτώνα π.χ. στην ανάγλυφη μορφή του Διονύσου στην τριγωνική βάση τρίποδος του Εθνικού Αρχαιολογικού Μουσείου αρ. ευρ. 1463, του β' μισού του 4ου αι. π.Χ.[17] Η ρυτιδωμένη επιφάνεια του χιτώνα που απλώνεται επάνω στο δεξί άκρο πόδι (εικ. 12) απαντάται στην ίδια θέση και σε αττικό επιτύμβιο άγαλμα στο Μουσείο του Λούβρου αρ. Ma 926, γύρω στο 325 π.Χ.[18]

Ανάμεσα στην πλίνθο και την παρυφή του χιτώνα στην κύρια όψη του αγάλματος διακρίνονται τα ίχνη του τρυπάνου. Ο χιτώνας στην πλάτη χάνει τη διαφάνειά του (εικ. 2). Οι πυκνές πτυχές στις ωμοπλάτες και οι κρεμαστές ημικυκλικές πτυχές ανάμεσα στα κορδόνια επιτείνουν την αφθονία του υφάσματος. Ως κοντινό παράλληλο μπορεί να αναφερθεί ένα γυναικείο άγαλμα του τελευταίου τετάρτου του 4ου αι. π.Χ. στο Μητροπολιτικό Μουσείο της Νέας Υόρκης.[19] Και εδώ ο λεπτός χιτώνας ζώνεται ψηλά και συγκρατείται γύρω από τους ώμους με κορδόνια που διασταυρώνονται στην πλάτη, όπου σχηματίζονται μεγάλες ημικυκλικές πτυχές. Με το άγαλμα αυτό διαπιστώνεται ομοιότητα και στη γενική απόδοση της

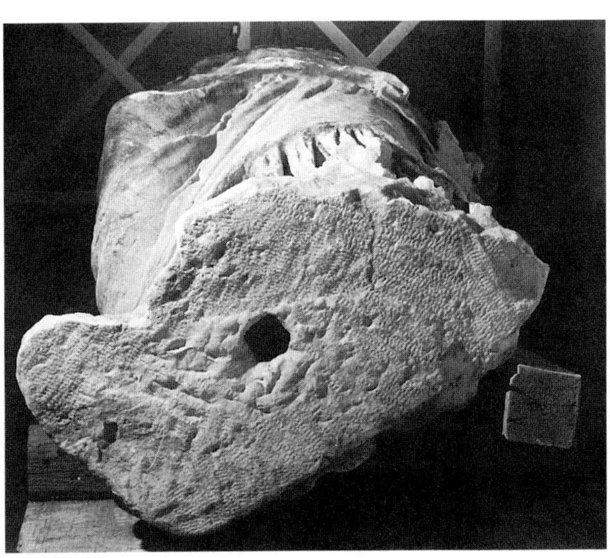

Εικ. 11. Άγαλμα Μουσείου Πειραιώς αρ. ευρ. 5935. Κάτω επιφάνεια πλίνθου.

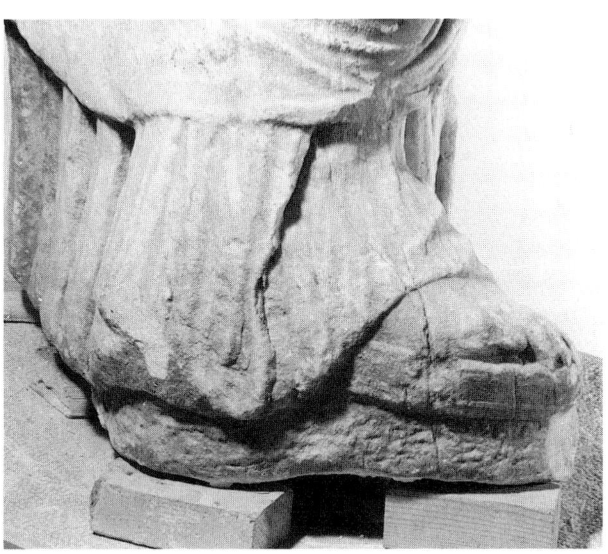

Εικ. 12. Άγαλμα Μουσείου Πειραιώς αρ. ευρ. 5935. Δεξιό άκρο πόδι.

πίσω όψης, δηλαδή στις πλατιές απτύχωτες επιφάνειες του ιματίου, στην κάπως σκληρή διατύπωση των στριμωγμένων πτυχών στο βαρύ επάνω τμήμα του και στον τονισμό του δεξιού γλουτού. Στο μαρμάρινο άγαλμα μικρού κοριτσιού στο Μουσείο Πειραιώς αρ. ευρ. 427, ένα έργο του πρώιμου 3ου αι. π.Χ.[20] και σαφώς υστερότερο από το νέο εύρημα, οι βαριές και άτακτες πτυχές του χιτώνα ανάμεσα στα κορδόνια στην πίσω όψη (εικ. 13) δείχνουν πώς ένα μοτίβο που έλκει την καταγωγή του από τον 4ο αι. π.Χ. αποδίδεται πλέον χωρίς την φυσικότητα και την οργάνωση των προγενέστερων δημιουργιών.

Το ιμάτιο στο άγαλμα του Μουσείου Πειραιώς περιβάλλει το κάτω τμήμα του κορμού και αφήνει ακάλυπτο το επάνω, επιτρέποντάς του να αναπνέει ελεύθερα (εικ. 1). Το επάνω τμήμα του ιματίου που είναι τυλιγμένο γύρω από τον αριστερό πήχυ και λίγο επάνω από τον αγκώνα διατρέχει συμμαζεμένο λοξά την πίσω όψη (εικ. 2). Στη συνέχεια επανεμφανίζεται επάνω από τον δεξιό γοφό (εικ. 3 και 7) και σχηματίζει εμπρός μια πλατιά τριγωνική αναδίπλωση με βαθιές τοξωτές πτυχές, κυματιστή παρυφή και το άκρο στο αριστερό πλάι (εικ. 1). Το ογκηρό επάνω τμήμα μετά από ένα ταραγμένο περιδίνισμα των πτυχώσεων στην κορυφή που σχηματίζει έναν ημιρόδακα, χαμηλώνει βαραίνοντας κάτω από τον αφαλό, για να υψωθεί και πάλι προς τον αριστερό γοφό, όπου συγκρατείται επάνω στο σώμα με τον καλυμμένο πήχυ. 'Ενα ατίθασο φούσκωμα του ιματίου στο σημείο αυτό τονίζει τον προτεταμένο γοφό.

Το τελευταίο μοτίβο απαντάται σε αρκετά επιτύμβια ανάγλυφα του 4ου αι. π.Χ., όπως π.χ. στο ανάγλυφο του Εθνικού Μουσείου αρ. ευρ. 966,[21] στη "στήλη του αποχαιρετισμού," στο ίδιο Μουσείο αρ. ευρ. 870,[22] στη στήλη της Φιλινώς, επίσης στο Εθνικό Μουσείο αρ. ευρ. 832,[23] κ.ά. Το ίδιο μοτίβο επανευρίσκεται και στην απεικόνιση της Περσεφόνης σε αποσπασματικά σωζόμενο ανάγλυφο του β' μισού του 4ου αι. π.Χ. στο Μουσείο Ελευσίνας αρ. ευρ. 17/5067.[24] Στη λεγόμενη Θέμιδα του Χαιρεστράτου από τον Ραμνούντα,[25] ως πρωτότυπη πηγή έμπνευσης για την οποία έχει υποστηριχθεί ότι υπήρξε ο κορμός της Αγοράς S 2370,[26] το περίτεχνο φούσκωμα του ιματίου ανάμεσα στον λυγισμένο πήχυ και τον γοφό έχει πάρει σκληρή οξύκογχη μορφή και ο ημιρόδακας στην κορυφή του αναδιπλωμένου τμήματος έχει μεταλλαχθεί σε αφύσικο διακοσμητικό στοιχείο.

Οι μεγάλες διαγώνιες πτυχές του ιματίου στο άγαλμα του Μουσείου Πειραιώς που καταλήγουν επάνω από τα σφυρά του δεξιού ποδιού (εικ. 1), οι οποίες απαντώνται συχνά σε έργα του τελευταίου τρίτου του 4ου αι. π.Χ.,[27] οι τοξωτές πτυχές στο πλάι της κνήμης και οι θηλειόσχημες πτυχές στο πλάι του μηρού (εικ. 3 και 7) προβάλλουν ιδιαίτερα την πλαστικότητα του σκέλους αυτού, κατά τρόπο ανάλογο με του λεγομένου φιλοσόφου των Δελφών (σελ. 62, εικ. 2).[28]

Την υπόδηση της μορφής αποτελούν σανδάλια, στα οποία οι ιμάντες είχαν αποδοθεί άλλοτε μόνο με

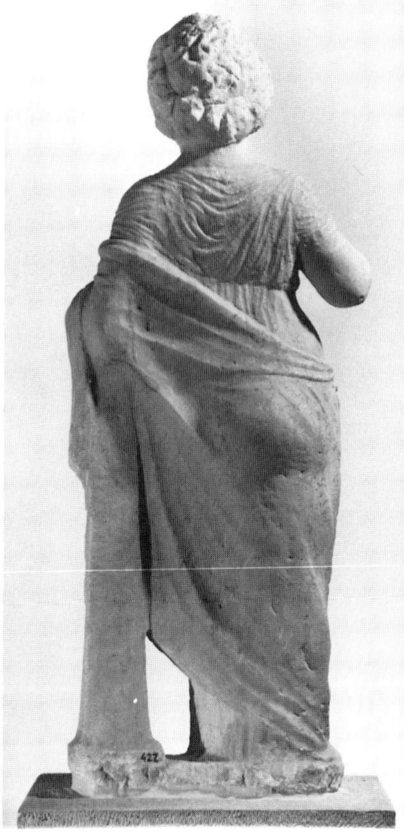

Εικ. 13. Άγαλμα Μουσείου Πειραιώς αρ. ευρ. 427.

χρώμα. Το κάττυμα είναι ψηλό και στολίζεται με δύο ανάγλυφες ταινίες (εικ. 12). Χτυπητή ομοιότητα διαπιστώνεται με το κάττυμα του σανδαλιού της καθιστής γυναίκας σε επιτύμβιο ανάγλυφο από το Πόρτο Ράφτη (Μουσείο Βραυρώνος αρ. ευρ. 125), που χρονολογείται μετά τα 330 π.Χ.[29] 'Αλλο παράλληλο προσφέρει η απόδοση των σανδαλιών της Δαμασιστράτης στην επιτύμβια στήλη του Εθνικού Μουσείου αρ. ευρ. 743, μετά τα μέσα του 4ου αι. π.Χ.[30]

Το νέο εύρημα έχει τη δροσιά και τη φρεσκάδα που χαρακτηρίζει τα πρωτότυπα έργα. Αψευδείς μάρτυρες είναι το μαλακό πλάσιμο, η ευφορία των όγκων, η προσεκτική και λογική διευθέτηση των πτυχών. Μικρή αμφιβολία μπορεί να υπάρξει ότι έχουμε προ οφθαλμών ένα αττικό δημιούργημα του τέλους του 4ου αι. π.Χ.

Ο γενικός αγαλματικός τύπος της γυναικείας μορφής με τον λεπτό και ψηλά ζωσμένο χιτώνα, με τα κορδόνια γύρω από τους ώμους ή χωρίς αυτά, και το φαρδύ ιμάτιο – το οποίο συνήθως καλύπτει τον αριστερό ώμο – με την τριγωνική αναδίπλωση ή χωρίς αυτήν χρησιμοποιήθηκε κατά το τελευταίο τρίτο του 4ου έως και τις αρχές του 3ου αι. π.Χ. για την απεικόνιση της Αρτέμιδος (π.χ. στο ανάγλυφο του Εθνικού Αρχαιολογικού Μουσείου αρ. ευρ. 3917),[31] της Κόρης (π.χ. το άγαλμα από την Καλλίπολη της Αιτωλίας [σελ. 52, εικ. 10–12]),[32] της Αφροδίτης (π.χ. το σύμπλεγμα Αφροδίτης και 'Ερωτος από το ιερό στο Δαφνί, στο Εθνικό Αρχαιολογικό Μουσείο αρ.

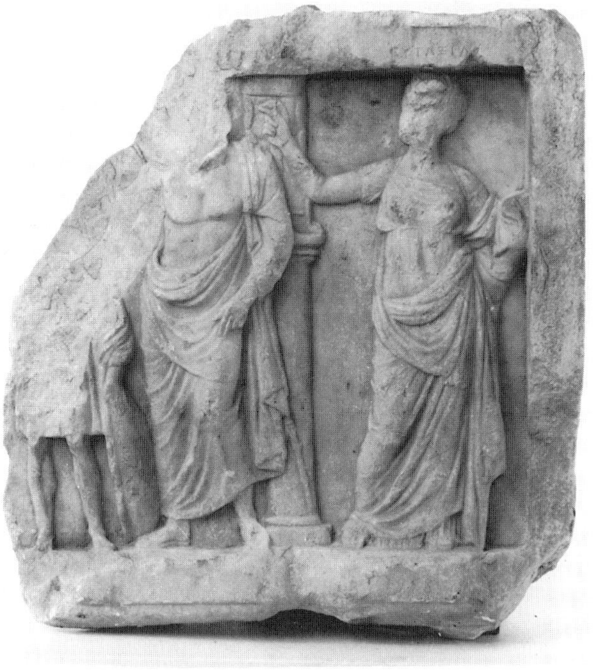

Εικ. 14. Ανάγλυφο Εθνικού Αρχαιολογικού Μουσείου αρ. ευρ. 2958.

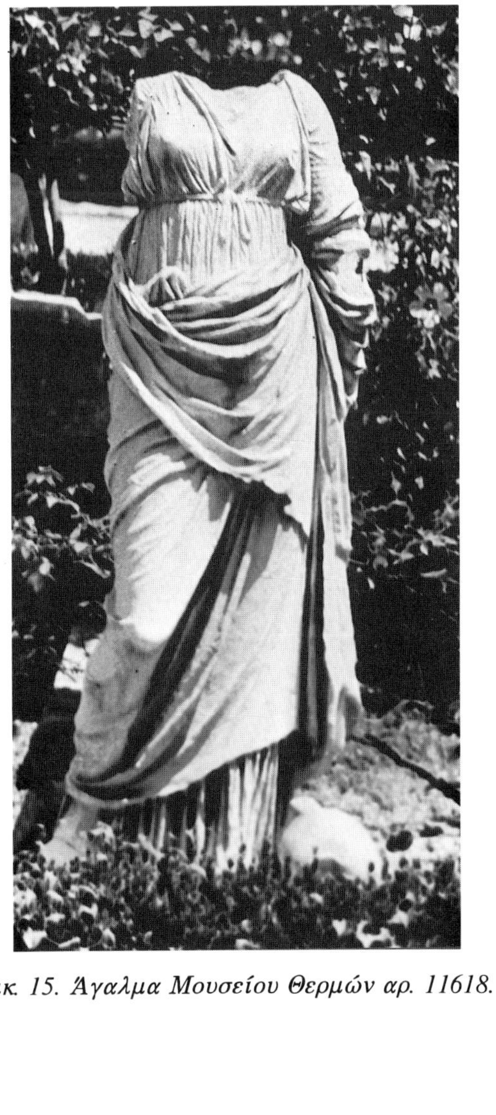

Εικ. 15. Άγαλμα Μουσείου Θερμών αρ. 11618.

ευρ. 2167),[33] Μουσών (π.χ. στην ανάγλυφη πλάκα από την Μαντίνεια η καθιστή Μούσα με την πανδούρα, στο Εθνικό Αρχαιολογικό Μουσείο αρ. ευρ. 216),[34] Νυμφών (π.χ. στο ανάγλυφο του Εθνικού Αρχαιολογικού Μουσείου αρ. ευρ. 2012)[35] και διαφόρων προσωποποιήσεων, όπως της Αγαθής Τύχης (π.χ. ο κολοσσικός κορμός της Αγοράς S 2370),[36] της Υγιείας (π.χ. στο ανάγλυφο του Εθνικού Αρχαιολογικού Μουσείου αρ. ευρ. 1335,[37] στο ανάγλυφο του ίδιου Μουσείου αρ. ευρ. 1330,[38] στο ανάγλυφο του Μουσείου Τεγέας αρ. ευρ. Ι 6524)[40] κ.ά.

Άξιο ιδιαίτερης προσοχής είναι ότι όλα τα κύρια τυπολογικά γνωρίσματα της μορφής του αγάλματος στο Μουσείο Πειραιώς τόσο ως προς τη στάση του σώματος όσο και ως προς τη διάθεση των ενδυμάτων, απαντώνται στη μοναδική έως σήμερα γνωστή απεικόνιση της προσωποποίησης της Ευταξίας σε ανάγλυφο από την Ακρόπολη, σήμερα στο Εθνικό Αρχαιολογικό Μουσείο αρ. ευρ. 2958 (εικ. 14), του τελευταίου τετάρτου του 4ου αι. π.Χ.[41] Η Ευταξία, το όνομα της οποίας είναι χαραγμένο στην ταινία επάνω από το ανάγλυφο, κρατάει πιθανώς δέλτο στο λυγισμένο αριστερό χέρι και εκτείνει στο πλάι το δεξί. Τα μαλλιά της είναι αναδεμένα στο πίσω μέρος του κεφαλιού. Δίπλα της απεικονίζεται ο Δήμος ή ένας από τους επώνυμους ήρωες της Αττικής και ένας οπλίτης. Ο τρίποδας επί του κίονος στο βάθος ίσως αποτελεί τοπογραφική δήλωση του Λυκείου γυμνασίου ή είναι το έπαθλο σε αγώνα.

Η Ευταξία ήταν η προσωποποίηση της κοσμιότητας και της πειθαρχίας, ιδιαίτερα στο γυμνάσιο και στην παλαίστρα.[42] Στα τελη του 4ου αι. π.Χ. αναφέρεται με το όνομα αυτό και μια λειτουργία, η οποία συσχετίσθηκε με εορταστικό αγώνα οπλιτών.[43] Δεδομένου ότι τα στοιχεία που διαθέτουμε για την Ευταξία είναι πολύ πενιχρά, η αναγνώριση της βραχύβιας αυτής προσωποποίησης στο άγαλμα του Μουσείου Πειραιώς φαίνεται παρακινδυνευμένη.

'Ενα φυσικού μεγέθους άγαλμα των μέσων του 2ου αι. μ.Χ. στο Μουσείο Θερμών αρ. 11618,[44] το οποίο βρέθηκε το 1905 στη Via Venti Settembre στη Ρώμη (εικ. 15), παρουσιάζει τόσο στενή ομοιότητα με το άγαλμα του Μουσείου Πειραιώς, ώστε επιτρέπεται να μιλήσουμε για σχέση αντιγράφου και πρωτοτύπου.

Το ρωμαϊκό άγαλμα, από λευκό ιταλικό μάρμαρο, σώζεται ακέφαλο και έχει ύψος χωρίς την πλίνθο 1.35 μ. Το κεφάλι και το αριστερό άκρο χέρι με τμήμα του πήχυ, τα οποία λείπουν, ήταν ένθετα. Ολόκληρο το δεξί χέρι είναι σπασμένο από τον ώμο. Το χέρι αυτό, κρίνοντας από τον ελαφρά προς τα επάνω ωθημένο μαστό, θα ήταν υψωμένο, όπως και στο αττικό ανάγλυφο με την Ευταξία. Στους ώμους δεν υπάρχουν βόστρυχοι. Καμιά ένδειξη δεν σώζεται για τα προσδιοριστικά σύμβολα που θα κρατούσε η μορφή. Η στάση του σώματος και η διάθεση των ενδυμάτων είναι όπως στο άγαλμα του Μουσείου Πειραιώς, αλλά με ορισμένες μικρές διαφορές. Το ρωμαϊκό αντίγραφο είναι κάπως στατικό και απλούστερο στη δομή. Το

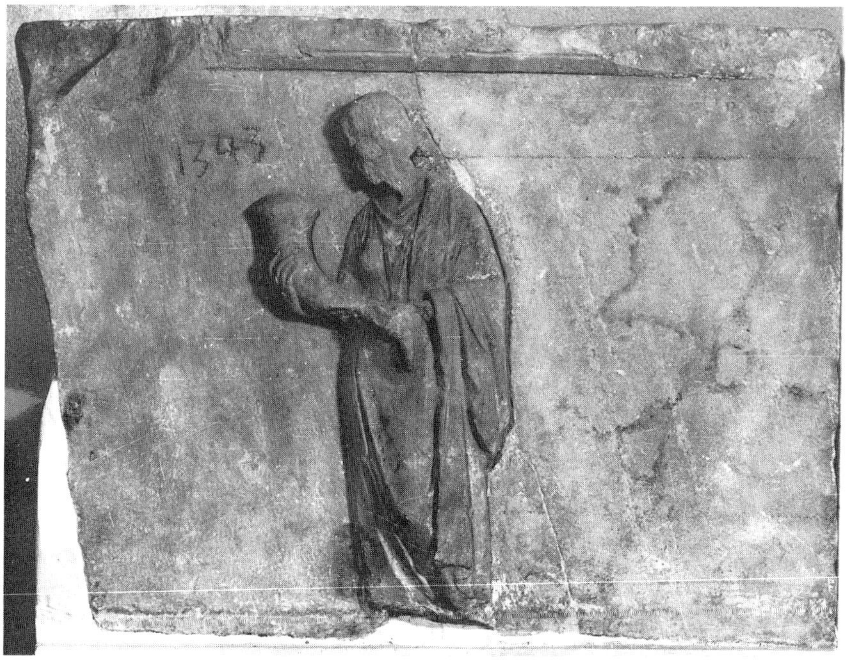

Εικ. 16. Ανάγλυφο Εθνικού Αρχαιολογικού Μουσείου αρ. ευρ. 1343.

κορδόνι που ζώνει τον λεπτό χιτώνα κάτω από το στήθος σχηματίζει εμπρός έναν φιόγκο. Οι πτυχές κάτω από το ζώσιμο είναι ξηρές και άκαμπτες. Το φούσκωμα του ιματίου ανάμεσα στον λυγισμένο πήχυ και το πλευρό έχει παραλειφθεί. Ωστόσο ο απόηχος της δροσιάς του πρωτοτύπου στο ρωμαϊκό αυτό αντίγραφο δύσκολα παραγνωρίζεται. Αξίζει να προσεχθούν και τα κορδόνια γύρω από τους ώμους που υπάρχουν και στα δύο έργα. Ήδη η Kabus-Jahn είχε σημειώσει πολύ ορθά την συμφωνία ως προς την τεχνοτροπία και τα τυπολογικά γνωρίσματα ανάμεσα στο αντίγραφο του Μουσείου Θερμών και το ανάγλυφο του Εθνικού Μουσείου αρ. ευρ. 2958 με την απεικόνιση της Ευταξίας.[45]

Το άγαλμα του Μουσείου Θερμών εντάσσεται από τους μελετητές, όπως από την R. Kabus-Jahn, την L Guerrini, την C. Nippe, σε μια πολυάριθμη σειρά ρωμαϊκών αντιγράφων και παραλλαγών, από τον 1ο αι. π.Χ. έως τον 3ο αι. μ.Χ., που απεικονίζουν την προσωποποίηση της Αγαθής Τύχης σύμφωνα με έναν αγαλματικό τύπο ιδιαίτερα αγαπητό στον ύστερο 4ο αι. π.Χ., ο οποίος όμως χρησιμοποιήθηκε ευρύτατα για την απεικόνιση διαφόρων θεοτήτων και προσωποποιήσεων.[46] 'Εχει υποστηριχθεί ότι ο κολοσσικός κορμός της Αγοράς S 2370 ήταν το πρότυπο, από το οποίο προέκυψαν τα ρωμαϊκά αντίγραφα.[47] Πάντως είναι άξιο σημειώσεως ότι η τριγωνική αναδίπλωση του ιματίου που απαντάται σε όλα τα αντίγραφα δεν υπάρχει στον κορμό της Αγοράς. Αντιθέτως τα κορδόνια γύρω από τους ώμους απουσιάζουν από όλα τα αντίγραφα, με μόνη εξαίρεση το άγαλμα στο Μουσείο Θερμών, το οποίο όμως παρουσιάζει αποκλίσεις από τον κύριο τύπο. Ο κορμός της Αγοράς, δύο μικροί τόρμοι στον αριστερό ώμο και στον πήχυ του οποίου υποδηλώνουν την προσάρτηση ενός χάλκινου συμβόλου, πιθανότατα του κέρατος της Αμαλθείας, αναγνωρίστηκε ως απεικόνιση της Αγαθής Τύχης από τον T. Leslie Shear, Jr.[48] O H.A. Tompson και η E.B. Harrison υποστήριξαν την ταύτιση με τη Θέμιδα.[49] Η Ο. Παλαγγιά αρχικά υπέθεσε ότι πρόκειται για απεικόνιση της Δημοκρατίας,[50] αλλά πρόσφατα υποστήριξε την άποψη της παράστασης της Τύχης ως θεάς της πόλεως.[51] 'Εχουν αναγνωριστεί δύο υπό κλίμακα ρωμαϊκά αντίγραφα του κορμού της Αγοράς, το ένα από την Leptis Magna, στο Μουσείο Τριπόλεως στη Λιβύη,[52] και το άλλο από την Παμφυλία, στο Μουσείο της Ατταλείας.[53]

Τα πρωταρχικά σύμβολα της Αγαθής Τύχης, σύμφωνα με την αποκατάσταση του τύπου από την R. Kabus-Jahn, ήταν το κέρας της Αμαλθείας στο λυγισμένο αριστερό χέρι και η σπονδική φιάλη στο χαμηλωμένο, ελαφρά προτεταμένο δεξιό.[54] Η αντικατάσταση της φιάλης με τον οίακα επί της σφαίρας οφείλεται στους ρωμαίους αντιγραφείς, οι οποίοι εξομοίωσαν την ελληνική προσωποποίηση της Αγαθής Τύχης με την Bona Fortuna.[55] Είναι απολύτως βέβαιο ότι τόσο στο άγαλμα στο Μουσείο Πειραιώς όσο και στο αντίγραφο στο Μουσείο Θερμών δεν μπορεί να αποκατασταθεί το κέρας της Αμαλθείας στο αριστερό χέρι. Συγχρόνως ενδείξεις για την διατύπωση οποιασδήποτε υπόθεσης ως προς τα σύμβολα που κρατούσε η μορφή και στα δύο έργα απουσιάζουν. Επί πλέον είναι άγνωστο τι κρατούσε με το κατά πάσαν πιθανότητα υψωμένο δεξί χέρι η μορφή στο Μουσείο Θερμών.

Εκτός από τη φιλολογική παράδοση που αναφέρει άγαλμα της Αγαθής Τύχης κοντά στο αθηναϊκό Πρυτανείο και αγάλματα της Αγαθής Τύχης που

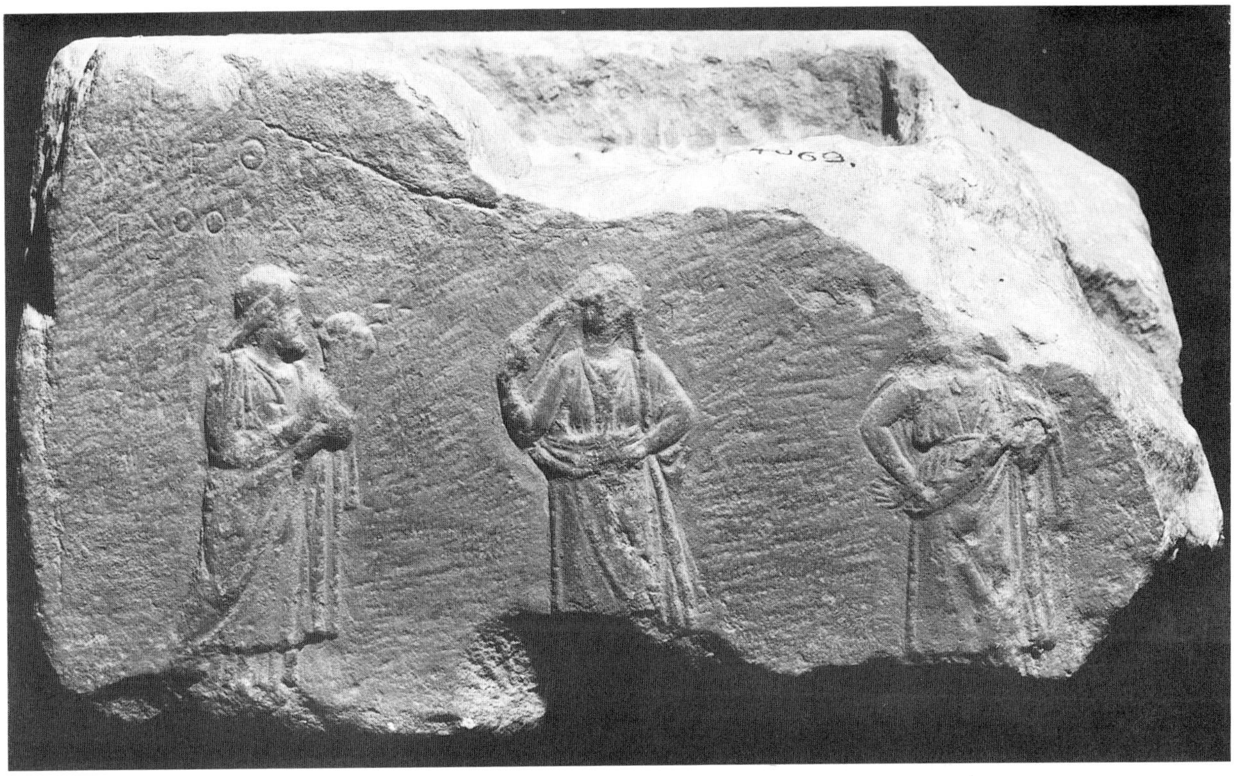

Εικ. 17. Ανάγλυφη βάση Μουσείου Ακροπόλεως αρ. ευρ. 4069.

κατασκεύασε ο Πραξιτέλης (ένα για το ιερό της στα Μέγαρα που πιθανώς απεικονίζεται σε ρωμαϊκά νομίσματα και ένα άλλο μαζί με τον Αγαθοδαίμονα που μεταφέρθηκε αργότερα στο Καπιτώλιο),[56] η λατρεία της Αγαθής Τύχης στην Αττική κατά την διάρκεια του 4ου αι. π.Χ. και η ύπαρξη ιερών της στην Αθήνα και τον Πειραιά, επιβεβαιώνονται από επιγραφικές μαρτυρίες, τις οποίες συγκέντρωσε τελευταία ο Stephen Tracy.[57] Πέραν τούτου, έχει υποστηριχθεί με βάσιμα επιχειρήματα ότι επειδή η Αγαθή Τύχη εξέφραζε το Αγαθό Πνεύμα – ήταν θεότητα που χάριζε την ευτυχία και ευνοούσε την ίαση – σπάνια λατρευόταν μόνη, αλλά κατά κανόνα σε συνάρτηση με μιαν άλλη θεότητα.[58] 'Ετσι είναι απόλυτα κατανοητή η λατρεία της Αγαθής Τύχης τόσο στο αθηναϊκό όσο και στο πειραιώτικο Ασκληπιείο.[59] Ωστόσο οι βέβαιες απεικονίσεις της Αγαθής Τύχης τον 4ο αι. π.Χ. στην Αττική παραμένουν ευάριθμες.[60]

Πιθανώς η Τύχη με το κέρας της Αμαλθείας στο αριστερό χέρι παριστάνεται σε Παναθηναϊκό αμφορέα.[61] Σε ενεπίγραφο αναθηματικό ανάγλυφο από το αθηναϊκό Ασκληπιείο (Εθνικό Αρχαιολογικό Μουσείο αρ. ευρ. 1343), του α' τετάρτου του 4ου αι. π.Χ., η Αγαθή Τύχη με χιτώνα και ιμάτιο χωρίς την τριγωνική αναδίπλωση κρατάει το κέρας της Αμαλθείας και με τα δύο χέρια (εικ. 16).[62] Σε ενεπίγραφη ανάγλυφη βάση από την Ακρόπολη αρ. ευρ. 4069, του β' μισού του 4ου αι. π.Χ., η Αγαθή Τύχη χωρίς σύμβολα, ντυμένη με αχειρίδωτο χιτώνα και ιμάτιο, το οποίο ανασύρεται επάνω στο κεφάλι και δεν παρουσιάζει την τριγωνική αναδίπλωση, απεικονίζεται ανάμεσα

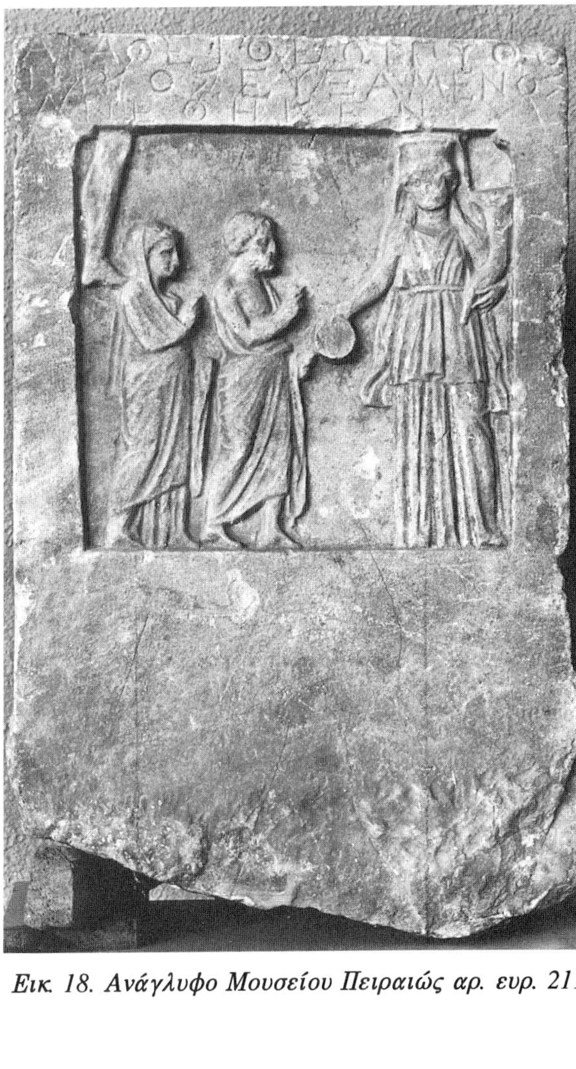

Εικ. 18. Ανάγλυφο Μουσείου Πειραιώς αρ. ευρ. 211.

στον Αγαθοδαίμονα και μια άλλη γυναικεία θεότητα (εικ. 17).[63] Σε αναθηματικό ανάγλυφο του Μουσείου Πειραιώς αρ. ευρ. 211, του τέλους του 4ου αι. π.Χ., η Αγαθή Τύχη, που αναφέρεται στην επιγραφή ως *'Αγαθὴ Θεός*, με πόλο στο κεφάλι και καλύπτρα και με ψηλά ζωσμένο πέπλο με μακρύ απόπτυγμα κρατάει στο αριστερό χέρι το κέρας της Αμαλθείας και στο δεξιό μια φιάλη (εικ. 18).[64] Από την επισκόπηση των απεικονίσεων αυτών συνάγεται ότι τον 4ο αι. π.Χ. δεν υπήρχε στην Αττική ένας μόνον εικονογραφικός τύπος για την παράσταση της Αγαθής Τύχης.

Η έλλειψη χαρακτηριστικών συμβόλων και το γεγονός ότι ο γενικός αγαλματικός τύπος είχε χρησιμοποιηθεί για την απεικόνιση αρκετών θεοτήτων και προσωποποιήσεων καθιστούν την αναγνώριση της θεότητας που εικονίζεται στο άγαλμα του Μουσείου Πειραιώς αρκετά προβληματική. Αμφιβολίες μπορούν να εκφραστούν και για το άγαλμα του Μουσείου Θερμών.

Εντέλει παρά τις δυσκολίες αναγνώρισης της μορφής που απεικονίζεται, το άγαλμα του Μουσείου Πειραιώς είναι σημαντικό απόκτημα, καθόσον πρόκειται για ένα πρωτότυπο και δροσερό έργο της Αττικής Σχολής του τέλους του 4ου αι. π.Χ.

Συντομογραφίες

Εκτός από τις καθιερωμένες συντομογραφίες χρησιμοποιούνται και οι εξής:

Palagia 1982: O. Palagia, "A Colossal Statue of a Personification from the Agora of Athens," *Hesperia* 51, 1982, 99–113, πίν. 29–36.

Palagia 1994: O. Palagia, "No Demokratia," στο W.D.E. Coulson, O. Palagia κ.ά. (επιμ.), *The Archaeology of Athens and Attica under the Democracy* 113–122.

Σημειώσεις

1. Ευχαριστώ θερμότατα και από την θέση αυτή τον επίτιμο Έφορο των Αρχαιοτήτων κ. Βασίλειο Πετράκο για την πρόθυμη άδεια δημοσίευσης του αγάλματος, τον καθηγητή κ. Γεώργιο Δεσπίνη για την πολύτιμη βοήθειά του στη διάρκεια της μελέτης μου και για τη διόρθωση του κειμένου που παρουσιάστηκε στο συνέδριο, τον καθηγητή κ. Άγγελο Δεληβορριά για το ενδιαφέρον και τη συζήτηση ορισμένων θεμάτων και τη ζωγράφο κ. Μανόλια Σκουλούδη για την εκπόνηση των σχεδίων. Ευχαριστώ επίσης για την χορήγηση φωτογραφιών και την άδεια δημοσίευσής τους την Β' Εφορεία Προϊστορικών και Κλασικών Αρχαιοτήτων Αττικής, το Γερμανικό Αρχαιολογικό Ινστιτούτο Αθηνών και το Εθνικό Αρχαιολογικό Μουσείο.

2. Για την πρώτη παρουσίαση του αγάλματος βλ. Μ.Ι. Πωλογιώργη, *ΑΔελτ* 46, 1991 (1996) Χρονικά, 58–59, πίν. 33 β-γ, όπου απεικονίζονται η κύρια και η πίσω όψη πριν από τις εργασίες καθαρισμού. Αρχικά ο κορμός έφερε λέκιασμα βαθυκάστανου χρώματος, ίσως από λάδια, στις πτυχές του αναδιπλωμένου τμήματος του ιματίου στην κύρια όψη, σε δύο οριζόντιες ζώνες στους γλουτούς και σε μεγάλη έκταση στη δεξιά πλευρά. Ο καθαρισμός έγινε μόνο με πράσινο σαπούνι και νερό από τους μαρμαροτεχνίτες του Μουσείου Πειραιώς κ. Αριστείδη Τριγώνη και κ. Γιάννη Σαμαντά.

3. Λοιπές διαστάσεις: Πλάτος στους ώμους 0.41 μ. και στην περιφέρεια 0.52 μ. κατά προσέγγιση. Τόρμος γόμφωσης στη δεξιά πλευρά: ύψος 0.03 μ., πλάτος 0.015 μ., βάθος 0.09 μ. Τόρμος στον αριστερό πήχυ: πλάτος 0.03 μ., βάθος 0.08 μ. Κοιλότητα για την ένθεση της κεφαλής: 0.25 Χ 0.21 μ., μέγιστο βάθος 0.15 μ. Πλίνθος: μέγιστο μήκος 0.57 μ., πλάτος 0.35 μ., μέγιστο πάχος 0.06 μ.

4. M. Flashar – R. von den Hoff, *BCH* 117, 1993, 407–433, ιδιαίτερα για τον τρόπο προσαρμογής του δεξιού χεριού στις μορφές αρ. ευρ. 1817 και 1820 βλ. σ. 415 κ.ε., εικ. 7 και 11 αντίστοιχα. Δες και την ανακοίνωση του W. Geominy, σελ. 61–68.

5. Για το άγαλμα αυτό βλ. W. Geominy, *Die Florentiner Niobiden* (διδακτορική διατριβή Bonn 1984) 274, εικ. 322. Palagia 1982, 102.

6. A. Stewart, *Greek Sculpture. An Exploration* (1990) 176–177, πίν. 497.

7. Stewart ό.π. (σημ. 6) πίν. 501.

8. Βλ. E.B. Harrison στο *Festschrift für Frank Brommer* (1977) 156. Για το *στρόφιον* βλ. και Ι.Α. Παπαποστόλου, *ΑΔελτ* 32, 1977, Μελέτες 303.

9. Βλ. σχετικά C. Nippe, *Die Fortuna Braccio Nuovo. Stilistische und typologische Untersuchung* (διδακτορική διατριβή Berlin 1989) 49 και παραδείγματα στη σημ. 322.

10. Βλ. σχετικά Harrison ό.π. (σημ. 8) 155 κ.ε. Palagia 1982, 110.

11. Διεξοδική παρουσίαση του κορμού έγινε από την Palagia 1982, 99–113, πίν. 29–30. Αναθεώρηση της ερμηνείας: Palagia 1994, 113–122, όπου και η παλιότερη βιβλιογραφία.

12. Palagia 1982, 101–103. Palagia 1994, 113.

13. Geominy ό.π. (σημ. 5) 273–274, εικ. 319. Ε. Βουτυράς, *Εγνατία* 2, 1990, 129–130, εικ. 5. Στα τέλη του 4ου αι. π.Χ. χρονολογείται ο κορμός της αθηναϊκής Αγοράς και από τον T. Lygkopoulos, *Untersuchungen zur Chronologie der Plastik des 4. Jhs. Chr.* (διδακτορική διατριβή Bonn 1983) 141–142.

14. R. Carpenter, *Hesperia* 2, 1933, 54–56 εικ. 15.

15. Palagia 1982, 104.

16. Γ. Δεσπίνης, *Παρθενώνεια* (1982) 94, αριθ. 8.33, όπου και η παλιότερη βιβλιογραφία.

17. Σ. Καρούζου, *'Εθνικὸν Ἀρχαιολογικὸν Μουσεῖον. Συλλογὴ γλυπτῶν* (1967) 155, αρ. 1463, πίν. 51 β. Flashar – von den Hoff ό.π. (σημ. 4) 429 και σημ. 76 με την παλιότερη βιβλιογραφία, εικ. 20.

18. M. Collignon, *Les statues funéraires dans l'art grec* (1911) 158, εικ. 90. M. Hamiaux, *Musée du Louvre. Les sculptures grecques* (1992) 206–207, αρ. 213.

19. G.M.A. Richter, *Catalogue of Greek Sculptures, Metropolitan Museum of Art, New York* (1954) 127, αρ. 126, πίν. XCVI. Η χρονολόγηση γύρω στα 340–330 π.Χ. φαίνεται υψηλή. Στο τελευταίο τέταρτο του 4ου αι. π.Χ. το εντάσσει η Harrison ό.π. (σημ. 8) 157 σημ. 18.

20. C. Vorster, *Griechische Kinderstatuen* (διδακτορική διατριβή Köln 1983) 349, αριθ. καταλ. 53, πίν. 16,2.

21. H. Diepolder, *Die attischen Grabreliefs des 5. und 4. Jahrhunderts v. Chr.* (1965) πίν. 43,2. Palagia 1982, 105 σημ. 39.

22. Diepolder ό.π. πίν. 47. Palagia ό.π. (σημ. 21).
23. S. Woodford, *An Introduction to Greek Art* (1986) 158, εικ. 232. Palagia ό.π. (σημ. 21).
24. G.E. Mylonas, *Eleusis and the Eleusinian Mysteries* (1961) 190, εικ. 63.
25. Καρούζου ό.π. (σημ. 17) 164, αρ. ευρ. 231. Lygkopoulos ό.π. (σημ. 13) 142 (του πρώιμου 3ου αι. π.Χ., μετά τον κορμό της Αγοράς S 2370). Stewart ό.π. (σημ. 6) 198, πίν. 602–603 (γύρω στα 300 π.Χ.). B.S. Ridgway, *Hellenistic Sculpture* I (1990) 55–57, πίν. 31. L. Todisco, *Scultura greca del IV secolo* (1993) 138–139, εικ. 306 (310–290 π.Χ.). Από τον Geominy ό.π. (σημ. 5) 243. 273 και σημ. 646, εικ. 266–267. 320 υποστηρίχθηκε η χρονολόγηση της Θέμιδος γύρω στο 315 π.Χ., πριν από τον κορμό της Αγοράς S 2370 (γύρω στα 310 π.Χ.). Palagia 1994, 118–119, εικ. 5. Για τη Θέμιδα δες και το άρθρο του Π. Θέμελη στον παρόντα τόμο, σελ. 47–59.
26. Harrison ό.π. (σημ. 8) 157. Palagia 1982, 105–106, πίν. 33 d-e.
27. B. Richter ό.π. (σημ. 19) 127, αρ. 126, με παραδείγματα.
28. Βλ. Flashar – von den Hoff ό.π. (σημ. 4) 409 κ.ε., εικ. 3.
29. Α.Γ. Καλογεροπούλου, *ΑΔελτ* 24, 1969, Μελέτες, 219–222, πίν. 122–124.
30. A. Conze, *Die attischen Grabreliefs* (1893–1922) αρ. 410, πίν. 97. K. Dohan Morrow, *Greek Footwear and the Dating of Sculpture* (1985) 72, πίν. 54.
31. Palagia 1982, 106. 108 και σημ. 43 με την παλιότερη βιβλιογραφία, πίν. 35 b.
32. Ν. Παπαχατζή, *Παυσανίου Ελλάδος Περιήγησης, Βοιωτικά-Φωκικά* (1981) 378–379, εικ. 414. Palagia 1982, 103–104. 108 και σημ. 58. Flashar – von den Hoff ό.π. (σημ. 4) 420 εικ. 18. Δες και την ανακοίνωση του Π. Θέμελη στον παρόντα τόμο, σελ. 47–59.
33. S. Wide, *ΑΕφημ*, 1910, 48–49, εικ. 6. Palagia 1982, 108 και σημ. 58.
34. Palagia 1982, 108 και σημ. 58, πίν. 36 b.
35. Palagia 1982, 108 και σημ. 47 και 58, πίν. 35 e.
36. T.L. Shear, Jr., *Hesperia* 40, 1971, 270–271, πίν. 56. Palagia 1994, 113–122, εικ. 1.
37. Palagia 1982, 101 και σημ. 8. 108 κ.ε., πίν. 31 c.
38. Palagia 1982, 105 σημ. 37, πίν. 34 a.
39. *LIMC* V (1990) λ. Hygieia, αρ. 59 (F. Croissant).
40. Palagia 1982, 109 και σημ. 58, πίν. 36 c.
41. Palagia 1982, 107 με σημ. 47.109, πίν. 35 c (329/8–317/08 π.Χ.). M. Meyer, *Die Griechischen Urkundenreliefs*, 13. Beih. *AM* (1989) 306, αρ. κατ. A 142, πίν. 42,1 (320–310 π.Χ.). C.L. Lawton, *Attic Document Reliefs. Art and Politics in Ancient Athens* (1995) 146, αρ. κατ. 150, πίν. 79 (τελευταίο τέταρτο 4ου αι. π.Χ.). Δες και παρακάτω, σημ. 43.
42. Β. Παπαδάκη-Αγγελίδου, *Αἱ προσωποποιήσεις εἰς τήν ἀρχαίαν ἑλληνικήν τέχνην* (1960) 55.
43. O. Palagia, *JHS* 95, 1975, 180–182. *LIMC* IV (1988) λ. Eutaxia (O. Palagia).
44. A. Pasqui, *NSc* 11 (1914) 143, εικ. 2–3. R. Kabus-Jahn, *Studien zu den Frauenfiguren des 4. Jahrhunderts vor Christus* (1963) 36–37 και σημ. 38, αριθ. 8. L. Guerrini, *StMisc* 22, 1974–1975, 110 σημ. 10, αρ. 11. Palagia 1982, 107, πίν. 34 b. *Museo Nazionale Romano. Le sculture* I,8 (1985) 494, αρ. IX, 18 (αρ. ευρ. 2001480) (D. Bonanome). Nippe ό.π. (σημ. 9) 18–20. 82–83, αρ. κατ. K 11, πίν. 5a.
45. Kabus-Jahn ό.π. (σημ. 44) 39 και σημ. 50.
46. Βλ. ιδιαίτερα Nippe ό.π. (σημ. 9) 49.
47. Shear ό.π. (σημ. 36) 271. Guerrini ό.π. (σημ. 44) 109–113.
48. Shear ό.π. (σημ. 36) 271.
49. H.A. Thompson, *The Athenian Agora Guide*[3] (1976) 204–205, εικ. 37. Harrison ό.π. (σημ. 8) 157.
50. Palagia 1982, 111–113.
51. Palagia 1994, 120. O. Palagia, *Yale University Art Gallery Bulletin* 1994, 65, εικ. 36.
52. Guerrini ό.π. (σημ. 44) 111, εικ. 25. Palagia 1994, 115. 117, εικ. 4.
53. Palagia 1994, 117, εικ. 8.
54. Kabus-Jahn ό.π. (σημ. 44) 38.
55. Kabus-Jahn ό.π. (σημ. 44) 38. Βλ. και J. Inan, *Roman Sculpture in Side* (1975) 108–109, αριθ. κατ. 45, πίν. L1,2. Για τα σύμβολα της Τύχης, το cornucopia και τον οίακα, βλ. κα. C.M. Edwards, *Hesperia* 59, 1990, 533–534.
56. Για τη λατρεία της Τύχης, τις απεικονίσεις και τις φιλολογικές μαρτυρίες των αγαλμάτων της βλ. F.W. Hamdord, *Griechische Kultpersonifikationen der Vorhellenistischen Zeit* (1964) 37–39. 97–100. Kabus-Jahn ό.π. (σημ. 44) 37–38. Guerrini ό.π. (σημ. 44) 113. Palagia 1994, 120. H.A. Shapiro, *Personifications in Greek Art* (1993) 227–228; *LIMC* VIII (1997) λ. Tyche (L. Villard) και λ. Tyche/Fortuna (F. Rausa).
57. S.V. Tracy, *Hesperia* 63, 1994, 241–244. Ας προστεθεί ακόμα τμήμα μαρμάρινου αναθήματος με την επιγραφή *'Αγαθῆι Τύχηι* που βρέθηκε σε επιχώσεις του μεσαιωνικού Ριζόκαστρου στη δυτική πάροδο του Διονυσιακού θεάτρου: Ν. Πλάτων, *ΑΔελτ* 21, 1966, Χρονικά, 39, πίν. 61 α (αρ. ευρ. Μουσείου Ακροπόλεως 14.902).
58. A. Effenberger, *Studien zur Tyche von Antiochia* (1969) 51. K. Bemmann, *Füllhörner in klassischer und hellenistischer Zeit* (1994) 56.
59. Bemmann ό.π. (σημ. 58) 56–58.
60. Hamdorf ό.π. (σημ. 56) 37–38. Palagia 1982, 109 σημ. 61.
61. Hamdorf ό.π. (σημ. 56) 38. Palagia 1982, 109 σημ. 58 και 61 με την παλιότερη βιβλιογραφία.
62. Palagia 1982, 109 σημ. 61. Bemmann ό.π. (σημ. 58) 215–216, αριθ. κατ. B 14, εικ. 35, με την παλιότερη βιβλιογραφία.
63. Palagia ό.π. (σημ. 62). Bemmann ό.π. (σημ. 58) 219, αριθ. κατ. B 19, με την παλιότερη βιβλιογραφία.
64. Palagia 1982, 109 σημ 61. Bemmann ό.π. (σημ. 58) 216–217, αριθ. κατ. B 15, εικ. 35, με την παλιότερη βιβλιογραφία. Ο Ι. Πετρόχειλος *ΑΕφημ* 1992, 35–36, εικ. 4 πιθανολογεί την συσχέτιση της *'Αγαθῆς Θεοῦ* του αναγλύφου αυτού με την Κυβέλη.

Attic Sculpture from Kallipolis (Aitolia): a Cult Group of Demeter and Kore

Petros Themelis

The fortified site of Velouchovo is in a strategical position in the mountainous region of eastern Aitolia. It covers the eastern flank of an isolated hill of Mt Vardousi commanding the confluence of four rivers. It is identified as ancient Kallion, also known as Kallipolis, mentioned in the literary sources as the polis of the Aitolian ethnos of the Ophioneis and their community of the Kallieis, and main target of the Celtic raid in 279 B.C. It was the only polis in eastern Aitolia and ranked among the major cities of the Aitolian territory, such as Kalydon, Trikhonion and Pleuron. Kallipolis was a convenient stop for Delphic theorias on their tours through western Greece.[1]

In the years 1977 to 1979 a rescue excavation was carried out by the author in collaboration with the French School at Athens, a Dutch survey team and an American team from the Loyola University of Chicago in a desperate attempt to bring to light as much as possible of the architectural remains of the city, the lower part of which was going to disappear under the waters of the huge artificial lake created by the dam of the Mornos River. A cluster of Hellenistic houses were uncovered at the lowest east terrace of the inhabited area; their fronts face a road running along the east wall and leading from the south gate to the agora. The agora, flanked by a stoa on its north side, was also accessible through the main gate in the middle of the east wall. On the upper terraces the scene and the proskenion of a theater, as well as a stoa and a large public building were excavated. During the Roman period (second century A.D.) a huge Bath was constructed in the area partly above the ruins of Houses IV and V.[2] A hoard of silver tetrobols of the early second century B.C. from the foundation trench of the theater and a second from the Bath comprising sestertii of Alexander Severus (231–235 A.D.) are worth mentioning.

Houses I and IV were destroyed by fire and were not rebuilt or reused as was the case with Houses II and III. The thick destruction layer with all the house furniture sealed the floors of the rooms. According to a selection of well-preserved fine ware from the destruction layer of House IV, so-called Archive, recently published by E. Valavani, the destruction should be dated to the late third or early second century B.C.,[3] and not related to the sack of the city by the Gauls in 279 B.C. as I had suggested in my first report.[4] This dating seems to be corroborated by Pantos' study of the 600 sealings found in House IV.[5] However, pottery, stamped amphora handles and particularly a considerable number of well-dated (late fourth – early third century B.C.) bronze and silver coins found in the destruction layers of Houses I and IV, as well as in their floor fills, foundation trenches and drainage conduits, have not been taken into consideration by Pantos and Valavani.[6] The building history of the habitation quarter of the lower terrace is thus much more complicated than it appears to be in the above publications. There is no doubt that all houses, including House IV, were first constructed in the late fourth century B.C.; Houses II and III were completely repaired and reinhabited after the destruction, while Houses I and IV were abandoned. The exact dates and the causes of their destruction should be reconsidered on the evidence of the coins and the rest of the finds.[7]

Two temples came to light outside the fortification walls of the city: a large peripteral one lying about 1.200 metres to the south[8] and a smaller one only 15 metres to the east of the southeastern tower.[9] The second temple with an east-west orientation is a square oikos measuring 4.80 × 4.80m in the inside (Figs. 1–2). No altar was found in front of the temple; the two rectangular structures close to its south side seem to be bases for votive monuments. A narrow, slightly raised chamber (opisthodomos), accessible through a staircase from the south, was added to the rear west side of the temple at a later period. It comprises two rooms, a large north one measuring 2.37m × 2.80m and a smaller, 0.95m × 1.45m, in its southwest corner.

Outside the temple, close to its north side, fragments of Laconian pan and cover tiles came to light; some of the tiles bear rectangular stamps with the ethnic ΚΑΛΛΙΠΟΛΙΤΑΝ to the right or left (Fig. 3), one of them preserving ΠΕ[---] (an official's name). The debris seems to be from a destruction layer removed from the temple area during repairs.[10] On the evidence of pottery, mainly lamp fragments and miniature vases, found in the

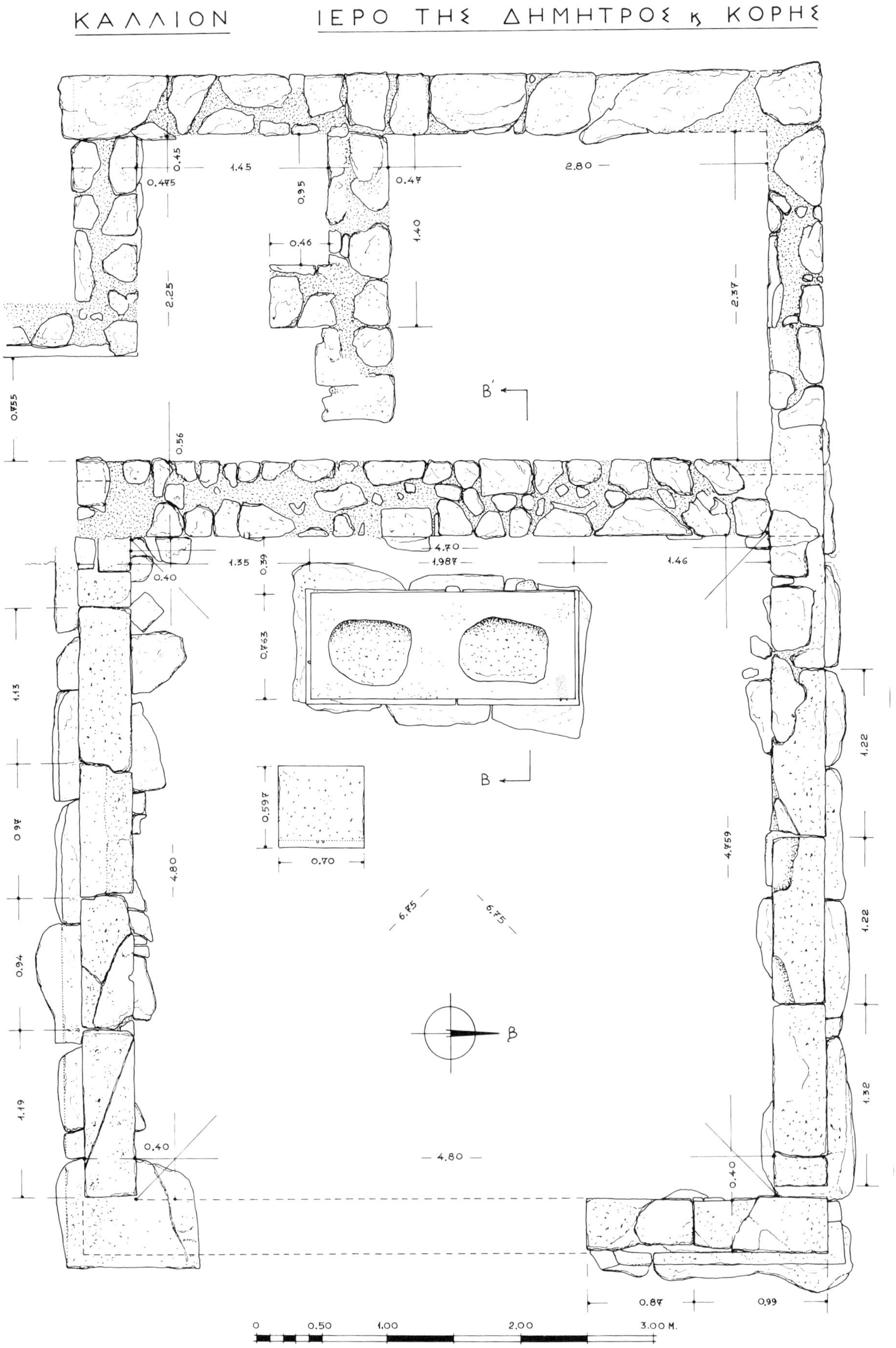

Fig. 1. Ground plan of the temple of Demeter, Kallipolis. Drawing Th. Thomaïdes.

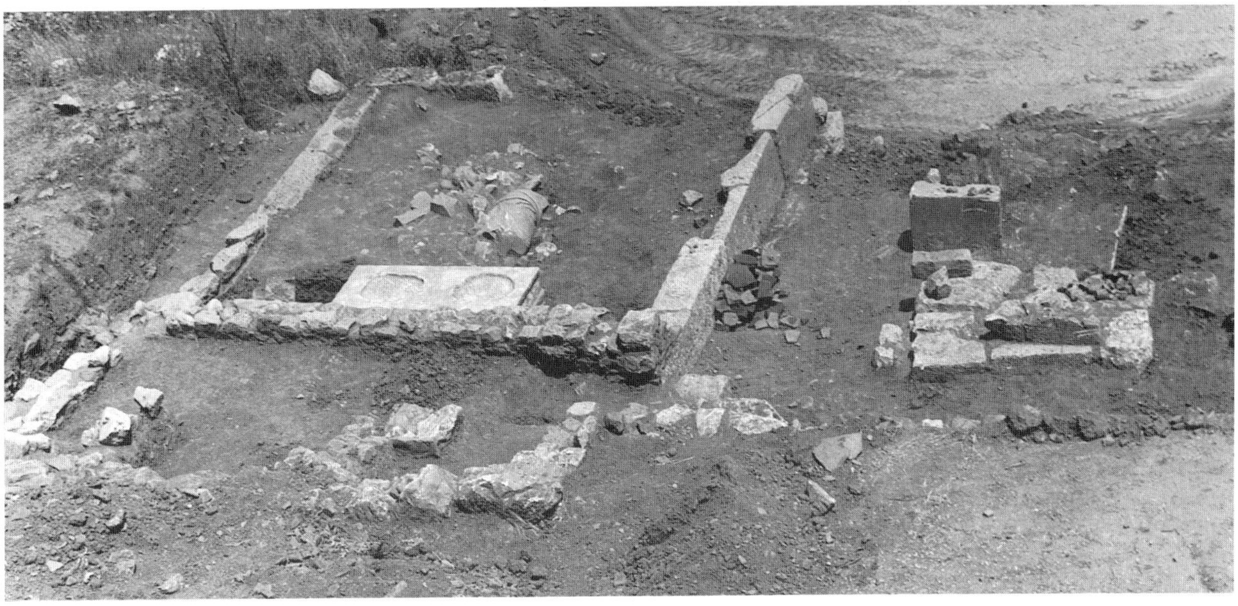

Fig. 2. General view of the temple of Demeter from the west. Photo V. Stamatopoulos.

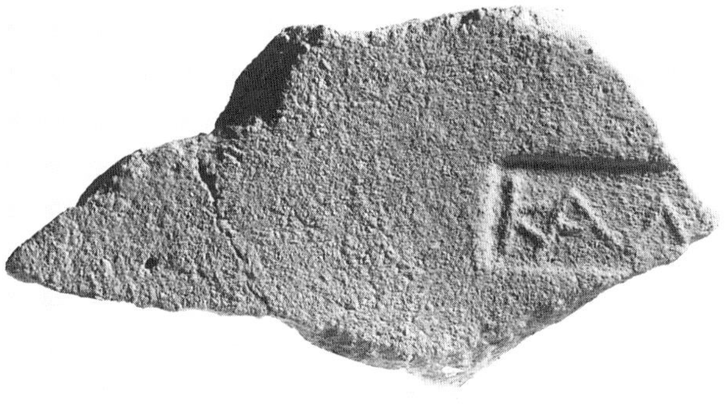

Fig. 3. Fragment of stamped roof tile. Photo S. Tsavdaroglou.

layer that covered the floor of the cella, it was clear that cult was practised in the temple at least from the early third century B.C. to the fourth A.D. without interruption. The final destruction of the temple does not seem to have been violent but was apparently due to a general decline and abandonment of the site. The roof of the Late Roman period with its superstructure collapsed gradually and covered the ruins.

One of a pair of marble cult statues (Fig. 4), a standing female figure, was the last to fall from the base above the layer of the roof tiles (Fig. 5).[11] Its exposure to rain while still standing outdoors caused the heavy weathering of its surface, mainly of the separately worked head and neck. The second statue of the cult group to the left of the standing figure disappeared almost completely, with the exception of a few fragments : part of the right hand holding a staff or scepter (Fig. 7), the right foot shod in a sandal (worked roughly underneath) (Fig. 6) and part of the separately carved foot-stool, indicating that she was seated. It seems that this massive seated figure did not fall from the base but was smashed into pieces and scattered in recent times. It was apparently female and represented Demeter as indicated by the iconography of the standing female figure identified with Kore (Fig. 4).

Part of an inscribed limestone block (Fig. 8), found in a modern terrace wall north of the temple, leaves no doubt about the identity of the deities: Delphi Museum 11869, 0.022m high, 0.55m long, 0.32m wide. The anathyrosis on top and the dowel hole in its left broken edge indicate that it was originally part either of a base constructed of several blocks or of the temple itself. The inscription on the face reads as follows:

[-- names? --]Δάματρι καὶ Κό[ραι] εὐ [---]
[-----] καὶ ἀνέθηκαν.

Height of letters 0.022–0.033m; third century B.C. The words KAI KO[PAI] were added above the first line with smaller letters of a later type as indicated by the broken horizontal line of A and the presence of more pronounced apices. The use of the plural in "dedicated" implies more than one dedicant. The word εὐ [---] could be completed as εὐ[ξάμεναι] or -οι]. The additive "and" in front of "dedicated" suggests the presence of a second verb in the plural, probably referring to construction or rather reconstruction of the monument to which the inscribed block belonged. Provided our suggestion is correct, we have to assume that in the missing part of the first line, not only the names of the dedicants but also the object of their dedication were mentioned.[12]

All the fragments of the statues, as well as the blocks of the base are now in the Delphi Museum.

The standing young goddess, 1.96m high, is of Pentelic marble (Figs. 10–24). Only the lower part of the left leg is missing. Fragments of the pendent folds of the himation join the left lower side (Fig. 15). The head and neck with

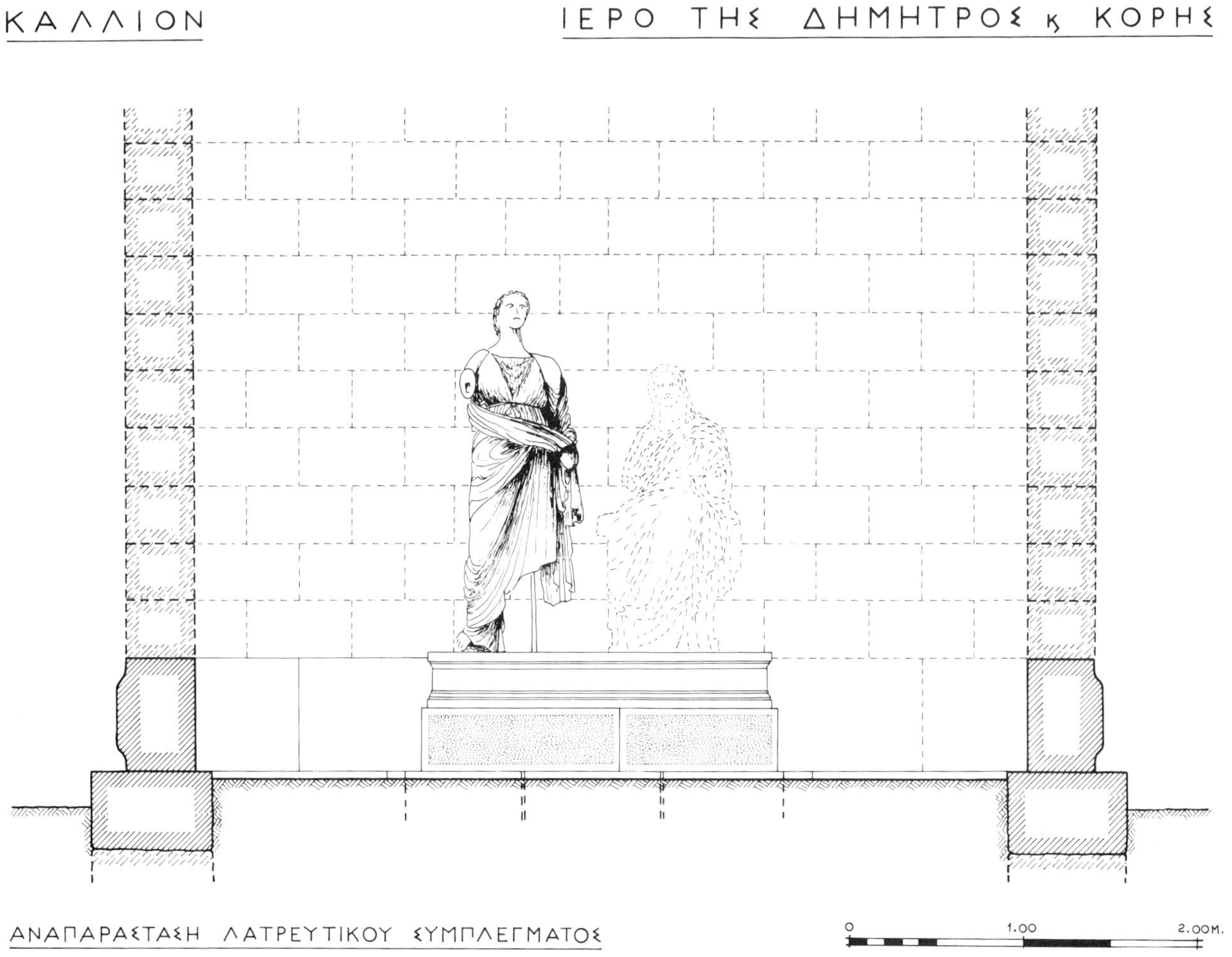

Fig. 4. Reconstruction of the cult group. Drawing by E. Olympios.

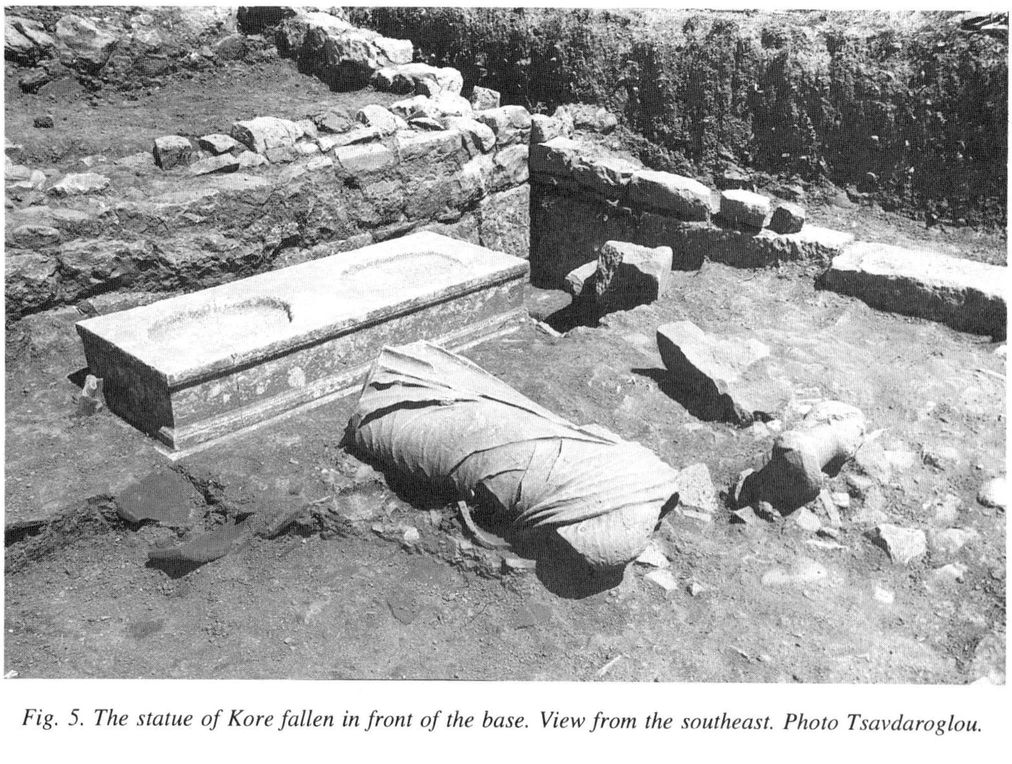

Fig. 5. The statue of Kore fallen in front of the base. View from the southeast. Photo Tsavdaroglou.

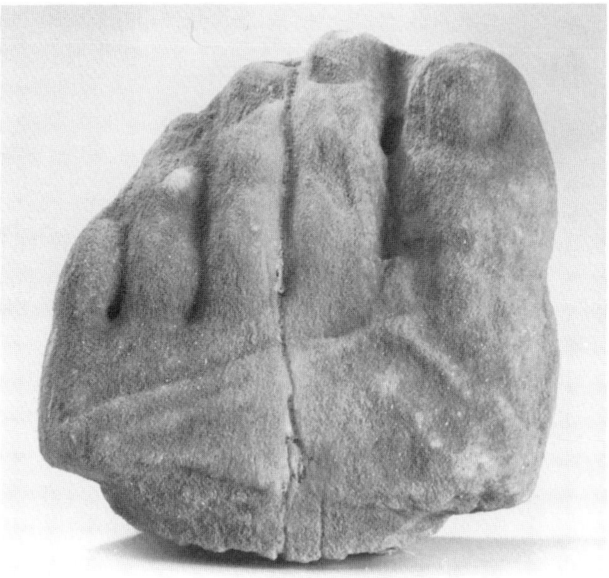

Fig. 6. Right foot of Demeter. Photo Stamatopoulos.

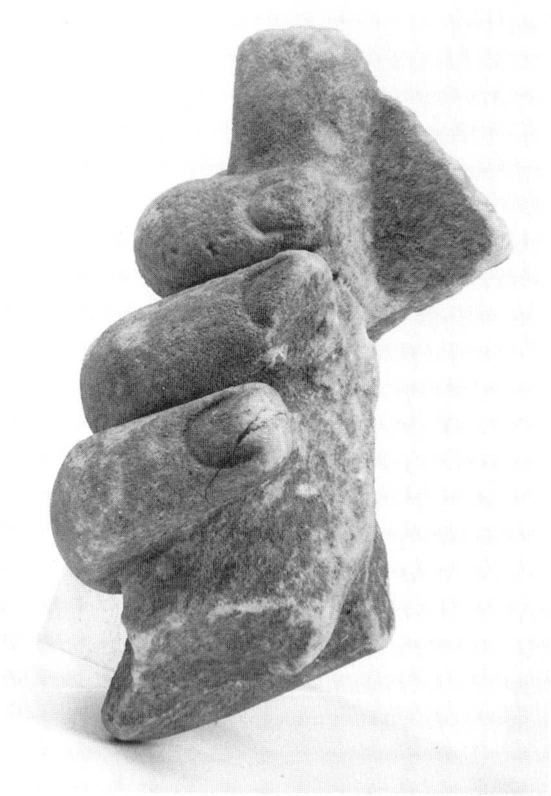

Fig. 7. Left hand of Demeter. Photo Tsavdaroglou.

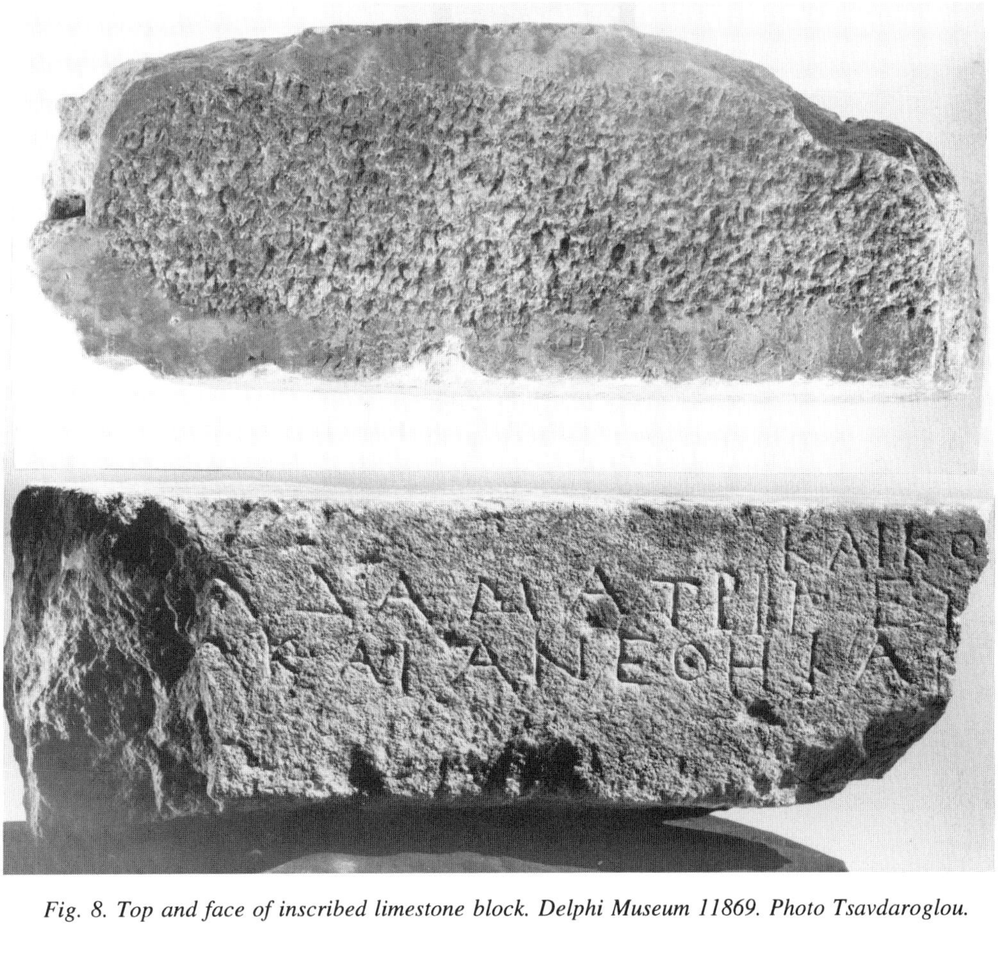

Fig. 8. Top and face of inscribed limestone block. Delphi Museum 11869. Photo Tsavdaroglou.

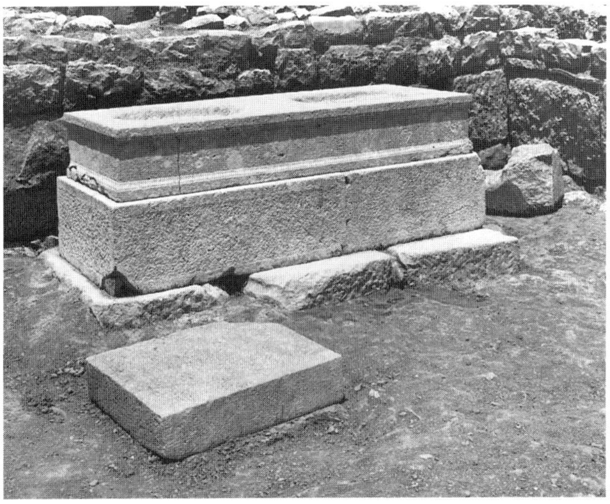

Fig. 9. The base of the cult group. View from the southeast. Photo Tsavdaroglou.

the upper part of the chest were separately carved and inserted into the deep cavity between the shoulders (Figs. 16–19). Also separately worked were the right arm (Figs. 20–21), free of the body, both hands and most of the fingers adjusted with iron dowels (Figs. 22–23). The back is roughly worked. The attribute she was holding is lost; it was probably a torch held with both hands across her body, as on the votive relief Athens National Museum 3917, depicting Artemis in a type of 330–320 B.C. similar to the Kallipolis Kore, but with opposite ponderation.[13]

The Kallipolis Kore is tall, with relatively small head and long neck (Figs. 10; 13). She stands with her right leg placed sideways on tiptoe; her foot is shod in a strapless sandal (Fig. 14). The chiastic pose (contrapposto) of legs and arms gives a rhythmic stance to the figure. Her shoulders are level. The body is almost frontal, while the head is turned upwards to her left. The waved hair is bound with a band behind and falls on the back (Figs. 16–19). Except for the front and side of the hair locks, the back is very rough and gives the impression of having been recut (Fig. 19).[14] The eyes, deep in their cavities and strongly shaded, look up. The lips are slightly parted, the face oval with triangular forehead. Despite the fact that she was grouped with Demeter seated at her left, the Kallipolis Kore is an isolated figure with no external or internal relation to her divine mother (Fig. 4).[15]

The Kore wears a transparent, short-sleeved chiton, allowing the prominent breasts to show through. A cord is fastened across the shoulders and under the breasts, forming a Herakles knot in keeping with late fourth-century fashion (Fig. 13). Two kolpoi fall over the girdle on the left and right. The crinkly chiton is modelled by

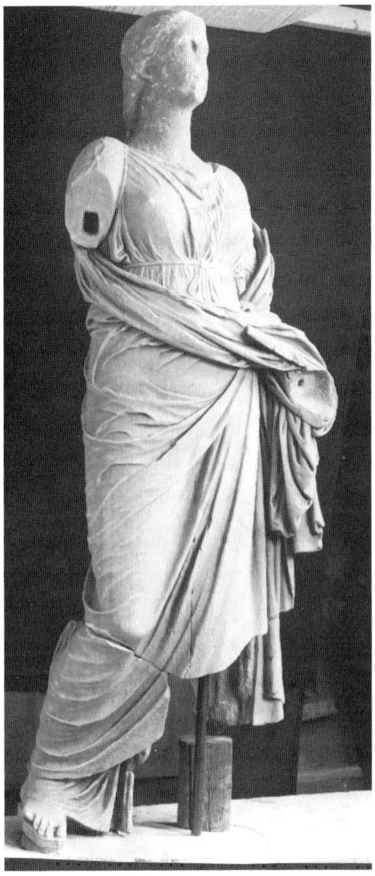

10

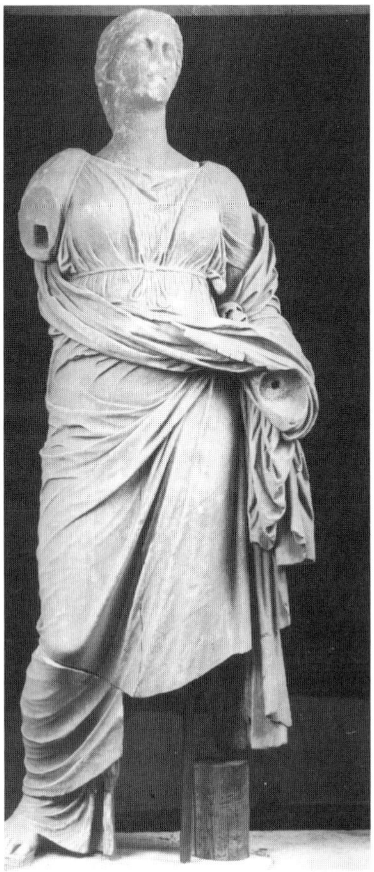

11

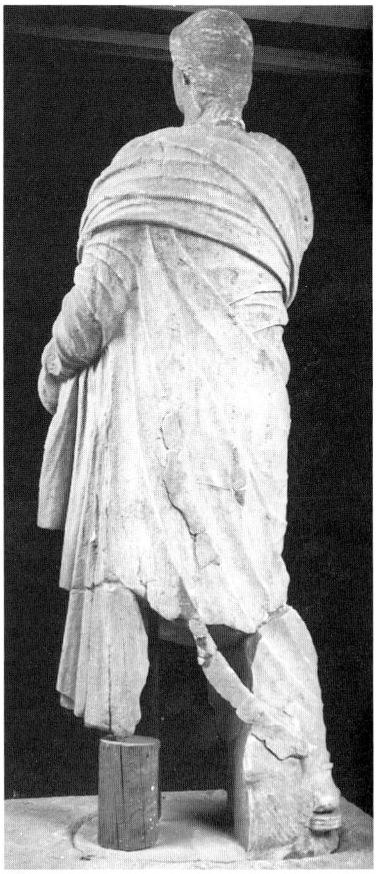

12

Figs. 10–12. Kore of Kallipolis. Delphi Museum. Photo Stamatopoulos.

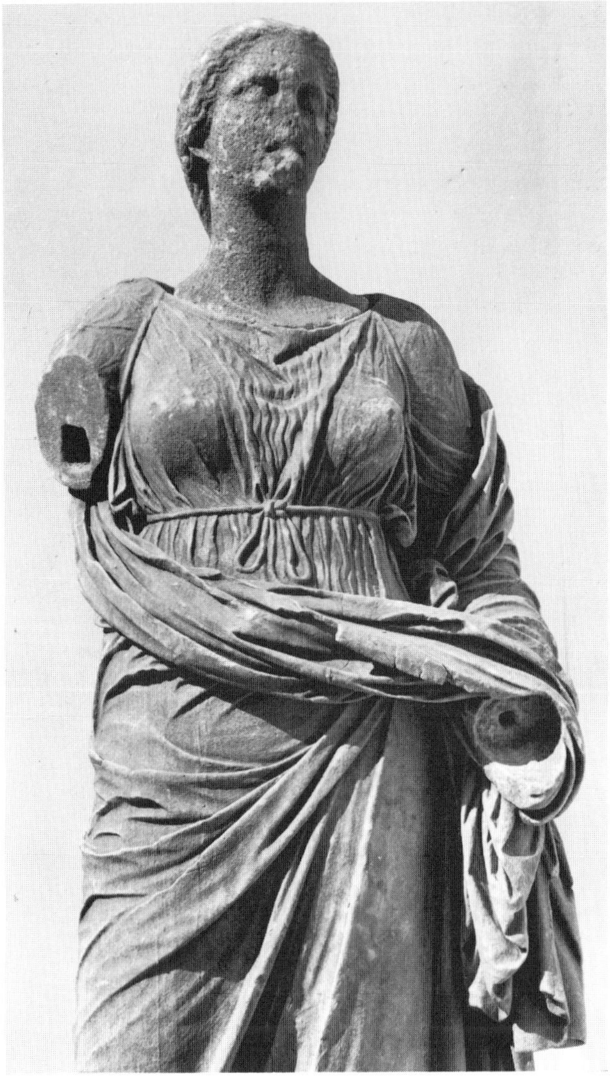

Fig. 13. Detail view of the Kore of Kallipolis. Delphi Museum. Photo Tsavdaroglou.

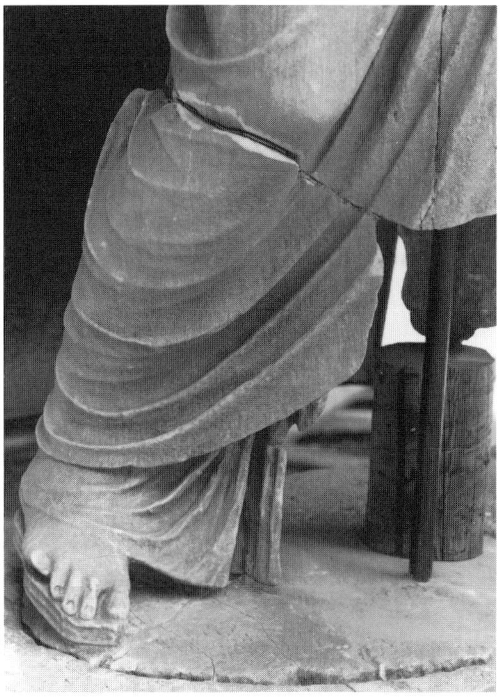

Fig. 14. Right lower leg and foot of the Kore of Kallipolis. Photo Stamatopoulos.

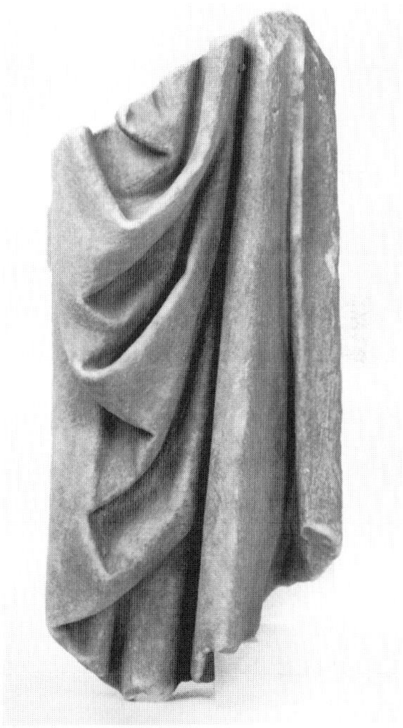

Fig. 15. Fragment of pendent folds of the himation from the left side of the Kore. Delphi Museum. Photo Tsavdaroglou.

vertical ridges, while rippling V-shaped folds fall between the breasts creating a distinct bunch from the neckline to the knot in the girdle. Above the girdle the cloth is articulated in sunken frets, a motif occurring in works of the late fourth century, the best known original being the female torso Agora Museum S 2370.[16] "Fluttering" folds sometimes occupy the entire chiton surface, notably in grave statues of women and in particular in votive statuettes of girls of the late fourth and early third centuries B.C.[17]

The himation draped over the left upper arm and covering her body in front from under the waist to above the feet, allowing the lower part of the chiton to appear, hangs over the left thigh forming a voluminous transverse roll of folds at hip level, from the left forearm to the right side. A fragment of folds (Fig. 24), not yet attached to the figure's garment, finds its parallel in the isolated puffed-up and rosette-like motif that fits into the middle of the similar transverse drapery roll formed by the himation of the Themis of Rhamnous, which gives the impression of "a different piece of cloth deposited in the figure's lap".[18] Three long folds of the himation starting from different parts of the right leg meet on the left thigh of the Kallipolis Kore (Fig. 11). The folds of her himation, interrupted by diagonal lines, give the drapery a creased and nervous effect; such a complex execution of folds

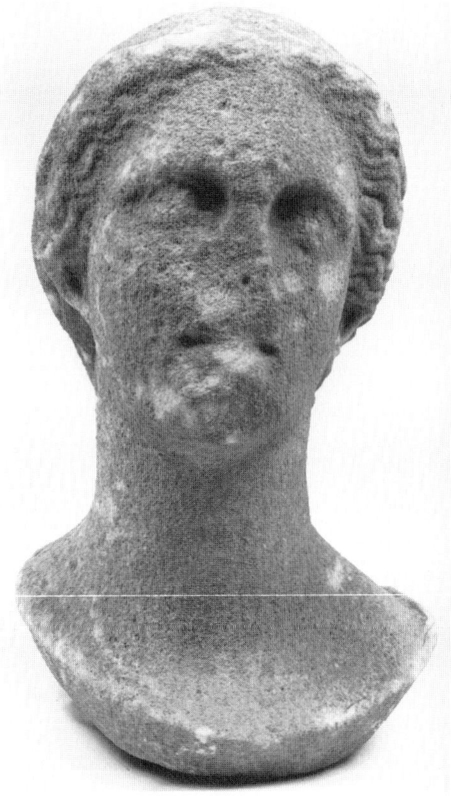

16

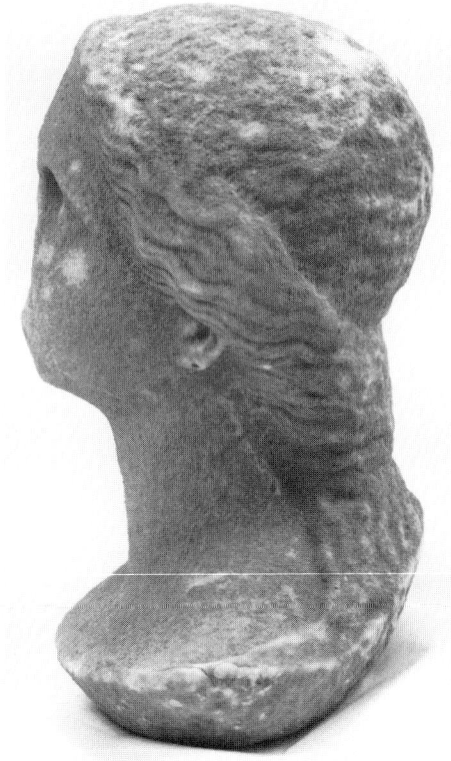

17

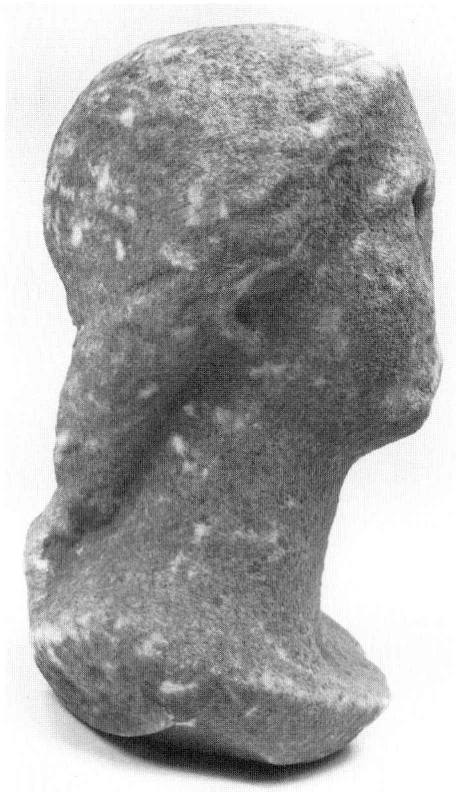

18

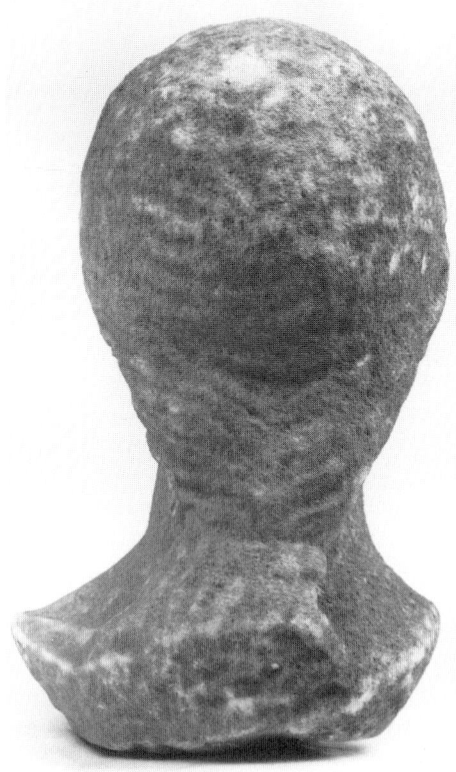

19

Figs. 16–19. Head of the Kore of Kallipolis. Delphi Museum. Photo Stamatopoulos.

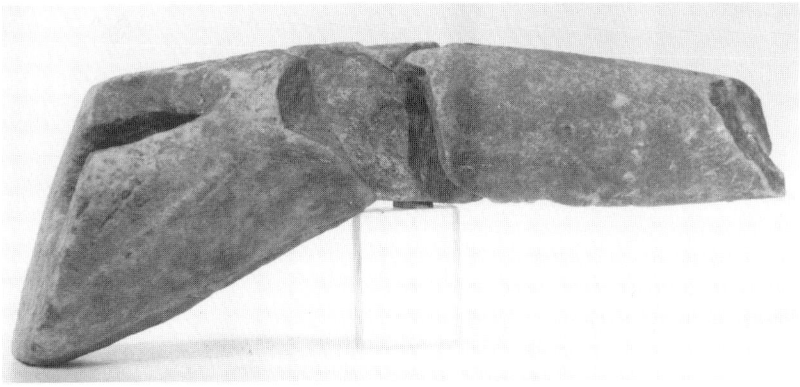

20

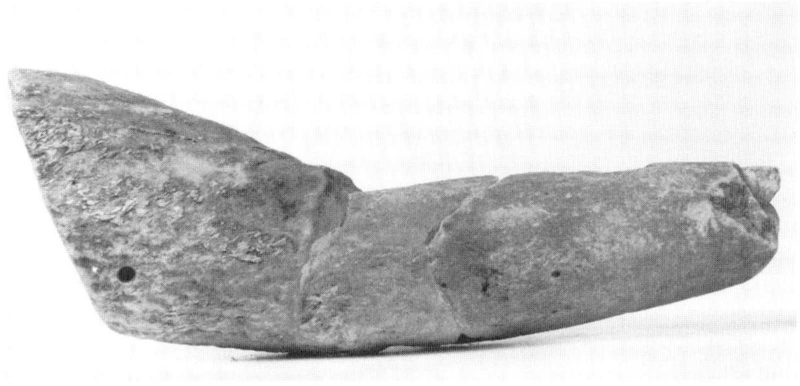

21

Figs. 20–21. Right arm of Kore. Delphi Museum. Photo Tsavdaroglou.

already occurs in document reliefs of about 320 B.C.[19]

The Kallipolis Kore appears momentarily posed, slightly moving to her left, although her elongated body remains almost frontal. Momentary movement, combined with elongated proportions characterizes the depiction of figures in the late 4th century B.C., emphasizing their heroization as in the grave stele of Hieron and Lysippe from Ramnous (Athens National Museum 833).[20] A characteristic parallel of this manner of representation is the figure of Demos on the document relief of Euphron of Sikyon, Athens National Museum 1482, dated to 318/7 B.C.[21] The momentary movement is particularly accentuated by the edge of the himation on the left arm of the Kallipolis Kore, appearing as if sliding down, a motif deriving from Praxitelean figures, for example the so-called Small Herculaneum Woman,[22] an excellent replica of which is the statue of an Artemis priestess from Aulis (Thebes Museum BE 64).[23]

The drama of the drapery and its restless rendering, the rhythmic stance, the exaggerated long neck and upturned head with the deeply shadowed eyes, the pathetic expression, betray a "baroque" tendency (Fig. 11). "... `baroque' tendencies of a sort were already present in Attic sculpture long before Phyromachos was born or turned his hand to portraiture ... This hankering after the grandiose and passionate seems to have begun around the middle of the fourth century and to have flourished in particular during the 'Alexanderzeit' and the period of the early Diadochi".[24]

The statuary type of the torso Athenian Agora S 2370, an important original of 330–320 B.C. probably representing Agathe Tyche, was employed for various deities and personifications.[25] The torso Agora S 2370 and its variants form a special group in the general category of "praying women", related to the Artemisia of Halicarnassus (London, British Museum 1001). The most important statue drawing on the Agora torso is the Themis of Rhamnous, signed by Chairestratos, son of Chairedemos, of Rhamnous (Athens National Museum 231).[26] A statue support in the form of a tree or rock with the folds of a garment on its upper part, found at Delphi in 1896 near the findspot of the Delphi Charioteer bears the inscription: Χαιρέστρατος | Ἀθηναῖος | [ἐποί]ησεν, confirming the activity of the sculptor of the Themis at Delphi (Delphi Museum 3620, height, 0.63m, width, 0.165m).[27]

The Themis of Chairestratos is now dated to 320–316 B.C. on the basis of stylistic and epigraphical evidence. Frel rightly argued that the Bouleutes Chairestratos honoured during the archonship of Euthykritos in 328/7 B.C. was the sculptor himself and not his grandfather.[28]

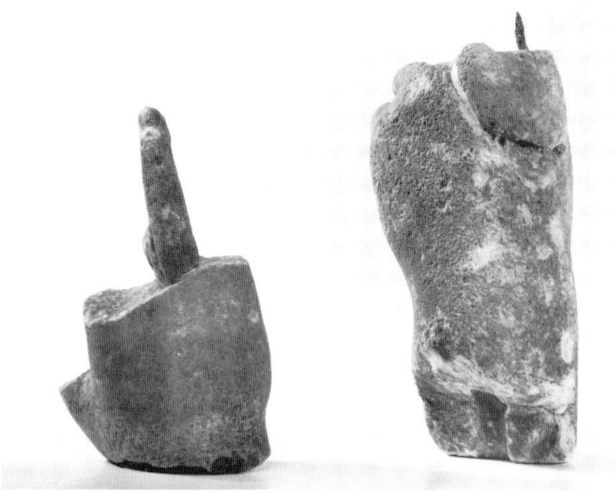

22

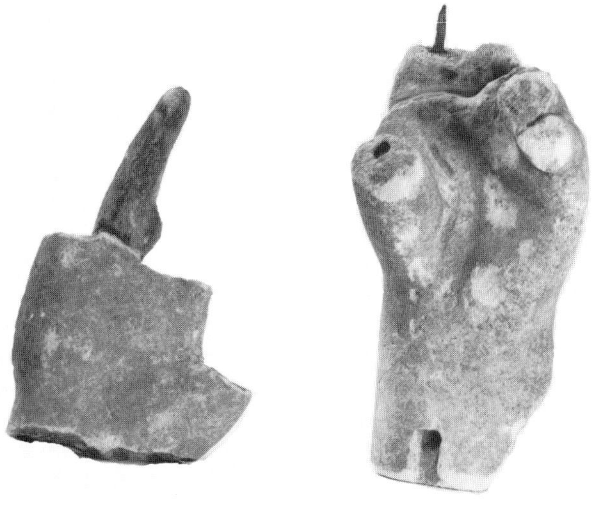

23

Figs. 22–23. Hands of Kore. Delphi Museum. Photo Tsavdaroglou.

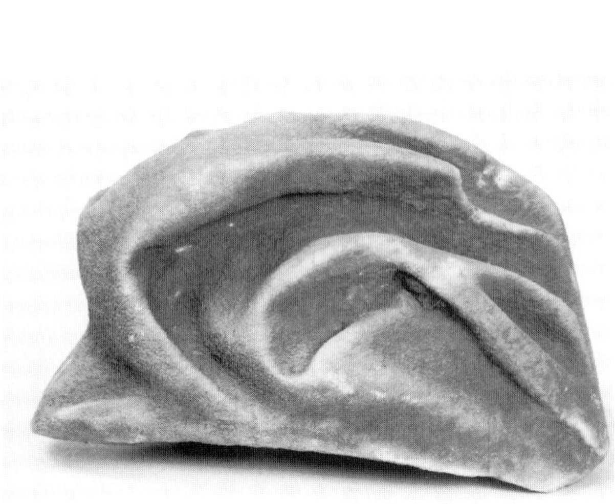

Figs. 24. Drapery fragment. Kore of Kallipolis. Delphi Museum. Photo Tsavdaroglou.

Chairedemos, father of Chairestratos, was priest at Rhamnous in 315/4 B.C. (*IG* II^2 2726). Geominy's stylistic evaluation of the Themis is in agreement with Frel's suggestion concerning the period of Chairestratos' artistic activity.[29] Evidence toward an "external" dating of the statue of Themis is also provided by her sandals, which display "the earliest true example of an indented sole" according to Morrow.[30] Furthermore, Chairedemos was choregos when he dedicated the statue according to the inscription on the base (*IG* II^2 3109). This testimony supports an absolute date for the Themis before 316 B.C., since the choregia, along with all other liturgies, was abolished around that time by Demetrios of Phaleron, all financial responsibilities henceforth falling on the city.[31]

The similarities betweem the Kallipolis Kore and the Themis of Rhamnous are close, not being confined to the pose and drapery but extending to formal details; the differences, however, in general conception and quality of execution are apparent. By comparison with the bulky, frontal and almost immovable Themis, the Kore of Kallipolis, by a first-rate master, turns and moves freely in space. It is clear that the Kallipolis Kore belongs to a more advanced stage than the Themis, while both represent successive phases in the evolution of the sculptural type adapted from the Agora torso S 2370. Except for the Themis of Rhamnous and the Kore of Kallipolis, two more originals of similar type, the headless statue in New York, Metropolitan Museum 07.12.17[32] and the headless Athena, 0.73 m high, in the Benavides Collection in Padova,[33] contribute to the reconstruction of a clearer evolutionary sequence. The transverse roll of the upper part of their himatia rises gradually from the right hip towards the waist on the same side, followed by a lowering of the left arm; thus, while in the Agora torso the transverse drapery roll is sloping to the right, it is almost horizontal in the Themis and sloping to the left in the Benavides Athena and particularly the Kallipolis Kore. This gradual change of direction (of the drapery motif) is accompanied by the appearance of more elongated proportions and prominent movements, thus confirming the chronological sequence: Agora torso, Themis (ca. 316 B.C.), Benavides Athena, Kallipolis Kore.

The upper chronological limit of our Kore is provided not only by the Themis which must be dated before the abolition of liturgies by Demetrios of Phaleron, but also by the Attic document relief of Euphron, dated to 318/17 B.C.,[34] while the lower limit is marked by the Attic document relief in honour of Herodoros, Athens, Acropolis Museum 4063+2307 (*IG* II^2 646), dated to 295/4 B.C.[35] The folds of Demos' himation on Euphron's relief stretch diagonally from ankle to hip in a way similar to the Kore of Kallipolis; also similar are, as stated above, his rhythmic stance and momentary movement; compare also Athena's high waist on the same relief, her height increased by her crested helmet. The Herodoros relief, on the other hand, displays all characteristics present in the statue from Kallipolis: isolation, frontality, elongated proportions, small head, high-girt chiton, but in a more advanced rendering. I would thus place the Kallipolis Kore between 310 and 295 B.C., anyhow before the sack of Kallipolis by the Gauls in 279 B.C. and before the statue made by Polyeuktos in 280/79 B.C. representing Demosthenes in a four-square static pose, his drapery arranged in simple lines.[36]

Three statues found at Delphi, the so-called Philosopher, Delphi Museum 1819 (here p. 62, Fig. 2),[37] the female statue Delphi Museum 1817 (here p. 62, Fig. 3)[38] and the male torso Delphi Museum 1820 (here p. 63, Fig. 4),[39] present striking stylistic and technical similarities with the Kallipolis Kore. Poulsen and Studniczka had dated the so-called Philosopher of Delphi after the middle of the fourth century B.C., Dohrn to 310–300 B.C., while Kleiner placed it before the static, closed and slender portrait statue of Demosthenes.[40] According to Waywell, the three statues should be considered later works of one of the Mausoleum ateliers.[41] M. Flashar and R. von den Hoff dated the statues to 310–290 B.C. and attributed them to the same sculptural group.[42] Stance, movement, contrapposto, proportions, drapery type and details, technical characteristics of all three statues find their closest parallels in the Kallipolis Kore, already noticed and discussed by Flashar and v. den Hoff. Their himatia form voluminous rolls at the waist. Three long distinct folds starting from their right leg meet on the left thigh. The folds of their himatia are intersected by sharp diagonal lines, giving the drapery the same creased and nervous effect as in the Kallipolis Kore; the right leg of all statues is brought to the side, their body being almost frontal. The only preserved head, belonging to the so-called Philosopher, is slightly turned to his right, the eyes are very deeply set. The high-laced *trochades* of the same male figure "help confirm the early hellenistic date".[43] The realistic rendering of his facial traits is not unprecentended.[44]

Two famous cult groups of the two Eleusinian goddesses are reported in the sources as made by Praxiteles, one with Triptolemos, probably located at Eleusis and later in Rome (Pliny, *NH* 36.23), another with Iakchos, seen by Pausanias in the Eleusinion near the Dipylon Gate (Pausanias 1.2.4; Cicero, *In Verr.* 4.60; Clem., *Protr.* 4.45).[45] A group of Demeter, seated and holding a sceptre, and Kore standing, depjcted on fragments of Panathenaic amphoras from Eleusis, dated between 359 and 348 B.C., seems to reproduce the Praxitelean group at Eleusis. They provide an important *terminus ante quem* for its creation.[46] The group on the amphoras seems to display certain compositional analogies to the Kallipolis cult group. The Kore on the amphoras, however, is wrapped tightly in her himation with its upper part covering the breasts in a type close to the so-called Kore of Florence (Florence, Uffizi 120). She is quite different from the Kallipolis Kore, thus excluding the possibility that the Florence type was the source of inspiration of our anonymous sculptor.[47] Variants are reproduced in an unpublished statuette from Brauron and a statuette from Kos, and on the votive reliefs from Mondragone (Naples, Museo Nazionale), Kyzicos (Paris, Louvre 2849), Eleusis (Paris, Louvre 752 and Eleusis Museum 5061 and 12), the Athenian Agora (Agora S 1251 and S 1646) and Piraeus (Athens, National Museum 1461), as well as on a document relief honoring the peripolarchos Smikythion (Eleusis Museum 5115).[48] The closest parallel to the Kore of Kallipolis is the Kore type in high-girt chiton and himation depicted on the votive relief Eleusis Museum 5067, next to Demeter seated on a cista.[49]

Notes

1. *IG* IX 1(2) 154–158; *SEG* 23.399; *SGDI* 2137; Polybios 20.11.11; Livy 36.30.4; Pausanias 10.22.4–6; Appian, *Syr.* 21; Stephanos Byzantios s.v. Korax; A. Plassart, *BCH* 45, 1921, 1–85.
2. P. Themelis, *AAA* 12, 1979, 245–279; id., *ASAtene* 61, 1983, 213–256; R. Laffineur, *ADelt* 32, 1977, Chron. 118, pl. 72; id., *BCH* 102, 1978, 840–847; *BCH* 103, 1979, 631–634; *BCH* 104, 1980, 742–747; S.C. Buchuizen, *ADelt* 32, 1977, Chron. 115–118;. id. in S. van de Maele and J. M. Fossey (edd.), *Fortificationes antiquae* (Amsterdam 1992) 171–184; J.A.C. Vroom, *Pharos* 1, 1993, 113–138; S. Herbert and E.W. Kase, *ADelt* 32, 1977, Chron. 114–115.
3. E. Baziotopoulou-Valavani in *Επιστημομονική συνάντηση γιά την ελληνιστική κεραμεική. Χρονολογημένα σύνολα-εργαστήρια*, September 1991, Thessaloniki (1994) 46–55, pls. 16–24.
4. P. Themelis, *AAA* 12, 1979, 270.
5. P. Pantos, *Τα σφραγίσματα της αιτωλικής Καλλιπόλεως* (1985) 454–458.
6. D. Kravartoiannos, "Κατάλογος νομισματικών ευρημάτων Καλλιπόλεως, ανασκαφής 1978," *Tetramina* 19–20 (Amfissa 1981) 1309–1340, especially nos. 1; 3; 8–11; 20; 29–33; 35; 42 (=coins from House IV).
7. The function of House IV as a Prytaneion and not as a private residence was suggested to me by J. Mck.Camp II in a letter of April 20, 1982. Cf. S.G. Miller, *The Prytaneion. Its Function and Architectural Form* (1978) 67–86.
8. P. Themelis, *ASAtene* 61, 1983, 248–254; F. Felten in *FREMDE ZEITEN, Festschrift für J. Borchhardt* II (1996) 141, figs. 1–2.
9. N. Papachatzis, *Παυσανίου Ελλάδος περιήγησις. Βοιωτικά, Φωκικά* (1981) 375–379, figs. 411–412; 414.
10. This destruction might be related to the Celtic raid; the letter-forms on the roof tiles do not preclude a date before 279 B.C.
11. The limestone base (Fig. 9) is composed of three superimposed parts: a) lower part=euthynteria, 2.22m × 1.13m, constructed from three irregular slabs; pairs of sockets at the joints without iron bonds, b) middle part=podium, 2.09m × 0.84m, h. 0.37m, made of two blocks joined by iron bonds, dowels at the short sides for attachment into the upper part, lifting elbow left at the back side, c) upper part of one block, 1.987m × 0.763m, h. 0.31m., projecting bands with mouldings around the edges at the front and

narrow sides, lifting elbow rear left, two oval cuttings on the surface measuring 0.61 × 0.48m and 0.63 × 0.48m respectively for the insertion of the plinths. Total height of base above ground level: ca. 0.70m. It belongs to the category of "simple block bases with profiles" esp. popular in the early Hellenistic period: I. Schmidt, *Hellenistische Statuenbasen* (1995) 21–26 and 200–201, cat. nos. I.2.1–I.2.3; I.2.15. The base of the Themis of Chairestratos is the closest parallel.

12. Cf. C. Antonetti, *Les Étoliens. Image et religion* (1990) 293–294, who illustrated and commented on the inscription without permission and without indicating its provenance.
13. O. Palagia, *Euphranor* (1980) 30–31, fig. 18.
14. Probably after the recostruction of the temple and the repair of the cult group damaged during the sack of the city by the Celts: cf. remarks concerning the debris of the stamped roof tiles and the inscribed block.
15. The Demeter of Knidos (London, British Museum 1300, height, 1.47 m), used for our reconstruction drawing Fig. 4, was probably grouped with a Kore of similar size and pose to ours: *LIMC* IV (1988) s.v. Demeter, no. 138 (L. Beschi) with bibliography, although its cult character is denied: cf. J. Boardman, *Greek Sculpture. The Late Classical Period* (1995) 71, pl. 49.
16. On the date and name of the pattern: Palagia (supra n. 13) 15 n. 70. Agora torso: T.L. Shear, Jr., *Hesperia* 40, 1971, 270–277; O. Palagia, *Hesperia* 51, 1982, 99–113, pls. 29–36; ead. in W.D.E. Coulson, O. Palagia et al. (edd.), *The Archaeology of Athens and Attica under the Democracy* (1994) 113–122, fig. 1; B.S. Ridgway, *Hellenistic Sculpture* I (1990) 54–55, pl. 29.
17. C.V. Hesse, *Griechische Kinderstatuen* (1983) nos. 28; 30; 41; 44; 51.
18. Ridgway (supra n. 16) 56.
19. M. Meyer, *Die griechischen Urkundenreliefs* (1989) 69; C.L. Lawton, *Attic Document Reliefs. Art and Politics in Ancient Athens* (1995) 72.
20. W. Fuchs, *Die Skulptur der Griechen* (1979) 479, fig. 579; B. Schmalz, *Griechische Grabreliefs* (1983) 205–207, fig. 3 on page 19; B. Petrakos, *Prakt* 1977, 3–18, fig. 5; id. in *ΣΤΗΛΗ, τόμος εις μνήμην Ν.Κοντολέοντος* (1980) 402–407, pls. 187–190; id., *AEphem* 1979, 39–42, figs. 17–18.
21. Schmalz (supra n. 20) 205; Lawton (supra n. 19) 107–108, no. 54 with earlier bibliography; pl. 28.
22. Ridgway (supra n. 16) 92, pl. 56b. The motif combined with the same type of drapery occurs on a Muse of the Mantineia base in the Athens National Museum 216: Ridgway (supra n. 16) pl. 132b (Muse in the middle).
23. K. Demakopoulou, D. Konsola, *Archaeological Museum of Thebes* (1981) 80, no. BE 64, fig. 28.
24. A. Stewart, *Attika. Studies in Athenian Sculpture of the Hellenistic Age* (1979) 11.
25. Palagia (1994, supra n. 16); cf. *The Athenian Agora Guide*[4] (1990) 209, fig. 133.
26. V. Stais, *AEphem* 1891, 47–48, pl. 4; *IG* II[2] 3109; R. Horn, *Stehende weibliche Gewandstatuen in der hellenistischen Plastik* (1931) 19; 95; A. Wilhelm, *ÖJh* 32, 1942, 200–209; J. Marcadé, *Recueil des signatures de sculpteurs grecs* I (1953) 12; M. Bieber, *The Sculpture of the Hellenistic Age*[2] (1961) 65–66, fig. 516; C.M. Havelock, *Hellenistic Art* (1971) fig. 111; A. Borbein, *JdI* 88, 1973, 41f.; J. Frel, *GettyMusJ* 6–7, 1978–79, 75–82; id., *GettyMusJ* 8, 1980, 206; K.D. Morrow, *Greek Footwear and the Dating of Sculpture* (1985) 91, fig. 8a; M. Corsano, *Themis* (1988), fig. 2; Travlos, *Attika,* fig. 499; A. Mantis, *Προβλήματα της εικονογραφίας των ιερειών και των ιερέων στην αρχαία ελληνική τέχνη* (1990) 104–115, pl. 46a; Ridgway (supra n. 16) 55–57, fig. 31; Palagia (1994, supra n. 16) 3, fig. 5; P. Moreno, *Scultura ellenistica* (1994) 169–173, figs. 216–218; 220. The impressionistic treatment of Themis' hairstyle and the triangular forehead find their closest parallel on a female head of the late fourth century B.C. from Brauron, whose hair is also outlined against the face : *Ergon* 1958, 37, fig. 39 (top right). On the Themis of Rhamnous see also I. Leventi, here p. 111 n. 18.
27. Discussed by Frel, *GettyMusJ* 6–7, 1978–79, 76–82.
28. Frel (supra n. 27); id., *GettyMusJ* 8, 1980, 206; cf. the inscription in B.D. Meritt, J.S. Traill, *Agora* XV, *Inscriptions. The Athenian Councillors* (1974) 59, no. 49.
29. H.W. Geominy, *Die Florentiner Niobiden* (1984) 243f. n. 646; 273f., fig. 320; cf. A. Stewart, *Greek Sculpture* (1990) 198, figs. 602f.
30. Morrow (supra n. 26) 91; 93; 108; 140, fig. 8a.
31. Plutarch, *Praec. ger. reip.* 31.3; E. Bauer, *Demetrios Phalereus der Athener* (1942) 61f.; A.W. Pickard-Cambridge, *The Dramatic Festivals of Athens*[2] (1988) 91–92. I owe this reference to Niki Makri who deals with the subject of choregia in her unpublished Oxford dissertation. On Demetrios' abolition of state liturgies see also here p. 26 n. 57.
32. Picard, *Manuel* IV.2, 91 n. 1, figs. 43–44.
33. L. Beschi in *Marco Mantova Benavides, Atti della giornata di studio nel IV centenario dalla morte, 1582–1982* (1984) 17–25, pls. I–II.
34. Lawton (supra n. 21).
35. Lawton (supra n. 19) 109, no. 59, pl. 31.
36. Bieber (supra n. 26) 66–68, figs. 214–225; Ridgway (supra n. 16) 225: "Although the pose is static, the position of the right leg, forward and to the side, suggests incipient movement ... The himation is worn approximately as on the ... Delphi philosopher, but no "apron" is created by the overfold." R.R.R. Smith, *Hellenistic Sculpture* (1991) 38, pl. 39; J. Onians, *Art and Thought in the Hellenistic Age* (1979) 46, fig. 44; Moreno (supra n. 26) 181–189, figs. 227; 230; 233; 237–239; 241.
37. Ridgway (supra n. 16) 223, pl. 106; R. Kabus-Jahn, *Studien zu den Frauenfiguren des 4. Jhs. v. Chr.* (1963) 42–43; Fuchs (supra n. 20) 132, fig. 119. See also here pp. 61–68.
38. Kabus-Jahn (supra n. 37) 46–48; G.B. Waywell, *The Freestanding Sculpture of the Mausoleum at Halicarnassus in the British Museum* (1978) 71; here pp. 61–68.
39. Waywell (supra n. 38) 70; here pp. 61–68.
40. F. Poulsen, *Orakel i Delfi* (1919); F. Studniczka, *Artemis und Iphigenie* (1926) 108 n. 2; G. Kleiner, *Tanagrafiguren* (1942) 149.
41. Waywell (supra n. 38) 69.
42. M. Flashar – R. von den Hoff, *BCH* 117, 1993, 107–433; cf. J. Pouilloux, *La région Nord du sanctuaire, FdD* II (1960) 13 attributed to the same workshop only the Philosopher and the woman but not the naked male figure

no. 1820 which he dated to the first century B.C.; Kabus-Jahn (supra n. 37) was the first to associate the Philosopher with the two statues.

43. Ridgway (supra n. 16) 224.

44. Cf. for example the ivory heads and the medallions at the bottom of the silver cups from the Macedonian tombs II and III at Vergina: M. Andronikos, *Βεργίνα* (1984) pls. 79–81; 85–86 (the ivory heads from the same tomb, pls. 76–78 and 83 are comparable to the head of the Kallipolis Kore as well); 112–114; 179–180; similar realistic renderings occur in silver bowl medallions from the tombs of Derveni and Toumba Pappa in Sebaste, Pieria: *Μακεδονία. Από τον Φίλιππο ως τη ρωμαϊκή κατάκτηση* (1993) nos. 2546 and 2548, figs. 204–205, dated to the period 310–280 BC : P. Themelis, J. Touratsoglou, *Οι τάφοι του Δερβενίου* (1997) 174.

45. The statue base Athens Agora I 4165, signed by Praxiteles, was found in the Kolonos Agoraios : A. Ajootian in O. Palagia, J.J. Pollitt (edd.), *Personal Styles in Greek Sculpture* (1996) 95–96; cf. N. Papachatzis, *Παυσανίου Ελλάδος περιήγησις. Αττικά* (1974) 154 n. 1; Palagia (supra n. 13) 28.

46. N. Eschbach, *Statuen auf panathenäischen Preisamphoren des 4.Jhs. v.Chr.* (1986) 71–80, pls. 20–21, cat. nos. 46–48; *LIMC* IV, s.v. Demeter, nos. 264–268, with earlier bibliography.

47. Lippold, *Plastik* 237; M. Bieber, *Ancient Copies* (1977) 196–197, fig. 795; Kabus-Jahn (supra n. 37) 2–4, recognizes more Greek variations; Eschbach (supra n. 46) 79, pl. 21,3; A. Peschlow-Bindokat, *JdI* 87, 1972, 137 n. 333; B. Vierneisel-Schlörb, *Klassische Skulpturen des 5. und 4. Jahrhunderts v. Chr. Glyptothek München. Katalog der Skulpturen* II (1979) 265 and n. 39. The type of dress of the Muse with the double flute on the base from Mantineia in the National Museum, Athens is identical to that of the Kore of Florence: Stewart (supra n. 29) 492.

48. See the discussion in Palagia (supra n. 13) 28–30, cat. nos. B1–B2; B10; B13 with earlier bibliography; cf. Bieber (supra n. 47) 197, fig. 797 (=Kyzicos); Peschlow-Bindokat (supra n. 47) no. R44, 121, fig. 44 (=Eleusis no. 12); *LIMC* IV, s.v. Demeter, no. 234, (=Louvre); no. 379 (=Eleusis); no. 412 (=Mondragone); nos. 413–414 (=Agora); no. 279 (=Smikythion); Lawton (supra n. 19) 147, no. 152, pl. 80; S. Papaspyridi, *Guide du Musée National d'Athènes* (1927) 144 (=Piraeus); Picard, *Manuel* IV 2, 381, fig. 167 (=Piraeus). Peschlow-Bindokat (supra n. 47) 154, no. R 52; *LIMC* IV, s.v. Demeter, no. 281.

The So-called Delphi Philosopher and his Context

Wilfred Geominy

In an old photograph (Fig. 1)[1] one can see, quite near the site of their excavation, the three statues which have played a considerable role during the conference.[2] They are the well-known statue of the so-called Philosopher (Fig. 2), a woman (Figs. 3 and 7), and a male figure which is larger in scale than the others (Figs. 4 and 6). Despite the photograph, and the fact that the excavation report mentions the circumstances of the discovery,[3] the attribution of all figures to one group was made only recently by Croissant[4] and Flashar/v.d. Hoff,[5] nearly 100 years after the excavation. These authors, as well as Hans-Ulrich Cain in his so far unpublished study on the iconography of Dionysos[5a] suggested the unity of the figures. They also suggested that the male figure dressed in chiton and himation (Fig. 4) could only be Dionysos in view of the costume, the overwhelming size which once reached to a height of 2.40 m., and the bare feet. A further observation by Despinis can be added to support the idea of a compositional grouping of god and mortals: in the cavities for the woman's head and the head of Dionysos, there is a lewis hole, not a dowel hole. This detail adds a technical argument in support of the proposed grouping.

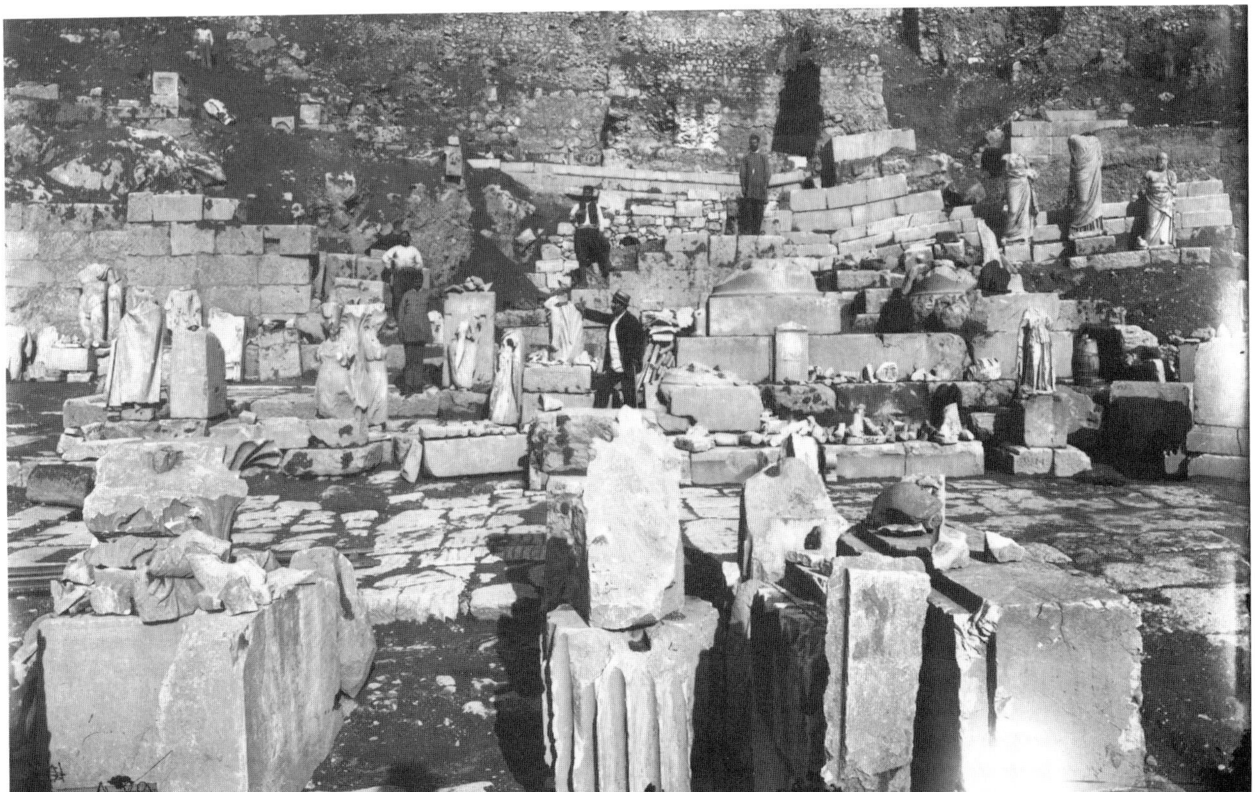

Fig. 1. The area to the north of the temple of Apollo, Delphi, after the excavations of 1894. The figures Delphi Museum 1817, 1819 and 1820 can be seen on the extreme right. The figure Delphi Museum 1793 is at the extreme left. Photo: École Française d' Athènes.

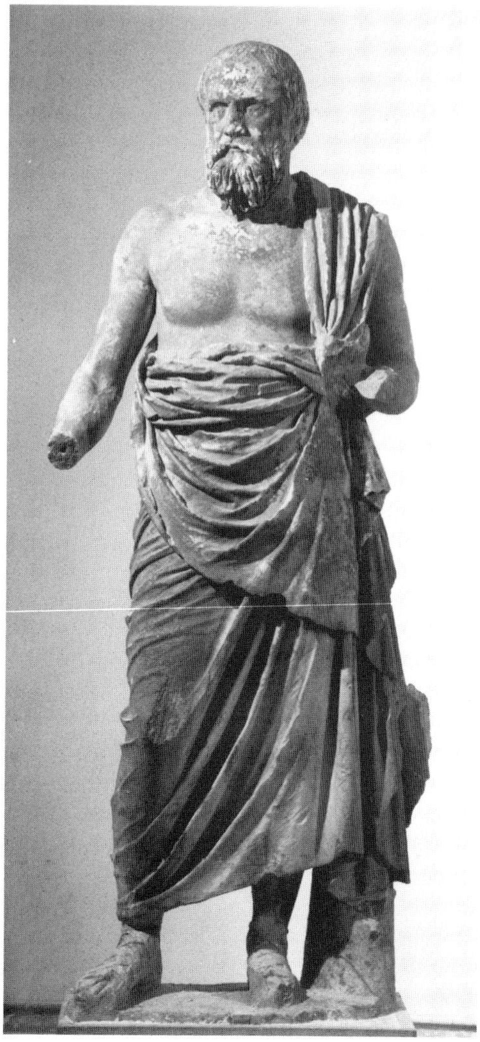

Fig. 2. So-called Philosopher. Delphi Museum 1819. Photo École Française d' Athènes.

While the grouping, therefore, is no longer in doubt, we must accept the fact that differences in quality existed between the statues; for example, the folds of the Dionysos (Fig. 4) project less sharply. Variation can also be observed on the back (Fig. 6), where the workmanship of the female figure (Fig. 7) is more skilful.[6] In addition to the differences in size, it was perhaps these differences in quality and style which hitherto prevented the Dionysos from being linked to the two mortals.

The stylistic dating of works of art which fall between late Classical and early Hellenistic times is characterized by a general uncertainty. Some scholars see a connection with the past; others are tempted to see the new, and as dated works of this period are rare, we have almost no means of verifying these views. The woman under discussion is normally assigned to the fourth century, while the 'Philosopher' is placed in the middle of the third century.[7] Flashar and v.d. Hoff suggest dating the group to about 300 B.C.[8] Two problems, however, emerge in connection with this proposal: first, the total lack of parallels for the head of the 'Philosopher' among the many grave reliefs,[9] and second the stylistic affinity of the woman to the Kore from Kallipolis (here p. 52, Fig. 10) discussed by Themelis in the present volume.[10] It has been suggested that in Kallipolis the destruction of the excavated area could be assigned to the invasion of the Gauls,[11] which would form a chronological *terminus ante quem* for the female figure. Yet, the clear signs of weathering on the surface of the head (here p. 54, Fig. 16) demand a long exposure to the open air. It is more likely, therefore, that the figure dates shortly after the repulsion of the Gauls than that it was spared from destruction by the Gauls.[12]

The problem of dating is connected with the question of the interpretation of the group. A Dionysos among mortals gives rise to the idea that it could be a votive offering, linked to the artists of Dionysos. It is not necessary to assume that the man and the woman (who is possibly his wife) were proper members of this guild; it is perhaps more convincing to suggest that both gave money for the celebration of a festival organized by the artists. We know of a similar case mentioned in a long, now lost inscription from Korkyra:[13] a couple gave funds to celebrate the Dionysia of Korkyra, and the inscription gives full details

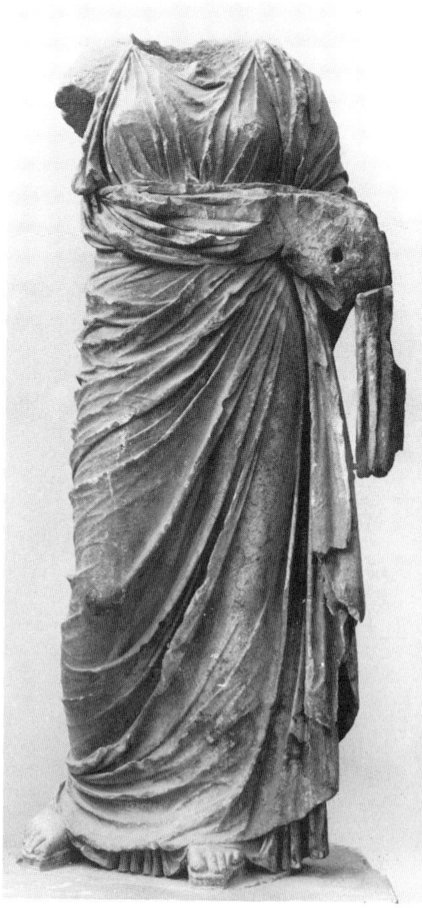

Fig. 3. Woman. Delphi Museum 1817. Bildarchiv Photo Marburg.

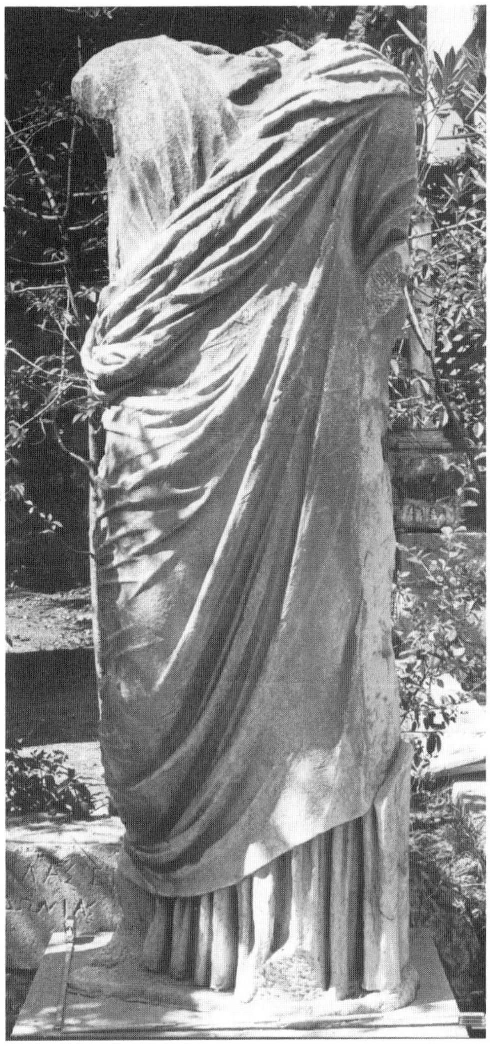

Fig. 4. Dionysos. Delphi Museum 1820.
Photo M. Flashar.

of how the money was to be spent. It may well be that a monument in the form of the Delphic one examined here would perfectly suit such an endowment.

Conventionally the artists of Dionysos are thought to have acquired a toehold in Delphi only after the invasion of the Gauls. Their appearance in Delphi seems to be linked with the festival of the *Soteria*, founded after the victory,[14] as it was they who gave the festival form and content.[15] The interpretation of the group as connected with the artists of Dionysos was considered by Flashar/ v.d. Hoff and Cain; Flashar and v.d. Hoff, however, rejected it immediately because it did not agree with their dating of the sculptures to about 300 B.C.[16] It would, perhaps be better to question their proposed dating rather than the attractive theory which sees the 'Philosopher' and the woman as benefactors of the artists, thus enabling the celebration of the *Soteria*.[17] Perhaps the Aetolians themselves, who at that time dominated the sanctuary and played a leading part in the repulsion of the Gauls, initiated the construction of the monument. Already from the beginning the *Soteria* seem to have been a special Aetolian invention; the Aetolians may have felt a particular reason to honor benefactors of their festival and to use a part of the endowment for the dedication of statues.[18]

Croissant discusses the addition of a further figure to this group,[19] as do Flashar and v.d. Hoff,[20] namely the nearly naked statue (Figs. 5 and 9) whose fragments can be seen on the left hand side of the old photograph (Fig. 1) mentioned above. They do not, however, investigate the meaning of this figure in the context of the other statues. It is admittedly difficult to demonstrate stylistic and technical connections, because a mostly naked figure cannot be compared directly with clothed ones. It has further been argued that the findspots were not identical (see Fig. 1, where the naked figure is separated from the others by a considerable distance).[21] Yet if we consult the detailed account of the discovery provided by Homolle, we can be sure that the different pieces of the naked man were all found in the same spot with the other figures.[22]

The following characteristics justify the reconstruction of a group of four figures. First, there can be no doubt that the three figures so far linked are made of Pentelic marble. This observation was made by Despinis when he examined the statues. The fourth figure is also of Pentelic

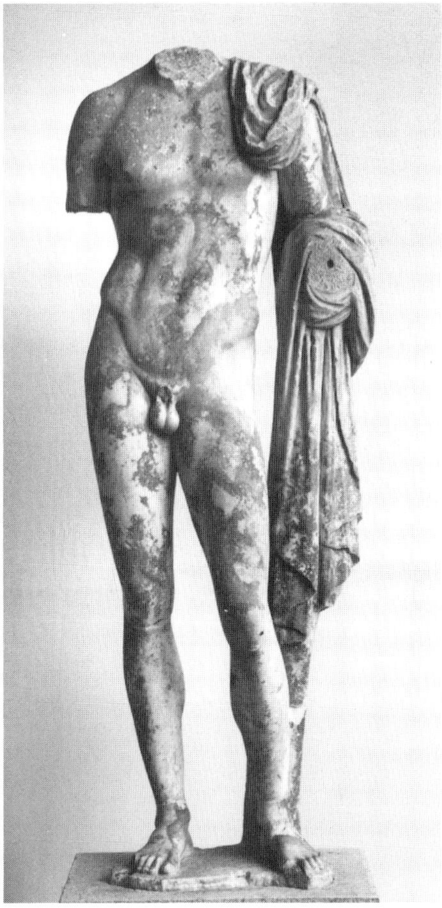

Fig. 5. "Hermes". Delphi Museum 1793.
Photo École Française d' Athènes.

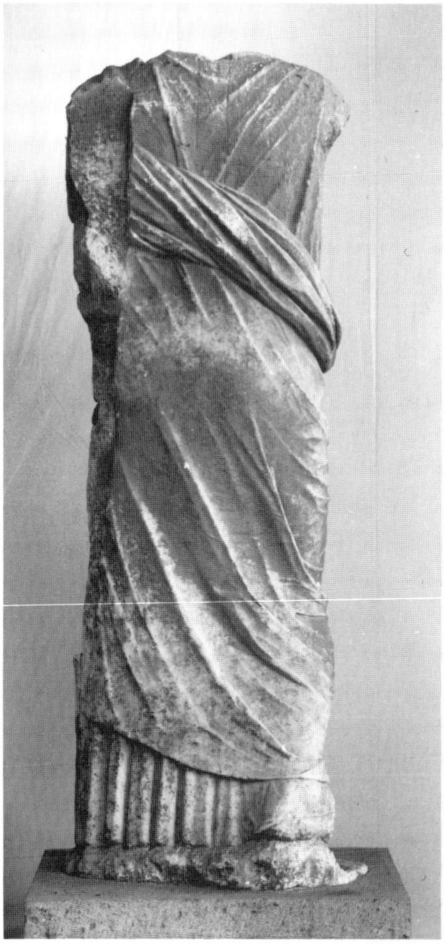

Fig. 6. Rear view of the Dionysos Fig. 4. Photo École Française d' Athènes.

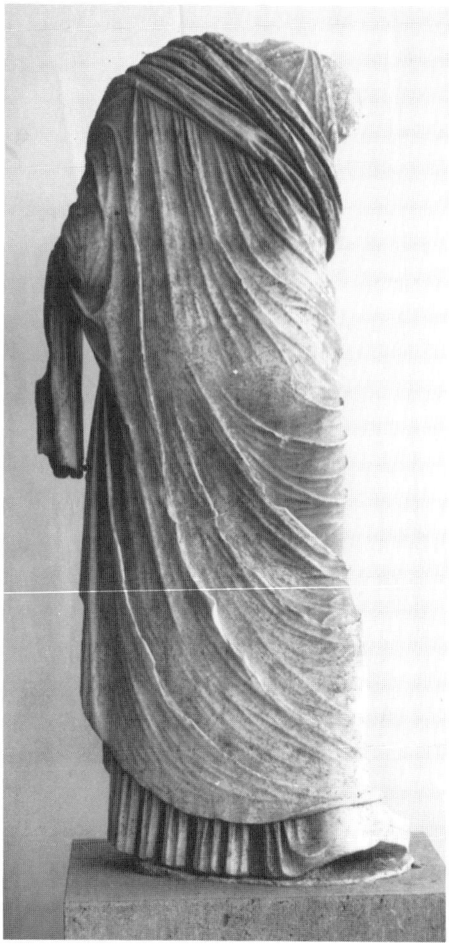

Fig. 7. Rear view of the woman Fig. 3. Photo École Française d' Athènes.

marble. Second, all figures show traces of weathering on the upper surface, on the shoulders and, in the case of the 'Philosopher', on the head. Third, the naked figure has – and this has also been observed by Flashar and v.d. Hoff[23] – the same chronological setting as the others. Fourth, the naked figure is as large as the Dionysos. Fifth, the rendering of the drapery is basically identical. The observation that the plinths of the four figures were once fastened by clamps to the base cannot be used as an argument, because it is doubtful whether this manner of attachment is the original one.[24]

Discussion will now center upon items 3–5 above, leaving aside questions of the identity of the marble and the state of preservation of the statues. The drapery of the nearly naked figure shows the same press folds and the same rough surface as the other figures. If the drapery seems somewhat carelessly worked, it shares this quality with the statue of Dionysos. But one cannot compare the parts of drapery which hang from the left arm, for these folds were once hidden by perhaps better worked drapery (Figs. 9–10). In any case, the folds around the place where the left forearm was attached do not continue.

Now comes the question of dating. The workmanship is certainly Greek, not Roman. The setting of the support, hidden behind the left leg (Figs. 4 and 9), is totally unknown in Roman practice. The right arm has no link with the body in the form of a strut, a technical detail which is never lacking in Roman statuary. The type is dependent on the Hermes Richelieu (Fig. 8), but stylistically our figure is more advanced.[25] The differences in proportion are conspicuous. Extremely striking are the long legs. A further quality is the vigorously curved form of the body which leads to the distortion of the classical structure. The classical torso always has a well-defined trunk and a separate pelvis. The pelvic region in the Delphi figure is unaccented and set so high that it starts almost directly beneath the breast. If we compare the body with that of the Agias from the Daochos monument (here p. 16, Fig. 3), the connections become clearer.[26] Both figures show generally the same proportions. Differences are explained by the fact that the Agias depends more closely on the structural principles of the fourth century. The Agias thus reveals its origins while the other figure is more remote from them. In any case, a link with the high-Hellenistic features of statues like the Terme Ruler in Rome is not yet to be seen.[27]

Now we come to the fourth point. The naked figure is of the same monumental size as the Dionysos (Fig. 5). The lack of pubes, however, indicates that it is not a ruler, but a god, who is represented. If so, the figure may be interpreted as a companion to Dionysos with the same size and stature. The type of drapery associated with the naked body suggests an identification as Hermes. But does Hermes in a group with mortals make sense? Dionysos in Delphi is a well-known figure. But with Hermes the situation is quite different. Because a funerary context is to be excluded, there exists only the possibility of an agonistic interpretation.[28] It is instructive to note that the Hermes Richelieu of almost the same type has been interpreted as *enagonios*.[29] The view that the Hermes Richelieu does not represent a Hermes at all has been convincingly rejected by Maderna who shows that two Hermes figures of later times are derivations of the Hermes Richelieu.[30] Our figure indicates that the Richelieu type was used as a model earlier than previously thought.

The interpretation as Hermes Enagonios is important for the explanation of the Dionysos, which is thus connected with the agonistic circle. It is thus no longer possible to see him in connection with a family votive such as the Daochos monument, or with a votive donated by a priest and his wife.[31] The link with the *Soteria* becomes inevitable, since the presence of Dionysos excludes every other agonistic context. But if the artists are involved with Dionysos, then the group can be dated only after the repulsion of the Gauls. This conclusion, which provides a *terminus post quem*, could be of great significance for our concept of the development of art in early Hellenistic times. But, is it possible to pin down the dating even more closely?

If we accept the hypothesis that the gymnastic contests of the *Soteria* were added to the dramatic and musical events rather late,[32] then the group must be dated after 246 B.C.,[33] the year of the reformation of the *Soteria* and the introduction of games equivalent to the panhellenic ones. Yet, the figures lack qualities typical for the second half of the third century B.C. It is difficult, for example, to see any connection with the Antium Girl or the Juno Cesi.[34] If we must decide in favor of an early date for the

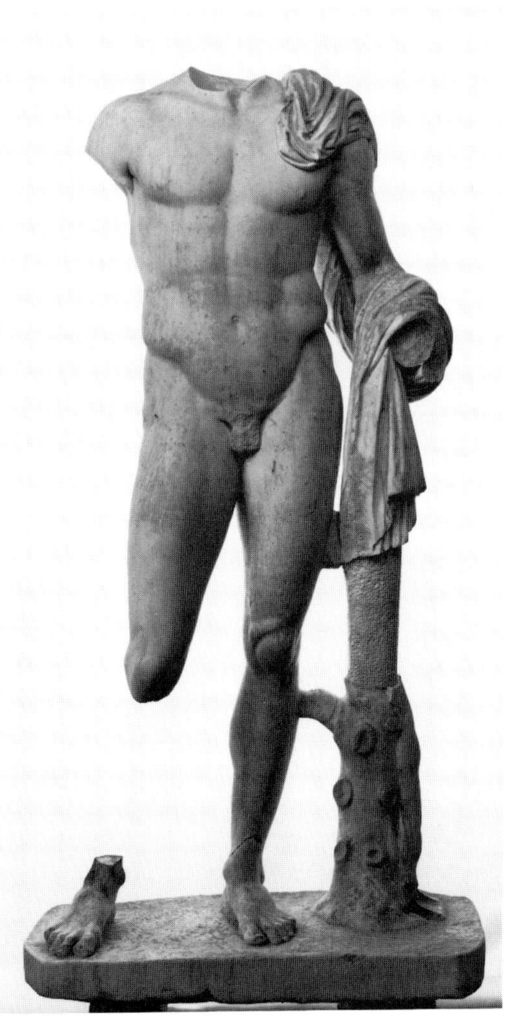

Fig. 8. Hermes Richelieu, copy. Munich, Glyptothek 290. Photo Museum.

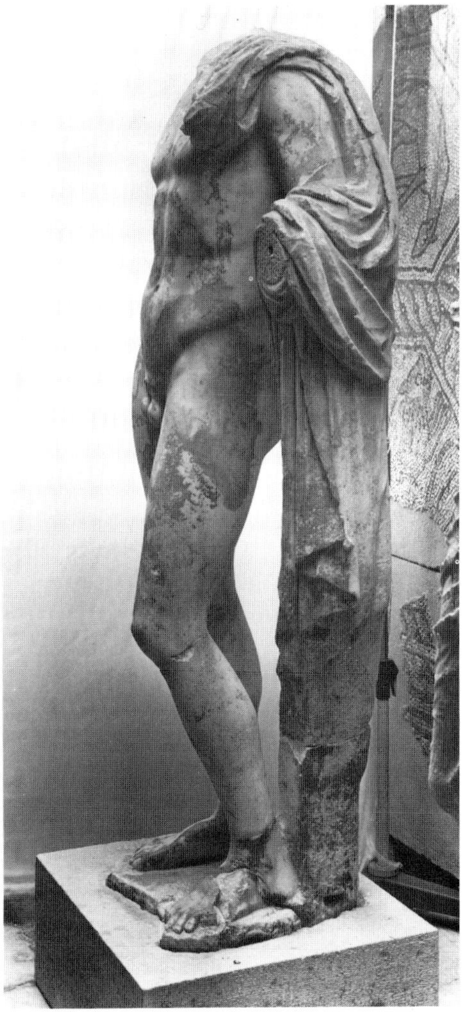

Fig. 9. Side view of "Hermes" Fig. 5. Photo German Archaeological Institute, Athens, 72/157.

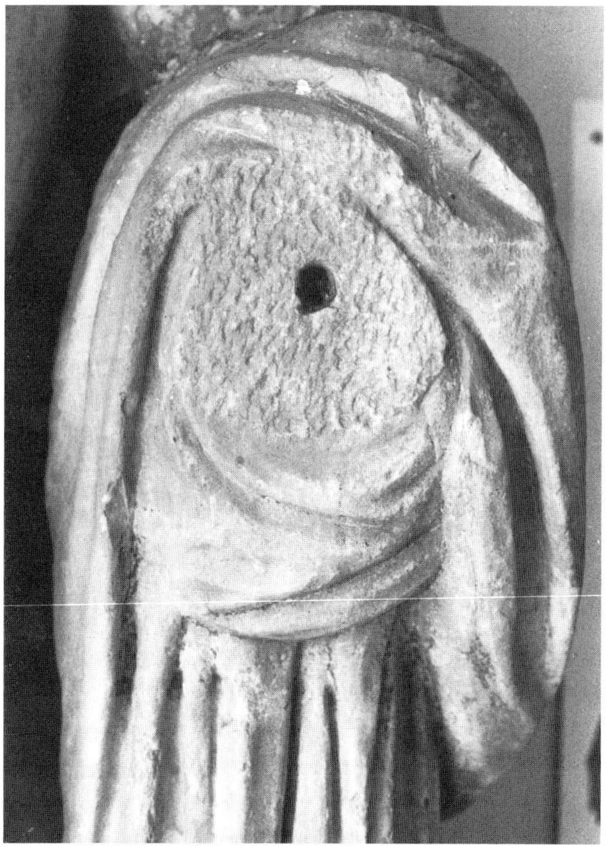

Fig. 10. Detail of "Hermes" Fig. 5. Photo M. Flashar.

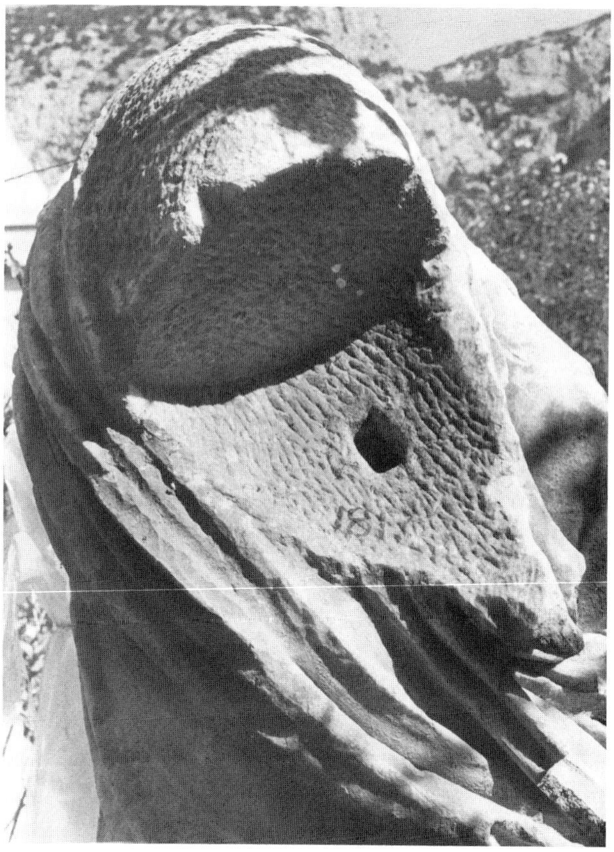

Fig. 11. Detail of the woman Fig. 3. Photo M. Flashar.

group, the hitherto suggested development of the games, based on historical arguments, may be incorrect; for under these circumstances, gymnastic competitions would have existed beside the dramatic ones from the very beginning of the festival.[35]

A few remarks must be made concerning the question of where this group might have been placed in the sanctuary. Naturally, someone not acquainted with the topographical details familiar to a Delphi specialist, can only make a suggestion, and if such a suggestion may be allowed here, then the most likely place appears to be the base of the Korkyraians, mainly because there is no other appropriate site in the neighbourhood.[36] It should be noted that the excavators, finding no other monument at hand, placed the 'Philosopher', his wife, and Dionysos on this base. Obviously different phases of this monument need to be distinguished; there seems to be a phase of the fifth century and another perhaps of later times.[37] The base is evidently too long for only four figures,[38] but other things may also have been placed on it. The top layer of the inscribed blocks contained, according to Pouilloux, round holes for objects made of bronze. Pouilloux thinks of animals,[39] but the existence of tripods cannot be excluded.[40] Furthermore, perhaps some of the blocks, now deposited in front of the base which is situated in the 'Neoptolemos' area, may also have belonged to the Korkyra base.[41] One of these blocks has a cavity; its measurements fit the plinth of our naked figure, and underscore the need for a general reexamination of the Korkyra monument.[42]

The material from which the group was made suggests that it is the product of Attic sulptors, perhaps employed by the Aetolians. It is possible to distinguish this Delphi workshop from the one which was busy in Kallipolis at about the same time. The piecing method used by the Kallipolis master differs from the practice in Delphi, where, for example, another technique was used in joining the forearm (Fig. 10). Characteristic is the method of attachment of the right arm (Fig. 11). The solution adopted in Delphi seems uncommon, but as M. Poligiorgi has shown, it is also known in the Piraeus statue (here p. 36, Fig. 5). In sum, if the Kallipolis figure and the Delphi ones are Attic, it would appear that there were several Attic workshops, using different methods, working at about the same time.

Acknowledgements

The author would like to thank J.A. Lloyd for assistance with the translation, M. Flashar for providing him with his personal notes and photographic material, R. Kolonia and F. Croissant for permission to study the figures, and G. Despinis for accompanying him to Delphi and for his most useful observations. He is also grateful for the scientific interchange which he had with R. v.d. Hoff.

Abbreviations

Pouilloux	J. Pouilloux, *La région Nord du sanctuaire, FdD* II (1960)
Flashar/v.d. Hoff	M. Flashar – R. v.d. Hoff, *BCH* 117, 1993, 400ff.
Croissant	F. Croissant in *Guide de Delphes, Le Musée* (1991)

Notes

1. The photograph in question has been published twice: École Française d'Athènes, *La redécouverte de Delphes* (1992) 169, fig. 80; Pouilloux pl. 4.
2. See the articles of M. Pologiorgi and P. Themelis in the present volume.
3. Now published in *La redécouverte de Delphes* (supra n. 1) 175.
4. Croissant 100ff.
5. 407ff.

5a. See now H.-U. Cain (ed.), *Dionysos – "Die Locken lang, en halbes Weib?"* (exh. cat. Munich 1997/98) 66ff.

6. The same observations were made by Croissant 108.
7. On different suggestions for the dating of the figures see Flashar/v.d. Hoff 410–412.
8. 418ff.
9. Noticed also by Flashar/v.d. Hoff 423.
10. The affinity has been observed by Flashar/v.d. Hoff 420. See also P. Themelis' paper here, pp. 47–59.
11. P. Themelis, *AAA* 12, 1979, 254ff.; N.D. Papachatzes, *Παυσανίου Ελλάδος περιήγησις* 5 (1981) 379, caption to fig. 414. These views are now revised by Themelis, here pp. 47–59.
12. Even the seals of Kallipolis do not belong to the period before the invasion, but seem to start after the destruction of the town. See P.A. Pantos, *Τα σφραγίσματα της Αιτωλικής Καλλιπόλεως* (1985) 444ff. For a different dating of the Kore see here p. 57.
13. *IG* IX 1, 694; B. Laum, *Stiftungen in der griechischen und römischen Antike* II (1914) 3ff.; M. Guarducci, *Epigrafia greca* III (1974) 250f.; A. Manzmann, *Griechische Stiftungsurkunden* (1962) 25ff.
14. The precise time of the foundation is not known. See G. Nachtergael, *Les Galates en Grèce et les Sôtéria de Delphes, Académie Royale de Belgique, Mémoires de la classe des lettres* 63,1 (1977) 295f. The lists of participants (Nachtergael 404ff.) do not start earlier than 265 B.C. See also here p. 126 n. 43.
15. G.M. Sifakis, *Studies in the History of Hellenistic Drama* (1967) 100, believes the inscription *SIG*³ 460 (privileges for the Isthmian and Nemean *koinon*) to be the first in which the artists of Dionysos are mentioned, and dates it before 280. According to R. Flacelière, *Les Aitoliens à Delphes* (1937) 433 n.18 the archon Ainesilas who appears in that inscription might have been in charge in the year 280/79 B.C., but Nachtergael (supra n. 14) 297 n. 1 says: "Dans l'état actuel de nos connaissances, il parait hasardeux de dater cet archontat à quelque dix ans près". The first inscription (*SIG*³ 399), which mentions the artists of Dionysos of Athens, is transmitted only in a later copy, of the year 130/29 B.C., and recalls the archon Hieron who is linked to the year 278/7. Nachtergael (supra n. 14) 196 n. 298 dates this decree to the spring of 277. It is commonly assumed that the Athenian and the Isthmian-Nemean guild came into being between 294 and 278. See A.W. Pickard-Cambridge, *The Dramatic Festivals of Athens*² (1968) 281ff.
16. Flashar/v.d. Hoff 432.
17. In the beginning the artists received payments for their victories. When the victorious artists refused to take money, this noble gesture was emphasized in the inscriptions. See Nachtergael (supra n. 14) 300; 339.
18. The Aetolians in Delphi are now generally regarded as usurpers. But at least at the beginning of the third century they would have seen themselves as defenders of the sanctuary against the illegal attempts of Macedonian rulers like Demetrios Poliorketes to take it over. It is not at all clear how the Delphi sanctuary, i.e. the Amphictyony, functioned in the late fourth and early third centuries, when the Thessalians were unable to fulfil their role as the legitimate leaders. Is it really possible to believe that the games in Delphi were organized as usual? It may be possible to suggest that the Aetolians needed the Gauls as an excuse to justify their involvement in the sanctuary but I doubt that it is right to see their part in the repulsion only as a result of later propaganda. Their renown must have been high from the beginning, as their victory monuments were almost immediately erected in Delphi. Therefore, I doubt whether the opinion originated with W.W. Tarn, *Antigonos Gonatas* (1913) 439ff. and sustained by others (recently C. Champion, *AJPh* 116, 1995, 218), that there were two versions of the events during the repulsion of the Gauls, can be right. The Aetolians started to emphasize their role at once and it is not likely that an independent local version could have been born while they were controlling the sanctuary. There is no evidence that they were at odds with the priests in Delphi: perhaps they were in total agreement. Naturally in later times, when their influence was absolute, they may have tried to inflate their own contribution in the affair.
19. Croissant 108f.
20. 426.
21. Croissant 105 n. 14: "... gisait, brisée en plusieurs morceaux, près de l'angle Nord-Est du temple, c'est-à-dire juste en contre-bas de la base en fer à cheval".
22. *BCH* 23, 1899, 426f.
23. 426.
24. It is likely that the plinth of the naked figure has been broken and worked in modern times, because the front border of the plinth runs underneath the broken big toe. This border cannot therefore be ancient and neither can the clamp which it holds.
25. I choose for comparison the statue in Munich: B. Vierneisel-Schlörb, *Skulpturen des 5. und 4. Jhs. v.Chr., Glyptothek München, Kat. der klassischen Skulpturen* II (1979) no. 27, pp. 283ff.
26. The similarities with the monument of Daochos have been observed by Flashar/v.d. Hoff 426. But they do not justify a dating to the fourth century. As I am going to show in a special study dedicated to the Daochos monument, this family group is a work of early Hellenistic times. For the Daochos Monument see also Palagia in this volume, pp. 18–19.
27. N. Himmelmann, *Herrscher und Athlet, exh. cat. Bonn* (1989) *passim*.

28. Hermes Enagonios may be attested in Delphi, but the relevant inscription is unfortunately damaged: É. Bourguet, *FdD* III 1 (1910) 163, no. 298.
29. D. Arnold, *Die Polykletnachfolge*, 25. Ergh. *JdI* (1969) 189. The so-called *Schulterbauschtypus* is often used in agonistic contexts. See, for example, many grave reliefs of the fourth century B.C.: H. Oehler, *Untersuchungen zu den männlichen römischen Mantelstatuen* (1961) 79 n. 22; N. Himmelmann, *Ideale Nacktheit in der griechischen Kunst*, 26. Ergh. JdI (1990) 67ff.
30. C. Maderna, *Iuppiter, Diomedes und Merkur als Vorbilder für römische Bildnisstatuen* (1988) 84. The Hermes figures are from Aigion and Atalanti, the latter certainly still belonging to the first century B.C., the former perhaps Flavian.
31. Both interpretations were taken in consideration by Flashar/v.d. Hoff 431f.
32. Sifakis (supra n. 15) 64; Nachtergael (supra n. 14) 328ff.; 339.
33. Nachtergael (supra n. 14) 339: "La première célébration des Sôtéria panhéllénique dut avoir lieu, avons-nous vu, en 245/4".
34. Antium Girl: A. Stewart, *Greek Sculpture* II (1990) fig. 721. Juno Cesi: A. Linfert, *Kunstzentren hellenistischer Zeit* (1976) pl. 48, 251.34.
35. For the problems concerning the *Soteria* see Sifakis (supra n. 15) 69ff.
36. I think that the description given in the *Journal des Fouilles* (supra n. 3) is in conformity with this location. Pouilloux, 49 and 52 confuses the issue by ascribing the three statues to the 'Neoptolemos' area. He has been misguided by the "base à assises légèrement en retrait les unes sur les autres" (so the relevant passage of the *Journal des Fouilles*) which he identifies with the base in the so called 'Neoptolemos' area. This base has courses of stone which are set progressively further back, but so slightly that this feature does not seem architecturally significant for the monument. The base of the Korkyraians, however, has stone courses which are set back very clearly giving a recognizable and characteristic stepped form. This makes it readily identifiable, a condition important especially at a time when the monuments were still unnamed. – Although Pouilloux says that at least three figures have been found in front of the base of the 'Neoptolemos' area and that it would be tempting to put them above the monument, he excludes the possibility because its surface is unfinished. Besides this unfinished state, which is also noted by J. Bousquet, *BCH* 88, 1964, 655 n. 2 and others, the base of the 'Neoptolemos' area seems too small for four figures, of which two are extremely tall. For a monument with four figures of the size of the Delphic ones a length of at least 4 m is needed (The base of the 'Neoptolemos' area is only 3.72 m). The base in the form of a horseshoe has cavities too small for our figures: see Flashar/v.d. Hoff 426ff. See Pouilloux 86.
37. J.-F. Bommelaer, *Guide de Delphes, Le Site* (1991) 198, no. 508: "Son premier état date du milieu du Ve s. d'après le travail des blocs (en calcaire blanc rosé). Mais elle a du être déplacée, si nous avons raison de dater d'après 373 le remblai sur lequel elle est en partie fondée. Aussi bien, sa dédicace est été refait au IVe s." If this is right, the hesitation of Flashar/v.d. Hoff in connecting the Korkyra base with our figures could be abandoned. Whether the dedicatory inscription is really to be dated to the fourth century is doubtful. Pouilloux corrects his earlier dating to the fourth century in *FdD* III 4 (1976) 132, no. 454 n. 1: "Cette date est peut-être trop haute. L'alpha de [Korkyr]aioi a un barre médian arrondie". Unfortunately, the two proxeny decrees do not give an obligatory *terminus ante quem* for the dating of the base: Courby, *FdD* II 3 (1927) 247; *FdD* III 4 (1976) 81ff., no. 406/07. According to G. Daux, *Chronologie Delphique, FdD* III (hors série) (1943) 22ff. both Delphic archons belong to the period between 315 and 280 B.C., but a wider chronological range seems possible. For *FdD* III 4 no. 407 see the comment of G. Daux, *BCH* 103, 1979, 472ff.
38. The monument has a length of 10.24 m. and is slightly shorter than the monument of Daochos. Without the antae, the remaining area for the placing of the figures would be 7.80 m.
39. Pouilloux 46 and 48: "Peut-être statues équestres, si l'on juge plus convenable à des animaux les encastrements circulaires et profonds que l'on rencontre sur les blocs de la corniche".
40. For the insertion of tripods rectangular holes are used: see, for example, P. Amandry, *BCH* 98, 1974, 171ff.; id., *BCH* 111, 1987, 79ff.; id., *BCH* Suppl. 1 (1973) 17ff. But there are a few exceptions: *BCH* 100, 1976, 28ff.; 91f.
41. Pouilloux' second Thessalian monument. To the five blocks mentioned by Pouilloux 78ff. is to be added a sixth, described and illustrated in J. Pouilloux, *FdD* III 4 (1976) 70, no. 392. The block with the cavity (Pouilloux 79, fig. 4) is large enough to receive the plinth of the Hermes figure. It should be noted that these six blocks, despite their similarity, have different heigths, i.e. 30.5 m, 35–37.5 m, and 42.5 m.
42. There are obvious contradictions between the chronological development of the excavation and the dating of the old photographs. When the PAN base is mentioned for the first time on August 16 (Pouilloux 60), then fig. 79 in *La redécouverte* (supra n. 1) cannot date from July 26, because in the photo the excavation had already reached the Daochos monument, which happened on August 28. The same problem arises with ibid. fig. 80. If I understand properly the caption to that photograph, fig. 80 is dated August 4. In my opinion both photographs represent the final state of the 1894 campaign. A reexamination of the documents would be desirable.

The Divine Circle: The Roundels of Mahdia

Hoyer von Prittwitz

Seventy years ago in 1926, Danish archaeologists made an unexpected discovery in Aetolia. While excavating a building in Calydon, they found fragments of unusual sculptures, busts and heads, which they described as "Wandprotome in kreisrundem Rahmen" (wall protomai in a circular frame).[1] The problem was, however, that fragments of a frame were not among the finds. Some years later, roundels from Delos were published; these had been dedicated in the sanctuary of the Great Gods of Samothrace in 102/1 B.C. by the Athenian priest Helianax in honor of King Mithridates VI Eupator Dionysus.[2] While the finds from Calydon include heads and busts of gods and a head of the founder of the Heroon, those from Delos include a few busts, one head, as well as the frames with various inscriptions. The persons portrayed can thus be identified as King Ariarathes VII Philometor, King Antiochus Epiphanes, and Diophantus, *strategos* of Mithridates. Since these discoveries of groups of roundels, only single Hellenistic examples have come to light.

The restoration of bronzes and marbles from the shipwreck of Mahdia in 1992–1993 in the Rheinisches Landesmuseum of Bonn provided a surprise when the

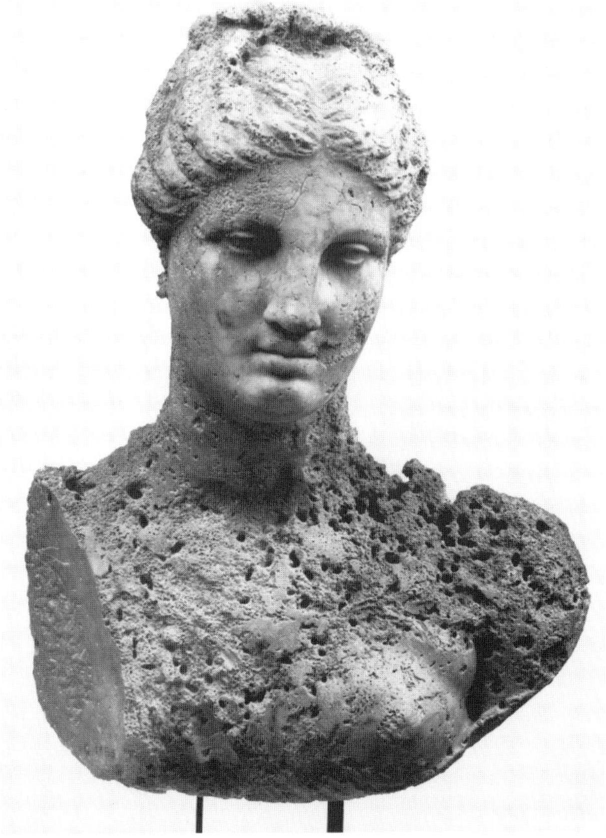

Fig. 1. Aphrodite or Ariadne. Tunis, Musée National du Bardo. Photo Rheinisches Landesmuseum Bonn/H. Lilienthal.

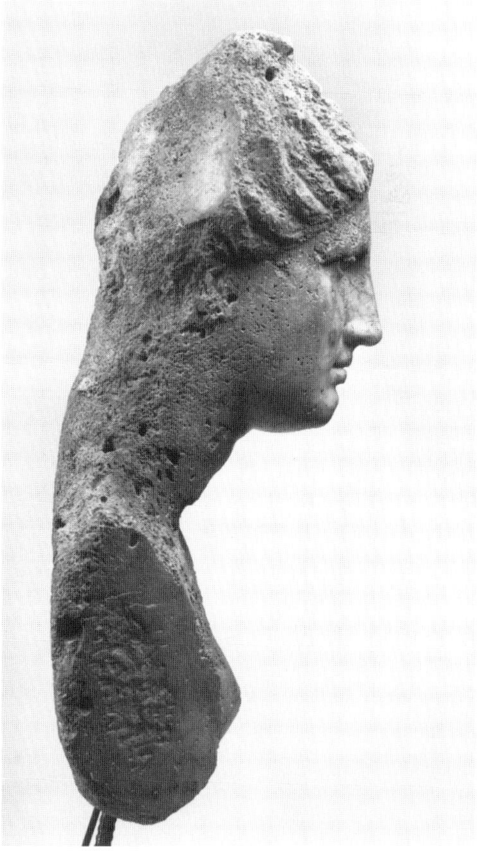

Fig. 2. Aphrodite or Ariadne. Tunis, Musée National du Bardo. Photo Rheinisches Landesmuseum Bonn/H. Lilienthal.

figure of Aphrodite was examined (Fig. 1).[3] When discovered, the sculpture was identified with Aphrodite because of the naked breast and was interpreted as the upper part of a statue. If this is so, the viewer would be puzzled about the thin profile at the shoulder (Fig. 2), the circularly cut bust, and the remains of a nail in the back of the head. In view of these details, the bust cannot be considered part of a statue, but instead as part of a medallion, also variously called a "tondo" or a roundel. A larger surface, cut at a slant from the back and narrowing towards the front of the bust, is smooth on the perimeter and in the center. It served for the attachment of the right breast and shoulder.

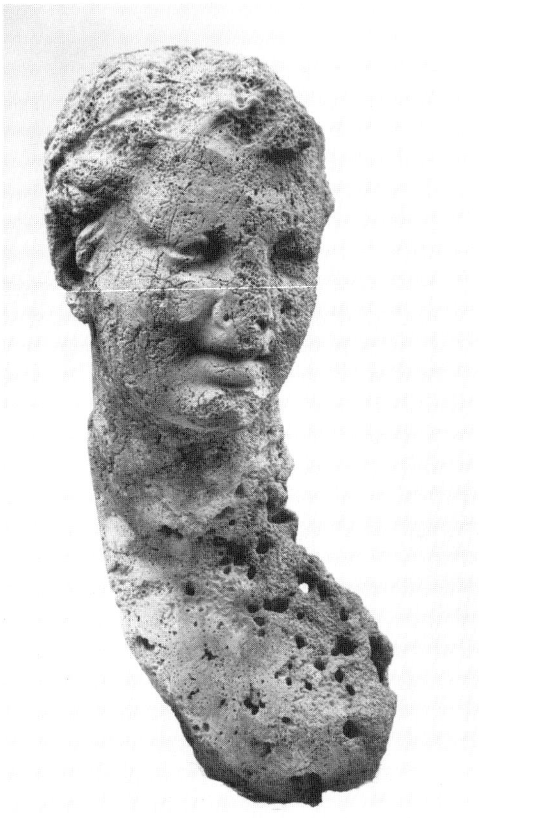

Fig. 3. Female satyr. Tunis, Musée National du Bardo. Photo Rheinisches Landesmuseum Bonn/H. Lilienthal.

Some of the features observed on this Aphrodite can be seen on other examples of busts found in the Mahdia shipwreck. The rather poorly preserved head and bust of a maiden can be identified as a female satyr because of her pointed ear (Fig. 3). Here the right shoulder and breast were attached directly below the neck. The round part of the head at the back was added separately; the seam is still visible on one side throughout the entire length. Here is preserved a massive lead dowel with a deep, square hole, which held the pin that attached the head to the wall. Another bust, immediately recognizable as a tondo, shows a male with the paw of a wild animal on his shoulder (Fig. 4). The paw had been considered that of a lion and the bust that of Herakles. Yet, after comparison with the satyr from the so-called "Stützgruppe" on the Borghese krater,[4] it becomes apparent that this bust is that of a satyr wearing a panther skin. In contrast to the busts of Aphrodite and the female satyr, the head of this satyr was sculpted separately and then set into a specially carved hollow in the neck. Although the head is missing, the bust can still throw light on the function of other heads found on the ship.

The best preserved of them was interpreted soon after its discovery as a replica of Niobe (Fig. 5), an interpretation which has recently been called into question.[5] Because of the cutting at the edge of the neck, the head was attached separately. A seven centimeter long dowel and the attached back part of the head confirm this fragment's identification as part of a tondo. Two other heads of females can be interpreted as tondi on the basis of the edge of the neck, the lead dowel, and the surface prepared for the attachment of the rear part of the head. One female represents a maenad (?) (Fig. 6); the other cannot be identified because

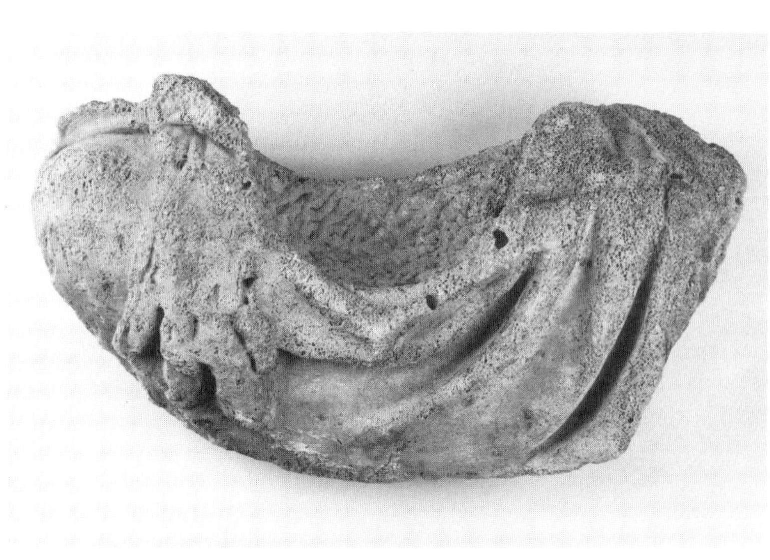

Fig. 4. Heracles or satyr. Tunis, Musée National du Bardo. Photo Rheinisches Landesmuseum Bonn/H. Lilienthal.

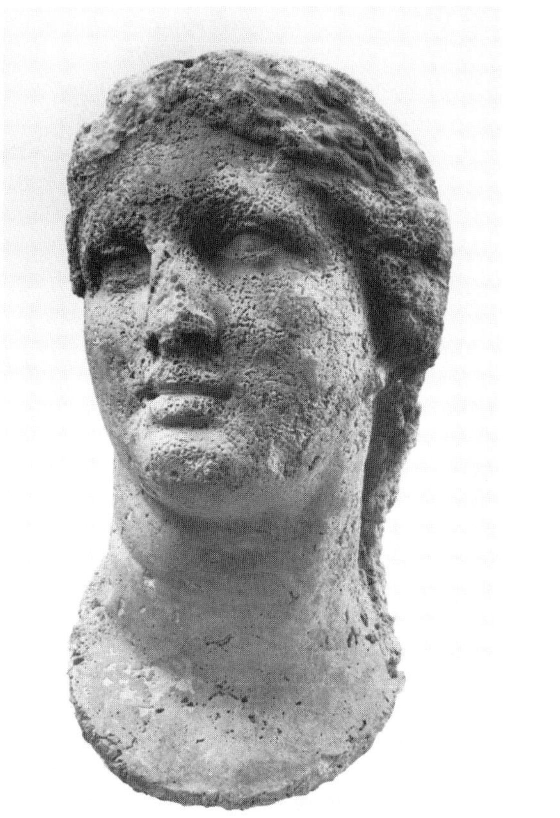

Fig. 5. Maenad. Tunis, Musée National du Bardo. Photo Rheinisches Landesmuseum Bonn/H. Lilienthal.

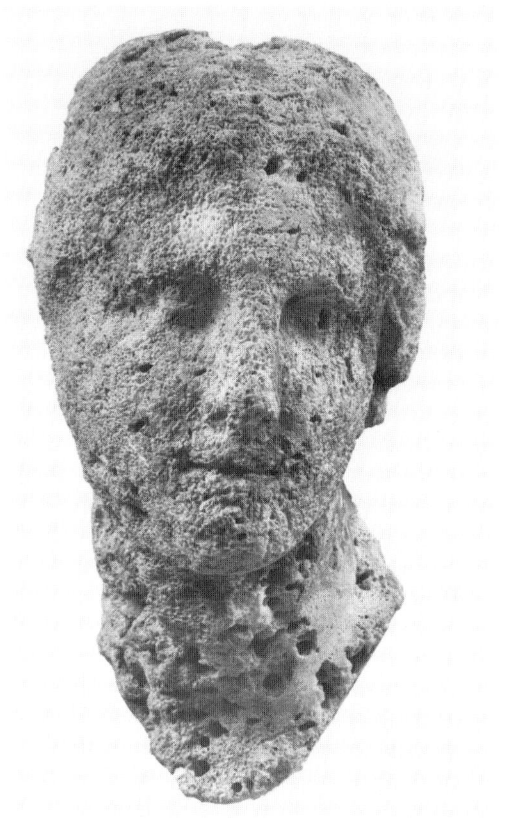

Fig. 6. Maenad. Tunis, Musée National du Bardo. Photo Rheinisches Landesmuseum Bonn/H. Lilienthal.

of the corrosion of the face by shells. Traces of a scraper on the right side, together with the rough finish of the neck's base, distinguish this head from the others (Fig. 7). In addition, the head was apparently adorned with a bronze ribbon or wreath, as indicated by two holes with lead remains, and with separate locks of hair behind the right ear, as seen by three small holes in a row for their attachment. Another head depicts a satyr with brush-like hair (Fig. 8). As with the other heads, it has a place for attachment at the back of the head and therefore belongs to a tondo. Two additional shoulder parts of male figures, as well as the back part of a head, were found in the shipwreck, providing evidence that more tondi had originally been carried on the ship.

Based on stylistic comparisons, scholars are in agreement in dating the tondi to ca. 120 B.C. One feature which supports this date is the movement which is expressed by the mouth, a trait which is also seen in the Aphrodite of Melos, dated to 130 B.C.[6] Comparison with Attic heads is also instructive, especially to those from the Lacrateides relief in Eleusis, dated to around 100 B.C.[7]

Nearly all the heads have in the back a dowel which held a pin for their attachment to a wall. The hole for the dowel was made about 4.5 cm deep; an iron pin was then inserted and the hole filled with lead. Upon cooling, the lead around the iron pin was hammered compact, thereby creating numerous small holes (Fig. 9).

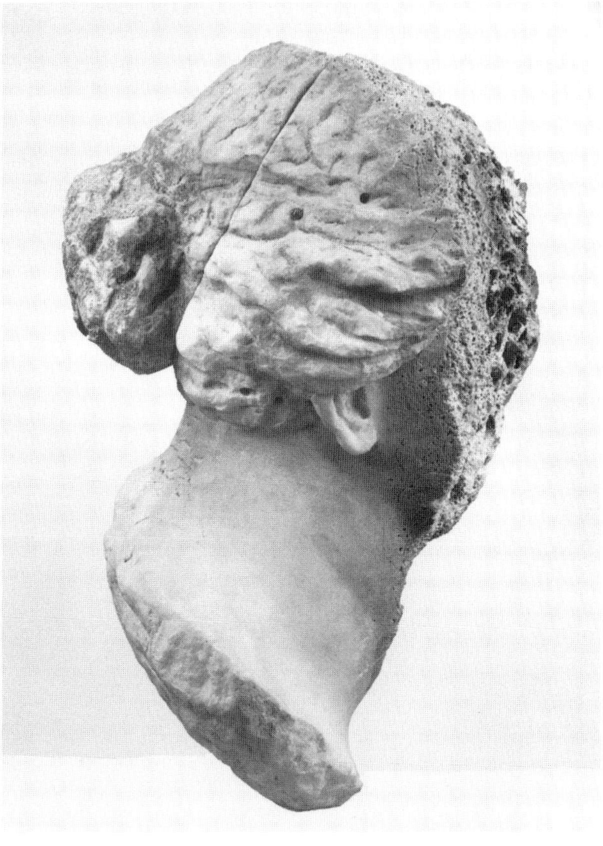

Fig. 7. Donor or donor's wife. Tunis, Musée National du Bardo. Photo Rheinisches Landesmuseum Bonn/H. Lilienthal.

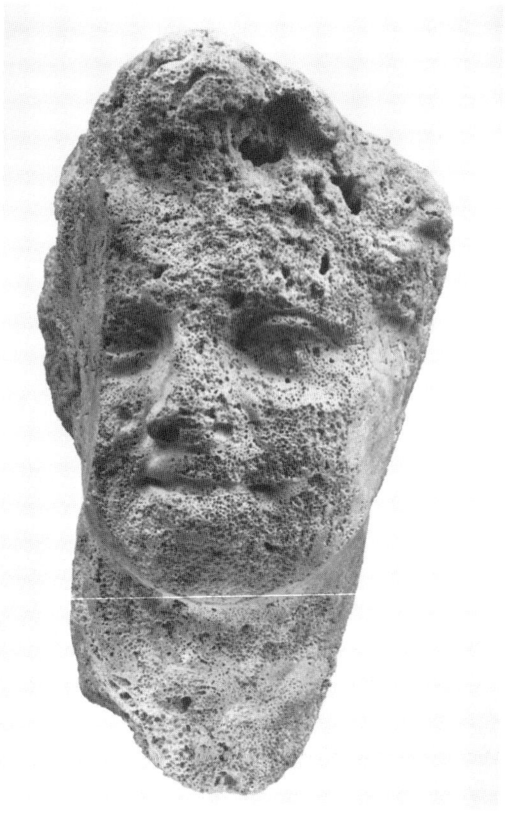

Fig. 8. Satyr. Tunis, Musée National du Bardo. Photo Rheinisches Landesmuseum Bonn/H. Lilienthal.

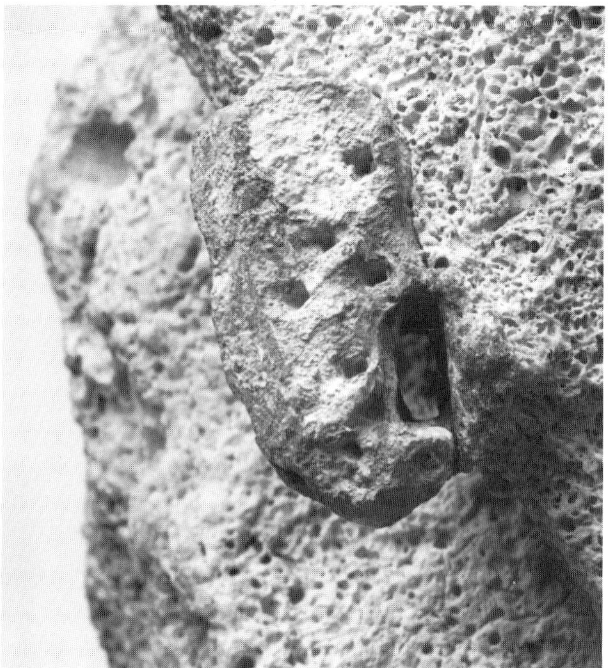

Fig. 9. Detail of female satyr. Tunis, Musée National du Bardo. Photo Rheinisches Landesmuseum Bonn/H. Lilienthal.

Busts for tondi from the Heroon of Calydon provide the closest parallels to the Mahdia busts and were fastened with dowels in similar fashion. However, there the dowels are located in the lower part of the bust, not at the back of the head. The Calydon busts and their context offer the most convincing explanation of both the purpose and the meaning of medallion busts. Eight more or less complete busts are known from Room VII, the so-called 'cult-room,' at the Heroon in Calydon. Almost all have additionally attached structural pieces. Similar to the Mahdia tondi, some of the Calydon busts were made with a separate head piece which was inserted into the neck, as for example, the heads of Apollo and Meleager.

Bol is the latest scholar to present a convincing interpretation of the Calydon tondi assemblage. The portrait of a young man with a beard is surrounded by gods in the divine circle: Zeus, Apollo, Eros, Aphrodite, and Herakles, as well as the local hero Meleager. Besides Meleager, the young man is the only figure wearing a bronze wreath. Unlike the other heads, however, the portrait does not display classisistic features. The person portrayed may thus be considered a hero, perhaps as Bol suggests, the hero Leon who is attested by epigraphical evidence. With this comparison in mind, one is tempted to recognize in the female head with corroded face from the Mahdia wreck the donor or donor's wife (Fig. 7). This head is distinguished by its workmanship and by the fact that it also wears a bronze wreath. Although general parallels between the two groups of tondi are many, specific comparisons must be made with caution. The few heads which can be identified, such as the satyr (Fig. 8) and the female satyr (Fig. 3), are concerned with a different theme from that of the gods from the Heroon in Calydon. The question arises, then, of whether the heads from Mahdia should be seen in a Dionysiac context.

The best preserved bust from the Mahdia ship was identified soon after its discovery as Aphrodite (Figs. 1 and 2) because of the hairstyle – the "krobylos" – and the naked left breast. In the late Hellenistic period, however, other goddesses had a similar hairstyle as, for instance, the Ariadne on the Borghese krater.[8] The bare breasted Ariadne is known from other examples and supports the identification of the Aphrodite from Mahdia as Ariadne.

Similar doubts have been expressed about the bust with animal skin (Fig. 4), whose identification as a satyr has been argued above. The identification, however, does not extend to the head of the satyr, which appears to be a copy of the satyr of the "Invitation to a Dance" group.[9] The satyr from this group is predestined for a tondo figure; the upper part of the body leans forward with slightly bowed head while dancing in front of a female companion. Geominy has rightly questioned the identification of both female busts as Niobe (Fig. 5) and a daughter (Fig. 6).[10] A comparison of this "Niobe" with the Niobe in Florence[11] is instructive. The Florentine Niobe is characterized by a thrust-up head with raised eyebrows and an extremely concentrated facial expression. Although the position of the head and the hairstyle of the Mahdia head are similar to the Florentine Niobe, the concentrated facial expression of the latter sets it apart from the Mahdia "Niobe." Specific arguments, however, against the identification as Niobe are not possible because of the poor state of preservation. It remains here only to suggest that, in view of the freely flowing hair, the heads could represent maenads.

The tondi from Mahdia, like those from Calydon, can be shown to be decorative elements for a heroon. In contrast to those from Calydon, however, those from Mahdia do not portray the Olympian gods, but deities of the Dionysiac realm. The features common to the Mahdia and Calydon tondi are further evidence in respect to their place of production. According to Bol, the tondi of Calydon are made of Pentelic marble. Their production in an Attic workshop is, therefore, most probable, since no school of marble sculpture is known in the region of Calydon. Equally probable is the origin of the Mahdia tondi in Athens. The ship from Mahdia loaded its cargo in Athens and contained, amongst other goods, some 60–70 columns of Pentelic marble, as well as the tondi. Even though the tondi are of Parian marble (except for the satyr with the paw, which is Pentelic), their production in an Athenian workshop still seems likely, given the close connection of Delos with Athens. The tondi for the Mithridates monument on Delos were ordered by the Athenian priest Helianax and were, thus, producted either in Athens or on Delos. Another individual tondo from Chalcis also probably originated from an Attic workshop.[12]

In the late Hellenistic period, examples of tondi occur frequently in Attica but are lacking in other regional schools. Even though they originate from one regional school, the tondi do not exhibit any common stylistic features. The question must, therefore, be asked of whether or not a regional school existed in Athens in the last quarter of the second century B.C. Recent studies have shown that there existed in the late Hellenistic period schools or workshops that produced grave reliefs.[13] Certain characteristic features were used repeatedly and suggest that these reliefs were made in one and the same cultural region, where sculptors carried out their traditional craft for a local market. Customers and contracts from abroad were an exception to the rule.

This local tradition, however, does not seem to apply to Athens, since at the end of the second century Athens and Delos were the major production centers. The extensive marble quarries on Mount Pentelicum and the great demand by Roman contractors resulted in a highly successful market. With such an international market in Athens, a traditional regional style was not likely to have survived.[14]

Acknowledgements

The author would like to express his gratitude to E. Schalk, Heidelberg, for making the translation from German to English and to M. Carrol-Spillecke, Cologne, for answering questions on the translation of technical archaeological terms.

Notes

1. For the Calydon busts see now P.C. Bol, *AntPl* XIX (1988) 35–47, pls. 24–33.
2. For the busts see F. Chapouthier, *Délos* XVI, *Le sanctuaire des dieux de Samothrace* (1935) 12–42.
3. For further information, see the author's paper in G. Hellenkemper Salies et al. (edd.), *Das Wrack. Der antike Schiffsfund von Mahdia* (1994) 303–328.
4. See now D. Grassinger in *Das Wrack* (supra n. 3) 267–268, fig. 12.
5. W.A. Geominy, *Die Florentiner Niobiden* (1984) 207ff.
6. A. Pasquier, *La Vénus de Milo et les Aphrodites du Louvre* (1985); for the dating see J.-P. Niemeier, *Kopien und Nachahmungen im Hellenismus* (1985) 32. See here 173, Figs. 12–13.
7. Prittwitz in *Das Wrack* (supra n. 3) 309 n. 14, fig. 29.
8. Grassinger (supra n. 4) 267; 269, fig. 16. Good photo in W. Fuchs, *Der Schiffsfund von Mahdia* (1963) pl. 69.
9. Prittwitz in *Das Wrack* (supra n. 3) 321.
10. Supra n. 5.
11. Prittwitz in *Das Wrack* (supra n. 3) 323, figs. 31–32.
12. G. Neumann, *AM* 103, 1988, 221–238.
13. S. Schmidt, *Hellenistische Grabreliefs* (1991).
14. For the Mahdia tondi see also here p. 187.

Hellenistic Sculpted Funerary Monuments from the Athenian Agora

Janet Burnett Grossman

Fourteen sculpted funerary monuments[1] that seem to be Hellenistic in date have been identified among the sculptures that have been found during the American excavations in the Athenian Agora.[2] All fourteen are extremely modest monuments, but they are of interest because in the corpora of sculpted Attic funerary monuments of all periods, Archaic through Roman, only a small number can be placed in the Hellenistic period.[3] This paper presents the fourteen monuments discussing their style and characteristics and, in many cases, comparing them to other small relief sculptures of the period such as votive and documentary reliefs.

"But he [Demetrius] also placed a limit upon newly erected monuments, providing that nothing should be built above the mound of earth except a small column no more than three cubits in height, or else a table or small basin."[4] This well-known and oft-quoted passage by Cicero describes the apparent restrictions on the size and appearance of funerary monuments by the sumptuary legislation of Demetrius of Phaleron, the pro-Macedonian ruler of Athens from 317 to 307 B.C.[5] The date 317/16 B.C. has been accepted by most scholars of Greek sculpture as a firm *terminus ante quem* for the production of Athenian grave monuments in the form of marble stelai and vessels with relief sculpture.[6] The archaeological record generally supports this view as evidenced by the hundreds of columellae excavated in the Kerameikos alone.[7] But there are columellae and stelai with sculpted reliefs that appear to belong to the post-Demetrian period and thus are exceptions to the currently held view of absolute restriction of monuments of this type after 317 B.C.

The inscriptions on twelve of the fourteen sculpted funerary monuments in the Athenian Agora can be dated to the Hellenistic period on the basis of their letter forms.[8] Six of the twelve inscribed monuments are the familiar columellae bearing in addition to the inscription a loutrophoros in relief.[9] The remaining six consist of one fragment of a mensa monument with a relief of a loutrophoros, and fragments of five stelai with reliefs.[10]

The earliest in date of the twelve inscribed monuments comes from the very last years of the fourth century B.C. (Fig. 1).[11] The preserved inscription reads: [----]ς Φίλωνο [ς----]. The fragment of the monument of the son of Philo is broken all round, but its thickness assures its identification as belonging to a mensa. This monument type is one of those permitted under Demetrius, that is after

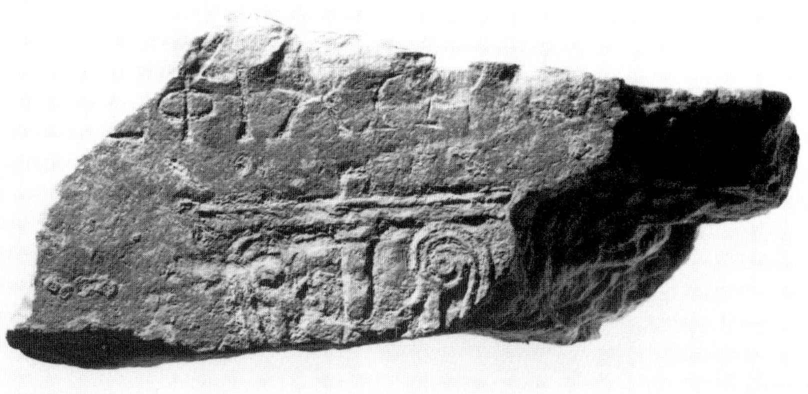

Fig. 1. Mensa monument of the son of Philon. From Athens. Athens, Agora I 4891. Photo Agora Excavations, American School of Classical Studies at Athens.

317 B.C., but the letter forms of the inscription keep it in the fourth century. Below the name, an amphora-loutrophoros is carved in shallow relief. It is comparable to the amphora-loutrophoros incised on the mensa of Euekes and Timagora in the Athens Epigraphical Museum, dated to the end of the fourth, beginning of the third century B.C.[12] The handles on both of the vessels are adorned with fillets.

Columnar monuments bearing reliefs of loutrophoroi have been dated to each century of the Hellenistic period, but the loutrophoroi on those of the third century B.C. are carved in higher relief and are generally of better sculptural quality than those in successive centuries.[13] An example from the third century B.C. is the monument of Apollonides, the son of Pythodoros of Erchia (Fig. 2).[14] Its inscription reads: Ἀπολλωνίδης / Πυθοδώρου / Ἐρχιεύς. From the first century B.C. is the monument of Apollonios (Fig. 3).[15] The inscription reads: Ἀπολλώνιος / χρηστός. Both columellae are among the grave monuments partially buried in the earth in that part of the Agora known as the sepulchral garden, which is south of the Hephaisteion and along the western boundary fence.[16] The amphora-loutrophoros on the monument of Apollonides measures 0.23 high and stands on a rectangular base. The body of the vessel is plain and there is a fillet hanging from the handles. The loutrophoros on the monument of Apollonios stands on a rectangular base and is placed within a niche. There is a decorative quality to the rendering of the vessel. The body is divided at its widest point by a horizontal band with closely spaced tongues occupying the lower half.

Other columnar monuments bearing loutrophoroi, either in relief or inscribed, include the four that follow. Again, those dated earlier show reliefs of better quality than those dated later. The monument of Nikostrate, the daughter of Simios, is dated by Kirchner to the third century B.C.[17] Its inscription reads: Νικοστρ[άτη] / Σιμί[ου] / θυγάτ[ηρ]. The monument of Nikostratos, son of Menekrates of Phlya, is dated by Meritt to the third to second centuries B.C.[18] The inscription reads: Νικόστρατ{τ}ος / Μεν⟨ε⟩κράτο / Φλυεύς. The monument of Apollonios is dated by Meritt to the second century B.C.[19] The inscription reads: Ἀπολλώ[νιος] / χρηστ̣[ός]. And the monument of Phila, daughter of Nikomachos of Phaleron, is dated by Kirchner to the first century B.C.[20] The inscription reads: Φίλα / Νικομάχου / Φαληρέως / θυγάτηρ.

There are five fragments that belong to stelai with relief sculpture. The earliest is a fragment of the stele of a slave, Kilikas, dated to the third century B.C. by Meritt (Fig. 4).[21] The inscription reads: Κιλικᾶς. Kilikas wears a himation in the manner of male figures on monuments

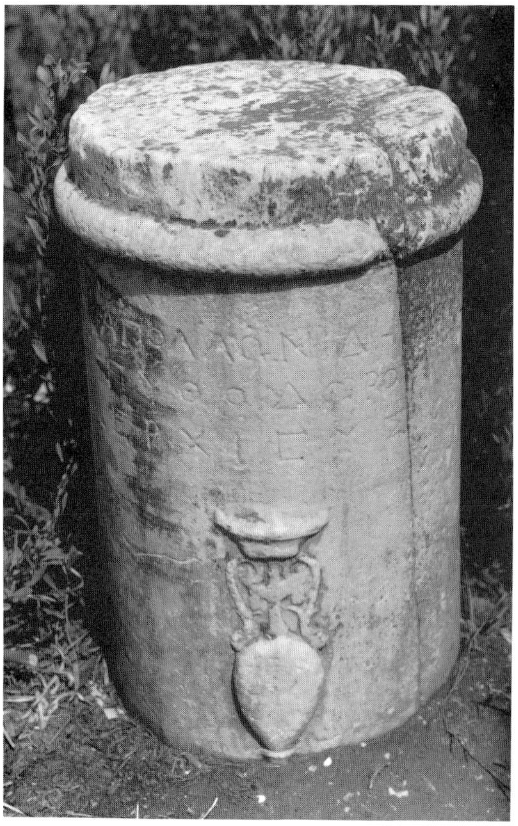

Fig. 2. Columnar monument of Apollonides. From Athens. Athens, Agora I 7038. Photo Agora Excavations, American School of Classical Studies at Athens.

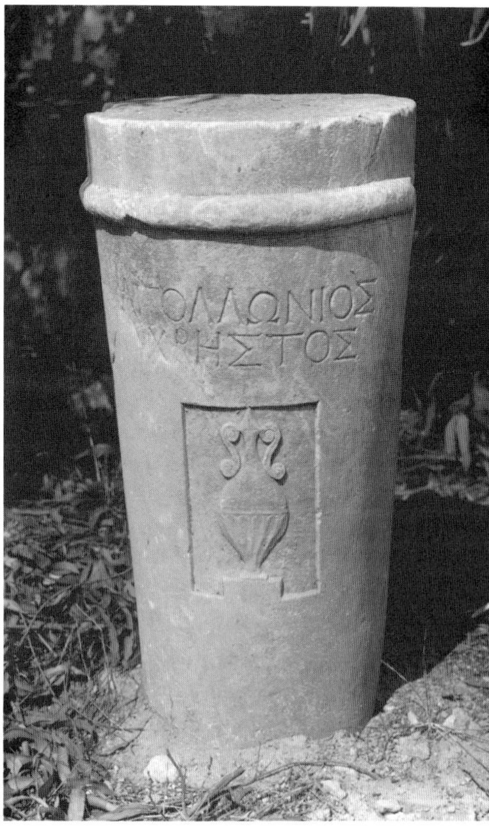

Fig. 3. Columnar monument of Apollonios. From Athens. Athens, Agora I 7037. Photo Agora Excavations, American School of Classical Studies at Athens.

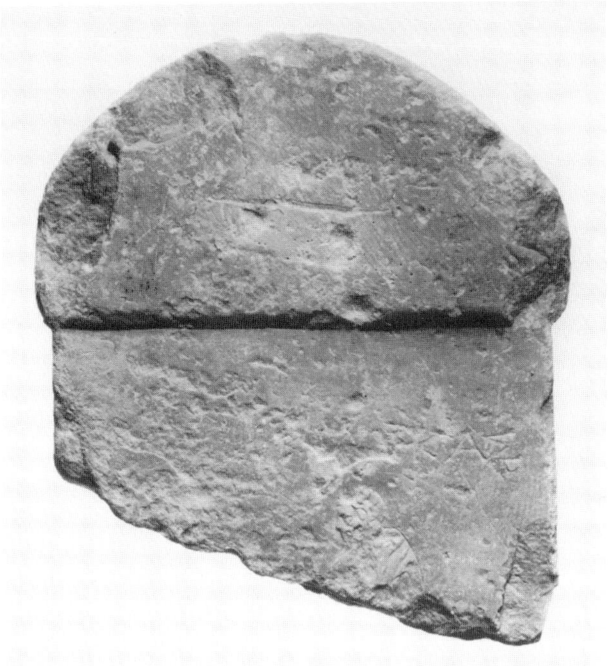

Fig. 4. Grave relief of Kilikas. From Athens. Athens, Agora I 6077. Photo Agora Excavations, American School of Classical Studies at Athens.

of the Classical period, that is, draped on the left shoulder with the right shoulder and chest bare. The form of the stele with its rounded pediment is simple and may be compared to the stele of Mikillos, the son of Achaios, from Aiga in the Athens Epigraphical Museum, dated to the early third century B.C. by Kirchner.[22] There was originally a second figure on the Agora stele, since the illegible traces of a second name occur at the left. The figure was probably seated because of the inclination of Kilikas' head and the lower placement of the second name on the stone. The small head and squat childlike quality of Kilikas are comparable to the figures on a votive relief to Pan and the nymphs in the Athens National Museum, dated by Edwards to 310–290 B.C.[23]

The second stele fragment belongs to a small relief of white marble that is placed in the third century on the basis of its style (Fig. 5).[24] At the right side of a shallow niche a woman wrapped in a mantle sits on what was probably originally a stool with a cushion. Her left hand is held to her chin while her right is extended in front of her to clasp the hand of an opposing figure who is missing. The figure is comparable to that on one of the votive reliefs from the Pankrates sanctuary dated by Vikela to the first half of the third century B.C.[25] Similar are the proportions of the two figures, the way they fill the space of the relief field, their awkward postures, and large hands. Additionally, both feature drapery carved in low relief with few folds.

From the mid second century B.C. is the fragment of a grave relief of a man from Herakleia, the Greek colony on the Black Sea (Fig. 6).[26] The inscription reads: [- ca. 4 -]ογένης / [- ca. 5 -]σίου / [Ἡρα]κλεώτης.[27] The ethnic is the second most common on Attic gravestones. The lower half of a male figure standing frontally is placed at the right of a shallow niche. His feet are bare and he wears a himation wrapped about him so that it ends in a diagonal line at the hem. The style of the figure with its closely wrapped himation with minimal folds may be compared to that of Amphikles, the son of Polynikes of Salamis, on a stele in Piraeus that is dated by Kirchner to the late second century B.C.[28] We see exhibited in both stelai the change in orientation of the figure that characterizes monuments of the later Hellenistic period.[29] That is, figures are placed frontally to confront the viewer with the inscription frequently placed below the figure field.

In the second century B.C., we begin to see monuments that recall those of the Classical period, such as a stele with an anthemion, the monument of Euthoinos, the son of Eudorides (Fig. 7).[30] The inscription reads: [Ε]ὔθοινος / [Εὐ]δωρίδ̣ου / [----?----]. The style of the anthemion is placed in the second century B.C. by

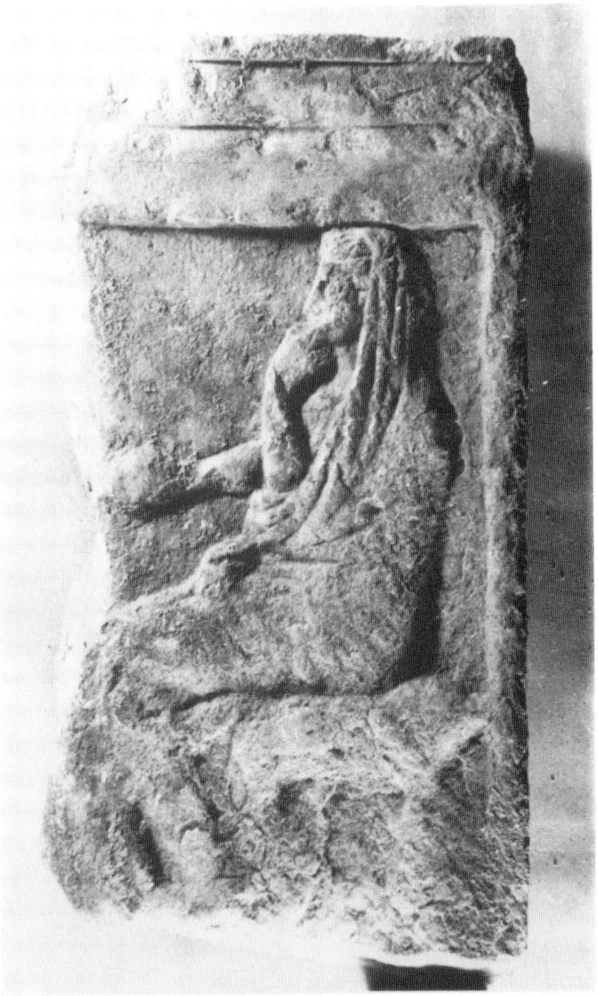

Fig. 5. Grave relief of a woman. From Athens. Athens, Agora S 782. Photo Agora Excavations, American School of Classical Studies at Athens.

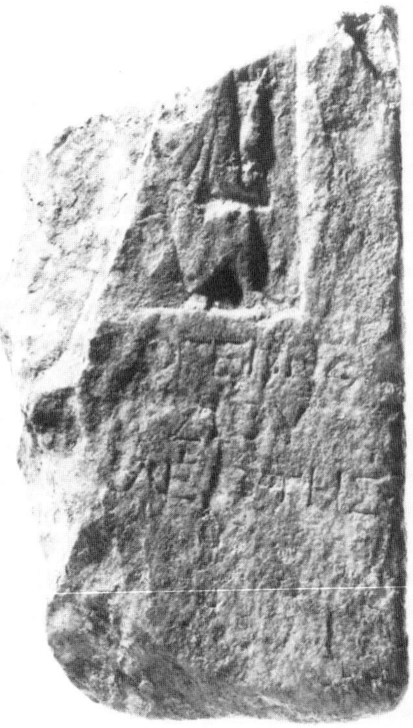

Fig. 6. Grave relief of a man from Herakleia. From Athens. Athens, Agora S 2462. Photo Agora Excavations, American School of Classical Studies at Athens.

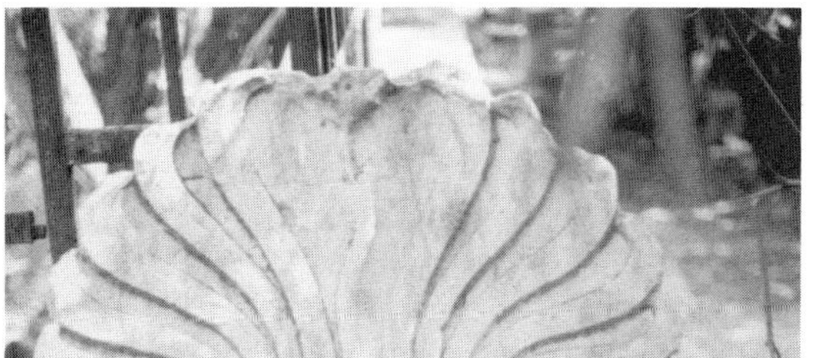

Fig. 7. Grave monument of Euthoinos. From Athens. Athens, Agora KTL 823. Photo author.

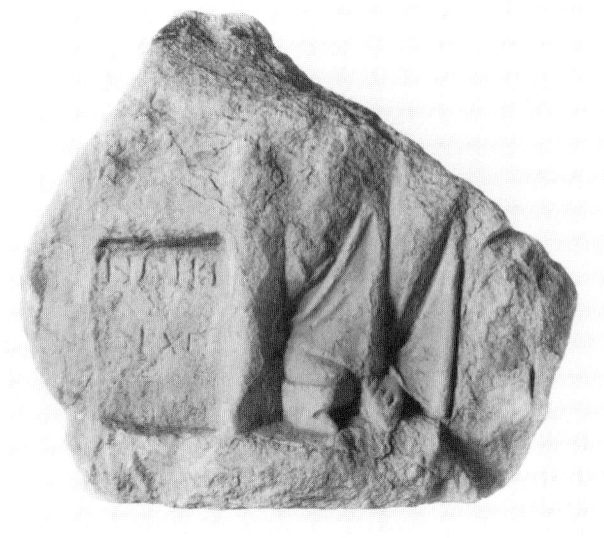

Fig. 8. Grave relief of Neikia. From Athens. Athens, Agora I 132. Photo Agora Excavations, American School of Classical Studies at Athens.

Möbius.[31] But both he and Kirchner date the inscription to the first century A.D., indicating a re-use of the monument.[32] The style and plastic quality of the anthemion is comparable to that seen on the stele of Thrasyxenos, the son of Dositheos, from Myrrhinoutta, dated by both its style and inscription to circa 150 B.C.[33]

Sculpted reliefs closely resembling their Classical counterparts become more numerous in the first century B.C.[34] The fragment of the monument of Neikia depicts a seated woman with a second woman standing nearby (Fig. 8).[35] At the left, the feet and lower legs remain of a seated woman facing right. The stool is rectangular with the front leg carved at an angle to the bottom of the niche, which slopes outward. The footstool is placed at an angle in relation to the back of the niche. A second woman stands at the right, behind the legs of the seated woman. Her right sandaled foot is placed frontally at the bottom of the niche. The drapery of both women falls in soft, broad planes. The anatomy of the lower leg of the standing woman is clearly indicated beneath her garment. The inscription is placed beneath the stool and reads: Νεικί / ας / Ἐρχε[---]. Comparable in the drapery style of broad planes with a few tent-like folds is the stele of Isidotos, the son of Isidoros of Miletos, in the Athens National Museum, dated by Muehsam to the first century B.C.[36]

The two remaining inscribed Hellenistic grave reliefs from the Agora are scrappy specimens, but they are included for the sake of completeness. The first is the monument of Skiros of the first century B.C. (Fig. 9).[37] The inscription reads: Σκίρος [------]. The left akroterion of the stele was formed by either a sphinx or a griffin, probably the former, whose hind quarters are seen crouching on the raking cornice of the pediment. Classical predecessors of the beasts rested on horizontal surfaces,

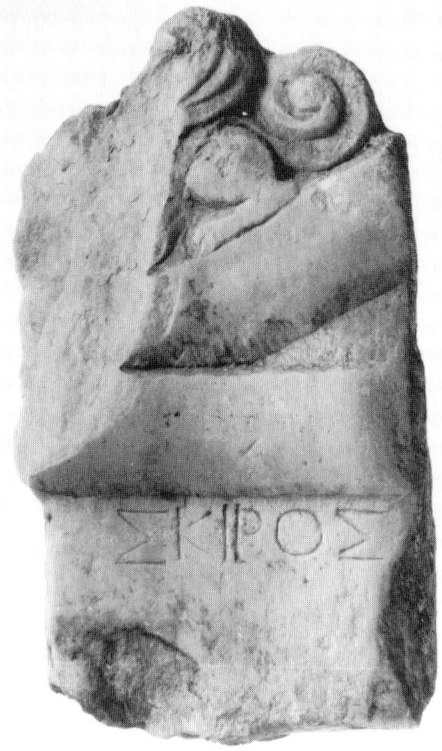

Fig. 9. Grave monument of Skiros. From Athens. Athens, Agora I 5021. Photo Agora Excavations, American School of Classical Studies at Athens.

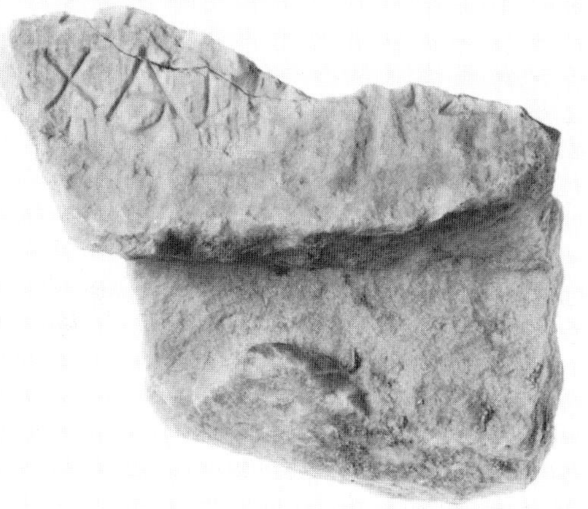

Fig. 10. Grave relief of an Acharnian. From Athens. Athens, Agora I 2294. Photo Agora Excavations, American School of Classical Studies at Athens.

as demonstrated by a sphinx akroterion in Berlin[38] and by the griffins on a stele in London.[39] The Agora stele is substantial, being carved from a thick slab of high grade white marble. The quality of the carving of both the figure and the lettering is good. Perhaps there was originally a carved or painted figure on the face of the stone.[40]

The final Hellenistic funerary relief from the Agora bears evidence of re-use. From the first century B.C. is the fragment of a stele that preserves the]tios of the first inscription with the top of a head carved in fairly high relief (Fig. 10).[41] The earlier inscription was erased and the area re-inscribed for an Acharnian. The inscriptions read:

a. ca. first century B.C. [------] / [------] / [----] ṭιος.
b. ca. first century A.D. [------] / [.]ọσα̣[---] / Ἀχαρṇεύς.

From the remains of the head, it appears that a frontal male figure was depicted, with his hair given a rough texture using a fine pointed chisel.

What conclusions may be drawn from this brief survey of some of the small group of funerary monuments from the excavations in the Agora that date from the Hellenistic period? First of all, it may be that the sumptuary law of Demetrius of Phaleron was not as restrictive as most scholars have interpreted it. In virtually every study of sculpture of this period there are statements such as the following example by Stewart: "The Attic market [for

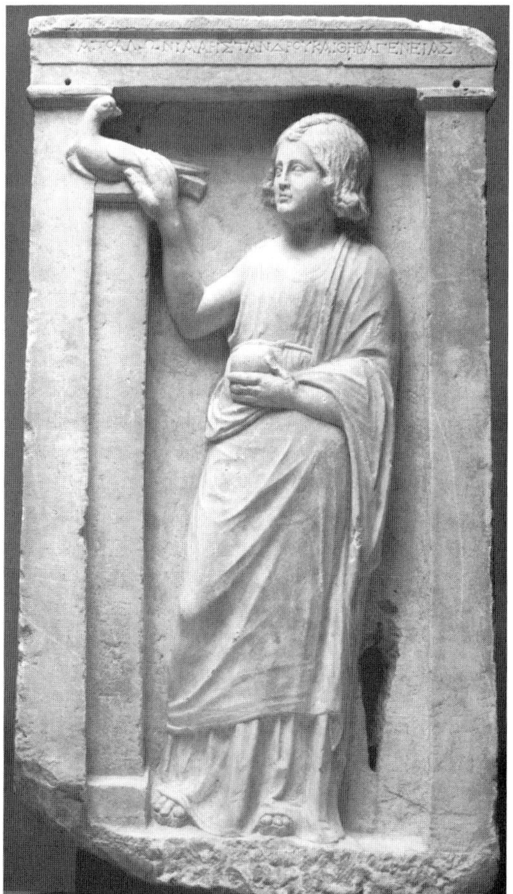

Fig. 11. Grave monument of Apollonia. Malibu, The J. Paul Getty Museum 74.AA.13. Photo courtesy of JPGM.

gravestones] was demolished at a stroke by Demetrios of Phaleron's sumptuary legislation of 317. Thereafter, it was apparently not until the second century that similar industry developed."[42]

While the production of large grave reliefs of high quality does indeed appear to have ceased at the end of the fourth century and does not seem to begin again before the second half of the second century B.C., there seems to have been a continuous production of very modest reliefs throughout the Hellenistic period.[43] Based on the quantity thus far identified as belonging to the Hellenistic period, they were not produced in great number. Vikela placed nine reliefs from the Pankrates sanctuary in the first half of the third century B.C.[44]

Higher quality funerary monuments re-appear in the late Hellenistic period, an example of which is in Malibu. The monument of Apollonia the daughter of Aristandros and Thebageneia is complete (Fig. 11).[45] The inscription reads: Ἀπολλωνία Ἀριστάνδρου καὶ Θηβαγενείας. Apollonia stands in a three-quarter frontal position facing left. In her left hand she holds a pomegranate and with her right she strokes a dove perched on top of a tall rectangular pillar. The stele is placed in the first half of the first century B.C. by Spiliopoulou-Donderer on the basis of drapery, hair, and shoe styles; of the spatial relationship between the figure and its architectural frame; and by the classicistic treatment of the body and face. It may be compared to an Attic gravestone of the first century B.C. in Grenoble.[46] Similar on the two are the high-girt dresses of Apollonia and the woman on the Grenoble stele and the simply carved hands that are large in proportion to the rest of the anatomy on Apollonia and on the male figure on the Grenoble stele.

It seems that a direct effect of the sumptuary legislation of Demetrius of Phaleron was that while the carvers and workshops of high quality funerary sculpture moved elsewhere not long after 317 B.C., possibly to work in the prosperous new Hellenistic courts such as Alexandria, Seleucia, and Thessalonike, the makers of modest monuments remained in Athens throughout the Hellenistic period.[47] There are document, votive and funerary reliefs that can be dated as early as the first half of the third century B.C. An example of a document relief is Athens honoring Herodoros of 295/294 B.C., in the Athens National Museum,[48] and of a votive relief one of those dedicated to Pankrates, dated by Vikela in the first half of the third century B.C.[49]

In his study on Attic letter cutters of 340 to 290 B.C., Stephen Tracy found that although there was certainly less inscribing under Demetrios, cutters remained active and found work where they could, inscribing deme decrees, inventories, boundary stones and simple grave markers.[50] In discussing prior sumptuary legislations, Shapiro noted that in Greece especially where there were laws, there were ways to circumvent them.[51] The end of the fourth century and beginning of the third century B.C. was a time of economic prosperity in Athens. Demetrius lowered taxation on the wealthy and curbed extravagance by private individuals.[52] Prior to Demetrius, burials in Athens had frequently consumed much of the wealth of the deceased's family. Humphreys noted in her study of commemoration practices from the Archaic to Hellenistic periods that by the end of the fourth century B.C. something more than an artistic representation of family solidarity was needed. She found that the history of commemoration of the dead in Athens was one of a progressive narrowing of the circle involved from outward-looking monuments of the Archaic period to intimate groups of kin and friends.[53] Perhaps this contrictive view resulted in a ready acceptance and continuation of nonfigural grave markers, an apt description for the columellae introduced by Demetrius. It might explain why depictions of family groups did not reappear as soon as Demetrius of Phaleron was deposed in 307 B.C.[54] Perhaps as we learn more about sculpture during the early Hellenistic period in Athens, boundaries that had seemed to be finite and definitive will blur.

Notes

1. It has been my privilege to study the sculpted funerary monuments in the Athenian Agora thanks to the initial suggestion of Evelyn Harrison, the support of past Directors of excavation, Homer Thompson and T. Leslie Shear, Jr., the present director of excavation, John Camp, and the permission of the successive Ephors in charge of the Agora, Petros Kalligas and Ismene Trianti. I wish to thank the organizers of the conference, William D.E. Coulson and Olga Palagia, for giving me the opportunity to participate.
2. Of the 3,455 sculptures inventoried through May 1995, there are approximately 325 that have been identified as belonging to funerary monuments. Most of the monuments are fragmentary and in a battered state of preservation, being found during the demolition of modern houses. They were brought into the Agora from cemeteries outside the city walls and used as building material. Thus, the original provenance of each monument included here is unknown. The 165 funerary sculptures of the classical period have been published in the author's dissertation, *The Sculptured Funerary Monuments of the Classical Period in the Athenian Agora* (1995). Eventually all the sculptures and fragments belonging to funerary monuments Classical through Roman will be published by the author as one of the volumes in the series *Agora*.
3. S. Schmidt, *Hellenistische Grabreliefs: Typologische und chronologische Beobachtungen* (1991) 43 ff.
4. Cicero, *Laws* 2.26.66.
5. Much has been written about Demetrius and his legislation. See S.V. Tracy, *Athenian Democracy in Transition: Attic Letter-Cutters of 340 to 290 B.C.* (1995) 36 n. 1, for a recent bibliography on the tyrant. See also Palagia in this volume, p. 19 with n. 36.
6. See, for example, D.C. Kurtz and J. Boardman, *Greek Burial Customs* (1971) 162 ff. C.W. Clairmont, *Classical Attic Tombstones* Intro. (1994) 2, seems unaccepting of 317 B.C. as the *terminus ante quem*, but offers no evidence for this opinion.

7. A field of columnar monuments has been created just north of the Kerameikos Museum. A study by A. Proukakis of the inscribed columnar monuments found during the Kerameikos excavations is forthcoming in the *Kerameikos* series. See K. Kübler, *AA* 1932, 189, for a description of the placement of a columella within a Hellenistic grave enclosure.
8. Some of the sculpted inscribed funerary monuments have been published previously by D.W. Bradeen, *Agora* XVII (1974) nos. 93 (I 2294), 126 (I 7038), 127 (I 132), 333 (I 3106), 347 (I 6049), 718 (I 7037), 719 (I 6910), 878 (I 6077), 935 (I 1184), 979 (I 5021), 1007 (I 4891). But since his focus was on the inscriptions and he did not study the sculptural aspects of the monuments, I include them in my study.
9. Agora inventory numbers I 1184, I 3106, I 6049, I 6910, I 7037, I 7038. See S.B. Franklin, *AJA* 4, 1900, 181, for the abstract of a paper delivered at the AIA general meeting in December, 1899, on reliefs on columellae.
10. Agora inventory numbers S 782, S 2462, I 132, I 2294, I 4891 (mensa), I 5021, I 6077. One of the monuments does not yet have an inventory number, but an interim designation, KTL 823.
11. I 4891. Bradeen (supra n. 8) no. 1007. PH: 15 cm; pW: 36 cm; pTh: 37 cm.
12. Athens EM 10501. A. Conze, *Die attischen Grabreliefs* IV (1922) 1769, pl. 378; *IG* II^2 5367; G. Kokula, *Marmorlutrophoren* (1974) 89 n. 73.
13. Conze (supra n. 12) includes a special section on columnar monuments with sculpted reliefs, nos. 1771–1830. The columnar monument with the finest sculpting, the monument of Hieronymos, bears a relief of ivy and berries and is dated to the third century. Conze (supra n. 12) 1790; *IG* II^2 11710 now in the Athens Epigraphical Museum 10895.
14. I 7038. Bradeen (supra n. 8) no. 126. H: 90 cm; Diam: 35 cm.
15. I 7037. Bradeen (supra n. 8) no. 718. H: 94 cm; Diam: 34.5 cm.
16. The sepulchral garden was created as part of the landscaping program of the mid-1950's. See H.A. Thompson – R.E. Wycherley, *Agora* XIV: *The Agora of Athens: The History, Shape and Uses of an Ancient City Center* (1972) 233. Funerary sculptures, mostly lekythoi and loutrophoroi, that had been on display in the Hephaisteion when it was a museum, were "planted". Unfortunately time and atmosphere have taken their toll on the monuments. Most are covered with black particulate soiling and lichen growth. Many are completely hidden among the bushes and trees that have now reached maturity.
17. I 1184. *IG* II^2 12302. Bradeen (supra n. 8) no. 935, pl. 74. PH: 15.2 cm; pW: 16 cm; pTh: 9.2 cm. It is of interest that part of only one handle is preserved above the break indicating that a hydria loutrophoros is pictured, a vessel associated with monuments for unmarried females.
18. I 6049. Bradeen (supra n. 8) no. 347; B.D. Meritt, *Hesperia* 17, 1948, 51, no. 55, pl. 22. PH: 32 cm; D: 28 cm. An impressionistic outline version of an amphora loutrophoros is incised into the surface of the stone below the inscription.
19. I 6910. Bradeen (supra n. 8) no. 719; B.D. Meritt, *Hesperia* 32, 1963, 53, no. 92, pl. 19. PH: 25 cm; D: 14 cm. A crudely rendered amphora loutrophoros is placed just below the inscription.
20. I 3106. *IG* II^2 7625. Bradeen (supra n. 8) no. 333, pl. 27. H: 105 cm; D: 36 cm. An amphora loutrophoros in low relief is placed below the inscription. It is well-proportioned and with the decorative quality of the later examples. Here the amphora loutrophoros, usually associated with markers for males, is used on a monument for a female.
21. I 6077. B.D. Meritt, *Hesperia* 30, 1961, 279, no. 138, pl. 57. PH: 33.5 cm; W: 28.5 cm; Th: 9.5 cm. Bradeen (supra n. 8) no. 878, dated it to possibly the second century B.C., but was perhaps influenced by his belief that no relief stelai were produced in Athens during the third century B.C. (p. 1). The whole question of third century Athenian funerary sculpture is a vexed one, but a small tumulus and perhaps a stone grave marker were erected in the Kerameikos in the third century, as well as more conventional monuments. W. Kovacsovics, *Kerameikos* 14 (1990) 54 ff.; J. Kirchner, *AEphem* 1937, 338 ff.
22. Athens EM 10979. Conze (supra n. 12) 1334a; *IG* II^2 8404.
23. Athens NM 2007. C.M. Edwards, *Greek Votive Reliefs to Pan and the Nymphs* (1985) 606 ff., no. 51.
24. S 782. PH: 35.5 cm; p.W: 20 cm; Th: 9.7 cm.
25. Athens, Fetiyie Tjami P 31 B. E. Vikela, *Die Weihreliefs aus dem Athener Pankrates-Heiligtum am Ilissos*, 16. Beih. *AM* (1994) no. A 20, pl. 16.2.
26. S 2462. PH: 35.5 cm; pW: 21 cm; Th: 7.4 cm.
27. I thank John Traill for his help with the inscription and the dating of this relief.
28. Piraeus Museum. Conze (supra n. 12) 1989; *IG* II^2 10172; E.J. Walters, *Attic Grave Reliefs that Represent Women in the Dress of Isis, Hesperia* Suppl. 22 (1988) 58 n. 5.
29. R.R.R. Smith, *Hellenistic Sculpture* (1991) 188 ff.; S. Dillon, *AJA* 100 (1996) 393.
30. KTL 823. PH: 116 cm; W: 70 cm; D: 33 cm.
31. H. Möbius, *Die Ornamente der griechischen Grabstelen* (1968) 113f. n. 181.
32. *IG* II^2 11390/1.
33. Conze (supra n. 12) 1833; *IG* II^2 6920.
34. Walters (supra n. 28) 58 f.
35. I 132. Bradeen (supra n. 8) no. 127. H: 27 cm; W: 31 cm; Th: 8.5 cm.
36. NM 1024. Conze (supra n. 12) 1973; A Muehsam, *Berytus* 10, 1952, 58.
37. I 5021. Bradeen (supra n. 8) no. 979. PH: 41.5 cm; pW: 24.3 cm; Th: 16 cm.
38. Staatliche Museen K 32. D. Woysch-Méautis, *La Représentation des animaux et des êtres fabuleux sur les monuments funéraires grecs* (1982) 134, no. 367.
39. British Museum 1905.5–18.1. Woysch-Méautis (supra n. 38) 136, no. 382.
40. An example of a stele crowned by a carved anthemion with a painted figural scene on the shaft is the monument of Tokkes in the Athens National Museum, inv. no. 1002. Clairmont I (supra n. 6) no. 1.388.
41. I 2294. Bradeen (supra n. 8) no. 93. PH: 21.5 cm; pW: 23.5 cm; Th: 11 cm.
42. A. Stewart, *Greek Sculpture* (1990) 62.
43. C.L. Lawton, *Attic Document Reliefs* (1995) 72 ff. Vikela

(supra n. 25) 226 ff.; 235 f.

44. Athens, Fetiyie Tjami P 5 A; P 12 A; P 31 B; P 32 B; P 38 B; P 42 B; P 44 B; P 78 A; P 81 A. Vikela (supra n. 25) nos. F 10; F 11; A 20; B 3; S 2; B 10; B 18; B 9; and B 6, respectively. See 235 f. for the dating of these nine.

45. J.Paul Getty Museum 74.AA.13. I. Spiliopoulou-Donderer, *Roman Funerary Monuments in the J. Paul Getty Museum* I (1990) 5 ff. *SEG* 40.229. H: 111cm; W: 61.5 cm.

46. Musée de Grenoble 376. M. Daumas – B. Holtzmann, *MonPiot* 73, 1993, 1 ff.

47. J.M. Williams, *Athens without Democracy: The Oligarchy of Phocion and the Tyranny of Demetrius of Phalerum, 322–307 B.C.* (Diss. Yale, 1982) 186.

48. Acropolis Museum 4063+2307. Lawton (supra n. 43) 109 f, no. 59. See also Palagia in this volume, p. 25 n. 40.

49. Athens, Fetiyie Tjami P 42 B. Vikela (supra n. 25) no. B 10.

50. Tracy (supra n. 5) 40.

51. H.A. Shapiro, *AJA* 95, 1991, 631.

52. Williams (supra n. 47) 209.

53. S.C. Humphreys, *JHS* 100, 1980, 122–123.

54. W.A. Geominy, *Die Florentiner Niobiden* (1984) 241 n. 638. See I. Morris, *Hephaistos* 11/12, 1992/3, 44 ff., who posits that restraint in funerary display could have served an ideological function for third century Athenians.

Goddess or Queen? A Colossal Marble Head in the Athenian Agora

Andrew Stewart

In 1935 the excavators of the Agora found a colossal female head in a late wall across the Panathenaic Way from the Stoa of Attalos.[1] The head (Figs. 1; 3–4; 6–7) is almost 40 cm high, so the statue it came from, if it stood upright, must have been around 3 m tall. It is made of a medium-grained crystalline white marble of good quality which should be Parian. It is almost unweathered, though the chin, lips, nose, and brows are battered. Much of the right side of the hair and a large portion of the left side of the crown of the head are missing, and the neck has split off at chin height. The eyes have been intentionally disfigured, and minor abrasions and bruises are to be found sporadically across the entire surface.

The top and back of the head (Fig. 6) are finished in an unusual way. At the top, a rough cutting about 3 cm wide and a few millimeters deep was made into the hair with the flat chisel and the claw (3 teeth/1 cm), encircling the skull about 10–12 cm above the hairline. At least two holes were drilled into this cutting, one above the parting of the hair and the other just over 12 cm to the left of it,

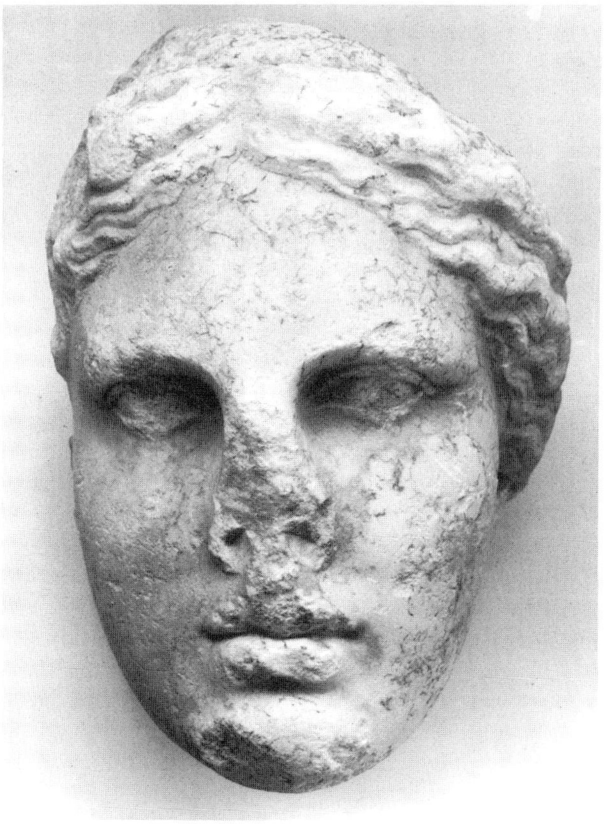

Fig. 1. Colossal head of a goddess from the Athenian Agora: frontal view. Agora S 551. Photo: American School of Classical Studies at Athens, Agora Excavations 5–2/3.

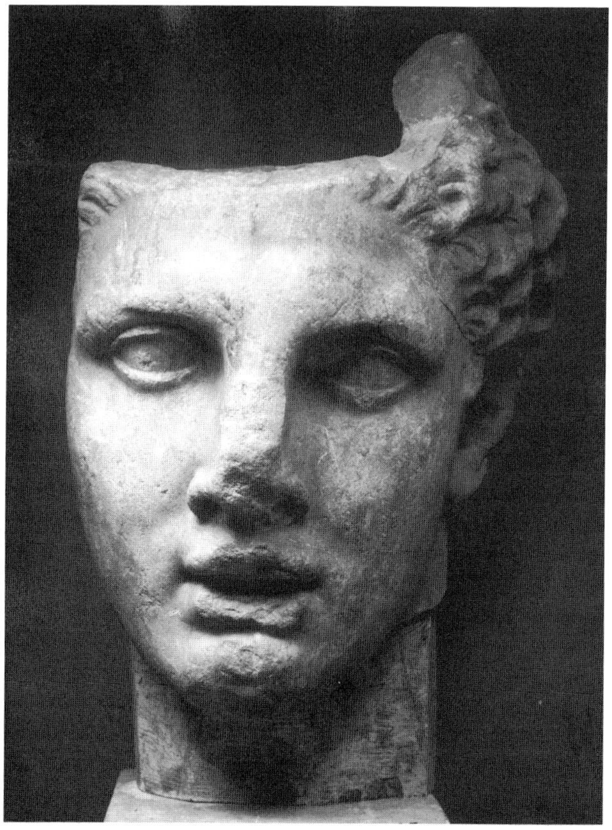

Fig. 2. Colossal head of Hercules attributed to Polykles of Athens, from the west side of the Capitoline Hill in Rome: frontal view. Rome: Palazzo dei Conservatori inv. 2381. Photo: DAI Rome 34.225.

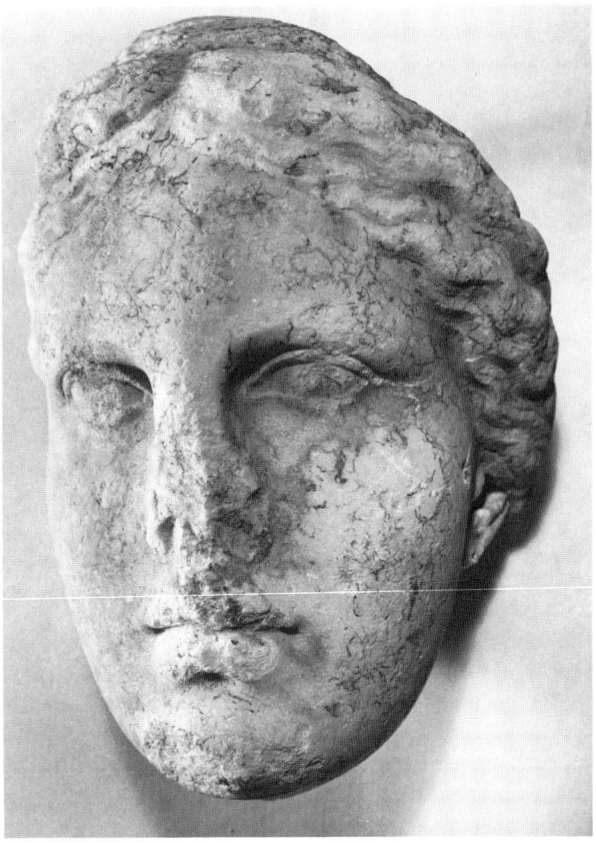

Fig. 3. Colossal head of a goddess, Agora S 551: left threequarter view. Photo: American School of Classical Studies at Athens, Agora Excavations I-10.

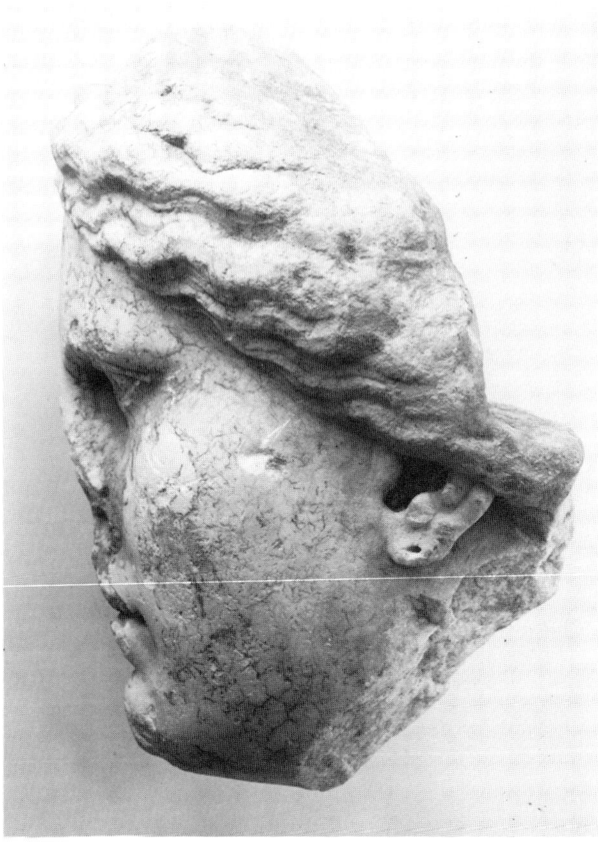

Fig. 4. Colossal head of a goddess, Agora S 551: left profile. Photo: American School of Classical Studies at Athens, Agora Excavations 5–2/2.

above the outer corner of the left eye; the former is 0.4 cm in diameter and 2 cm deep, and the latter (just visible above the hair in Fig. 3) still has the remains of a 3 mm-diameter bronze pin embedded into it. If any corresponding hole existed on the right side, the damage to this area (Fig. 5) has obliterated it. This arrangement clearly served to secure an object, presumably also of metal, that was set into the cutting. Above and behind it, to judge by what little remains, the hair was never carved, only vaguely sketched with the flat chisel.

All this seems too complicated for a flat fillet or *tainia*, which would hardly need such a secure anchorage; more likely, perhaps, is a metal crown or *stephane* (cf. Figs. 8–9). A colossal early Hellenistic head of a goddess or perhaps (from its findspot in northern Epirus) one of Pyrrhos's four queens, now in Ioannina, offers an exact parallel, though employs four dowels, not three.[2]

As for the back of the head, this is cut into an irregular step by coarse punching from a pointed chisel. This step is not vertical and oriented parallel to the plane of the face but slopes forward a little and is set at a twenty-degree angle to it, beginning just behind the left ear but slicing off the right one somewhat above the lobe (Figs. 4 and 7). The remains of a rectangular hole, 2 cm across, 3.8 cm high, and 3.7 cm deep, are to be found at the lower edge of this step, high on the break at the back (Fig. 6). Although the bottom of the hole is completely broken away, the flat chisel marks on its upper surface, horizontal punch-marks on its sides, and dents from the same tool on its rear surface (clearly visible in Fig. 6) show that it was not cut vertically from below, but horizontally from the back of the head. So the dowel that it held must have been horizontal also, securing the head to another piece of marble at the back rather than to the body below (cf. Fig. 8).

This step is unlikely to be a weight-saving device, for although the heads of many colossal Hellenistic cult statues were truncated at the back for this reason, the normal practice was to cut down the occiput (safely beyond the spectator's normal line of vision) into a single, flat, sloping plane, which was then hollowed out.[3] The Agora head's step and dowel, on the other hand, look like they were intended to carry some kind of headgear, now lost. By process of elimination, the best candidate is a separately-carved veil, whose front edges would have concealed the rough finish of the join and the uncarved portion of the top of the head, as in Figs. 8–9. The cutting's diagonal alignment supports this reconstruction, for it would angle the head somewhat to its right and into the veil – a common way of breaking the otherwise rather staid frontality of the type.

Whereas archaic and classical sculptors carved head

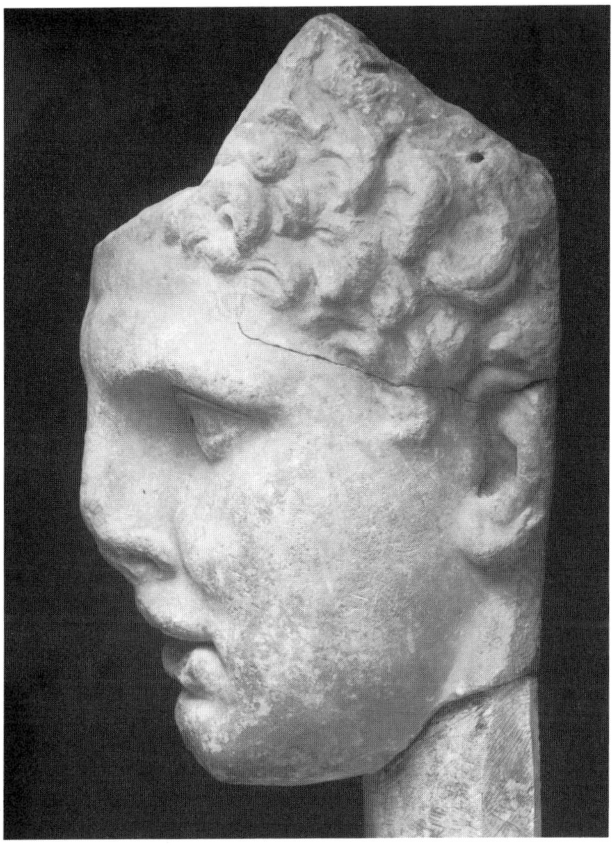

Fig. 5. Colossal head of Hercules from the Capitoline: left profile. Photo: DAI Rome 33.808.

and veil in one piece even when the ensemble was to be inset into the body, their Hellenistic successors increasingly preferred to insert the head into a previously hollowed-out veil, often cutting it down at the back and top for the purpose. Good examples of the earlier technique are the "Hera" of Cheramyes, the Demeter of Knidos, and a battered head of a goddess in Boston – of which more below. The later one can be seen on many of the portraits of the third-century Ptolemaic queens assembled by Helmut Kyrieleis.[4] The early third-century Ioannina "queen", once completed with a veil in at least three pieces secured by dowels (top and two wedge-shaped sides), perhaps represents a transitional stage – unless, given its colossal size and remote location, the sculptor was merely trying to economize on marble. Although I cannot find an exact parallel to the Agora head's "step," the back of the head of one of the women from the early first-century Mahdia wreck (here p. 71, Fig. 6) was added using a very similar cutting. Here, though, the addition is not dowelled and the neck is modelled wholly in the round.[5]

The horizontal dowel is, however, to be found in the center of the head-cavity of the veiled statue of Saufeia from the Baebia group from Magnesia-on-the-Meander, which was almost certainly made in 62 (Fig. 8). Here, though, the veil – carved in one piece with the body – is simply chiselled out into a rough concavity, as normal.[6] The true reason for the Agora head's step – clearly an experimental device – now becomes clear: regardless of whether the statue's body and veil were made in one piece or two, it enabled the veil to counterbalance the

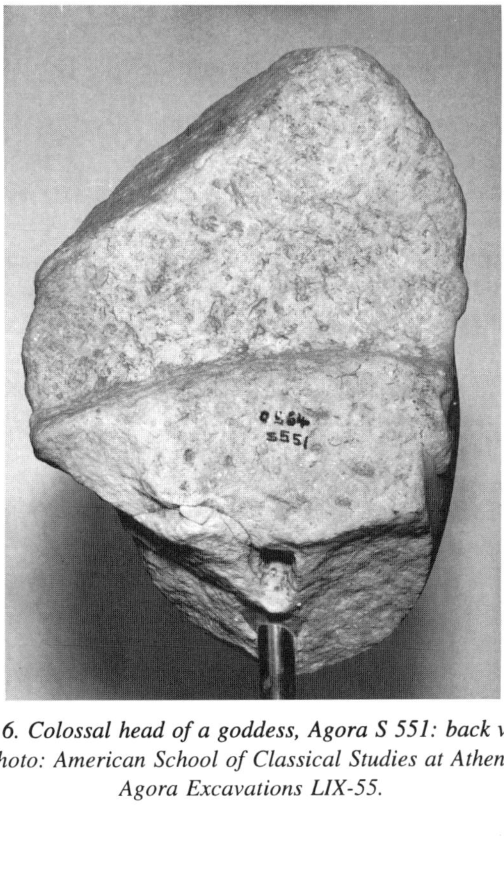

Fig. 6. Colossal head of a goddess, Agora S 551: back view. Photo: American School of Classical Studies at Athens, Agora Excavations LIX-55.

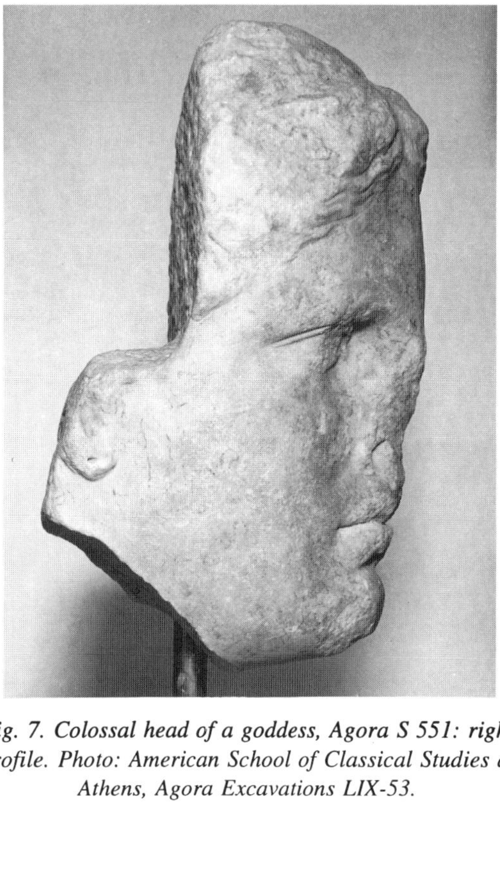

Fig. 7. Colossal head of a goddess, Agora S 551: right profile. Photo: American School of Classical Studies at Athens, Agora Excavations LIX-53.

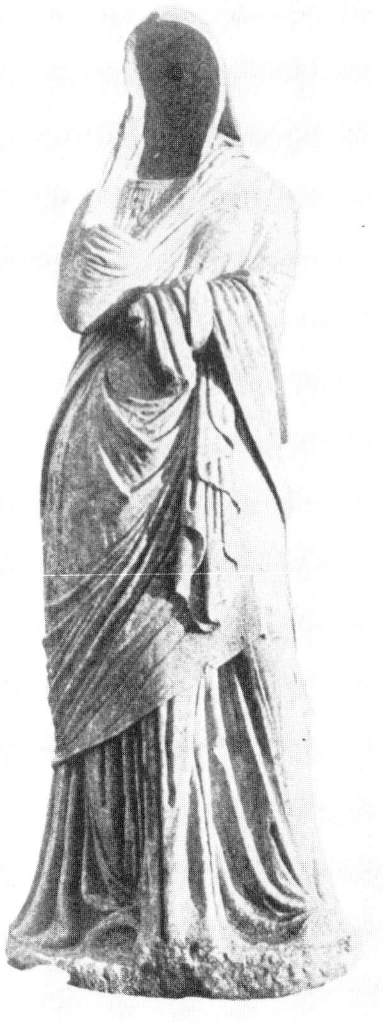

Fig. 8. Saufeia from Magnesia on the Meander. Istanbul inv. 606. Photo from C. Humann, Magnesia am Mäander *(1904) fig. 199.*

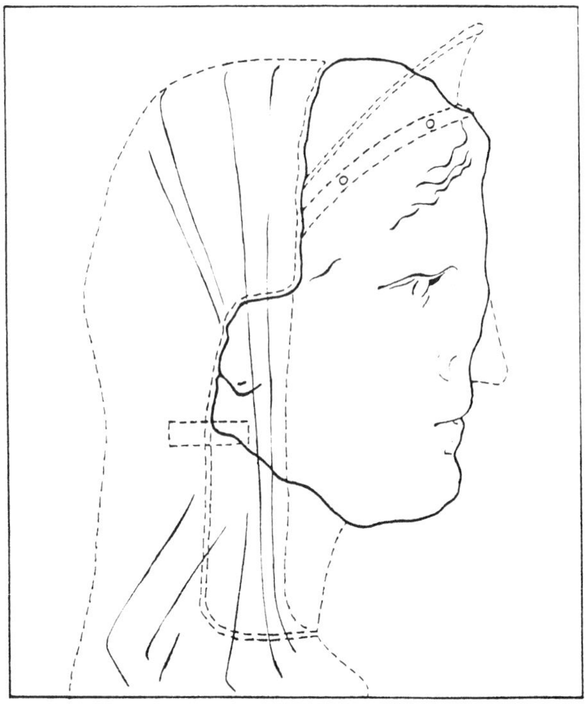

Fig. 9. Conjectural reconstruction of the Agora goddess, S 551. Drawing by Bao Vo.

projecting mass of the face (figs. 4, 7, and 9). In the one-piece arrangement, the head would have slid into its two-tier cutting mortise-and-tenon style (Fig. 9), forming a snug fit that even without the dowel would have stopped it falling forward over the breast. Yet even if the sculptor had cut the veil from a separate block and dowelled it to the body, the sheer weight of it pressing on the "step" would still have acted as a fairly efficient anchor.

In contrast to the semi-worked state of the back and top of the head, the modelled surfaces were treated with great care. Traces of tool-marks are few. A flat chisel was used to facet the hair into separate strands and to cut the ocular portion of the upper eyelids. The lips were separated with the aid of a very fine running drill, only 2 mm in diameter; a drill-bit of the same size was used to pierce the earlobes, though not all the way through. A 4 mm drill hollowed out the corners of the mouth and the canthus of the left eye, and a 5 mm one may have been used on the nostrils, though the damage here makes this uncertain. Finally, patches of delicate rasp work are also visible in the nostrils, and the hair was smoothed with medium-grade abrasives.

The face is slightly asymmetrical. Its right side is fractionally broader than the left, and the parting of the hair lies a little off-center, towards the inner corner of the right eye. The axes of the eyes and mouth also converge gently towards the right, reinforcing the turn of the head in this direction. This turn could indicate that the Agora statue was grouped with another standing to its right (the spectator's left). Unfortunately, the head's findspot offers no help concerning either this or its orig-

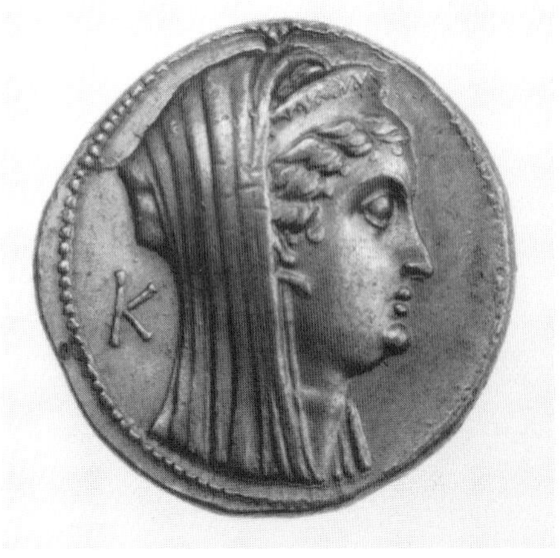

Fig. 10. Silver tetradrachm of Kleopatra II of Egypt. New York, American Numismatic Society. Photo: ANS 82–0463.

inal location, though the lack of primary weathering suggests that it was protected from the elements, perhaps inside a portico or temple. This building is likely, though not certainly, to have been in the Agora itself. For though the complex of walls in which the head was found have yielded sculptural fragments that originally stood elsewhere in Athens, our head's relatively well-preserved surface suggests that it may have wandered only a short distance prior to re-use.

The structure of the head is a heavy oval. The deep, full chin is slightly flattened at the tip, the cheeks are firm and broad, the forehead wide and smooth. The hair, a homogeneous mass, is combed to the sides from the central parting into long, undulating locks, each sharply divided into several strands. The features are strong, well-defined, and firmly embedded into the flesh of the face. The mouth is rather wide, with full, slightly parted lips that appear to pout a little when seen in profile; this impression is strengthened by the pronounced dimple under the lower lip, which is itself a little shorter than the upper. The corners of the mouth, turned down a little, are indented and surrounded with soft pads of flesh. Enough survives of the nose to show that it was broad and rounded along its ridge, which in profile forms a slight angle with the plane of the forehead. The almond-shaped eyes are quite deeply set, especially at the inner corner, and canted forward somewhat. The eyeballs, intentionally damaged by iconoclasts or other vandals, are slightly hollowed. The ocular portions of the upper and lower lids were sharply faceted, though their orbits are soft and fleshy; the upper lid crosses the lower in both cases. The brow is clearly defined at the inner end, where it swings into the ridge of the nose, but softens towards the outside and eventually merges imperceptibly into the side of the skull without meeting the cheekbone at all. What can be seen of the left ear is large, soft, and fleshy, with a pronounced tragus, antitragus, and lobe.

The treatment of all flesh surfaces is deep and expansive, with almost imperceptible transitions between the major muscles; these form complex swellings that gently rise and fall in harmony with the bone structure below. The cheekbones are slightly undercut by the naso-labial furrow's almost horizontal upper border, greatly increasing the volume of flesh around the mouth. The overall impression is one of maturity and authority, as the strong contours, broad planes, and imposing features fuse to create a composition that is both majestic and dignified yet neither remote nor unfeminine, at least when seen from the angle intended by the sculptor (Fig. 3).

Like the technique, the style of the head also suggests a Hellenistic date. The heavy, full face with its prominent chin, rather wide mouth, and ample cheeks recalls late fifth-century Pheidian types such as the Erechtheion korai (Fig. 11). It is also reminiscent of the head associated with the Prokne of Alkamenes, and what little remains of the head of the Nemesis of Rhamnous.[7] Yet the flesh surfaces are too tenderly modelled, the coiffure too insouciant, the forehead too triangular, the eyes too narrow, the cheekbone and brow too widely separated at the temples, and the lips too petite, to support such a date.

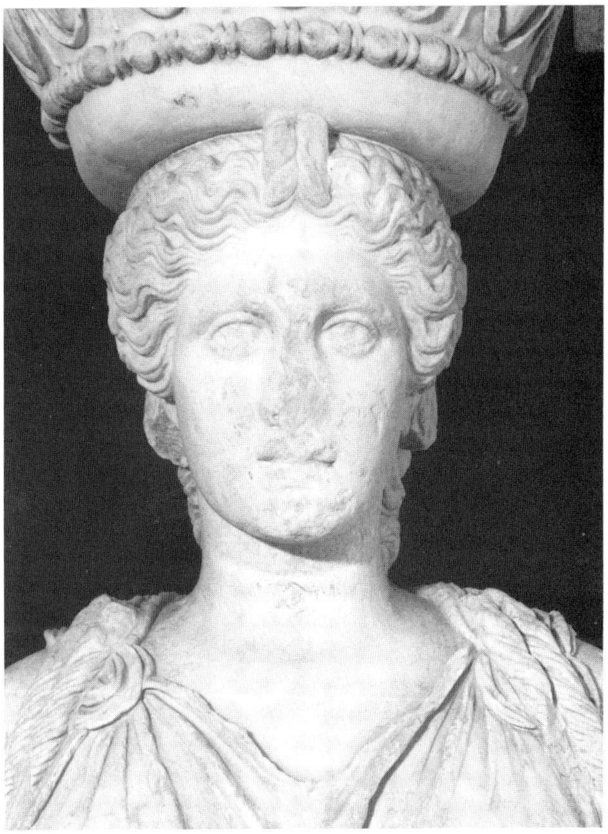

Fig. 11. Head of a kore (Caryatid) from the Erechtheion at Athens. London, BM 407. Photo: BM B 8379.

These details look to Attic fourth century sculpture. While the coiffure echoes the Demeter of Knidos and the Boston head, mentioned above, the tender modelling directly recalls Praxiteles' late style, as preserved for us today in the Leconfield head in Petworth House (Fig. 12).[8] The eyes, too, are conceived somewhat in his manner. Yet even here the rapport is by no means complete. In the Agora head, the muscles are more mobile and the features more dominant in proportion to the face as a whole; furthermore, the slurred, at times almost pulpy handling of the mouth, ears, and cheeks accords ill with the crisp transitions that define them. The thick lower lip, fleshy surround to the mouth, and strongly-marked, almost horizontal transition from this to the cheek are particularly striking. These find no parallel in the fourth century: instead, one must look to a later period, where a combination of various classical traits with an up-to-date surface manner was eagerly sought by sculptors of quality. For this head is a fine piece of work, carefully crafted by a deft and discriminating hand.

A number of Hellenistic neoclassic marbles have survived that show a similar blend of old and new, though not always in the same proportion as here. Among those from Athens itself, perhaps the closest is a colossal statue

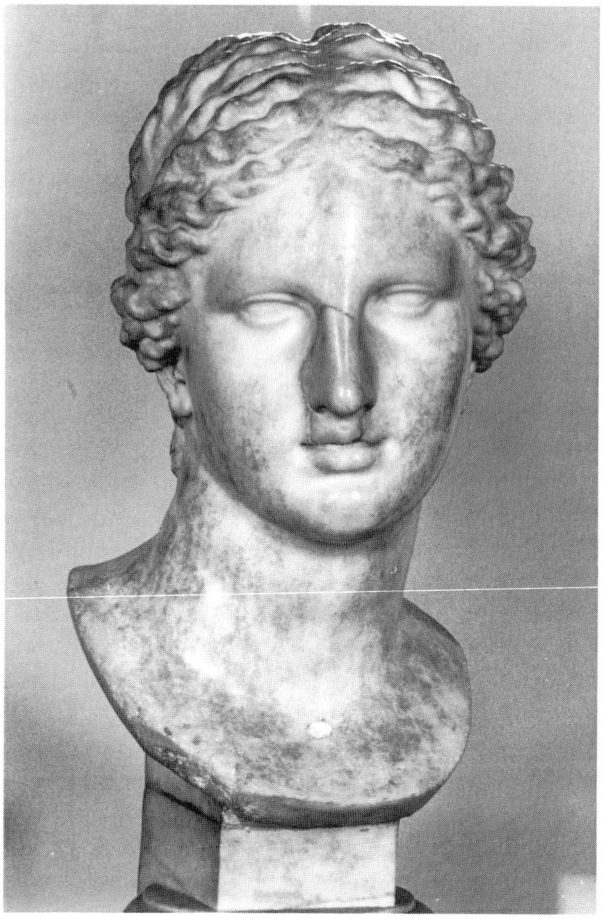

Fig. 12. Head of the Leconfield Aphrodite, attributed to Praxiteles or his school. Petworth House, Sussex. Photo: author.

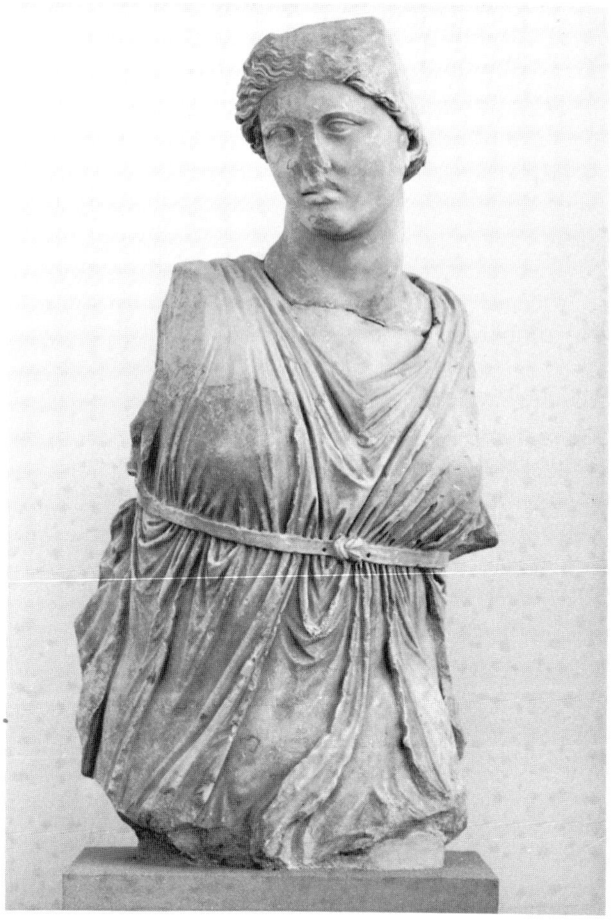

Fig. 13. Colossal statue attributed to Euboulides, from the inner Kerameikos, Athens. Athens NM 233. Photo: author.

of a woman from a cache of sculptures found near a large base located between the Agora and the Sacred Gate. This statue is unanimously dated to the later second century (Fig. 13). Unfortunately, its attribution to the Attic sculptor Euboulides on the strength of a signed block found on-site and a note in Pausanias is problematic at best.[9]

Among those pieces found outside Athens but definitely carved by Athenian sculptors, a female head from Pheneos in the Argolid is the closest. Part of a colossal akrolithic group of Asklepios and Hygieia, it was found with an inscribed signature of Attalos son of Lachares of Athens.[10] Its scale, proportions, and modelling are all similar, though its mouth is somewhat shorter and the overall effect – despite its inlaid eyes – is blander and considerably more mannered.

Yet the nearest relative to the Agora head is not female but male, and comes not from Greece but from the edge of the Capitoline Hill in Rome: a colossal Hercules in the Palazzo dei Conservatori (Figs. 2 and 5).[11] Becatti and Coarelli have shown that on stylistic grounds this head belongs to the mid second century, and that it might well be the Hercules by the Athenian sculptor Polykles that stood near the Capitoline temple of Ops. Given the difference in gender, the affinities between the two pieces are really quite striking. Similar in structure, proportions, and profile views, they share the same form of the lips, eyes, naso-labial furrow, and (where preserved) the nose; the same mixture of linear definition and softened detailing in the features; and the same slurred modelling of the flesh. Though I would not necessarily argue that they were carved by the same hand, they might well come from the same Athenian workshop.

But in the flush of enthusiasm for an attribution one must not overlook the differences between them, or rather, the varying degrees of success with which they master the problems occasioned by their subjects and modes of rendering. Both of them graft fourth-century modelling and detailing upon a basically fifth-century formal scaffolding. Yet in the Hercules the selfconsciously simplified geometry, mobile flesh, slurred transitions, and somewhat contrived pathos coexist uneasily at best. Structure and surface, idealism and rhetoric compete for the spectator's attention.

The Agora head avoids this basic incoherence. By definition, its sculptor had no need to articulate a sense of heroic pathos through wide-ranging manipulation of surface. In his work the formal perfection, softly undulating flesh, and contained expression are not only appropriate to the subject, but absolutely complementary to each other. If a sense of complete interiority, of an inner life pulsating deep down behind the classical mask, has not been achieved, it is probably because no retrospective style that seeks to apply the outer forms of one age to the structures of another can ever succeed in fusing the two completely. Some feeling of disjunction, and thus of lack of depth, will always remain.

If the style of the Agora head is difficult to penetrate, its identity is even more problematic. It has long been recognized as an Aphrodite if only because of its distinctively mature features and coiffure, to which we may now tentatively add its *stephane* and veil. But though the *stephane* would certainly characterize its subject as (in some sense) a queen, was she really a goddess or a mortal assimilated to a goddess, a cult statue or a heavily-idealized portrait?

In Athens, three Olympian goddesses may wear a *stephane* and sometimes a veil: Hera, Demeter, and Aphrodite.[12] Of these, Hera had no specific cult in the city, so may be safely put aside.

Demeter was worshipped with Persephone in a sanctuary just inside the Dipylon Gate and in the City Eleusinion in the Agora, but in neither case has her temple been excavated. On the single battered document relief from Athens that shows the two goddesses, Demeter was veiled and Kore not, but neither appears to wear a *stephane*.[13] And if the colossal fifth-century peplophoros found in the Agora's Southeast Temple in 1959 was also a Demeter, its Roman replicas show that it only wore a simple narrow *tainia*.[14]

Yet the fourth-century Boston head, bought in Athens and allegedly found near the Eleusinion, wears both *stephane* and veil; when L.D. Caskey acquired it in 1915, he at once identified it as a Demeter. If its provenance is to be believed, our sculptor could very well have been imitating it. Yet its marble seems not to be Pentelic (as one would expect in fourth-century Athens) and Athenian dealers' provenances, never particularly reliable, should be especially suspect at a time when the turmoil of the Balkan Wars had been feeding the city's antiquities market with many such pieces from all over Greece.[15] So since this head really offers no help either way, those who would identify the Agora head as Demeter must argue *faut de mieux* that its sculptor was augmenting the goddess' traditional Athenian headgear for added effect.

Aphrodite, on the other hand, regularly wears a *stephane* but adds a veil only when marriage, or some semblance of it, is in the offing – as in, for example, the Judgment of Paris. Presumably for this reason, fifth-century Attic sculptors showed her as veiled in at least one statue type and on two sets of votive reliefs.

The statue type is the so-called Leaning Aphrodite, best known from a well-preserved replica in Naples. This is usually regarded as post-Pheidian, and is often connected with Athens – either with the Aphrodite Pandemos on the southwest slope of the Akropolis, or with Alkamenes' Aphrodite in the Gardens.[16] Yet in this case the goddess wears only a flat *tainia* with her veil, not a *stephane*. The reliefs, on the other hand, honor Aphrodite Ourania; not only has her altar been discovered in the Agora, but she was represented both in hermaic form and in a cult statue made (according to Pausanias) by Pheidias. Both of these images are lost, but the reliefs show her in action: in one series, demurely descending a ladder from her bridal bed-chamber, and in the other, triumphantly riding a she-goat, her veil billowing above her head like a cloud.[17] In neither case does the goddess wear a *stephane*, and neither activity seems indicated for the Agora statue. Yet once again, it could still have been an elaboration of the Leaning Aphrodite or of some other Aphrodite type, or even a hybrid divinity or a personification such as Tyche.

An alternative suggestion, tentatively advanced by Antje Krug, is that she might be a Hellenistic queen, specifically a Ptolemaic one. As we know from coins and sculpture, these ladies often wore *stephane* and veil (Fig. 10).[18]

As it happens, Pausanias tells us that portraits of Ptolemy II Philadelphos and Arsinoe II actually stood in the Agora, but fails to specify their material or to describe them further. He also notes that the Athenians set up honorary portraits of Ptolemy IX Philometor Soter II and his daughter Berenike after Ptolemy's death in 80, but says that they were of bronze.[19] Unfortunately, these brief notices represent the sum total of the evidence for the portraits of the Hellenistic queens in Athens. Indeed, given the Agora head's probable second-century date, the best candidates are three that Pausanias does *not* mention: Kleopatra II, wife of Ptolemy VI Philometor of Egypt (Fig. 10), and two Attalids: Apollonis (wife of Attalos I) and Stratonike (wife of Eumenes II and then, when he died in 159, of Attalos II).[20] Yet once again, several objections come to mind.

To begin with, in Hellenistic Athens marble was usually reserved for temple-statues or *agalmata*, while honorary portraits were of bronze. We know of only one Hellenistic monarch who was accorded an *agalma* at Athens: Ariarathes V of Cappadocia, by the Dionysiac Artists.[21] And although his wife Nyssa was certainly mentioned in the same decree, it pointedly withholds this honor from her. Second, almost no portraits of the Hellenistic queens found outside their own kingdoms are over lifesize, regardless of their location and function, and – as in the case of temple statues – we may expect Athens to have been among the most conservative in such matters.[22] Third, the Agora head lacks the strongly arched eyebrows of the Ptolemies, their wide-open, almost thyroid eyes, and their omnipresent smiles (Fig. 10) – though one could argue that these unclassical features might have been muted or even suppressed entirely by the strongly classicizing taste of mid Hellenistic Athens. And fourth, as remarked earlier, the Agora head's own eyes have been deliberately hacked about, which certainly shows that one late Roman iconoclast *thought* she was a pagan goddess rather than some long-dead woman who could do him no harm.

In conclusion, then, the Agora head is much more likely to be a goddess rather than a mortal, and marginally more likely to be Demeter rather than Aphrodite. But even if the former's two temples within the city walls are excavated and more evidence discovered, the piece's exact identity may always remain a mystery.

Acknowledgements

My thanks to Homer Thompson and Evelyn Harrison for allowing me to study and publish this piece, and for discussing its manifold problems with me. I am also grateful to Antje Krug for generously waiving her prior claim to publication and for freely sharing her thoughts on it, and to Amanda Claridge, Mary Lee Coulson, Christian Habicht, Margaret Miles, Olga Palagia, Phillip Stanley, Anne Stewart, Nancy Tersini, and the late Charles Edwards for their generous assistance on particular points. And finally, I must thank Olga Palagia and William D.E. Coulson for giving me the opportunity to present it in this volume. None of them should be considered responsible for the shortcomings of the final product.

Abbreviations

Bieber	M. Bieber, *The Sculpture of the Hellenistic Age*^{2} (1961)
Boardman	J. Boardman, *Greek Sculpture: The Classical Period* (1985)
Kyrieleis	H. Kyrieleis, *Bildnisse der Ptolemäer* (1975)
Moreno	P. Moreno, *Scultura ellenistica* (1994)
Smith, *HRP*	R.R.R. Smith, *Hellenistic Royal Portraits* (1988)
Smith, *HS*	R.R.R. Smith, *Hellenistic Sculpture: A Handbook* (1991)
Stewart, *Attika*	A. Stewart, *Attika: Studies in Athenian Sculpture of the Hellenistic Age* (*JHS* Suppl. 14, 1979)
Stewart, *GS*	A. Stewart, *Greek Sculpture: An Exploration* (1990)

Notes

1. Found 4–9–1935 in Section O (just to the south of the central axis of the Stoa) in a late Roman wall; no. 0.564; inv. S 551; unpublished. Height, 39.5 cm; width, 28 cm; depth, 22 cm. The lower "riser" of the cutting at the back measures 12 x 26 cm; the flat step, 5 x 27 cm; and the upper "riser," 19 x 28 cm.
2. Ioannina inv. 15, though the head is not recut as they believe, but completed with a three-piece veil (see p. 85); see I. Vokotopoulou, *Οδηγός Μουσείου Ιωαννίνων* (1973) 91f., pl. 37; and esp. F. Krinzinger and K. Rakatsanis, *Mitteilungen der anthropologischen Gesellschaft in Wien* 123–24 (1993–94) 349–357, pls. 1–4. I am most grateful to Peter Ruggendorfer for alerting me to the existence of this piece, and for the reference to Krinzinger's and Rakatsanis's article.
3. See e.g. Stewart, *GS* figs. 787–793; Smith, *HS* figs. 299–302; the most convenient illustration of the technique is Bieber fig. 667; cf. also Moreno fig. 648.
4. Stewart, *GS* figs. 93–96; 571–572; Kyrieleis pls. 72–74; 76–80; 83–87; 94–97; Smith, *HRP* pls. 35–37; for the Boston head (15.856) see M. B. Comstock and C. Vermeule, *Sculpture in Stone: The Greek, Roman, and Etruscan Collections of the Museum of Fine Arts, Boston* (1976) no. 47 – where, as in the earlier publications (infra n. 16), the *stephane* is overlooked. But even in the Hellenistic period, the older one-piece method is still to be found: see, e.g., the Attalid queen from Pergamon (Smith, *HRP* pl. 23,2), and the head perhaps of Kleopatra II in Berlin (Kyrieleis pl. 105).
5. Tunis, Bardo Museum C 1186: G. Hellenkemper Salies and H.-H. von Prittwitz und Gaffron (eds.), *Das Wrack: Der antike Schiffsfund von Mahdia* 1 (1994) 313ff., figs. 14–17 and p. 71 of the present volume; my thanks to Amanda Claridge for alerting me to this parallel.
6. E.g. Saufeia, Istanbul inv. 606: C. Humann, *Magnesia am Mäander* (1904) 199f., fig. 199, whence my Fig. 8. I thank Evelyn Harrison for this reference; the dowel is now invisible, for a cast of her sister Baebia's head has been inserted into the cavity: cf. D. Pinkwart, *AntPl* XII (1973) 150 pls. 52f.; Smith, *HS* fig. 116.
7. See esp. H. Lauter, *AntPl* XVI (1976); H. Knell, *AntPl* XVII (1979) pl. 9; G. Despinis, *Συμβολή στη μελέτη του έργου του Αγορακρίτου* (1971) pls. 54f.
8. See Stewart, *RA* 1977, 195–202; Stewart, *GS* fig. 500.
9. Athens NM 233: Stewart, *Attika* 52 pl. 16d; Stewart, *GS* fig. 805; Smith *HS* 240; Moreno 553f. with further references; the signature is *IG* II^2. 4298. It, the sculptures, and the base were found on the north side of the intersection of Adrianou and Ermou Streets, right by the church of Aghioi Asomatoi, in 1837 and 1874. Pausanias 1.2.5 lists "an image of [Athena] Paionia, Zeus, Mnemosyne, the Muses, and Apollo, the dedication and work of Euboulides" at or near this location; but if read strictly (so, e.g., Beschi and Musti's new edition, ad loc.), this gives Euboulides only the (now lost) Apollo; yet in *IG* II^2. 4298 he signs only as sculptor, not as dedicator too. The base, a monumental stepped construction 2.87m. high and at least 8 m. long, was reburied shortly after its discovery, and only the inscription and sculptures – two Roman portraits and NM 233 – were saved; see L. Ross, *Le monument de Eubulides dans le Céramique intérieur* (1837) (=*Archäologische Aufsätze* 1, 143ff.); for a map showing the exact location of the find see id., *Das Theseion und der Tempel des Ares in Athen* (1852), endplate; and on the nineteenth-century controversy, E. Loewy, *Inschriften griechischer Bildhauer* (1885) 167ff. For the latest examination of the remains, see G. Despinis, in *Akten des XIII. internationalen Kongresses für klassische Archäologie, Berlin 1988* (1990) 151, who argues that of the extant marbles only NM 233 comes from the group. I now think that the Athena, NM 234, found in

1874 on the same site (see L. Julius, *AM* 7, 1882, 81–95, pl. 5; Despinis, *Ακρόλιθα* [1975] 33, pl. 37; Stewart, *Attika* 52, pl. 16c; Stewart, *GS* fig. 804; Moreno fig. 668), is Roman, as her incised irises would in any case suggest.

10. E. Protonotariou-Deilaki, *ADelt* 17. 2, 1961–62, 57–61, pls. 62–66; Smith, *HS* fig. 300; Moreno 554f., figs. 670; 672, with further references. The (presumed) cult statue of Fortuna Primigenia at Praeneste (Palestrina) is even closer, but its author is unknown: see H.G. Martin, *Römische Tempelkultbilder* (1987) 177 ff., pl. 31, who dates it to ca. 120–100.
11. Pal. Cons. inv. 2381: D. Mustilli, *Il Museo Mussolini* (1939) no. 11; pl. 44, 177–178; G. Becatti, *RIA* 7, 1940, 7–116, at 38f. and figs. 16–17; F. Coarelli, *StMisc* 15, 1970, 75–89, at 8f. and pls. 18–20; Stewart, *Attika* 42ff.; Stewart, *GS* fig. 858; Moreno 524ff., figs. 648–649; the attribution is based on Cicero, *ad Atticum* 6.1.17. On the Polykles family see most recently Stewart, *GS* 304ff.; Moreno 522ff.
12. For convenience, see *LIMC* q.v.
13. C. L. Lawton, *Attic Document Reliefs: Art and Politics in Ancient Athens* (1995) 46; 152, no. 165, pl. 86; she tells me that the Agora votive reliefs add little to this picture: "I have two possible Eleusinians, veiled and holding torch or scepter, both of them unpublished. One, probably Kore, late fifth- or fourth-century, has a veil over the back of her head. The other, very worn, probably fourth-century, wears a polos with a veil over it" (personal communication, 4.5.1996).

    For the Dipylon sanctuary see Pausanias 1. 2. 4, attributing the cult statues to Praxiteles; and for an early second-century refurbishment of the temples in the Eleusinion see the inscription *Hesperia* 11, 1942, 265, no. 51; R.E. Wycherley, *Agora* III: *Literary and Epigraphical Testimonia* (1957) 81, no. 225. My thanks to Margaret Miles for her generous help with this topic, and for furnishing me with an advance copy of part of her publication of the City Eleusinion.
14. E.B. Harrison, *Hesperia* 29, 1960, 339ff.; 371f., pl. 81c; for convenient pictures of the best (presumed) copy, in the Museo Capitolino, see *LIMC* IV (1988) s.v. Demeter, no. 55 (L.Beschi); Boardman fig. 212.
15. But, as remarked earlier (supra n. 4), Caskey overlooked the *stephane*, which he identified as a part of the veil drawn tight about the hair: *MFA Annual Report* (1915) 96; *AA* 1916, cols. 78f.; *AJA* 20, 1916, 369; 383–390; *BMusFA* 14, 1916, 9ff.; 28; *Catalogue of Greek and Roman Sculpture* (1925) no. 27. The marble is consistently given in the publications as Parian; at any rate, it does not look Pentelic to either Olga Palagia, whom I also thank for the caution about Athenian dealers' provenances, or myself.
16. Naples G 136: *LIMC* II (1984) s.v. Aphrodite, no. 185 (A.Delivorrias), with bibliography; Boardman fig. 216; M. Brinke, *Kopienkritische und Typologische Untersuchungen zur statuarischen Überlieferung der Aphrodite Typus Louvre-Neapel* (1991)(non vidi); A. Delivorrias, *MEFRA* 103, 1991, 129–157; E.D. Reeder, *Pandora: Women in Classical Greece* (1995) no. 17; cf. Pausanias 1.22.3.
17. For the Athenian temple and candidates for the herm and Pheidian statue of Aphrodite Ourania (Paus. 1.14.7 and 19.2) see J. Travlos, *Pictorial Dictionary of Ancient Athens* (1971) 79–82, figs. 102–105 with *LIMC* II s.v. Aphrodite, nos. 174–181; yet E.B. Harrison, *Agora* XI : *Archaic and Archaistic Sculpture* (1965) no. 218 identifies Travlos's herm as Artemis-Hekate, and in *Hesperia* 53, 1984, 379–388, pls. 73–75 links the so-called Sappho type with Pheidias's *Elean* Ourania; she also rejects Pausanias' attribution of the Athenian Ourania to him on the grounds that by the time the Periklean building program shifted to the Agora, he was already in exile. For the two types of votives see C.M. Edwards, *Hesperia* 53, 1984, 59–72, pls. 17–19; these two types represent the totality of Aphrodite votive reliefs in the Agora storerooms (personal communication from Carol Lawton, 4.5.1996).
18. A. Krug, as quoted in H.A. Thompson, *The Athenian Agora: A Guide to the Excavations and Museum* (1976) 288ff.; 325; for comparanda see Kyrieleis and Smith, *HRP*.
19. Pausanias 1.8.6 and 9.5.
20. On Athens' relationships with these two dynasties see M. Thompson, *ANS-MusNotes* 11, 1964, 119–129 and C. Habicht, *Hesperia* 59, 1990, 561–577.
21. *IG* II^2. 1330.
22. On Hellenistic colossal portraits see D. Kreikenbom, *Griechische und römische Kolossalporträts bis zum ersten Jahrhundert nach Christus* (27. Ergh. *JdI*, 1992); the Ioannina head (supra n. 2), if truly a queen, may be an exception, as are the three colossal heads from Delos, an island where the normal rules evidently did not apply.

Atticism, Classicism, and the Origins of Neo-Attic Sculpture

Mark D. Fullerton

As the last speaker on Athens and Attica in a conference on "Regional Schools in Hellenistic Sculpture," it is only logical that I should discuss the phenomena of classicism, retrospection, eclecticism and Romanization. In an era when the traditional structures for the classification of Hellenistic sculpture are eroding, one concept has remained fixed – that of a characteristically classicizing Late Hellenistic era beginning around 150 B.C., centered in Athens, and brought about by the demands of a Roman predator culture.[1] That even one such concept might be fixed is certainly an attractive prospect, given the difficulty of pinning down Hellenistic sculptures and sculptors – whether stylistically, thematically, geographically, or chronologically. Yet, as useful as such models are for the organization of physical remains, one has to be aware of the degree to which they are deduced from historical circumstances rather than induced from the sculptures themselves. In an indisputably circular manner, the *assumption* of such a model can frame our understanding of the evidence used to support it and thus dictate the terms of interpretation. With that in mind, I would like to turn our attention to one aspect of late Hellenistic production which weaves together all of these concepts and problems: the origin of Neo-Attic relief.

Although definition of the term is notoriously elusive,"Neo-Attic" most often refers to a corpus of Roman marble objects with relief decoration portraying a variety of themes drawn from Greek mythology. The styles of the reliefs vary, but many figures show formal features characteristic of sculptures of Classical or even earlier times. The *term* "Neo-Attic" itself was first used by Heinrich Brunn, who designated a small group of late Hellenistic sculptors as *neu-attische* in order to distinguish them from the *alt-attische* sculptors of Classical Athens.[2] While Brunn praised the later sculptors for their respect for Classical form, his term does not yet seem to connote a consciously revivalist attitude, and his designation as Attic refers only to the ethnic of the sculptor himself. Brunn's Neo-Attic group included a handful of signed statues and three works of relief sculpture[3] which formed the core of Friedrich Hauser's study of Neo-Attic reliefs. Collecting over 150 examples, Hauser demonstrated that many of the various figures found among these reliefs derive from a relatively limited number of figural types.[4] At a time when scholars like Furtwängler were refining the art of reconstructing lost Greek Classical statuary on the basis of assumed Roman copies, the term "type" necessitated a Classical prototype and "Neo-Attic" came to imply decorative schemes which copied figures from conspicuous monuments in Athens. This is the assumption which forms both the method and the objective of Werner Fuchs' still standard study, as is manifest in his definition of Neo-Attic as the "reproduction and decorative employment of Classical works in Athens."[5]

The canonical status of Fuchs' treatment is attested by the quarter-century of relative silence on Neo-Attic which follows his work, but in the last ten years there has been an upsurge of interest in the topic. Separate monographs on candelabra, kraters, and bases have recently appeared, and the monumental publication of the Mahdia wreck material in 1994 has caused reassessment of the critical early examples.[6] Much of the recent work was inspired by the groundbreaking research on classicism and archaism by such scholars as Ridgway and Zanker,[7] and informed by Hölscher's model for Roman sculptural style, published a decade ago.[8] This highly influential work presents a view of Roman sculpture which postulates the existence of a palette of forms, wherein an entire spectrum of distinct stylistic features was available synchronically for particular subjects and purposes. Thus, in these recent studies there is movement away from Fuchs' monolithic assertion of the necessity of a specifically Classical prototype behind nearly every image. In Grassinger's book on kraters, for example, one finds a detailed articulation of figural types according to the era of the prototype – High Classical, Late Classical, or Hellenistic. Other works concern themselves with the way in which Neo-Attic artists have *varied* from the Classical prototypes or *combined* Classical images with those of Hellenistic origin.[9] Yet, what has seldom – if ever – been proposed is that the very concept of prototype should be abandoned.

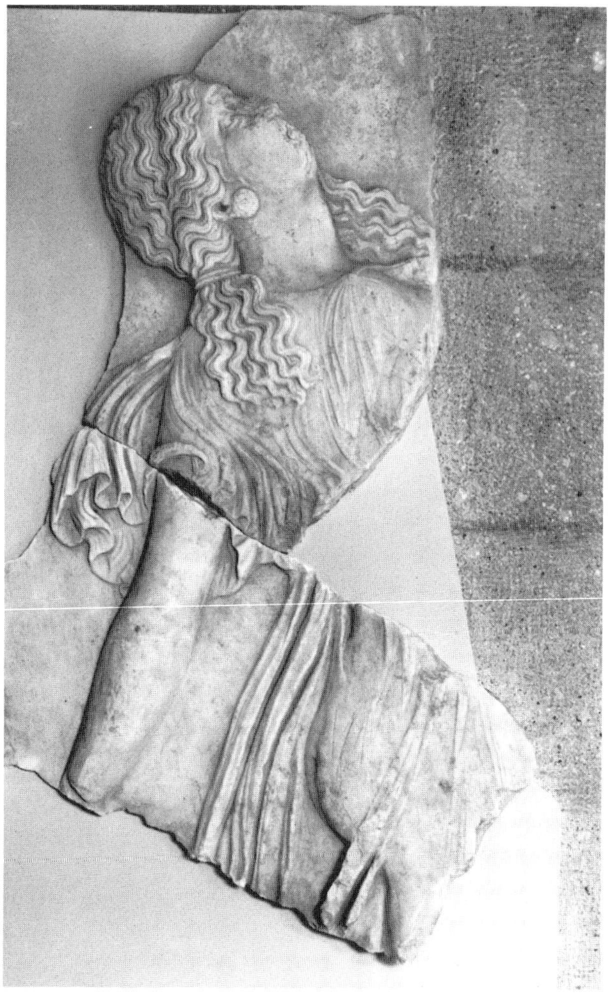

Fig. 1. Relief of dancing maenad. Corinth Museum S 2597. Photo American School of Classical Studies – Corinth Excavations.

One reason why this concept is so ingrained in our attitudes toward Neo-Attic is the replicative nature of the art itself. Similar images and even comparable compositions are reiterated on a number of different objects – a situation which suggests some sort of model. However, it is essential to recognize that the prototype in question is a model used by Neo-Attic artists for practical reasons of production, and it need not antedate the beginning of that production. Recent works on the copying of statuary are beginning to overturn entrenched notions of copy and prototype. It is well-accepted now that close reproductions and multiple originals were created in Classical times.[10] It has also been established that Roman replica series can derive from a Roman original.[11] Copying in and of itself, therefore, does not indicate the existence of a significantly *earlier* prototype.

It is true that some of the figures found on Neo-Attic objects resemble figures from Classical art and a very small handful do seem to copy Classical models.[12] But to assume from the latter group (which is small in number and late in date) a universality for the phenomenon overall is not prudent. Concerning the prototypes of the most commonly encountered Neo-Attic types – such as the dancing maenad reliefs (Fig. 1) or the archaistic four-gods group (Fig. 2) – there is no agreement, nor is any likely to emerge soon.[13] It may be better to consider the previous Classical and Hellenistic traditions of figural production as a *source* for the creation of Neo-Attic types rather than as necessarily containing specific *prototypes* copied on the later reliefs just as the Belvedere torso – another of Brunn's *neu-attische* works – reflects Classical *sources* but is equally a work which reflects the personality of its own time.

A useful example drawn from the realm of Neo-Attic relief is the four-gods type, which is known from late Hellenistic reliefs found on Delos (Fig. 2) and in Athens and recurs frequently in the Neo-Attic repertoire.[14] For generations, it has been assumed that these figures copy a fourth century prototype, based largely on the archaistic drapery of the Athena emblem on late Classical Panathenaic amphorae and supported by the existence of generally similar figures on the Samothrace frieze.[15] On the other hand, Becatti and Havelock have proposed that such archaistic figural types could have been created only in late Hellenistic times, when a presumed copying mentality would have permitted the use of cartoons – a process suggested by the reiterative outline of the figures.[16] While differing on the issue of chronology, both views take for granted the concept of prototype and the necessity of fixing that prototype in time. Yet if we are willing to rethink our conceptions of source and citation and look strictly at the extant images, a solution to the impasse might be found.

The striding archaistic image of Athena existed already in the later fifth and fourth centuries on Panathenaic amphorae.[17] Examples from around 400 B.C. already show archaistic patterns in the overfold drapery, and the fourth century examples display every variety of mannered archaistic linear device. Similar Athena images also occur on early Hellenistic coins.[18] It is now agreed that the frieze of archaistic dancers from Samothrace *must* date to the second half of the fourth century, and these figures are clearly related to the general type of the Athena.[19]

It is clear then that already in Classical times there existed, within a figural repertoire shared by various two-dimensional media, a general type of archaistic draped striding figure. By Hellenistic times, examples also exist in sculpture in the round, with varying degrees of archaism.[20] At some point, and most probably around the time of the beginning of the production of Neo-Attic reliefs, the types of the four-gods reliefs were created and quickly extended to other subjects. I would not argue that they copy a "prominent original in Athens," as Fuchs and others would generally have it, nor even any specific prototype at all. On the other hand, I would also not assert that the creation of these types took place in total ignorance of the archaistic figures which did exist from

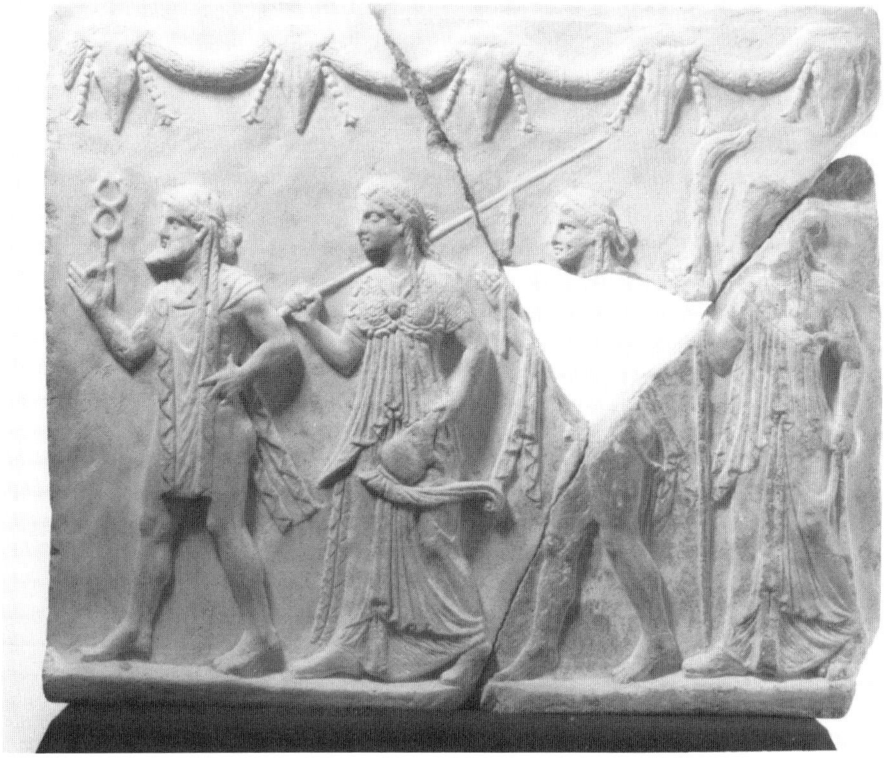

Fig. 2. Archaistic relief of four gods. Delos Museum A 9. Photo École Française d' Athènes.

earlier times. The Neo-Attic workshops simply drew on a general figural repertoire, which included the striding archaistic draped figure, and adapted figures from this repertoire to suit their own purposes. Moreover, the existence of a figural type within the Neo-Attic repertoire indicates nothing *a priori* about its genealogy other than its availability at the time of its first employment.

To return to our initial point, although this alternative model for the origin of Neo-Attic figural types emerges logically from a reading of the material evidence, it is not consistent with the prevailing concept of a classicizing, retrospective, even nostalgic late Hellenistic Athens. While the use of idealized styles similar to those found in Classical art is clearly documentable in Hellenistic art, and Classical allusion unquestionably existed in some monuments, the assertion of a characteristically classicizing style period in late Hellenistic Athens is problematic on at least three counts.[21]

First, there is the general problem of periodization in Hellenistic art. As mentioned, recent work on Neo-Attic proposes pushing back Hölscher's semantic system of contemporaneously available styles into late Hellenistic times. That such a system was already in place by late Classical times is suggested not least by the utter impossibility of establishing accepted Hellenistic style-periods.[22] To choose just one example from among the plurality of styles found in Hellenistic times, one could consider the case of the baroque. As is now well-recognized, exaggeration of contrast and chiaroscuro for dramatic effects originates in the arts of the fourth century, as for example in the pedimental sculptures at Epidauros and Tegea.[23] The most famous examples in Hellenistic Pergamon differ little from Roman works like the Sperlonga sculptures or the Laocoon by the same artists.[24] One could trace analogous sequences for the other styles which consititute the Hellenistic palette. In fact, it is quite clear that the various styles of Hellenistic times – including not only the baroque, but also the realistic, rococo, and, for lack of a better term, the classicizing – depend for their signification upon the play of difference among themselves. To borrow linguistic terminology, the idealism of the deities on the Pergamon Altar draws meaning *syntagmatically* from its relationship to the baroque of the juxtaposed giants.[25] Similarly, the unstinting realism of a Hellenistic grotesque signifies *paradigmatically* through its *not* employing, for example, Classical idealism.[26]

The second problem follows directly from the first. If there exists in Hellenistic times a system of mutually dependent and continuously available stylistic alternatives, the existence of style-periods becomes unlikely, if not impossible. A look at the "afterlife" of Classical styles and style features suggests that this phenomenon too is not chronologically limited but rather occurs throughout the era in question. There are at least two related but distinct impulses behind the continued use of Classical forms in Hellenistic sculpture. The first – a kind of religious conservatism – entails the continuing appeal of Classical idealism for the depiction of Olympian deities – especially, but not only, in cult statues. Perhaps the most obvious example is the cult statue group from the Sanctuary of Despoina and Demeter at Lykosoura; these works of Damophon were once used to bolster the concept of late Hellenistic classicism but are now shown to date to the middle of the Hellenistic period.[27] The second impulse is more specifically historical: the continuing role of Athens as a source of inspiration or a model for emulation in each era following the fifth century. In late Classical times one encounters the diffusion of elements of Athenian High Classical style throughout Greece[28] (and beyond) at the same time that the Macedonians come to incorporate High Classical figural types and stylistic features into their new royal arts.[29] As we saw in the case of the striding Athena above, the early Hellenistic rulers, true to their Macedonian background, sought to share in the cultural authority of Athens[30] – an objective which was subsequently pursued with even greater zeal by the Attalids of Pergamon and the Romans themselves. It is conventional in the study of reiterative styles like the archaizing and classicizing to seek to divide the retentive from the imitative.[31] Such division is itself no easy task; both imperatives are clearly at work here, and both indicate a continuity in the usage of Classical forms in late and post-Classical art.

This conflation of the traditional and the retrospective brings us immediately to the third problem with the prevailing concept of late Hellenistic classicism – the inherent inadequacy of "classicism" itself, both as a term and as a concept. It is a label which is applied indiscriminately on the basis of visual analysis, yet it is charged with connotative force. Once a work is classified as classicizing in style, it is almost invariably read as a direct and deliberate allusion to the Classical era itself. Yet if classical forms are used continuously from the Classical era onward, how can we be so confident in assigning a specific referent to such a form? To cite just one example, is the contrapposto of the Primaporta Augustus an allusion to the work or even the era of Polykleitos, as is generally assumed, or does it situate the image in a tradition of heroic forms, like that of Augustus' own divinized father, which would have been far more familiar to the intended viewer?[32]

To sum up so far, we have seen that there are two basic views of the origin of types in Neo-Attic art. One privileges the *notion* of specific prototypes although admits considerable variety in the chronological range allowed these prototypes. The other suggests that in most cases specific prototypes should *not* be sought, but rather that the entire figural and stylistic repertoire of Greek art up to the point in time when the Neo-Attic type was first employed was present and available as a source. The mining of such sources did not *necessarily* indicate a deliberate or even perceived referentiality; the latter is a relationship which needs to be demonstrated apart from pure visual analysis. Once, however, we view Neo-Attic art as neither necessarily nor even primarily retrospective and we see the era after ca. 150 B.C. as neither exclusively nor even characteristically classicizing, the usefulness of type for fixing the origins of Neo-Attic sculpture becomes limited. That is to say, such a view has much to offer concerning *how* Neo-Attic objects came to be made, but very little about when. On the other hand, we are now freed from the conventional view which places the beginning of Neo-Attic production in the second half of the second century simply because that is the era in which classicism begins. In the end, what distinguishes Neo-Attic work from the rest of Hellenistic sculpture is not to be found in the styles or figural types of its decorative relief, but rather in the nature of the works decorated – utilitarian objects carved from marble for domestic display and decorated through a process of relatively precise, perhaps even mechanical, copying. We must, in short, look at the Neo-Attic sculptures themselves.

The archaeological evidence is limited in quantity but quite clear in its implications. The earliest datable Neo-Attic works are those found among the Mahdia wreckage. Despite, or perhaps because of, the enormous work recently done on this cargo, the acceptable dates have a rather wide span, but it seems generally agreed that the ship went down somewhere between 80 and 60 B.C.[33] How much earlier than this did Neo-Attic production begin?

For this question we are dependent on more circumstantial evidence. The use of copying in production suggests a date not far from that of the wreck. While certain forms of reiteration and "multiple originals" were long known, the earliest copies of statuary like those found in Imperial times seem to date from the first half of the first century, and extant examples are rare before the second half.[34] One can also invoke the figure of Pasiteles – about whom the literary sources suggest a number of features reminiscent of Neo-Attic: that he was a maker of vessels, a user of models, and a writer of art history. As a contemporary of Pompey the Great, as Pliny tells us, Pasiteles' *floruit* must have been around the second quarter of the first century B.C.[35]

As for the cultural context in which Neo-Attic arose, there is little hard evidence, but it is tempting to cite as a parallel, with no causative implications in either direction, the rise of Atticism in rhetoric.[36] As a movement which arose in reaction to the excesses of so-called Asianism, which advocated strongly the close following of privileged models, and which sought a purity of form through rather rigid strictures, Atticism reflects a sorting out, by the Romans, of the multiple rhetorical traditions inherited from the now subject Greeks. As works of art, the Neo-Attic vases and candelabra seem modest, especially when compared in cultural importance to a phenomenon like rhetoric, but the consumers of these objects were just the same bilingual elite – like Cicero – who concerned themselves with such metarhetorical issues. Again, as with Neo-Attic, the origins of Atticism are obscure and the question itself has been obscured by the assumption of a second century retrospective *zeitgeist*, but most recent studies seem to agree that it originated in a Greco-Roman context within a generation before its first occurrence in Ciceronian writings of 46 B.C., and that it became widespread during the Augustan principate.[37] Although I would not argue that either phenomenon directly influenced the other, the parallels between Neo-Attic sculpture and Atticism in rhetoric are compelling and would suggest at least that both arose in the same cultural context.

In conclusion, acknowledging for the moment the dangers inherent in any argument *ex nihilo*, there seems to be no evidence which would place the beginnings of Neo-Attic production earlier than the first century B.C. – perhaps even a generation into that century. The Mahdia material might very well be among the first such objects produced. The placement of this production in the second century, encountered in every work on Neo-Attic known to me, seems based entirely on the assumption that Hellenistic art following the battle of Pydna enters an era typified by a retrospective and eclectic appropriation of earlier, especially Classical, stylistic forms. More important than the chronological suggestion, which could in fact be overturned by a single archaeological discovery, is the demonstration that this characterization of late Hellenism is, at best, both incomplete and misleading. It oversimplifies what is in fact a highly complex situation and obscures the dynamic stylistic system which was essential to the significative power of Hellenistic art. If my thesis has eliminated our last generally accepted fixed point for a chronology of Hellenistic sculpture, I hope that this offence has been vindicated by offering a new avenue of inquiry and by suggesting that it is only through the questioning and possible rejection of traditional assumptions that such new paths might be opened.

Acknowledgements

I would like to thank Professor Olga Palagia for inviting me to participate in this conference and in this publication. I am grateful to the many members of the audience who responded to the ideas I presented, at once correcting, expanding and encouraging my work. Most of all, I thank my wife, Monica Barran Fullerton, for her support and for her critical comments on the various drafts of this paper, both as delivered in Athens and as published here.

Notes

1. The classic statement of this position is, of course, to be found in G. Becatti, *RIA* 7, 1940, 71–116 and many valuable observations are to be found in A.Stewart, *Attika: Studies in Athenian Sculpture of the Hellenistic Age* (1979), esp. ch. 2. A useful recent overview of Athenocentric classicism in late Hellenistic sculpture can be found in Stewart, *Greek Sculpture: An Exploration* (1990) 219–233.
2. H. Brunn, *Geschichte der griechischen Künstler* I (1853) 559–570, esp. 560.
3. Brunn (supra n. 2) 550. The best-known of the statues were the Belvedere torso, the Herakles Farnese, and the bronze Doryphoros head from the Villa of the Papyri. The relief vessels were the Salpion krater in Naples, the Pontios rhyton in the Conservatori and the Sosibios krater in the Louvre. These remain the only signed Neo-Attic vases.
4. F. Hauser, *Die neuattischen Reliefs* (1889). See especially his line drawings pl. I.
5. W. Fuchs, *Die Vorbilder der neuattischen Reliefs* (1959) 2.
6. Candelabra: H.-U. Cain, *Römische Marmorkandelaber* (1985); kraters: D. Grassinger, *Römische Marmorkratere* (1991); bases and altars: O. Dräger, *Religionem significare: Studien zur reich verzierten römischen Altaren und Basen aus Marmor*, 33. Ergh. *RM* (1994). The Neo-Attic sculptures from the Mahdia wreck include kraters of the Pisa and Borghese types: Grassinger in G. Hellenkemper Salies et al. (edd.), *Das Wrack* (1994) 259–283; and several undecorated candelabra: Cain and Dräger in *Das Wrack* 239–257. The same two authors in *Das Wrack* 809–829 have also included a useful summary of current thinking on various issues concerning Neo-Attic workshops.
7. P. Zanker, *Klassizistische Statuen* (1974) is fundamental. B.S. Ridgway has included chapters on imitations and revivals in each of her books on period styles: *The Severe Style in Greek Sculpture* (1970) ch. 8–9; *Fifth Century Styles in Greek Sculpture* (1981) ch. 9; *The Archaic Style in Greek Sculpture*[2] (1993) ch. 11. Ridgway, *AJA* 78, 1974, 1–17 on the Plinian Amazon contest at Ephesos, remains a model for establishing distinctions between a copy and a classicizing creation.
8. T. Hölscher, *Römische Bildspracher als semantisches System* (1987).
9. See especially Grassinger (1991, supra n. 6) 44–141; Cain (1985, supra n. 6) 23–142.
10. Ridgway (1981, supra n. 7) 193–198; ead. in *Retaining the Original, Studies in the History of Art* 20 (1989) 13–26.
11. See M. Fullerton, *AA* 1989, 57–67 on the Roman date of the Herculaneum Athena type. More generally on copies after Roman orginals see M. Marvin in *Retaining the Original* (supra n. 10) 29–45 and E. Gazda, *JRA* 8, 1995, 529–534.
12. Especially the shield of the Athena Parthenos. V.M. Strocka, *Piräusrelief und Parthenosshild* (1967); Θ. Στεφανίδου-Τιβερίου, *Νεοαττικά* (1979).
13. On the dancing maenads see now L.-A. Touchette, *The Dancing Maenad Reliefs*, *BICS* Suppl. 62 (1995). For the four-gods relief see Fuchs (supra n. 5) 45–51; M.-A. Zagdoun, *La sculpture archaïsante dans l'art hellénistique et dans l'art romain du haut-empire* (1989) 83–97; the latter treats the group as a subset of an archaistic group of twelve gods rather than as a type in and of itself.
14. For the Athens and Delos pieces: E.B. Harrison, *Agora* XI: *Archaic and Archaistic Sculpture* (1965) 81–84; J. Marcadé, *Au Musée de Délos* (1969) 292–293.
15. For this dating based on Panathenaics see E.Schmidt, *Archaistische Kunst in Griechenland und Rom* (1922) esp. 70–86. For the Samothrace frieze and its interpretation: Ph. Lehmann and D. Spittle, *Samothrace* V: *The Temenos* (1982) 172–266.

16. For a summary of Becatti's and Havelock's chronology, with bibliography, see M.Fullerton, *The Archaistic Style in Roman Statuary* (1990) 3.
17. For this development see also Fullerton, *AA* 1989, 63–64; J.D. Beazley, *The Development of Attic Black Figure*² (1986) 81–92.
18. C.M. Havelock, *AJA* 84, 1980, 331–340.
19. Lehmann and Spittle (supra n. 15) 267–273.
20. See, for example, the "dancer" from the Attalid palace of Pergamon and related figures: Fullerton, *AM* 102, 1987, pl. 18,1.
21. I will not deal here with the more broadly contextual evidence for late Hellenistic classicism, including such historiographic and art critical issues as idealism and the "fantasia" theory, Pliny's sources, the latter's "cessavit... revixit" model of Hellenistic development, or the philosophical parallel of the Middle Stoa. Although these issues do touch on the topic of Atticism in rhetoric (discussed below), they would expand the discussion far beyond the parameters of this paper and are the topic of an article in progress. J.J. Pollitt, *The Ancient View of Greek Art* (1974) 9–85, provides a good introduction to most of these issues. In sum, it seems that the interpretation of the evidence concerning specifically "retrospective" or "revivalist" attitudes in second century rhetoric and philosophy may also be conditioned by the pre-existing notion of characteristically classicizing late Hellenistic era; thus the situation parallels that of the sculpture.
22. Attempts at establishing Hellenistic chronology focus primarily on establishing a sequence of dated monuments, from which a dating system can be inferred. See, for example, B. Andreae in H.-U. Cain, H. Gabelmann, D. Salzmann (edd.), *Festschrift N. Himmelmann* (1989) 237–244 or, somewhat more circumspect, J.J. Pollitt, *Art of the Hellenistic Age* (1986) 265–271. Few of these monuments so invoked are in fact externally datable. However, the problem goes far beyond that of "fixed points," since the process itself assumes a linear development such as that conventionally detected in Archaic through High Classical art. As we see here, anther paradigm seems to prevail for Hellenistic styles.
23. Epidauros: most recently: N. Yalouris, *AntPl* XXI (1993). Cf. especially the "Priam" head pp. 26–27, pl. 17a. Tegea: A.F. Stewart, *Skopas of Paros* (1977) 5–84; also, a more recent summary with updated bibliography: Stewart (supra n. 1) 182–184; 286.
24. A recent discussion of the meaning(s) of Hellenistic baroque: Stewart in P. Holliday (ed.), *Narrative and Event in Ancient Art* (1993) with specific reference to the Pergamon gigantomachy pp. 153–169. The bibliography on the Laocoon and Sperlonga is enormous; for overviews: Pollitt (supra n. 22) 120–126; N. Himmelmann, *Sperlonga: die homerische Gruppen und ihre Bildquellen* (1995); for the artists: Stewart (supra n. 1) 309–310. See also Andreae, *Laokoon und die Gründung Roms* (1988) and the review article by Ridgway, *JRA* 2, 1989, 171–181.
25. R. Carpenter, *Greek Sculpture* (1960) 198–227. He long ago recognized the Classical origins of Hellenistic baroque. Stewart (1993, supra n. 24) 169–172, discusses the co-existence on the Altar of baroque and Classical elements and summarizes the traditional explanations and interpretations. He stresses the hybrid nature of the Altar's style, the inherent conflict which arises from the difference between the two styles, and how this conflict contributes to the Altar's meaning. Many, then, have recognized the normative quality of the Classic as an historically fixed and remote model (or foil) for the baroque. This however differs considerably from the recognition that the Classical style was a continuously available (and employed) stylistic option (as were the other styles) which could contribute to the semiosis of a monument through either its presence or its absence. The chronological (and semiological) implications of this are developed below.
26. Among the best-known and best-dated of these are the pair of bronzes from the Mahdia wreck. See S. Pfisterer-Haas in *Das Wrack* (supra n. 6) 483–504.
27. P. Themelis, *AntK* 36, 1993, 24–40; id. in O. Palagia and J.J. Politt (edd.), *Personal Styles in Greek Sculpture*, *YaleClSt* 30 (1996) 154–185: his studies suggest a date as early as the late third century and no later than the beginning of the second.
28. On Atticism at Epidauros, for example: Yalouris (supra n. 23) 75–81.
29. For example, the Pella mosaics and the Alexander Sarcophagus share several ultimately High or Early Classical figural types; Pollitt (supra n. 23) 37–46. Most conspicuous, perhaps, is the "Harmodios" figure on the Lion Hunt (Pollitt, fig. 34) and Stag Hunt (fig. 35) mosaics as well as on the battle scene of the sarcophagus' short side (fig. 38) (here p. 282, Fig. 1). One could also cite the many High Classical stylistic features in the figural decoration of the Derveni krater, especially the "rich style" mannerisms of the maenads' drapery.
30. Havelock (supra n. 18).
31. Fullerton (supra n. 16) 2–6, on the controversies surrounding the question of the origin of the archaistic style, which in many ways depends on the broader issue of imitation vs. retention. Since the question is inevitably one of intention and/or reception and thus subjective and/or irretrievable, definitive answers might never be possible. I treat this issue explicitly in an article, "Description vs. Prescription: A Semantics of Sculptural Style," in K.J. Hartswick & M.C. Sturgeon (edd.), *ΣΤΕΦΑΝΟΣ: Studies in Honor of Brunilde S. Ridgway* (1998) 69–77.
32. J. Pollini in W.G. Moon (ed.), *Polykleitos, the Doryphoros, and Tradition* (1995) 262–282. This article thoroughly explores the referentiality of the Prima Porta Augustus. While its peculiarly Roman qualities are emphasized, the prevailing view that it was intended and perceived as an allusion specifically to the Doryphoros of Polykleitos is supported. On the type of Divus Julius, Fullerton, *AJA* 89, 1985, 479, esp. n. 50.
33. For a summary of the dating evidence see Hellenkemper Salies in *Das Wrack* (supra n. 6) 21–22. The most diagnostic material seems to be the pottery, the latest types of which date ca. 80–70 B.C., and bronze vessels dated 90–60 B.C.
34. J.P. Niemeier, *Kopien und Nachahmungen im Hellenismus* (1985) argues for a continuous tradition of exact copying beginning in the mid-second century B.C. It is not at all clear at what point the tradition of reiteration and multiple originals, traceable to the beginning of Greek art, gives way to the copying industry of Roman times,

not least because of the difficulty of deciding what a copy is. The early examples cited by Niemeier (pp. 94–106) have stylistic features, especially surface treatments, strongly affected by contemporary Hellenistic works and thus are only subjectively separated from, for example, the Pergamon Athena Parthenos, which all agree is a classicizing variant. The first copy in the sense of a mechanically produced replica would still seem to be the Delos Diadoumenos, generally placed around 100 B.C. Niemeier 106–107; cf. Stewart (supra n. 2) 25. There have, however, been some recent challenges to the idea that complex mechanisms for producing copies – specifically the "pointing machine" envisioned by Richter and others – ever were used in antiquity; M. Pfanner, *JdI* 104, 1989, 531–532; P. Rockwell, *The Art of Stoneworking* (1993) 122; Gazda (supra n. 11). These arguments seem to revolve around the issue of exactitude, which is less a measure of the mechanisms used than the way the mechanisms are applied. The salient issue, however, may not be one of equipment but rather one of mass production. Neo-Attic reliefs seem to imply something of the sort, and there is no real evidence for the production of *numbers* of statuary copies after a single original until the Roman era, prompted no doubt by demands of state portraiture and the embellishment of elaborate public buildings.

35. Sources on Pasiteles are collected in Stewart (supra n. 1) 306–307 with bibliography.
36. For a recent summary with full bibliography: J. Wisse in J. Abbenes, S. Slings, I. Sluiter (edd.), *Greek Literary Theory after Aristotle* (1995) 65–82.
37. Wisse (supra n. 36) 80–81.

Η Υγεία του Νικηράτου του Αθηναίου. Συμβολή στη μελέτη της πρώιμης γλυπτικής της Περγάμου

Ιφιγένεια Κ. Λεβέντη

Ο αγαλματικός τύπος της Υγείας Conservatori-Βερολίνου, όπως τον ονομάζουμε εδώ από τα δύο αντιπροσωπευτικότερα αντίγραφά του, δεν έχει ώς σήμερα αποτελέσει αντικείμενο μιας συστηματικής έρευνας. Ως πρωτότυπο συνήθως θεωρείται ένα μαρμάρινο άγαλμα της θεάς που χρονολογείται στον 4ο ή στο α'μισό του 3ου αι. π.Χ., και μόνον η Kabus-Jahn, υποστήριξε ότι πρόκειται για μία εκλεκτική ρωμαϊκή δημιουργία.[1]

Τον τύπο παραδίδουν κατ' αρχήν τέσσερα αγάλματα: α) άγαλμα συμπληρωμένο ως Υγεία στη Galleria Chiaramonti στο Βατικανό, του 1ου αι. μ.Χ. (εικ.1),[2] β) άγαλμα γυναικείας μορφής, άλλοτε στο Velletri, Palazzo Ginetti, σήμερα χαμένο (εικ.2),[3] γ) πιθανόν εικονιστικό άγαλμα στο Palazzo dei Conservatori, τραϊάνειων – αδριάνειων χρόνων (εικ. 3–4),[4] και δ) άγαλμα Υγείας στο Βερολίνο, Altes Museum, αντωνίνειων χρόνων (εικ. 5–6).[5] Τρία ακόμη αγάλματα Υγείας του 2ου αι. μ.Χ., στο Μουσείο Επιδαύρου, στο Μουσείο Λευκωσίας από τη Σαλαμίνα της Κύπρου, και στην Αρχαιολογική Συλλογή Ιεράπετρας στην Κρήτη, αποτελούν εκλεκτικές παραλλαγές του ίδιου τύπου.[6] Θραύσματα από αγάλματα του ίδιου πιθανότατα τύπου έχουν βρεθεί

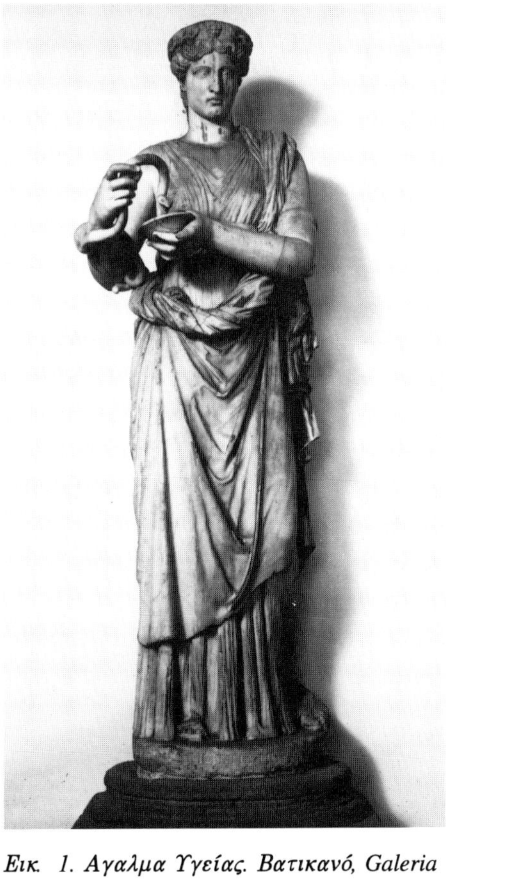

Εικ. 1. Αγαλμα Υγείας. Βατικανό, Galeria Chiaramonti 1246. Φωτογραφία: Musei Vaticani, Archivio Fotografico XXXIV.14.40.

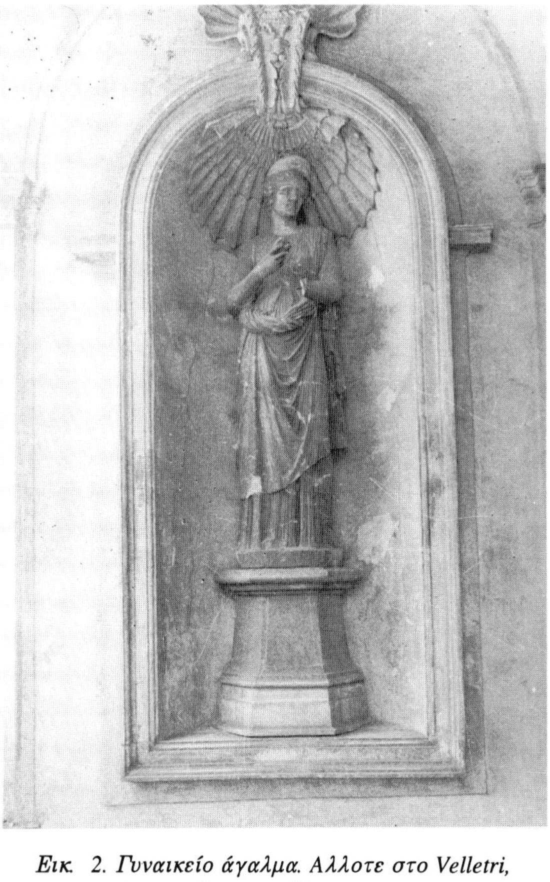

Εικ. 2. Γυναικείο άγαλμα. Αλλοτε στο Velletri, Palazzo Ginetti. Φωτογραφία: DAI Rom 38.1291.

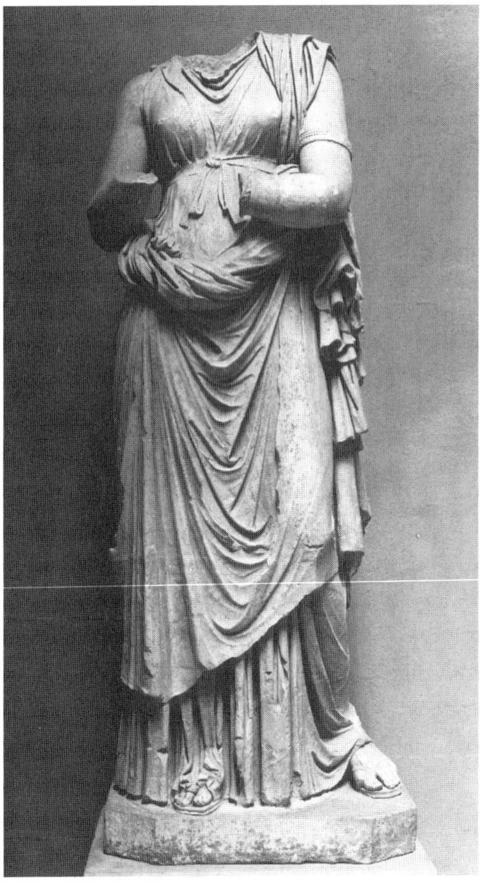

Εικ. 3. Γυναικείο άγαλμα. Ρώμη, Palazzo dei Conservatori, Museo Nuovo 899. Φωτογραφία: DAI Rom 60.1256.

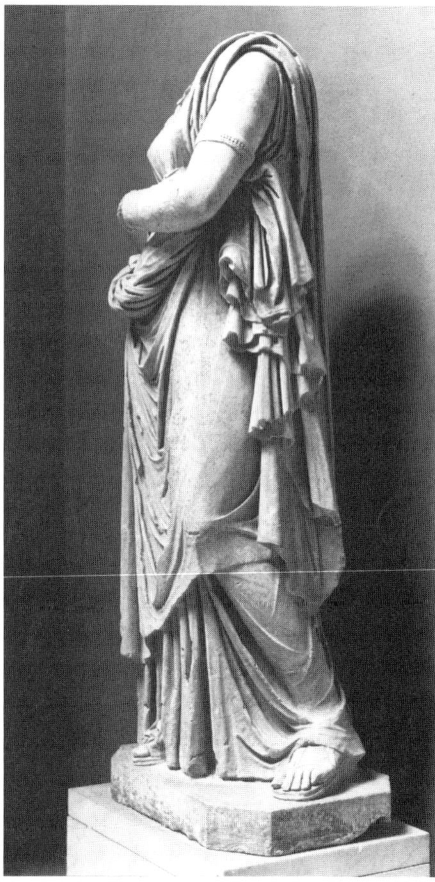

Εικ. 4. Γυναικείο άγαλμα. Ρώμη, Palazzo dei Conservatori, Museo Nuovo 899. Αριστερή όψη. Φωτογραφία: DAI Rom 60.1257.

στη Σαλαμίνα της Κύπρου και πάλι, καθώς και στη Ρώμη. Τέλος, το χάλκινο αγαλμάτιο της Υγείας στη Συλλογή Fleischman άλλοτε στη Νέα Υόρκη, τώρα στο Malibu, J.Paul Getty Museum, είναι ένα ίσως νεώτερων χρόνων μικρογραφικό αντίγραφο του αγάλματος της Υγείας στο Βερολίνο.[7]

Αν και μόνον η Υγεία του Βερολίνου διατηρεί το αρχαίο φίδι το οποίο και κρατά με τα δυό χέρια της, είναι γενικά αποδεκτό στην έρευνα ότι το πρωτότυπο άγαλμα παρίστανε τη θεά αυτή. Τα αγάλματα στο Velletri και στο Palazzo dei Conservatori, όπου τα χέρια είναι λυγισμένα στο ύψος του στομάχου, επιβεβαιώνουν ότι στο πρωτότυπο η Υγεία κρατούσε με αυτά το φίδι. Και στο άγαλμα του Βατικανού τα χέρια, σήμερα συμπληρωμένα μαζί με το φίδι, θα πρέπει να είχαν την ίδια θέση.[8] Οι τρείς παραλλαγές από τον ελληνικό χώρο έφεραν επίσης το φίδι, αν και σε διαφορετική θέση από αυτήν που υποθέτουμε για την πρωτότυπη σύνθεση.[9]

Το πρωτότυπο άγαλμα της Υγείας, μεγαλύτερο του φυσικού, στρεφόταν ελαφρά προς τα δεξιά του, με στηρίζον σκέλος το δεξιό, και το άνετο αριστερό φερόμενο προς τα πίσω και στο πλάι. Το περιβραχιόνιο με μετάλλιο στα αντίγραφα Conservatori (εικ. 7),[10] και Βατικανού (εικ. 1) μαρτυρεί ότι στην πρωτότυπη σύνθεση η Υγεία φορούσε πιθανότατα πέπλο,[11] ο οποίος θα ήταν ζωσμένος κάτω από τα στήθη με ζώνη που σχημάτιζε μακρύ "φιόγκο".[12] Η Υγεία φορά επίσης ιμάτιο με κυλινδρική, τοξοειδή αναδίπλωση στο ύψος των ισχίων, και το συγκρατεί με τη βοήθεια του αριστερού χεριού στο αντίστοιχο πλευρό. Οι παρυφές του δίπλα στο αριστερό σκέλος δημιουργούν συστάδες πτυχών πλούσιων σε όγκο, οι οποίες και αναδεικνύονται με τη στροφή της θεάς (εικ. 4).

Πλησιέστερα στην πρωτότυπη δημιουργία βρίσκεται το άγαλμα στο Βερολίνο (εικ. 5–6) ως προς την απόδοση της στροφής του κορμού και των πτυχών του ιματίου ανάμεσα στα σκέλη, και ιδίως εκείνο του Palazzo dei Conservatori (εικ. 3–4), ως προς την απόδοση της σωματικότητας και της υφής των ενδυμάτων.[13] Και τα δύο παραπάνω αντίγραφα μας ανάγουν σε ένα χάλκινο πρωτότυπο άγαλμα. Προβληματικό παραμένει εν τούτοις το ζήτημα της ορθής παράδοσης της κεφαλής του πρωτοτύπου. Η κεφαλή του αγάλματος της Υγείας του Βερολίνου (εικ. 8) είναι ιδεαλιστική με κόμη σύνθετη που ίσως απηχεί σε γενικές γραμμές εκείνη του πρωτοτύπου.[14] Τα αγάλματα Βατικανού (εικ. 1) και Velletri (εικ. 2), όπως και η Υγεία στην Κύπρο, έχουν κλασικιστικές

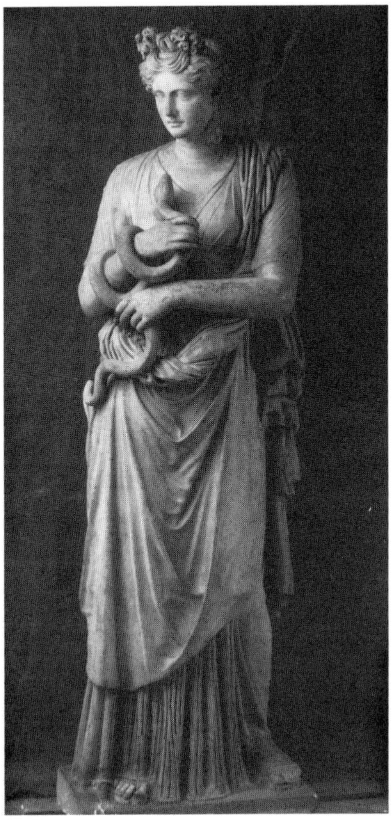

Εικ. 5. Αγαλμα Υγείας. Βερολίνο, Altes Museum, Rotunda Sk 353. Φωτογραφία: Staatliche Museen zu Berlin, Sk 7286.

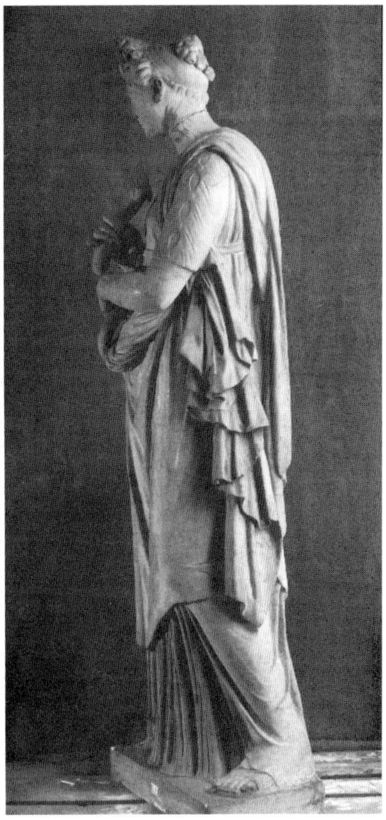

Εικ. 6. Αγαλμα Υγείας. Βερολίνο, Altes Museum, Rotunda Sk 353. Αριστερή όψη. Φωτογραφία: Staatliche Museen zu Berlin, Sk 7286.

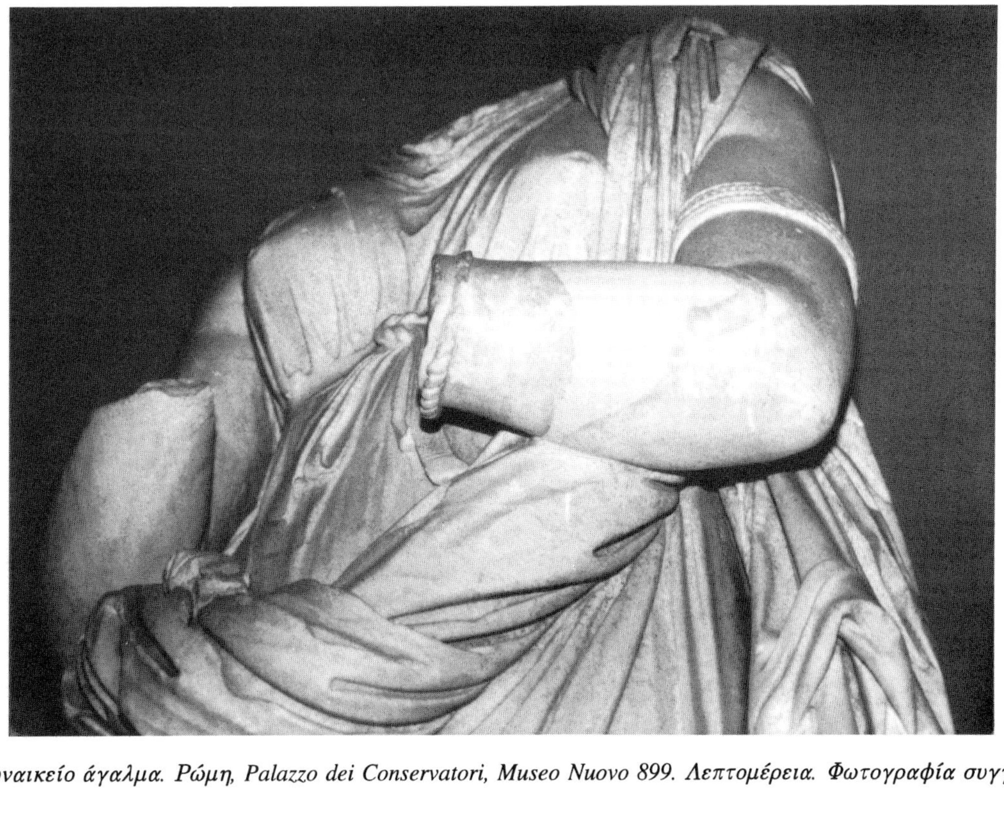

Εικ. 7. Γυναικείο άγαλμα. Ρώμη, Palazzo dei Conservatori, Museo Nuovo 899. Λεπτομέρεια. Φωτογραφία συγγραφέως.

κεφαλές με διάδημα, που στρέφονται αντίθετα με την κίνηση της πρωτότυπης σύνθεσης, και η παραδοσή τους δεν είναι ενιαία.[15]

Το άγαλμα της Υγείας Conservatori-Βερολίνου εξαρτάται τυπολογικά από γυναικείες μορφές της αττικής πλαστικής του β' μισού του 4ου αι. π.Χ., όπως είναι η Αγαθή Τύχη του Μουσείου της Αγοράς των Αθηνών, η γυναίκα του επιτύμβιου αναγλύφου στην Αγγλία, Brocklesby Park, και η Υγεία τύπου Broadlands-Conservatori.[16] Επιπλέον ανάλογα μοτίβα πτύχωσης του ιματίου παρουσιάζουν ορισμένες Μούσες από τη βάση της Μαντίνειας στο Εθνικό Μουσείο της Αθήνας, καθώς και οι υστεροκλασικοί αγαλματικοί τύποι της Μεγάλης Ηρακλειώτισσας και της λεγόμενης Υγείας Zara.[17]

Επίσης η ανάπτυξη της σύνθεσης στην Υγεία με την έμφαση στον κατακόρυφο άξονα που διακόπτεται από άλλους εγκάρσιους, θυμίζει τη λεγόμενη Θέμιδα από το Ραμνούντα στο Εθνικό Μουσείο της Αθήνας, του ύστερου 4ου ή πρώιμου 3ου αι. π.Χ., το πορτραίτο του Δημοσθένους, σταθερά χρονολογημένο γύρω στο 280 π.Χ., καθώς και την περίπου σύγχρονη με αυτό μορφή της Μηδείας στη γνωστή τοιχογραφία στο Μουσείο της Νεαπόλεως.[18] Παραβάλλοντας ιδιαίτερα την Υγεία με τη λεγόμενη Θέμιδα διαπιστώνουμε έναν κοινό μετακλασικό χαρακτήρα, φανερό στην αυτονόμηση από το σώμα ορισμένων μοτίβων του ιματίου. Επίσης, το ίδιο διακοσμητικό στοιχείο εμφανίζεται σε επαφή με την καμπύλη αναδίπλωση του ιματίου και στα δύο αγάλματα.[19]

Ωστόσο η πυραμιδοειδής σωματική δομή της Υγείας και η στροφή της στο χώρο δείχνουν υπέρβαση της κυβικότητας και στατικότητας των παραπάνω μορφών, και συγγένεια περισσότερο με έργα του β' μισού του 3ου ή και του πρώιμου 2ου αι. π.Χ., όπως με τη λεγόμενη κόρη από το Άντιο στο Μουσείο Θερμών στη Ρώμη.[20] Αυτή εμφανίζει εντονότερη περιστροφική κίνηση, αλλά όπως και η Υγεία, ιδιαίτερο όγκο των ενδυμάτων και ανεξαρτησία τους από το σώμα. Η κόρη βέβαια πλησιάζει χρονολογικά και τεχνοτροπικά στις θεές της Γιγαντομαχίας του Βωμού της Περγάμου (περ. 160 π.Χ.).[21]

Συγγενής επίσης με την Υγεία Conservatori-Βερολίνου είναι ως προς τη σωματική δομή, τη στροφή του σώματος και τη σχέση σώματος-ενδύματος η βασίλισσα-Τύχη στην πτολεμαϊκή οινοχόη της Βερενίκης Β' Ευεργέτιδος περ. του 240 π.Χ. στο Μουσείο Αττάλειας,[22] και ιδίως το σύγχρονο γυναικείο αγαλμάτιο από τις Τράλλεις στο Μουσείο του Αϊδινίου (εικ. 9).[23] Ακόμη, η εναλλαγή της πτυχολογίας με τις λείες επιφάνειες στα ενδύματα της Υγείας έχει το αναλογό της στις μορφές της ζωφόρου του βωμού της Αρτέμιδος Λευκοφρυηνής στη Μαγνησία, η οποία χρονολογείται πειστικότερα στις τελευταίες δεκαετίες του 3ου αι. π.Χ.[24] Τέλος, τεχνοτροπικές ομοιότητες διαπιστώνονται ως προς την ανάπτυξη του σωματικού όγκου και τη σχέση

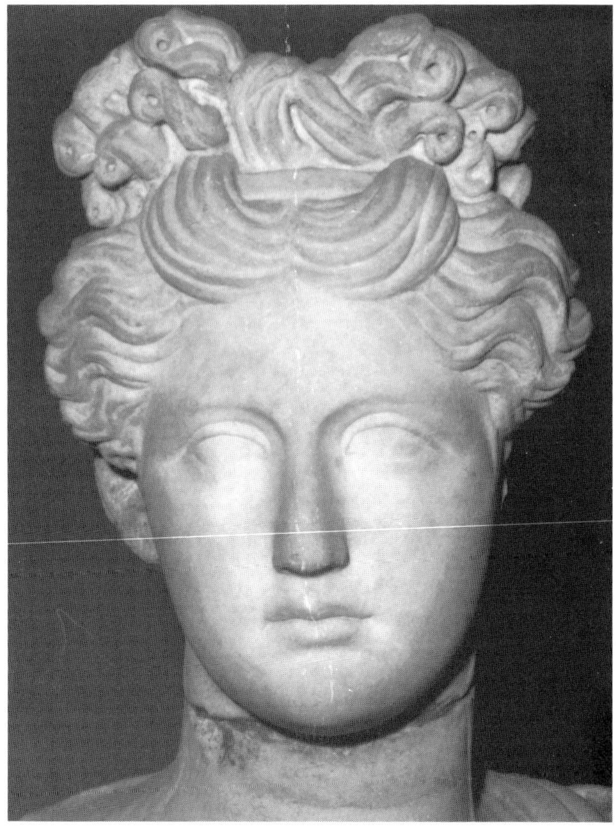

Εικ. 8. Κεφαλή αγάλματος Υγείας. Βερολίνο, Altes Museum, Rotunda Sk 353. Φωτογραφία: Staatliche Museen zu Berlin, Karin März.

σώματος-ενδύματος ανάμεσα στην Υγεία και τους κορμούς των γυναικείων θεοτήτων από το σύνταγμα του Δαμοφώντος στο Μουσείο της Λυκόσουρας, που μπορεί να χρονολογηθεί στον ύστερο 3ο ή πρώιμο 2ο αι. π.Χ. με βάση νέα επιγραφική μαρτυρία.[25] 'Οπως στα αγάλματα του συντάγματος της Λυκόσουρας, έτσι και στο άγαλμα της Υγείας διαπιστώνουμε την επιβίωση κλασικών στοιχείων που συνδυάζονται με την εμφάνιση περισσότερο εξελιγμένων, "μπαρόκ" χαρακτηριστικών.[26]

Συνεπώς, η χρονολόγηση του αγάλματος της Υγείας στο διάστημα 240–220 π.Χ. προκύπτει αβίαστα, ενώ ενισχύεται και από την παρατήρηση ότι το σπειροειδές ψέλιο του αγάλματος στο Palazzo dei Conservatori (εικ.7) έχει παράλληλα στον προχωρημένο και ύστερο 3ο αι. π.Χ.[27]

Στην προσπάθειά μας να εντοπίσουμε το καλλιτεχνικό περιβάλλον δημιουργίας του πρωτότυπου αγάλματος της Υγείας Conservatori-Βερολίνου στρεφόμαστε αρχικά στη γλυπτική παραγωγή της Αττικής, στην κλασική παράδοση της οποίας εντοπίσαμε ήδη τις τυπολογικές καταβολές του. Όμως η σπανιότητα σε γλυπτά από την Αττική στους χρόνους της μακεδονικής κατοχής (263–229 π.Χ.),[28] συνιστά ήδη ένα πρόβλημα. Οπωσδήποτε, ορισμένα αγάλματα του α' μισού του 3ου αι. π.Χ. που

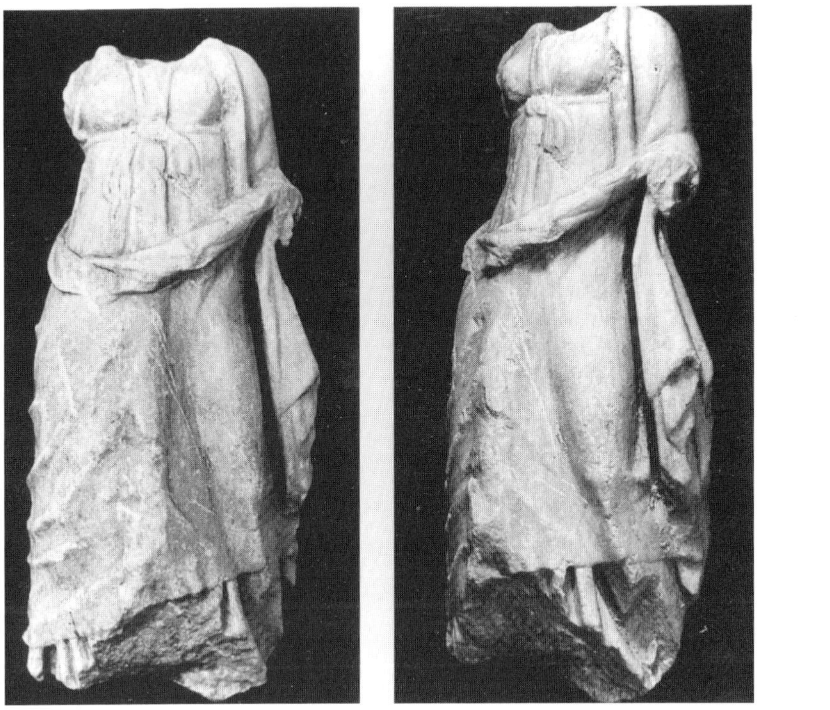

Εικ. 9. Γυναικείο αγαλμάτιο. Μουσείο Αϊδινίου 571. Φωτογραφία: R. Özgan, Die griechischen und römishen Skulpturen aus Tralleis *(1995) πίν. 1,1–2.*

αποδίδονται σε Αθηναίους γλύπτες, αλλά βρέθηκαν εκτός Αττικής, παρουσιάζουν τεχνοτροπικές διαφορές από την Υγεία. Τέτοια είναι τα αγάλματα της Κωμωδίας και του Διονύσου στο Μουσείο της Θάσου, που διακρίνονται για την εξαρτημένη ως επί το πλείστον από τις μορφές του σώματος απόδοση της πτυχολογίας.[29] Επίσης διαφορές από την Υγεία, παρά τα κοινά σημεία στην ανάπτυξη της σύνθεσης, διαπιστώνονται και με το άγαλμα της Κόρης του α' μισού του 3ου αι. π.Χ. που βρέθηκε στην αιτωλική Καλλίπολι, το οποίο διακρίνεται για μία περισσότερο "καλλιγραφική" απόδοση της πτυχολογίας.[30]

Αντίθετα, το πρωτότυπο άγαλμα της Υγείας, όπως παραδίδεται από τα πιστότερα αντίγραφα, χαρακτηρίζεται από μεστή σωματικότητα, θεατρικότητα στο στήσιμο, καθώς και από τον όγκο και την πλαστικότητα των ενδυμάτων της, που αυτονομούνται σε τέτοιο βαθμό από το σώμα ώστε υποκαθιστούν εν μέρει τις λειτουργίες του. Αυτά τα στοιχεία υποδηλώνουν μία "μπαρόκ" τεχνοτροπία.[31] Και είναι ακριβώς ορισμένες γυναικείες μορφές της περγαμηνής τέχνης του 2ου αι. π.Χ. με τις οποίες η Υγεία παρουσιάζει ομοιότητες, όπως η Κυβέλη του Μεγάλου Βωμού (εικ. 10),[32] ή ένα γυναικείο άγαλμα στο Βερολίνο, Μουσείο Περγάμου.[33] Επίσης συγγενές, ιδίως ως προς την πτύχωση του ιματίου, είναι ένα αποσπασματικό πήλινο γυναικείο ειδώλιο από το τέμενος των ηγεμόνων στην Πέργαμο (εικ. 11).[34]

Επιπλέον η στρεπτή αναδίπλωση του ιματίου της Υγείας, είναι χαρακτηριστική ιδίως σε περγαμηνά γλυπτά, όπως η Juno Cesi, η κόρη από το Άντιο, η λεγόμενη Τραγωδία και θεές της Γιγαντομαχίας.[35] Και ο μακρύς "φιόγκος" στη ζώνη της Υγείας είναι αγαπητός σε μορφές της περγαμηνής γλυπτικής, όπως και πάλι στην Κυβέλη (εικ. 10), και στην Ηώ του Μεγάλου Βωμού.[36] Εξάλλου το περίτεχνο περιβραχιόνιο της Υγείας απαντάται στην καλύτερα σωζόμενη χορεύτρια του περγαμηνού ανάγλυφου κυκλικού μνημείου στο Μουσείο Κων/πόλεως (εικ. 12),[37] και το σπειροειδές ψέλιο των αντιγράφων Conservatori (εικ. 7) και Velletri (εικ. 2), στη λεγόμενη Νύχτα της Μεγάλης Ζωφόρου.[38] Ακόμη, τον καταρράκτη των κυλινδρικών πτυχών του ιματίου στο αριστερό πλευρό της Υγείας (εικ. 4.6) συναντάμε στη χλαμύδα του Γαλάτη στο Μουσείο Θερμών από το μεγάλο ανάθημα του Αττάλου Α'.[39] Αλλά και οι λεπτομέρειες της υφής του ενδύματος στο άγαλμα Conservatori, με τις πτύξεις και τις σκληρές, τονισμένες και με την εγχάραξη παρυφές είναι χαρακτηριστικά που απαντούν σε περγαμηνά γλυπτά,[40] καθώς και σε μιμήσεις τους.[41]

Ένα παράλληλο για την κόμη της Υγείας στο αντίγραφο του Βερολίνου (εικ. 8) με το χαρακτηριστικό "φιόγκο" προσφέρει η υστεροελληνιστική κεφαλή γυναικείας μορφής από την Πέργαμο στο Μουσείο της Σμύρνης.[42] Παρά το ψυχρό πλάσιμο της κεφαλής της Υγείας του Βερολίνου, τα μικρά χαρακτηριστικά του προσώπου, ο όγκος της κόμης με τους κυματιστούς βοστρύχους πάνω από τους κροτάφους, και ο κρωβύλος στον αυχένα (εικ. 6) μπορούν να συγκριθούν με γυναικείες κεφαλές από τη ζωφόρο της Γιγαντομαχίας του περγαμηνού Βωμού.[43] Οι συγκρίσεις αυτές

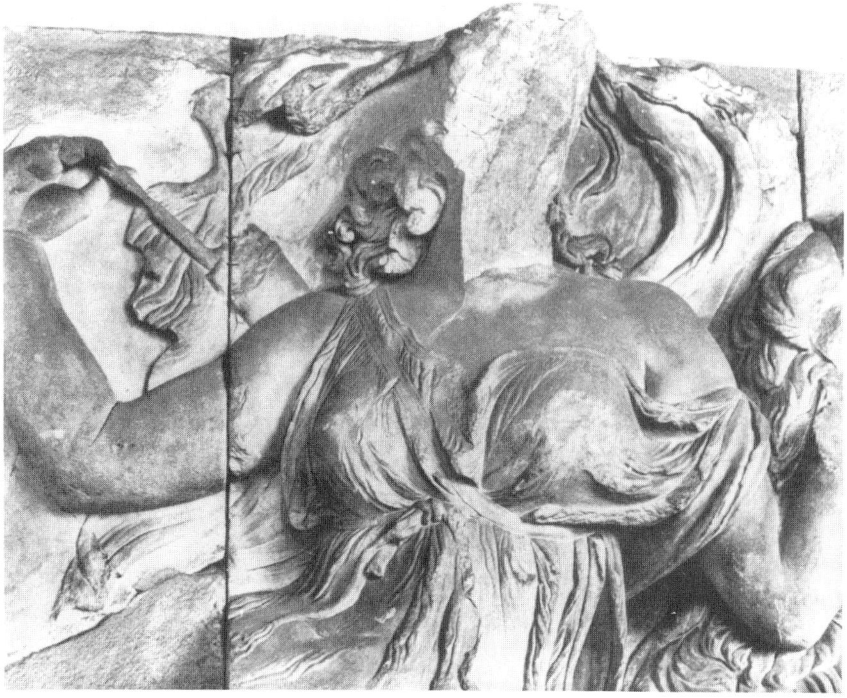

Εικ. 10. Κυβέλη από τη ζωφόρο του βωμού της Περγάμου. Βερολίνο, Μουσείο Περγάμου. Φωτογραφία: W. Müller, Der Pergamon-Altar *(1964) πίν. 38.*

ενισχύουν παράλληλα την πιθανότητα πιστότητας της κεφαλής του αγάλματος στο Βερολίνο.

Από τα παραπάνω είναι φανερό ότι το πρωτότυπο άγαλμα της Υγείας μπορεί από την άποψη της τεχνοτροπίας αλλά και της εικονογραφίας του να συσχετισθεί στενότερα με τη γλυπτική παραγωγή της Περγάμου.

Ο Πλίνιος, *N.H.* 34.80, αναφέρει ότι τα αγάλματα του Ασκληπιού και της Υγείας, τα σπουδαιότερα έργα του χαλκοπλάστη Νικηράτου, βρίσκονταν στο ναό της Ομονοίας στη Ρώμη.[44] Ο Νικήρατος Ευκτήμονος Αθηναίος είναι γνωστός κατ'αρχήν από τις υπογραφές του, στην πλειοψηφία τους από κοινού με το γλύπτη Φυρόμαχο, που τον συγκαταλέγουν στους επήλυδες αττικούς καλλιτέχνες που εργάσθηκαν στην αυλή των Ατταλιδών.[45]

Το έργο του Νικηράτου μπορεί να ενταχθεί στο β' μισό του 3ου αι. π.Χ. με βάση τη χρονολόγηση των υπογραφών του.[46] Ιδιαίτερα σημαντικό θεωρείται το επίγραμμα του αναθήματος του Σωσικράτους στη Δήλο που εξυμνεί τη δόξα ενός Φιλεταίρου στους Γαλατικούς πολέμους και τα έργα του Νικηράτου που τη διαιωνίζουν.[47] Ο Φιλέταιρος έχει ταυτισθεί με τον ιδρυτή της περγαμηνής δυναστείας (283–263 π.Χ.),[48] αλλά και με το νεώτερο ομώνυμό του, τον αδελφό των Ευμένους Β' (197–158 π.Χ.) και Αττάλου Β' (158–138 π.Χ.).[49] Ωστόσο ορισμένοι ερευνητές υποστήριξαν ότι το ανάθημα είναι δυνατόν να οφείλεται σε πρωτοβουλία του Αττάλου Α' (241–197 π.Χ.) προς τιμήν του πρεσβύτερου Φιλεταίρου για λόγους δυναστικής προπαγάνδας.[50]

Την τελευταία αυτή άποψη θεωρούμε ορθότερη, καθώς η λέξη *ἄναξ* δεν μπορεί να είναι απλώς μία επική επίκληση για τον Φιλέταιρο σύμφωνη με το ύφος του επιγράμματος, αλλά θα πρέπει να παρέπεμπε στον υπάρχοντα τότε στην Πέργαμο βασιλικό θεσμό.[51] Οπως είναι όμως γνωστό ο βασιλικός τίτλος φέρεται για πρώτη φορά από τον Άτταλο Α' στη δεκαετία 240–230 π.Χ.,[52] οπότε αποκτάμε ένα *terminus post quem* για την ίδρυση του αναθήματος. Παράλληλα έχει ήδη επισημανθεί στην έρευνα ότι η βαρύτητα που αποδίδεται στο επίγραμμα στη Γαλατική νίκη αλλά και ο βασιλικός τίτλος *ἄναξ* δύσκολα αρμόζουν στο λιγότερο επιφανή νεώτερο Φιλέταιρο, που δεν είχε κυβερνητική εξουσία.[53] Στο επίγραμμα επομένως, η αναφορά του βασιλικού τίτλου στο πρόσωπο του ιδρυτή του κράτους της Περγάμου αποτελεί μάλλον τιμητικό αναχρονισμό της εποχής του Αττάλου Α'.[54]

Η χρονολόγηση του επιγράμματος του Σωσικράτους στο β' μισό του 3ου αι. π.Χ. φαίνεται επίσης πιθανότερη με κριτήριο τη μορφή των γραμμάτων του.[55] Εξάλλου στο ίδιο διάστημα, και όχι αργότερα, ανάγονται και τα υπόλοιπα μνημειώδη αναθήματα των Ατταλιδών στη Δήλο, ορισμένα από τα οποία εξαίρουν επίσης ακριβώς την προσωπικότητα του πρεσβύτερου Φιλεταίρου.[56] Συνεπώς το επίγραμμα του Σωσικράτους, τοποθετεί την καλλιτεχνική δραστηριότητα του Νικηράτου στην περίοδο βασιλείας του Αττάλου Α' (241–197 π.Χ.). 'Ισως μάλιστα ο γλύπτης να εργαζόταν ώς τις αρχές της βασιλείας του Ευμένους Β' (197–158 π.Χ.),

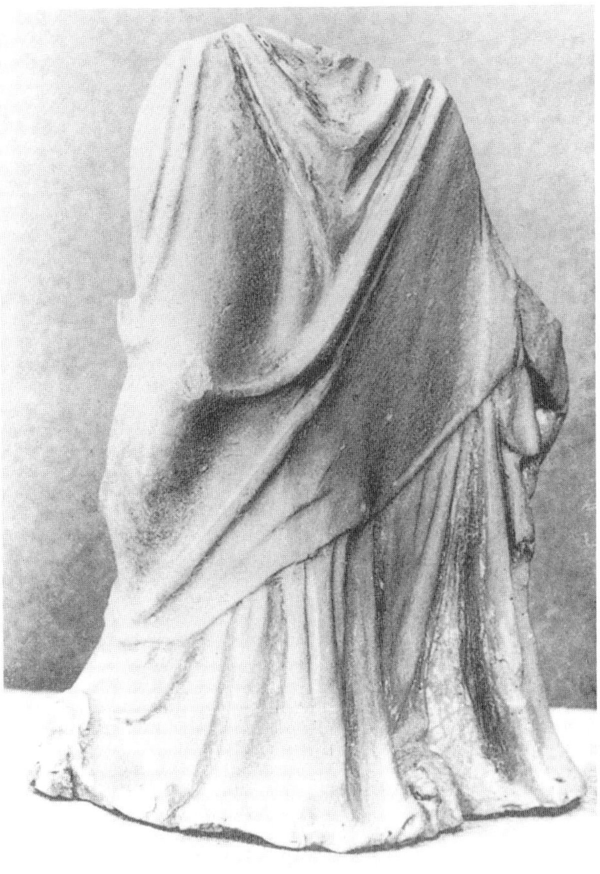

Εικ. 11. Κατώτερο τμήμα πήλινου γυναικείου *αγαλματίου. Πέργαμος (Bergama) Αρχαιολογικό Μουσείο Τ 43. Φωτογραφία: E. Boehringer-F. Krauss,* AvP *IX (1937) πίν. 53b.*

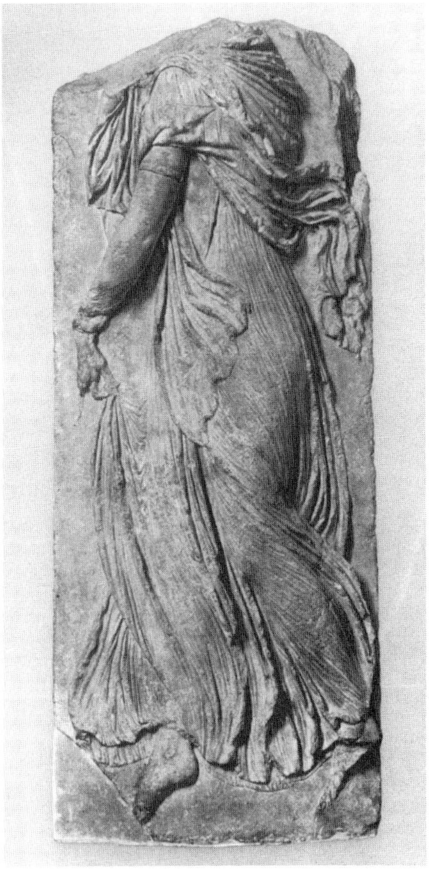

Εικ. 12. Χορεύτρια από ανάγλυφο βωμό (;). Μουσείο Κωνσταντινουπόλεως 764. Φωτογραφία: M. Schede, Meisterwerke der türkischen Museen zu Konstantinopel *I.* Griechische und römische Skulpturen des Antikenmuseums (1928) πίν. 25.

κατόχου επίσης του βασιλικού τίτλου σε αντίθεση με τον Ευμένη Α' (263–241 π.Χ.), αν ένα σχέδιο μάλλον του Κυριακού της Αγκώνας (15ος αι. μ.Χ.) παραπέμπει πραγματικά σε ένα έργο του Νικηράτου από τους χρόνους του βασιλέως αυτού, όπως δηλώνει η φράση της παραδιδόμενης επιγραφής *Eumen<est>is regis*.[57]

Εξίσου σημαντικός για τη χρονολόγηση της καλλιτεχνικής δραστηριότητας του Νικηράτου είναι ο καθορισμός της περιόδου δημιουργίας του στενού συνεργάτη του, του γλύπτη Φυρομάχου. Στη μελέτη του έργου του τελευταίου και ιδίως στο πρόβλημα της χρονολόγησής του έχει αφιερώσει εμπεριστατωμένες μελέτες ο Andreae, ο οποίος καταλήγει στην ένταξή του κυρίως στο β' τέταρτο του 2ου αι. π.Χ.[58] Ο Andreae ειδικότερα χρονολογεί τον Ασκληπιό του Φυρομάχου στη δεκαετία 170–160 και το πορτραίτο του Αντισθένους στη δεκαετία 160–150 π.Χ., ενώ υποθέτει συμμετοχή του στο λεγόμενο μικρό ανάθημα των Ατταλιδών που αποδίδει στους βασιλείς Ευμένη Β' και Άτταλο Β,' σύμφωνα με το δυσερμήνευτο και πολυσυζητημένο χωρίο του Πλίνιου, *N.H.* 34.84.[59]

Ωστόσο εναλλακτική χρονολόγηση για τον Ασκληπιό και το εικονιστικό άγαλμα του κυνικού Αντισθένους έχει προταθεί στο διάστημα 200–180 π.Χ.[60] Επίσης άλλοι ερευνητές δέχονται ότι το παραπάνω χωρίο του Πλίνιου αναφέρεται στη συμμετοχή του Φυρομάχου στο λεγόμενο μεγάλο ανάθημα των Ατταλιδών (230–220 π.Χ.), ή στο μικρό Γαλατικό ανάθημα, που όμως το χρονολογούν περί το 200 π.Χ.[61] Τελικά, και για τον Φυρόμαχο μπορεί να υποστηριχθεί χρονολόγηση στον ύστερο 3ο και στο α' τέταρτο του 2ου αι. π.Χ.[62] Επιπλέον η σταθερή σειρά των ονομάτων των δύο καλλιτεχνών στις κοινές υπογραφές τους με πρώτο το Νικήρατο, παρά τη μεγαλύτερη φήμη που φαίνεται ότι απολάμβανε ο Φυρόμαχος, υποδηλώνει ίσως ότι ο Νικήρατος ήταν ο πρεσβύτερος, και πιθανότατα ο δάσκαλος του Φυρομάχου.[63]

Επομένως, το πρωτότυπο της Υγείας τύπου Conservatori – Βερολίνου που ήταν ένα έργο του τρίτου τετάρτου του 3ου αι. π.Χ. και δημιουργήθηκε σε ένα περγαμηνό εργαστήριο, με αναμφίβολα αττικές καταβολές στη σύνθεσή του, μπορεί να ταυτιστεί με την Υγεία του Αθηναίου γλύπτη Νικηράτου, ο οποίος εργαζόταν για την Περγάμο στο ίδιο χρονικό διάστημα. Για την ταύτιση με την Υγεία από το ασκληπιακό ζεύγος του Νικηράτου στο ναό της Ομονοίας σημασία έχει και το γεγονός ότι τα περισσότερα αντίγραφα βρέθηκαν στην Ιταλία.[64]

Αν η θέση που υποστηρίζουμε για την αναγνώριση της Υγείας του Νικηράτου στον αγαλματικό τύπο της Υγείας Conservatori-Βερολίνου είναι εύλογη,[65] μένει να εξετάσουμε στη συνέχεια ποιό θα ήταν το χάλκινο άγαλμα του Ασκληπιού του ίδιου γλύπτη με το οποίο η μορφή της θεάς αποτελούσε προφανώς σύνταγμα. Ήδη οι Heiderich και Becatti αναγνώρισαν τον Ασκληπιό του Νικηράτου στο πρωτότυπο του λεγόμενου Ασκληπιού Pitti, που μας είναι γνωστός κυρίως από αγάλματα που βρέθηκαν αποκλειστικά στη Ρώμη. Σημαντικότερα για την αντιγραφική παράδοση του τύπου είναι το άγαλμα στο Palazzo Pitti στη Φλωρεντία (εικ. 13), και ο Ασκληπιός του λεγόμενου διπτύχου Gaddi στο Liverpool, Merseyside County Museum.[66] Το πρωτότυπο άγαλμα του Ασκληπιού χρονολογήθηκε από τους παραπάνω μελετητές στον 2ο αι., εν τούτοις η τοποθέτησή του στον ύστερο 3ο αι. π.Χ. φαίνεται πιθανότερη, καθώς η κεφαλή του θυμίζει εκείνη του Ποσειδώνος σε νόμισμα του Αντιγόνου Δώσωνος λίγο μετά το 230 π.Χ.[67] Ο Ασκληπιός τύπου Pitti παρουσιάζει επίσης τεχνοτροπική συγγένεια με το άγαλμα του κυνικού φιλοσόφου στο Μουσείο Καπιτωλίου που χρονολογείται στον ύστερο 3ο ή αρχόμενο 2ο αι. π.Χ. και αποδίδεται στο περγαμηνό εργαστήριο.[68]

Το άγαλμα του Ασκληπιού παρουσιάζει αξιοσημείωτες ομοιότητες με εκείνο της Υγείας τύπου Conservatori-Βερολίνου. Αυτές εντοπίζονται στην ίδια κλίμακα, στην αντίστοιχη στροφή του σώματος, στην παρουσία κυλινδρικής αναδίπλωσης και στην οριοθέτηση της αριστερής πλευράς του σώματος από συστάδες πτυχών του ιματίου. Στο δίπτυχο Gaddi όμως, ο Ασκληπιός τύπου Pitti συνοδεύεται από μία ελάχιστα πρωτότυπη, κλασικιστική Υγεία που εξαρτάται τυπολογικά από παράγωγες δημιουργίες της φειδιακής Αφροδίτης Ουρανίας.[69] Γενικά, η ανεξάρτητη αντιγραφική παράδοση του Ασκληπιού τύπου Pitti και της Υγείας Conservatori-Βερολίνου δεν αποτελεί πρόβλημα, καθώς μπορεί να αποδοθεί στη μεταγενέστερη κατάλυση του λατρευτικού πιθανότατα συντάγματος του Ασκληπιού και της Υγείας, όταν τα αγάλματά τους τοποθετήθηκαν ξεχωριστά στα μετακιόνια του ναού της Ομονοίας στη Ρώμη.[70]

Αξιοσημείωτο είναι ότι τόσο ο Ασκληπιός όσο και η Υγεία εξαρτώνται από την κλασική αττική εικονογραφική παράδοση,[71] η παράστασή τους όμως εμπλουτίζεται με νέο περιεχόμενο, καθώς ο Ασκληπιός χαρακτηρίζεται ως φιλόσοφος και η Υγεία κρατά το φίδι και με τα δύο χέρια της (δρακοντοφόρος).

Αν η Υγεία Conservatori-Βερολίνου αποτελούσε πράγματι σύνταγμα με τον Ασκληπιό τύπου Pitti (εικ. 14), αυτό θα έμοιαζε ως προς την τοποθέτηση των δύο αγαλμάτων με τις επίσης αγαλματικές μορφές της Νίκης και ίσως του Αττάλου Α' σε πομπηιανή τοιχογραφία στο Μουσείο Νεαπόλεως, που ανάγεται πιθανότατα σε περγαμηνό πρότυπο (εικ. 15).[72]

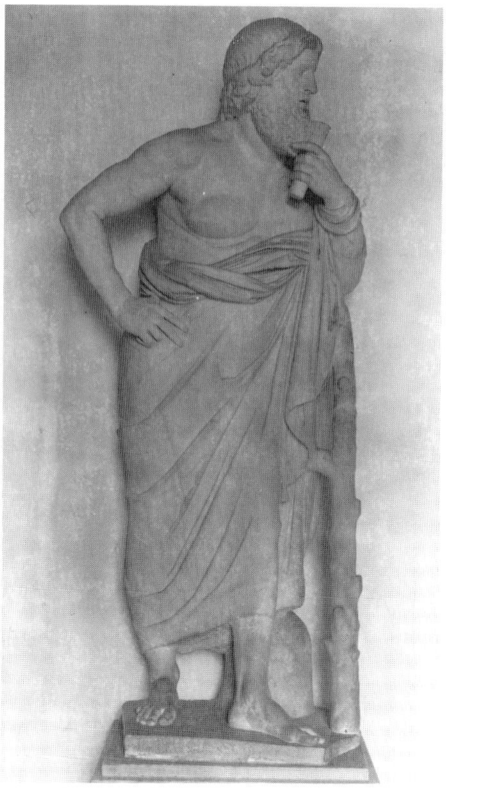

Εικ. 13. Άγαλμα Ασκληπιού Pitti. Φλωρεντία, Palazzo Pitti. Φωτογραφία: Gab. Fotografico Soprintendenza beni artistici e storici di Firenze 154763.

Τελευταίο μένει να εξετασθεί το πρόβλημα της αρχικής θέσεως του ασκληπιακού συντάγματος του Νικηράτου. Ρητή μαρτυρία ότι ήταν στημένο στην Πέργαμο δεν υπάρχει, αν και αυτή η υπόθεση φαίνεται η πιθανότερη.[73] Ακριβώς στους χρόνους του Αττάλου Α', οπότε δημιουργήθηκαν η Υγεία και ο Ασκληπιός του Νικηράτου, οικοδομείται στο Ασκληπιείο της Περγάμου ο πρώτος μαρμάρινος δωρικός ναός αφιερωμένος σύμφωνα με όλες τις ενδείξεις στους δύο αυτούς θεούς. Σε αυτόν θα μπορούσε εύλογα να στεγαζόταν το χάλκινο σύνταγμα του Νικηράτου.[74] Αλλά εξίσου δεν μπορούμε να αποκλείσουμε ότι τα δύο αγάλματα ήταν στημένα εκτός του Ασκληπιείου, σε έναν άλλο χώρο λατρείας αυτών των θεών στην Πέργαμο.[75]

Οι αγαλματικοί τύποι της Υγείας και του Ασκληπιού που υποθέτουμε ότι αποτελούσαν το σύνταγμα του Νικηράτου δεν μαρτυρούνται ανάμεσα στις παραστάσεις των δύο θεών στα αναθηματικά αγαλμάτια και τα νομίσματα της Περγάμου. Η απήχηση βέβαια γενικότερα περγαμηνών λατρευτικών αγαλμάτων στα αναθηματικά μνημεία όπως και στους νομισματικούς τύπους της πόλεως φαίνεται να είναι περιορισμένη.[76] Το ζήτημα της αρχικής θέσεως της Υγείας και του Ασκληπιού παραμένει τελικά ανοικτό, όπως άγνωστο είναι και το πότε μεταφέρθηκαν στη Ρώμη.[77]

Οπωσδήποτε αναμφισβήτητη είναι η συνάντηση στον αγαλματικό τύπο της Υγείας Conservatori-Βερολίνου της αττικής γλυπτικής παράδοσης και των νεωτερισμών που εμφανίζονται κυρίως στο πλαίσιο της περγαμηνής γλυπτικής στον ύστερο 3ο αι. π.Χ. Γίνονται φανερές για μία ακόμη φορά οι αττικές ρίζες της τελευταίας.[78] Επιπλέον όμως η Υγεία μαρτυρεί με τις σχέσεις που παρουσιάζει και με έργα άλλων περιοχών, κάποια ρευστότητα στον καθορισμό των εργαστηρίων στη μετάβαση από την πρώιμη στην ώριμη φάση της ελληνιστικής γλυπτικής.

Θερμές ευχαριστίες οφείλω στους καθηγητές Ο.Παλαγγιά, A.Stewart και F.Queyrel, στον διευθυντή του Επιγραφικού Μουσείου Χ.Κριτζά και την Δρ. A.Herrmann καθώς και στην αρχαιολόγο C.Zimber γιά χρήσιμες παρατηρήσεις και υποδείξεις. Επίσης ευχαριστώ τη Soprintendenza Archeologica di Roma και τον καθηγητή E.La Rocca, τον Δρ. P.Liverani των Μουσείων του Βατικανού, την Δρ. H.Heres των Κρατικών Μουσείων του Βερολίνου, την ΚΔ' Εφορεία Προϊστορικών και Κλασικών Αρχαιοτήτων, τον Προϊστάμενο της Διεύθυνσης Προϊστορικών και Κλασικών Αρχαιοτήτων Δρ. Γ.Τζεδάκι, το DAI στη Ρώμη, το Forschungsarchiv für die römische Plastik στην Κολωνία, καθώς και την Διεύθυνση του Palazzo Pitti στη Φλωρεντία, γιά την παροχή άδειας μελέτης ή φωτογραφιών γλυπτών που αναφέρονται εδώ. Τέλος, ευχαριστώ τον αρχιτέκτονα Σ. Παρασκευόπουλο γιά το σχέδιο της εικ. 14 και την M.Mauzy, φωτογράφο της Αμερικανικής Σχολής Κλασικών Σπουδών στην Αθήνα γιά τις φωτογραφίες των εικ. 9–12 και 15.

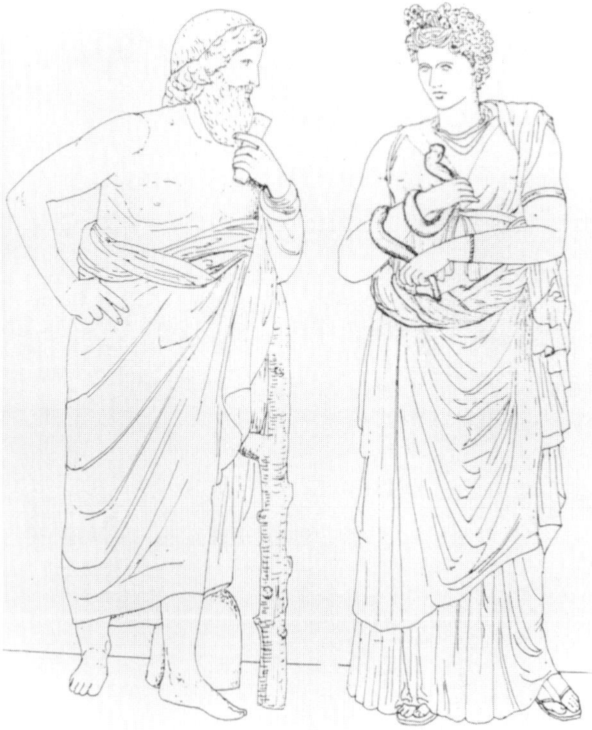

Εικ. 14. Σχεδιαστική αναπαράσταση της θέσεως των αγαλμάτων Υγείας και Ασκληπιού στο σύνταγμα του Νικηράτου. Όχι ακριβής ως προς τις λεπτομέρειες των δύο γλυπτών. Σχέδιο: Σταύρος Παρασκευόπουλος.

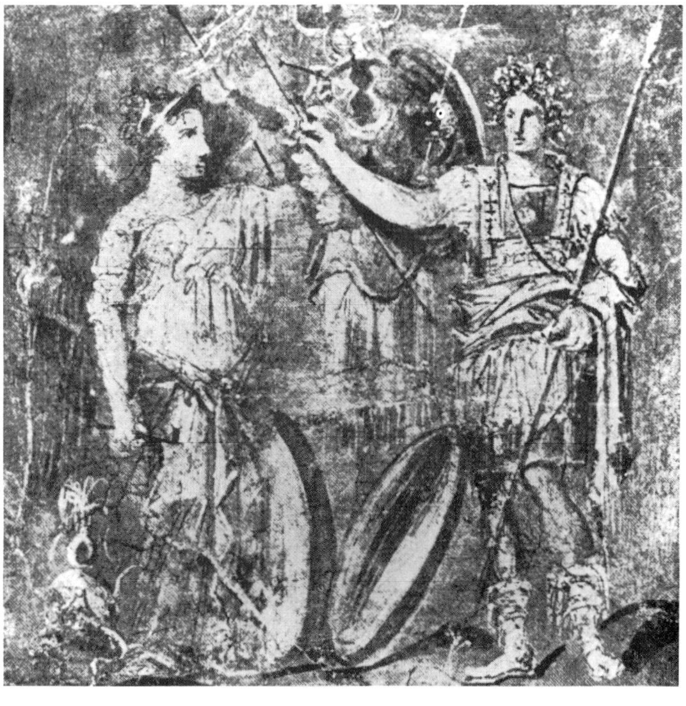

Εικ. 15. Τοιχογραφία από την Πομπηΐα. Μουσείο Νεαπόλεως 8843. Νίκη και Άτταλος Α' (;). Φωτογραφία: Wenning πίν. 9,1.

Συντομογραφίες

Andreae, *Phyromachos-Probleme*:	B.Andreae (επιμ.), *Phyromachos-Probleme*, 31.Ergh. *RM* (1990)
Andreae:	B.Andreae στο Andreae, *Phyromachos-Probleme*, 45–100
Becatti:	G.Becatti, *ArchCl* 25–26, 1973–74, 18–53
Croissant:	*LIMC* V (1990) λ. Hygieia (F.Croissant)
Heiderich:	G.Heiderich, *Asklepios* (1966)
Himmelmann:	N.Himmelmann στο Andreae, *Phyromachos-Probleme*, 13–23
Holtzmann:	*LIMC* II (1984) λ. Asklepios (B. Holtzmann)
Marcadé:	J.Marcadé, *Recueil des signatures de sculpteurs grecs* II (1957)
Moreno:	P.Moreno, *Scultura ellenistica* (1994)
Ridgway:	B.S.Ridgway, *Hellenistic Sculpture* I (1990)
Wenning:	R.Wenning, *Die Galateranatheme Attalos* I, *PF* 4 (1978)

Γιά την τέχνη της Περγάμου κατά τον 3ο αι. π.Χ. καθώς και το έργο του Φυρομάχου και του Νικηράτου βλ. και την ανακοίνωση του Marszal στον παρόντα τόμο, σελ. 117–127.

Σημειώσεις

1. A. Flasch, *Annali dell' Instituto di Corrispondenza Archeologica* 6, 1873, 17–19. Amelung, *Vat. Kat.* II 230–232. Mustilli 88. Stuart Jones, *Pal. Cons.* 112. Lippold, *Plastik* 333 και σημ. 2. R. Kabus-Jahn, *Studien zu den Frauenfiguren des 4. Jhs. v. Chr.* (1963) 54–56. Croissant 571. B. Andreae (επιμ.), *Bildkatalog der Skulpturen des Vatikanischen Museums* I. *Museo Chiaramonti* (1995) 33, αρ. II 85. O Croissant αρ. 191–194, αναφέρει τον αγαλματικό αυτό τύπο ως Υγεία Belvedere, και εντάσσει την παραλλαγή του στο Μουσείο Επιδαύρου (παρακ. σημ. 6) σε άλλον αγαλματικό τύπο Υγείας. Επίσης, ο Croissant αρ. 194, κατατάσσει στον τύπο της Υγείας Belvedere τη μορφή της θεάς σε ανάγλυφο επίκρανο ψευδοπαραστάδας στο Μουσείο Θεσσαλονίκης 6690: τελευταία, Θ. Στεφανίδου-Τιβερίου, *Το Μικρό Τόξο του Γαλερίου στη Θεσσαλονίκη* (1995) 92–95, πίν. 31β, η οποία παρουσιάζει απλώς κάποια εξάρτηση από αυτόν.
2. Αρ. ευρ. 1246 (παλαιότερα βρισκόταν στο Cortile del Belvedere). Υ.:2,13 μ.: Flasch ό.π. (σημ. 1) 5–19, πίν. A. Amelung, *Vat. Kat.* II 227, αρ. 85, πίν. 22. Helbig[4] I, αρ. 298 (W. Fuchs). Croissant αρ. 191*. Andreae ό.π. (σημ. 1) πίν. 382–383.795, με χρονολόγηση στα μέσα του 1ου αι. μ.Χ. Το άγαλμα θα μπορούσε ίσως να χρονολογηθεί στους χρόνους του αυτοκράτορα Τιβερίου, καθώς παρουσιάζει πολλές ομοιότητες στην απόδοση της πτυχολογίας με την κόρη του Βάλβου στον τύπο της Μικρής Ηρακλειώτισσας στο Μουσείο Νεαπόλεως 6244: M. Bieber, *Ancient Copies* (1977) 150, πίν. 116, εικ. 683–684. C. Nippe, *Die Fortuna Braccio Nuovo. Stilistische und typologische Untersuchung* (1988) 10 και σημ. 25.
3. E.E. Schmidt, *Römische Frauenstatuen* (διατριβή, Berlin, Freie Universität 1957) 152, αρ. 6. Kabus-Jahn ό.π. (σημ. 1) 55 σημ. 106. Σήμερα γνωστό μόνον από τις φωτογραφίες του DAI Ρώμης 1932.1585 και 38.1291. Φαίνεται ότι ήταν επίσης πρώιμων αυτοκρατορικών χρόνων λόγω της τεχνοτροπικής ομοιότητάς του με το άγαλμα στο Βατικανό.
4. Αρ. ευρ. 899. Υ.:1,80 μ. χωρίς την πλίνθο: Stuart Jones, *Pal. Cons.* 112, αρ. 64, πίν. 38 (συμπληρωμένο με κεφαλή του τύπου του Απόλλωνος Λυκείου). Mustilli 88, αρ. 10, πίν. 52, εικ. 211. Helbig[4] II, αρ. 1724 (H.v. Steuben). Croissant αρ. 192*. Συγγένεια στην απόδοση της πτυχολογίας των ενδυμάτων παρουσιάζει το άγαλμα αυτό με τα λεγόμενα ανάγλυφα Traiani/Hadriani στη Ρώμη, Forum Romanum (περ. 118 μ.Χ.): U. Rüdiger, *AntPl* XII (1973) 161–173, πίν. 67–72. G.M. Koeppel, *Bjb* 186 (1986) 2–5. 17–24, αρ. 1–2, εικ. 1–2 (χρόνοι Τραϊανού), καθώς και με το πρώιμο αδριάνειο εικονιστικό άγαλμα της Σαβίνας στο Μουσείο της Vaison: M. Wegner, *Herrscherbild* (1956) 130, πίν. 41b.
5. Αρ. ευρ. Sk 353. Υ.:2,13 μ.: Reinach, *RSt* II,1 298, αρ. 3. C. Blümel, *Römische Bildnisse* (1933) 16, αρ. R 38, πίν. 19. 21. Schmidt ό.π. (σημ. 3) 26–27 (με χρονολόγηση στους χρόνους Αυγούστου-Τιβερίου). H. Heres – G. Heres, *FuB* 20, 1980, 107. 144 (χρόνοι Τραϊανού-Αδριανού). H.J. Kruse, *Römische weibliche Gewandstatuen des 2. Jhs. n. Chr.* (1975) 360, αρ. D 65 (ορθότερα, πρώιμη εποχή Αντωνίνων). Croissant αρ. 193*. Βλ. επίσης, M. Bieber, *Griechische Kleidung* (1928) πίν. LII,1–2.
6. 'Αγαλμα Υγείας στο Μουσείο Επιδαύρου 16: A. Defrasse – H. Lechat, *Épidaure* (1895) 173. Kruse ό.π. (σημ. 5) 387, αρ. D 119, με χρονολόγηση γύρω στο 160 μ.Χ. Croissant αρ. 122. Σ. Κατάκης, *Η πλαστική των ρωμαϊκών χρόνων από το ιερό του Απόλλωνα και του Ασκληπιού στην Επίδαυρο* (διδακτορική διατριβή Αθήνα 1992) 71, αρ. 31, πίν. 153–155. 'Αγαλμα από τη Σαλαμίνα της Κύπρου: V. Karageorghis – C.C. Vermeule, *Sculptures from Salamis* I (1964) 35, αρ. 33, πίν. XXXV,1–2. II (1966) 27, αρ. 94, πίν. XIII,1–3 (125–150 μ.Χ.). V. Karageorghis – J. Frel, *AAA* 3, 1970, 237–238, εικ. 1. Στο άγαλμα αυτό παραλαμβάνονται στοιχεία από τον υστεροκλασικό αγαλματικό τύπο της Υγείας Broadlands-Conservatori: Croissant αρ. 63*.66*, που εντοπίζονται στη χρήση του χειριδωτού χιτώνα, στην αναδίπλωση του ιματίου που περνά πάνω από το αριστερό χέρι, και στη θέση του φιδιού που κατευθυνόταν από το δεξιό μηρό με τη βοήθεια του δεξιού χεριού προς τη φιάλη που πιθανότατα κρατούσε η Υγεία με το αριστερό. Άγαλμα στην Αρχαιολογική Συλλογή Ιεράπετρας 58: αδημοσίευτο. Παρουσιάζει ομοιότητες με εκείνο της Σαλαμίνας, ιδίως στη θέση του δεξιού χεριού που πιθανότατα κρατούσε το φίδι, όπως εικάζεται από την ύπαρξη ενός puntello.
7. Σαλαμίς Κύπρου: Karageorghis – Vermeule ό.π. (σημ. 6) I, 31, αρ. 23, πίν. XXVIII,2. Ρώμη, Palazzo dei Conservatori, Museo Nuovo: γνωστό από τη φωτογραφία DAI Ρώμης 7469. Αγαλμάτιο της Υγείας Fleischman, J.Paul Getty Museum 96.AB.195.2: A. Herrmann στο M. True – A. Kozloff κ.ά., *A Passion for Antiquities. Ancient Art from the Collection of Barbara and Lawrence Fleischman* (1994) 298, αρ. 156, την οποία ευχαριστώ για την υπόδειξη και από τη θέση αυτή.
8. O Flasch ό.π. (σημ. 1) 14–15, πίν. A, υπέθεσε ότι αρχικά το φίδι βρισκόταν στο άγαλμα αυτό στην ίδια θέση με το αντίγραφο στο Βερολίνο, αν και στο άγαλμα του Βατικανού δεν σώθηκαν ίχνη του.

9. Για τη θέση του φιδιού στα αγάλματα της Σαλαμίνας της Κύπρου και της Ιεράπετρας, βλ. παραπ. σημ. 6. Το άγαλμα στην Επίδαυρο έχει το φίδι περασμένο γύρω από τους ώμους, στην πλάτη. Αυτή η θέση του φιδιού απαντά και σε ορισμένες άλλες παραστάσεις της Υγείας αυτοκρατορικών χρόνων και τόνιζε τη μετωπικότητα της σύνθεσης που συχνά υπογραμμιζόταν και με την τοποθέτηση του αγάλματος εντός κόγχης. Βλ. το αγαλμάτιο της Υγείας άλλοτε στη Συλλογή Melchett, αργότερα στη Ρώμη, εμπόριο αρχαιοτήτων: E. Strong, *Catalogue of the Greek and Roman Antiquities in the Possession of the Honorable Lord Melchett* (1928) αρ. 5, πίν. 13. Croissant αρ. 119. Ακόμη, το αγαλμάτιο της Υγείας στο Μουσείο του Δίου: Δ. Παντερμαλής, *Οι αρχαιολόγοι μιλούν για την Πιερία* (1986) εικ. εξωφύλλου. Επίσης, το άγαλμα της Υγείας από κόγχη του Νυμφαίου της Βύβλου στο Μουσείο Βηρυτού: J. Lauffray, *BMusBeyr* 4, 1940, 27–18, πίν. 4. Kruse ό.π. (σημ. 5) 380, αρ. D 100 (150–160 μ.Χ.). Croissant αρ. 43. Τέλος, βλ. την Υγεία του δίπτυχου Gaddi: παρακ. σημ. 69. Και το άγαλμα της Υγείας της Επιδαύρου ήταν πιθανότατα στημένο σε κόγχη: Κατάκης ό.π. (σημ. 6) 577.

10. Ιδιαίτερα περίτεχνο και με δισδιάκριτη ανάγλυφη μορφή στο μετάλλιο. Κατά τον Stuart Jones ό.π. (σημ. 4), απεικονίζεται ο Διαδούμενος του Πολυκλείτου.

11. Ο πέπλος μαρτυρείται από το άγαλμα Conservatori, και από την προσοχή που έχει δοθεί σε ορισμένες λεπτομέρειές του, πιστεύουμε ότι αυτό πρέπει να ήταν το ένδυμα του πρωτότυπου αγάλματος. Ο χειριδωτός χιτώνας της Υγείας στο Βερολίνο, συνηθέστερος στην εικονογραφία της θεάς, οδήγησε αναγκαστικά τον αντιγραφέα στην παράλειψη του περιβραχιόνιου.

12. Ο "φιόγκος" εμφανίζεται σε όλα τα αντίγραφα πλην εκείνου στο Βερολίνο, όπου η θέση των χεριών πολύ κοντά στο σώμα δεν επέτρεψε την απόδοσή του. Στο άγαλμα της Επιδαύρου (παραπ. σημ. 6) διατηρούνται puntelli που μάλλον στήριζαν τα έξεργα τμήματά του.

13. Το άγαλμα Conservatori δεν αποφεύγει εντελώς τα εμβόλιμα στοιχεία της εποχής που δημιουργήθηκε, συγκεκριμένα τη μετωπική ανάπτυξη της σύνθεσης και την επιφανειακή απόδοση των πτυχών του ιματίου ανάμεσα στα σκέλη. Για τα χαρακτηριστικά αυτά σε ιδεαλιστικά αγάλματα των τραϊάνειων και αδριάνειων χρόνων, Nippe ό.π. (σημ. 2) 12–13. 16–17.

14. Εσφαλμένα η κεφαλή του αναγνωρίσθηκε ως εικονιστική από τον Blümel ό.π. (σημ. 5). Πρβ. αντίθετα, Kruse ό.π. (σημ. 5). Εμβόλιμο στοιχείο του αντιγραφέα είναι ο "μηνίσκος" της κόμης εμπρός και ίσως η οπισθοσφενδόνη. Ο "φιόγκος" στην κορυφή είναι συνήθης σε αγάλματα Αφροδίτης από τον 3ο αι. π.Χ. ώς τον 2ο αι. μ.Χ., και ίσως εμφανίζεται στο αντίγραφο αυτό κατ' αναλογία με συγκρητιστικές παραστάσεις Αφροδίτης-Υγείας των αυτοκρατορικών χρόνων: βλ. παρακ. σημ. 69.

15. Η κεφαλή του αντιγράφου στο Βατικανό μολονότι αρχαία, δεν συνανήκει: Amelung ό.π. (σημ. 2) 229–230. Ο Flasch ό.π (σημ. 1) 10–12. θεώρησε ότι απηχεί τον τύπο κεφαλής της Αθηνάς Υγείας του Πύρρου εξαιτίας των ανάγλυφων φιδιών που κοσμούν το διάδημα. Η κεφαλή της Υγείας στο Βατικανό εξαρτάται μάλλον από την κεφαλή της Αθηνάς τύπου Velletri του ύστερου 5ου αι. π.Χ. Πρβ. την πρώιμη αντωνίνεια προτομή στη Γλυπτοθήκη του Μονάχου 213: B. Vierneisel-Schlörb, *Glyptothek München* II. *Klassische Skulpturen des 5. und 4. Jhs v. Chr.* (1979) 136, αρ. 12, εικ. 64. Παρόμοιο τύπο κεφαλής παρουσιάζει το αντίγραφο της Υγείας στο Velletri, που ίσως προέρχεται από ένα κοινό εργαστήριο με εκείνο του Βατικανού. Για το συνδυασμό στα εκλεκτικά εργαστήρια της Ρώμης κλασικιστικών κεφαλών που παραπέμπουν στην τέχνη του 5ου αι. π.Χ. με κορμούς αγαλμάτων ελληνιστικής, και μάλιστα περγαμηνής τεχνοτροπίας, βλ. M. Fuchs, *RM* 89, 1982, 78. Αντίστοιχα, η κεφαλή του αγάλματος στη Σαλαμίνα της Κύπρου εξαρτάται από εκείνη της Αρτέμιδος τύπου Βερσαλλιών, που σχετίζεται με το Λεωχάρη: *LIMC* II (1984) λ. Artemis-Diana, αρ. 27a* (E. Simon).

16. Αγαθή Τύχη, Μουσείο Αγοράς S 2370: O. Palagia, *Hesperia* 51, 1982, 99–113, πίν. 29 (άγαλμα της Δημοκρατίας). Η ίδια, στο W. Coulson, O. Palagia κ.ά. (επιμ.), *The Archaeology of Athens and Attica Under the Democracy. Proceedings of an International Conference December 4–6, 1992* (1994) 113–122, εικ. 1 (ταύτιση ως άγαλμα της Αγαθής Τύχης). Επιτύμβιο ανάγλυφο στο Brocklesby Park: D. Woysch-Méautis, *La représentation des animaux et des êtres fabuleux sur les monuments funéraires grecs de l'époque archaïque à la fin du IVe siècle av. J-C.* (1982) 130, αρ. 324, πίν. 50. Για την Υγεία τύπου Broadlands – Conservatori βλ. παραπ. σημ. 6. Πρβ. επίσης την Υγεία στο ανάγλυφο Εθνικό Μουσείο 1335: Holtzmann αρ. 96*. Croissant αρ. 34.

17. Οι δύο Μούσες στα δεξιά στην πλάκα από τη βάση της Μαντίνειας Εθνικό Μουσείο 217 (330–300 π.Χ.): G. Rizzo, *Prassitele* (1932) 86–89, πίν. 130–132. Ridgway πίν. 132c. Για τη βάση γενικά, R. Horn, *Stehende weibliche Gewandstatuen in der hellenistischen Plastik*, 2. Ergh. *RM* (1931) 16–17. Θ. Στεφανίδου-Τιβερίου, *Νεοαττικά. Οι ανάγλυφοι πίνακες από το λιμάνι του Πειραιά* (1979) 153 σημ. 2. A.Ajootian στο O.Palagia – J.J.Pollitt (επιμ.), *Personal Styles in Greek Sculpture* (1996) 122–124, εικ. 68. Μεγάλη Ηρακλειώτισσα (περ. 320 π.Χ.): Rizzo 100–103, πίν. 135. Bieber ό.π. (σημ. 2) 148. I.Linfert-Reich, *Musen und Dichterinnenfiguren des 4. und frühen 3. Jhs. v. Chr.* (1971) 51–57. Kruse ό.π. (σημ. 5) 41–42. Ridgway 92–93. Αγαλματικός τύπος της λεγόμενης Υγείας Zara: Kabus-Jahn ό.π. (σημ. 1) 9–10 και σημ. 38–39. Linfert-Reich 62–63. 65–70. F. Ghedini, *ASAtene* 47, 1985, 119–120 και σημ. 149, εικ. 42.

18. Η χρονολόγηση της λεγόμενης Θέμιδας από το Ραμνούντα, Εθνικό Μουσείο 231, εξαρτάται κυρίως από το εάν ο γλύπτης της Χαιρέστρατος Χαιρεδήμου ταυτίζεται με τον Αθηναίο βουλευτή του 328/7 π.Χ., ή ήταν εγγονός του. Η παραδοσιακή άποψη τοποθετεί το άγαλμα αυτό λίγο μετά το 300 π.Χ.: Nippe ό.π. (σημ. 2) 50 και σημ. 326. Ridgway 55–57 και σημ. 40, πίν. 31. Νεώτερες κυρίως απόψεις το χρονολογούν στη δεκαετία 320–310 π.Χ.: W. Geominy, *Die Florentiner Niobiden* (1984) 243–244 και σημ. 646, 273–274, εικ. 320. M. Flashar – R.v. den Hoff, *BCH* 117, 1993, 420 και σημ. 32. Βλ. εδώ, Θέμελης, σελ. 55–56. Για την ταύτιση της μορφής, Α. Μάντης, *Προβλήματα της εικονογραφίας των ιερειών και των ιερέων στην αρχαία ελληνική τέχνη* (1990) 104–113. Εικονιστικό άγαλμα Δημοσθένους του Πολυεύκτου: A. Michaelis, *Die Bildnissse des Demosthenes* (1887) στο K. Fittschen (επιμ.), *Griechische Porträts* (1988) 78–100, πίν. 114–116.

G.M.A. Richter, *The Portraits of the Greeks* (abridged and revised by R.R.R. Smith, 1984) 108–113, εικ. 74. Ridgway 224–226 σημ. 17, πίν. 107. Η Μήδεια της τοιχογραφίας από την Ηράκλεια στο Μουσείο Νεαπόλεως 8976 ανάγεται από πολλούς ερευνητές στη χαμένη ζωγραφική σύνθεση του Τιμομάχου από το Βυζάντιο του α' μισού του 3ου αι. π.Χ.: Horn ό.π. (σημ. 17) 14–15, πίν. 3,2. *LIMC* VI (1992) λ. Medeia, αρ. 7. 11* (M. Schmidt). Πρβ. επίσης την προσωποποίηση της Αρετής ή της Μακεδονίας στο μακεδονικό τάφο II της τούμπας Μπέλλα στη Βεργίνα, του πρώιμου 3ου αι. π.Χ.: Μ. Ανδρόνικος, *Πρακτ* 1982, 53–54. Ο ίδιος, *ΑΕφημ* 126, 1987, 367–368. Ν. Σταμπολίδης, *ΑΕφημ* 131, 1992, 140 και σημ. 34.36.

19. Πρβ. και τη μορφή της Υγείας σε ένα αναθηματικό ανάγλυφο από το Αμύνειο, στο Εθνικό Μουσείο της Αθήνας 3530 (310–300 π.Χ.): U. Hausmann, *Kult und Heiltum* (1948) 171, αρ. 64 (A 16), εικ. 8.

20. H. Kenner, *SBWien* 274:1, 1971, 1–38, εικ. 1–7. H. Lauter, *AM* 86, 1971, 147–161, πίν. 72. 74,1. 75,1. 77. L. de Lachenal στο A. Giuliano (επιμ.), *Museo Nazionale Romano* I,1 (1979) 186, αρ. 121. Ridgway 228–230, εικ. 111a-c. Για την ταύτισή της με άγαλμα Πυθίας και την απόδοση στη σχολή της Περγάμου τελευταία, Moreno 316–318, εικ. 395. 399–402.

21. Η παραδοσιακή χρονολόγηση της μεγάλης ζωφόρου με τη Γιγαντομαχία του Βωμού του Διός στην Πέργαμο είναι στη δεκαετία 180–170 π.Χ., και της μικρότερης ζωφόρου με την Τηλέφεια στη δεκαετία 170–160 π.Χ. ή λίγο αργότερα: J.J. Pollitt, *Art in the Hellenistic Age* (1986) 97. 198. W. Hoepfner, *AA* 1989, 633–634. Με βάση κυρίως τη μελέτη της κεραμεικής από τη θεμελίωση του βωμού ο P.J. Callaghan, *BICS* 28, 1981, 115–121, υποστήριξε τη χρονολόγηση και των δύο ζωφόρων στο διάστημα 165–159 π.Χ. Την άποψη αυτή δέχονται ο T.M. Schmidt, στο Andreae, *Phyromachos-Probleme* 141–162, ο Σταμπολίδης ό.π. (σημ. 18) 143 και σημ. 51 και ο W. Hoepfner στο W. Hoepfner – G. Zimmer (επιμ.), *Die griechische Polis. Architektur und Politik* (1993) 117. Ο ίδιος, *AA* 1996, 133 σημ. 42. Ο C. Börker, *Akten des XIII. internationalen Kongresses für klassische Archäologie. Berlin 1988* (1990) 591–592, θεωρεί ότι οι εργασίες στο μνημείο συνεχίσθηκαν στη δεκαετία 140–130 π.Χ.

22. Αρ. ευρ. 571: D.B. Thompson, *Ptolemaic Oinochoai and Portraits in Faience. Aspects of the Ruler Cult* (1973) 149, αρ. 75, πίν. XXV-XXVII.

23. Αρ. ευρ. 571: R. Özgan, *IstMitt* 32, 1982, 204 και σημ. 35, πίν. 48,2, ο οποίος υποστηρίζει την εξάρτησή του από έργα της μνημειώδους πλαστικής. Ο ίδιος, *Die griechischen und römishen Skulpturen aus Tralleis* (1995) 12, αρ. TR 1, πίν. 1,1–2.

24. Βερολίνο, Μουσείο Περγάμου: A. Linfert, *Kunstzentren hellenistischer Zeit* (1976) 28–29. 164–167, εικ. 18–19. R. Özgan, *IstMitt* 32, 1982, 196–209, πίν. 45,1–2. 47,1–2.

25. Βλ. E. Lévy – J. Marcadé, *BCH* 96, 1972, 967–1004, εικ. 1–6. Τελευταία για το σύνταγμα της Λυκόσουρας, Moreno 508–514 και σημ. 812. P. Themelis στο Palagia – Pollitt ό.π. (σημ. 17) 167 και σημ. 63–68, και για τη χρονολόγηση με *terminus ante quem* το 190 π.Χ. στην πρώτη δεκαετία του 2ου αι. π.Χ., που προκύπτει από το τιμητικό ψήφισμα της Λυκόσουρας, σελ. 169–171. Ο Θέμελης θέτει την ακμή του Δαμοφώντος στο διάστημα 223–190 ή 214–182 π.Χ.: Π. Θέμελης, στο O. Palagia – W.D.E. Coulson (επιμ.), *Sculpture from Arcadia and Laconia* (1993) 100–104. Ο ίδιος, *AntK* 36, 1993, 34–38. Ο ίδιος στο Palagia – Pollitt ό.π. (σημ. 17) 167–172. Πρβ. αντίθετα, Moreno 808 σημ. 814, που επανέρχεται στην παραδοσιακή χρονολόγηση του έργου του Δαμοφώντος στο α' μισό του 2ου αι. π.Χ.

26. Για τον κλασικισμό των λατρευτικών αγαλμάτων στον ύστερο 3ο αι. π.Χ. και ιδίως στο έργο του Δαμοφώντος, βλ. Themelis, *AntK* 36, 1993, 39 και σημ. 69. Για τη σύζευξη κλασικιστικών στοιχείων που συνεχίζουν την παράδοση του 4ου αι. π.Χ. και "μπαρόκ" στοιχείων στο έργο του Δαμοφώντος βλ. Themelis στο Palagia – Pollitt ό.π. (σημ. 17) 179–181.

27. Πρβ. M. Pfrommer, *Untersuchungen zur Chronologie früh- und hochhellenistischen Goldschmucks* (1990) 340, αρ. TA 106, πίν. 19,1–2 (Αίγυπτος, 275–250 π.Χ.), 331, αρ. TA 4, πίν. 10,3 (Ιταλία, 250–200 π.Χ.).

28. A. Stewart, *Attika: Studies in Athenian Sculpture of the Hellenistic Age, JHS* Suppl. 14 (1979) 6.

29. Η Κωμωδία, αρ. ευρ. 652, προέρχεται από το χορηγικό μνημείο A' του Διονυσίου, και ο Διόνυσος, αρ. ευρ. 1473, από το λίγο μεταγενέστερο χορηγικό μνημείο B': βλ. γενικά, P. Bernard – F. Salviat, *BCH* 83, 1959, 288–335. F. Salviat, *Thasiaka, BCH Suppl.* V (1979) 155–167. Στην έρευνα γίνεται σήμερα αποδεκτή η χρονολόγηση των γλυπτών των δύο μνημείων στο τέλος του 4ου – αρχές του 3ου αι. π.Χ.: A.H. Borbein, *JdI* 88, 1973, 48–55. Βλ. και Ridgway 50–54 και σημ. 35, πίν. 27a-b (Κωμωδία). 28 (Διόνυσος).

30. Στο Μουσείο Δελφών. Βλ. εδώ, Θέμελης, σελ. 52, εικ. 10–12 και Geominy, σελ. 62. Επίσης, Ν.Δ. Παπαχατζής, *Παυσανίου Ελλάδος Περιήγησις. Βοιωτικά και Φωκικά* (1981) εικ. 414.

31. Τη διαγραφή των πλούσιων σωματικών όγκων κάτω από τα ενδύματα που έχουν ωστόσο και δική τους ιδιαίτερη πλαστική υπόσταση συναντάμε στα αττικά πήλινα αγαλμάτια του "μνημειώδους ρυθμού" (monumental style) ήδη στο α' μισό του 3ου αι. π.Χ. Ακριβώς σε αυτά τα μικρής κλίμακας έργα παρατηρείται το πέρασμα από τον κλασικισμό στο "μπαρόκ": Βλ. D.B. Thompson στο H.A. – D.B. Thompson, *Hellenistic Pottery and Terracottas* (1987) 314–315, αρ. 13. 15, πίν. 26. 337–339, αρ. 6, πίν. 30 (Agora T 139 και Agora T 1339). J.P. Uhlenbrock στο J.P. Uhlenbrock (επιμ.), *The Coroplast's Art. Greek Terracottas of the Hellenistic World* (1990) 52 και σημ. 43–44, εικ. 39. Πιθανότατα η σπανιότητα μνημειώδους πλαστικής στην Αττική του προχωρημένου 3ου αι. π.Χ. (βλ. παραπ. σημ. 28) οδήγησε στην πλήρη ανάπτυξη της νέας τεχνοτροπίας στα μικρασιατικά εργαστήρια γλυπτικής, ιδιαίτερα σε αυτό της Περγάμου όπου εργάσθηκαν Αθηναίοι γλύπτες. Για το περγαμηνό "μπαρόκ", A. Schober, *Die Kunst von Pergamon* (1951) 168–169. Για την εμφάνιση της "μπαρόκ" τεχνοτροπικής γλώσσας σε μικρασιατικά γλυπτά ήδη του ύστερου 3ου αι. π.Χ., Özgan ό.π. (σημ. 24) 203–204.

32. H. Kähler, *Der Grosse Fries von Pergamon* (1948) πίν. 8. E.M. Schmidt, *The Great Altar of Pergamon* (1962) πίν. 25–26.

33. F. Winter, *AvP* VII 1 (1908) 87, αρ. 53, πίν. XX (λίγο πριν από το Μεγαλο Βωμό). Horn ό.π. (σημ. 17) 51–53. Schober ό.π. (σημ. 31) 110 και σημ. 174. 172–173, εικ. 78.

34. Πέργαμος (Bergama) Αρχαιολογικό Μουσείο Τ 43: E. Boehringer - F. Krauss, *AvP* IX (1937) 114, πίν. 53b. E. Töpperwein, *Terrakotten von Pergamon*, *PF* 3 (1976) 20. 203, αρ. 45, πίν. 7.

35. Juno Cesi, στη Ρώμη, Μουσείο Καπιτωλίου: Stuart Jones, *Mus. Cap.* 340, αρ. 2, πίν. 85. Linfert ό.π. (σημ. 24) 108 και σημ. 401, εικ. 251–253. Özgan ό.π. (σημ. 24) 202 και σημ. 26–27, πίν. 46. Για την κόρη από το Άντιο (παραπ. σημ. 20), βλ. ιδίως Moreno εικ. 402. Τραγωδία, στο Βερολίνο, Μουσείο Περγάμου: Winter ό.π. (σημ. 33) 76, αρ. 47, πίν. XIV-XV. Schober ό.π. (σημ. 31) 107–108, εικ. 64. Linfert 109 και σημ. 424. Özgan 199 και σημ. 11. Για την άποψη ότι η Τραγωδία όπως και το γυναικείο άγαλμα παραπ. σημ. 33, ανήκουν στη διακόσμηση του Μεγάλου Βωμού, βλ. τελευταία W. Hoepfner, *AA* 1996, 123, εικ. 5 και 16. Στη μεγάλη ζωφόρο του περγαμηνού Βωμού βλ. τη Λητώ, την Αρτέμιδα, τη Φοίβη και τη Νύκτα: Schmidt ό.π. (σημ. 32) πίν. 14–15. 17. 36, αντίστοιχα.

36. Για την Κυβέλη βλ. παραπ. σημ. 32. Ηώς: Schmidt ό.π. (σημ. 32) πίν. 23. Επίσης βλ. και τη Μοίρα: Schmidt πίν. 35. Πρβ. και τη Νίκη της πομπηιανής τοιχογραφίας στο Μουσείο της ιταλικής Νεαπόλεως που έχει θεωρηθεί ότι αποδίδει ένα περγαμηνό άγαλμα: παρακ. σημ. 72.

37. Αρ. ευρ. 764. F. Winter, *AvP* VII 2 (1908) 272, αρ. 344A, πίν. XXXVIII. Mendel II 298, αρ. 575 με σχέδιο. M. Schede, *Meisterwerke der türkischen Museen zu Konstantinopel I. Griechische und römische Skulpturen des Antikenmuseums* (1928) πίν. 25. Schober ό.π. (σημ. 31) 146, εικ. 147. Πρβ. απλούστερα αλλά ανάλογης μορφής περιβραχιόνια σε αγαλματικούς τύπους Αφροδίτης από τον κύκλο του Πραξιτέλους (την παρατήρηση οφείλω στην ευγενή υπόδειξη του F. Queyrel): E. Kelperi, στο H.v. Steuben κ.ά., *IstMitt* 39, 1989, 558–560, πίν. 55. Ειδικά, για το περιβραχιόνιο της Κνιδίας Αφροδίτης ως σύμβολο ομορφιάς της θεάς, C. Blinkenberg, *Knidia* (1933) 99–101. 100 σημ. 2. Το περιβραχιόνιο της Υγείας ίσως υποδήλωνε συγγένεια προς την Αφροδίτη. Άλλωστε ο γενικός εικονογραφικός τύπος με την καμπύλη αναδίπλωση του ιματίου ανακαλεί κλασικές παραστάσεις Αφροδίτης, όπως ο περίφημος αγαλματικός τύπος της Ηρας Borghese: *LIMC* IV (1988) λ. Hera, αρ. 102 (A. Kossatz-Deissmann). A. Delivorrias, *MEFRA* 103, 1991, 129–157, εικ. 34–36. Ο ίδιος στο H. Beck - P.C.Bol (επιμ.), *Polykletforschungen* (1993) 221–252, εικ. 1–16. Πρβ. την εικονογραφική προσέγγιση της Υγείας προς την Αφροδίτη σε κλασικά αττικά ανάγλυφα, λ.χ. Εθνικό Μουσείο 1338: Holtzmann αρ. 86*. Croissant αρ. 41. Βλ. και παρακ. σημ. 69.

38. H. Winnefeld, *AvP* III 2 (1910) 73, εικ. 16–17. Kähler ό.π. (σημ. 32) πίν. 43,1. Πρβ. επίσης το ψέλιο σε ένα διπλάσιο του φυσικού γυναικείο χέρι από την Πέργαμο: Winter ό.π. (σημ. 37) 241, αρ. 296.

39. Αρ. ευρ. 8608. E. Künzl, *Frühhellenistische Gruppen* (1968) 118–127, εικ. 18. Ο ίδιος, *Die Kelten des Epigonos von Pergamon* (1971) 7–9. B. Palma στο A. Giuliano (επιμ.), *Museo Nazionale Romano* I 5 (1983) 146, αρ. 64. Το τμήμα αυτό της χλαμύδας είναι σε μεγάλο μέρος του συμπληρωμένο, ωστόσο πλούσια σε αναδιπλώσεις πρέπει να ήταν και η αρχική μορφή του: Wenning πίν. 4,3–5.

40. Βλ. Winter ό.π. (σημ. 33) 69, αρ. 45, πίν. XII (άγαλμα Κυβέλης). Επίσης βλ. την Τραγωδία: παραπ. σημ. 35 και τη γυναικεία μορφή παραπ. σημ. 33.

41. Πρβ. Fuchs ό.π. (σημ. 15) 78 και πίν. 21,2–3. 24,3. 25,2. 28,3.

42. Winter ό.π. (σημ. 33) 124, αρ. 104, εικ. 104a-b. D. Pinkwart στο *Pergamon Ausstellung, 22. April-4. Juni 1972 in Erinnerung an E. Boehringer* (1972) αρ. 29 (150–100 π.Χ.).

43. Πρβ. τη Σελήνη, τη Νύκτα, την πρώτη από τις Μοίρες, και την Εκάτη: Schmidt ό.π. (σημ. 32) πίν. 19. 56. 58–59 αντίστοιχα. Επίσης βλ. την κεφαλή ενός αγάλματος στη Συλλογή Stroganoff: Schober ό.π. (σημ. 31) 173, εικ. 144.

44. *Niceratus (fecit) Aesculapium et Hygiam, qui sunt in Concordiae templo Romae.* M. Pape, *Griechische Kunstwerke aus Kriegsbeute und ihre öffentliche Aufstellung in Rom* (1975) 155, αρ. 1. 215. Σχετικά με τη μετατροπή του ναού αυτού σε ένα είδος Μουσείου στους χρόνους του αυτοκράτορα Τιβερίου: Becatti 30–31. 42.

45. Δύο επιγραφές του βρίσκονται στη Δήλο, μία στην περιοχή της Κυζίκου, και τρείς στην Πέργαμο: Marcadé αρ. 79–82, πίν. XXXVIII,1–2. H. Lauter, *Erlanger Forschungen, R.A. Geisteswissenschaften* 23, 1974, 19 σημ. 45 (Κύζικος, υπογραφή μαζί με τον Φυρόμαχο). Επίσης, M. Wörrle στο M.N. Filgis - W. Radt, *AvP* XV 1 (1986) 157–160, που αμφισβητεί την απόδοση της υπογραφής αυτής της Περγάμου στο γνωστό γλύπτη. Πρβ. αντίθετα, F. Queyrel, *RA* 1989, 289–290. Ο Νικήρατος είναι γνωστός και από χωρία του Πλίνιου και του Τατιανού: Πλίνιος, *N.H.* 34.88. Τατιανός, *Oratio ad Graecos* 33. Βλ. και J.J. Pollitt, *The Art of Ancient Greece: Sources and Documents*[2] (1990) 113–114.

46. Το Νικήρατο τοποθετούν στον 3ο, ή στον 3ο προς 2ο αι. π.Χ. οι: A. Reinach, *Mélanges Holleaux* (1913) 233–255. G. Lippold, *RE* 33 (1936) 314–316, λ. Nikeratos 4 (και οι δύο α' μισό 3ου αι.). A. Schober, *ÖJh* 32, 1940, 76–79 (μέσα 3ου – αρχές 2ου αι.). B. Schweitzer, *AA* 1939, 407–413. Conticello, *EAA* 5 (1963) 475 λ. Nikeratos (3ος-2ος αι.). Pollitt ό.π. (σημ. 21) 84. Himmelmann 20.22 και σημ. 44–45.59 (β' μισό 3ου). F. Queyrel, *RA* 1992, 379–380 (β' μισό 3ου αι.). Moreno 262–265 (α' μισό 3ου αι.). Πρβ. και M.J. Osborne - S.G. Byrne (επιμ.), *A Lexicon of Greek Personal Names* II. *Attica* (1994) λ. Nikeratos 332, αρ. 12. Στο 2ο αι. π.Χ. τον τοποθετούν οι: A. Mahler, *JdI* 20, 1905, 26–31. A. Schober, *ÖJh* 31, 1939, 142–148 (2ος αι.). Heiderich 94. Wörrle ό.π. (σημ. 45) 159 και σημ. 38. Andreae 60–62. 68–69. 93. Βλ. και παρακ. σημ. 48–50.

47. Ὦ μάκαρ, ὦ Φιλέταιρε, σὺ καὶ θείοισιν ἀοιδοῖς
καὶ πλάστῃσιν, ἄναξ, εὐπαλάμοισι μέλεις·
οἳ τὸ σὸν ἐξενέπουσι μέγα κράτος, οἱ μὲν ἐν ὕμνοις,
οἱ δὲ χερῶν τέχνας δεικνύμενοι σφετέρων,
ὥς ποτε δυσπολέμοις Γαλάταις θοὸν Ἄρεα μείξας
ἤλασας οἰκείων πολλὸν ὕπερθεν ὅρων·
ὧν ἕνεκεν τάδε σοι Νικηράτου ἔκκριτα ἔργα
Σωσικράτης Δήλῳ θῆκεν ἐν ἀμφιρύτῃ,
μνῆμα καὶ ἐσσομένοισιν ἀοίδιμον · οὐδέ κεν αὐτὸς
Ἥφαιστος τέχνην τῶν γε ὀνόσαιτ' ἐσιδών.

Βρίσκεται κατά χώραν στα ΒΔ. του ναού των Αθηναίων (Ε 67): *IG* XI,4, 1105. Marcadé αρ. 79, πίν. XXXVIII,1. P. Bruneau - J. Ducat, *Guide de Delos*[3]

(1983) 128, αρ. 10 (β' μισό 3ου αι. π.Χ.). F. Chamoux, *REG* 101, 1988, 499, αρ. 2. Queyrel ό.π. (σημ. 45) 287–288, εικ. 31–32. Αν το ανάθημα του Σωσικράτους ήταν μάχη Ατταλιδών και Γαλατών ή σειρά δυναστικών πορτραίτων παραμένει άγνωστο, αν και η πρώτη άποψη φαίνεται πιθανότερη: Βλ. Moreno 262.

48. Chamoux ό.π. (σημ. 47). Queyrel ό.π. (σημ. 45) 288. Moreno 262 και σημ. 505 (με συγκέντρωση απόψεων). Στους χρόνους 277–239 π.Χ. χρονολογεί το επίγραμμα ο A. Stewart, *Greek Sculpture: An Exploration* (1990) 302, αρ. T 153.

49. Ο H.J. Schalles, *Untersuchungen zur Kulturpolitik der pergamenischen Herrscher im dritten Jahrhundert v. Christus* (1985) 39–40 και σημ. 263, επισημαίνει ότι δεν μαρτυρείται άμεση συμμετοχή του πρεσβύτερου Φιλεταίρου σε πολεμικές επιχειρήσεις κατά των Γαλατών. Πρβ. B. Hintzen-Bohlen, *Herrscherrepräsentation im Hellenismus: Untersuchungen zu Weihgeschenken, Stiftungen und Ehrenmonumenten in den mutterländischen Heiligtümern, Delphi, Olympia, Delos und Dodona* (1992) 167–168 και σημ. 1258.

50. Wenning 44 και σημ. 289. R.E. Allen, *The Attalid Kingdom: A Constitutional History* (1983) 22 σημ. 46. 31 σημ. 8. 136–137, που ενισχύει τη θέση του και με το επιχείρημα της μορφής των γραμμάτων του επιγράμματος. Pollitt ό.π. (σημ. 21) 84. Επίσης τελευταία η I. Schmidt, *Hellenistische Statuenbasen* (1995) 83–87. 439, αρ. VII 10, θεωρεί πιθανή τη χρονολόγηση του αναθήματος του Σωσικράτους στους χρόνους του Αττάλου Α' λόγω της αρχιτεκτονικής μορφής της βάσης του (αν και στον κατάλογό της θέτει ως *terminus ante quem* to 171 π.Χ.). Ο Himmelmann 20 και σημ. 44, θεωρεί πιθανή τη χρονολόγηση του αναθήματος στο β' μισό του 3ου αι. π.Χ., πιστεύει όμως ότι το επίγραμμα χαράχθηκε στο 2ο αι. π.Χ.

51. Αντίθετα, Moreno 262. Αντίστοιχα, η λέξη *μάκαρ* του επιγράμματος είναι δυνατόν να αναφέρεται στο νεκρό πλέον Φιλέταιρο: Schweitzer ό.π. (σημ. 46) 409. Αντίθετα, για την άποψη ότι χαρακτηρίζει και αυτή ως επικό επίθετο το ζώντα ιδρυτή της περγαμηνής δυναστείας, βλ. Chamoux ό.π. (σημ. 47) και Moreno 262 σημ. 506.

52. Βλ. Chamoux ό.π. (σημ. 47) 494 σημ. 7. Schalles ό.π. (σημ. 49) 145 και σημ. 323. O. Mørkholm, *Early Hellenistic Coinage from the Accession of Alexander to the Peace of Apamea (336–188 B.C.)* (1991) 129 (περ. 240 π.Χ.).

53. Πρβ. Himmelmann ό.π. (σημ. 50).

54. Και το *μέγα κράτος* της Περγάμου του επιγράμματος οδηγεί στους χρόνους του Αττάλου Α': Pollitt ό.π. (σημ. 21) 81. Hintzen-Bohlen ό.π. (σημ. 49) 119–120 και σημ. 910.

55. Πρβ. αντίθετα, Andreae 68–69 Τα γράμματα του επιγράμματος του Σωσικράτους είναι παρόμοια με αυτά της επιγραφής του 239/8 π.Χ. από την Αγορά των Αθηνών: M. Crosby, *Hesperia* 6, 1937, 444, αρ. 2A (την υπόδειξη οφείλω στο διευθυντή του Επιγραφικού Μουσείου Χ. Κριτζά), καθώς και με εκείνα της επιγραφής του λεγόμενου αναθήματος της Τευθρανίας στη Δήλο από τον ύστερο 3ο αι. π.Χ.: παρακ. σημ. 56. Το επίγραμμα τοποθετεί στο β' μισό του 3ου αι. π.Χ. και ο F. Durrbach, *Choix d' inscriptions de Délos* I (1921) 38, αρ. 31, που ανεβάζει όμως τη χρονολόγηση του Νικηράτου στο α' μισό του 3ου αι. με βάση την άλλη υπογραφή της Δήλου: παραπ. σημ. 45, και θεωρεί ότι το επίγραμμα είναι μεταγενέστερο της δημιουργίας του αναθήματος.

56. Αυτά είναι: α) Εικονιστικό άγαλμα του πρεσβύτερου Φιλεταίρου, που ανέθεσε ο Ευμένης Α' (263–241 π.Χ.): *IG* XI,4, 1106. Hintzen-Bohlen ό.π. (σημ. 49) 110 και σημ. 809. β) Γαλατικό ανάθημα του Αττάλου Α' και έφιππος ανδριάντας του στρατηγού του Επιγένους μπροστά από τα άκρα της Ν. στοάς στην ιερά οδό, που στήθηκαν σύμφωνα με τα επιγραφικά δεδομένα των βάσεών τους γύρω στο 228 π.Χ.: *IG* XI,4, 1109 και 1110. R. Vallois, *L' architecture hellénique et hellénistique à Délos* I: *Les monuments* (1944) 66–67 και σημ. 3. Β. Σμιτ-Δούνα, *Εγνατία* 1, 1989, 117–118. Hintzen-Bohlen 120–121, εικ. 11. K. Bringmann – H.v. Steuben (επιμ.), *Schenkungen hellenistischer Herrscher an griechischer Städte und Heiligtümer* I (1995) 221, αρ. 173–174. γ) Το ανάθημα με τους ανδριάντες των Ευμένους Α', Αττάλου Α', και πιθανόν και του πρεσβύτερου Φιλεταίρου, καθώς και μυθικούς ήρωες της Τευθρανίας, από το οποίο σώζονται ενεπίγραφες πλάκες, του ύστερου 3ου αι.: *IG* XI,4 1107–1108 και 1206–1208: Schalles ό.π. (σημ. 49) 127–135. Bringmann – v. Steuben 218, αρ. 172, και γενικά για τα αναθήματα των Ατταλιδών στη Δήλο, 218–226, αρ. 172–182.

57. Πρόκειται για απεικόνιση αγάλματος μιας ενδεδυμένης μορφής με ξίφος (παράσταση Νίκης;) πάνω σε βάθρο με τη λατινική επιγραφή: *Opus Nicerati. Fertur autem imaginem fuisse Eumen<est>is regis*: Marcadé αρ. 81. Πρβ. T. Hölscher, *Victoria Romana* (1967) 14–15. Moreno 263–265, που ανάγουν το συγκεκριμένο έργο του Νικηράτου στους χρόνους του πρεσβύτερου Φιλεταίρου ή και του Ευμένους Α,' αντίστοιχα. Πρβ. Wörrle ό.π. (σημ. 45) 48 σημ. 310. 101 σημ. 620. Αντίθετα, Queyrel ό.π. (σημ. 46) 380, με χρονολόγηση στους πρώιμους χρόνους του Ευμένους Β'. Επίσης ο B. Andreae στο B. Andreae – C.P. Presicce (επιμ.), *Ulisse. Il mito e la memoria* (1996) 69, εικ. 24–25. Στο β' τέταρτο του 3ου αι. τοποθετεί τη δραστηριότητα του Νικηράτου ο Stewart ό.π. (σημ. 28) 7–8, που στηρίζεται κυρίως στη χρονολόγηση ενός γλύπτη Μικίωνος Νικηράτου που εργάστηκε στην Ολυμπία για τον Ιέρωνα των Συρακουσών και τους γιούς του στο γ' τέταρτο του 3ου αι. π.Χ. (Παυσανίας 6.12.4 και 15.6. Πλίνιος, *N.H.* 34.88. Τατιανός, *Adversus Graecos* 52–53). Marcadé, αρ. 76. Ωστόσο, οπωσδήποτε δεν είναι πολύ πιθανό ο πατέρας του Μικίωνος – που έφερε και το εθνικό Συρακόσιος – Νικήρατος, να ήταν ο εν λόγω γλύπτης. Γενικά για το όνομα Νικήρατος στην Αττική, Osborne – Byrne ό.π. (σημ. 46) λ. Nikeratos 332.

58. B. Andreae στο *Eikones. Festschrift H. Jucker*, 12 Beih. *AntK* (1980) 40–48. Andreae 57–100. Η χρονολόγηση του Φυρομάχου συμπαρασύρει για πολλούς ερευνητές και εκείνη του Νικηράτου είτε στο α'μισό του 3ου είτε στο 2ο αι. π.Χ. Βλ. παραπ. σημ. 46 και παρακ. σημ. 62.

59. Για τον Ασκληπιό και τον Αντισθένη, βλ. Andreae ό.π. (σημ.58). Για την ερμηνεία του χωρίου του Πλίνιου, Andreae 62, αρ. 10. 65–70.

60. Για τη χρονολόγηση των έργων αυτών του Φυρομάχου στο β' μισό του 3ου αι. π.Χ., Stewart (ό.π. σημ. 28)

8–16. Ειδικότερα, για το άγαλμα του Αντισθένους, Himmelmann 13. Για την ανασκευή των θέσεων του Andreae βλ. Queyrel ό.π. (σημ. 46) 379–380.

61. Για τη χρονολόγηση του μικρού αναθήματος των Ατταλιδών γύρω στο 200 π.Χ., Pollitt ό.π. (σημ. 21) 91. Queyrel ό.π. (σημ. 46) 371 και σημ. 12. Πρβ. και Queyrel ό.π. (σημ. 45) 278–285. Το μικρό ανάθημα των Ατταλιδών μπορεί να θεωρηθεί επίσης δημιούργημα του εργαστηρίου του Φυρομάχου χωρίς προσωπική συμμετοχή του ίδιου, λίγο πριν από τα μέσα του 2ου αι. π.Χ. Για τη χαμηλή χρονολόγηση με απόδοση στο Μεγάλο Βωμό βλ. Hoepfner ό.π. (σημ. 35) 129 και σημ. 34, εικ. 4 και 14. Με αυτόν τον τρόπο ερμηνεύεται η τεχνοτροπική συγγένεια που επισημαίνει ο Andreae 49–54 και 92–94, ανάμεσα στο κεφάλι του λεγόμενου Γίγαντα από το μικρό ανάθημα στο Μουσείο Νεαπόλεως (εδώ σελ. 122, εικ. 2) και στα άλλα αποδιδόμενα στον Φυρόμαχο έργα που γνωρίζουμε από ρωμαϊκά αντίγραφα.

62. Queyrel ό.π. (σημ. 46) 379. Για την ύπαρξη περισσοτέρων του ενός γλυπτών με το όνομα Φυρόμαχος βλ. Himmelmann *passim.* Queyrel 372–380. Πρβ. και Wenning 44 σημ. 286. Εξάλλου η εξαιρετικά δημιουργική και μακρόχρονη σταδιοδρομία του Φυρομάχου που διαγράφει ο Andreae 89–94, ο οποίος πρόσφατα υποστήριξε τη συμμετοχή του γλύπτη αυτού και στη μεγάλη ζωφόρο του περγαμηνού Βωμού, φαίνεται υπερβολική. Πρβ. Queyrel 371 και σημ. 14.

63. Οπως ορθά επισήμανε ήδη ο Stewart ό.π. (σημ. 28) 7.18. Πρβ. Queyrel ό.π. (σημ. 46) 379–380. Για συνεργασία δασκάλου και μαθητή στο ίδιο έργο βλ. την περίπτωση των γλυπτών Ονάτα και Καλλιτέλους (Παυσανίας 5.27.8 και 10.13.10): E. Walter-Karydi, *Alt-Ägina* II,2 19, αρ. 4. 21, αρ. 9, 23.26. Αν η διαφορά ηλικίας μεταξύ Νικηράτου και Φυρομάχου ήταν περίπου 20 χρόνια, και ο Νικήρατος άρχισε την καριέρα του γύρω στα μέσα του 3ου αι., η συνεργασία του με το Φυρόμαχο μπορεί να τοποθετηθεί γύρω στο 220. Ο Νικήρατος πιθανότατα ολοκλήρωσε την καλλιτεχνική σταδιοδρομία του στη στροφή προς τον 2ο αι.: βλ. παραπ. σημ. 57. Τον Φυρόμαχο η νεώτερη έρευνα αποσυνδέει αποφασιστικά από την ακμή του στην 121η Ολυμπιάδα (296–292) που παραδίδει ο Πλίνιος, *N.H.* 34.51: Andreae 69–70. Πρβ. Himmelmann 21–22.

64. Εκτός από το άγαλμα άλλοτε στο Velletri, το άγαλμα του Βερολίνου προέρχεται από τη λεγόμενη έπαυλη του Μάριου στο Frascati: βλ. παραπ. σημ. 5. Η Υγεία Chiaramonti αγοράσθηκε στην Νεάπολη: C.Pietrangeli, *Bolletino. Monumenti, musei e gallerie Pontificie* 11, 1991, 164.

65. Ο E. Thraemer στο Roscher, *ML* I (1886–1890) 2779 λ. Hygieia, αναγνώρισε το ζεύγος των θεών του Νικηράτου στα συντάγματα Ασκληπιού και Υγείας στην Κοπεγχάγη, Γλυπτοθήκη Ny Carlsberg 535: Holtzmann αρ. 38*. Croissant αρ. 21, και στο Βατικανό 571: Holtzmann αρ. 39. Croissant αρ. 22*, τα οποία θεωρούνται σήμερα ότι αποδίδουν το σύνταγμα του Σκόπα στην αρκαδική Γόρτυνα, 4ου αι. π.Χ. (Παυσ. 8.28.1): Holtzmann. Croissant 59. Επίσης βλ. S. Lattimore, *AJA* 91 (1987) 413. Ο L. Mariani, *BullCom* 42, 1914, 3–12, ταύτισε τα αγάλματα του Νικηράτου με την Υγεία τύπου Broadlands-Conservatori: βλ. παραπ. σημ. 6, και τον Ασκληπιό τύπου Giustini: Holtzmann 894, αρ. 154–233. M. Meyer, *AM* 103, 1988, 119–159, που ανάγονται όμως στον 4ο αι. π.Χ. Επίσης, ο Marcadé αρ. 81 σημ. 2, πρότεινε την ταύτιση με το εκλεκτικό ρωμαϊκό σύνταγμα Ασκληπιού και Υγείας στο Τορίνο: Croissant αρ. 128*.

66. Heiderich 86–96. Becatti *passim* πίν. VI-XII. Την ταύτιση δέχονται επίσης οι Holtzmann 893 και Croissant 570. Για τα μνημεία που παραδίδουν τον αγαλματικό τύπο του Ασκληπιού Pitti: Holtzmann αρ. 382–393. Άγαλμα Pitti: Holtzmann αρ. 382*. Δίπτυχο Gaddi: Holtzmann αρ. 388*.

67. C. Boehringer, *AMuGS* 5, 1972, πίν. 11,2. Stewart ό.π. (σημ. 28) 6, πίν. 2a. Ισως ο τύπος της κεφαλής του Ασκληπιού Pitti αποδίδεται σε νόμισμα της Περγάμου του ύστερου 3ου ή πρώιμου 2ου αι.: Stewart εικ. 7. Η αντίστοιχη κοπή με την κεφαλή της Υγείας ωστόσο θυμίζει ελάχιστα την κεφαλή της Υγείας του Βερολίνου, και δεν φαίνεται να διασώζει τον τύπο της κεφαλής της Υγείας του Νικηράτου. Για τους νομισματικούς τύπους βλ. και C. Boehringer στο *Pergamon Ausstellung, 22. April-4. Juni 1972 in Erinnerung an E. Boehringer* (1972) αρ. M 35 (Ασκληπιός), M 51 (Υγεία).

68. Αρ. ευρ. 737: Stuart Jones, *Mus.Cap.* 347, αρ. 8, πίν. 86. G.M.A. Richter, *The Portraits of the Greeks* II (1965) 185, εικ. 1071. 1074 (περ. 240 π.Χ.). Helbig[4] II, αρ. 1431. Βλ. και C. Zimber, *Studien zu hellenistischen Philosophenporträts* (αδημοσίευτη μεταπτυχιακή εργασία, Βερολίνο, Freie Universität 1988) 24–34, με χρονολόγηση στο 200–180 π.Χ. R. von den Hoff, *AntPl* 25 (1996) 65–73, πίν. 51–58 (περίπου 240 π.Χ.).

69. Για την Υγεία του διπτύχου Gaddi: Heiderich 96–98. Becatti 26–28, πίν. XIII. Croissant αρ. 38* και σ. 570. Για τις υστερότερες μεταπλάσεις της φειδιακής Αφροδίτης Ουρανίας: *LIMC* II (1984) λ. Aphrodite, αρ. 176*-184* σελ. 43 κ.ε., αρ. 307*-316* (A. Delivorrias). Βλ. και την Αφροδίτη τύπου Κάπουας από τον ύστερο 4ο αι. π.Χ.: *LIMC* ό.π. αρ. 627–642. H. Knell, *AntPl* 22 (1993) 117–139, πί. 43–63. Για τον λατρευτικό και εικονογραφικό συγκρητισμό ανάμεσα στην Υγεία και στην Αφροδίτη στους προχωρημένους αυτοκρατορικούς χρόνους, G. de Luca, *IstMitt* 41, 1991, 344 και σημ. 68.

70. Βλ. Becatti 34, πίν. 17,2. Το άγαλμα της Υγείας στο Βερολίνο συνδυαζόταν στο εικονογραφικό πρόγραμμα της έπαυλης όπου βρέθηκε, με ένα άγαλμα Ασκληπιού που εξαρτάται από τον τύπο Pitti σήμερα επίσης στο Βερολίνο Sk 68: Blümel, *KatSkulptBerlin* V (1938) 11, αρ. K 211, πίν. 25. Heiderich 95–96. Holtzmann αρ. 385. Βλ. και σημ. 5.

71. Για τον Ασκληπιό πρβ. τη μορφή του θεού στο αναθηματικό ανάγλυφο Εθνικό Μουσείο 1331: Holtzmann 386. Ακόμη πρβ.τον Ραδάμανθυ στη ζωγραφική σύνθεση της πρόσοψης του μακεδονικού τάφου των Λευκαδιών (πρώιμος 3ος αι.): Φ.Μ. Πέτσας, *Ο Τάφος των Λευκαδίων* (1966) 132–134, πίν. Α',Θ',Γ' και 8. *LIMC* VII (1994) λ. Rhadamanthys, αρ. 3 (M. Xagorari). Ο εικονογραφικός τύπος του θεού απαντά επίσης σε διάφορες παραλλαγές στις ανάγλυφες επιτύμβιους ληκύθους των κλασικών χρόνων: B. Schmaltz, *Untersuchungen zu den attischen*

Marmorlekythen (1970) αρ. A 21, πίν. 11, αρ. A 34, πίν. 15, A 80, πίν. 25, A 99, πίν. 28, A 108, πίν. 30, A 176, πίν. 36. Για την Υγεία βλ. παραπ. σημ. 16. Επίσης, στο επιτύμβιο ανάγλυφο στο Brocklesby Park (παραπ. σημ. 16) συνδυάζεται μία γυναικεία μορφή στον εικονογραφικό τύπο του αγάλματος της Υγείας Conservatori-Βερολίνου με μία ανδρική μορφή στον τύπο του Ασκληπιού Pitti.

72. Αρ. ευρ. 8843: A. Reinach, *REG* 26, 1913, 391–396, εικ. 6; K. Woelcke, *BJb* 120, 1911, 182–188, εικ. 8. E. Pfuhl, *Malerei und Zeichnung der Griechen* II (1923) 816. 892, εικ. 658. Wenning 39 και σημ. 259, πίν. 9,1. Σταμπολίδης ό.π. (σημ. 18) 162, αρ. 8 και σημ. 177, εικ. 24, 141–142 και σημ. 38–40.

73. Την προέλευση αυτή θεώρησε πιθανή ήδη ο Bursian, *SBMünchen* (1854) 172 κ.ε. (όπως αναφέρεται στο Lippold, ό.π. [σημ. 46] 314). Αμφισβήτηση για την προέλευση από την Πέργαμο εκφράζει ο H.v. Fritze, *Die Münzen von Pergamon* (1910) 49 σημ. 1.

74. Το ενεπίγραφο επιστύλιο αυτού του ναού διασώζει το όνομα της Υγείας: C. Habicht, *AvP* VIII 3 (1969) 155, αρ. 158, πίν. 46. G.de Luca στο Andreae, *Phyromachos-Probleme* 39 και σημ. 54. Η ίδια ό.π. (σημ. 69) 333–334 και σημ. 31–32. Ο ναός καταστράφηκε το 201 π.Χ. κατά την επιδρομή του Φιλίππου Ε'της Μακεδονίας: Schalles ό.π. (σημ. 49) 144–145. Πρβ. Stewart ό.π. (σημ. 28) 15, οπότε τίθεται το πρόβλημα τί απέγιναν τα αγάλματα του Ασκληπιού και της Υγείας του Νικηράτου που βρίσκουμε αργότερα στη Ρώμη. Και ο Stewart 14–15, πιστεύει ότι στο ναό αυτό ήταν στημένο ένα ασκληπιακό ζεύγος, τις κεφαλές του οποίου αναγνωρίζει σε ελληνιστικούς νομισματικούς τύπους της Περγάμου: βλ. παραπ. σημ. 67. Η de Luca ό.π. (σημ. 69) 340–345, αναγνωρίζει το λατρευτικό άγαλμα της Υγείας του ναού στο πρωτότυπο της Υγείας τύπου Μόναχο 310: Croissant 566, αρ. 195–205 και σ. 571 (ύστερος 4ος αι. π.Χ.). de Luca 325–332 σημ. 18–21. 346–348, πίν. 39–42.43,1. Ο αγαλματικός τύπος της Υγείας του Μονάχου – που μαρτυρείται στην Πέργαμο, όπως και σε άλλες ελληνικές περιοχές – ανάγεται λόγω της κλειστής σύνθεσής του μάλλον στον πρώιμο 3ο αι. π.Χ., οπότε παρουσιάζεται δυσκολία για την απόδοσή του στον παραπάνω ναό. Πρβ. εξάλλου de Luca 341–342.

75. Πρβ. G. de Luca στο Andreae, *Phyromachos-Probleme* 32. 38–39. Η ίδια ό.π. (σημ. 69) 340–342.

76. Βλ. γενικά de Luca ό.π. (σημ. 75) 34–35. Επίσης πρβ. v. Fritze ό.π. (σημ. 73) 48 για τους συμβατικούς νομισματικούς τύπους του Ασκληπιού στην Πέργαμο. Συμβατικός είναι εξάλλου και ο συνηθέστερος νομισματικός τύπος της Υγείας στην Πέργαμο που την απεικονίζει να ταΐζει το φίδι: v. Fritze πίν. V,12–14. Επίσης η μορφή της Υγείας σε νόμισμα της Περγάμου κοπής του Μάρκου Αυρηλίου δεν αποδίδει ένα περγαμηνό άγαλμα της θεάς, όπως πιστεύει η de Luca ό.π. (σημ. 69) 342–343, αλλά τον υστεροκλασικό αγαλματικό τύπο της λεγόμενης Fortuna Braccio Nuovo: Kabus-Jahn ό.π. (σημ. 1) 33–38, πίν. 7. Nippe ό.π. (σημ. 2). Η γενική εικόνα των λατρευτικών αγαλμάτων στην Πέργαμο δεν είναι καθόλου ξεκαθαρισμένη, και ενδεικτικά αναφέρουμε το πλήθος εικονογραφικών τύπων του Ασκληπιού και το πρόβλημα της σχέσης τους με λατρευτικά οικοδομήματα της πόλεως, συμπεριλαμβανόμενου και του περίφημου αγάλματος του Ασκληπιού του Φυρομάχου. Βλ. σχετικά H.v. Fritze, *Nomisma* II (1908) 19–35. Ο ίδιος ό.π. (σημ. 73) 39–41. 47–54. Stewart ό.π. (σημ. 28) 12–14, εικ. 7a-d. P. Kranz στο *Festschrift N. Himmelmann* (1989) 290–292 και σημ. 18–22.28–30. Για τον Ασκληπιό του Φυρομάχου ειδικότερα πρβ. τις εκ διαμέτρου αντίθετες απόψεις των Andreae 85–89, και E.L. Schwandner στο Andreae, *Phyromachos-Probleme* 41–43, με αυτή του Kranz 289–295, πίν. 47.

77. Η Pape ό.π. (σημ. 44) υποθέτει ότι η μεταφορά στη Ρώμη έγινε λίγο μετά το 133 π.Χ., οπότε το βασίλειο της Περγάμου κληροδοτήθηκε στους Ρωμαίους, ενώ ο Becatti 41, πιστεύει ότι ο Τιβέριος έφερε τα αγάλματα αυτά στη Ρώμη από την Κω ή την Πέργαμο. Η πρώτη άποψη ίσως είναι πιθανότερη, αν λάβουμε υπόψιν μας ότι η μορφή της Valetudo στο δηνάριο του Μν. Ακιλίου Γλαβρίου του 50/49 π.Χ. (Croissant αρ. 39*) παρουσιάζει εξάρτηση από τον αγαλματικό τύπο της Υγείας Conservatori-Βερολίνου, στη στάση, στη διάταξη των ενδυμάτων και στη θέση του φιδιού, παρά τις αλλαγές που επιφέρει το μοτίβο της στήριξής της σε κιονίσκο. Πρβ. H.A. Grueber, *Coins of the Roman Republic in the British Museum* I (1910/1970) 497 σημ. 3, για την άποψη ότι η Valetudo αποδίδει την Υγεία του Νικηράτου. Το ότι τα αγάλματα του Νικηράτου δεν αντιγράφηκαν από τα νεοαττικά εργαστήρια πριν από τους αυτοκρατορικούς χρόνους θα μπορούσε ίσως να αποδοθεί στην έλλειψη ενδιαφέροντος για την περγαμηνή τέχνη πριν από την εποχή του Αυγούστου. Βλ. σχετικά, Fuchs ό.π. (σημ. 15) 78–79.

78. Πρβ. Schweitzer ό.π. (σημ. 46) 406–412. Stewart ό.π. (σημ. 28) 16–17 για τις αττικές ρίζες του περγαμηνού "μπαρόκ." Βλ. και παραπ. σημ. 31.

Tradition and Innovation in Early Pergamene Sculpture

John R. Marszal

Today Pergamon is widely recognized as one of the major centers for the arts in the Hellenistic period, and the reputation is well deserved. The German excavations over the past more than a century have revealed that the Attalid kings spent lavishly to outfit their citadel, city and outlying sanctuaries.[1] Other cities of western Anatolia, even if not directly under Pergamene control, such as Pitane and Kyzikos, received Attalid material and monetary contributions, possibly also royal dedications.[2] Further afield, Pergamene monuments, entire buildings as well as statuary dedications, were erected at the major Hellenic centers; those at Delphi, Delos and especially Athens are the best known,[3] but we should also assume that Olympia, where the horses of an Attalos are said to have won much fame,[4] sported a Pergamene dedication or two. Pergamon's contribution to, and resulting reputation in the arts was truly exceptional. Their achievements seem all the more impressive in the early period, given the small size of the city and its still incipient role on the international political scene.

Today Pergamon is also widely recognized as one of the leading *innovative* centers in the arts, at the latest from the time Attalos I declared himself king, shortly after the middle of the third century B.C. The dedications (and attributed statues), especially those celebrating the victory over the Gauls, have been viewed as the bridge leading directly from the classical and Hellenistic art of Greece to that of Rome, and noted as the key turning points in our periodization of Hellenistic sculpture; they are still credited as playing a crucial role in the development of the Hellenistic baroque, and cited as being among the first to express the pathos and nobility of the fallen (barbarian) enemy.[5]

This second general point, the emphasis on innovation, is questionable, and for several reasons. First, Pergamon has not been adequately viewed against the background of the early Hellenistic period, for the earlier, pre-Pergamene works are not sufficiently, and certainly not comparably preserved. Second, several of the sculptural works generally associated with early Pergamon, and on which the reputation is to a large degree based, including the barbarian statues, are dubious attributions. A third, albeit lesser issue must also be addressed: when considering royal dedications, it is necessary to differentiate the lavish and impressive from the truly innovative.

Before I turn my attention to these points and through them to the monuments, it will be useful to establish the terms of the argument, and take note of a few observations on the subject. First, the time frame – my focus is on the early period of Pergamene production, which I define as extending to the end of or a little beyond the reign of Attalos I, who died in 197 B.C. This termination will leave us before 188, that is before the Battle of Magnesia (Pergamon together with Rome, victorious against the Seleukid king Antiochos III) and the resulting Treaty of Apameia, which left Pergamon with the favor of Rome and in control of much of Anatolia west of the Tauros mountains.[6] With these events Pergamon suddenly achieved the status of a major power. This rise in the fortunes of the kingdom most likely stood behind the extensive building campaigns begun by Eumenes II, which led to the elaborate citadel that is so well-known.

Second, the terms tradition and innovation – the two might seem polar opposites, but are perhaps better viewed as tendencies that lead to varying degrees of change; even a conservative work, unless it is a slavish copy, introduces new qualities or at least presents them in a new arrangement or form, and even the most experimental must to some extent build on established practice. By traditional I mean the production of new works that present relatively minor variations on a theme, ones that fit well within established genres of production. Such conservative practice does not necessarily yield negative results, for works manufactured within a tradition may be masterpieces artistically and politically very assertive. It is clear that most Pergamene works can be understood in the context of the genres commonly in use at the time. Moreover, Pergamon was not alone in erecting such works, for similar, albeit rival monuments were set up also by the older, established centers; it seems arguable that most Hellenistic art is essentially conservative. Innovation, on the other hand, demands a greater departure from the norm; variations may be introduced in response to specific historical circumstance or for artistic reasons, or they may result, quite simply, from a lavish scale of presentation. To judge from the remains and descriptions, the Gallic dedications of Attalos I both at Pergamon and on the Acropolis of Athens quite clearly have special qualities and introduce important variations, regardless of how one ultimately conceives their form.

Third and to conclude this preface, it seems pertinent and necessary to comment at least briefly on the common perception of the Attalid kings in Hellenistic history. Allen, in his study of Pergamene administrative affairs, has quite rightly noted that ancient commentary on the Pergamene rulers is almost invariably favorable, and that this assessment is reflected in the modern approval of the Attalids in politics.[7] The Pergamene rulers were particularly savvy in that they did not too soon or too openly challenge the major Hellenistic powers, and that they maintained generally the good will of Rome. They were commendable for their loyalty to one another, and this loyalty permitted them to avoid the internal conflict that so plagued the other Hellenistic kingdoms. Also, the attendance of the Attalids, as young princes, in the philosophical schools of Athens (the ancient equivalent of the leading modern universities) and their "support for the arts" has permitted us to treat them as a bunch of good fellows, in many ways just like us.[8] This favorable assessment of the Attalids in politics and history has trickled down into the modern treatment of their involvement with the arts, for here too may be perceived an uncritically favorable account. Pergamene art is perceived as very influential and widely copied, even in Hellenistic times, and when the Pergamenes take a statue or two from an older Greek city, it is as collectors and connoisseurs of the arts, but when the Romans do the same, on a larger scale to be sure, it is plunder.[9] We seem too readily to expect and to accept that all good things, and only good things, should flow from this one source.

Turning to the main topic, although it will be difficult absolutely to separate the various lines of the argument, we may begin by reviewing the background of the earlier but now lost pre-Pergamene Hellenistic works. Among the several developments of the early Hellenistic period that may be discerned from the literature and the scant remains, two stand out as particularly noteworthy. First is the emergence of new portrait types, especially that of the dynamic and ultimately divine, although still living ruler; and second is the appearance of a type of *tableaux-vivants*, that is large, multifigured, in the round, sculptural monuments that commemorate the achievements of still living individuals by presenting idealized renderings of the events. In both cases we find an emphasis on the individual and an enhanced specificity of representation that are, to my mind, highly characteristic of the times. In both cases the innovations are very strongly to be linked to the changing forms of art patronage, with the far greater influence of a few powerful individuals, usually the kings and their favorites.

The developments in portraiture were foreshadowed in later Classical art of the very late fifth and fourth centuries, with monuments celebrating the achievements of the still living. Best known and most important perhaps is the Lysander dedication that once stood at Delphi, on which Lysander, one of the reigning kings of Sparta, was crowned by a god for his non-athletic achievement; unfortunately, we cannot assess the individuality of the portrait, for it has long since disappeared.[10] The expression of dynamism and divinity in royal portraiture was achieved as soon as the new patronage system was in place, within the lifetime of Alexander the Great. The dynamic potential was suggested by the dramatic stance, the godlike status by the appropriation of divine attributes, such as the thunderbolt of Zeus in the painting of Alexander by Apelles,[11] possibly also by the use of the colossal scale, even if Deinokrates' suggestion to carve Mount Athos as Alexander may be considered exceptional.[12] One key variation, the sprouting of horns, whether to look like or to express the power and nature of the god, is explored at the latest in works for Alexander's Successors.[13]

The *tableaux-vivants* seem to be new creations of the Hellenistic period. The Granikos monument, commissioned of Lysippos by Alexander, even though it probably did not show the actual combat, may be considered the model for these large multifigured and very specific dedications.[14] The earliest known example certainly to have shown the event is the lion hunt, made by Lysippos and Leochares, that was commissioned by Krateros to celebrate his assistance to Alexander; unfortunately the remains are unimpressive.[15] Within the generation, cavalry battles were also being erected, for example one by Euthykrates, the son and pupil of Lysippos.[16] The multifigured form may find its conceptual precedence in large-scale painting, or in the very specific depiction of royal achievements in Near Eastern art, but again it is only in the Hellenistic period that the specific and individual subject matter comes to the fore in the Greek world. We may consider, for example, the four paintings that were hung about the coffin of Alexander the Great, which showed him in suitably kingly activities.[17]

These earlier, now lost Hellenistic monuments provide the minimal requisite background to the question of Pergamene art. To discuss works that no longer exist, discerning their character and contribution, is always a somewhat curious practice, and I must admit some discomfort in treating the subject in this manner. Yet to dwell on these earlier monuments, as I have, is necessary to be able to confront the power of the images that have been found at or attributed to one art center. The most elaborate of early Hellenistic royal monuments, and many more than those mentioned here, have not survived because they were either delicate (the paintings) or were made of a very recyclable material (the bronze statues).

The most elaborate of Pergamene royal monuments are also now lost, and for the same reasons. Yet the art of Pergamon has retained a much greater visibility. The relatively good state of preservation at the site (when compared to the capitals of the Ptolemies, Antigonids and Seleukids), the reconstruction of highly visible and standard textbook monuments (such as the Stoa of Attalos in the Athenian Agora) and the attribution of several very well-known statues (especially the Gauls, which are again standard textbook monuments) give to the Pergamene dedications a palpability that no other Hellenistic center can hope to match.

Such visibility can too easily lead to a misreading of, by over-emphasizing, the importance of any art tradition. The assessment of Pergamon, discernible in current scholarship, has exactly this positivistic quality, for it too directly connects-the-dots from the restrained works of the Greek classical period to the known and presumed known monuments of the Attalid kings. Even if the commonly attributed statues are pertinent, the current view of early Pergamon is skewed and in need of review.

The other side of the argument considers the works actually or allegedly produced for the Pergamene kings, the statues and statuary attributions. I begin with some of the less problematic pieces.

The portraits of the Attalids present the usual difficulties of precise identification and date, yet as examples within the genre of Hellenistic royal portraiture they have been well discussed and are well understood.[18] Among the early Pergamene portraits may be detected a limited range of styles. Mature male figures seem not to be overly idealized. The bust from the Villa of the Papyri, generally identified as Philetairos, has relatively small facial features set into a massive structure, as also found on the coin portraits.[19] The very large, even verging on colossal head from Pergamon, commonly recognized as Attalos I (Fig. 1), possesses a similar fleshiness.[20] Both are dramatically turned, in the manner of Alexander, but eschew the most obvious characteristics of divinity, excepting of course the size of the Attalos head. Women and youths are more strongly idealized, as seemed proper to their depiction. A queen, possibly Apollonis, is of a scale comparable to the Attalos and may have been displayed together with it.[21] Several unidentified young princes, for example one wearing the royal diadem, have been found on the site and might belong to the early period, although the idealization leaves these figures unfortunately difficult to date.[22]

These portraits are excellently manufactured pieces, presumably expressing the will of the ruling family. Some may indeed have been part of a family display, as such practice was not out of keeping with the period.[23] Although these portraits are stylistically restrained, they may be understood as being quite assertive politically. The issue of coins with the portrait of Philetairos may be read as a statement on the independence of the city and could have been perceived by the Seleukids as an affront; such practice became possible only after the victory of Eumenes

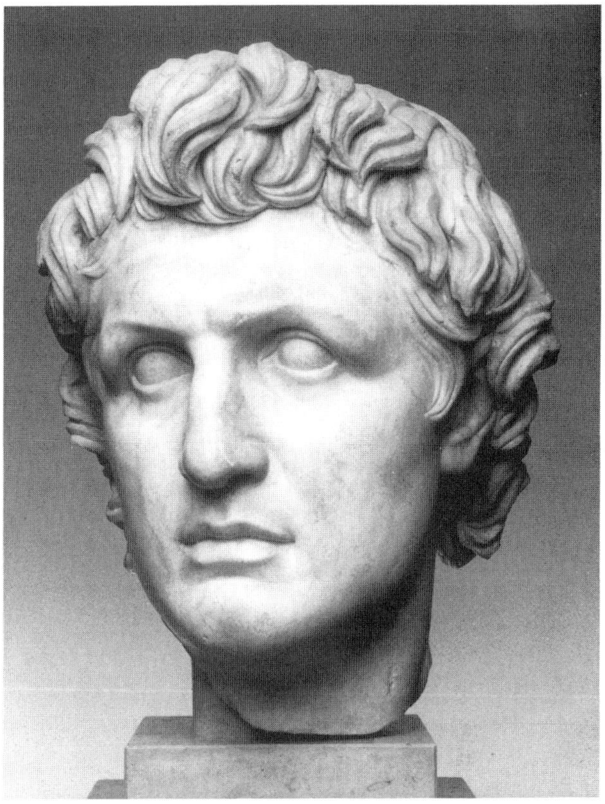

Fig. 1. Head of Attalos I (?). Berlin, Pergamonmuseum P 130. From Pergamon. Photo after Die Antikensammlung im Pergamonmuseum und in Charlottenburg *(1992) no. 71.*

I against Antiochos I in 261, and because Seleukid attention was diverted from the small Pergamene state by the difficulties of ruling the east. With the scale of the Attalos portrait, it is clear that he wanted to make his newly acquired royal status known to all. A similar intent likely stood behind the dedication of portrait statues of the king or the ancestors, known today only from the bases, especially when erected at the major Hellenic sanctuaries, such as Attalos on a pillar before his stoa at Delphi,[24] or the figures of the Philetairos base, signed by Nikeratos of Athens,[25] and the Teuthrania Monument(s?) on Delos.[26]

Similar qualities may be recognized in the statues of gods, heroes and the favorite philosophers, although here it is even more difficult to ascertain, whether the surviving and attributed works are to be dated to the period under consideration. A few examples will have to suffice.

A colossal head of Herakles found at Pergamon (here pp. 129–130, Figs. 1–3) is probably best set here; it is certainly an impressive piece, yet whatever its correct date, it is hardly to be viewed as an experimental work, for it exhibits features that are generally associated with the style of Lysippos.[27] Nikeratos worked for the Attalids also at Pergamon, and possibly made the Asklepios and Hygieia there that were later taken to Rome, but nothing remains to tell us about their appearance and not any of the attributions is secure.[28] More physical evidence survives concerning the works of Phyromachos of Athens, a younger contemporary and co-worker of Nikeratos, whose career spans the reigns of Attalos I and Eumenes II.[29] Phyromachos made a statue of Asklepios for the extramural sanctuary of the god sometime before the attack in 156 by Prousias of Bithynia.[30] The statue may have stood until late antiquity and was considered a most impressive work, yet bronze civic coins of Pergamon show the god standing in a common pose and with his usual attributes. Another coin shows the god's head, with strongly marked features (probably enhanced on the coin) and with thick hair and beard, as is not uncommon at the time for mature male divinities.[31] An inscription discovered at Ostia tells us that Phyromachos also created a portrait of Antisthenes; the well-known portrait series of the philosopher has subsequently been ascribed to him.[32] Yet it is difficult to know whether the known copies reflect his version of the philosopher, and if the statue was indeed a new creation, or one merely updated by the addition of luxuriously turbulent locks (as had been done for the type B of Sokrates, commonly assigned to Lysippos).[33]

Finally and most importantly, we turn to the monuments of Attalos I that commemorated his military achievements, both those erected at Pergamon, in the Athena sanctuary in the 230s and 220s, and those on the Acropolis of Athens at the very end of the century. I begin with the set at Pergamon.

The two monuments raised by Attalos I in the Athena sanctuary of the Pergamene acropolis to celebrate his military achievements are well-known. One stood on a large round base near the middle of the sanctuary; the other, a long battle monument that was divided into sections, one for each victory, stood on a base parallel to the old south wall and its foundations are still in situ (Fig. 4).[34] The two statues, both found at Rome, that have stood behind all attempts to visualize these dedications are equally well-known, the Ludovisi Group of a Gallic chieftain killing himself and his wife in the Palazzo Altemps and the Dying Trumpeter in the Capitoline.[35] The two were identified as Gauls early in the nineteenth century; attributed to the Pergemene school, as originals, by Brunn in 1853, even before the excavation of the site had begun; and associated with the dedications, as copies, shortly after the first excavation reports were made public.[36] All other attributions to the monuments are based on an assessed similarity to these two.[37] Even more importantly, these statues stand at the core of the modern perception of early Pergamene art. They present a naturalism in the depiction of the barbarian type that has become virtually synonymous with the Pergamene style. They render the pathos and nobility of the figures, even though they depict a defeated and barbarian foe.

The two statues have been variously connected to the bases. Schober (whose reconstruction is best known), Coarelli (in a slight variation) and Andreae (although he has not published the details of his version) have suggested compositions on the round base.[38] Künzl, Wenning and Schalles have proposed slightly varying ways of aligning the figures (although only Künzl has provided us with a reconstruction drawing) one in each section of the long battle monument.[39] But neither association is credible, for the statues do not suit the scale of the monuments. Each figure stands about two meters tall, a common height for free-standing mythological or honorary statuary of the time, and head-and-shoulders taller than the average Greek; I consider such statues to be "heroically" proportioned. The scale is certainly appropriate to the subject, but it leaves the figures too small for the round base, which typologically demands a colossal figure (or figures) and too big for the battle monument, which to judge from the remains, specifically the two at least partially preserved "footprints" (I shall consider these momentarily), had figures about life-size.

In addition to the difficulty of scale, many of the commonly presented justifications for attribution are problematic. Brunn's arguments on the originality of the statues and his view of the pertinent history were logical in the mid-nineteenth century, but cannot be maintained today. Attempts to explain when and where the figures were "copied" are unsatisfactory, and the marble type, even if the often suggested Anatolian provenance is correct, is unmatched at Pergamon.[40] The image of barbarian suicide is otherwise unattested until the historically justified suicide of Decebalus on Trajan's Column.[41] The attribution is dubious at best, even though these figures have been long and often linked to Pergamon, they must disappear not only from our consideration of the dedications, but also from our assessment of Pergamene art in general.

Fortunately, the bases provide important clues to the figural display. The large round base imitates in its dedication to Athena, its scale and location before the temple the base of the Pheidian Athena Promachos on the Athenian Acropolis. It seems likely, as has been frequently posited, that a similarly colossal statue of the goddess, inspired by the Promachos, once stood on the base.[42] An imitation of the Pheidian Athena would not be artistically new, we should nonetheless recognize the monument as being surprisingly presumptuous politically, especially since it appeared so early in the reign of Attalos, and it does give an interesting twist to a developing iconography. The defeat of the Gauls had already been given a special significance as the victory of Greek civilization over barbarity, and compared to the Greek achievement against the Persians. The Aitolians who defended Delphi commemorated their victory by hanging Gallic shields (very similar in shape to Persian ones) on the architrave of the temple of Apollo at Delphi, where the Persian shields from Marathon had already long hung, and there was established at Delphi a festival of the Soteria.[43] Ptolemy II, who had beaten some of his own Gallic mercenaries, admittedly rebellious, cited divine precedent and had his deed compared to the victory of the gods over the Titans.[44] All such equations are clear reflections of an overblown history, for the Gauls did not constitute a threat to Greek civilization comparable to that of the Persians, and far less than that of the Titans.

The imitation of Athens (with respect to the Athena cult) was already a well established practice in the Greek cities of western Asia, but Pergamon may have been the first to quote Athens in this way, mimicking a monument (itself rather ostentatious) raised specifically to celebrate the Battle of Marathon. By comparing their victory to Marathon, they set it, as the Athenians had done, into a sequence leading from the mythological past of gods and heroes directly to the recent event. The model of Marathon is more obvious for the Attalid dedication at Athens, but it seems to be also implied here. A colossal statue would have appeared even more dramatic in the Pergamene Athena sanctuary, where it would have dominated the much smaller precinct and temple.

The imitation of Athens may seem odd for a Hellenistic king, for our perception of Athens is strongly shaped by the city's role as the leading democratic state of ancient Greece, but in antiquity the Athenians were more famous for their learning (which was not necessarily democratic) and for their military prowess. After the Persian wars, Athens had been one of the leading powers of Greece and it was the first Greek state successfully to establish an empire. The Pergamenes, even after defeating the Gauls, could not claim such a status, but a monument like this one suggests that they considered it highly desirable.

Attalos' battle dedication on the long base, made by the local Pergamene artist Epigonos, should likely be included among the actual representations of battle, as is suggested by Pliny's brief comment on the Pergamene *proelia*.[45] As such, it follows comfortably within the genre of *tableaux-vivants*. For this monument it is particularly unfortunate that so much emphasis has been laid on the supposedly pertinent statues, for it has distracted from the truly unusual, perhaps even singular features of this dedication, obvious from the remains of the base, that reflect its historically justified variation on the theme of the battle.

The base provides evidence in two forms, the inscriptions and the attachment traces for the bronze statues. The inscriptions are presented at two levels, a dedication by Attalos at one end for the entire display, and along the length, the mention of several battles, six preserved and eight commonly postulated against not only the Gauls but also Antiochos Hierax and the generals of a Seleukos, probably III, in sections divided by shallowly cut stripes.[46] The two fragmentary capping blocks show two footprints for the attachment of the figures, one circular for the setting of a horse's hoof, the other, only half preserved, oblong for a human foot.[47] The remains suggest that the conflicts were in some manner actually depicted, probably between cavalry and foot soldiers, and that the figures were about life-size;[48] these features should not be seen as unusual. From a distance the battle would have appeared unified. But the division of the monument into sections must demand a fragmentation of the battle scene. Since each section was to be read independently, the image cannot have been so complex as to have fallen figures sprawled across the entire composition, like those on the Alexander Sarcophagus (here p. 282, Figs. 1–2); rather the battle must have appeared as a series of independent skirmishes, more like a line-up of grave stelai, with the figures grouped in two's or three's, and with a Pergamene victor in each section. This fragmentation is curious and the universality of the victory may be new; it is certainly not evident in battle scenes of the Classical period, although it is impossible to assess this quality on the earlier, now lost Hellenistic examples.

The Athenian dedication of Attalos I is for me the most difficult to imagine, despite the seemingly precise comments of Pausanias, who mentions four mythological and historical battles (against the giants, amazons at Athens, Persians at Marathon and Gauls in Mysia), as well as the two-cubit dimension.[49] The four battle groups were erected near, not on, the south wall, probably ca. 200 B.C., when Attalos visited the city and was hailed as an eponymous hero.[50] There is a similar pattern in the scholarship concerning this dedication, beginning with the attribution of statues of appropriate subject and scale, and then proceeding to the reconstruction principles.[51] But again there are problems with the statuary attributions. Particularly difficult for these figures is the so-called Asiatic marble, and the related questions of when and where the "copying" might have occurred, since the originals were still standing on the Acropolis of Athens when Pausanias passed through the city in the 160s or 170s A.D. The hypothesis of a second set at Pergamon is not convincing, and the marble is still unmatched there.[52] The most comprehensive study of the figures is by Palma, who listed 42 statues and variants, but accepted only ten as likely to belong;[53] it seems that size and subject are not sufficient to guarantee pertinence. Moreover, her accepted ten are questionable; a few examples will suffice to demonstrate.

The "Persian" in Aix wears a garment without sleeves, very curious for a Persian, and has the flaps of his hat (if there are flaps at all) drawn up, more in the style of a Dacian.[54] Of the three figures in Venice, one, already deceased, seems properly a Gaul wearing only a belt, but the older, bearded barbarian wears an exomis that is stylistically much like the tunic of Decebalus on Trajan's Column and he falls into the same position, his hand resting on a conveniently located rock;[55] there is a conflation of barbarian traits that could not have occurred before Roman Imperial times. Even the crucial set of four figures in Naples with the proper four subjects (giant [Fig. 2], amazon, Persian and Gaul [Fig. 3]) is problematic.[56] The Persian costume is again curiously sleeveless and cap unusually fastened; and the hair of the amazon does not respond to gravity, falling to her shoulders and not the ground. Although I suspect that these statues are likely to have been inspired ultimately from the Attalid dedication (with the Romans substituting themselves as

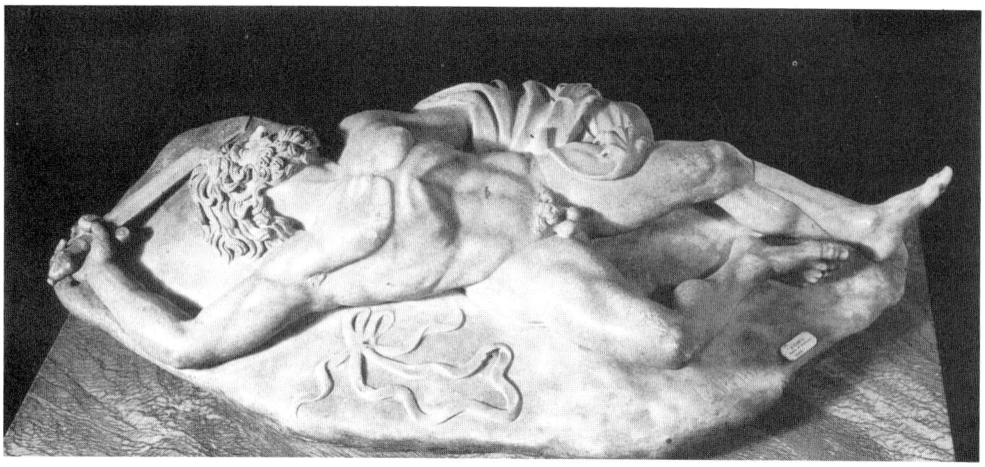

Fig. 2. Giant. Naples, Museo Nazionale 6013.
Photo after Le collezioni del Museo Nazionale di Napoli *(1989) 48.*

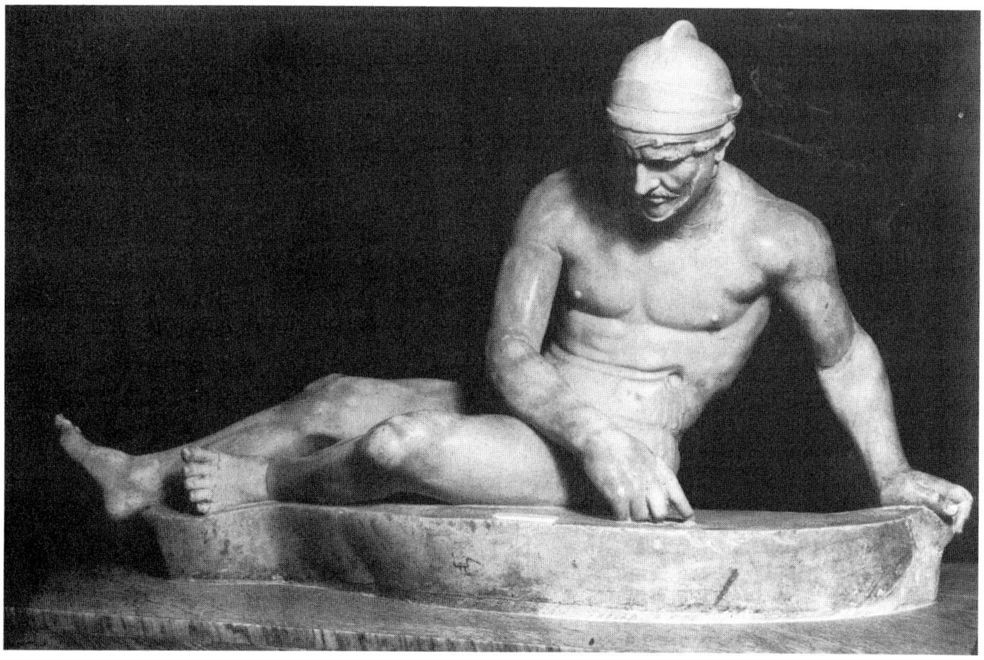

Fig. 3. Gaul. Naples, Museo Nazionale 6014.
Photo after Le collezioni del Museo Nazionale di Napoli *(1989) 46.*

the final defenders of civilization), they cannot be assessed as accurate copies of the lost figures. Since there is no trace of the base and the "copies" are not useful, the questions of the composition (the number and arrangement of the figures, and the presence or absence of the victors) are moot, and all attempts to restore the monument from these figures, or to date it from their style, cannot convince.[57]

Yet the description of Pausanias does make it clear that this dedication was inspired by those celebrating the Athenian victory at Marathon. The presentation of battles in a sequence from the mythological to the recent past was originally an Athenian practice. Even the scale that has been considered so unusual may well have been inspired from the Athenian monuments; two cubits is about the size of the figures on the shield of the Athena Parthenos (perhaps also on that of the Promachos) or on the metopes of the Parthenon. The monument, whatever its form, may not have been artistically innovative, but it does seem to have been lavish and with it Attalos could express his desired position in the post-Alexander Hellenistic world.

In conclusion – the monuments of Pergamon from the beginning of its independence should be recognized as lavish and politically assertive, although not as the crux artistically innovative works of the time. It is no con-

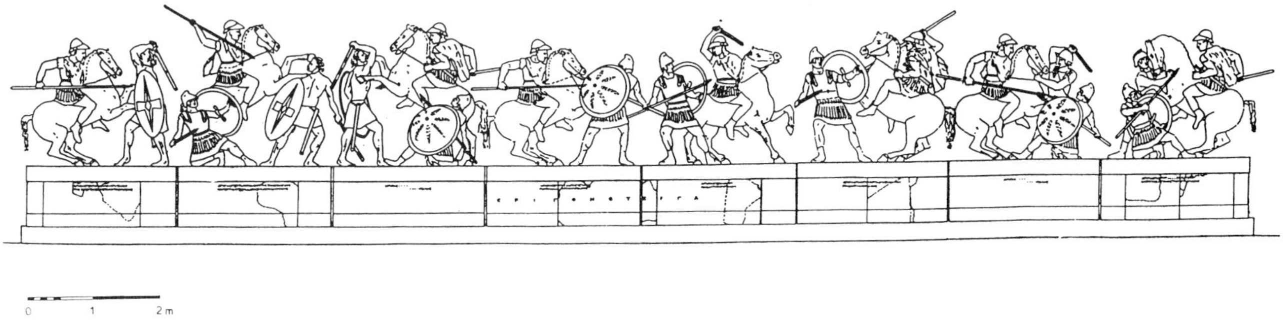

Fig. 4. Pergamon Battle Monument, reconstruction author.

demnation that the Pergamenes were not the first to commission such monuments, for they were *opsigonoi*, that is, late-comers into the world of the Hellenistic kings. And very much to their credit, we must acknowledge that they certainly made up for the late start and added a number of their own distinctive variations in at least one genre of production, the *tableaux-vivants*. The works seem, however, to have been very assertive politically, showing the new-found status of the Pergamene rulers, and eventually kings, for all the world to see. This political function, rather than the purely artistic, even though they sought the leading artists of the day, probably lies closer to the thinking of the Attalids as they commissioned their monuments.

Turning back to the theme of the conference, the question of schools, I must present a negative conclusion, for the type of commemorative monuments ordered by the Pergemene kings, within the established genres of production, or imitative of earlier, specifically Athenian, works will not allow us readily to identify them as products of a distinctive Hellenistic school. The sculpture of Pergamon, at least in its early phase, is not to be distinguished from others of the time. There is, however, a positive side to this conclusion. Specific historical circumstance, local traditions and the personality of the individual patrons would strongly influence the exact form of production. Yet if the School of Pergamon is viewed as somewhat less experimental than it usually is, its production may be considered more typical of the Hellenistic period and thus more valuable to help us envision the many lost works of the less well-preserved centers.

Abbreviations

Bringmann	W. Ameling – K. Bringmann – B. Schmidt-Dounas in K. Bringmann – H.v. Steuben (edd.), *Schenkungen hellenistischer Herrscher an griechische Städte und Heiligtümer* I (1995)
IvP	M. Fraenkel, *Die Inschriften von Pergamon*, *AvP* VIII 1–2 (1890–95)
Moreno	P. Moreno, *Scultura ellenistica* (1994)
Schober, *KvP*	A. Schober, *Die Kunst von Pergamon* (1951)

Notes

This text both draws from and responds to my dissertation, *The Representation of the Gauls in the Hellenistic and Roman Imperial Periods* (Bryn Mawr 1991), in which I concluded that the several well-known statues of the Gauls could not be copies of Pergamene originals. Having worked, theoretically, with Pergamon for so long, I wished to understand the sculpture and so turned to the works excavated at the site, and to the remains of the statuary bases, both at Pergamon and abroad. It is curious how seldom the original sculpture of Pergamon is illustrated and discussed (excepting, of course, that associated with the Great Altar and a few portrait heads, notably that identified as Attalos). I have an article ready for publication with my reconstructions of the victory monuments of Attalos I, and hope soon to find a journal willing to take it.

I have not attempted to provide full references for each statue or argument, rather a selection of the original, important, accessible and recent opinions.

1. J.J. Pollitt, *Art in the Hellenistic Age* (1986) 79–110, for a concise summary of the art; Schober, *KvP*, for a more comprehensive view; W. Radt, *Pergamon* (1988) for a good account of the site as a whole.
2. Pitane, money: *OGIS* 335; *IG* XII Suppl. 142; Bringmann, 295, no. 257.

   Kyzikos, money, horses, grain, freedom from taxes: *OGIS* 748; Bringmann, 272–274, no. 241 E1; and a temple of Apollonis, possibly erected by Eumenes II and Attalos II: *AP* 3 (introduction to the epigrams 1–19); Bringmann, 424–426, no. 355, considers Attalid participation doubtful, despite the Attalid tradition of building dedications.
3. The best known Attalid gifts were the stoai, certainly at Delphi and Athens, and possibly on Delos; for the statuary infra nn. 24–26.

   Delphi, Stoa of Attalos I: J.J. Coulton, *The Architectural Development of the Greek Stoa* (1976) 234, fig. 61,2; G. Roux, *La terrasse d'Attale I, FdD* II (1987); J.-F. Bommelaer, *Guide de Delphes. Le site* (1991) 191–195, nos. 402–405; 501–503, figs. 80–81; A. Jacquemin – D. Laroche, *BCH* 116, 1992, 229–258; Bringmann, 143–146, no. 91, figs. 48–53.

   Athens, Stoa of Eumenes II: Vitruvius 5.9.1; Coulton 225, fig. 55,6; M. Korres in *Bauplanung und Bautheorie der Antike, DiskAB* 4 (1983) 201–207, demonstrates that the major building elements were finished at Pergamon of local marble and shipped to Athens; Bringmann 62–

63, no. 28, figs. 6–7; and: Stoa of Attalos II: *OGIS* 318; *IG* II^2 317; Coulton 219, fig. 54,10; Bringmann 63–66, no. 29, figs. 9–14.

Delos, South Stoa: Coulton 234, fig. 60,12; P. Bruneau – J. Ducat, *Guide de Délos* (1983) 118, no. 4, fig. 17,4; Bringmann 477–478, no. 415.

4. *IvP* 10–12; Diogenes Laertios 4.6.30.
5. Literature on the monuments is difficult to characterize, for it is complex with the many subtle variations in the arguments. Virtually every statue of a Gaul, and many representations of barbarians (even those on Roman historical reliefs) have been linked to these as originals, copies, or works under the influence; on Pergamene influence, e.g. P.R.v. Bienkowski, *Die Darstellung der Gallier in der hellenistischen Kunst* (1908) 29–36; 79–85, suggests the Pergamene statues stand behind the galatomachies on Etruscan sarcophagi; B. Andreae, *Motivgeschichtliche Untersuchungen zu den römischen Schlachtsarkophagen* (1956) 74–83, sees a Pergamene painting as the model for Roman battle sarcophagi; R. Wenning, *Die Galateranatheme Attalos I. Eine Untersuchung zum Bestand und Nachwirkung pergamenischer Skulptur, PF* 4 (1978) 52–63, finds Pergamene motifs in Trajanic reliefs; H.P. Laubscher, *AntK* 30, 1987, 138–140, dates a colossal head of a Gaul in Cairo before the Pergamon monuments but reconstructs the figure as suicidal, on the model of the Ludovisi group. For a discussion that sets Pergamene representation of the Gauls into the broader context of Hellenistic production, J.R. Marszal in N.T. de Grummond and B.S. Ridgway (edd.), *Pergamon and Sperlonga: Sculpture in Context* (forthcoming).

   G. Krahmer, *RM* 38/39, 1923/24, 138–184, remains a crucial discussion of the chronology; he viewed the "large Gauls" as the turning point monument between the early quiet style of Hellenistic sculpture and the ensuing baroque. Although his periodization has been critiqued, the beginning of the baroque is still often set very close to his proposal; B.S. Ridgway, *Hellenistic Sculpture* I (1990) 5–6, for a sound commentary on chronology.
6. The death of Attalos I is the usual point of division between the first and second Schools of Pergamene sculpture (for the moment leaving the final period aside), e.g. Schober, *KvP* 49–76/77–120; Moreno, 255–319; 415–499. Moreno provides the fullest account of the sculpture of the early period, which is extremely useful for recent bibliography, but I find him somewhat optimistic in the attribution game.
7. R.E. Allen, T*he Attalid Kingdom. A Constitutional History* (1983) 9.
8. M.I. Finley, foreword to P.E. Easterling – J.V. Muir (edd.), *Greek Religion and Society* (1985) xviii, comments on the tendency to view at least the educated elite of the Greeks as "good chaps basically like us," and the difficulties thus created for understanding ancient Greek society. Cf. also J. Gould, ibid., 1–33.
9. Radt (supra n. 1) 312–315; H.-J. Schalles in *Akten des XIII. internationalen Kongresses für klassische Archäologie, Berlin 1988* (1990) 598, who also promises a comprehensive study, on the Pergamene collections. Pollitt (supra n. 1) 150–155, on Roman "acquisition" of Greek works. Supra n. 5, on Pergamene influence.
10. Lysander Dedication: Pausanias 10.9.7–9; Plutarch, *Lysander* 18.1; J.-F. Bommelaer, *BCH* 95, 1971, 43–64; id. (supra n. 3) 108–110, no. 109, fig. 37.
11. Pliny, *NH* 35.92.
12. Vitruvius 2, praef. 2.
13. E.g. the well-known coin portraits of Alexander minted by Ptolemy I and Lysimachos: R.R.R. Smith, *Hellenistic Royal Portraits* (1988) 12–13, pl. 74, 1 and 4. Smith 40–41, for comments on horn types and use.
14. Granikos Monument: Pliny, *NH* 34.64; Arrian, *Anabasis* 1.16.4; Velleius Paterculus 1.11.3; Plutarch, *Alexander* 16.7; G. Calcani, *Cavalieri di bronzo, La torma di Alessandro, opera di Lisippo* (1989); B.S. Ridgway, *JRA* 4, 1991, 206–209; Bringmann, 179–181, no. 112.
15. Krateros Monument: Pliny, *NH* 34.64; Plutarch, *Alexander* 40.4–5; *FdD* III 4, 137; F. Courby, *La Terrasse du temple, FdD* II (1927) 237–240, figs. 187–191; Bommelaer (supra n. 3) 225–227, no. 540, fig. 99; C. Saatsoglou-Paliadeli, *Egnatia* 1, 1989, 79–100; Bringmann, 141–143, no. 90. See also Palagia in this volume, p. 21.
16. Pliny, *NH* 34.66.
17. Diodoros 18.26.3.
18. Smith (supra n. 13) 9–53, on the character and function of royal portraiture.
19. Philetairos bust, Naples, Museo Nazionale 6148: Schober, *KvP* 51–52, fig. 4; Smith (supra n. 13) 74–75; 159, no. 22, pl. 17; A. Stewart, *Greek Sculpture: An Exploration* (1990) 205, figs. 662–663; Moreno 259–262, figs. 333; 380. Coin portraits: Schober, *KvP* 27; 52, figs. 2–3; U. Westermark, *Das Bildnis des Philetairos von Pergamon. Corpus der Münzprägung* (1961); Smith 74, pl. 74,12; Stewart 205, fig. 664; Moreno 260, fig. 332.
20. Berlin, Pergamonmuseum P 130: Schober, *KvP* 117–118, fig. 92; Smith (supra n. 13) 79–81; 160, no. 28, pls. 22–23,1; Stewart (supra n. 19) 209, figs. 680–682.
21. Berlin, Pergamonmuseum P 87: Schober, *KvP* 136, fig. 123; Smith (supra n. 13) 81; 160, no. 29, pl. 23,2.
22. Berlin, Pergamonmuseum P 137: Schober, *KvP* 135; 143, fig. 120; Smith (supra n. 13) 79; 176, no. 113, pl. 64,1–2.
23. Family groups seem an effective means to present the dynastic legitimacy of a royal house. They appeared at the latest by the time of Philip II, e.g. in the Philippeion at Olympia with Philip, his son, wife and parents rendered in gold and ivory (Paus. 5.20.9–10). Pergamene family groups may appear on Delos, infra nn. 25–26. B. Hintzen-Bohlen, *JdI* 105, 1990, 129–154. J.-P. Niemeier, *Kopien und Nachahmungen im Hellenismus* (1985) 164–165, suggested, rhetorically, that a very large, verging on colossal, head of Herakles (infra n. 27; here pp. 129–136, Figs. 1–3) joined the Attalos head as a divine ancestor; although the idea seems attractive and gods and mortals may appear together on a monument (Lysander dedication, supra n. 10), the inclusion of a mythological progenitor with a mortal ruler is otherwise unattested (cf. infra n. 26) and should be treated with caution.
24. Delphi, Pillar of Attalos I: Bommelaer (supra n. 3) 193, no. 404; B. Schmidt-Dounas, *Egnatia* 1, 1989, 117–118; Jacquemin – Laroche (supra n. 3) 231–233; 244–246, figs. 12–13a; Bringmann 447. The pillar has long been

perceived as a monument for but not by Attalos I, since it bore an amphiktyonic inscription (*FdD* III3, 238) that mentioned the image of Attalos, but Jacquemin – Laroche have demonstrated that the pillar was likely part of the original plan, and thus Attalid. Bringmann 404; 447; Schmidt-Dounas, 101–125, deny that any king erected his own image, preferring always to see the contribution of a local individual or council. They may be right in general, but carry the hypothesis too far, for they even deny the contribution of Philip to the Philippeion at Olympia (Paus. 5.20.9–10, supra n. 23), citing a locally funded Philippeion at Megalopolis (Paus. 8.30.6). But Pausanias seems capable of distinguishing, in exactly this case, royal from local (non-royal) contributions.

25. Delos, Philetairos base (with signature of Nikeratos): *IG* XI.4, 1105; J. Marcadé, *Recueil des signatures de sculpteurs grecs* II (1957) 79; Bruneau – Ducat (supra n. 3) 128, no. 10; Moreno 262–263. The base is ca. 8 m long and so may be restored as having 7–8 standing figures, including a Philetairos. The suggestion that the Gaul from Delos (Athens NM 274) was once located on it (P. Wolters *AM* 15, 1890, 188–198; Bienkowski [supra n. 5] 28; M. Bieber, *The Sculpture of the Hellenistic Age*[2] [1961] 107, figs. 420–422) is denied by the attachment traces of quietly standing figures (cf. Marcadé for an illustration).

    There is considerable controversy about the identity of the Philetairos honored and the date (which Pergamene king stood behind Sosikrates in the dedication). E.g. F. Chamoux, *REG* 101, 1988, 498–499; and Moreno 262–263, suggest that Philetairos, founder of the dynasty, had the monument erected in his own honor, before 261. Marcadé; A. Stewart, *Attika. Studies in Athenian Sculpture of the Hellenistic Age* (1979) 7–8; id. (supra n. 19) 302–303, date the monument after 261, or about mid-century. Bienkowski (supra n. 5) 28; A. Schober, *ÖJh* 31, 1939, 142–149; *KvP* 124–126, identify Philetairos as the younger brother of Eumenes II and Attalos II and date Nikeratos to the second century.

    It seems most likely that the monument celebrated Philetairos the founder and that it was erected in the reign of Attalos I. Letter styles suggest a third-century date, but are inconclusive, for similar letter forms were employed at Pergamon (intentionally recalling earlier monuments?) in the time of Attalos III, cf. *IvP* 245–248. In the inscription the honored Philetairos is called *makar*, blessed, suggesting that he had died, and *anax*, great king. It seems unlikely that any ruler of Pergamon would be called *anax* before Attalos assumed the royal title, and unlikely that a younger brother who never ruled would be so labeled (or said to have *mega kratos*). Chamoux and Moreno note that Agamemnon was called *makar* in his life-time (*Iliad* 3.182) but Agamemnon was recognized as a *basileus* and *anax* in his life, while Philetairos was only *kurios tou frouriou kai ton hrematon* (Strabo 13.4.1; 623), master of the fortress and the money. A date in the reign of Attalos I would permit another signature of Nikeratos at Pergamon (Marcadé II, 81) on a monument of king Eumenes, now lost, to pertain to Eumenes II, which would justify the royal title of the inscription. On Nikeratos' other literarily attested works, Lippold, *Plastik* 320–321; Overbeck, *Schriftquellen* 917–920. On his relation to Phyromachos and the debate on the latter's dates, infra nn. 29; 31. See also Leventi in this volume, pp. 101–116.

26. Delos, Teuthrania Monument: *IG* XI.4, 1107–1108; 1206–1208; A. Wilhelm, *AM* 39, 1914, 148–156; L. Robert in *Etudes Déliennes, BCH* Suppl. 1 (1973) 478–485; Bringmann 218–221, no. 172, figs. 97–105. Wilhelm first identified the three inscriptions (1206–1208) as referring to Mysian heroes, Midios, Teuthras and Phaleros, and linked them to those of two Pergamene rulers, Eumenes I and Attalos I. The script character is similar, but the letters are not the same size, 0.014 m (1107–1108) and ranging between 0.016–0.022 m (1206–1208), and the blocks with ruler incriptions have a recessed band at the bottom. Athough the two sets may have been cut at about the same time and displayed in proximity, they do not form part of a single monument. Nonetheless, we have ruler portraits presenting a dynastic sequence, as well as Mysian heroes, set up somewhere on the island.

27. Berlin, Pergamonmuseum 1675: E. Rohde, *Pergamon. Burgberg und Altar* (1982) 134, fig. 114; Pollitt (supra n. 1) 110, fig. 110; Damaskos in this volume, pp. 129–136, Figs. 1–3. The head is commonly dated in the second century, for it has a classicizing quality, but imitation of a Classical style should not be so limited chronologically.

28. Pliny *NH* 34.80. Moreno 795 n. 515, lists the attributions. On the Vatican-Berlin (Belvedere) type Hygieia see Leventi in this volume, pp. 101–116, Figs. 1–8.

29. Phyromachos signed together with Nikeratos on Delos (Marcadé II, 82), Kyzikos (H. Lauter, *Zur gesellschaftlichen Stellung des bildenden Künstlers in der griechischen Klassik* [1974] 19 n. 45) and possibly at Pergamon (*IvP* 132–134); both were Athenians, and Phyromachos seems to be the younger; Stewart (supra n. 25) 7, suggested that Nikeratos was the teacher, possibly even the father of Phyromachos.

    On Phyromachos' other literarily attested works, Lippold, *Plastik* 321; Overbeck, *Schriftquellen* 921; 1994; 1998–2001; F. Queyrel, *RA* 1992, 367–380, gives a good account of the sources on the two or three sculptors named Phyromachos.

30. Polybios 32.15; Diodoros 31.35.

31. H.v. Fritze, *Die Münzen von Pergamon* (1910) 41–42, pl. 1,15 and 17; C. Boehringer in *Pergamon Ausstellung in Erinnerung Erich Boehringer* (1972) nos. M43; M49; Stewart (supra n. 25) 13–14, pl. 7 c–d. Pergamene coins also show a seated image of the god: Fritze pl. 1,29; Boehringer M32; Stewart pl. 7 a. Both are said to be inspired after cult statues. Some scholars have favored the seated version as that of Phyromachos, e.g. Fritze 41–42, although most, I believe rightly, prefer the standing type.

    The statue was certainly created before 156, but how long before is controversial. The extramural sanctuaries of Pergamon were sacked by Philip V in 201 (Polyb. 16.1) and again by Seleukos, son of Antiochos III in 190 (Polyb. 21.10; Livy 37.18–21); a date before 190 is thus unlikely. Moreno 265–268, dates Phyromachos in the third century and has the statue survive the destruction. Stewart (supra n. 25) 12–18; id. (supra n. 19) 207, fig. 679; Queyrel (supra n. 29) 379–380, date the statue in the 180s, shortly after the attack of Seleukos, which seems right to me. Schober (supra n. 25) 142–149; *KvP* 124; B. Andreae in Andreae (ed.), *Phyromachos-Probleme*, 31. Ergh. *RM* (1990) 60–70; id., *RM* 100, 1993, 83–106, suggest later in the second century, 167–156.

Andreae (1990) 49–54, pls. 20–23; 25–35; (1993) 83–106, pls. 12; 14–15, attributes a colossal head in Syracuse, Museo Regionale 693, based on a perceived similarity to the coin images, which to me does not seem credible.

32. F. Zevi, *RendPontAc* 42, 1967–70, 110–114, fig. 20.

G.M.A. Richter, *Portraits of the Greeks* (1965) 179–181, figs. 1037–1056, even before the discovery of the inscription dated the portrait series to the second century; Stewart (supra n. 19) 207, fig. 678; Andreae in R.A. Stucky – I. Jucker (edd.), *Eikones. Festschrift Hans Jucker*, 12. Beih. *AntK* (1980) 40–48; N. Himmelmann, in *Phyromachos-Probleme* (1990) 13–23; Moreno 268–271, figs. 343; 562; R. von den Hoff, *Philosophenporträts des Früh- und Hochhellenismus* (1994) 136–150, figs. 140–157.

33. G.M.A. Richter (R.R.R. Smith), *Portraits of the Greeks*[2] (1984) 198–202; Stewart (supra n. 19) 188, figs. 557–558; von den Hoff (supra n. 32) 28–32. See also Palagia in this volume, p. 23. If the commonly accepted sequence of the Socrates types is correct (type A early fourth century, type B to Lysippos) then even an artist of the caliber and reputation of Lysippos makes only mild variations on a theme, adding more turbulent hair and beard, when commissioned to do so.

34. Round base: *IvP* 20; R. Bohn, *Das Heiligtum der Athena Polias Nikephoros, AvP* II (1895) 84–87, pl. 39; Schober, *KvP* 53–55, figs. 20–21 (with his restored figures); infra n. 38.

Long base foundations: Wenning (supra n. 5) 39–41, pls. 17–19.

35. Ludovisi Group, Rome, Palazzo Altemps: Schober, *KvP* 57–60, figs. 6–7; 17; Stewart (supra. n. 19) 206, figs. 671–674; M. Mattei, *Il Galata capitolino* (1987) 47–55, figs. 33–42, pls. 24–27 (with illustrations after the recent cleaning); Moreno 274–284, figs. 331; 349. Dying Trumpeter, Rome, Museo Capitolino 747: Schober, *KvP* 57–60, figs. 11–12; Stewart (supra n. 19) 205–206, figs. 667–670; Mattei 23–37, figs. 18–29, pls. 1–23; M. Mattei in S. Moscati (ed.), *I Celti* (1991) 70–71; Moreno 274–284, figs. 342; 344; 351; 353.

36. Both statues are first recorded in the collection of the Ludovisi family in 1623, and were probably discovered shortly before. A. Nibby, *Effemeridi literarie di Roma* III (April 1821) 49–76, first identified the Capitoline trumpeter as a Gaul; E.Q. Visconti, *Opere varie* IV (1831) 325–326, the Ludovisi Group. F. Haskell and N. Penny, *Taste and the Antique: The Lure of Classical Sculpture 1500–1900* (1981) 224–227; 282–284, for a summary of the earlier identifications. H. Brunn, *Geschichte der griechischen Künstler* I (1853) 443–459, first linked the two to Pergamon; and Bienkowski (supra n. 5) 1–2, noted (without citation) Furtwängler as the first to recognize the statues as Roman period copies. Both are today generally recognized as Roman copies of the second century A.D., but F. Coarelli in P. Santoro (ed.), *I Galli e l'Italia* (1978) 231–234, considers them Caesarian, 46–44 B.C., and Mattei (supra n. 35, 1991) suggests that they might be Pergamene originals.

37. Wenning (supra n. 5) 64–65, for a list of the attributions.

38. A. Schober, *RM* 51 (1936) 104–124, figs. 4–5; *KvP* 53–55, figs. 20–21; Coarelli (supra n. 36) 231–234, figs. 6; 8; 10–12; id., *Da Pergamo a Roma. I Galati nella città degli Attalidi* (1995); Andreae in Moscati (ed.), *I Celti*, 64–66. L. Hannestad in P. Bilde et al. (edd.), *Centre and Periphery in the Hellenistic World: Studies in Hellenistic Civilization* 4 (1993) 21–24, has supported a reconstruction on the round base, though without offering a specific solution.

39. E. Künzl, *Die Kelten des Epigonos von Pergamon, Beiträge zur Archäologie* (1971) 11–18; 24–30, fig. 6; Wenning (supra n. 5) 37–42; H.-J. Schalles, *Untersuchungen zur Kulturpolitik der pergamenischen Herrscher im dritten Jahrhundert vor Christus, IstForsch* 36 (1985) 68–104.

40. Bienkowski (supra n. 5) 2, gave a fine description of the marble and recognized it as different from that of the original Pergamene statues; he retained the label already commonly employed in his day "Asia Minor" although he was uncertain of the source. G. Lippold, *Kopien und Umbildungen griechischer Statuen* (1923) 108–113, acknowledges that the marble does not point to Pergamon, but then labels it as "Pergamene", that is, Asia Minor. Mattei (supra n. 35, 1987) 149, announced that samples had been taken from both statues, and (supra n. 35, 1991) 71, that a scientific study had concluded the marble must come from an Asia Minor quarry, but she does not specify. Amanda Claridge convinced me in a discussion before the statues that the most likely source is Dokimeion, which is in Anatolia, but the fine-grained stone remains unmatched at Pergamon.

41. J.R. Marszal, *AJA* 98, 1994, 335 (abstract).

42. J.L. Ussing, *Pergamos, seine Geschichte und Monumente* (1899) 12; 72; E. Ohlemutz, *Die Kulte und Heiligtümer der Götter in Pergamon* (1940) 26–28 n. 31; Künzl (supra n. 36) 21–22.

43. Pausanias, 10.19.4; B. Hintzen-Bohlen, *Herrscherrepräsentation im Hellenismus, Arbeiten zur Archäologie* (1992) 62–63. The Athenians had shortly before, probably in 294, rehung the Persian shields, cf. the Psephisma of Dromokleides of Sphettos: Plutarch, *Demetrios* 13; C. Habicht, *Untersuchungen zur politischen Geschichte Athens im 3. Jahrhundert v. Chr., Vestigia. Beiträge zur Alten Geschichte* (1979) 34–44; Hintzen-Bohlen, 52.

The Soteria established immediately after the events was apparently organized by the priests (amphiktyony) of Delphi; the Aitolians revived and reorganized the festival in 246/5 B.C., cf. G. Nachtergael, *Les Galates en Grèce et les Sôtéria de Delphes* (1977) 295–382. See also here p. 63.

44. Kallimachos, *Hymn* 4 (to Delos) 171–185.

45. Pliny, *NH* 34.84. A. Schober, *JdI* 53, 1938, 126–149, on the career of Epigonos.

46. Schober (supra n. 45) 126–149; *AnzWien* 78, 1941, 1–14; *KvP* 55–57.

47. Schober (supra n. 45) 133, figs. 4–5. Wenning (supra n. 5) 39 n. 256, denies the pertinence of the capping blocks because the division stripes are said to be wider, 0.026 and 0.032 m, but both in fact measure 0.029 m; Schalles (supra n. 39) 78 n. 484, dismisses the importance of the blocks, mentioning them in an only tangentially related

footnote. I thank Prof. W.D. Heilmeyer and his staff for assistance with the blocks in the storerooms of the Pergamon museum.

48. Schober, *KvP* 55, suggested a composition of 25–30 life-size figures. For a reconstruction on the noted compositional principles, Marszal (supra n. 5).
49. Pausanias 1.25.2.
50. Polybios 16.26.2; Livy 31.15.2; Pausanias 1.5.5, 8.1. Schalles (supra n. 39) 136–143; C. Habicht, *Athen in hellenistischer Zeit* (1994) 114; 183–185; id., *Athen. Die Geschichte der Stadt in hellenistischer Zeit* (1995) 225–229, on the relations of Attalos with Athens and his eponymous status.

    The visit of Attalos to Athens, in 200, is widely accepted by scholars who reject the stylistic down-dating of the monument to the mid-second century (cf. infra n. 57) as the most likely reason for its erection, e.g. Pollitt (supra n. 1) 91.
51. H. Brunn, *AdI* 42, 1870, 292–323.
52. On the marble supra n. 40. Lippold (supra n. 40) 112–113, suggested the second group at Pergamon, to avoid the conflict with the marble type, which seems widely accepted in German scholarship, e.g. A. Schober, *RM* 54, 1939, 95–98; Schober, *KvP* 125; Radt (supra n. 1) 198; also Stewart (supra n. 19) 210; Moreno 586. W. Hoepfner, *AA* 1996, 104–130; id. in R. Dreyfus and E. Schraudolph (edd.), *Pergamon: The Telephos Frieze from the Great Altar* (1996) 55; 64–67, has recently suggested placing the second set on the Great Altar; Ridgway (supra n. 5) 291, notes that the Athenian amazonomachy and Marathonomachy make sense as dedications only at Athens, perhaps only on the Acropolis.
53. B. Palma, *Xenia* 1, 1981, 45–84, esp. 54–55, for a table of the attributions.
54. Aix-en-Provence, Musée Granet 246: Schober, *KvP* 127, figs. 117–118; Palma (supra n. 53) 77–78, no. 23; F. Queyrel, *RA* 1989, 253–296, figs. 1–10; 27.
55. Venice, Museo Archeologico nos. 56 (belted), 57 (bearded): Schober, *KvP* 126; 129–30, figs. 100–102; Palma (supra n. 53) 60–61; 65–66, nos. 6; 10; G. Traversari, *La statuaria ellenistica del Museo Archeologico di Venezia* (1986) 84–89, no. 26 (bearded), 93–94, no. 28 (belted).
56. Naples, Museo Nazionale 6012 (amazon), 6013 (giant), 6014 (Persian), 6015 (Gaul): Schober, *KvP* 126–127; 130–131, figs. 106–111; 114–115; Palma (supra n. 53) 56–59; 60–61, nos. 1–3; 7; Stewart (supra n. 19) 210, figs. 685–688.
57. E.g. R. Horn, *RM* 52, 1937, 140–163, from an analysis of the head structure concluded the originals must date to the second century; Schober (supra n. 51) 95–98, argues a late date from the one-sided (*einansichtig*), hence classicistic quality; T. Hölscher, *AntK* 28, 1985, 123–128, noting that the presence of victors would demand over 100 figures in the four groups, suggests that nearby colossal statues of the Pergamene kings (Eumenes II and Attalos II) could take the place of the victors, and so reduces the number of requisite figures to a minumum of 20; Andreae (supra n. 32) 46–48, attributes the dedication to Phyromachos on the basis of a perceived similarity of the Naples giant to the portraits of Antisthenes; id. (supra n. 31, 1993) 97–98, pl. 16, sets the figures on, not by or toward, *pros*, the south wall; Bringmann 66–68, no. 30, figs. 18–19.

Ένα κολοσσικό κεφάλι Ηρακλή από το Πέργαμο

Δημήτρης Δαμάσκος

στο Γιώργο Δεσπίνη,
μικρό αντίδωρο

Κατά τη διάρκεια των ανασκαφών στις αρχές του αιώνα στο Πέργαμο βρέθηκε στο βυζαντινό τείχος στη νότια πλαγιά της ακρόπολης ένα κολοσσικό κεφάλι Ηρακλή, το οποίο δε συμπεριλήφθηκε στο διπλό τόμο της δημοσίευσης των περγαμηνών γλυπτών από τον F. Winter, αλλά δημοσιεύθηκε με μια σύντομη περιγραφή το 1910 από τον G. Schröder.[1] Έκτοτε φυλάσσεται στην αποθήκη του Μουσείου Pergamon του Βερολίνου (αρ. ευρ. Sk. 1675). Το γλυπτό απεικονίστηκε στα εγχειρίδια ελληνιστικής πλαστικής, έτυχε μικρού σχολιασμού σε μεμονωμένες μελέτες, αλλά ουδέποτε μελετήθηκε διεξοδικά.[2]

Το κεφάλι (εικ. 1) έχει μέγιστο ύψος 48 εκ. (32 εκ. από τη ρίζα των μαλλιών μέχρι το πηγούνι). Σώζεται ολόκληρο το κεφάλι με το λαιμό καθώς κι η αρχή των ώμων. Ολόκληρη η μορφή θα είχε μέγεθος τουλάχιστον διπλάσιο του φυσικού. Το πλάτος της μορφής είναι 28 εκ. και το μέγιστο βάθος 38 εκ. Η κάτω διάμετρος του λαιμού είναι 30 εκ.[3]

Η πολύ καλά σωζόμενη κεφαλή είναι από λευκό, λεπτόκοκκο μάρμαρο με γκριζωπή πάτινα. Ίχνη κόκκινου χρώματος σώζονται στα μαλλιά μπροστά καθώς και στους βοστρύχους πάνω από τ' αυτιά. Παρουσιάζει αποκρούσεις στη μύτη, στο δεξί αυτί και στην αριστερή πλευρά του αυχένα, ενώ δύο αποθραύσεις υπάρχουν πίσω από το αριστερό αυτί μεγέθους περίπου 5 x 6 εκ. Το γλυπτό βρέθηκε σε τρία τμήματα. Στο κομμάτιασμά του συνέτεινε το γεγονός ότι το κεφάλι ήταν συνδεδεμένο με τον κορμό μ' ένα μεγάλο τόρμο, τώρα αθέατο λόγω της στερέωσης του γλυπτού στη βάση του. Το ένα σπάσιμο ξεκινούσε από τη μέση του αυχένα, ανέβαινε μέχρι το ύψος της στεφάνης και περνούσε κάτω από το αριστερό αυτί και μια συστάδα βοστρύχων κι έφτανε μέχρι το μέσον του λαιμού. Το δεύτερο ξεκινούσε από τη δεξιά πλευρά του αυχένα, συνέχιζε πίσω από το κεφάλι, περνούσε πάνω από το δεξί αυτί και κατέληγε επίσης στο μέσον του λαιμού (εικ. 2). Το τρίτο κομμάτι συμπεριλάμβανε το πρόσωπο μαζί με τμήμα του κεφαλιού. Στο ύψος του λαιμού το κεφάλι, για τη σύνδεσή του με τον κορμό, είναι κομμένο πλαγίως, από τη ρίζα του λαιμού και τις αρχές των ώμων μπροστά μέχρι το επάνω μέρος του αυχένα πίσω (εικ. 3). Το κόψιμο αυτό, το οποίο σώζεται ακέραιο, έχει μια κλίση περίπου 30°. Η επιφάνεια σύνδεσης είναι πολύ καλά λειασμένη. Στην περίμετρο της τομής διακρίνεται καθαρά η αναθύρωση που την διέτρεχε.

Το κεφάλι είναι αμελώς δουλεμένο μόνο με ντισιλίδικο στην πίσω καθώς και στην επάνω πλευρά (εικ. 4). Το μέγεθος της μορφής καθώς κι η πιθανή τοποθέτησή του μπροστά από έναν τοίχο δε θα επέτρεπαν στο θεατή να δει την πίσω όψη του

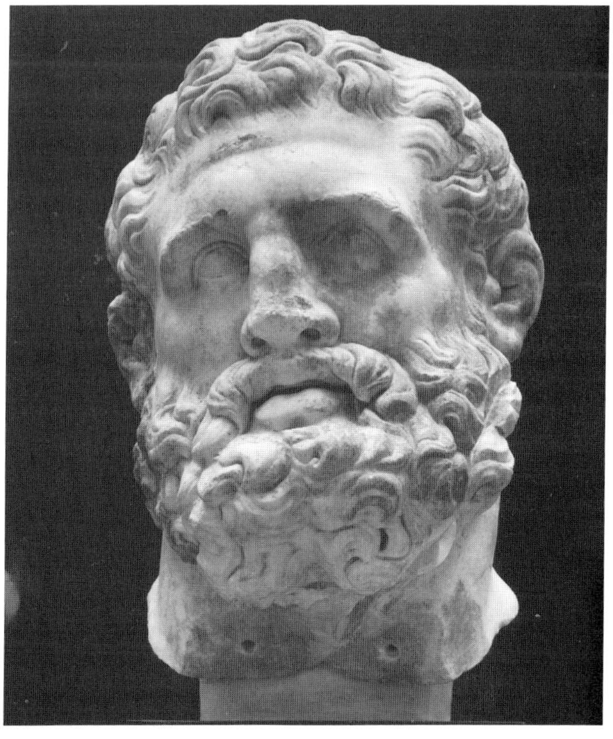

Εικ. 1. Μπροστινή όψη κεφαλής Ηρακλή Sk 1675. Antikensammlung, Staatliche Museen zu Berlin – Preussischer Kulturbesitz. Φωτογραφία: Johannes Laurentius.

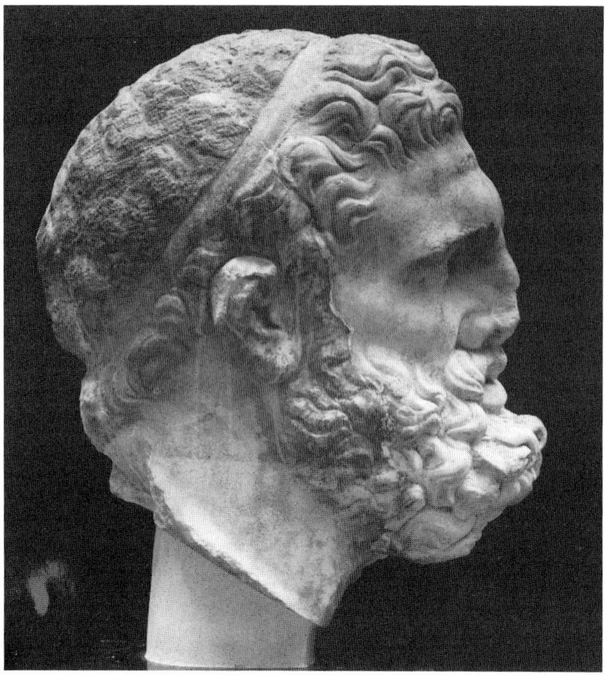

Εικ. 2. Πλάγια όψη κεφαλής Ηρακλή Sk. 1675. Antikensammlung, Staatliche Museen zu Berlin – Preussischer Kulturbesitz. Φωτογραφία: Johannes Laurentius.

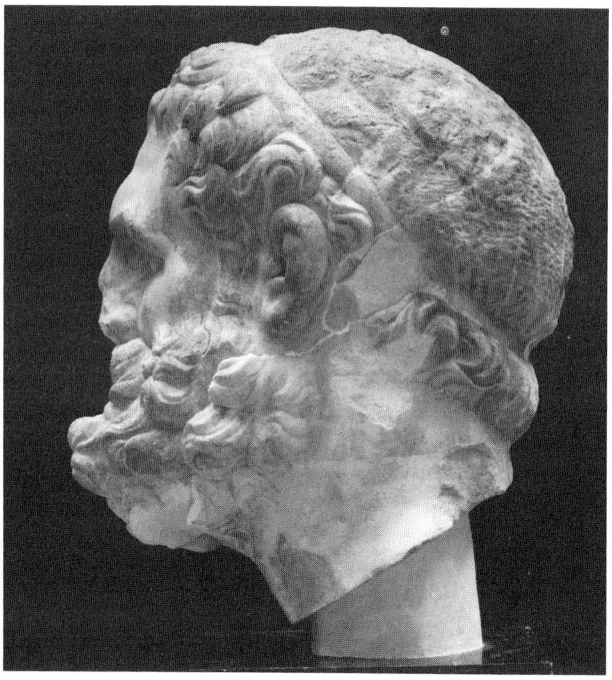

Εικ. 3. Πλάγια όψη κεφαλής Ηρακλή Sk. 1675. Antikensammlung, Staatliche Museen zu Berlin – Preussischer Kulturbesitz. Φωτογραφία: Johannes Laurentius.

αγάλματος. Η μορφή φορά κυλινδρική στεφάνη (Wulstbinde).[4] Η χρήση ενός μικρού τετράγωνης τομής τόρμου διαστάσεων 3,3 x 1,7 εκ. και βάθους 4,5 εκ. στο επάνω μέρος της κεφαλής δεν είναι δυνατόν να διαπιστωθεί, είναι πάντως πολύ μικρός για να χρησίμευε στην ανύψωση και στερέωση του κεφαλιού στον κορμό. Δύο μικροί κυλινδρικοί τόρμοι στο λαιμό του Ηρακλή είναι νεώτεροι και οφείλονται στις συμπληρώσεις με γύψο των χαμένων τμημάτων από τους συντηρητές του Μουσείου στις αρχές του αιώνα.

Ο Ηρακλής απεικονίζεται γενειοφόρος, προχωρημένης ηλικίας κι έχει τα χαρακτηριστικά πρησμένα αυτιά του παλαιστή. Το κεφάλι έχει μια έντονη κλίση προς τα επάνω και δεξιά, κάτι που τονίζεται κι από την κατεύθυνση του βλέμματος του ήρωα. Το κάτω τμήμα του μετώπου του, περίπου τα δύο τρίτα του συνολικού του ύψους, είναι προτεταμένο, χωρίζεται από το πάνω τμήμα με μια χαρακτηριστική οριζόντια, αβαθή αύλακα και ιδωμένο σε τομή είναι έντονα κυρτό. Τα μικρά μάτια του είναι βαθιά τοποθετημένα μέσα στις κόγχες τους κι ο κανθός αποδίδεται έντονα πλαστικά. Τα επάνω βλέφαρα αποδίδονται με μια λεπτή ταινία κι ένα αυλάκι τα διαχωρίζει από την περιοχή των φρυδιών. Τα βαριά φρύδια προβάλλουν έντονα πάνω από τα μάτια, δημιουργώντας έντονες φωτοσκιάσεις, και είναι πλαστικά αποδοσμένα με λεπτές, κυματοειδείς εγχαράξεις. Η μύτη είναι σαρκώδης και πλατιά και τα πτερύγιά της δημιουργούν δύο χαρακτηριστικές δρεπανοειδείς καμπύλες και χωρίζονται από τις παρειές με μια βαθιά εγχάραξη στη ρίζα τους. Το στόμα είναι μικρό, τα χείλη μισάνοιχτα και χωρίζονται από το μουστάκι με δύο μικρές κάθετες αυλακώσεις. Τα μαλλιά και τα γένια του προσώπου είναι δουλεμένα με τρυπάνι. Σε αρκετά σημεία μάλιστα οι αύλακες από το τρυπάνι στην περίμετρο των βοστρύχων είναι τόσο βαθιές, με αποτέλεσμα να προβάλλει ο κάθε βόστρυχος χωριστά. Μια βαθιά αύλακα με τρυπάνι περίπου στο μέσον του πηγουνιού τέμνει το γένι σε δύο μέρη. Η κοντοκουρεμένη κόμη και το γένι αποτελούνται από κυματοειδείς ή και ημισεληνοειδείς βοστρύχους που αναπτύσσονται σε ομάδες των δύο ή και των τριών. Παρά το ότι δεν αποδίδονται σ' όλη την επιφάνεια του κεφαλιού κατά τον ίδιο τρόπο είναι στο σύνολό τους χωρίς έντονες πλαστικές εξάρσεις και δουλεμένοι σε στενή συνάφεια με το κρανίο και το πρόσωπο. Στις παρειές, όπου και είναι περισσότερο πλαστικά αποδοσμένοι, αναπτύσσονται προς μια κατεύθυνση, από πίσω προς τα μπρος, ενώ μπροστά οι βόστρυχοι αποδίδονται άτακτα, ακριβώς όπως κι αυτοί της κόμης. Οι τελευταίοι μάλιστα, κι ιδίως αυτοί στο μπροστινό κι επάνω μέρος του κεφαλιού μέχρι τη στεφάνη, αποδίδονται σχεδόν καλλιγραφικά, γραμμικά με αβαθείς εγχαράξεις.

Το εξεταζόμενο κεφάλι είναι ένα χαρακτηριστικό δείγμα της περγαμηνής πλαστικής, για τη χρονολόγηση του οποίου προκύπτει το γενικό και γνωστό πρόβλημα της χρονολόγησης ολόκληρης ουσιαστικά της ελληνιστικής πλαστικής, η έλλειψη δηλαδή σίγουρων χρονολογημένων μνημείων που βοηθούν στην κατασκευή ενός ασφαλούς

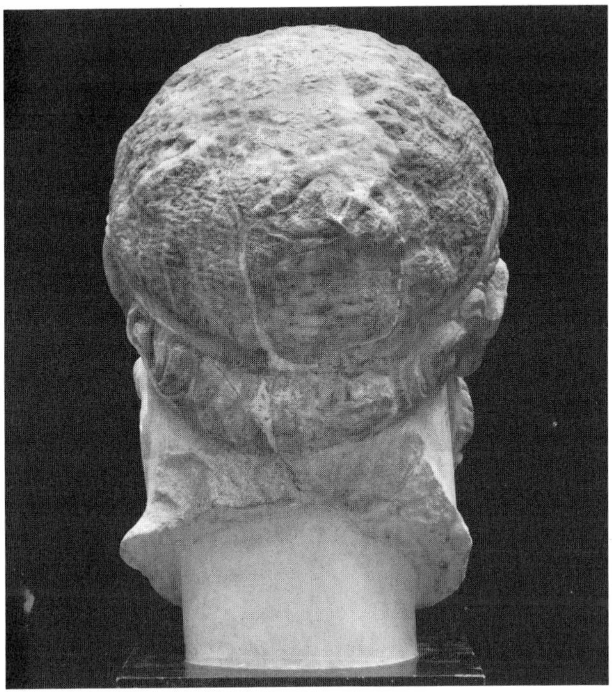

Εικ. 4. Κεφαλή Ηρακλή Sk. 1675. Antikensammlung, Staatliche Museen zu Berlin – Preussischer Kulturbesitz. Φωτογραφία: Johannes Laurentius.

χρονολογικού πίνακα. Για τη χρονολόγηση του μεγαλύτερου μέρους της περγαμηνής τέχνης οι μελετητές καταφεύγουν, όπως είναι φυσικό, στο γλυπτό διάκοσμο των δύο ζωφόρων του περγαμηνού βωμού, η ακριβέστερη χρονολόγηση του οποίου, πέρα από την από τους πάντες αποδεκτή χρονολόγησή του από τις αρχές του δεύτερου τετάρτου του 2ου αι. π.Χ. και μετά, βασίζεται προς το παρόν σε υποθέσεις που έχουν να κάνουν με γεγονότα συναφή με την αφορμή ανέγερσής του.[5] 'Ετσι λοιπόν τα περισσότερα έργα χρονολογούνται, πριν, παράλληλα ή μετά τη μεγάλη ή τη μικρή ζωφόρο. Το ίδιο σύστημα χρονολόγησης ισχύει και για το κεφάλι του Ηρακλή.

Παρά το γεγονός ότι όλοι οι μέχρι τώρα μελετητές θεωρούν αναμφισβήτητη τη χρονολόγηση του έργου μέσα στον 2ο αι. π.Χ., υπάρχει ασυμφωνία απόψεων για μια ακριβέστερη χρονολόγηση. Οι G. Schröder,[6] P.C. Bol[7] και E. Rohde[8] έχουν υποστηρίξει μια χρονολόγηση γύρω στα μέσα του αιώνα ή ίσως και λίγο αργότερα, στηριζόμενοι στο "λυσιππικό" – κλασικίζοντα χαρακτήρα του έργου, κάτι που κατά τη γνώμη τους εμφανίζεται στο Πέργαμο από τη ζωφόρο του Τηλέφου και μετά. Μια χρονολόγηση στις πρώτες δεκαετίες του αιώνα υποστήριξε αντίθετα ο J.P. Niemeier,[9] συνεπικουρούμενος αργότερα από τον R. von den Hoff.[10] Ο Niemeier συνέκρινε το κεφάλι με το πορτραίτο που σύμφωνα με την επικρατούσα άποψη θεωρείται ότι απεικονίζει τον Άτταλο Α' και χρονολογείται στα χρόνια της μεγάλης ζωφόρου ή και λίγο αργότερα (σελ. 119, εικ. 1.[11] Τονίστηκε η ομοιότητα των δύο έργων στη διάπλαση της περιοχής των ματιών, των παρειών και της μύτης καθώς και στη διάρθρωση του εσωτερικού τους σκελετού.

Αν εξετάσει κανείς λεπτομερέστερα τις δύο παραπάνω απόψεις, θα διαπιστώσει ότι κι οι δύο ευσταθούν, αν και βασίζονται μόνο σε μεμονωμένες παρατηρήσεις. Η σύγκριση του κεφαλιού με το περγαμηνό ηγεμονικό πορτραίτο μας παρέχει στυλιστικές ομοιότητες. Τα μικρά οβάλ μάτια, η έντονα πλαστική απόδοση των υπερκείμενων φρυδιών καθώς και η διάρθρωση της μύτης με τα χαρακτηριστικά της πτερύγια αποτελούν κοινά στυλιστικά στοιχεία όχι όμως μόνο των δύο έργων, αλλά και κεφαλιών από τη μεγάλη ζωφόρο.[12]

Δυσκολίες παρουσιάζει ωστόσο η ανεύρεση έργων για τη στυλιστική κατάταξη των βοστρύχων του κεφαλιού, μια που γενειοφόρες κεφαλές με παρόμοια περίπου απόδοση του γενιού και των μαλλιών από την περγαμηνή τουλάχιστον τέχνη, απ' όπου και αν προέρχονται τα πλησιέστερα στυλιστικά μνημεία προς σύγκριση, δεν υπάρχουν. Το γεγονός μάλιστα ότι η σωζόμενη περγαμηνή πλαστική του 2ου αι. και μετά είναι άφθονη, ενώ τα πρωιμότερα έργα ουσιαστικά σπανίζουν, δυσχεραίνει τη στυλιστική μελέτη, μια που όλα τα έργα προς σύγκριση ανήκουν ουσιαστικά στην περίοδο της μεγάλης ζωφόρου και μετά. Οι βόστρυχοι των μορφών από τη μεγάλη ζωφόρο αποδίδονται κατά κανόνα ολόγλυφα, έντονα κινημένοι και με δική τους υπόσταση, ανεξαρτητοποιούμενοι έτσι από το κεφάλι, κάτι που δεν συμβαίνει με τους βοστρύχους του κεφαλιού του Ηρακλή, όπου οι βόστρυχοι αποδίδονται σφιχτά ο ένας κοντά στον άλλον, αλλά και στη σχέση τους με το πρόσωπο και το κρανίο. 'Ισως είναι αυτή η διαπίστωση που παρακίνησε ορισμένους μελετητές να τονίσουν τον κλασικιστικό χαρακτήρα του έργου, μια που παρόμοια απόδοση απαντάται σε υστεροκλασικά αττικά έργα.[13] Αν δεχθούμε ότι ο κλασικισμός στο Πέργαμο είναι η κυρίαρχη τάση στην περγαμηνή τέχνη από τη ζωφόρο του Τηλέφου και μετά, δηλαδή κάπου γύρω στα μέσα του 2ου αι. π.Χ., προκύπτει το ερώτημα αν το εξεταζόμενο κεφάλι μπορεί να ενταχθεί στην περίοδο αυτή.

Η σύγκριση του κεφαλιού με τα γλυπτά της ζωφόρου αποβαίνει άκαρπη, μια που και πάλι μεγάλες ομοιότητές του με παραδείγματα από το πλαστικό σύνολο δεν είναι δυνατόν να διαπιστωθούν.[14] Η σύγκρισή του όμως μ' ένα φυσικού μεγέθους κεφάλι Ηρακλή από το Γυμνάσιο (εικ. 5), το οποίο μπορεί με σχετική βεβαιότητα να χρονολογηθεί στο δεύτερο μισό του αιώνα, αποδεικνύει τις στυλιστικές αλλά και χρονολογικές διαφορές των δύο κεφαλιών.[15] Τα γένια στο μικρό κεφάλι είναι αποδοσμένα περισσότερο διακοσμητικά (βλ. π.χ. τη μανιεριστική απόδοση του μουστακιού), τα οποία επικολλώνται απλώς παρατακτικά στις παρειές, χωρίς να υπάρχει ιδιαίτερη συνάφεια ανάμεσα στα γένεια και το πρόσωπο. Η ίδια παρατακτική απόδοση παρατηρείται εξάλλου και στη σύνδεση των μελών του προσώπου, με αποτέλεσμα ο εσωτερικός σκελετός να χάνει τη συνοχή του και το πρόσωπο να είναι μια μάσκα, όπου κάθε μέλος παρατάσσεται μήν έχοντας οργανική σχέση το ένα με το άλλο. Στο κολοσσικό κεφάλι αντίθετα το κάθε μέλος του προσώπου διατηρεί την αυτοτέλειά του, η μετάβαση όμως από το ένα μέλος στο άλλο γίνεται μαλακά χωρίς ν' αποβαίνει εις βάρος του συνόλου, έτσι ώστε το πρόσωπο νά διατηρεί την εσωτερική του συνοχή. Μια άλλη διαφορά που παρατηρείται ανάμεσα στο εξεταζόμενο κεφάλι και σε άλλα υστεροελληνιστικά έργα εκτός Περγάμου, όπως π.χ. στο κεφάλι του Δία από την Αίγειρα,[16] είναι η στυλιζαρισμένη απόδοση των βοστρύχων στο πηγούνι κατά τη χαρακτηριστική διαίρεση του γενιού στα δύο. Η διαφορά ανάμεσα στη μή νατουραλιστική απόδοση των σπειροειδών βοστρύχων του Δία και στην αντίστοιχη αυτών του Ηρακλή είναι εμφανής. Από την άλλη πλευρά όμως η επίπεδη, σχεδόν καλλιγραφική απόδοση της κόμης στο πάνω μέρος του κεφαλιού, στοιχείο που συναντάμε π.χ. στο υστεροελληνιστικό, επονομαζόμενο "ωραίο κεφάλι" από το Πέργαμο,[17] δεν συναντάται στις μορφές της μεγάλης ζωφόρου και θα μπορούσε να θεωρηθεί ένα υστερότερο χρονολογικό στοιχείο.

Μπορούμε επομένως να διακρίνουμε στο έργο αυτό τόσο στοιχεία που μας οδηγούν σε μια χρονολόγησή του στα χρόνια της δημιουργίας της μεγάλης ζωφόρου, όσο και στοιχεία που θα επέτρεπαν μια υστερότερη χρονολόγησή του. Από το δίλημμα αυτό μπορούν ίσως να μας βγάλουν στοιχεία εικονογραφικά και ίσως ιστορικά. Επίσης και ο τόπος εύρεσής του μπορεί πολύ πιθανόν να οριοθετήσει ένα σχετικό terminus post quem για τη χρονολόγησή του. Η εξαιρετικά καλή διατήρηση της επιφάνειας του γλυπτού φανερώνει ότι το άγαλμα δεν θα μπορούσε να ήταν στημένο πολύ μακριά από κει που βρέθηκε, δηλαδή τη νότια πλαγιά της ακρόπολης. Είναι πολύ πιθανόν επομένως ότι θα μπορούσε να ήταν στημένο στο παρακείμενο Γυμνάσιο, μια που ο Ηρακλής θεωρούνταν μαζί με τον Ερμή οι θεοί των γυμνασίων.[18] Εκεί μάλιστα βρέθηκαν και μερικά άλλα αγάλματα Ηρακλή, πολύ αποσπασματικά σωζόμενα.[19] Η σχέση του ήρωα με τα γυμνάσια τονίζεται εξάλλου εικονογραφικά και με τ' αυτιά παλαιστή που έχει το εξεταζόμενο κεφάλι. Το περγαμηνό γυμνάσιο κτίστηκε επί Ευμένη Β',[20] είναι επομένως πολύ λογικό να υποθέσουμε ότι το άγαλμα θα στήθηκε στο γυμνάσιο μετά το 197 π.Χ., χρονιά που ο Ευμένης ανέλαβε την εξουσία. Ο ακριβής τόπος ανέγερσής του είναι όμως δύσκολο να διαπιστωθεί. Η πολύ καλή διατήρηση της επιφάνειας του γλυπτού συνηγορεί στο γεγονός ότι το άγαλμα θα μπορούσε να ήταν στημένο σε στεγασμένο χώρο, όπως π.χ. μέσα σε μια κόγχη. Η πιθανότητα, το κεφάλι να ήταν τμήμα λατρευτικού αγάλματος, δεν είναι δυνατόν ν' αποδειχθεί.[21]

Άλλο ένα στοιχείο που μπορεί να μας βοηθήσει σημαντικά είναι το μέγεθός του. Το κεφάλι αυτό είναι ένα από τα ελάχιστα σωζόμενα κολοσσικά ολόγλυφα περγαμηνά κεφάλια. Τα αμέσως μεγαλύτερα σε μέγεθος γλυπτά είναι ο Αλέξανδρος[22] και ένα κεφάλι Αθηνάς από το άνδηρο του ναού της.[23] Αποτελεί αυτό τυχαίο γεγονός; Στην απάντηση αυτού του ερωτήματος συμβάλλει η αποκατάσταση του αγάλματος και τα ερμηνευτικά προβλήματα που προκύπτουν.

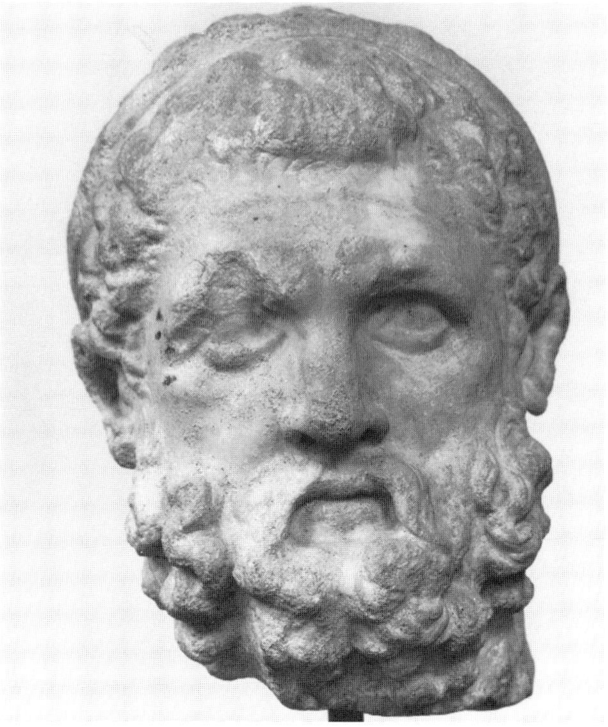

Εικ. 5. Κεφαλή Ηρακλή από το περγαμηνό Γυμνάσιο. Μουσείο Σμύρνης 551. Φωτογραφία: Γερμανικό Αρχαιολογικό Ινστιτούτο Κωνσταντινούπολης. Αρ. αρνητικού 64/651.

Βοηθητικό στοιχείο για την αποκατάσταση του τύπου του αγάλματος είναι η χαρακτηριστική κλίση της κεφαλής, κάτι που απαγορεύει, κατά τη γνώμη μου, την υπόθεση ότι το κεφάλι θα ανήκε σε ένα όρθιο άγαλμα. Εάν υποθέσουμε ότι ο Ηρακλής απεικονιζόταν όρθιος, έχουμε τότε να κάνουμε με ένα άγαλμα ύψους πάνω από τρία μέτρα. Το μέγεθος αυτό αυξάνεται με τη βάση του αγάλματος, η οποία θα ήταν τουλάχιστον μισό μέτρο. Ο θεατής θα μπορούσε με δυσκολία να δει το πρόσωπο του αγάλματος, το οποίο θα ήταν στραμμένο προς τα επάνω, πέρα μόνο ίσως από το πηγούνι του. Δυσκολίες παρουσιάζει επίσης η κατάταξη του αγάλματος σε κάποιον από τους γνωστούς αγαλματικούς τύπους του Ηρακλή, μια που δε μας σώζεται κανένας τύπος όρθιου Ηρακλή που να παρουσιάζει αυτή την κλίση προς τα επάνω και δεξιά.[24] Αντιθέτως υπάρχουν αντίστοιχα παραδείγματα από αγάλματα καθιστού Ηρακλή.

Από την εποχή που ο Λύσιππος έπλασε τον Ηρακλή για πρώτη φορά στην ολόγλυφη πλαστική καθιστό και ηλικιωμένο,[25] οι λυσίππειοι τύποι επηρέασαν

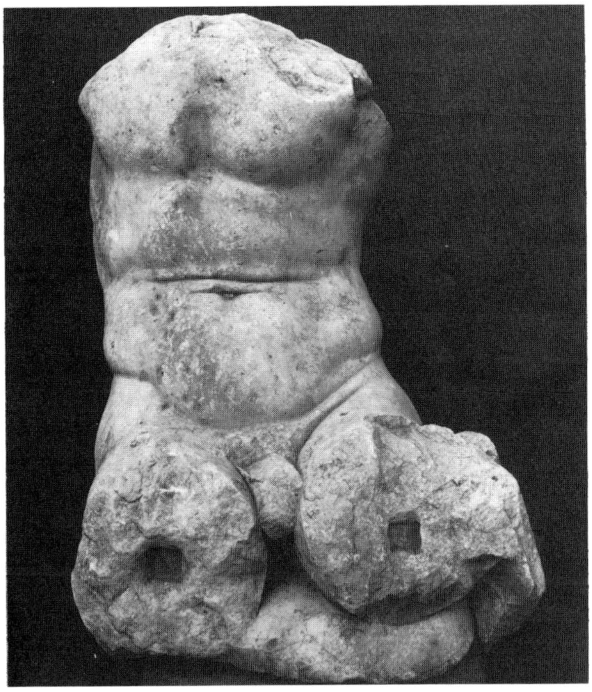

Εικ. 6. Κορμός καθιστού Ηρακλή από το περγαμηνό Γυμνάσιο. Φωτογραφία: Γερμανικό Αρχαιολογικό Ινστιτούτο Αθήνας. Αρ. αρνητικού Perg. 761c.

σημαντικά τη μετέπειτα εικονογραφία του ήρωα, ιδιαίτερα στη μεγάλη πλαστική, όπου τα ελάχιστα σωζόμενα πρωτότυπα γλυπτά έργα του Ηρακλή από τα τέλη του 4ου αι. π.Χ. κ.εξ., όπως π.χ. το πρώιμο ελληνιστικό κολοσσικό κεφάλι από τη Σπάρτη,[26] μαρτυρούν την επίδρασή του.[27] Από τους δύο μαρτυρημένους τύπους του, τον Ηρακλή Επιτραπέζιο και το "σκεπτόμενο" ή Ηρακλή του Τάραντα, το κεφάλι του τύπου του Επιτραπέζιου ταιριάζει με το περγαμηνό κεφάλι απόλυτα. Δεν είναι μόνο η ταυτόσημη κλίση της κεφαλής αλλά και το στεφάνι, χαρακτηριστικό εικονογραφικό στοιχείο του Ηρακλή Επιτραπέζιου, μια που απαντάται σε όλες τις μεταπλάσεις του.[28] Θα μπορούσε επομένως το περγαμηνό γλυπτό να αποτελεί κατά κάποιο τρόπο μια ελληνιστική μετάπλαση του υστεροκλασικού έργου. Δεν αποτελεί εξάλλου το μοναδικό παράδειγμα αυτού του τύπου που μας σώζεται από την πρωτεύουσα των Ατταλιδών. 'Ενας κορμός καθιστού Ηρακλή από το Γυμνάσιο (εικ. 6) μπορεί να αποκατασταθεί σύμφωνα με τα σωζόμενα παραδείγματα.[29] Δύο λόγια όμως για τον αγαλματικό τύπο είναι απαραίτητα πριν προχωρήσουμε στη συνέχεια.

Σύμφωνα με τους ρωμαίους συγγραφείς του 1ου αι. μ.Χ., το Στάτιο και το Μαρτιάλη,[30] ο Λύσιππος έφτιαξε μετά από παραγγελία του Μ. Αλεξάνδρου ένα καθιστό άγαλμα Ηρακλή, το οποίο ο βασιλιάς έφερε μαζί του καθ' όλη τη διάρκεια της εκστρατείας. Από τον συνδυασμό των φιλολογικών μαρτυριών και των σωζόμενων μεταπλάσεων, μικρού μεγέθους κυρίως, μπορούμε να αποκαταστήσουμε τον ήρωα ως στεφανωμένο συμποσιαστή, καθισμένο σε ένα βράχο, με τα δύο χέρια τεντωμένα μπροστά, κρατώντας στο ένα χέρι το ρόπαλο και στο άλλο έναν κάνθαρο. Φιλολογικές μελέτες κατέδειξαν ότι το επίθετο "επιτραπέζιος" απαντάται μεν σε κείμενα των ρωμαϊκών χρόνων, όχι όμως σε πρωιμότερα από αυτά των παραπάνω συγγραφέων.[31] Ο όρος είναι δηλαδή επινόησή τους και αναφέρεται στην ιδιότητα του ήρωα ως προστάτη των συμποσίων. Ως γνωστόν το συμόσιο έπαιξε μεγάλο ρόλο για τον ήρωα: όταν αυτός έφερε εις πέρας τους δώδεκα άθλους, αποθεώθηκε, έλαβε μέρος στο συμπόσιο των δώδεκα θεών στον Όλυμπο και παντρεύτηκε την Ήβη. Οι παραλληλισμοί που μπορούν να γίνουν ανάμεσα στον Ηρακλή και τον Αλέξανδρο έχουν μια λογική βάση, αν αναλογιστεί κανείς ότι ο Αλέξανδρος ταυτιζόταν μαζί του και εμφανιζόταν ως ο νέος Ηρακλής που ακριβώς όπως κι αυτός έσωζε με την εκστρατεία του τους Έλληνες και κέρδιζε την αθανασία.

Ας γυρίσουμε στο περγαμηνό γλυπτό. Έχοντας υπόψιν τις κολοσσικές διαστάσεις του έργου καθώς και την ιστορία του προτύπου του προκύπτει το ερώτημα, εάν η επιλογή του τύπου αυτού μπορεί να συνδεθεί με ένα συγκεκριμένο ιστορικό γεγονός.

Η λατρεία του Ηρακλή στο Πέργαμο συνδέεται με τη λατρεία του γιού του, Τηλέφου, γενάρχη της ατταλικής δυναστείας και ιδρυτή της πόλης.[32] Από την πλευρά της η συστηματική καλλιέργεια της γενεαλογίας τους αρχίζει την εποχή του Ευμένη Β', από όπου και οι πρώτες μαρτυρίες από την πόλη, όταν ο Ηρακλής απεικονίζεται τόσο στη μεγάλη ζωφόρο του Βωμού, δίπλα στον πατέρα του Δία,[33] όσο και στη μικρή ζωφόρο, την Τηλέφεια, όπου απεικονίζεται στο επεισόδιο της ανεύρεσης του γιού του και μάλιστα σε έναν εικονογραφικό τύπο άμεσα επηρεασμένο από τον λυσιππικό Ηρακλή Farnese.[34]

Η σημαντική όμως ώθηση της λατρείας του Ηρακλή μαρτυρείται στα χρόνια του Αττάλου Β', όταν μετά την απόκρουση των δυνάμεων του Προυσία το 154/3 π.Χ., ο οποίος ένα χρόνο πριν είχε καταστρέψει το Ασκληπιείο και το Νικηφόριο και παραλίγο να εισβάλλει στην πόλη, καθιερώθηκε διπλή γιορτή προς τιμήν του Ασκληπιού και του Ηρακλή, τα Σωτήρια και τα Ηράκλεια, η οποία τελούνταν πιθανότατα κάθε τέσσερα χρόνια. Η γιορτή αυτή είναι γνωστή από δύο επιγραφές που βρέθηκαν στην πόλη.[35] Η χρονολόγηση της καθιέρωσής της οφείλεται σε σχετική μελέτη του Louis Robert, ο οποίος συνέδεσε επίσης πολύ πειστικά ένα επίγραμμα της Ανθολογίας του Μάξιμου Πλανούδη με τη νίκη των Ατταλιδών.[36] Σύμφωνα με αυτό, ο Ηρακλής κατεβαίνει από την περγαμηνή ακρόπολη για να νικήσει τους εχθρούς των απογόνων του, αφού πρώτα απαριθμηθούν οι άθλοι που του χάρισαν την αθανασία. Η εμφάνιση του ήρωα στην περγαμηνή λατρεία έτσι όπως διαγράφεται τα χρόνια αυτά του προσδίδει μια δεύτερη ιδιότητα. Για πρώτη φορά απ' όσο γνωρίζουμε, δεν λατρεύεται μόνον ως ο πατέρας του Τήλεφου, αλλά ως ο σωτήρας τους από τις συμφορές που είχε προξενήσει ο Προυσίας και κατ' επέκταση από τα δεινά που μπορεί να προκαλέσει οποιοσδήποτε εχθρός.

Είναι δυνατόν η ανέγερση του κολοσσικού αγάλματος να συμπίπτει με την καθιέρωση αυτής της γιορτής; Σημαντικές ενστάσεις για τη χρονολόγηση του έργου στα μέσα του αιώνα θεωρητικά δεν υπάρχουν. Η μορφή διατηρεί στοιχεία από μορφές της μεγάλης ζωφόρου – ένα τέτοιο έργο θα είχε σαφέστατα επηρεάσει κι άλλους γλύπτες, αν ο Ηρακλής δεν ανήκει σε κάποιον γλύπτη που δούλεψε στη ζωφόρο -, αλλά και μας προϊδεάζει για τις έντονες κλασικιστικές τάσεις από τα χρόνια που έρχονται. Ενστάσεις μπορεί όμως κανείς να εγείρει όσον αφορά σε άλλα προβλήματα του έργου. Οι γνώσεις μας για το γλυπτό δεν είναι τόσες πολλές για να μπορέσουμε να το συνδέσουμε με κάποιο συγκεκριμένο γεγονός, όταν μάλιστα δεν είναι δυνατόν να επιτευχθεί μια ασφαλής χρονολόγησή του. Αν θέλαμε να εξαντλήσουμε όλες τις πιθανές περιπτώσεις, θα διαπιστώναμε ότι υπάρχουν και άλλες αφορμές ανέγερσής του. Το άγαλμα θα μπορούσε να είχε στηθεί στο Γυμνάσιο ήδη από την αρχή λειτουργίας του – και τότε προκύπτει το ερώτημα, πότε τελείωσε η ανέγερσή του; – ή ακόμα επ' ευκαιρία της οριστικής απόκρουσης των Γαλατών το 166 π.Χ.[37] Στις δύο τελευταίες περιπτώσεις εμφανίζεται και πάλι ο Ηρακλής ως ο σωτήρας των Περγαμηνών – μόνο που γι' αυτό δεν υπάρχει η αντίστοιχη φιλολογική ή άλλη μαρτυρία. Μια πιθανότητα ανέγερσής του μετά τα μέσα του 2ου αι. π.Χ. βασισμένη σε ιστορικά γεγονότα δε μπορεί να υποστηριχθεί με τις μέχρι τώρα υπάρχουσες πηγές, στυλιστικά όμως δε θα μπορούσε το έργο να κατέβει πολύ μετά τα μέσα του αιώνα. Θα μπορούσαμε επομένως, να αφήσουμε ανοιχτή την ημερομηνία ανέγερσης του γλυπτού, κι επομένως της χρονολόγησής του, και να ορίσουμε απλώς τα χρονολογικά πλαίσια μέσα στα οποία θα μπορούσε να είχε φιλοτεχνηθεί το άγαλμα. Κατ' αυτόν τον τρόπο αποφεύγεται το σφάλμα, η χρονολόγηση του γλυπτού μόνο με στυλιστικά κριτήρια να αντιτάσσεται σε μια χρονολόγησή του με βάση ιστορικά ή άλλα στοιχεία και το αντίστροφο. Μια χρονολόγησή του ανάμεσα στα χρόνια 180–150 π.Χ. είναι πολύ πιθανή. 'Οσο για την εμφάνιση του ήρωα ως συμποσιαστή, μπορούμε να πούμε ότι ταιριάζει απόλυτα σε ένα Γυμνάσιο, αν αναλογιστεί κανείς ότι τα συμπόσια ήταν αφορμή φιλοσοφικών συζητήσεων, ακριβώς όπως το Γυμνάσιο ήταν πολύ συχνά τόπος φιλοσοφικής διδασκαλίας. Κατ' αυτόν τον τρόπο συνοψίζεται στο συγκεκριμένο εικονογραφικό τύπο η προσφιλής στα ελληνιστικά χρόνια διπλή ιδιότητα του Ηρακλή ως φιλοσόφου και πάτρωνα των γυμνασίων.

Εάν η προτεινόμενη χρονολόγηση που προκύπτει από το συνδυασμό όλων των δυνατών μαρτυριών για το ρόλο του Ηρακλή στην περγαμηνή κοινωνία ισχύει, καταλήγουμε τότε στο εξής συμπέρασμα: ο κλασικιστικός χαρακτήρας του έργου δεν είναι απαραίτητο να είναι απόρροια στυλιστικών μεταβολών στην περγαμηνή τέχνη, αλλά να οφείλεται σε μια σκόπιμη υιοθέτηση ενός παλιού εικονογραφικού τύπου με συγκεκριμένη ιστορία και συγκεκριμένο πολιτικό μήνυμα για το Πέργαμο την εποχή εκείνη. Η λατρεία του Ηρακλή δεν είναι επομένως υποχρεωτικό να συνδέεται μόνο με τη λατρεία του γιού του Τηλέφου, αλλά να πηγάζει από μια πολύ συγκεκριμένη ιστορική και πολιτική κατάσταση. Οι διαπιστωθείσες δε στυλιστικές διαφορές ανάμεσα στο κεφάλι και τις μορφές της ζωφόρου φανερώνουν την πολυμορφία στις υπάρχουσες τεχνοτροπικές τάσεις την εποχή κατασκευής του γλυπτού διακόσμου του Μεγάλου Βωμού.

Για την παραχώρηση του δικαιώματος δημοσίευσης του γλυπτού ευχαριστώ τη δρ. H. Heres (Antikensammlung Berlin), όπως επίσης και τα Γερμανικά Αρχαιολογικά Ινστιτούτα Κωνσταντινούπολης και Αθήνας για την παραχώρηση των φωτογραφιών των εικόνων 5 και 6 αντιστοίχως. Σημαντική βοήθεια προσέφεραν επίσης οι A.H. Borbein, Ο. Παλαγγιά, Δ. Πλάντζος, Α. Σαββαντίδου. Τους ευχαριστώ. Η μελέτη αυτή δεν θα ήταν δυνατόν να πραγματοποιηθεί χωρίς τη σημαντική αρωγή και τη σε όλους γνωστή γενναιοδωρία του Γιώργου Δεσπίνη σε όλα τα στάδια της εργασίας.

Σημειώσεις

1. G. Schröder, *Amtliche Berichte aus den königlichen Kunstsammlungen* 31, 1909–10, 197 κε. Βλ. επίσης *Aus dem Berliner Museum. Festschrift R. Kekulé von Stradonitz* (1909) 1, πίν. 1.
2. Οι μέχρι τώρα αναφορές των ερευνητών στο έργο είναι οι εξής: M. Bieber, *The Sculpture of the Hellenistic Age*[2] (1961) 119, εικ. 476. F. de Visscher, *Héraklès Epitrapezios* (1962) πίν. 8, εικ. 12. P.C. Bol, *AntPl* 10 (1970) 86, εικ. 16. E. Rohde, *Pergamon. Burgberg und Altar* (1982) 134, εικ. 114. J.-P. Niemeier, *Kopien und Nachahmungen im Hellenismus* (1985) 164 κε. J.J. Pollitt, *Art in the Hellenistic Age* (1986) 108, εικ. 110. N. Himmelmann, *Herrscher und Athlet. Ausstellungskatalog Bonn* (1989) 162. R. von den Hoff, *Philosophenporträts des Früh- und Hochhellenismus* (1994) 86 σημ. 271.
3. 'Αλλες μετρήσεις: ύψος μετώπου 9 εκ.˙ πλάτος 20 εκ.˙ ύψος βοστρύχων κεφαλής 6 εκ.˙ μάτια 4 εκ. μήκος 2 εκ. ύψος˙ μήκος μύτης 9 εκ.˙ πλάτος μύτης 4 εκ. (επάνω), 8 εκ. (κάτω)˙ κέντρο μύτης-παρειές 10 εκ.˙ μήκος χειλιών 7 εκ.˙ σωζόμενο ύψος λαιμού 9–10 εκ.˙ μήκος αυτιών 10 εκ.˙ πάχος 6 εκ.˙ απόσταση αυτιών από κέντρο μύτης 16 εκ. (αριστερά), 19 εκ. (δεξιά)˙ πάχος λαιμού 21 εκ.˙ πάχος σβέρκου 20,5 εκ.˙ πλάτος στεφάνης 1–2,5 εκ.˙ απόσταση αυχένα-μαλλιών 4 εκ.
4. Για τη μορφή της στεφάνης βλ. A. Krug, *Binden in der griechischen Kunst* (1968) 41 κε. 102 κε. 129 κε.
5. Τον τελευταίο καιρό έχουν διατυπωθεί απόψεις που

τείνουν να χρονολογήσουν την αρχή ανέγερσης του Βωμού μετά το 166 π.Χ., χρονιά οριστικής απόκρουσης των Γαλατών (βλ. τη βιβλιογραφία στο άρθρο του Ν. Σταμπολίδη, *ΑΕφημ* 131, 1992, 142 σημ. 51).

6. Schröder ό.π. (σημ. 2).
7. Bol ό.π. (σημ. 2).
8. Rohde ό.π. (σημ. 2).
9. Niemeier ό.π. (σημ. 2).
10. von den Hoff ό.π. (σημ. 2).
11. F. Winter, *AvP* VII_1 (1908) 147, αρ. 131, πίν. 33, παράρτημα 21. Η άποψη του Niemeier ότι το άγαλμα του Ηρακλή και το πορτραίτο του Αττάλου ήταν στημένα στην κόγχη του "Τεμένους για την ηγεμονική λατρεία" δεν είναι δυνατόν να αποδειχθεί.
12. Πρβλ. H. Winnefeld, *AvP* III_2 (1910) πίν. 29 καθώς και E. Schmidt, *Der Große Altar von Pergamon* (1961) πίν. 43 (Πορφυρίων). 44 (Κλυτίος). 45 (αντίπαλος της Άρτεμης).
13. Δες π.χ. την απόδοση των μαλλιών του θωρακοφόρου στο αττικό επιτύμβιο, παλαιότερα στη συλλογή Lonckorowski, σήμερα το κεφάλι στο Βερολίνο (Antikensammlung 1972.15) και ο κορμός στην Αθήνα (Εθνικό Μουσείο 3668). Καλές φωτογραφίες του κεφαλιού στο άρθρο του B. Schmaltz, *MarbWPr.* 1985, 41 κε. πίν. 12, 2. 15, 2. 16, 1. Βλ. επίσης τη βιβλιογραφία στον κατάλογο έκθεσης K. Stemmer (επιμ.), *Standorte. Kontext und Funktion antiker Skulptur* (1994) 56 κε. (F. Öczan).
14. Πρβλ. την απόδοση των γενειοφόρων μορφών από τη μεγάλη και τη μικρή ζωφόρο (Winnefeld ό.π. [σημ. 12] πίν. 29 και 36 αντίστοιχα).
15. H. Hepding, *AM* 32, 1907, 380 κε. πίν. 20 (ύψος προσώπου 24 εκ.).
16. R. Trummer, *AntPl* 22 (1993) πίν. 64.
17. Winter ό.π. 117 κε., αρ. 90, πίν. 25, παράρτημα 15. Βλ. επίσης καλή φωτογραφία της μπροστινής όψης στο Pollitt ό.π. (σημ. 2) 108, εικ. 111.
18. Για την πορεία του βυζαντινού τείχους βλ. W. Radt, *Pergamon* (1988) 322, εικ. 158. Σχετικά με τη λατρεία του Ερμή και του Ηρακλή στο Πέργαμο βλ. E. Ohlemutz, *Die Kulte und Heiligtümer der Götter in Pergamon* (1940, ανατύπωση 1968) 230 κε. Επίσης γενικά J. Delorme, *Gymnasion* (1960) 339 κε. καθώς και *RAC* 13 (1986) 169 κε. (W. Speyer).
19. Αξιοπρόσεκτο είναι ότι στο Γυμνάσιο, εκτός από την προαναφερόμενη κεφαλή (ό.π. σημ. 15) βρέθηκαν ακόμη μόνο δύο θραύσματα αγαλμάτων Ηρακλή, βλ. Hepding ό.π. (σημ. 15) 381 κε., εικ. 1 (κορμός καθιστού Ηρακλή: σωζ. ύψος 84 εκ., βλ. επίσης παρακάτω σημ. 29). 382 (θραύσμα αριστερού κάτω χεριού με τμήμα λεοντής). Για τα υπόλοιπα σωζόμενα παραδείγματα, τα οποία δημοσιεύονται από τον F. Winter, δεν υπάρχει ακριβής τόπος εύρεσης.
20. Radt ό.π. (σημ. 18) 103 κε. (για την επέκταση της πόλης την εποχή του Ευμένους Β'). 131 κε. (για το Γυμνάσιο). Βλ. επίσης τελευταία U. Wulf, *IstMitt* 44, 1994, 142 κε.
21. Ο κύριος ναός του Γυμνασίου (ναός R, βλ. σχετικά W. Doerpfeld, *AM* 33, 1908, 349 κε. επίσης P. Schazmann, *Das Gymnasion* [1923] 69 κε.) σώζει μέρος του λατρευτικού αγάλματός του (για το άγαλμα βλ. προσεχώς στη διατριβή του γράφοντος με τίτλο "Untersuchungen zu hellenistischen Kultbildern" [Freie Universität Berlin]). Ο σε κακή κατάσταση σωζόμενος κορινθιακός ναός στο μεσαίο άνδηρο του Γυμνασίου (Schazmann ό.π. 40 κ.εξ.) δεν είναι δυνατόν να διαπιστωθεί σε ποιά θεότητα ήταν αφιερωμένος. Η υπόθεση ότι θα μπορούσε να ήταν αφιερωμένος στον Ερμή και τον Ηρακλή δεν μπορεί να αποκλειστεί, παραμένει όμως προς το παρόν αναπόδεικτη.
22. Winter ό.π. (σημ. 11) 147, αρ. 131 (ύψος προσώπου 35 εκ.).
23. Winter ό.π. (σημ. 11) αρ. 25, εικ. 25. M. Weber, *JdI* 108, 1993, 100 κε., εικ. 23–25 (ύψος προσώπου 46 εκ.).
24. Η περίπτωση το κεφάλι να ανήκει σε κάποιον άγνωστο, ελληνιστικό αγαλματικό τύπο θα πρέπει μάλλον να απορριφθεί. Η εικονογραφία του γενειοφόρου καθιστού Ηρακλή στα ελληνιστικά χρόνια δεν παρουσιάζει κανένα νεωτερισμό, αλλά αναπλάθει τους παλαιότερους κλασικούς τύπους (βλ. τη συλλογή παραδειγμάτων στο *LIMC* IV [1988] λ. Herakles, σ. 773 κε., αρ. 927 κε. [O. Palagia] καθώς και τα σχόλια αυτόθι σ. 793 κε.).
25. Ο τύπος του καθιστού Ηρακλή στην ολόγλυφη πλαστική απαντάται ήδη από τον 5ο αι. π.Χ., μια που αναφέρεται ότι ο Μύρωνας έπλασε ένα άγαλμα καθιστού Ηρακλή, αλλά νέου και αγένειου (βλ. *LIMC* IV λ. Herakles, σ. 772 κε., αρ. 911 κε.).
26. M.N. Tod – A.J.B. Wace, *Catalogue of the Sparta Museum* (1906) 142, αρ. 52. H.G. Martin, *Römische Tempelkultbilder* (1987) 169 κε., εικ. 41.
27. Για το Λύσιππο τελευταία με όλη τη σχετική βιβλιογραφία βλ. τον κατάλογο έκθεσης P. Moreno (επιμ.), *Lisippo. L'arte e la fortuna* (1995).
28. Για τα σωζόμενα παραδείγματα του τύπου βλ. E. Bartman, *Ancient Sculptural Copies in Miniature* (1992) 147 κε.
29. Hepding ό.π. (σημ. 15) 38 κε., εικ. 1. Από το άγαλμα λείπουν τα χέρια, τα κάτω άκρα από τα γόνατα και κάτω και το κεφάλι. Ο ήρωας απεικονίζεται καθιστός πάνω σε βράχο σκεπασμένο με λεοντή. Ο κορμός παρουσιάζει μια έντονη στροφή προς τα δεξιά. Τα χέρια θα ήταν απλωμένα προς τα εμπρός. Με το αριστερό του χέρι κρατούσε το ρόπαλο, όπως φανερώνουν οι τόρμοι στερέωσής του στο πλάι της μορφής. Μια καλή εικόνα για την πιθανή όψη ολόκληρου του αγάλματος μας δίνει το πολύ καλά σωζόμενο χάλκινο αγαλματίδιο στο Μουσείο της Βιέννης (Kunsthistorisches Museum, Antikensammlung Inv. VI 342. Βλ. Moreno ό.π. [σημ. 27]. 146 κε.).
30. Mart. *Epigr.* 9. 43. 44. Stat. Silv. 4. 6. 32 κε.
31. H. Cancik-Lindenmaier, *Die altgriechische Unterricht* 3, 1971, 43 κε. Martin ό.π. (σημ. 26) 165 κε. S. Ritter, *Herakles in der römischen Kunst. Von den Anfängen bis Augustus* (1995) 92 κε. Ακόμα την παλιά ερμηνεία του όρου χρησιμοποιεί η Bartman ό.π. (σημ. 28) 151.
32. Η μέχρι πρότινος άποψη ότι ο Διόνυσος και όχι ο Ηρακλής ήταν ο γενάρχης των Περγαμηνών αντικρούστηκε με σημαντικά επιχειρήματα από τον H. Müller, *Chiron* 19, 1989, 539 κε. Σχετικά με τις πρώτες μαρτυρίες για τη λατρεία του Ηρακλή από τους Ατταλίδες βλ. T.S. Scheer, *Mythische Vorväter zur Bedeutung griechischer Heroenmythen im Selbstverständnis kleinasiatischer Städte. Münchener Arbeiten zur alten Geschichte* 7 (1994) 110 κε.
33. Μόνο μικρά θραύσματα της μορφής σώζονται, βλ. E.

Simon, *Pergamon und Hesiod* (1975) πίν. 15 (ανατολική ζωφόρος).

34. Winnefeld ό.π. (σημ. 12) 159 κε., πίν. 31,2 και 170 κε., πίν 31,6. Βλ. επίσης *LIMC* VII (1994) λ. Telephos, σ. 857 κε., αρ. 1, πλάκες 3 και 12 (H. Heres). Για τις επιρροές από τα έργα του Λυσίππου στην Τηλέφεια βλ. K.P. Stähler, *Das Unklassische im Telephosfries* (1966) 59 κε.

35. P. Jacobsthal, *AM* 33, 1908, 406, αρ. 35. Ch. Habicht, *AvP* VIII_3 (1969) 26, αρ. 3.

36. *Anth. Gr.* 16. 91. L. Robert, *RPh*[3] 58, 1984, 1 κε. (=*Opera Minora Selecta* VI [1989] 457 κε.). Λανθασμένα χρονολογεί η Scheer ό.π. (σημ. 32) 141 κε. την καθιέρωση της γιορτής στα χρόνια του Ευμένη Β'.

37. Για τα γεγονότα βλ. J. Hopp, *Untersuchungen zur Geschichte der letzten Attaliden. Vestigia. Beiträge zur alten Geschichte* 25 (1977) 51 κε.

Παρατηρήσεις σχετικά με τη θεματική παραγωγή της 'Σχολής' της Ρόδου

Βασιλική Μαχαίρα

"... of notes and studies
put together against books unwritten..."
L. Durrell, *Reflections on a Marine Venus* (1953)

Η διάκριση της ελληνιστικής πλαστικής σε σχολές, με κέντρα το Πέργαμο, τη Ρόδο, την Αλεξάνδρεια, συνιστά τον άξονα στις σχετικές μελέτες.[1] Είναι παράλληλα αποδεκτό στην βιβλιογραφία ότι η Ρόδος και η Κως από κοινού με τις μικρασιατικές πόλεις (Πριήνη, Πέργαμο, κλπ.) (εικ. 1) παίζουν σημαντικό ρόλο στη διαμόρφωση και εξέλιξη των τάσεων που χαρακτηρίζουν την ελληνιστική τέχνη. Εξέχουσα είναι η θέση της Ρόδου κυρίως σύμφωνα με τη φιλολογική παράδοση.[2] Όσον αφορά τα μνημεία που έχουν σωθεί

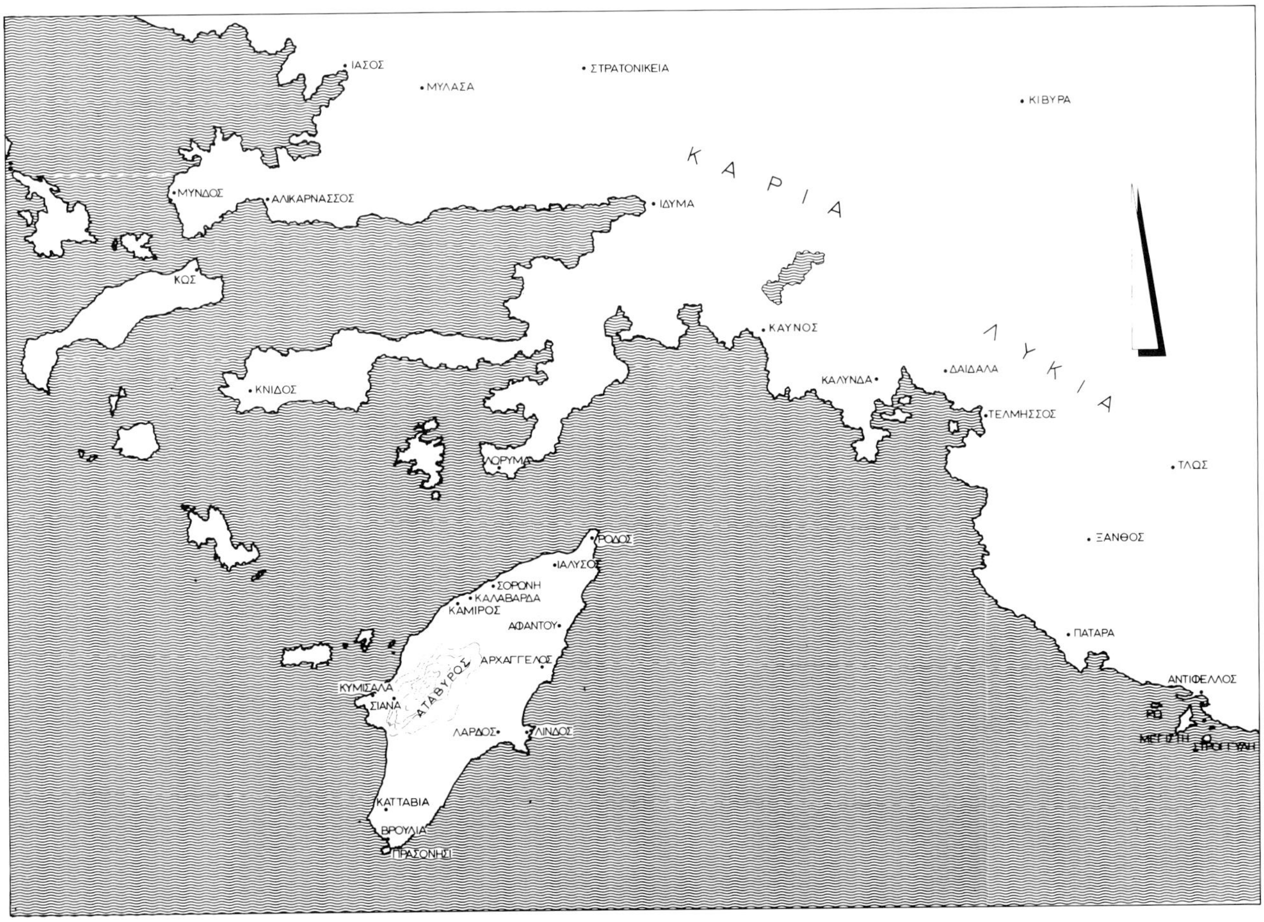

Εικ. 1. Η Ρόδος και η Μικρασιατική ακτή. Σχέδιο Ε. Λαμπρινού.

ως τις μέρες μας, αξιοσημείωτη είναι η παραγωγή μαρμαρίνων έργων κυρίως κατά τα ύστερα ελληνιστικά χρόνια, πράγμα που έχει οδηγήσει στην υπόθεση ότι ως μεγάλο πολιτιστικό κέντρο θα μπορούσε να θεωρηθεί έδρα σχολής.[3] Θα μας απασχολήσει εδώ το κατά πόσο αυτή η θέση στοιχειοθετείται με βάση το ίδιο το υλικό, δηλαδή τα γλυπτά που έχουν βρεθεί σε ανασκαφές στην πόλη της Ρόδου και στην ευρύτερη περιοχή της.[4] Επιλεκτικά θα αναφερθούμε σε συγκεκριμένα θέματα που φωτίζουν υποθέσεις της παλαιότερης και νεώτερης έρευνας.

Εντάσσουμε το υλικό μας στις ακόλουθες *δύο* κατηγορίες, οι οποίες δεν είναι ισότιμες ποσοτικά: Α. *αντίγραφα* με την ευρεία έννοια, έργα δηλαδή στα οποία αντανακλώνται γνωστές κλασικές δημιουργίες[5] και Β. *νέες δημιουργίες*, έργα δηλαδή θεωρούμενα αντιπροσωπευτικά της "ροδιακής σχολής." Σε ιδιαίτερη θέση θα αναφερθούμε στην μετάπλαση ενός πρώιμου ελληνιστικού τύπου σε μεταγενέστερα χρόνια. Η επιλογή των παραδειγμάτων μας έγινε με βάση την εύρεσή τους στη Ρόδο, σε ορισμένες περιπτώσεις τη χρήση του τοπικού λίθου.[6]

Α. Στην πρώτη κατηγορία περιλαμβάνονται αγαλμάτια, με μικρότερο του φυσικού μέγεθος, τα οποία συσχετίζονται με πραξιτελικές κυρίως δημιουργίες. Εξέχουσα σημασία προσδίδουμε στον κορμό από γκρίζο λάρτιο λίθο με αρ. ευρετηρίου Γ 1010 (εικ. 2),[7] που στάθηκε η αφορμή μας για τη θεώρηση της γλυπτικής παραγωγής της Ρόδου όπως ακολουθεί. Βρέθηκε στην πόλη της Ρόδου, στην αρχαία οδό Ρ 17. Σώζεται σε ύψος 24,5 εκ. Το αγαλμάτιο ακέραιο δεν θα υπερέβαινε τα 50–55 εκ. Διακρίνουμε απολεπίσεις και ρηγματώσεις σε διάφορα σημεία του κορμού. Ο γκρίζος αυτός λίθος από την περιοχή Λάρτος ή Λάρδος της κεντρικής Ρόδου χρησιμοποιείται σπάνια στη γλυπτική εξαιτίας της δυσκολίας που παρουσιάζει στη λάξευση.[8] Πρόκειται για ελληνιστικό αντίγραφο, το πρωιμότερο που σώζεται, του Απόλλωνος Σαυροκτόνου του Πραξιτέλους. Η μεταφορά στον ευτελέστερο λάρτιο λίθο καθώς και η σμίκρυνση του αρχικού μεγέθους έχουν ως συνέπεια τη συνοπτικότερη απόδοση των όγκων και των λεπτομερειών. Ακολουθείται το σχήμα του πρωτοτύπου, όπως το γνωρίζουμε από τα ρωμαϊκά αντίγραφα.

Ο όρος αντίγραφο χρησιμοποιείται εδώ για να δηλώσει την περιληπτική, σε σμίκρυνση απόδοση του αρχικού τύπου. Ανάλογες μεταπλάσεις πραξιτελικών έργων θεωρούνται και τα δύο αγαλμάτια 'Ερωτος που ακολουθούν. Είναι κατασκευασμένα από λευκό χονδρόκοκκο μάρμαρο, που χαρακτηρίζεται ως νησιωτικό, και σε λίγο μεγαλύτερη κλίμακα από το προηγούμενο.

Το ένα, με αρ. ευρετηρίου Ε 530 (εικ. 3), σώζεται σε ύψος 35 εκ. ενώ η ταυτότητά του πιστοποιείται από τις δύο οπές στην ωμοπλάτη (εικ. 4) για την ένθεση φτερών.[9] Αρχικά ο Laurenzi ανεγνώρισε

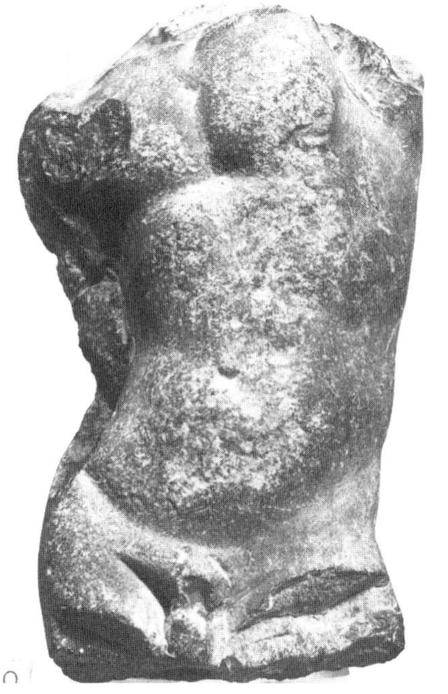

Εικ. 2. Μουσείο Ρόδου, αρ. ευρ. Γ 1010. Φωτ. Μουσείου.

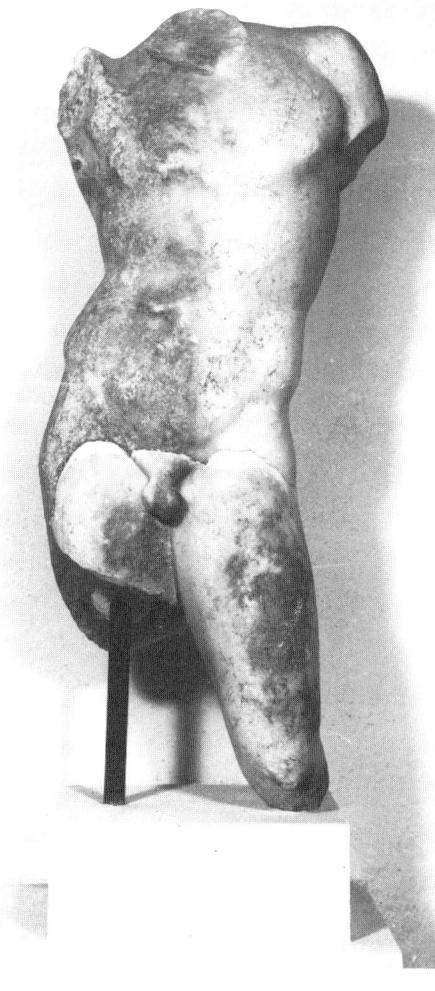

Εικ. 3. Μουσείο Ρόδου, αρ. ευρ. Ε 530 – πρόσθια όψη. Φωτ. Μουσείου, αρ. αρνητικού 1701.

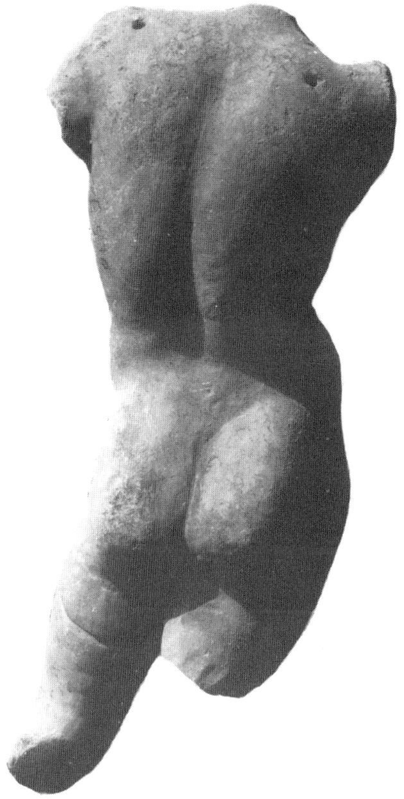

Εικ. 4. Μουσείο Ρόδου, αρ. ευρ. Ε 530 – πίσω όψη. Φωτ. Ιταλικής Αρχαιολογικής Σχολής, αρ. αρνητικού 3262.

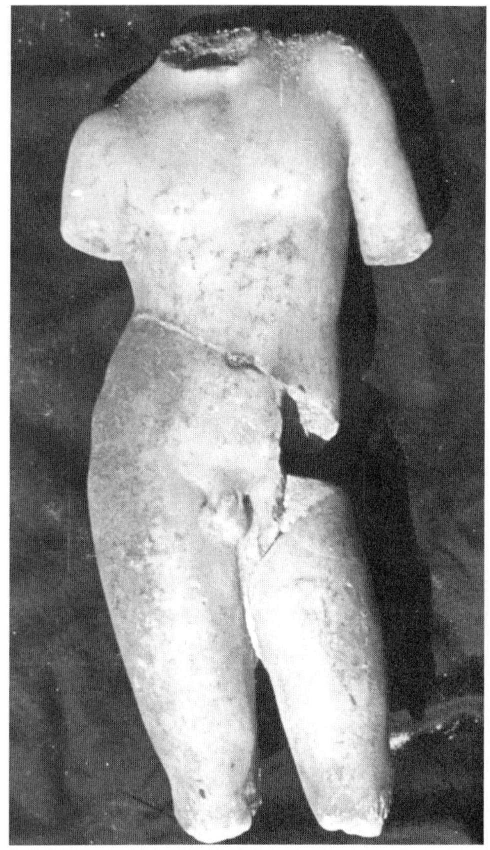

Εικ. 5. Μουσείο Ρόδου, αρ. ευρ. Ε 498. Φωτ. Ιταλικής Αρχαιολογικής Σχολής, αρ. αρνητικού 3376.

σ'αυτόν ένα ελληνιστικό αντίγραφο πραξιτελικού Έρωτος, με βάση τη απεικόνισή του σε νομισματικό τύπο του Περγάμου κατά τα αυτοκρατορικά χρόνια.[10] Το ροδιακό αγαλμάτιο βρίσκει εγγύτερα πρότυπα στις εκθηλυσμένες μορφές των Σατύρων και του Απόλλωνος Σαυροκτόνου παρά στη σειρά των Ερώτων που αποδίδονται από τη φιλολογική παράδοση στον Πραξιτέλη. Η Merker αναγνωρίζει στο αγαλμάτιο Ε 530 "έναν γυμνό νέο κατά την τεχνοτροπία που συνήθως αποδίδουμε στον Πραξιτέλη," χωρίς μνεία σε συγκεκριμένο έργο του.

Το άλλο, με αρ. ευρετηρίου Ε 498, σώζεται σε ύψος 36,5 εκ. και φέρει επίσης οπές στις ωμοπλάτες (εικ. 5).[11] Όπως και το προηγούμενο αγαλμάτιο συσχετίζεται και αυτό με την πραξιτελική παράδοση και προφανώς με κάποιον Έρωτα.[12] Τυπολογικά βρίσκεται ωστόσο πλησιέστερα στον Σάτυρο και στον Απόλλωνα Σαυροκτόνο, του οποίου παραλλάσσει τη στάση των σκελών. Στο ροδιακό αυτό έργο, εκτός από τον γενικότερο εκλεκτικισμό, χαρακτηριστικές είναι και οι αναμνήσεις σχημάτων κλασικών, πιο συγκεκριμένα πραξιτελικών, που εντάσσονται στην πλαστική αντίληψη των υστεροελληνιστικών χρόνων.

Αγάλματα που αντιγράφουν παλαιότερους τύπους στα ελληνιστικά και κυρίως στα ρωμαϊκά χρόνια χρησιμεύουν αφ' ενός ως αναθήματα σε ιερά, αφ' ετέρου για τη διακόσμηση δημοσίων (θέατρα, αγορές)[13] ή ιδιωτικών (οικίες και πολυτελείς επαύλεις) χώρων.[14] Ο ακριβής τόπος εύρεσης των τριών αγαλματίων σε οικίες της πόλης της Ρόδου φαίνεται να επιβεβαιώνει αυτή την άποψη. Το μέγεθός τους, 1/3 περίπου του φυσικού για το πρώτο, μισό του φυσικού για τους δύο Έρωτες, δείχνει ότι η σμίκρυνση των αναλογιών για την παραγωγή διακοσμητικών έργων, από κοινού με την αντιγραφή γνωστών και δημοφιλών σχημάτων από την κλασική αρχαιότητα, μοιάζει να είναι ο κανόνας.[15] Η τάση αυτή απαντά κατά πρώτον στα ελληνιστικά, συνηθέστερα στα πρώτα ρωμαϊκά χρόνια, κυρίως στον ελλαδικό χώρο.

Όσον αφορά τις γυναικείες μορφές, που συσχετίζονται άμεσα ή έμμεσα με την πραξιτελική παράδοση, θα σταθούμε σε δύο χαρακτηριστικά θέματα. Το ένα αφορά άγαλμα Αφροδίτης χωρίς αριθμό ευρετηρίου που σώζεται σε ύψος 66 εκ. (εικ. 6).[16] Το λευκό κρυσταλλικό μάρμαρο φέρει πάτινα καφε-κόκκινη, που ανευρίσκεται και σε άλλα ροδιακά έργα. Ακολουθεί το σχήμα της πραξιτελικής ημίγυμνης Αφροδίτης, της Αφροδίτης Arles, διαφοροποιείται όμως στο άνω τμήμα του σώματος και έχει πιθανώς ως θέμα την ανάδυση της θεάς. Εκτός από την εκλεκτική υιοθέτηση επί μέρους εικονογραφικών μοτίβων, χαρακτηριστική για τη χρονολόγηση του ροδιακού γλυπτού είναι η έντονη βράχυνση της αριστερής πλευράς. Ο Laurenzi προτείνει τον 1ο αιώνα π.Χ. για τη δημιουργία του πρωτοτύπου,[17] ενώ η Merker πιστεύει ότι ίσως δεν είναι τυπικά ροδιακό αλλά ότι δημιουργήθηκε στην Αλεξάνδρεια.[18] Μια ιδέα για τη συνολική εικόνα του έργου μας δίνει το ακέραιο αγαλμάτιο από την Πριήνη (Μουσείο Κωνσταντινουπόλεως, αρ. ευρ. 1053),[19] που σώζεται σε ύψος 46 εκ. και χρονολογείται στον 2ο αιώνα π.Χ. Η χαρακτηριστική βράχυνση της αριστερής πλευράς ως να ήθελε με αυτό τον ανορθόδοξο τρόπο να συγκρατήσει το ιμάτιο στον γοφό και η ανύψωση του δεξιού χεριού για να στίψει τα μαλλιά της είναι τα κοινά στοιχεία των δύο αγαλματίων. Πιστεύουμε λοιπόν ότι η καλλιτεχνική γλώσσα, κοινή στη Ρόδο και στα μεγάλα μικρασιατικά κέντρα,[20] απλώνεται και στο σύνολο του εξελληνισμένου κόσμου κατά τα ύστερα ελληνιστικά χρόνια. Υπ' αυτή την έννοια κατανοούμε και την διάδοση του θέματος στην Αίγυπτο, στην Κυρήνη κ.α.

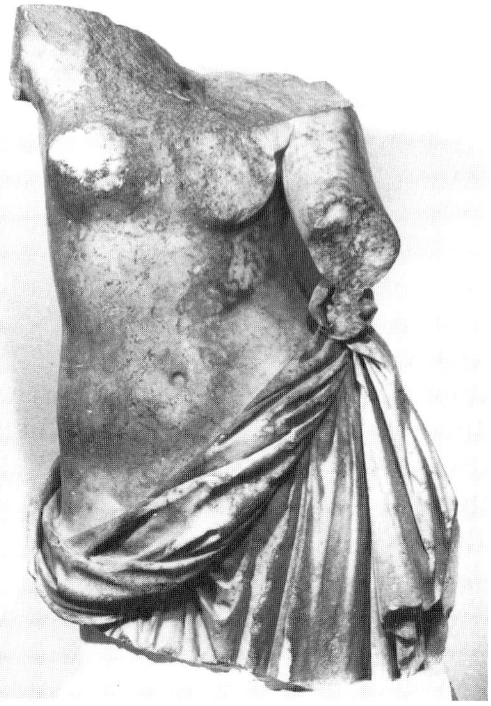

Εικ. 6. Μουσείο Ρόδου, ά.α. Φωτ. Μουσείου, αρ. αρνητικού 3730.

Το δεύτερο θέμα αφορά μια σειρά αγαλματίων Αρτέμιδος, γνωστών από παλαιότερα[21] και νεώτερα ευρήματα.[22] Αντανακλάται πιθανότατα σε αυτά – όσον αφορά το γενικό τους σχήμα – έργο του 4ου αιώνα, μάλλον πραξιτελικό. Εκτός από το ένα,[23] που βρέθηκε στην Κάμιρο και για το οποίο δεν έχουμε σαφείς πληροφορίες για το ακριβές σημείο εύρεσής του, τα λοιπά βρέθηκαν στην πόλη της Ρόδου. Το μεγαλύτερο της σειράς με αρ. ευρετηρίου 1224 (εικ. 7) σώζεται σε ύψος 65 εκ., είναι λίγο μικρότερο από το φυσικό. Ως υλικό χρησιμοποιείται το λευκό κρυσταλλικό μάρμαρο. Η θεά, ντυμένη τον κοντό χιτωνίσκο με απόπτυγμα και ιμάτιο που δένεται στη μέση, φέρει φαρέτρα στην πλάτη. Η ήρεμη κυρίως στάση και η ένδυση της θεάς ανακαλεί το πραξιτελικό θεωρούμενο πρωτότυπο της Αρτέμιδος Gabii. Τα επί μέρους ωστόσο μοτίβα, όπως π.χ. το ιμάτιο που σφίγει τη μέση[24] ανεξάρτητα αν ο χιτωνίσκος είναι ή όχι ζωσμένος, συνιστούν την ελληνιστική "συμβολή" στο θέμα. Στην πρώτη δημοσίευση, ο Maiuri τη θεωρεί *derivazione* της Αρτέμιδος Λαφρίας των Πατρών, η οποία αποδίδεται στον Δαμοφώντα από τη Μεσσήνη. Το εικονογραφικό σχήμα ωστόσο, που μας είναι γνωστό από τα αυτοκρατορικά νομίσματα των Πατρών,[25] δεν βοηθά σε εγγύτερη τυπολογική προσέγγιση του θέματος. Και τα αγαλμάτια της Ρόδου παρουσιάζουν σημαντικές τυπολογικές διαφοροποιήσεις μεταξύ τους, κάτι που δεν θα μας απασχολήσει εδώ. Τυπολογική μελέτη αυτών αλλά και των πολυαρίθμων ρωμαϊκών αντιγράφων με αυτό το θέμα μπορεί να οδηγήσει σε ενδιαφέροντα συμπεράσματα. Δεν πρέπει να ανάγονται όλα σε κοινό πρωτότυπο. Απλώς επισημαίνουμε τις σαφείς αναφορές στην υστεροκλασική παράδοση, που ενσωματώνονται όμως σε ένα έργο καταφανέστατα εκλεκτικά κλασικίζον.

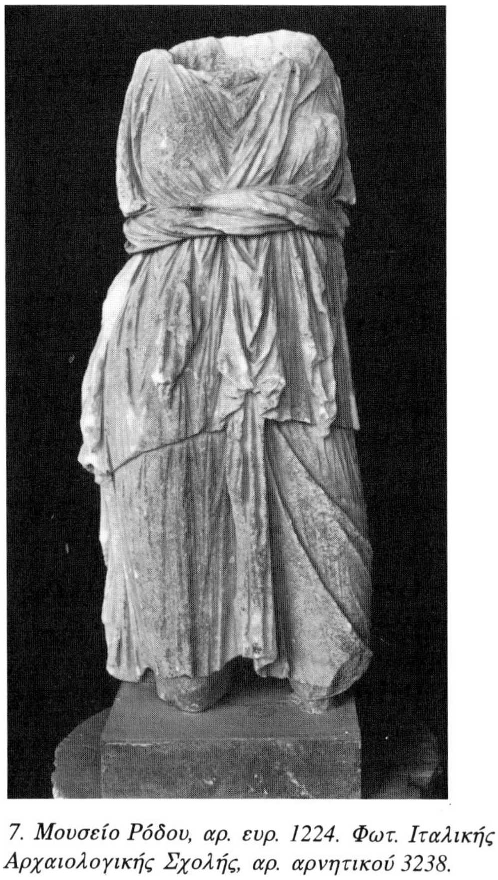

Εικ. 7. Μουσείο Ρόδου, αρ. ευρ. 1224. Φωτ. Ιταλικής Αρχαιολογικής Σχολής, αρ. αρνητικού 3238.

Ο τύπος είναι δημοφιλής στη Ρόδο χωρίς επαρκείς ενδείξεις για πρωτότυπη ροδιακή δημιουργία. Έχει υποστηριχθεί ότι αρχικά δημιουργήθηκε στο Πέργαμο, όπου υπήρχε και επίσημη σχολή αντιγραφέων από τα ώριμα ελληνιστικά χρόνια.[26] Είναι δύσκολο να αποδειχθεί με ασφαλή

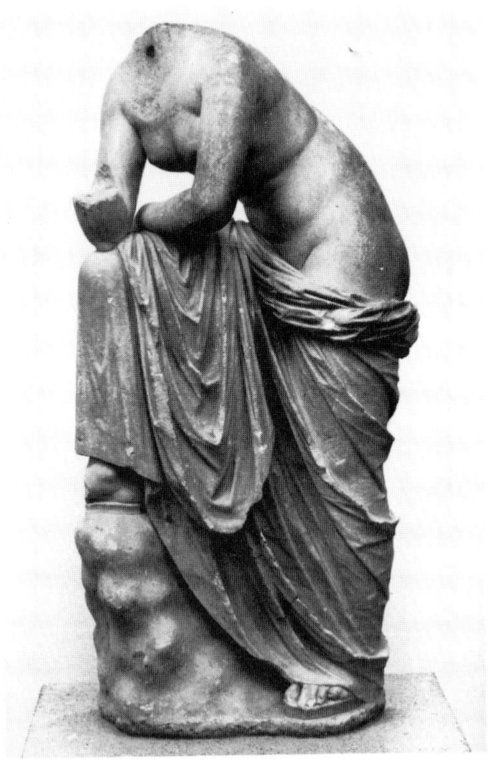

Εικ. 8. Μουσείο Ρόδου, αρ. ευρ. 13635. Φωτ. Μουσείου, αρ. αρνητικού 1709–7.

επιχειρήματα πού αρχικά δημιουργήθηκε το ελληνιστικό πρωτότυπο. Διαπιστώνουμε όμως ότι απαντά εξίσου στη Ρόδο, στη Δήλο,[27] στην Κυρηναϊκή,[28] αλλά και, στα ρωμαϊκά χρόνια, στην Κρήτη,[29] όπου συνοδεύεται από έναν καθιστό σκύλο. Ο Maiuri, χωρίς να συζητά καθόλου το θέμα της χρονολόγησής τους, υποθέτει ως προς τη λειτουργικότητά τους ότι είτε ήταν λατρευτικά έργα για μικρά αγροτικά ιερά ή -πιο πιθανόν- διακοσμητικά έργα ιδιωτικών οικιών.[30]

Οι γυναικείες μορφές, που συνήθως αναπαράγονται στα ελληνιστικά χρόνια στη Ρόδο, τόσο η αυστηρή, λιτή Άρτεμις σε στιγμή ανάπαυσης, όσο και η Αφροδίτη σε σκηνή λουτρού ή καλλωπισμού, επαναλαμβάνονται είτε απευθείας από τα κλασικά τους πρότυπα είτε με επιλεκτική προσθήκη νέων μοτίβων χωρίς να επηρεάζεται δραστικά το αρχικό σχήμα. Αυτή η δημιουργική επανάληψη ενός παλαιότερου τύπου μένει για την ώρα αμφίβολο αν λαμβάνει χώρα στην ίδια την Ρόδο ή στο Πέργαμο ή στην Αλεξάνδρεια. Θα μπορούσαμε ενδεχομένως να υποστηρίξουμε την άποψη ότι υπάρχει κάποια κοινή αντίληψη όσον αφορά την αντιγραφή.[31]

Όλα τα αγαλμάτια, ανδρικά και γυναικεία, που περιελήφθησαν σε αυτή την κατηγορία και στα οποία αντανακλώνται λιγότερο ή περισσότερο πιστά συγκεκριμένα κλασικά πρότυπα, προορίζονταν για τη διακόσμηση ιδιωτικών οικιών, είτε πρόκειται για οικιακά ιερά, είτε για αυλές και μικρά αίθρια, αφού στο μεγαλύτερο ποσοστό τους προέρχονται από την οικιστική ζώνη της πόλης της Ρόδου (βλ. σημ. 14).

Β. Στη δεύτερη κατηγορία περιλαμβάνονται αγαλμάτια, τα οποία έχει καθιερωθεί στην έρευνα να θεωρούνται ροδιακές δημιουργίες, χαρακτηριστικά δηλαδή έργα της "ροδιακής σχολής."

Στη λυσιππική παράδοση[32] και ακολουθώντας ένα σχήμα γνωστό κυρίως από ανδρικές μορφές[33] εντάσσεται το άγαλμα Αφροδίτης ή Νύμφης με αρ. ευρετηρίου 13635 (εικ. 8).[34] Λείπει το κεφάλι και σώζεται σε ύψος 78,5 εκ. Χρησιμοποιείται λευκό κρυσταλλικό μάρμαρο. Η Αφροδίτη (ή Νύμφη) φοράει το ιμάτιο μόνο στο κάτω τμήμα του σώματος ενώ ο κορμός μένει γυμνός. Πατάει με το δεξί της πόδι σε βράχο, καθώς γέρνει τον κορμό προς τα εμπρός για να ακουμπήσει με τα δύο χέρια της στο υψωμένο δεξί της γόνατο. Ο βράχος αποτελεί συστατικό στοιχείο της σύνθεσης. Για τη βάση ωστόσο δεν έχουμε επαρκείς ενδείξεις αν θα είχε και αυτή μορφή βράχου. Χρονολογείται στον 2ο αιώνα π.Χ. Στους Κήπους (το Taman της νότιας Ρωσίας) έχει τη θέση του λατρευτικού αγάλματος στο ιερό της Αφροδίτης.[35]

Ένα άλλο εξαιρετικά δημοφιλές σχήμα είναι αυτό μιας ντυμένης με ιμάτιο γυναικείας μορφής, που μισοκάθεται σε βράχο. Απαντά σε μια σειρά μαρμάρινων αγαλματίων και πηλίνων ειδωλίων με μέγεθος από 10–20 εκ. Ορισμένα αγαλμάτια έχουν βρεθεί στα λατομεία του Άη-Γιάννη στην πόλη της Ρόδου, το ένα στην Αρχάγγελο.[36] Το μεγαλύτερο, με αρ. ευρετηρίου 13614 σώζεται σε ύψος 63 εκ. (εικ. 9).[37] Ταυτίζεται με Αφροδίτη, Νύμφη ή Μούσα. Ο βράχος, όπως και στο προηγούμενο έργο, αποτελεί συστατικό στοιχείο της σύνθεσης και θεωρείται απευθείας αναφορά στο περιβάλλον. Αυτά τα αγαλμάτια της Αφροδίτης σε βράχο, πολυάριθμα στη Ρόδο, βρέθηκαν επίσης σε σπίτια της Πριήνης (εικ. 10),[38] αλλά και στην Κω, στην Casa Romana,[39] της οποίας θα κοσμούσαν το μικρό περιστύλιο μαζί με άλλα αγάλματα. Με βάση εξωτερικά στοιχεία χρονολογούνται περί τα μέσα του 2ου αιώνα π.Χ. Εκτός από την Κω και την Πριήνη, το θέμα απαντά εξίσου όχι μόνο στην Αλεξάνδρεια,[40] στη Δήλο,[41] στον αθηναϊκό Κεραμεικό[42] και στη Ρήνεια ως επιτύμβιο(;),[43] αλλά αντανακλάται και σε έργα στη γειτονική Ιταλία.[44]

Εκτός από τη θέση ότι πρόκειται για ροδιακή δημιουργία,[45] έχει επίσης διατυπωθεί η υπόθεση ότι ίσως σ' αυτό το θέμα αποκρυσταλλώνεται κατά τον πιο εύγλωττο τρόπο αυτό που η Bieber αποκαλεί *Asianism*,[46] την κοινή δηλαδή καλλιτεχνική γλώσσα των νησιών του νοτιοανατολικού Αιγαίου και της Μ. Ασίας. Όποιος και αν αποδειχθεί ότι είναι ο τόπος δημιουργίας του αγαλματικού αυτού τύπου, θεωρούμε ιδιαίτερης σημασίας την ευρύτατη διάδοσή του.

Με συστατικό στοιχείο της σύνθεσης τον βράχο, αλλά και με άμεση αναφορά στο νερό, έχουμε και το άγαλμα με αρ. ευρετηρίου 5288, που βρέθηκε στην Ακρόπολη της Ρόδου (εικ. 11).[47] Σώζεται σε ύψος 70 εκ. και είναι από λευκό κρυσταλλικό μάρμαρο. Η

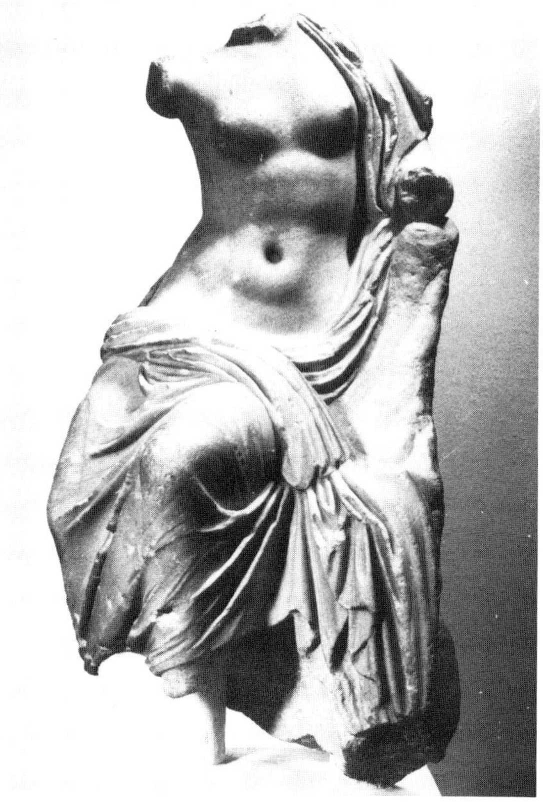

Εικ. 9. Μουσείο Ρόδου, αρ. ευρ. 13614. Φωτ. Μουσείου, αρ. αρνητικού 3181.

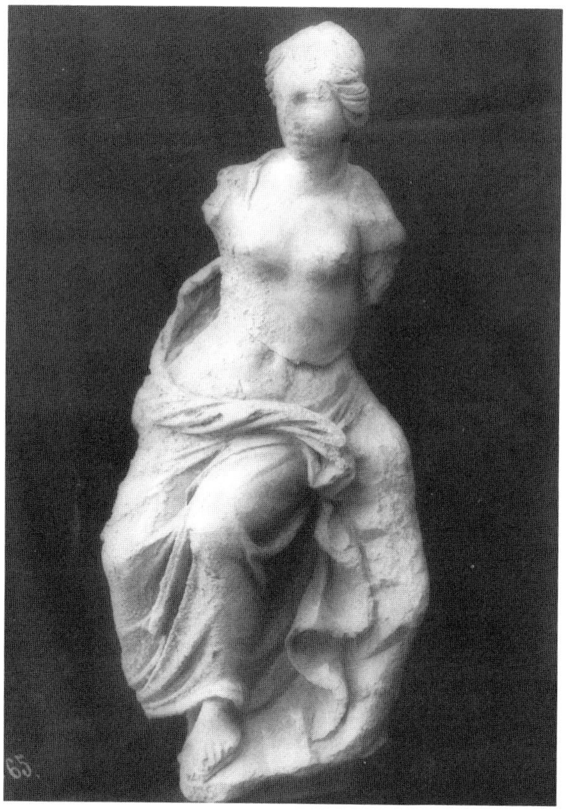

Εικ. 10. Αρχαιολογικό Μουσείο Κωνσταντινουπόλεως, αρ. ευρ. 746. Φωτ. Μουσείου.

Αφροδίτη, ή Νύμφη, μοιάζει σαν να γλυστράει προς τα εμπρός, προς μια λιμνούλα ή λεκάνη. Το θέμα αυτό, δύσκολο να βρεθεί στην ελεύθερη πλαστική, προοριζόταν πιθανώς για χρήση σε κρήνες ή πάντως σε βραχώδεις διαμορφώσεις κοντά σε υδάτινο περιβάλλον. Η σύλληψη είναι απολύτως ζωγραφική,[48] πράγμα σύνηθες στα υστεροελληνιστικά χρόνια, όπου και χρονολογείται το έργο. Χωρίς να έχει αυτόνομη θεματολογική υπόσταση στο χώρο,[49] έρχεται ως εξελικτική βαθμίδα του προηγούμενου θέματος. Η ακόμα εντονότερη δήλωση του τοπίου και η εύρεσή του σε περιοχή, όπου υπάρχουν νυμφαία, κάνει εύλογη την υπόθεση για τοποθέτησή του μάλλον σε δημόσιο χώρο αναψυχής και όχι σε ιδιωτική κατοικία.

Κοινό χαρακτηριστικό των αγαλματικών τύπων αυτής της κατηγορίας είναι ο βράχος, αναπόσπαστο στοιχείο της σύνθεσης. Και στα τρία οι μορφές συνιστούν χαρακτηριστικές δημιουργίες των υστεροελληνιστικών χρόνων, παρότι ως προς τα επιμέρους μοτίβα θα μπορούσαμε να διακρίνουμε και αναμνήσεις παλαιοτέρων εποχών. Σε αντίθεση προς τα έργα της πρώτης κατηγορίας, στα οποία ο αγαλματικός τύπος, η μορφή, έχει αυθύπαρκτη υπόσταση, εδώ γίνεται φανερή η ζωγραφική, διηγηματική κατά κάποιον τρόπο διάθεση. Πρόκειται για έργα που δίνουν την αίσθηση ότι αποτελούν τμήμα ενός συνόλου, εντάσσονται απολύτως στο τοπίο σε ένα ευρύτερο σκηνικό.[50]

Καταφανώς διακοσμητικά έργα και τα αγαλμάτια αυτής της κατηγορίας, βρίσκουν τη θέση τους στα περιστύλια των οικιών της Ρόδου. Οι αναφορές ωστόσο στο περιβάλλον υποδεικνύουν θέσεις όπως κρήνες, τα νυμφαία στην ακρόπολη της Ρόδου, τα άλση στο Ροδίνι, τεχνητά δηλαδή διαμορφωμένους χώρους αναψυχής στις παρυφές της αρχαίας πόλης.[51] Το νέο στοιχείο, που συνιστά και την κατεξοχήν συμβολή των ροδίων καλλιτεχνών, είναι η διαμόρφωση και διακόσμηση του φυσικού περιβάλλοντος όχι αποκλειστικά για λατρευτικούς σκοπούς.[52] Ίσως αυτός να είναι ο λόγος που οδηγεί με τόση αληθοφάνεια στη Ρόδο ως τόπο δημιουργίας των γλυπτών της δεύτερης κατηγορίας, δηλαδή ως απαραίτητο συμπλήρωμα των κάθε είδους τεχνητών διαμορφώσεων.

Σε ιδιαίτερη κατηγορία εντάσσεται η Αφροδίτη οκλάζουσα με αρ. ευρετηρίου 4685, η οποία βρέθηκε στην πόλη της Ρόδου (εικ. 12).[53] Σώζεται ακέραια και έχει ύψος μόλις 49 εκ. Το υλικό είναι λευκό μάρμαρο που από τον Jacopi θεωρήθηκε παριανό. Με ιδιαίτερη επιμέλεια έχει λειανθεί η επιφάνεια. Πρόκειται για μικρογραφική μετάπλαση του τύπου της Αφροδίτης οκλάζουσας, που δημιούργησε ο Δοιδάλσας στις αρχές του 3ου αιώνα π.Χ. Στην πραγματικότητα έχουμε τον συγκερασμό δύο ελληνιστικών εικονογραφικών θεμάτων, δηλαδή της Αφροδίτης οκλάζουσας από τη μια και της Αφροδίτης

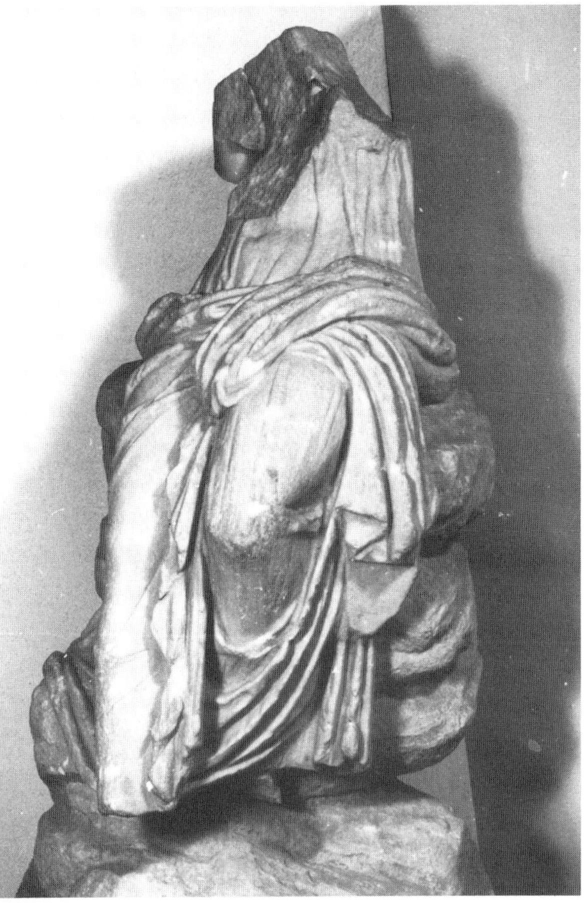

Εικ. 11. Μουσείο Ρόδου, αρ. ευρ. 5288. Φωτ. Μουσείου, αρ. αρνητικού 1700.

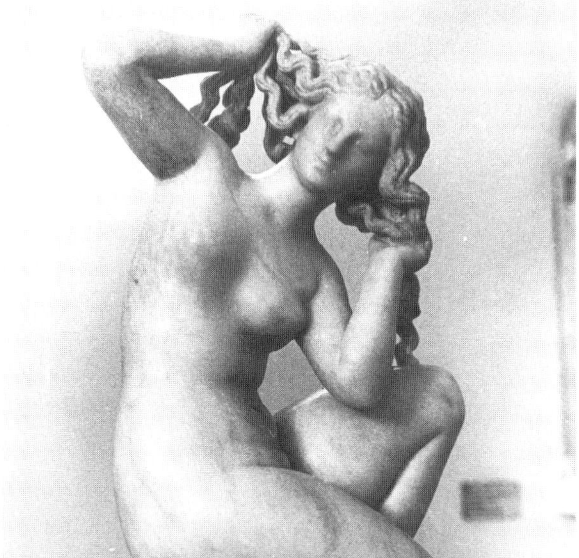

Εικ. 12. Μουσείο Ρόδου, αρ. ευρ. 4685. Φωτ. Μουσείου..

αναδυομένης από την άλλη. Εντάσσεται και αυτό το αγαλμάτιο στην αέναη δημιουργικότητα που διαπιστώνεται στο νησί κατά τους δύο τελευταίους προχριστιανικούς αιώνες. Έτσι ένα θέμα γνωστό και φημισμένο αναπαράγεται με την υιοθέτηση νέων μοτίβων αλλά και των νέων τάσεων. Υπακούει στη ζωγραφική διάθεση και από πολυεπίπεδο έργο, *vielansichtig*, εξελίσσεται στη μια μόνο διάσταση *einansichtig*. Οι κεντρόφυγες δυνάμεις, που οδηγούν σε άνοιγμα της μορφής, σε μια επιπεδικότητα, την *Einansichtigkeit*, χρονολογούν τη δημιουργία του αγαλματίου στα ύστερα ελληνιστικά χρόνια.[54] Παρότι αυτό το -ροδιακό- παράδειγμα είναι το γνωστότερο και δημοφιλέστερο στην αρχαιολογική βιβλιογραφία, πατρίδα του έχει θεωρηθεί η Αλεξάνδρεια,[55] όπου και απαντά ο τύπος με περισσότερα παραδείγματα.[56] Στην Αλεξάνδρεια εξάλλου προσγράφεται, σύμφωνα με μια υπόθεση, και η δημιουργία του τύπου της Αφροδίτης Αναδυομένης (βλ. σημ. 18).

Αξίζει να παρατηρήσουμε ότι αντίγραφα του τύπου της Αφροδίτης οκλάζουσας είναι εξαιρετικά σπάνια στην κυρίως Ελλάδα κατά τα ελληνιστικά χρόνια.[57] Στον 1ο αιώνα π.Χ. και στο ανατολικό τμήμα της Μεσογείου πιστεύουμε ότι δημιουργείται και η παραλλαγή της Αφροδίτης οκλάζουσας με τον Έρωτα. Υιοθετούνται και σε αυτήν, με άλλον τρόπο (την προσθήκη δηλαδή μιας ακόμα μορφής), οι αρχές της επιπεδικότητας που διαπιστώνουμε στη ροδιακή οκλάζουσα. Ο αρχικός τύπος αντιγράφεται κυρίως στην Ιταλία κατά τα ρωμαϊκά χρόνια.[58]

Καταλήγοντας μπορούμε να συνοψίσουμε ότι τα χαρακτηριστικά της ύστερης ελληνιστικής εποχής διακοσμητικά έργα -σε ιδιωτικούς είτε σε δημόσιους χώρους- δείχνουν και τη ροπή προς επίδειξη της ροδιακής κοινωνίας. Κοσμούσαν εσωτερικούς χώρους ή αίθρια, οικιακά ιερά ή περιστύλια, κρήνες, νυμφαία ή άλση (εικ. 13). Χωρίς να λείπουν από το θεματολόγιο οι θεϊκές μορφές, ακολουθούν και αυτές τον συρμό της εποχής με μεγέθη μικρότερα, είτε αυτό οφείλεται στην ιδεολογία -ή στην τοπική μόδα- είτε στην έλλειψη πρώτης ύλης, όπως έχει συχνά επισημανθεί. Προτιμώνται συνήθως σε ένα τέτοιο πλαίσιο τύποι Απόλλωνος, Αφροδίτης, Έρωτος, ή Αρτέμος (αποκλειστικά ως αναπαυομένη κυνηγέτις). Και ακολουθούν οι Μούσες, οι Νύμφες και οι Σάτυροι.

Για όλα αυτά τα θέματα είναι εξαιρετικά επισφαλές να ορισθεί η μια ή η άλλη πόλη ως τόπος δημιουργίας τους. Μπορεί τα περισσότερα αντίγραφα της Αφροδίτης οκλάζουσας να έχουν βρεθεί στην Αλεξάνδρεια, αναμφισβήτητα όμως εξέχουσα είναι η ποιότητα του ροδιακού παραδείγματος. Εξίσου επισφαλής μας φαίνεται και η υπόθεση της δημιουργίας του ελληνιστικού τύπου της Αρτέμιδος στο Πέργαμο. 'Εχει εξάλλου διατυπωθεί από μερίδα ερευνητών η υπόθεση ότι στη Ρόδο γεννήθηκε το μπαρόκ πριν την εκτεταμένη εφαρμογή του στα μνημειώδη οικοδομήματα του Περγάμου.[59] Η ροδιακή

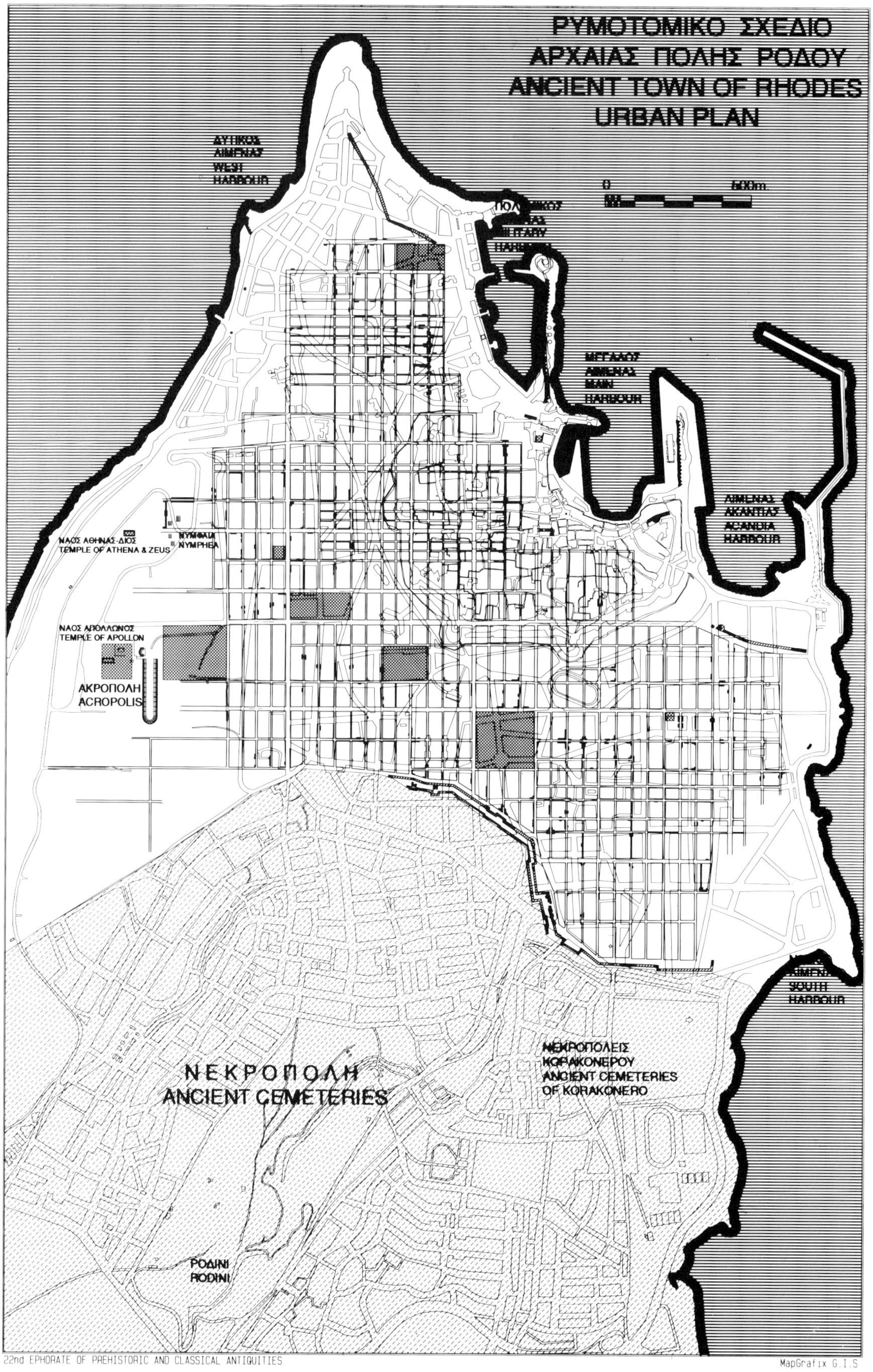

Εικ. 13. Ρυμοτομικό σχέδιο της αρχαίας πόλης της Ρόδου. ΚΒ' Εφορεία Προϊστορικών και Κλασικών Αρχαιοτήτων – επεξεργασία των δεδομένων σε Η/Υ από τον αρχιτέκτονα Νικόλαο Ζαρίφη.

θεματολογία μοιάζει ωστόσο πλησιέστερη στην αλεξανδρινή παραγωγή χωρίς να λείπουν και αναλογίες προς το Πέργαμο και την Πριήνη.[60] Η αποστροφή όμως ότι "η Ρόδος είναι αποδέκτης ως προς την Αλεξάνδρεια, δότης ως προς τη Δήλο" μένει προς το παρόν τουλάχιστον γενικόλογη.[61]

Από όσα επιλεκτικά και μόνο αναφέραμε συνάγεται η μεγάλη ρευστότητα που υπάρχει όσον αφορά την απόδοση σε συγκεκριμένη "σχολή" ενός έργου.[62] Επιλέξαμε παραδείγματα με βέβαιη προέλευση και αντιπροσωπευτικά της ροδιακής παραγωγής κατά τα ύστερα ελληνιστικά χρόνια. Και στην πρώτη κατηγορία, όπου διαπιστώνεται η πιστότερη συνέχεια της κλασικής παράδοσης, έχουμε έργα, που ανευρίσκονται ως τύποι και σε άλλες ελληνικές πόλεις. Αλλά και στη δεύτερη, όπου αναγνωρίζουμε τη δημιουργία νέων τύπων στο νησί της Ρόδου, περιλαμβάνονται έργα όχι μόνο με ιδιαίτερη εξάπλωση εκεί, αλλά και με ακτινοβολία που ξεπερνά τα όρια του ενός μόνο κέντρου. Για την περίπτωση, συνεπώς, της Ρόδου, εκτός από το γεγονός ότι δεν γνωρίζουμε, έως τώρα τουλάχιστον, τη μνημειώδη τέχνη της, αν πράγματι υπήρξε τέτοια,[63] μπορούμε να πούμε ότι αφομοιώνει δημιουργικά την κλασική παράδοση, αντιγράφει παλαιότερα έργα, αλλά και υιοθετεί παλαιότερα επί μέρους μοτίβα για τη δημιουργία νέων τύπων. Μακριά από τον ακαδημαϊσμό του Περγάμου πειραματίζεται με την καθημερινότητα, παίζει με τους όγκους, τις αναλογίες, τα μοτίβα.

Όπως διαπιστώνει ο J. Marcadé για τη γλυπτική παραγωγή της Δήλου,[64] έτσι και για τη Ρόδο κρίνουμε το σύνολο της γλυπτικής παραγωγής από τα μαρμάρινα έργα μόνο -αφού τα χάλκινα δεν έχουν σωθεί-[65]από τις προτιμήσεις κυρίως ορισμένων οικογενειών[66] και όχι από την επίσημη τέχνη[67] και, το σημαντικότερο, από τα μικρά έργα και όχι από τα "αριστουργήματα." Με αυτά τα δεδομένα λοιπόν είναι μάλλον δύσκολο να αναγνωρισθεί η ύπαρξη ή μή σχολής. Μένουμε συνεπώς στη συστηματική μελέτη του ίδιου του υλικού, το οποίο και μόνον θα μας κατευθύνει στην αναζήτηση των σχέσεων μεταξύ των κέντρων/πόλεων, της κοινής γλώσσας ή των κατά τόπους ιδιολέκτων σε αυτό το χωνευτήρι, που φαίνεται ότι έχουμε στα ελληνιστικά χρόνια.

Θερμές ευχαριστίες οφείλω στον Προϊστάμενο κ. Ιωάννη Παπαχριστοδούλου και σε όλους τους αρχαιολόγους της ΚΒ' Εφορείας Προϊστορικών και Κλασικών Αρχαιοτήτων για την πάντα εγκάρδια φιλοξενία και βοήθειά τους. Ιδιαίτερα θα ήθελα να ευχαριστήσω τις κυρίες Αγγελική Γιαννικουρή για τις κάθε είδους διευκολύνσεις στο Μουσείο της Ρόδου, Μαρία Κόλλια για την επίσκεψη στο χώρο των νυμφαίων, Βασιλική Πατσιαδά για τους περιπάτους στις περιοχές των νεκροταφείων και στο Ροδίνι αλλά και για την προθυμία της να διαβάσει αυτό το χειρόγραφο. Την κυρία Ηώ Ζερβουδάκη ευχαριστώ θερμά για τις χρήσιμες παρατηρήσεις της σε όλα τα στάδια αυτής της μελέτης.

Σημειώσεις

Εκτός από τις καθιερωμένες συντομογραφίες υιοθετούνται και οι ακόλουθες:

Merker, *Studies*:	G.S. Merker, *Studies in the Hellenistic Sculpture of the Island of Rhodes* (διδ. διατριβή, Bryn Mawr College 1970- Ann Arbor Microfilms 1979)
Merker:	G.S. Merker, *The Hellenistic Sculpture of Rhodes*, *SIMA* 40 (1973)
Gualandi:	G. Gualandi, *ASAtene* 54, N.S. 38, 1976, 7–259

1. L. Alscher, *Griechische Plastik* 4. *Hellenismus* (1957). Lippold, *Plastik*, 293–387. M. Bieber, *The Sculpture of the Hellenistic Age*² (1961): ιδιαίτερη διαπραγμάτευση για την τέχνη της Αλεξάνδρειας, της Πριήνης, του Περγάμου, της Ρόδου και νοτιοδυτικής Μ. Ασίας. A. Linfert, *Kunstzentren hellenistischer Zeit* (1976). P. Moreno, *Scultura ellenistica* (1994). Merker, *Studies*, 457: διακρίνει πολλά στοιχεία κατά του εντοπισμού τοπικών σχολών γλυπτικής κατά τα ελληνιστικά χρόνια.
2. Οι φιλολογικές πηγές, κυρίως Πλίνιος *NH* 34.36, 34.42, παραδίδουν ότι η Ρόδος ήταν η πόλη των κολοσσών, των μεγάλων συμπλεγμάτων, του μπαρόκ. 'Οπως η ρητορική και η λογοτεχνία έτσι και η τέχνη είχε τάση προς το κολοσικό και το επιδεικτικό.
3. Gualandi 14: κυρίως κατά τον 1ο και 2ο αιώνα π.Χ. Διϊστάμενες στην έρευνα είναι οι απόψεις σχετικά με αυτό το θέμα. Γενικά τα σωζόμενα γλυπτά δεν τεκμηριώνουν "ροδιακή σχολή:" πρβλ. και G.M.A. Richter, *Three Critical Periods in Greek Sculpture* (1951) 31. *EAA* VI (1965) 760 λ. Rodia, arte ellenistica (L. Laurenzi), ο οποίος επισημαίνει επί πλέον ότι η σχολή μόνο κατά σύμβαση θα μπορούσε να ονομαστεί ροδιακή. Συσχετίζει αυτή τη ροδιακή σχολή προς μιαν ευρύτερη νησιωτική-ασιατική, θέση που υιοθετεί και η Bieber ό.π. (σημ. 1) κεφάλαιο 9. J. Isager, *RM* 102, 1995, 115–131, με εκτενή αναφορά στη φιλολογική παράδοση αλλά μνεία μόνο των μνημειωδών συνθέσεων. Βλ. και την ανακοίνωση της Mattusch στον παρόντα τόμο, σελ. 149–156.
4. Το παλαιότερο υλικό των ιταλικών ανασκαφών δημοσιεύεται κυρίως από τους Maiuri, Jacopi, Laurenzi στα τεύχη του Clara Rhodos ως εξής: A. Maiuri – G. Jacopich, *ClRh* I (1928) 21–27. A. Maiuri, *ClRh* II, 1 (1932) 7–76. G. Jacopi, *ClRh* V, 1 (1931). Ο ίδιος, *ClRh* V, 2 (1932) 1–36. Ο ίδιος, *ClRh* VI-VII (1932–33) 265–278. L. Laurenzi, *ClRh* IX (1938) 9–122. Ο ίδιος, *ClRh* X (1941) 1–24. Κατάλογος όλων των ευρημάτων των ιταλικών ανασκαφών αλλά και συνθετική άρτια ενημερωμένη βιβλιογραφικά μελέτη είναι το άρθρο του G. Gualandi, *ASAtene* 54, N.S. 38, 1976, 7–259. Λίγο νωρίτερα δημοσιεύτηκαν η διδακτορική διατριβή (*Studies in the Hellenistic Sculpture of the Island of Rhodes*) και μια μονογραφία της G.S. Merker, *The Hellenistic Sculpture of Rhodes* το 1970 και 1973 αντίστοιχα. Για το νεώτερο υλικό των ελληνικών ανασκαφών έχουμε μόνο μνείες των ευρημάτων στο *Έργον*, στα *Πρακτικά της εν Αθήναις Αρχαιολογικής*

Εταιρείας, στο *Αρχαιολογικό Δελτίο*, στα *Αρχαιολογικά Ανάλεκτα εξ Αθηνών* (βλ. Gualandi 11 σημ. 1).

5. Αντιγραφική παράδοση κατά τον 2ο αιώνα π.Χ. είναι γνωστή κυρίως από το Πέργαμο: J.-P. Niemeier, *Kopien und Nachahmungen im Hellenismus* (1985). Και για τη Ρόδο έχουν ήδη επισημανθεί τάσεις μίμησης / αντιγραφής: η Merker, *Studies*, 425, διαπιστώνει ότι η επιρροή της κλασικής αττικής γλυπτικής πραγματώνεται στο μεν Πέργαμο κυρίως ως "αρχαιοδιφικό ενδιαφέρον" (antiquarian interest), ενώ στη Ρόδο κυρίως ως στυλ παρά ως εικονογραφία.

6. Δεν μαρτυρούνται λατομεία με καλής ποιότητας μάρμαρο στο νησί. Ο Isager, ό.π. (σημ. 3) 120, παρατηρεί ότι η Ρόδος δεν αναφέρεται μεταξύ των γνωστών για τα μάρμαρά τους τόπων. Εκτός από τον γνωστό λάρτιο λίθο, ο οποίος είναι γκριζωπός και μάλλον όχι κατάλληλος για την γλυπτική, διαπιστώνεται και χρήση χρωματιστών λίθων, καλύτερης δηλαδή ή μετριότερης ποιότητας ασβεστολίθων. Βλ. σχετικά A. Herrmann στο *Kanon*, Festschrift E. Berger, 15. Beih. *AntK* (1988) 244–246, πίν. 68–69.

7. Η. Ζερβουδάκη, *ΑΔελτ* 25, 1970, Χρον. Β 2, 513, πίν. 437 ε. Gualandi, 12–13 σημ. 2, 255. *LIMC* II (1984) λ. Apollon, αρ. 81k (O. Palagia). Για εκτενέστερη διαπραγμάτευση σχετικά με τον αγαλματικό τύπο βλ. Β. Μαχαίρα, "Κεφαλή Απόλλωνος Σταυροκτόνου," *Κατάλογος της Συλλογής των Γλυπτών του Μουσείου Μπενάκη* (υπό έκδοση).

8. Κυρίως κατασκευάζονται βάσεις αγαλμάτων που μιμούνται τον φυσικό βράχο, βλ. H. Lauter, *AntK* 15, 1972, 51, πίν. 15.2. I. Schmidt, *Hellenistische Statuenbasen* (1995) 193.195: τέτοιες βάσεις είναι γνωστές κατά τα ελληνιστικά χρόνια μόνο από τη Ρόδο και έχουν κυρίως βρεθεί στη Λίνδο και στην Κάμιρο.

9. L. Laurenzi, *ArchCl* 10, 1958, 172–175, πίν. 57–58. Merker, *Studies*, 240, αρ. 58, εικ. 33. Merker 29, αρ. 62, εικ. 40–41.

10. L. Lacroix, *Les reproductions de statues sur les monnaies grecques* (1949) 311–312. G.E. Rizzo, *Prassitele* (1932) 85, πίν. 118, 4–5.

11. Merker, *Studies*, 304, αρ. 83. Gualandi 196–197, αρ. 200, εικ. 250.

12. Έικάζεται πιθανότατα ο Έρωτας στο Πάριον της Τρωάδος. Πλίνιος, *NH* 36.23. Overbeck, *SQ* αρ. 1263–1267: για τους Έρωτες στο έργο του Πραξιτέλους. Βλ. επίσης το αγαλμάτιο Έρωτος από την Casa Romana στην Κω: L. Laurenzi, *ASAtene* 33–34, N.S. 17–18, 1955–56, 66–69, αρ. 2.

13. Κόρινθος: *Mind and Body* (1989) 332, αρ. 222 (Β. Μαχαίρα). T. L. Shear, *AJA* 30, 1926, 462, εικ. 15. B.S. Ridgway, *Hesperia* 50, 1981, 434 σημ. 50: συνήθως αντιγράφονται "standard Greek originals." Βλ. γενικότερα E. Bartman, *Ancient Sculptural Copies in Miniature* (1992) 4.26–27.

14. V.J. Harward, *Greek Domestic Sculpture and the Origins of Private Art Patronage* (1982). M. Kreeb, *Untersuchungen zur figürlichen Ausstattung delischer Privathäuser* (1988). W. Hoepfner – G. Brands (επιμ.), *Basileia. Die Paläste der hellenistische Könige* (1996). Η ανασκαφική έρευνα στη Δήλο και την Πριήνη σε εκτεταμένες οικιστικές ζώνες έκανε εύλογη την ταύτιση.

15. Η γενίκευση αυτή συνάγεται όχι μόνο από τα λίγα παρουσιαζόμενα έργα, αλλά από το σύνολο των ροδιακών γλυπτών. Η επανάληψη των τύπων προκύπτει χωρίς σημαντικούς εικονογραφικούς ή μορφολογικούς νεωτερισμούς. Βλ. σχετικά Gualandi 18. 229. Η. Ζερβουδάκη, *ΑΔελτ* 33, 1978, Μελ., 38–39.

16. L. Laurenzi, *ClRh* IX (1938) 50, εικ. 31. Merker, *Studies*, 98–100, αρ. 11. Merker 26, αρ. 4, πίν. 2, εικ. 6. Linfert ό.π. (σημ. 1) 159 σημ. 634, εικ. 390. *LIMC* II (1984) λ. Aphrodite, αρ. 542 (A. Delivorrias). Β. Μαχαίρα, "Δύο αγαλματικοί τύποι της ροδιακής πλαστικής των υστεροελληνιστικών χρόνων," στο *Πόλη Ρόδου. Από την ίδρυσή της μέχρι την κατάληψη από τους Τούρκους. Ρόδος 1993* (υπό έκδοση).

17. Ακαδημαϊσμός του 1ου αιώνα π.Χ. Διακρίνει ανάλογες αρχές με αυτές που διέπουν και τη δημιουργία της ροδιακής οκλάζουσας Αφροδίτης (βλ. παρακάτω).

18. Ό.π. (σημ. 16). Βλ. γενικά για έργα από την Αίγυπτο σε αυτό τον τύπο: Bieber ό.π. (σημ. 1) 98–99. A. Adriani, *Repertorio d'arte dell'Egitto greco-romano* A II (1961) 23, αρ. 85. 25, αρ. 95.97.

19. T. Wiegand – H. Schrader, *Priene* II (1904) 371, εικ. 467. Mendel II, 103–104, αρ. 362. *LIMC* II, λ. Aphrodite, αρ. 541. Το αγαλμάτιο έχει κατασκευαστεί από δύο κομμάτια μάρμαρο.

20. Η ακμή της ροδιακής ελληνιστικής πλαστικής θεωρείται από τον Linfert ό.π. (σημ. 1) 97, σύγχρονη με της γειτονικής της Κω και της Μαγνησίας του Μαιάνδρου.

21. A. Maiuri, *ClRh* II (1932) 16–18, αρ. 3–4, εικ. 6–7. Merker, *Studies*, 119–123, αρ. 17–19, εικ. 12. Merker 27, αρ. 15–17. Gualandi 53–56, αρ. 14, εικ. 27–30. *LIMC* II (1984) λ. Artemis, αρ. 194 a-b (L. Kahil).

22. Κ.Χ. Φατούρου, *ΑΔελτ* 19, 1964, Χρον. Β 3, 467, πίν. 550α. *BCH* 91, 1967, 768, εικ. 5. Βλ. και Gualandi 55 σημ. 4. *LIMC* II λ. Artemis, αρ. 194 c.

23. Gualandi 53–54, αρ. 14, εικ. 27.

24. Χαρακτηριστικό που διαφοροποιεί τα αγάλματα από τον τύπο που απαντά στα νομίσματα (βλ. παρακάτω σημ. 25). Αντίθετα στον τύπο Gabii η 'Αρτεμις φορά το ιμάτιο.

25. Lacroix ό.π. (σημ. 10) 232–238. 233, αρ. 4–6. 8. 10, πίν. 19, 8–9, 11. 238 αναφέρει ότι το πρωτότυπο δεν είναι παλαιότερο των ελληνιστικών χρόνων και μάλιστα το αποδίδει ειδικότερα στον Δαμοφώντα ή τη σχολή του.

26. Niemeier ό.π. (σημ. 5) 154: από τα 180/170 π.Χ. αρχίζει η διαδικασία αναπαραγωγής έργων τέχνης παλαιοτέρων χρόνων, και 157–163 για τη σημασία του Περγάμου στην πρώιμη αντιγραφική δραστηριότητα.

27. J. Marcadé, *Au Musée de Délos* (1969) 217 σημ. 5–6, πίν. 39. *LIMC* II, λ. Artemis, αρ. 195. Το αγαλμάτιο με αριθμό ευρετηρίου A 4152, αντιστοίχου μεγέθους προς το ροδιακό, φέρει τελαμώνα, όπου θα προσαρμοζόταν φαρέτρα, πράγμα που ισχύει και για το A 5481 μια και στη δεξιά ωμοπλάτη υπάρχει τένων.

28. E. Paribeni, *Catalogo delle sculture di Cirene; statue e rilievi di carattere religioso* (1959) 70, αρ. 157–158, πίν. 93. *LIMC* II, λ. Artemis, αρ. 199.

29. *LIMC* II, λ. Artemis, αρ. 242.

30. Ό.π. (σημ. 21). Η Merker, *Studies*, 122–123, θεωρεί τον τύπο αυτό ιδιαίτερα δημοφιλή στη Ρόδο, αμφιβάλλει

ωστόσο αν έχουμε πρωτότυπη ροδιακή δημιουργία.

31. Πρβλ. και Marcadé ό.π. (σημ. 27) 485 σημ. 1: υποδεικνύει αντίστοιχα έργα στη Δήλο επισημαίνοντας ότι σε κάθε ροδιακό έργο θα μπορούσε να παρατεθεί ένα δηλιακό.
32. Gualandi 27 σημ. 3.
33. Όπως π.χ. ο Ποσειδών: C. Vorster, *Museo Gregoriano Profano. Katalog der Skulpturen* II 1 (1993) 68–74, αρ. 27, πίν. 246–249, εικ. 125–132 με πλήρη βιβλιογραφία για τον τύπο του Λατερανού. Για την αναπαραγωγή αυτού του τύπου σε νομίσματα, κυρίως του Δημητρίου του Πολιορκητού, βλ. E.T. Newell, *The Coinages of Demetrius Poliorcetes* (1927). P.R. Franke – M. Hirmer, *Die griechische Münze*^{2} (1972) 117, αρ. 573, πίν. 174. O. Mørkholm, *Early Hellenistic Coinage from the Accession of Alexander to the Peace of Apamea (336–186 B.C.)* (1991) 80, πίν. X, αρ. 173.
34. G. Jacopi, *ClRh* V, 1 (1931) 16–22, εικ. 9–12, πίν. 2. Merker 26–27, αρ. 12, εικ. 9–12. Linfert ό.π. (σημ. 1) 91, πίν. 38, εικ. 199. *LIMC* II, λ. Aphrodite, αρ. 648. H.-H. von Prittwitz und Gaffron, *Der Wandel der Aphrodite* (1988) 61–89.
35. Μόσχα, Ιστορικό Μουσείο, αρ. ευρ. 99.553. *LIMC* II, λ. Aphrodite, αρ. 646. Prittwitz ό.π. (σημ. 34) 71–73, εικ. 23.
36. Gualandi 57–58, εικ. 33.
37. G. Jacopi, *ClRh* V, 2 (1932) 30–35, εικ. 19–21, πίν. 3–4. Gualandi 56–63, αρ. 15–17, εικ. 31–35. Linfert ό.π. (σημ. 1) 87. *LIMC* II, λ. Aphrodite, αρ. 879. Prittwitz ό.π. (σημ. 34) 30–60.
38. Κωνσταντινούπολη, Αρχαιολογικό Μουσείο, αρ. ευρ. 746. Wiegand – Schrader ό.π. (σημ. 19) 372, εικ. 468 (πρβλ. και εικ. 469 για την κατεύθυνση του δεξιού χεριού). Mendel II, 102–103, αρ. 361. *LIMC* II, λ. Aphrodite, αρ. 880.
39. L. Laurenzi, *ASAtene* 33–34, N.S. 17–18, 1955–56, 74–75 αρ. 6–7 (συναρμόζεται από δύο κομμάτια). 85, αρ. 28.
40. Σήμερα στη Στουτγάρδη, Württembergisches Landesmuseum, αρ. ευρ. 1.18 (10). *LIMC* II, λ. Aphrodite, αρ. 881. V. Machaira, *Les groupes statuaires d'Aphrodite et d'Éros* (1993) 79–80, αρ. 52. Για τον συσχετισμό με τα ροδιακά αγάλματα βλ. Gualandi 59 σημ. 3.
41. Marcadé ό.π. (σημ. 27) 484, πίν. 44 (αρ. ευρ. A 1722).
42. Αθήνα, Μουσείο Κεραμεικού, αρ. ευρ. P 53. H. Riemann, *Kerameikos* II (1940) 85, αρ. 111, πίν. 23. Machaira ό.π. (σημ. 40) 44, αρ. 8, πίν. 14.
43. Αθήνα, Εθνικό Αρχαιολογικό Μουσείο, αρ. ευρ. 380. Σ. Καρούζου, *'Εθνικό 'Αρχαιολογικό Μουσεῖο. Συλλογή γλυπτῶν* (1967) 174, πίν. 65. M.-Th. Couilloud, *Délos* 30 (1974) 232, αρ. 2, πίν. 89.
44. Νεάπολη, Αρχαιολογικό Μουσείο, αρ. ευρ. 150.386. Από την Baiae. *EAA* I (1958) λ. Amore e Psyche, 323, εικ. 462 (M. Napoli). O Gualandi 59, το θεωρεί ως produzione rodia.
45. Το άγαλμα της Ρόδου με αρ. ευρ. 13614 (βλ. σημ. 37) θεωρείται το καλύτερο από τη σειρά των αντιγράφων της Δίρκης στη σύνθεση του Toro Farnese και έργο των γλυπτών Απολλωνίου και Ταυρίσκου από τις Τράλλεις: Merker 26. Gualandi 57–58.
46. Ό.π. (σημ. 1) κεφ. 9. Βλ. επίσης Laurenzi ό.π. (σημ. 3): σχολή "per convenzione rodia ma ... per verità insulare-asiatica."
47. A. Maiuri, *ClRh* II (1932) 23, αρ. 7, εικ. 10. Merker 27, αρ. 13, εικ. 13–15. Gualandi 60 σημ. 4. Linfert ό.π. (σημ. 1) 90 σημ. 296.
48. Βλ. κυρίως την απεικόνιση του μύθου της Ανδρομέδας: *LIMC* I (1981) λ. Andromeda I (K. Schauenburg), η οποία συνήθως ακολουθεί τους εικονογραφικούς τύπους της Αφροδίτης καθώς και Νυμφών, Μουσών.
49. Βλ. αντίστοιχα για τα αγαλμάτια του Γανυμήδους, Η. Ζερβουδάκη, *ΑΔελτ* 33, 1978, Μελ., 34–35 σημ. 71. 37.
50. Βλ. Ρόδος, αρ. ευρ. 13635 (σημ. 34) το οποίο θα μπορούσε να βρίσκεται ανάμεσα στις μορφές του αναγλύφου του Αρχελάου: D. Pinkwart, *AntPl* IV (1965) 55–65. Κατά τον Lauter ό.π. (σημ. 51) 53, "στην πλαστική απαντάται σε συντετμημένη μορφή η τοπιογραφική σκηνογραφία."
51. G. Konstantinopoulos, *Archaeology* 21, 1968, 117–120 (για τα νυμφαία της ακρόπολης). H. Lauter, *AntK* 15, 1972, 53–58, εικ. 4–5, πίν. 15,4–16 (για τις διαμορφώσεις στο Ροδίνι). Η. Ζερβουδάκη, *ΑΔελτ* 33, 1978, 38–39. A. Dreliossi-Herakleidou στο Hoepfner – Brands (επιμ.) ό.π. (σημ. 14) 191. Για τη Ρόδο χαρακτηριστική είναι η γειτνίαση στην περιοχή του Ροδινιού αφενός των νεκροταφείων με τις μνημειώδεις προσόψεις των τάφων και αφετέρου του άλσους με τις ποικίλες τεχνητές διαμορφώσεις. Βλ. αντίστοιχα στην Αλεξάνδρεια και στην Αντιόχεια: Lauter 56.
52. Βλ. τελευταία E.E. Rice, *BSA* 90, 1995, 383–404, όπου όμως υπάρχει σύγχυση μεταξύ τεχνητά διαμορφωμένων άντρων και φυσικών σπηλαίων. Αντίθετα υπαίθρια ιερά με διαμορφωμένες κόγχες στον φυσικό βράχο απαντούν από τα κλασικά χρόνια και στην Αττική, τα ιερά της Αφροδίτης στο Δαφνί και στη βόρεια κλιτύ της Ακροπόλεως των Αθηνών.
53. G. Jacopi, *ClRh* I (1928) 22–25, εικ. 5–6. Merker, *Studies*, 111–115, αρ. 14. *LIMC* II, λ. Aphrodite, αρ. 1027.
54. R. Lullies, *Die kauernde Aphrodite* (1954) 84. A. Maiuri, *BdA* 1924, 390: έργο ροδιακών εργαστηρίων όχι μεταγενέστερο του 1ου αι. π.Χ. "costituiva la variante principale e più geniale della Venere di Doedalsas."
55. Κυρίως οι A. Adriani, *ASAE* 44, 1944, 68, και L. Laurenzi, *ASAtene* N.S. 8–10, 1946–48, 172 σημ. 3, την θεωρούν έργο *αλεξανδρινού περιβάλλοντος*. E. de Miro, *ArchCl* 8, 1956, 48–52. Πρόκειται για διαφορετικό από την Αφροδίτη του Δοιδάλσα πρωτότυπο, που δημιουργήθηκε στην Αλεξάνδρεια στο δεύτερο ήμισυ του 1ου αιώνα π.Χ. Η Merker, *Studies*, 114, την θεωρεί *μή* ροδιακή δημιουργία.
56. Adriani ό.π. (σημ. 18) 27–28, αρ. 106–111, πίν. 60–61.
57. Marcadé ό.π. (σημ. 27) 232: στη Δήλο απαντά μόνο σε ένα αποσπασματικό αγαλμάτιο και ένα ειδώλιο, στα οποία όμως δεν μπορεί να αναγνωριστεί η ακριβής στάση.
58. Βλ. επιλεκτικά *LIMC* II, λ. Aphrodite, αρ. 1018–1023 με πλήρη βιβλιογραφία. Καλύτερο και πιστότερο στο πρωτότυπο είναι το αντίγραφο της Villa Hadriana στο Tivoli (αρ. 1018).
59. Bieber ό.π. (σημ. 1) 124. J.J. Pollitt, *Art in the Hellenistic Age* (1986) 110. 113. Κατά τον Marcadé, ό.π. (σημ. 27) 485, σημαντικός είναι ο ρόλος της Ρόδου και στην επιβίωση των περγαμηνών τάσεων.
60. Marcadé ό.π. (σημ. 27) 481: έντονη δράση μικρασιατών καλλιτεχνών στη Ρόδο διαπιστώνεται κατά τους 3ο-1ο αι. π.Χ. Η V.C. Goodlet, *AJA* 95, 1991, 679, σημειώνει ότι οι ξένοι καλλιτέχνες στη Ρόδο κατάγονται στην πλειοψηφία τους από τη Μ. Ασία, ενώ Αθηναίοι δεν απαντούν μετά το 184 π.Χ.

61. Merker 14. Marcadé ό.π. (σημ. 27), 483–496 για τις αναλογίες και τις διαφορές στη γλυπτική της Δήλου και της Ρόδου.
62. Βλ. και πρόσφατα, Isager ό.π. (σημ. 3).
63. Με βάση επιγραφικά στοιχεία διαπιστώνονται πολλά εργαστήρια ακμαία στη Ρόδο: Goodlet ό.π. (σημ. 60) 669–681. Πάντως όσα μνημειώδη έργα αποδίδονται στη "ροδιακή σχολή" βρίσκονται εκτός Ρόδου (πρβλ. και το άρθρο της Ι. Τριάντη στον παρόντα τόμο). Δεν αποκλείεται όμως να μας επιφυλλάσει εκπλήξεις η ροδιακή γη. Βλ. πρόσφατα Ε. Κανίνια, *ΑΔελτ* 43, 1988, Χρον. Β 2, 610, πίν. 369 β: το μνημειώδες ανάγλυφο με αρ. ευρετηρίου Γ 1499, που βρέθηκε στη διάρκεια εργασιών της Δ.Ε.Υ.Α.Ρ.
64. Marcadé ό.π. (σημ. 27) 34.
65. Isager ό.π. (σημ. 3) 118–120. Μόνο η φιλολογική παράδοση δίνει στοιχεία, ενώ μαρτυρούν το μέγεθος οι βάσεις των ανδριάντων που έχουν σωθεί ως τις μέρες μας.
66. Τον κατ' εξοχήν διακοσμητικό, ανεπίσημο και ιδιωτικό χαρακτήρα της ροδιακής πλαστικής έχουν επισημάνει όσοι ερευνητές ασχολούνται με τα θέματα αυτά. Βλ. κυρίως Merker, *Studies*, 243, 423, 459. Gualandi 18. 229–230. Η. Ζερβουδάκη, *ΑΔελτ* 33, 1978, Μελ. Α, 39. Goodlet ό.π. (σημ. 60) 673: περγαμηνή μπαρόκ, ροδιακή διακοσμητική γλυπτική.
67. Merker, *Studies*, 459: δηλαδή την αρχιτεκτονική γλυπτική, παραγγελίες έργων ευρείας κλίμακας (από την πλούσια μοναρχία).

Rhodian Sculpture: A School, A Style, or Many Workshops?

Carol C. Mattusch

The only bronze statue that was included among the seven wonders of the world stood in Rhodes. A colossal statue of Helios, it stood seventy cubits in height and cost three hundred talents to produce, money that was raised by selling the siege machinery which Demetrios Poliorketes left behind when he gave up his siege of Rhodes in 305 B.C.[1]

How important is it that Chares, who made the Colossus of Rhodes, was a pupil of Lysippos? It may be that Chares learned what he knew about making a bronze colossus from Lysippos, who came from a family of bronze-casters. We have no way of knowing whether Chares was influenced by the style of Lysippos when he made the famous Colossus. Indeed, we learn from Pliny that there were one hundred other colossal statues in Rhodes, five of them by Bryaxis.

It took Chares twelve years to finish his enormous statue of Helios, and it toppled over about sixty years later, during an earthquake in 224 B.C. For most of its existence, then, the Colossus lay on the ground, which is why Pliny happened to notice that its fingers were larger than most statues. Strabo reports that the Colossus had broken at the knees when it fell.[2] Philo of Byzantium mentions the stone blocks and iron supports inside the statue, and tries to explain how it was made, a subject which has continued to be of interest.[3] In recent years, Herbert Maryon has suggested that the Rhodian Colossus was made of cast plates of bronze, but Denys Haynes's proposal that the statue was built up and cast in layers is far more likely.[4]

When the Saracens conquered Rhodes in 653 A.D., they carted off 980 camel-loads of bronze from this Colossus alone.[5] There was certainly a great deal more scrap metal than that still in Rhodes, considering the 3,000 lifesize statues that Pliny had estimated were still standing there in his day.[6]

What is known about the bronzeworking industry in Rhodes comes partly from ancient workshops, and partly from inscribed statue bases. Charis Kantzia and Gerhard Zimmer have studied the ancient foundries in the city.[7] So far, six casting pits have been found, all of them at the east foot of the akropolis, and all of them Hellenistic in date. They all lie near a sanctuary, which is presently unidentified, but which was in use between the third century B.C. and late imperial times. Statue bases from the area are inscribed with the names of priests and of athletes.

The two largest casting pits, seven and eight meters long, are bigger than any that have yet been excavated in Greece. Both were apparently part of one workshop, dating to the first half of the third century B.C. They were both used more than once. This means, unfortunately, that the debris from them was carted away after each casting, leaving no mold fragments to support the argument that in one of these pits (no. 1), part of a colossal statue was cast, one that stood ten meters in height. In the course of their excavations, Kantzia and Zimmer found the foot of a kantharos that had been inscribed with the name of Euboulos, and were tempted to assign this workshop to the bronze sculptor of that name whom Pliny credits with a statue of a praying woman.[8]

The well-known lifesize bronze Praying Boy in Berlin is known to have come from Rhodes (Fig. 1).[9] The statue represents a nude boy, weight on the left foot, the right foot trailing. His head is raised, as are his arms, elbows and wrists bent, palms upwards, fingers loosely extended as if in supplication. But this is not the way the statue looked when it was found, and it may not be the way in which the bronze was originally designed. The statue's history is known from 1503, when it arrived in Venice from Rhodes: an agent of Isabella d'Este recorded that the statue had come from the excavations of the Medieval city wall near the port of Rhodes and near the sanctuary of Helios. The agent described the statue as being well-preserved except for the hair, and noted that it was missing half of either arm and half of the right foot. The foot was soon restored, and a copy of the statue was cast with both feet but without the arms. That copy is now in the Museo Archeologico in Venice.[10]

The ancient statue of the Praying Boy had left Italy by the first half of the seventeenth century, and in 1639 it was owned by Charles I of England, when a drawing was

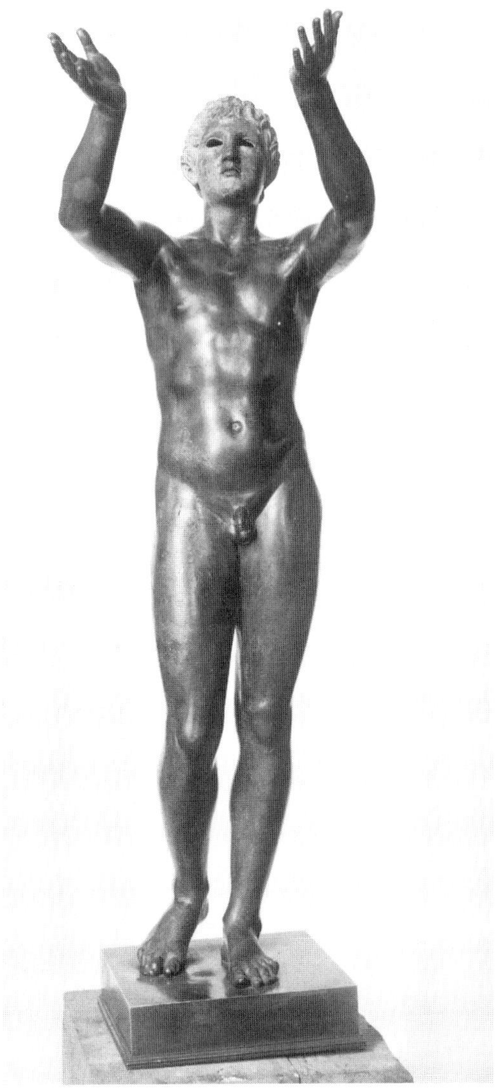

Fig. 1. Statue of Praying Boy, probably Hellenistic. H. 1.28 m. Antikensammlung, Staatliche Museen zu Berlin, Sk 2. Courtesy Antikensammlung, Staatliche Museen zu Berlin, Preussischer Kulturbesitz.

made of it, still without arms. One hundred years later, the bronze belonged to Frederick II: when he installed it at Sans Souci it had been restored to the state in which we see it today. The notion that the youth might be praying to Helios fits neatly with the raised head and with the fact that the statue originated in Rhodes, where the colossal statue of Helios stood. But this is a curious statue, one that does not lead the viewer to immediate associations.

Were the arms correctly restored? The position of the shoulders leaves no doubt that the arms were raised, which is not unknown, but it is difficult to find an antique parallel for the position of the hands. If the hands were to be turned slightly, however, and the angle of the elbows straightened just a little bit, the statue would become a familiar Classical type of athlete – a jumper or a runner. Since the front of the left foot is a Renaissance restoration, it might even be possible to raise the left heel slightly. There are excellent parallels for this now-familiar type in the small bronze runner from Olympia (Fig. 2), in the illustration of the bronze athlete being assembled on the Berlin Foundry Cup (Fig. 3), and in the illustration of a jumper on a calyx krater in Copenhagen (Fig. 4).[11] All have outstretched arms, raised head, and an open mouth, and none has the palms turned upwards, for theirs are active poses, not spiritual ones. In fact, there is ample evidence for statues of athletic victors being erected in Rhodes. It seems likely that the Praying Boy is, in fact, a young athlete.

A great deal of valuable information about the bronze-statue-industry in Rhodes is now available in Virginia Goodlett's recent study of signed Rhodian statue bases, and her identification of individual workshops practicing that industry.[12] Goodlett found that a family was the core of each Rhodian workshop and that the family-members stayed together, though their shop might be joined by others, including foreigners. The largest second-century-B.C. workshop was founded by Artemidoros of Tyre by 150 B.C. Sixty years later, his family-members were signing their names as Rhodians. It would be next to impossible to attempt to assign a particular artistic style to this Rhodian family. Menodotos, for example, the son of the workshop's founder, signed bases jointly with his father, his uncle, his cousin, and with another Rhodian to

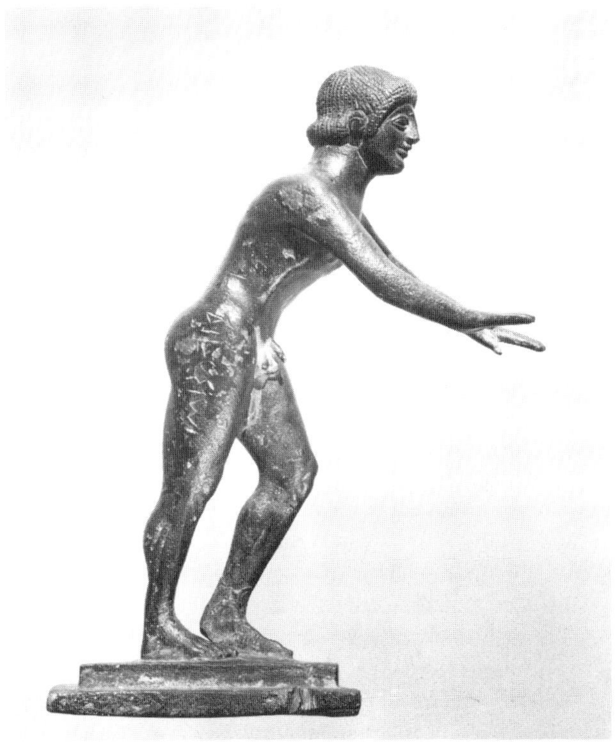

Fig. 2. Bronze statuette of runner, first half of the fifth century B.C. H. 10.2 cm. Olympia B 26. Courtesy Deutsches Archäologisches Institut, Athens, neg. no. OL 811.

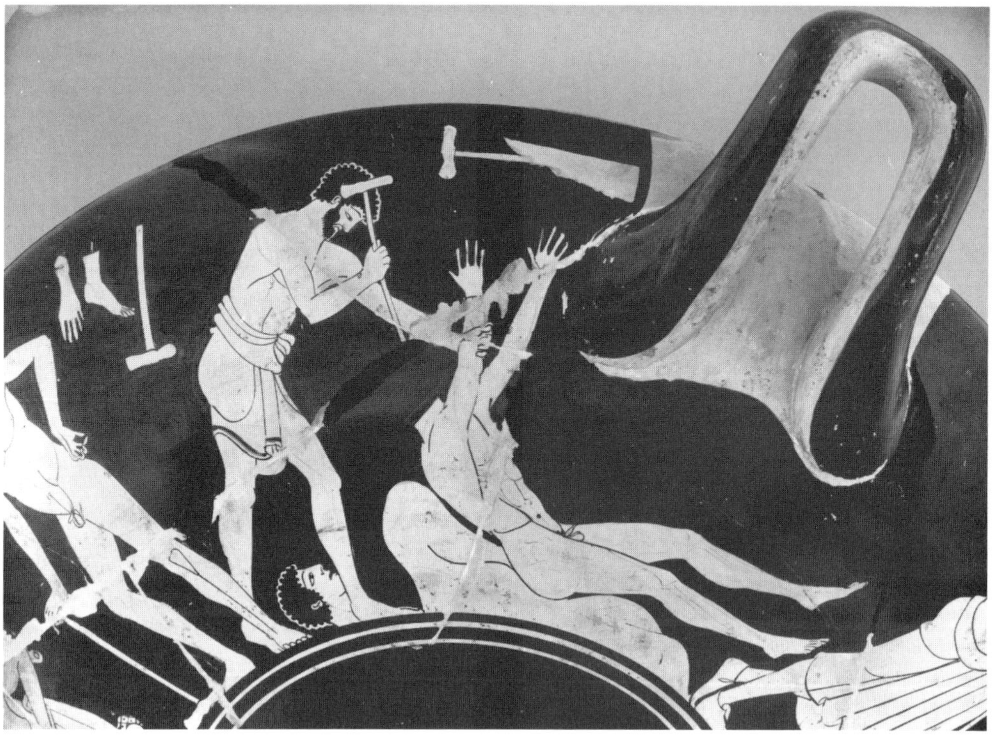

Fig. 3. Detail of red-figure kylix attributed to the Foundry Painter, early fifth century B.C. Antikensammlung, Staatliche Museen zu Berlin F 2294. Photo: Jutta Tietz-Glagow. Courtesy Antikensammlung, Staatliche Museen zu Berlin.

whom he was not related. Menodotos and his cousin made a statue that stood in Athens. His younger brother worked at Delphi; his father signed a base at Halikarnassos. Furthermore, Menodotos made three entirely different types of statues, which we would be likely to describe as having quite different styles. In Athens, he and his cousin made a statue of a pankratiast, which would have been nude, naturalistic, and doing something to alert viewers to his athletic victory. Menodotos also made portrait-statues for the local Rhodian market, which would have been fairly standardized, to judge from Dio Chrysostom's criticism of the Rhodians for their practice of reusing portrait statues.

"Whenever you vote to honor anyone with a statue – and the idea of doing this comes to you quite easily because you have a vast supply of statues on hand ... presto! there he stands before a vote is even taken! Your strategos simply points to the first statue he sees among those that have previously been dedicated, and then, once the inscription that was on the base has been removed and another name has been engraved, the job is finished!"[13] If they were this freely reused, portrait statues probably looked very much like one another, and the familiar type of image would have fit whatever name was inscribed beneath it.

The third style which Menodotos used for statues was archaistic. An archaistic statue of Apollo which was found in the sea near Piombino in 1812 or 1832 was purchased for the Louvre in 1834, and cleaned in 1842 (Fig. 5).[14] The stiffly standing, frontal statue, arms extended forwards from the elbows, used to be included in all of the

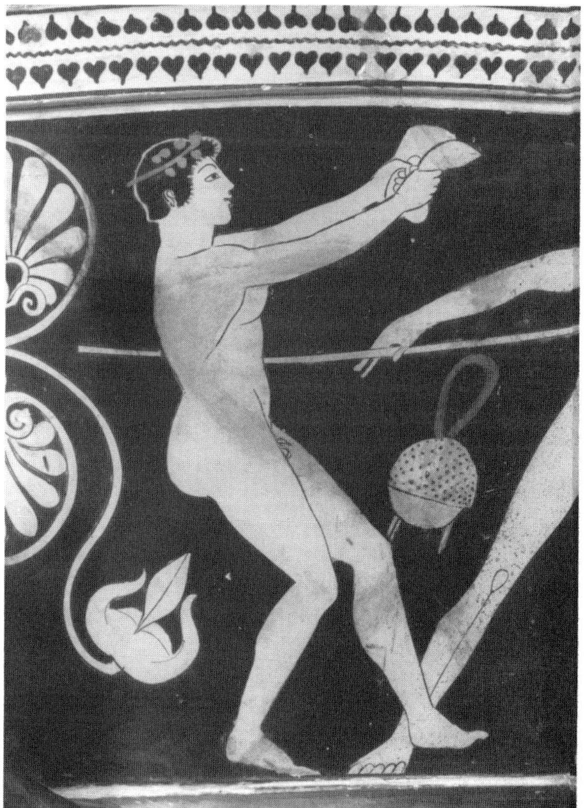

Fig. 4. Detail of red-figure calyx krater, early fifth century B.C. National Museum Copenhagen, no. 126. Courtesy National Museum Copenhagen.

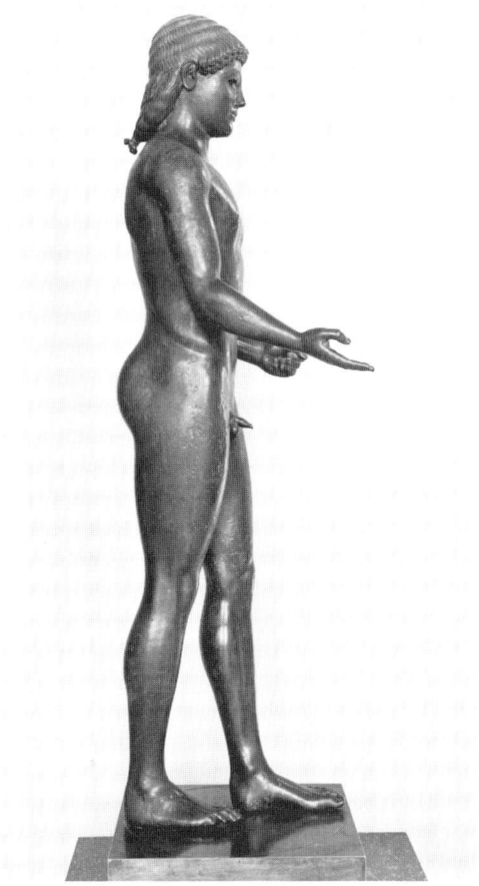

Fig. 5. Bronze statue of Apollo from Piombino, probably first century B.C. Paris, Louvre Br. 2. Courtesy Louvre, Musées Nationaux.

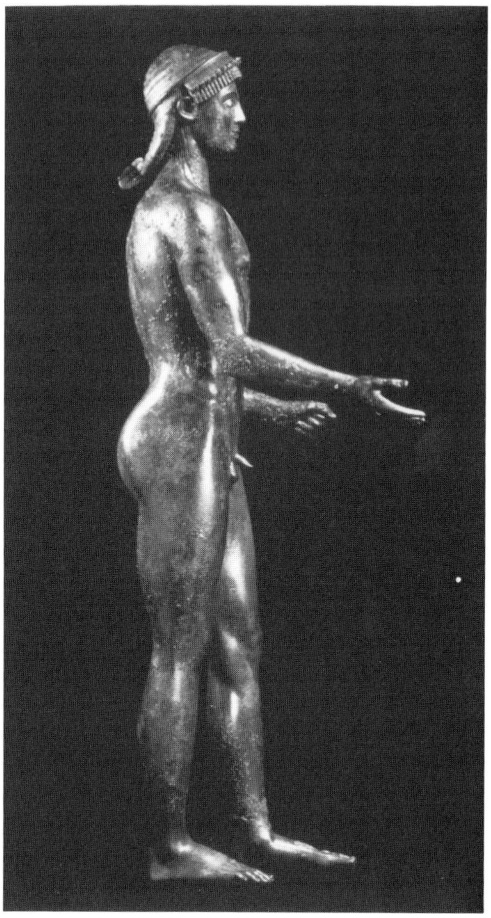

Fig. 6. Bronze statue of Apollo from the house of C. Julius Polybius at Pompeii. Pompeii inv. 22924. Courtesy "L'Erma" di Bretschneider.

textbooks as an example of an early fifth-century B.C. bronze original by a Sikyonian or a South Italian artist. An ancient lead tablet that was found inside the Piombino Apollo appears to read: "Menodotos and ..phon of Rhodes made it." Sterling Dow thought that Menodotos and ...phon had reattached the statue's left foot in the first century B.C. and recorded their repair on the tablet.[15]

The fronts of the feet did not just break off: they had been cast separately and flow-welded into place, as was relatively common practice in ancient foundries.[16] So it was the weld-metal that broke. As a rule, the arms of statues were also separately cast: bare arms were usually joined, again by flow-welding, just below the shoulders. These joins have held firm on the Piombino Apollo, unlike those on the statue of the young athlete in Berlin, which lost its arms in the area of the join.

The head of a statue was the other major portion that was cast separately, and very often a significant amount of detail was added to the wax working model for the head. On the Piombino Apollo, the details of the hair were cut and modeled directly in the wax working model. The knot of hair on the back of the neck and also the genitals were separately cast and welded into place. The eyes, now missing, were inserted from outside, copper eyebrows, lips, and nipples were inlaid, and silver was laid into an inscription that had been cut in the wax on the top of the left foot: "...os dedicated it to Athena as a tithe." The tablet found inside the statue can surely be taken literally as a record of the names of the men who made the bronze.

On stylistic grounds, Brunilde Ridgway has argued convincingly that the entire statue was made in the first century B.C., and now it is difficult to see how we ever thought otherwise.[17] But we can go even further than Ridgway did, and propose that once a type or a style exists, it is available for use at any time in any place. We can expect to see that type or style either in the form of a reproduction or in the form of a reflection, that is, a later variation upon an earlier theme. The Piombino Apollo could be described as an Archaic-Revival bronze that was made in a Rhodian workshop during the first half of the first century B.C. and was being shipped to a buyer, but was lost at sea off the west coast of Italy.

Just because modern scholars at first misidentified the statue certainly does not mean that it was intended to deceive the buyer. The argument that it was not a first-century B.C. forgery is strengthened by the fact that this was not the only statue made in the series. At least one other Archaic-Revival Apollo was cast from the same basic model. The second bronze statue was excavated at Pompeii in 1977 in the house of C. Julius Polybius (Fig. 6). It is the same size as the Piombino Apollo, but the surface details, like the hair, were finished a little differently.[18]

What might Pliny have said about the 'style' of an artist like Menodotos? Maybe nothing at all, if, as seems to have been the case, production in the family's workshop was driven by market demand, not by a single recognizable style. It is an interesting question whether the Piombino and Pompeii statues were of a type produced by that workshop alone, or whether one could order the Apollo from another shop as well. You could certainly order a herm from a particular series from more than one workshop. For example, the herm of Dionysos from the Mahdia shipwreck is signed by the person who made it, Boethos of Kalchedon (Fig. 7). The herm was being shipped somewhere during the first quarter of the first century B.C., about the same time as the Piombino Apollo was made and shipped. Another bronze herm, just like it, having the same measurements and the same bronze alloy, must come from the same workshop (Fig. 8). But a marble version of the same Dionysos, found at Pompeii, must have been produced in a marble workshop (Fig. 9).[19] It appears that the purchaser chose the kind of object to buy as well as the medium, and probably different sizes were also available. This style of Dionysos-herm was popular

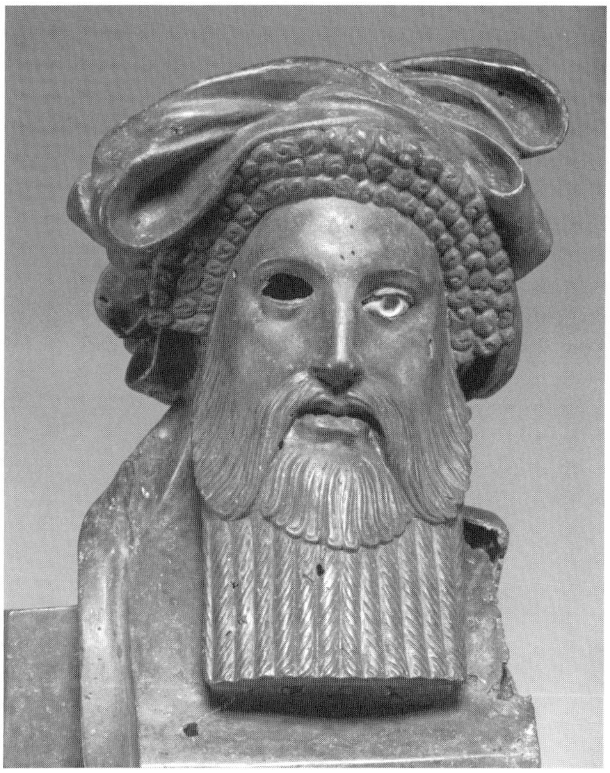

Fig. 8. Bronze Dionysos herm. H. 1.03 m. Malibu, J. Paul Getty Museum. Courtesy J. Paul Getty Museum.

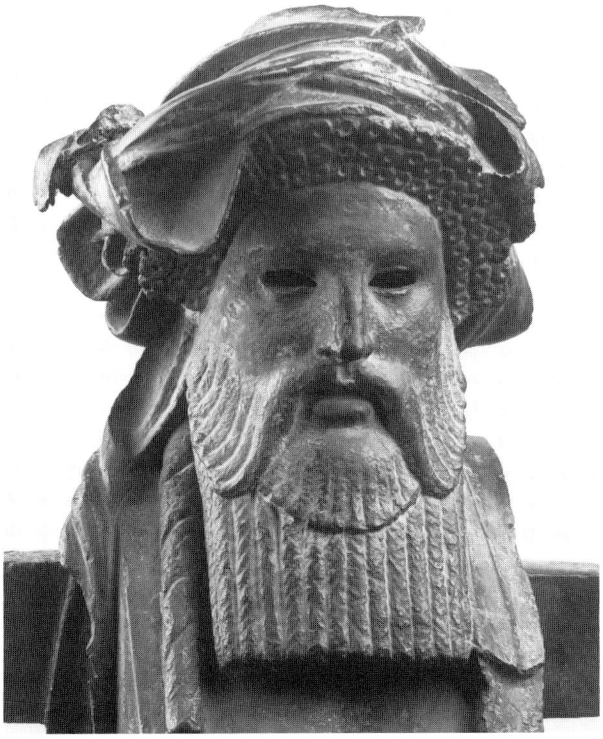

Fig. 7. Bronze Dionysos herm signed by Boethos, from the Mahdia shipwreck. H. 1.03 m. Tunis, Bardo Museum F 107. Photo H. Lilienthal. Courtesy Rheinisches Landesmuseum Bonn.

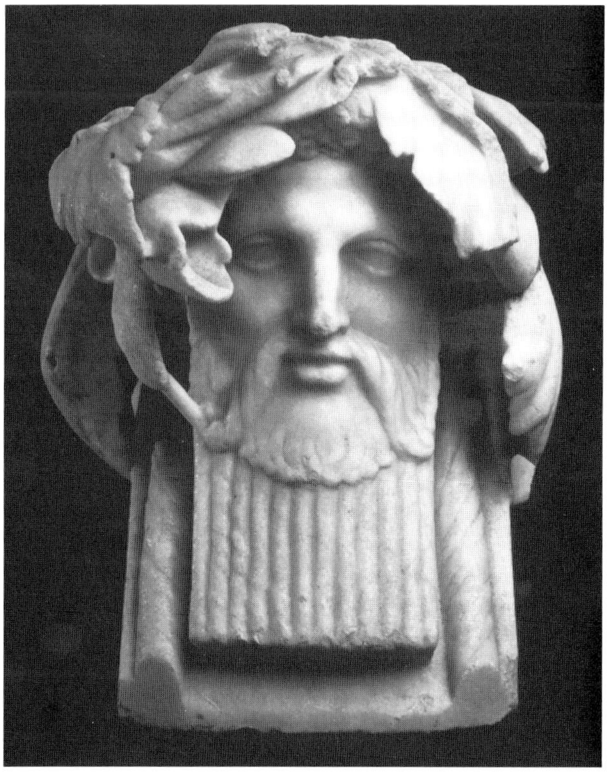

Fig. 9. Marble wreathed Dionysos head, excavated in the peristyle of a house at Pompeii. H. 27.5 cm. Pompeii inv. 2914. Courtesy "L'Erma" di Bretschneider.

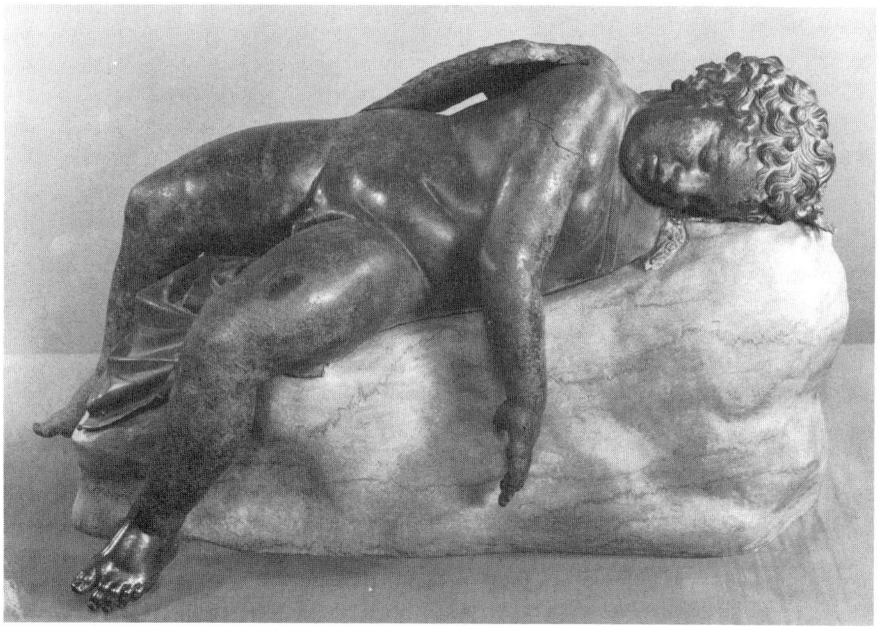

Fig. 10. Lifesize bronze sleeping Eros, L. 85 cm. New York, Metropolitan Museum of Art 43.11.4. Rogers Fund, 1943. Courtesy Metropolitan Museum of Art.

for a long time – from at least the early first century B.C. to 79 A.D., which is nearly two hundred years.

Sleeping Erotes were widely popular throughout antiquity. The statues and statuettes that are known to date all appear to be different. It is impossible to date them on the basis of style alone. There are three or more marble sleeping Erotes in Rhodes, and one bronze sleeping Eros is reported to have come from Rhodes (Fig. 10).[20] Because the bronze Eros is lifesize and of very high quality, exhaustive attempts have been made to date it, and scholars have placed it anywhere from the early third to the late second century B.C. Attributions to famous artists have also been made. The statue has been called 'an original,' or 'the original' sleeping Eros, that is, the inspiration for all other such images, whether they come from Greece, Italy, Cyprus, Turkey, North Africa, Spain, or France, or from somewhere in northern Europe. The statue was cast superbly in five or more pieces (the left arm and the original base are missing), the underside intentionally left open, its cast edges undulating so as to fit an uneven base. Much of the interior is visible, and the statue is a relatively thin-walled and even casting, with a smooth and nearly flawless surface, indications that this bronze could easily have been produced as one in a series of similar castings. Because it is undeniably a magnificent statue, scholars have felt the need to give it an identity. Is it Rhodian? Pergamene? Athenian? Pliny, our mainstay in such cases, does not even mention an artist who made a sleeping Eros. Why do we ask who made it, where, and when? Why do we seek to make it the first of all sleeping Erotes? After all, this type of statue was universally popular during Classical antiquity, and it is highly unlikely that of the relatively few examples surviving today, this could be the prototype. Furthermore, the Metropolitan Eros is the only one of its specific kind that now exists.

Another universally popular type of garden statue was the standing bronze child. It happens that there are a number of them from Pompeii and Herculaneum, where they functioned as garden ornaments. A buyer could choose a single one, or a matched pair, or a set of four to decorate a rectangular fountain, and they could be alike or different (Fig. 11).[21] The seated child was also a common and widespread type, but one that was evidently made of marble. These small statues have been found in the first-century A.D. villa at Sperlonga, and in the cargo of the early first-century B.C. Mahdia ship (Fig. 12). There is another one in a New York private collection.[22] The date for these groups of marble fountain-figures can only be described as **continuous**, from at least the early first century B.C. through at least the first century A.D., the same broad span of time to which we can securely date the marble and bronze Dionysos-herms and the Piombino and Pompeii Apollo-statues. In other words, they were produced for as long as they remained popular. The style for such images was surely not regional: it was ubiquitous, and the actual places of production no doubt depended upon the market demand. It is easy to imagine that a bronze foundry and a marble shop in one city could have stocked the same types of images and been in competition with others.

At Sperlonga, the small marble fountain-figures could easily have been made by the same marble workshop that produced the massive groups of marble sculptures for the grotto. Those carvers were Rhodians who, like Rhodian bronze-casters, signed their work. There was

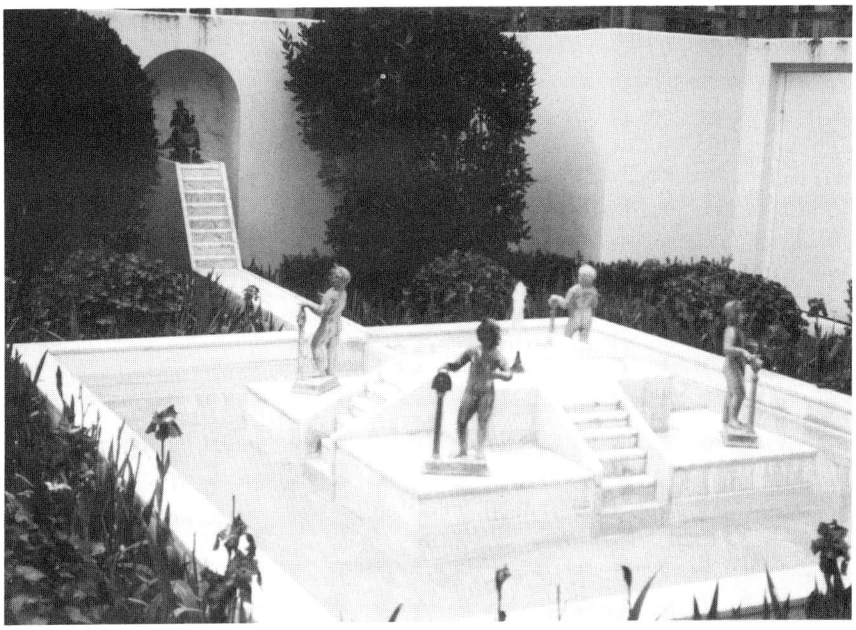

Fig. 11. Lifesize standing bronze babies used as fountain ornaments. Modern reproduction of a fountain at Herculaneum. Malibu, J. Paul Getty Museum. Photo C. Mattusch.

no white marble on Rhodes, nor were groups of such size and complexity as those for the grotto likely to have been moved very far after they were fully carved. In other words, the men who signed the Scylla group at Sperlonga – Athanodoros the son of Hagesandros, Hagesandros the son of Paionios, and Polydoros the son of Polydoros – must have been working in Italy. Pliny mentions these same three men.[23] They were marble-carvers, and good enough to be well-known for their work in the flamboyant style of the Laokoon group, the same style as that of the even more complex Scylla group. Indeed, five signatures of an artist named Athanodoros, son of Hagesandros, have been found on statue bases in Italy, all of them of standard types, and all of them apparently supporting nothing more elaborate than statues of standing figures, some of which were under lifesize.[24]

None of the marble babies for the fountain at Sperlonga is signed, but then these sculptures are not of the same complexity as the large sculptural groups at Sperlonga, and they were clearly produced in large numbers. After all, the fountain figures were of a common type, and they must have come from a less expensive line of production, albeit from the same workshop. We must remember that in antiquity, as today, a marble workshop or a bronze foundry which was a successful business was not likely to produce only one style or type of work. Did the same workshop that made the Sperlonga sculptures make the unsigned Laokoon group? We have only one ancient example of the latter, so we cannot be sure. In contrast, another torso of Scylla, smaller, but from the Dokimeion quarry in Turkey – the same type of marble as the Sperlonga Scylla – has been used convincingly to reconstruct part of the Sperlonga group, and the evidence

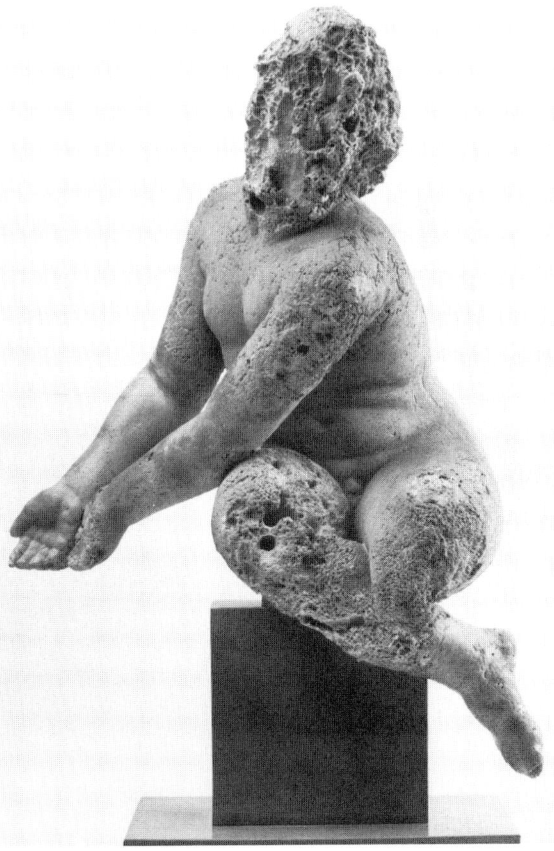

Fig. 12. Lifesize seated marble baby intended to ornament a fountain, from the Mahdia shipwreck. Tunis, Bardo Museum C 1178. Courtesy Rheinisches Landesmuseum Bonn.

suggests that even more examples of this particular group may have been carved.[25] It is interesting to conjecture what, if any, production rights there might have been for a work that was widely produced in more than one scale and medium. Could one easily buy a model-book, or were they closely-guarded property?

During antiquity, as today, if one wanted a bronze Scylla or Laokoon, one would go not to a particular school of sculptors, but, simply, to a bronzeworkers' shop that could produce the image.[26] For a marble statue, one would go to a marble shop. The information that there were Rhodian artists working at home and abroad means only that there were workshops, not a 'school' of sculptors or a certain style of sculpture. We have no evidence for a Rhodian 'school' of sculpture, but we have plentiful evidence for a Rhodian sculptural industry. Rhodians at home and abroad were skilled at producing statues in a variety of popular styles to meet the demands of the Greco-Roman market. Some of these artisans worked in marble; many others worked in bronze. Indeed, when Pliny speaks of places where there are still many bronzes to be seen, he mentions Rhodes first, before Athens, Olympia, and Delphi.[27] It is significant that he notes there must be 3,000 bronzes on Rhodes, but he does not comment upon any individual works beyond the colossi, nor does he detect a universal artistic style employed for making those sculptures.

Notes

1. Pliny, *NH* 34.41. For the Colossus of Rhodes see R. Higgins in P. Clayton and M.J. Price (edd.), *The Seven Wonders of the Ancient World* (1988) 124–137.
   I am very grateful to Olga Palagia and to W.D.E. Coulson for allowing me to participate in this fascinating conference.
2. 14.2.5.
3. *De septem orbis spectaculis* 4.
4. H. Maryon, *JHS* 76, 1956, 68–86; D.E.L. Haynes, *The Technique of Greek Bronze Statuary* (1992) 121–128.
5. Constantine Porphyrogennetos, *De administrando imperio* 20–21.
6. *NH* 34.36.
7. C. Kantzia and G. Zimmer, *AA* 1989, 497–523.
8. *NH* 34.88. Another graffito scratched on the outside of a cup found in the workshop gives Agathokles as the patronymic, a name found fairly often on Rhodes (supra n. 7, p. 522). Kantzia and Zimmer also mention a statue base inscribed, "Asklapon Phyromachou," from a nearby late antique wall and raise the question (supra n. 7, p. 505) of whether this could be the son of the Phyromachos whom Pliny places in the early third century B.C. (*NH* 34.51). For discussion of evidence for this artist, see A. Stewart, *Attika: Studies in Athenian Sculpture of the Hellenistic Age* (1979) 3–33 and here, pp. 106–107 and 119–120..
9. Berlin, Antikensammlung Sk 2. H. 1.28 m. See M. Kunze et al., *Die Antikensammlung im Pergamonmuseum und in Charlottenburg* (1992) 163–164, no. 66.
10. R. Kabus-Preisshofen, *AA* 1988, 687. For the statue's early reputation, and the sixteenth-century copy of it, see M. Perry, *BurlMag* 117, 1975, 204–211.
11. Olympia B 26; first half of the fifth century B.C. H. 10.2 cm. Kylix in Berlin, early fifth century B.C.; Antikensammlung F 2294, side A. Calyx krater in Copenhagen, early fifth century B.C.: National Museum 126.
12. V.C. Goodlett, *AJA* 95, 1991, 669ff.
13. Dio Chrysostom 31.9.
14. Piombino Apollo: Paris, Louvre 61. H. 1.15 m. For a detailed treatment of the statue, its appearance, and its early modern history, see B.S. Ridgway, *AntPl* VII (1967) 43–74.
15. S. Dow, *Hesperia* 10, 1941, 357–359.
16. For the piecing of statues and for flow-welding, see C.C. Mattusch, *The Fire of Hephaistos: Large Classical Bronzes from North American Collections* (1996) *passim*.
17. Supra n. 14.
18. Pompeii inv. 22924. See *Riscoprire Pompei* (1993) 262–264, no. 193. H. of Pompeii statue, 1.28 m; h. of head, 18 cm; w. of shoulders, 33 cm. H. of Piombino statue, 1.16 m; h. of head, 18 cm; w. of shoulders, 32 cm. (I have not measured either of the statues myself.)
19. C.C. Mattusch, *Classical Bronzes: The Art and Craft of Greek and Roman Statuary* (1996) 168–190. See also here p. 185, Fig. 1. For the second bronze herm, which is in Malibu (J. Paul Getty Museum inv. 79.AB.138), see also Mattusch (supra n. 16) 186–191, no. 3. For the marble example (Pompeii inv. 2914), which also appears to be of the same size, see *Riscoprire Pompei* 226f., no. 123.
20. New York, Metropolitan Museum of Art inv. 43.11.4. L. 85.2 cm. The statue was discovered in the center of the city of Rhodes, near the hospital, on the north side of the ancient akropolis, during the years of the Italian occupation (1912–1947): G. Konstantinopoulos, *Αρχαία Ρόδος* (1986) 123. I am grateful to Eos Zervoudaki for alerting me to this reference, and for further information that the mayor of Rhodes either found or reported the Sleeping Eros in 1936. The statue has been published repeatedly since its acquisition by the Metropolitan Museum in 1943. For references and for discussion of this statue and of a few related images, see Mattusch (supra n. 19) 160–168; for extensive stylistic treatment of the type, see M. Söldner, *Untersuchungen zu liegenden Eroten in der hellenistischen und römischen Kunst* (1986) 605, no. 17 and *passim*.
21. For discussion of variations on a theme within a series of castings, see Mattusch in G. Hellenkemper Salies et al. (edd.), *Das Wrack : Der antike Schiffsfund von Mahdia* 2 (1994) 789–800.
22. Sperlonga : B. Andreae, *RM* 83, 1976, 287–309. Mahdia (Bardo Museum inv. II 42 C 1178–1181): see B. Andreae in *Das Wrack* 1, 365–374. New York : D.v.Bothmer (ed.), *Glories of the Past: Ancient Art from the Shelby White and Leon Levy Collection* (1990) 236, no. 171.
23. *NH* 36.37.
24. E.E. Rice, *BSA* 81, 1986, 233–250.
25. Afyon, Archaeological Museum inv. 1875, H. 34 cm. See B. Conticello in B. Andreae and C.P. Presicce (edd.), *Ulisse : il mito e la memoria* (1996) 280ff.; also Andreae and S. Bertolin, ibid., 298ff., and Andreae, ibid., 362ff.
26. J. Isager has pointed out that there is no ancient reference to Rhodes as an artistic center : *RM* 102, 1995, 115–131. I am grateful to Olga Palagia for alerting me to this article.
27. *NH* 34.36.

The Victory of Samothrace

Ira S. Mark

Three well-known studies, the first two by Hermann Thiersch, published in 1930 and 1931,[1] the third by Christian Blinkenberg, published in 1938,[2] transformed the Victory of Samothrace into a much needed reference point for the understanding of regional style in the Hellenistic period (Fig. 1). Thiersch, citing a report of the geology department of the University of Copenhagen, announced that the distinctive gray-blue marble used for the prow of the Victory came from the ancient quarries near Lartos on Rhodes.[3] This conclusion, arrived at likely by thin section, needs now to be checked using additional, more modern techniques, importantly stable isotopic analysis and geochemistry. In conjunction with a full publication of the monument, we are currently undertaking this analysis. The marble is highly distinctive, visually and geologically, however, and I do not anticipate that the tie to Lartos will be put in doubt.

Blinkenberg's contribution was an equally important step. He identified the distinctive warship of the monument as a *trihemiolia.* It is narrow, low, and lightweight, with an enclosed deck and two banks of oars at nearly the same level, both projecting through the outrigger.[4] To judge from inscriptions, Rhodes took special pride in her deployment of this class of vessel. Other Hellenistic navies had *trihemioliai* in their fleets, including Macedon, Pergamon, Athens, and Egypt, but the *trihemiolia* was the Rhodian vessel *par excellence*. Building on the work of Thiersch and Blinkenberg, experts in the study of regional style in Hellenistic sculpture, including Ludger Alscher, Margarete Bieber and Andreas Linfert, have made the Victory the cornerstone in an attempt to understand a distinctive Rhodian approach to representation.[5]

In a talk at the annual meeting of the Archaeological Institute of America in 1995, I stressed the importance of the Rhodian connection for dating the work.[6] In this I find myself in substantial agreement with a view that Heinz Kähler set out in his classic study of the Great Frieze of the Altar of Zeus at Pergamon.[7] To give a full account of the historical criteria for dating would require too great a diversion, but it may be worthwhile to review the evidence in outline. It begins from a recognition that there are important stylistic similarities between the Victory and High Pergamene sculpture. Within the general period of the Pergamene Baroque, that is the later third and second centuries,[8] written sources attest only one occasion when the dedication of a ship monument in the form of a *trihemiolia* would be appropriate on Samothrace. In 190 B.C. Rome, in alliance with Rhodes, won a pivotal naval battle over Antiochos the Great off Myonnesos, a small city about thirty kilometers up the coast from Ephesos. We know about that battle from Livy (37.29–30) and learn that it was the swiftness and manoeuver-

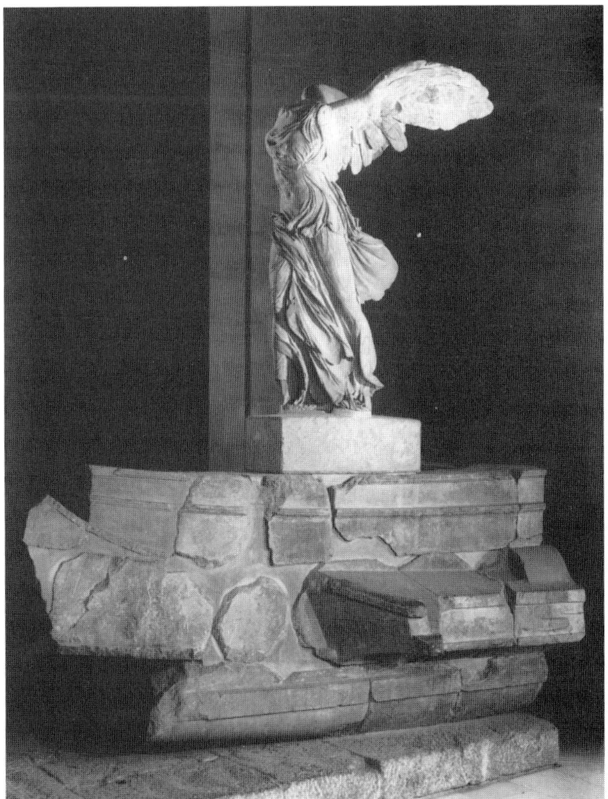

Fig. 1. Victory of Samothrace, Louvre. Photo R.M.N. neg. 87EN2200.

ability of Rhodes' warships that won the day (Livy 37.29.9: *et erant Rhodiae longe omnium celerrimae tota classe*; 37.30.2: *Robore navium et virtute militum Romani longe praestabant, Rhodiae naves agilitate et arte gubernatorum et scientia remigum*).[9] The Peace of Apamea that followed two years later stripped Antiochos of his navy. Rome had already decreed the destruction of virtually all of the fleet of Philip V in 196 B.C. With the Peace of 188, the Aegean became essentially a Roman lake with Rhodes as her police. The Peace was to mark the end of the seemingly endless naval triangles and intrigues of the Hellenistic powers in the Aegean.

Already before the Peace of Apamea, Rhodes had been extending her sphere of influence into the Northern Aegean. A Thasian decree honors the demos of Rhodes, apparently in gratitude for Rhodes' active support in maintaining the independence that Thasos won from Macedon in 196 B.C.[10] The Peace of Apamea returned Thasos and Samothrace to Macedonian control, but it apparently also allowed a rapprochement between Rhodes and Macedon. In preparation for the marriage of Perseus, son of Philip V, to Laodike, daughter of Seleukos IV, Perseus presented Rhodes with a quantity of wood for shipbuilding. In 178 B.C. the Rhodian fleet escorted Laodike to Macedon in full regalia (Polybios 25.4.9–10).

For Rhodes to celebrate her victory off Myonessos with a resplendent dedication on Samothrace, the premier sanctuary of the Northern Aegean, seems a fitting tithe for the turn of events that made possible her naval hegemony in that region.

The (presumably) Rhodian stone of the prow of the Victory does not of itself identify the monument as a Rhodian dedication and secure its date. Any Hellenistic power could have employed Rhodian sculptors, and the sculptors might have chosen Rhodian stone as a proud badge of their school or as a result of their working methods. It is the representation of the *trihemiolia* that is significant. Ship monuments in this form were not exclusive to Rhodes, but they are attested by especially prominent monuments there, namely the relief of Hagesandros carved in the living rock of the acropolis of Lindos and the free-standing Lindos prow.[11] And, as we have said, ancient sources attest only one battle, the Roman and Rhodian victory of 190 B.C., where this class of vessel, proud contingent of the Rhodian fleet, is likely to have played a leading role.

We come now to the style of the Victory, a statue too familiar to need lengthy introduction (Figs. 2–3).[12] The figure is striking, first, for its pose, at once forceful and precarious. In current display the Victory is raised on a

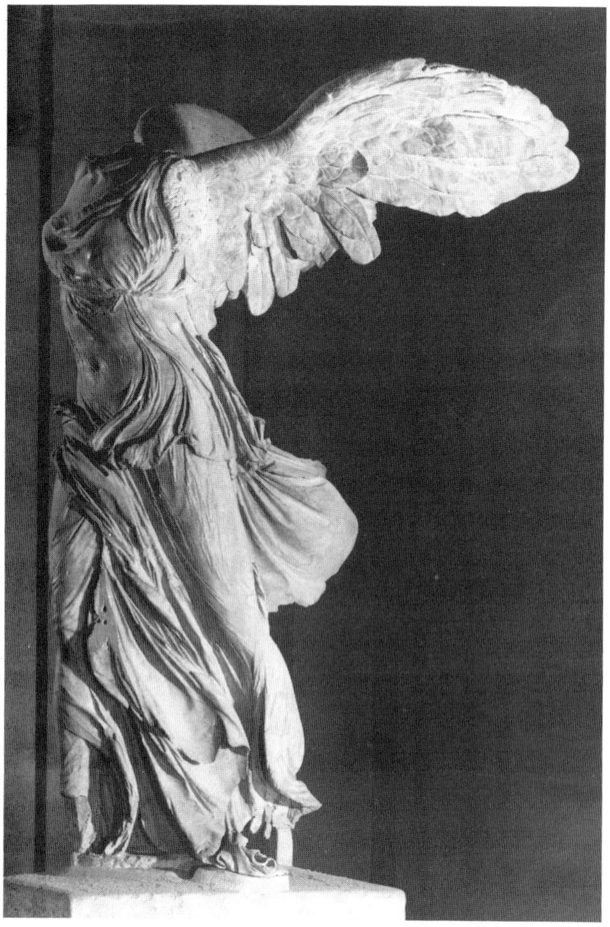

Fig. 2. Victory. Photo R.M.N. neg. 87EN2198.

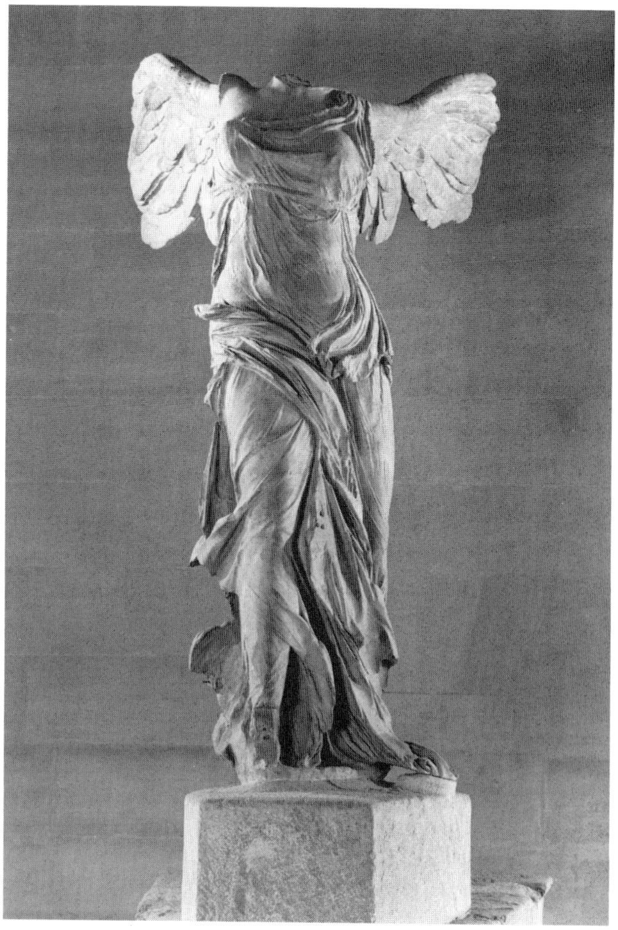

Fig. 3. Victory. Photo R.M.N. neg 87EN2220

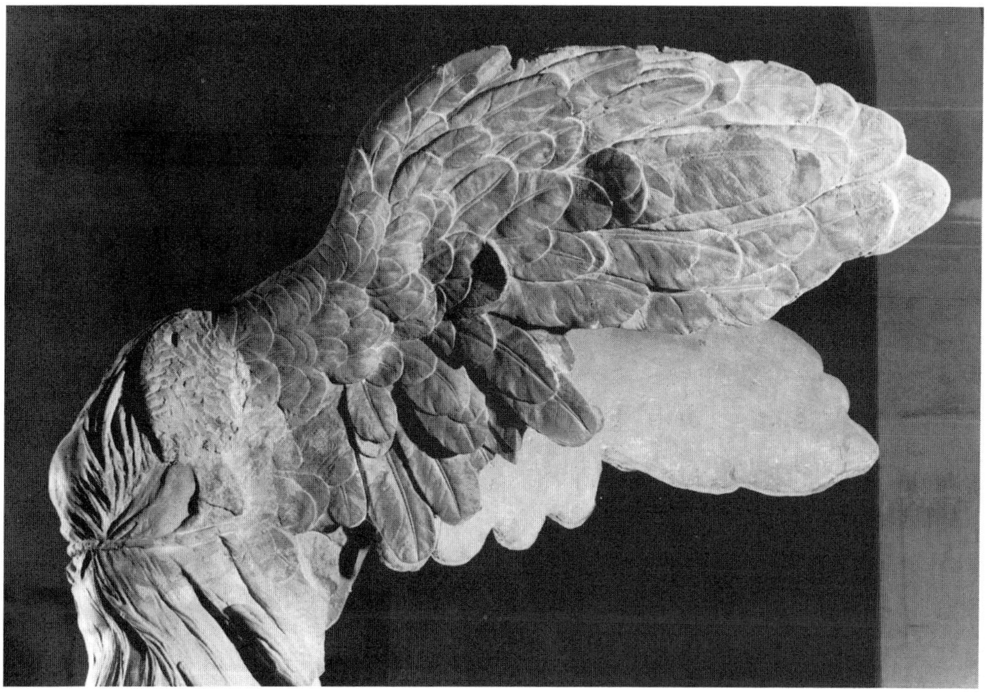

Fig. 4. Victory, detail of left wing. Photo R.M.N. neg. 87EN2205.

low modern base for better viewing from the foot of a monumental museum stair. Originally she stood directly on the deck, and her pose has to be understood in this light.[13] She takes a broad stride and half extends her wings for balance. As the ship rides the waves, she shifts her upper body in response. The resulting contrapposto is fleeting and uncontrived.

When scholars relate the Victory to High Pergamene Baroque, they are thinking above all of her stylistic similarity to figures on the Great Frieze of the Altar of Zeus at Pergamon, a monument sculpted apparently in the 60s of the second century.[14]

The relation resides partly in stylistic details, for example the form of the feathers on the preserved wing of the Victory (Fig. 4) and on the winged figures on the Great Frieze (Fig. 5). The two renderings share a distinctive hyper-naturalistic plasticity seen, to my knowledge, nowhere else in Greek art. There is, further, the forceful stance and muscular physique that the Victory shares with figures on the frieze. We can compare the muscularity and broad stride of the Athena from the east side of the Altar (Fig. 6).

These stylistic ties are undeniable, but there are also important differences. The figures on the Great Frieze tend to be organized in what German scholarship has labeled a closed style of composition. The gods and Giants tend to separate out into balanced two-, three-, and four-figure groups whose elements are compositionally interrelated.[15] The Athena and Giant (Fig. 6) are a particularly clear example. The two diverge axially, and the dominant "V" of their bodies is closed into a triangle

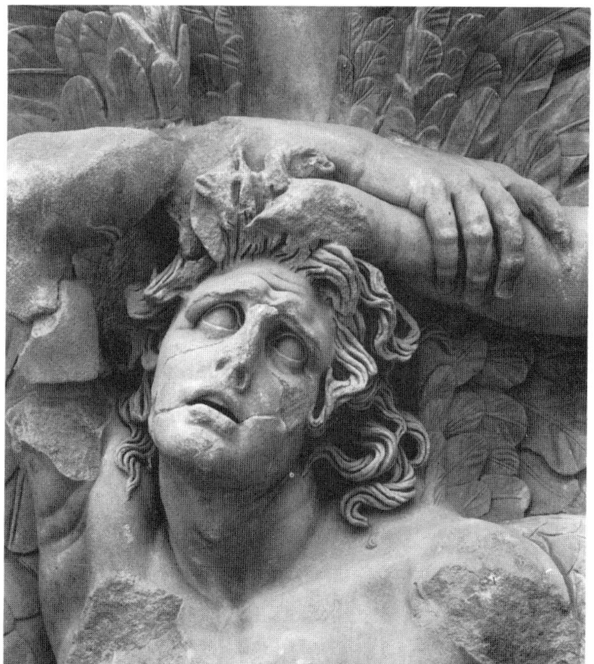

Fig. 5. Giant who opposes Athena. Great Frieze, Altar of Zeus at Pergamon. Staatl. Museen zu Berlin, Antikensammlung. Photo courtesy of Staatl. Museen zu Berlin – Preussischer Kulturbesitz, Antikensammlung, neg. PM 227.

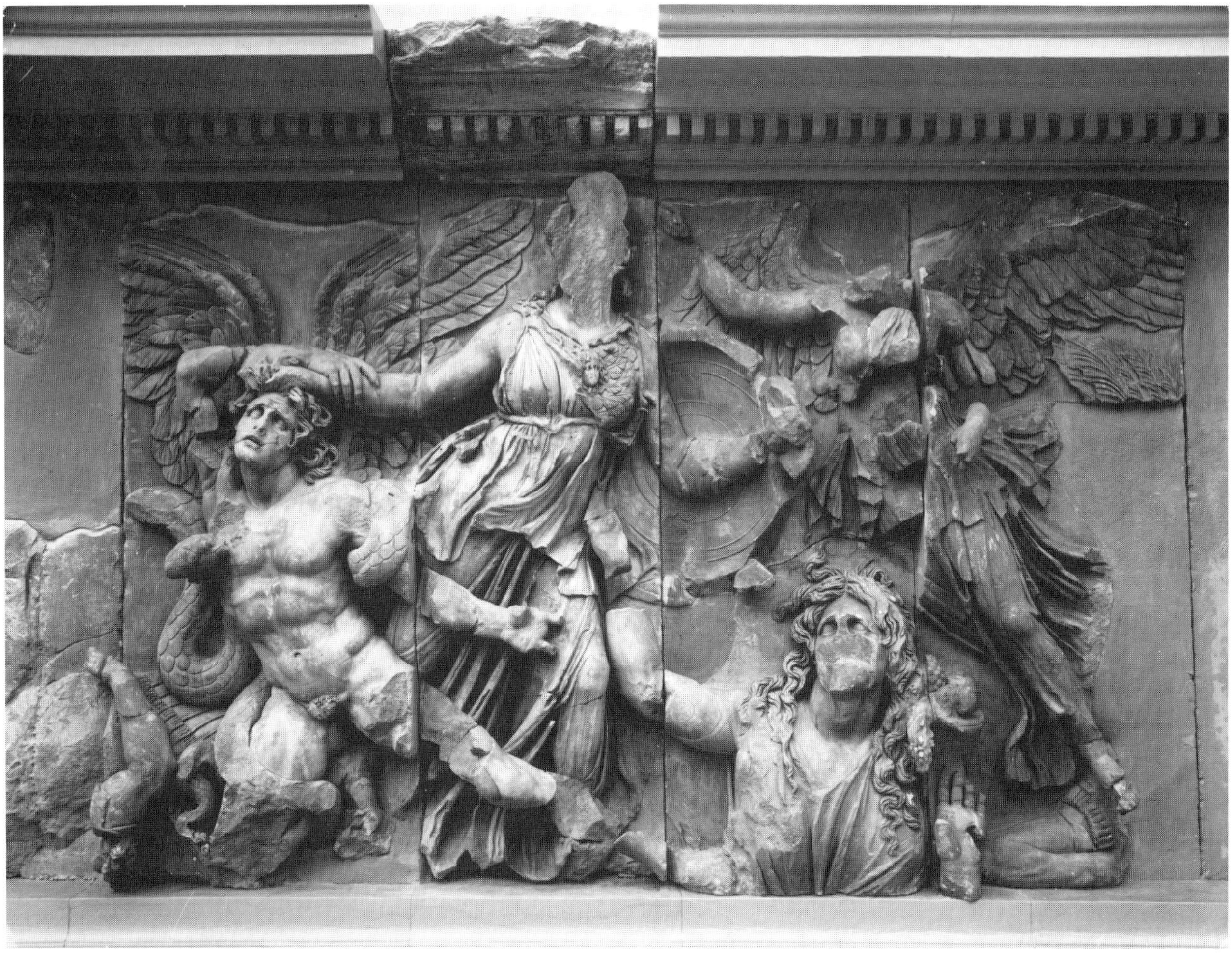

Fig. 6. Athena and Giant. Great Frieze, Altar of Zeus at Pergamon. Staatl. Museen zu Berlin, Antikensammlung. Photo courtesy of Staatl. Museen zu Berlin – Preussischer Kulturbesitz, Antikensammlung, neg. PM 7328.

by their linked arms. The artful closure of compositions was handled with great sophistication in the fifth century B.C., and the Athena and Giant are meant to evoke fifth-century sculpture.[16]

The formalist tradition applies the same terminology, closed versus open, both to groups and single figures in isolation. By its criteria the Victory, unlike the figures on the Frieze, is open.[17] The artist has taken care that the legs and torso, and as best we can reconstruct, the head, arms and wings do not align themselves in simple balanced and rhythmical patterns.[18]

There are also important differences in drapery style. Like the composition, the drapery style of the frieze also evokes the fifth century, specifically the style developed at Athens in the generation of Pheidias.

In that period, the rendering of cloth is distilled into a dichotomy of background and raised ridge, and the raised ridges form long continuous lines so that drapery design has a draftsmanly, calligraphic quality. We would never mistake the Pergamon frieze for actual fifth-century work, but it wraps itself, as it were, in the Classical Athenian manner.

These same formal qualities are evident in free-standing sculptures from Pergamon that appear to be close in date to the Great Altar. We can compare, for example, a life-size Victory from the precinct of Athena Nikephoros (Fig. 7),[19] and as a foil the fifth-century Nike of Paionios at Olympia (Fig. 8).[20] The latter work would appear to have been still standing in the Hellenistic period and may well have been known to the Pergamene sculptor.

The muscularity and strongly moved contrapposto of the Pergamene work are unmistakably Hellenistic, but although exaggerated, the pose invites comparison to its Classical predecessor, with the proper left leg forward and the line of the breasts angled down to the right. The clinging drapery of the Pergamon Victory, with raised linear folds, also strongly recalls the fifth century.

The drapery of the Victory of Samothrace belongs to a rather different tradition. There is clinging drapery with raised linear ridges. But these areas, over the torso and the legs, are counter-balanced by other areas where drapery has its own independent mass: the bunched drapery of the himation and the deep folds between the legs.

Much late fifth-century and early fourth-century sculpture contrasts clinging and bunched drapery, in the so-called damp-fold style and in the generation of Timotheos. However there are closer precedents in the Hellenistic period itself. Compare, for example, the Dionysos from a choregic monument on Thasos (Fig. 9).[21] The monument is difficult to date closely, but is usually, and I think correctly, put in the early third century.[22]

On both the Thasos figure and the Victory, drapery mass is rendered as line to some degree. We can note on the Thasos figure the deep, narrow furrows of the mantle as it sweeps around the proper right side and the linear fall of drapery over the right leg. Without going into detail, let me say that here we are dealing, not with a revival of the Classical tradition, but with its survival. Emerging from this linear tradition, however, there is a different, more plastic conception of gathered drapery where line is less regular and calligraphic. The style is nascent on the Thasos monument, and done with far greater skill and consistency on the Victory. The fabric projects boldly into space and recedes deeply into shadow falling in irregular, uncontrived patterns. It is particularly evident in the sweep of the mantle of the Victory over the thigh, where the furrows lie at odd angles to one another and are irregular in width, and in the plastic and highly complex formations of folds between the figure's legs. This is an "open" style of drapery, the complement in drapery to the open (uncontrived) stance.

Style in the Hellenistic period did not follow a unilinear path, and one cannot line up works one after another in one continuous stylistic series. A comparison between the Victory of Samothrace and another third-century work, the figure atop the ship monument in the agora of Cyrene, clarifies this, and at the same time helps to further define the special qualities of the Victory's style. The archaeologist who published the ship monument, A.L. Ermeti, argues from details in the construction of the warship and especially from the vessel's figural embellishment that the monument commemorates a naval victory at a time when the royal houses of Cyrene and Egypt were allied, namely under the marriage of Ptolemy III and Berenike of Cyrene.[23] She puts the monument in the third quarter of the third century.

Like a great deal of third-century sculpture, the Cyrene figure perpetuates with little change styles first developed in the late fourth century. The Apollo Patroos by Euphranor offers a good comparison.[24] The Cyrene figure's overfall seems to echo the earlier work: where the cloth is pinched in by the belt the folds loop one inside the next and fall in widely-spaced vertical ridges to either side.

The Cyrene figure and the Dionysos each offer a

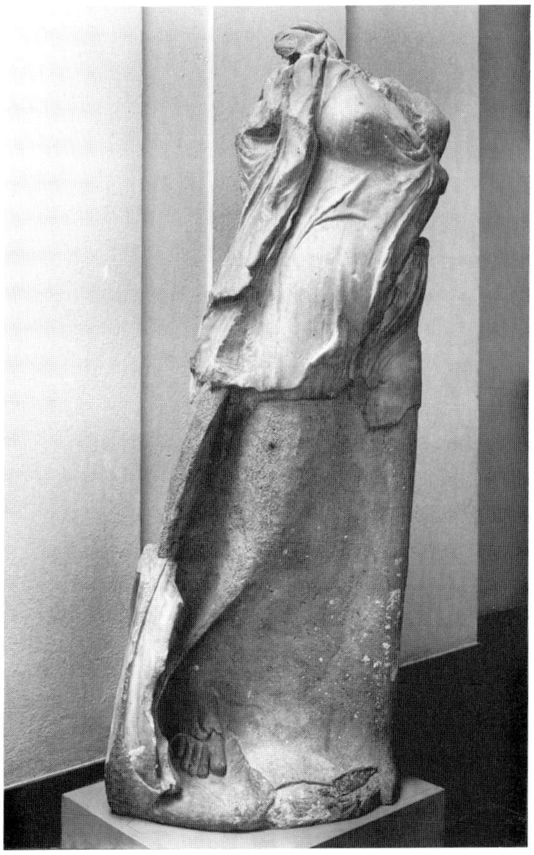

Fig. 7. Victory from the precinct of Athena Nikephoros, Pergamon. Staatl. Museen zu Berlin, Antikensammlung. Photo courtesy of Staatl. Museen zu Berlin – Preussischer Kulturbesitz, Antikensammlung, neg. PM 1350.

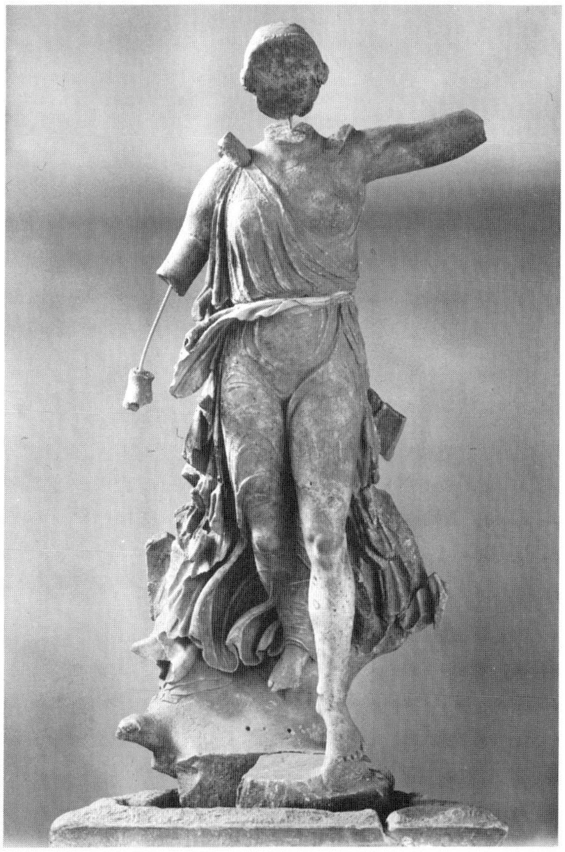

Fig. 8. Victory of Paionios. Olympia, Archaeological Museum. Photo courtesy of DAI Athens, neg. Hege 665.

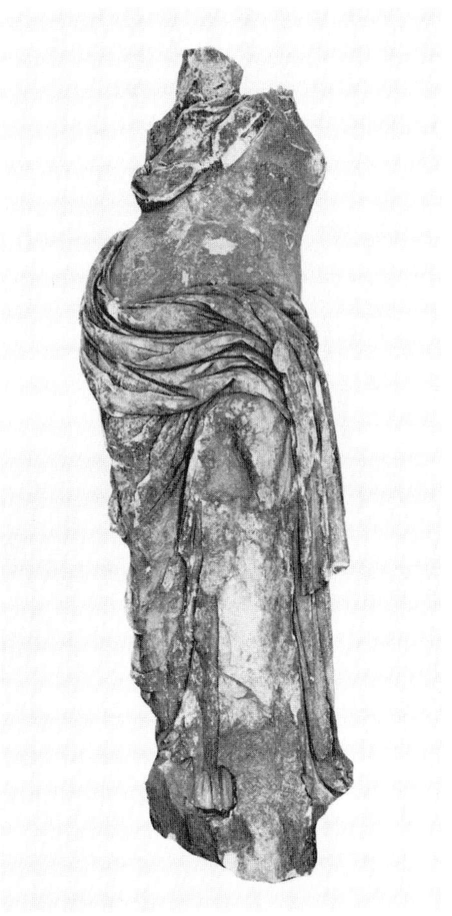

Fig. 9. Statue of Dionysos. Choregic monument, Thasos. Thasos, Archaeological Museum. Photo: École Française d'Athènes, neg. 27869.

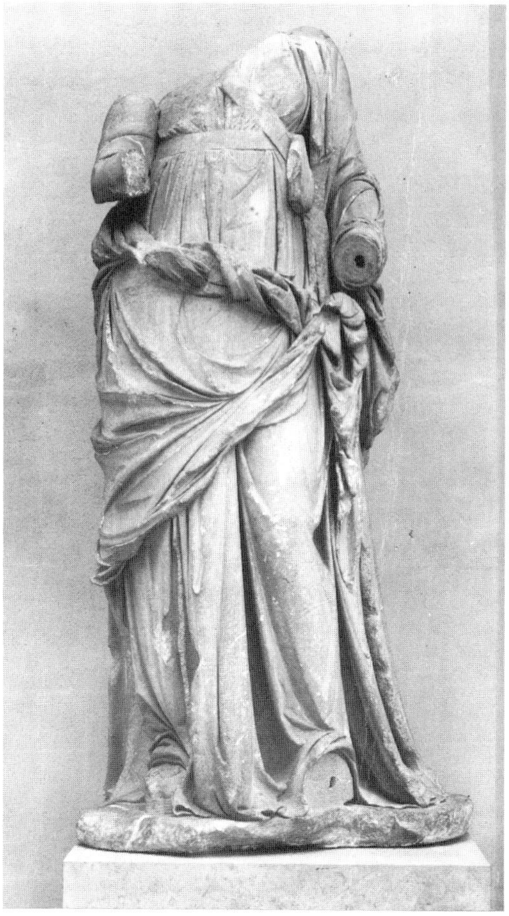

Fig. 10. Statue of Tragedy from the acropolis of Pergamon. Staatl. Museen zu Berlin, Antikensammlung. Photo courtesy of Staatl. Museen zu Berlin – Preussischer Kulturbesitz, Antikensammlung, neg. PM 1338.

different perspective on the Victory. The Dionysos and the Victory appear to show different stages within a developing tradition of drapery style. The comparison to the Cyrene figure is typological, not stylistic. Both are wind-swept figures with the right leg forward and the himation falling down the proper right side and over the thigh. The contrast exemplifies how the Samothrace Victory transforms the expectable into something emotive and highly dramatic.

The development of bold ideas in large scale appears to have been a signature of the Rhodian School, from the third century B.C. Colossus of Rhodes through the Punishment of Dirce, the Sperlonga sculptures and the Laocoon.[25] The Victory of Samothrace is evidence that by the early second century the school was distinguishing itself not only through scale and technical virtuosity. It was boldly furthering nascent stylistic directions to form a decisive style of its own.

I want to introduce one final issue before closing: the question of the stylistic relation of Rhodes and Pergamon in the early second century.

The down-dating of the Great Frieze substantially alters the established picture of the development of second-century art, and it will be some time before scholars can sort out the various implications. There is, I believe, one well-known work whose proper stylistic interpretation is key: the Tragedy from the acropolis of Pergamon (Fig. 10).[26]

The Tragedy is normally dated to the period of the Great Frieze,[27] but there are in fact important differences. Although the contrapposto is closed, as in High Pergamene art, it is free of Baroque exaggeration. The figure's drapery is also unmistakably different from that on the Great Frieze, more plastically conceived and less contrived. In these qualities it approaches that of the Victory. The rolling of the mantle across the waist breaks up the regularity of the folds in a manner not as radical, but similar to the staccato folds of the mantle of the Victory, and the deeply shadowed folds falling at the legs have a clear relation.

It would be premature to suggest more than an art historical scenario, but if the Samothrace Victory and the Tragedy are close in date, it suggests that in the early second century there were significant ties between the arts of Rhodes and Pergamon, presumably because the arts of Pergamon were taking form under strong Rhodian influence. The Great Altar would manifest a later formal language, rooted in Rhodian style but unmistakably Pergamon's own, reflective of that kingdom's own distinctive self-concept in the referentiality of its form.

Notes

1. *Pro Samothrake, Akademie der Wissenschaften in Wien, Philosoph.-hist. Kl., SB* 212, 1 (1930); "Die Nike von Samothrake: Ein rhodisches Werk und Anathem," *Nachrichten von der Gesellschaft der Wissenschaften zu Göttingen, Philolog.-Hist. Kl. 1931* (1931) 337–378. A number of talks in the Athens symposium dealt with issues directly relevant to mine. I would like to draw attention particularly to Iphigeneia Leventi's paper on the Hygeia of Nikeratos (here pp. 101–116), Vana Machaira's (here pp. 137–148) and Carol Mattusch's (here pp. 149–156) on Rhodian sculpture. I have also had the advantage of a research assistant who, at her own insistence, will remain anonymous.
2. *Triemiolia: Étude sur un type de navire rhodien, Lindiaka* 7 (1938).
3. I want to thank Scott Pike, former Acting Director of the Wiener Laboratory of the American School of Classical Studies at Athens, for examining the stone of the prow with me on Samothrace in 1996. Its character, both to the eye and under magnification, is remarkably consistent one sample to the next. The crystals are anhedral calcite with considerable elongation on the foliate plane. Grain size varies from 1 to 3 mm. The fabric contains some vein calcite, a sign of incomplete metamorphosis, but there are no evident fossils. For the geology of Lartian stone see G.P. Marinos (ed.), *Annales géologiques des pays helléniques*, ser. 1, vol. 22 (1970) 110–112. In the region of the quarries, on the coast about a kilometer to the south of modern Lartos, there are two formations: Lartian limestone and the metamorphic state of the same stone, Lartian marble. The putative match is to the metamorphic state.
4. Among more recent work on the *trihemiolia*, I would single out J.S. Morrison, *International Journal of Nautical Archaeology and Underwater Exploration* 9, 1980, 121–126. Morrison upholds Blinkenberg's conclusion. In contrast, L. Casson, *Ships and Seamanship in the Ancient World* (1971) 102–103, identifies the prow as a *quadrireme*. *Quadriremes*, larger than *triremes*, were apparently configured in the Hellenistic period with four files of rowers on each side arranged two men to an oar in two banks. The Samothrace prow, in contrast to the *quadrireme*, is an exceedingly low and narrow vessel, as is evident from the placement of both banks of oars in the outrigger, the relative proportion of the topside and deck to the beam, and the proportion of the beam to the width of the outrigger. The vertical proportions on the Hagesandros relief (infra n. 11), roughly contemporary with the Samothrace prow, are closely analogous. The Lindos prow (infra n. 11), firmly identified by inscription as a *trihemiolia* and a round half a century earlier, is not as sleek. The later design appears to make every effort to bring the center of gravity down. The outrigger and the rowers are positioned slightly lower, and the inner file of rowers, who had a bit more leg room, are some ten centimeters below the outer. On the Lindos prow the two banks appear to have been at the same level. The highly distinctive appearance of the ships represented, however, and their close similarity in cross-section put their identification as the same class of vessel beyond reasonable doubt. In my opinion A.L. Ermeti, *RendLinc* ser. 8, 33, 1978, 175–197, forces the evidence beyond recognition. She identifies the Hagesandros relief and the Samothrace prow as *trihemioliai*, but cites the slightly different form of the Lindos prow and labels it (notwithstanding the inscription) as a different class.

   Without attempting to echo the full controversy about rowing schemes, we make a few comments. Based on the Samothrace prow, the Lindos prow, and the Hagesandros relief, I strongly doubt that *trihemioliai* could have accommodated either of Morrison's proposals (*op. cit.*, 124–126). The two banks of oars on the Samothrace prow, nearly at the same level, had to have been manned side by side. The beam of the ship is far too narrow for Morrison's Arrangement B, which places eight rowers across in the stern, two to an oar in two banks. Arrangement A is better: it is asymmetrical with six across, two men to an oar on one side, one man on the other, in two banks. However, I far prefer one man to an oar, with one full bank extending bow to stern and a second half-bank from the bow to midship. This is the arrangement that L. Casson posits for the *hemiolia*, although not, we may note, for the *trihemiolia*: *JHS* 78, 1958, 14–18. In suggesting this arrangement, I do not wish to imply that *hemioliai* and *trihemioliai* were one and the same. Literary sources strongly suggest that they are distinct classes of vessel. Rather they appear to have had the same essential arrangement of oars. This lends credence to the view that the latter, attested only in naval warfare, was modeled on the former, the characteristic pirate vessel.
5. L. Alscher, *Griechische Plastik* IV: *Hellenismus* (1957) 162–163; M. Bieber, *The Sculpture of the Hellenistic Age*[2] (1961) 125–126; A. Linfert, *Kunstzentren hellenistischer Zeit* (1976) 83–86. Cf. G.S. Merker, *The Hellenistic Sculpture of Rhodes, SIMA* 40 (1973), who confines herself to finds from the island. G. Gualandi, *ASAtene* 54, 1976, 7–259, centers his study on finds from the island, but also discusses large-scale works of other provenience, including the Victory.
6. I.S. Mark, *AJA* 100, 1996, 398 (abstract).
7. *Der grosse Fries von Pergamon* (1948) 173–175 n. 75.
8. On the emergence of Pergamon as a sculptural center in the late third century, e.g. Bieber (supra n. 5) 107–122; J.J. Pollitt, *Art in the Hellenistic Age* (1986) 83–110; R.R.R. Smith, *Hellenistic Sculpture* (1991) 155–180. The most thorough review of the third century evidence is B.S. Ridgway, *Hellenistic Sculpture* I: *The Styles of ca. 331–200* (1990). Ridgway (e.g. p. 357) accepts a late third century date for the emergence of a school at Pergamon, but cites the metopes of the so-called Ptolemaion at Limyra as possible evidence for the Baroque style in the first half of the century. In preliminary publication, the excavators at Limyra have suggested an early third century date for the Ptolemaion: J. Borchhardt, *ÖJh* Beibl.

61, 1991–1992, 151–166. This placement of the Ptolemaion remains to be argued in detail, but even if convincing, it will not affect the dating of the Samothrace Victory. There is no attested occasion for the dedication of a *trihemiolia* on Samothrace in the first half of the third century.

9. Also Appian, *Syr.* 27. For an account of the battle R.M. Berthold, *Rhodes in the Hellenistic Age* (1984) 159–61. Other naval victories of the same general date have been considered, but they are comparatively poor candidates. (1) Polybios (5.101.1) recounts that Philip V pursued the pirate Skerdilaïdas with a fleet of twelve "enclosed" (*kataphraktoi*) vessels, eight "unenclosed" (*aphraktoi*) vessels and thirty *hemioliai*. Some scholars (most notably Blinkenberg [supra n. 1] 6) have thought that the terms *hemiolia* and *trihemiolia* refer to the same class of vessel, but in his account of the battle of Chios, fought in 201 BC, Polybios distinguishes between the two (cf. e.g. 16.3.4 and 16.6.4). Almost certainly the term in widespread use for the deck with enclosed sides, the type seen on the prow of the Victory, was *kataphraktos*. Not all *trihemioliai* were so enclosed, but this was a common configuration of the later Hellenistic period. Because of the small size of the *trihemiolia*, the deck that enclosed the rowers was at a height well above the gunwales, and the full woodwork of deck and sides raised the center of gravity appreciably making the boat far less stable. It would have required unusual skill and training to maneuver. The added weight would also have slowed the vessel down. As I mentioned, literary sources attest the *trihemiolia* only in naval warfare, and the *kataphraktos trihemiolia* must surely have been intended specifically for that use. *Hemioliai* on the other hand had a range of uses, and as best we know, were never decked in. (2) The battle of Chios: According to Polybios (16.2.1–16.8.10), the fleets of Philip V and Attalos I both included *trihemioliai*. The battle is described at length, and *trihemioliai* did not play a decisive role. Both Philip and Attalos claimed victory, but in truth the former suffered heavy losses, and the outcome was inconclusive. Philip was in control of Samothrace at the time, and Polybios lists one *trihemiolia* among the ships that he captured from Attalos (16.7.3), but the Samothrace prow is depicted afloat and underway. It is not a captured vessel. It is also worth noting that Polybios' wording at 16.2.10 and 16.7.1 suggests that the *trihemioliai* in both Philip's and Attalos' fleets were not *kataphraktoi*.

10. For the text, J. Pouilloux, *Études Thasiennes* 3: *Recherches sur l'histoire et les cultes de Thasos* I (1954) 437 n. 3. For the historical context, C. Friedrich, *IG* XII, 8 (1909) p. 79; *RE* ser. 2, V A (1934) 1820, s.v. Thasos (F. Hiller von Gärtringen). There is other evidence of Rhodes' northern interests from around the same date. In 197 at the conference at Nicaea, Rhodes listed among her requests of Flamininus that Philip be forced to give up control of two strategic Hellespontine cities, Sestos and Abydos. See Polybios 18.2.3; Livy 33.6–7. See further Berthold (supra n. 9) 135–137.

11. Relief of Hagesandros: Blinkenberg (supra n. 1) 22–30; E. Dyggve, *Lindos* III, 1 (1960) 56–57, fig. III, 27–28, pls. IIIA–B. Lindos prow: J. Marcadé, *RA* 25, 1946, 147–152; A.L. Ermeti, *L'Agorà di Cirene* III, 1, *Il Monumento navale*, *Monografie di archeologia Libica* 16 (1981) 62–64, fig. 8, pls. 4–5; A. Göttlicher, *Materialien für ein Corpus der Schiffsmodelle im Altertum* (1978) no. 367. K. Lehmann, in P.W. Lehmann and K. Lehmann (edd.), *Samothracian Reflections* (1973) 194 n. 19, fig. 11, draws attention to the fragmentary survival of a third major monument that, judged from the cross-section of its hull, appears also to have represented a *trihemiolia*. The fragment, in the collection of the Rhodes Archaeological Museum, is currently on display in the Palace of the Knights of St. John. It is listed in the museum without provenience, but Lehmann notes that he was told in 1953 that it came from the island. The fragment is published in full by Ermeti (op. cit.) 54, fig. 5, pls. 26–27; add now P. Moreno, *Scultura ellenistica* (1994) 369, fig. 464.

12. A recent monograph, H. Knell, *Die Nike von Samothrake: Typus, Form, Bedeutung und Wirkungsgeschichte eines rhodischen Sieges-Anathems im Kabirenheiligtum von Samothrake* (1995) 14–26, gives in-depth, stylistic analysis.

13. The plinth cutting for the statue is preserved on a large fragment of gray-blue (Rhodian) marble (Samothrace, Archaeological Museum 78.11). That fragment joins a second large fragment, 78.10, to preserve five sides of a massive block: P.L. 1.65, W. 0.708, H. 0.608 m. The block can be firmly attributed to the upper course of the deck by its width and course height, and the position of its one preserved clamp cutting. Marianne Hamiaux, who is preparing a report on the campaigns of Charles Champoiseau on Samothrace and a full publication of the statue, has drawn my attention to a block of roughly equivalent dimensions that Champoiseau reports having left behind when he shipped the other remains of the prow to Paris. C. Champoiseau, *RA* 39, 1880, 14: "Nous décidâmes toutefois d'abandonner une énorme cube de 1 m, 73 de long sur 0 m, 67 de large et 0 m, 53 de haut, complètement brut sur ses six faces, dont la masse rendait le transport difficile et qui, n'occupant dans le monument qu'une place insignifiante, invisible à l'extérieur, pouvait être, sans inconvénient, remplacé lors de la restauration." Photographs of 78.10 and 78.11 dating from 1923 appear in J. Bouzek and Iva Ondřejová (edd.), *Samothrace* 1923/1927/1978 (1985) pls. 27 (78.10) and 28 (78.10, 70.11). The photo captions however wrongly identify the two as coming "from the foundations of the Nike Fountain."

I am grateful to the Département des Antiquités Grecques, Etrusques et Romaines, Musée du Louvre, for allowing me to examine a fragment of Rhodian marble (Paris, Louvre 2373; *IG* XII, 8, no. 239) found in the vicinity of the Victory Monument by Champoiseau. The fragment is from the upper course of a base and preserves one corner of a plinth cutting for a statuette. Across the front are the letters ---]'Ρόδιος. Thiersch (supra n. 1) 341–364 identified the block as part of a low course that raised the Victory above the deck. He restored the inscription as the signature of the Rhodian sculptor Pythokritos, son of Timocharis: Pythokritos Timochario]s Rhodios/[epoiese]. Most scholars have doubted the attribution to the monument because of the small scale of the plinth cutting, but now that the actual plinth cutting has been identified in the deck itself, the attribution of 2373 is firmly ruled out. A restoration of the prow reproduced by Lehmann (supra n. 11) 188, fig. 5, pictures the Victory on a small cabin. This must also be erroneous.

14. The Altar is dated by pottery, specifically by molded bowls of the so-called long-petal type, recovered from the podium. On the date of these molded bowls, P.J. Callaghan, *BICS* 28, 1981, 115–121; id., *BICS* 29, 1982, 63–68; S. Rotroff, in J.P. Uhlenbrock (ed.), *The Coroplast's Art* (1990) 22–30. Some scholars continue to argue an earlier date for the Altar. Cf., for example, T.-M. Schmidt, in B. Andreae (ed.), *Phyromachos-Probleme* (1990) 141–162, who feels that a date as early as 175 BC is not excluded. W. Radt, *AA* 1995, 575–589, reporting on new excavations in the Altar foundations, is more conservative in his evaluation. He does not publish any of his recent ceramic finds, but since one dates by the latest recovered pottery, the new finds cannot establish a date *earlier* than that attested so far. I was surprised to read his opinion (p. 588) that the context pottery does not rule out a date as early as 185 B.C.

15. The term "closed" is derived from the German "geschlossene Form," coined as a descriptive label by Heinrich Wölfflin at the beginning of this century. See H. Wölfflin, *Kunstgeschichtliche Grundbegriffe*[13] (1963) 147–180.

16. On this see particularly Kähler (supra n. 7) 118–120.

17. The terms "closed" and "open," devised by Wölfflin in order to contrast sixteenth- and seventeenth-century European art, were introduced into the study of Hellenistic art above all by Gerhard Krahmer, *RM* 38–39, 1923–24, 138–184. Krahmer used the distinction as a way to date works, arguing that sculptures from ca. 300–150 were closed; from ca. 150–100, open. I do not believe that the contrast is a reliable chronological indicator. The Hellenistic period is too stylistically complex and diverse for such a simple formula. But the terms remain a useful short-hand to help differentiate one artistic language from another. Wölfflin thought of "closed" and "open" as polar opposites, but this is not true for the Hellenistic period. There are a plethora of formal strategies, with works extending from one extreme to the other. For Krahmer such works as the Poseidon of Melos were "open." The Poseidon is in fact more open than typical fifth- and fourth-century works. But the contrapposto, though it involves abrupt, emotive changes of direction, is still self-consciously contrived. Such a work as the Victory, and I would think also the Barberini Faun (Pollitt [supra n. 8] fig. 146), are composed in a wholly different, less perceptibly contrived manner.

18. The upper torso of the Victory is fragmentary and exact reconstruction of the pose is difficult. For the state of preservation, M. Hamiaux, *Les sculptures grecques* 2: *La période hellénistique (IIIe–Ier siècles avant J.-C.)* (1998) 27. Initial publication of the statue in A. Conze, A. Hauser and O. Benndorf, *Neue archaeologische Untersuchungen auf Samothrake* 2 (1880) 49–88, figs. 25a, 25b, restores the left arm down and the right raised. The head turns slightly to the right. The right wing, almost entirely lost, is restored as higher and more extended than the left.

19. *AvP* 7, no 46, pl. 13.

20. On the Nike of Paionios, A. Stewart, *Greek Sculpture: An Exploration* (1990) 89–92 with bibliography.

21. P. Devambez, *MonPiot* 38, 1941, 93–116; P. Bernard and F. Salviat, *BCH* 83, 1959, 288–335.

22. For a discussion of the date, Ridgway (supra n. 8) 50–53. Ridgway hesitates between a late fourth or early third-century dating, but includes the work in her late fourth-century chapter.

23. Ermeti (supra n. 22) 127–134. Ridgway (supra n. 8) 215–217, supports this date although with caution. The dating has been questioned by H.G. Martin and G. Caputo, among others. H.G. Martin, *Gnomon* 55, 1983, 117–122 (review of Ermeti). G. Caputo, in N. Bonacasa and A. di Vita (edd.), *Alessandria e il mondo ellenistico-romano: Studi in onore de Achille Adriani* 3 (1984) 451–460. Caputo argues that the monument commemorates the battle of Actium. The form of the galley, decorative program aside, can only be dated within broad limits, but it is unquestionably a Greek vessel of Hellenistic date. It seems an implausible commemoration for Actium. A fragment from a large-scale strongly moved figure found on Tenos but now lost appears closer in date to the Victory. See R. Etienne and J.-P. Braun, *Ténos* I: *Le Sanctuaire de Poseidon et d'Amphitrite* (1986) 271 n. 9; 286 n. 35; pl 164, 6.

24. O. Palagia, *Euphranor* (1980) 12–30, pls. 6–9; Stewart (supra n. 20) 179, fig. 512.

25. Also Pliny, *NH* 34.18.42, who, after discussing the Colossus of Rhodes, states: "There are a hundred other lesser *colossi* in the same city, which, if displayed somewhere each on its own, would have brought fame to that place. Besides these there are five *colossi* of gods made by Bryaxis."

26. *AvP* 7, no. 47, pp. 76–80.

27. E.g. Bieber (supra n. 5) 119; Stewart (supra n. 20) 213. The figure was excavated in the spring of 1879 on the northern border of the Great Altar, and this may have led some to view it as contemporaneous with that major project. The wholesale reterracing and architectural embellishment of the citadel under Eumenes II almost certainly entailed the resiting of preexisting dedications, however, so that the findspot does not of itself provide a date.

Ελληνιστικά αγάλματα της Μήλου

Ισμήνη Τριάντη

Στο βόρειο μέρος της Μήλου, στο ανατολικό σκέλος του μεγάλου κόλπου του Αδάμαντα, όπου σώζονται τα ερείπια της αρχαίας πόλης της Μήλου,[1] έχουν βρεθεί κατά καιρούς πολλά και σημαντικά γλυπτά, όπως είναι γνωστό. Πρώτο από όλα βρέθηκε το 1820 από έναν χωρικό, τον Γεώργιο Κεντρωτά, το άγαλμα της Αφροδίτης της Μήλου (εικ. 12–13) που μεταφέρθηκε στο Λούβρο μαζί με τρεις ερμαϊκές στήλες, τρία χέρια και τρεις επιγραφές, που βρέθηκαν επίσης στον ίδιο χώρο, στον οποίο τοποθετείται το Γυμνάσιο της πόλης.[2]

'Ενα δεύτερο σύνολο γλυπτών ανακαλύφθηκε επίσης τυχαία το 1877, όταν ο γεωργός Γιάννης Νοστράκης πήγε να φυτέψει ελιές στο κτήμα του στο Κλήμα, κοντά στη θάλασσα. Εκτός από το άγαλμα του Ποσειδώνα,[3] ανακαλύφτηκαν τότε μαζί ένα γυναικείο άγαλμα που ερμηνεύτηκε ως Αμφιτρίτη,[4] μια μικρότερη γυναικεία μορφή που στηρίζεται με το αριστερό της χέρι σε ένα αρχαϊστικό γυναικείο αγαλματάκι με πόλο,[5] ένας έφιππος ανδριάντας[6] και ένας ιματιοφόρος που ήταν στημένος πάνω σε μια ενεπίγραφη τετράπλευρη βάση.[7] Η επιγραφή αναφέρει ότι ήταν ανάθημα στον Ποσειδώνα και επιβεβαιώνει μαζί με το άγαλμα του ίδιου του θεού την ύπαρξη ιερού σε αυτή τη θέση.[8] Τα παραπάνω αγάλματα αγοράστηκαν το 1878 από την Αρχαιολογική Εταιρεία και μεταφέρθηκαν στο Εθνικό Αρχαιολογικό Μουσείο.

Τέλος, το 1896 ο Duncan Mackenzie, αρχαιολόγος της Αγγλικής Σχολής, έσκαψε συστηματικά στη θέση "Τρεις εκκλησιές" και έφερε στο φώς οκτώ αγάλματα ελληνιστικών επίσης χρόνων.[9] Στη θέση αυτή ο Mackenzie υποθέτει ότι θα βρισκόταν η Αγορά της Μήλου. Τα αγάλματα αυτά παρέμειναν στη Μήλο.[10] Εκτός από τα τρία παραπάνω σύνολα γλυπτών που πιστεύεται ότι προέρχονται από το ιερό του Ποσειδώνα, το Γυμνάσιο και την Αγορά της αρχαίας πόλης της Μήλου, έχουν βρεθεί και μεμονωμένα ευρήματα που επίσης προέρχονται από την αρχαία πόλη, για τα οποία όμως δεν υπάρχουν περισσότερες πληροφορίες για την ακριβή θέση ανεύρεσής τους.

Η έρευνα, ξεκινώντας από τα μεγαλύτερα από τα παραπάνω αγάλματα, έθεσε το ερώτημα αν είναι έργα ενός ντόπιου εργαστηρίου ή αν προέρχονται από άλλα καλλιτεχνικά κέντρα. Για την πρώτη υπόθεση έχουν διατυπωθεί αντιρρήσεις γιατί στο νησί αυτό δεν υπάρχει μάρμαρο. Αλλά ούτε και γλύπτης από τη Μήλο μαρτυρείται, πράγμα που θα αποτελούσε ένδειξη για την ύπαρξη ενός τοπικού εργαστηρίου. Αντίθετα οι υπογραφές που έχουν σωθεί δείχνουν προς διαφορετικά κεντρα του ελληνιστικού κόσμου.

Ο Πολυάνθης Σωκράτους, που σύμφωνα με την υπογραφή σε μια βάση (εικ. 1) του Μουσείου Μήλου έκανε το χάλκινο άγαλμα της Ρώμης,[11] είναι γνωστός από τη Δήλο, όπου υπογράφει ένα από τα έργα του ως Κυρηναίος.[12] Η υπογραφή του στη βάση της Μήλου χρονολογείται στα μέσα του 2ου αι. π.Χ. και το άγαλμα της Ρώμης θα ήταν ένα από τα πρώτα που είχαν κατασκευαστεί στην Ελλάδα.

Ο Αντιφάνης Θρασωνίδου Πάριος[13] υπογράφει στο στήριγμα του αγάλματος που φυλάσσεται στο Μουσείο του Βερολίνου και είναι αντίγραφο του τύπου του τέλους του 4ου αιώνα π.Χ. του γνωστού ως Ερμή Richelieu.[14] Το άγαλμα βρέθηκε το 1827 στην ίδια περίπου θέση με την Αφροδίτη της Μήλου. Η επιγραφή χρονολογείται στο α' μισό του 1ου αιώνα π.Χ.

Μια δεύτερη επιγραφή στη Μήλο, χαμένη σήμερα, αναφέρει έναν γλύπτη ----]ήναιο Διονύ[--. Το όνομά του συμπληρώνεται ως Αθήναιος Διονυσίου και συσχετίζεται από τον Rubensohn[15] με την υπογραφή σε ένα στήριγμα αγάλματος από την Γόρτυνα της Κρήτης όπου υπογράφει ένας γλύπτης "Αθήναιος Διονυσίου Πάριος". Με βάση τις επιγραφές, θεωρεί ο Rubensohn ότι στην Πάρο σε αυτά τα χρόνια λειτουργούσε ένα εργαστήριο κατασκευής αντιγράφων αγαλμάτων, το οποίο αποκαλεί μάλιστα νεοπαριανό.[16] Προς αυτό το εργαστήριο προσανατολίζεται ο Schäfer για την κατασκευή του Ποσειδώνα της Μήλου.[17]

Μαζί με την Αφροδίτη βρέθηκε και μεταφέρθηκε στο Μουσείο του Λούβρου η βάση με την επιγραφή --]ανδρος --]ηνίδου |--]ιοχεύς από Μαιάνδρου | εποίησεν.[18] Η βάση, χαμένη ήδη από τον περασμένο αιώνα, εξακολουθεί να απασχολεί την έρευνα σε σχέση με το όνομα του γλύπτη, αν είναι δηλαδή Αγήσανδρος ή Αλέξανδρος, καθώς και για το αν συνδέεται ή όχι με το άγαλμα της Αφροδίτης.[19]

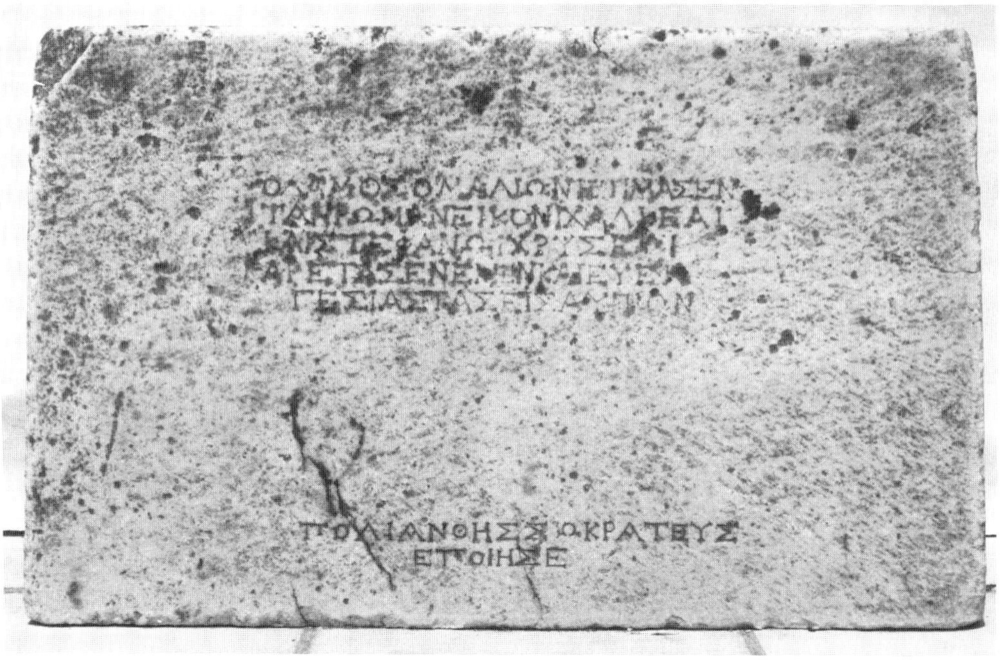

Εικ. 1. Βάση αγάλματος Ρώμης. Μήλος, Μουσείο, αρ. ευρ. 146. Φωτογραφία Μουσείου.

Στους παραπάνω γλύπτες από τη Μικρά Ασία, την Κυρήνη και την Πάρο που δούλεψαν για τη Μήλο, προστίθεται πιθανώς και ένας διάσημος πελοποννήσιος γλύπτης των ελληνιστικών χρόνων, ο Δαμοφών από τη Μεσσήνη.[20] Στον ενεπίγραφο κίονα που βρέθηκε στη Μεσσήνη το 1972,[21] στον οποίο αναγράφονται τιμητικά ψηφίσματα επτά ελληνικών πόλεων, περιλαμβάνεται, όπως έδειξε η πρόσφατη ανάγνωση, και ένα ψήφισμα του Δήμου των Μηλίων που τιμά τον Δαμοφώντα ως πρόξενο και ευεργέτη.[22] Χωρίς να είναι εντελώς σίγουρο ότι δούλεψε ως γλύπτης στη Μήλο, δεν μπορεί να είναι χωρίς σημασία η τιμή που του αποδίδεται.

Από τους παραπάνω γλύπτες που μαρτυρείται ότι δούλεψαν στη Μήλο, φαίνεται πιο πιθανό ότι ένα μεγάλο μέρος από την ως τώρα γνωστή καλλιτεχνική παραγωγή της Μήλου πρέπει να σχετιστεί με ξένους καλλιτέχνες. Θα προσπαθήσω και εγώ να προσεγγίσω αυτά τα ζητήματα ξεκινώντας όχι από τα ονόματα, αλλά από τα ίδια τα μνημεία.

Το πάνω μέρος μιας γυναικείας μορφής με αρ. ευρ. **28** σώζεται με το λαιμό (εικ. 2–5).[23] Είναι δουλεμένη σε χοντρόκοκκο μάρμαρο που μοιάζει με το παριανό. Το άγαλμα απαρτιζόταν από δύο κομμάτια μαρμάρου και ενωνόταν λίγο κάτω από τη μέση.[24] Η γυναίκα φοράει έναν χιτώνα με χαρακτές κατακόρυφες πτυχές και ραμμένη ταινία στο τελείωμα του λαιμού. Το ιμάτιο της καλύπτει όλο το σώμα. Το έντονα λυγισμένο στον αγκώνα δεξί χέρι της φέρεται μπροστά στο στήθος. Το αριστερό, κατά μήκος του κορμού, κάμπτεται ελαφρά, ενώ το άκρο χέρι έχει κατεύθυνση προς τα εμπρός. Ανάμεσα στο σώμα της και στον πήχη είναι συγκεντρωμένες πτυχές. Και τα δύο άκρα χέρια ήταν πρόσθετα, όπως φαίνεται από τις τρύπες και την προεργασία στο κάτω μέρος των πήχεων. Το ιμάτιο περνά με λοξές πτυχές διαγώνια από το σώμα, και πέφτει από τον αριστερό ώμο πίσω στη ράχη. Το πτυχωμένο άκρο του θα κολλούσε στην κατακόρυφη επίπεδη επιφάνεια πίσω, χωρίς γόμφο σε αυτό το τμήμα.

Το άγαλμα δεν κατατάσσεται σε ένα γνωστό τύπο. Όσον αφορά τη γενική διάταξη των πτυχών του ιματίου, όπως έρχεται γύρω από το λαιμό και μπροστά στην περιοχή κάτω από το στήθος, μοιάζει με έναν τύπο που παραδίδεται σε ένα αγαλματάκι από τη Μαγνησία στο Μουσείο της Σμύρνης.[25] 'Οσον αφορά τη θέση του δεξιού χεριού μπροστά στο στήθος, το οποίο είναι σε κάποια απόσταση ώστε να φαίνεται ο χιτώνας, θυμίζει τον τύπο της λεγόμενης Ήρας Campana.[26] Το ιμάτιό της είναι διαφανές, ιδιαίτερα στην μπροστινή πλευρά, και αφήνει να διαγράφονται οι κατακόρυφες πτυχές του χιτώνα όπως π.χ. στην Κλεοπάτρα της Δήλου[27] ή στη γυναίκα με το ένθετο κεφάλι στο Μουσείο της Κώ[28] που χρονολογείται στα τελευταία χρόνια του 2ου αιώνα π.Χ., όπου χρονολογείται και το γυναικείο άγαλμα της Μήλου. Στον γυναικείο κορμό της Μήλου βλέπουμε ότι κάποιες πτυχές του ιματίου είναι ιδιόμορφες. Είναι πλατειές, και σχηματίζουν γωνίες. Βλέπουμε μία στην περιοχή κάτω από το στήθος και δύο πλάι στο αριστερό χέρι.

Τέτοιες πτυχές βρίσκουμε και στο κάτω μέρος της ιματιοφόρου μορφής με αρ. ευρ. **60** (εικ. 6–7), που βρέθηκε στις "Τρεις εκκλησιές", στην ανασκαφή του Mackenzie.[29] Ο ανδρικός κάτω κορμός είναι δουλεμένος και αυτός σε χοντρόκοκκο νησιωτικό μάρμαρο, που παρουσιάζει και κομούς.[30] Το πάνω τμήμα του αγάλματος ήταν πρόσθετο από χωριστό κομμάτι μαρμάρου.[31] Τα πόδια του σώζονται ως το κάτω μέρος των κνημών και δείχνουν ότι η μορφή

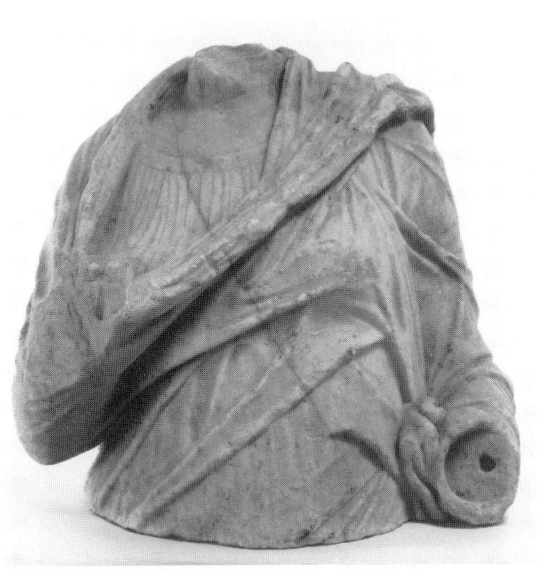

2

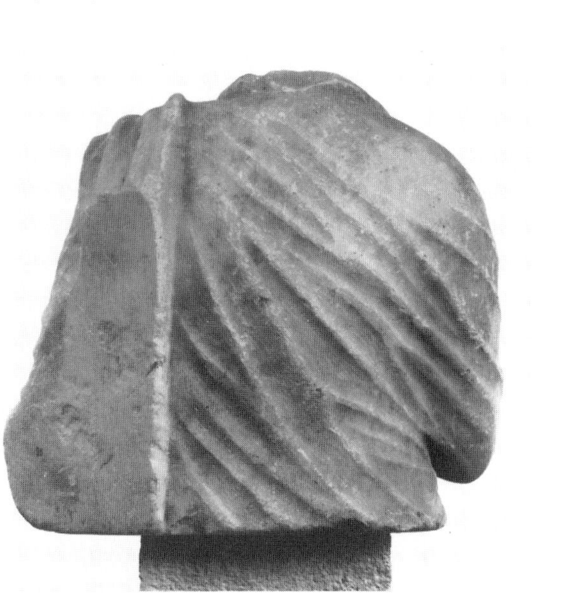

4

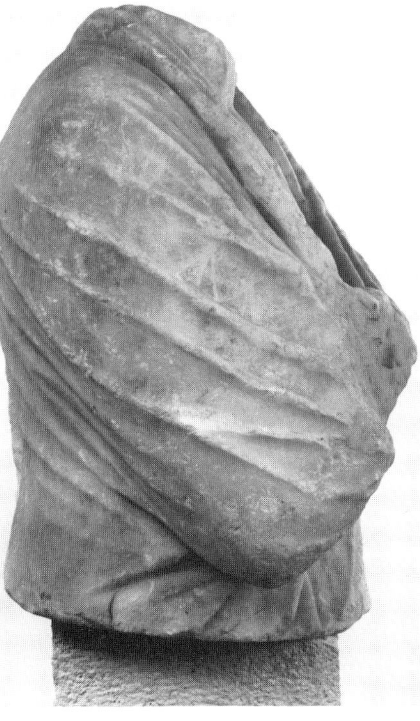

3

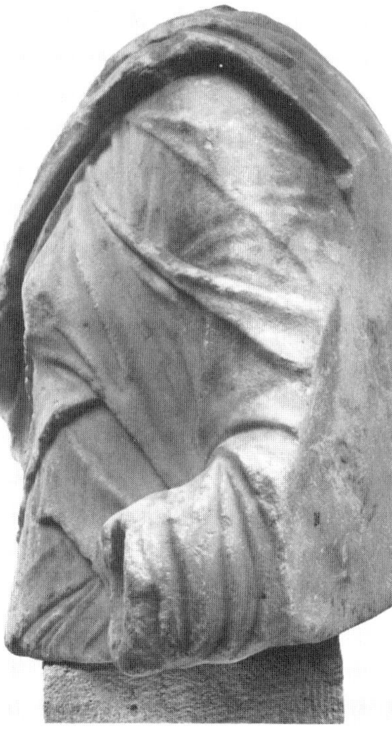

5

Εικ. 2–3. Γυναικείο άγαλμα. Μήλος, Μουσείο, αρ. ευρ. 28.

Εικ. 4–5. Γυναικείο άγαλμα. Μήλος, Μουσείο, αρ. ευρ. 28.

στηριζόταν στο δεξιό πόδι, ενώ το αριστερό, λυγισμένο στο γόνατο, φερόταν προς τα μπροστά. Το ιμάτιο είχε και μια τριγωνική απόληξη πάνω στην κοιλιά προς την αριστερή πλευρά. Αριστερότερα έπεφταν τα άκρα του, που σχημάτιζαν δύο ομάδες από κατακόρυφες πτυχές. Η μεγαλύτερη ομάδα πτυχών, η προς τα πίσω, στο πάνω μέρος σχηματίζει καμπύλη σα να συγκρατιόταν, ενώ πιο κάτω πέφτει κλιμακωτά ως την κάτω παρυφή. Η άλλη ομάδα, η προς τα μπροστά, φτάνει ως το μέσο του μηρού. Οι ιδιόρρυθμες πτυχές, που ανέφερα παραπάνω, σχηματίζονται, η μια στο τριγωνικό τμήμα του ιματίου στην κοιλιά και η άλλη στο εσωτερικό πλάι του αριστερού ποδιού.

Παρόμοιες πτυχές με γωνίες συναντούμε και σε έναν άλλο ιματιοφόρο, από τον οποίο σώζεται το δεξό στάσιμο σκέλος (εικ. 8). Το σκέλος με αρ. ευρ. **61** βρέθηκε επίσης στην ανασκαφή του Mackenzie.[32] Το άκρο του πόδι με σάνταλο με αρ. ευρ. **14** δεν αναφέρεται στη δημοσίευση της ανασκαφής και δεν

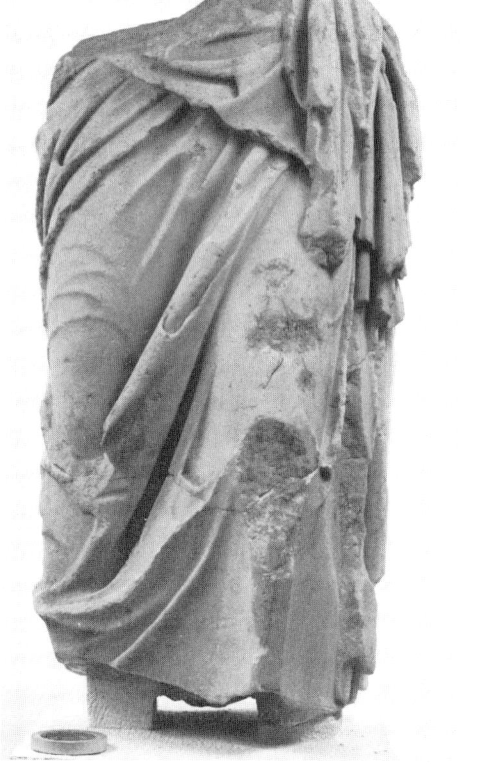

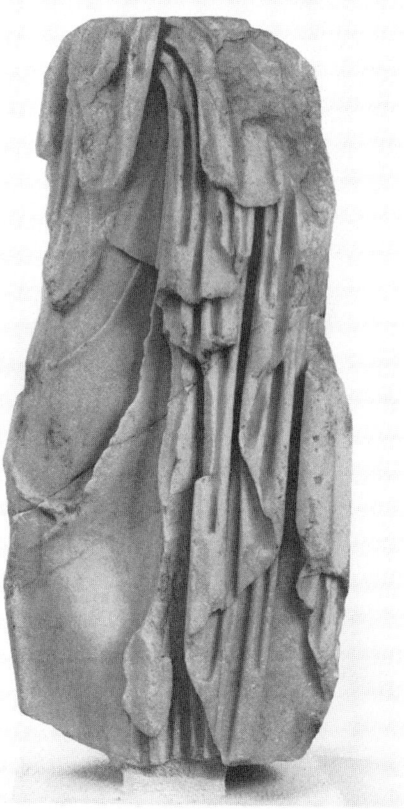

Εικ. 6–7. Κάτω κορμός ιματιοφόρου. Μήλος, Μουσείο, αρ. ευρ. 60. Φωτογραφία Μουσείου.

ξέρω αν βρέθηκε μαζί με τα υπόλοιπα γλυπτά. Το αναγνώρισα στην αποθήκη της Αρχαιολογικής Συλλογής Μήλου και το συγκόλλησα το 1984.[33] Το σάνταλο, του τύπου με τους πλεγμένους ιμάντες, έχει ένα καρδιόσχημο κόσμημα στο μετατάρσιο.[34] Η ομοιότητα των δύο γλυπτών, του κάτω κορμού του ιματιοφόρου **60** και του σκέλους **61**, είναι εμφανής. Η Lewerentz μάλιστα θεωρεί ότι οι δύο ιματιοφόροι είναι όχι μόνο χρονολογικά σύγχρονοι, αλλά προέρχονται και από το ίδιο εργαστήριο αν δεν έχουν κατασκευαστεί και από τον ίδιο γλύπτη.[35] Ο ιματιοφόρος αυτός με το σαντάλι δεχόταν και αυτός πρόσθετο το πάνω μέρος του κορμού, όπως συνάγεται από ένα μικρό τμήμα επίπεδης επιφάνειας στο πάνω μέρος του θραύσματος του σκέλους. Στο πίσω μέρος αυτού του σκέλους, ψηλά κοντά στο σημείο ένωσης με το πάνω κομμάτι, υπάρχει μια άλλη τεχνική λεπτομέρεια, τμήμα από έναν τόρμο για κάθετο σύνδεσμο.[36] 'Ενα τμήμα παρόμοιου τόρμου υπάρχει όμως και στον κολοσσικό κορμό του Μουσείου Μήλου που έχει αρ. ευρ. **127** (εικ. 9–10),[37] στο κατώτατο τμήμα της πίσω πλευράς του κορμού περίπου στο μέσον.[38] Από τα υπολείμματα των δύο αυτών τόρμων που συμπίπτουν και από άλλα στοιχεία που είναι κοινά, όπως π.χ. το μάρμαρο που είναι ίδιο, οι διαστάσεις που ταιριάζουν απόλυτα, η εργασία που είναι παρόμοια και στα δύο γλυπτά, συμπεραίνεται ότι ο κορμός **127** και το σκέλος **61** συνανήκουν και είχαν συνδεθεί στην πίσω πλευρά για ενίσχυση της στήριξης του αγάλματος με ένα σιδερένιο κάθετο σύνδεσμο, που στερεωνόταν στους τόρμους που σώζονται στα δύο τμήματα του αγάλματος.

Το άγαλμα **127**, όπως φαίνεται σε φωτομοντάζ στην εικόνα 11, θα είχε ύψος περίπου 3,30 μ., σχεδόν διπλάσιο δηλαδή από το φυσικό μέγεθος. Η μορφή στηρίζεται στο δεξιό πόδι ενώ το αριστερό ήταν λυγισμένο. Φοράει ένα ιμάτιο που πορπώνεται μπροστά στο στέρνο σα χλαμύδα και φέρεται στη ράχη, ενώ ένα τμήμα του από αριστερά, τυλίγει τα σκέλη αφήνοντας ακάλυπτα τα γεννητικά όργανα. Το δεξί του χέρι ήταν παράλληλο προς το σώμα, ενώ το αριστερό του πρόσθετο από χωριστό κομμάτι μαρμάρου, θα ήταν υψωμένο. Η επιβεβαίωση της απόδοσης αυτής έρχεται από ένα έργο της μικροτεχνίας, τον χρυσό ναΐσκο της Συλλογής Σταθάτου στο Εθνικό Μουσείο,[39] που απεικονίζει έναν Διόνυσο, ίδιο με τον μαρμάρινο κολοσσό της Μήλου.

Με το άγαλμα **127** παρουσιάζει ομοιότητες η Αφροδίτη της Μήλου (εικ. 12–13).[40] Εκτός από το γενικό ρυθμό της σύνθεσης που είναι ίδιος στα δύο αγάλματα, ίδια είναι και τα περιγράμματά τους, με τη συσπείρωση της αριστερής πλευράς, την έκταση

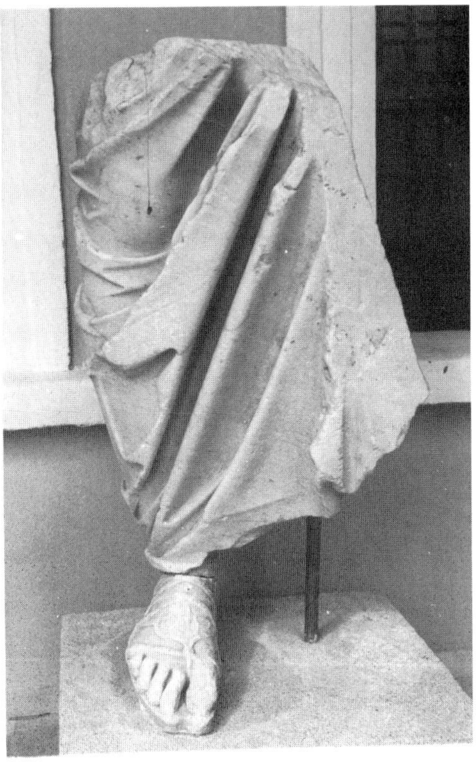

Εικ. 8. Σκέλος ιματιοφόρου. Μήλος, Μουσείο, αρ. ευρ. 61+14. Φωτογραφία Μουσείου.

της δεξιάς και τα σταματήματα στους μηρούς, στη μέση και στο θώρακα. Σχετική είναι και η πλαστική απόδοση παρολονότι ο ένας κορμός είναι γυναικείος και ο άλλος ανδρικός. Αυτό φαίνεται στη γενική διαμόρφωση των όγκων και των επιπέδων και σε λεπτομέρειες. Π.χ. η περιοχή της κοιλιάς, με τον αφαλό είναι και στα δύο αγάλματα σχεδόν ίδια σχεδιασμένη και πλασμένη, το ίδιο και ο δεξιός βραχίονας με την καμπύλη της μασχάλης κοντά στο σώμα. Αλλά και οι πτυχές του ιματίου της Αφροδίτης έχουν κοινά στοιχεία με τις πτυχές των άλλων αγαλμάτων της ομάδας. Π.χ. οι δύο διπλές λοξές πτυχές που έρχονται από το δεξί της πόδι προς το αριστερό γόνατο συγκρίνονται με τις λοξές διπλές πτυχές του ιματίου της γυναίκας αρ. ευρ. **28** από το δεξί χέρι στον αριστερό ώμο (εικ. 2). Η τριγωνική πτυχή πλάι από το λυγισμένο δεξιό γόνατο της Αφροδίτης υπάρχει στην ίδια θέση στον ιματιοφόρο **60** (εικ. 6). Σχετική είναι η τριγωνική πτυχή στο πάνω μέρος του δεξιού μηρού κάτω από το τύλιγμα του ιματίου με το τσάκισμα στο μέσο της πάνω πλευράς. Παρόμοια στους δύο είναι και τα άκρα των ιματίων, της Αφροδίτης, αυτό που φέρεται από τον αριστερό λυγισμένο μηρό, και του ιματιοφόρου, το άκρο που πέφτει πάνω στο μηρό και το άλλο πάνω άκρο του ιματίου πίσω.

'Εχουμε λοιπόν τέσσερα έργα που βρέθηκαν στη

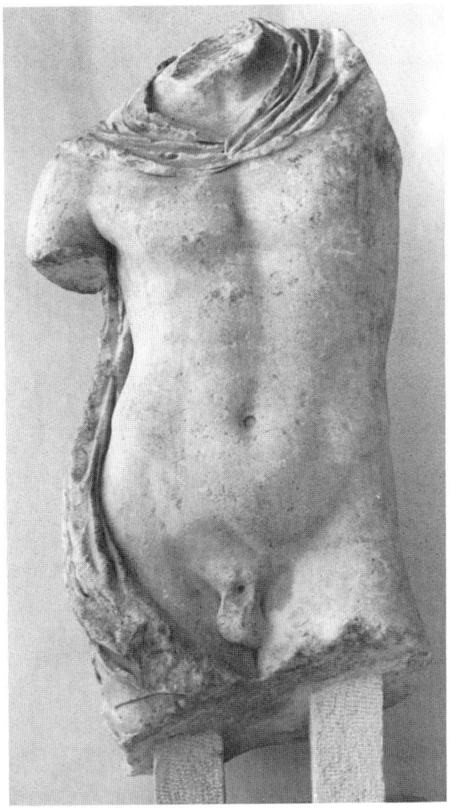

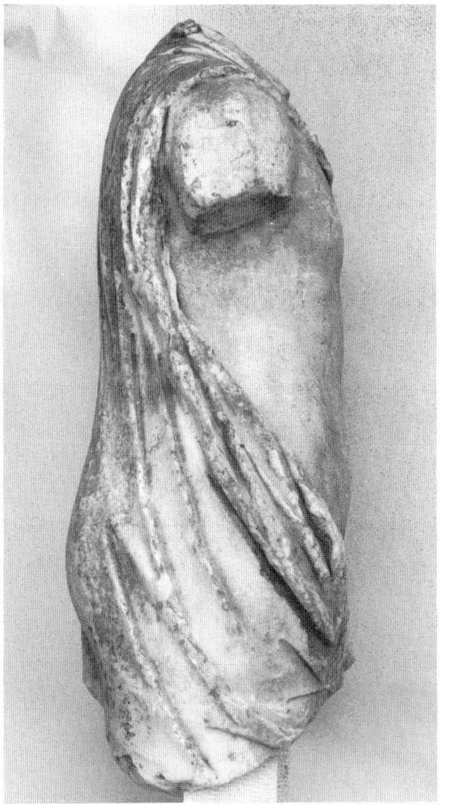

Εικ. 9–10. Ανδρικός κορμός με ιμάτιο. Μήλος, Μουσείο, αρ. ευρ. 127. Φωτογραφία Μουσείου.

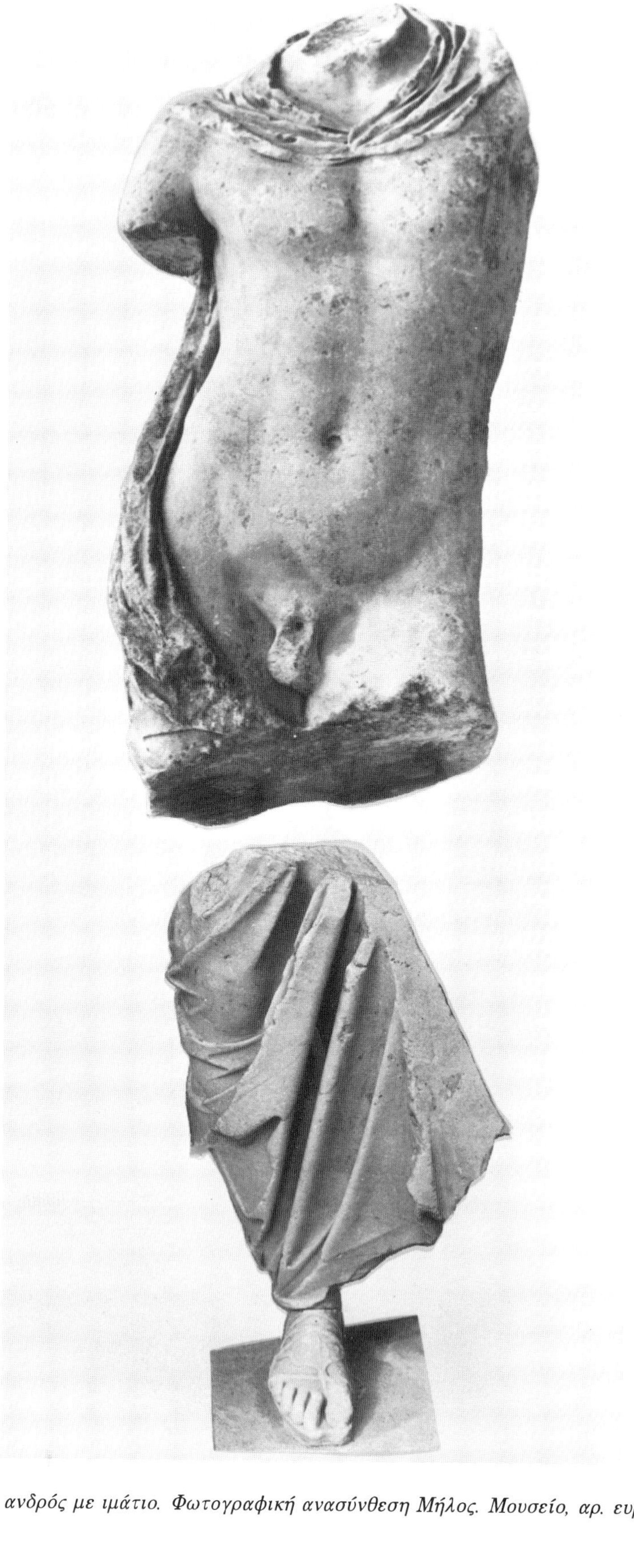

Εικ. 11. Άγαλμα ανδρός με ιμάτιο. Φωτογραφική ανασύνθεση Μήλος. Μουσείο, αρ. ευρ. 61+14+127.

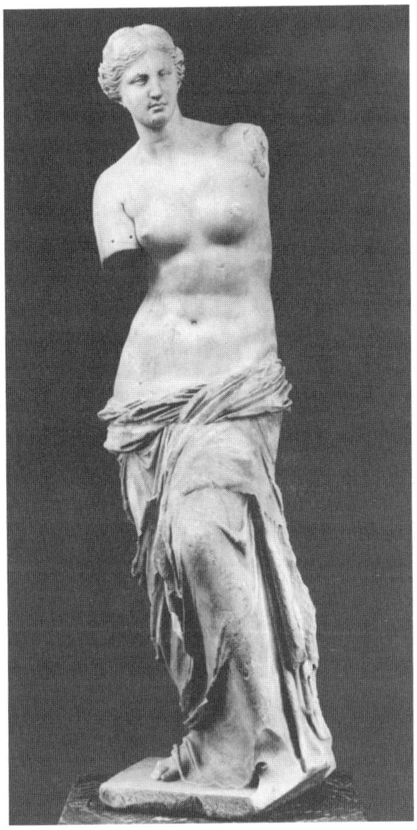

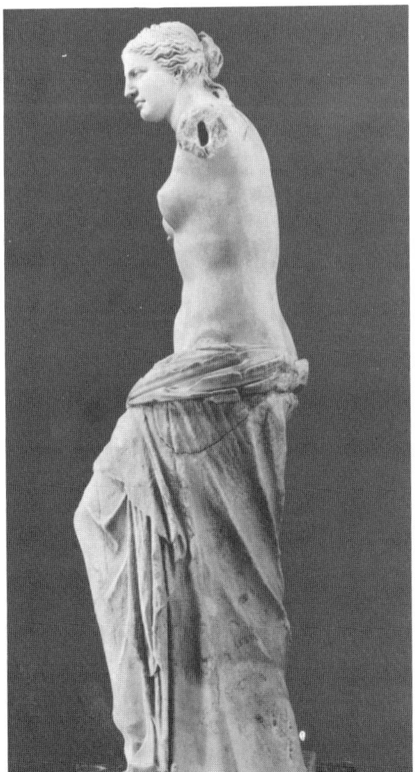

Εικ. 12–13. 'Αγαλμα της Αφροδίτης της Μήλου. Παρίσι, Μουσείο του Λούβρου. MA 54. Φωτογραφία Μουσείου.

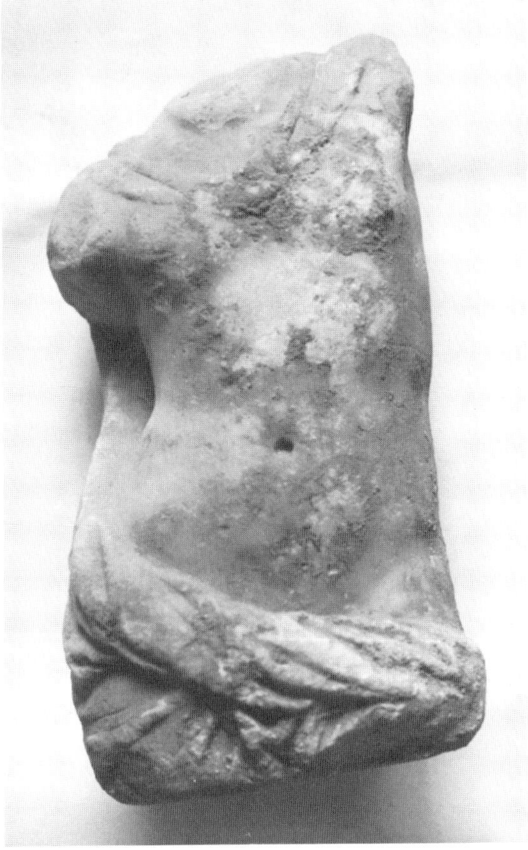

Εικ. 14. Κορμός ανδρικού αγαλματίου. Ρόδος, Αρχαιολογικό Μουσείο, αρ. ευρ. Ε 415. Φωτογραφία Μουσείου.

Μήλο, που είναι σύγχρονα ή περίπου σύγχρονα, χρονολογούνται στο τελευταίο τέταρτο του 2ου ή τις αρχές του 1ου αιώνα π.Χ., είναι κατασκευασμένα από το ίδιο υλικό, ένα χοντρόκοκκο νησιώτικο μάρμαρο, παρουσιάζουν ιδιαίτερα τεχνικά γνωρίσματα και έχουν κοινά και ορισμένα στυλιστικά στοιχεία. Δεν είναι παράτολμο, νομίζω, να υποστηρίξει κανείς ότι τα τέσσερα αυτά έργα προέρχονται από ένα εργαστήριο και είναι πιθανώς έργα του ίδιου γλύπτη.

Αναζητώντας στυλιστικές συγγένειες με τα έργα αυτά, μπορεί να οδηγηθεί κανείς στο Ρόδο. Ήδη, η σχέση της Μήλου με την πλαστική της Ρόδου έχει συζητηθεί με βάση τις στυλιστικές συγγένειες που παρουσιάζουν ορισμένα άλλα γλυπτά της Μήλου με γλυπτά της Ρόδου, όπως π.χ. το γυναικείο άγαλμα από τη Μήλο στο Εθνικό Μουσείο με αρ. ευρ. 238 που θεωρείται ότι αποδίδει ελαφρώς παραλλαγμένη τη Μούσα Κλειώ από το σύνταγμα των Μουσών του Φιλίσκου.[41] Η επίδραση της ροδιακής τέχνης στα νησιά αναγνωρίζεται και από τον Marcadé, που υποστηρίζει ότι η ροδιακή σχολή που κτίστηκε με γερές κλασσικές βάσεις, αφού δέχτηκε τις ελληνιστικοανατολικές επιδράσεις, επηρέασε όλο το νησιωτικό κόσμο του Αιγαίου.[42]

Σε ενίσχυση αυτών των απόψεων μπορεί να

προσθέσει κανείς τώρα και ενδείξεις από τα γλυπτά. Συγκεκριμένα, τις ίδιες ιδιόρρυθμες γωνιώδεις πτυχές που χαρακτηρίζουν τα αγάλματα της Μήλου της ομάδας που συζητήσαμε, αλλά και την ίδια αντίληψη για την απόδοση της σάρκας συναντούμε και σε έναν κάτω κορμό από ένα άγαλμα Νίκης στο Μουσείο της Ρόδου (ΒΕ 1174)[43] με τον οποίο συγκρίνεται από τους μελετητές και η Αφροδίτη, και μάλιστα με τη σύγκριση αυτή τονίζεται η σχέση της με τη ροδιακή πλαστική.[44] Με βάση αυτές τις ομοιότητες δεν μπορεί παρά να σκεφτεί κανείς ότι υπάρχει μια εξάρτηση της ομάδας αυτής των γλυπτών της Μήλου από ένα εργαστήριο της Ρόδου. Συνηγορεί σε αυτήν την υπόθεση και το γεγονός ότι ο τύπος του κορμού **127** επαναλαμβάνεται στο μικρό αγαλματάκι Ε 415 από τη Ρόδο,[45] κατά τον Gualandi πραξιτελική ανάμνηση υστεροελληνιστικών χρόνων (εικ. 14).

Σε ένα συνέδριο που έγινε πριν δύο χρόνια στη Ρόδο υπέθεσα ότι το άγαλμα της Μήλου απεικόνιζε πιθανώς τον Μιθριδάτη, ως Διόνυσο. Η υπόθεση αυτή είχε ως αφετηρία την προσπάθεια ερμηνείας του αγάλματος. Το άγαλμα της Μήλου, όπως δείχνει το κολοσσικό μέγεθός του, θα μπορούσε να παριστάνει έναν θεό, τον Διόνυσο πιθανώς, αφού ο τύπος του είναι ίδιος με τον Διόνυσο, όπως απεικονίζεται στο χρυσό ναΐσκο της Συλλογής Σταθάτου. 'Εχει όμως κάποια στοιχεία που δεν ταιριάζουν στο θεό, τα σάνδαλα π.χ. που φοράει, αφού είναι γνωστό ότι ο θεός συνήθως απεικονίζεται με εμβάδες ή κοθόρνους,[46] αλλά και η έλλειψη των βοστρύχων εκατέρωθεν του λαιμού που συνήθως έχουν αγάλματα του Διονύσου. Αν όμως δεν εικονίζεται ο Διόνυσος, τότε θα πρέπει να σκεφτεί κανείς ότι απεικόνιζε έναν ηγεμόνα.[47] 'Ενας ηγεμόνας που δέσποζε αυτή την εποχή στα νησιά[48] και μάλιστα είχε θεοποιηθεί ως Διόνυσος στη Δήλο,[49] δεν ήταν άλλος από το Μιθριδάτη. Ο Κικέρωνας μας πληροφορεί ότι ένα άγαλμα του Μιθριδάτη ήταν στημένο στη Ρόδο και δεν το κατέστρεψαν οι Ρόδιοι όταν ο Μιθριδάτης πολιόρκησε το νησί.[50] Η πλαστική του αγάλματος της Μήλου, όπως είδαμε, είναι σχετική με γλυπτά της Ρόδου. Είναι λοιπόν πολύ ελκυστική η υπόθεση ο τύπος του κολοσσικού αγάλματος της Μήλου, να ήταν ίδιος με τον τύπο του αγάλματος του Μιθριδάτη, που ήταν στημένο στη Ρόδο. Το αγαλμάτιο Ε 415 του Μουσείου της Ρόδου αποτελεί μια ένδειξη ότι αυτός ο τύπος δεν ήταν άγνωστος στο νησί.

Σημειώσεις

1. C. Renfrew (επιμ.), *An Island Polity* (1982) 53–58 (J.F. Cherry and B.A. Sparkes).
2. A. Pasquier, *La Vénus de Milo et les Aphrodites du Louvre* (1985) όπου είναι συγκεντρωμένη όλη η παλαιότερη βιβλιογραφία.
3. Εθνικό Μουσείο 235. A. Linfert, *Kunstzentren hellenistischer Zeit* (1976) 117 σημ. 467. J. Schäfer, *AntPl* VIII (1968) 55 κ.ε., πίν. 38–41.
4. Εθνικό Μουσείο 236. Linfert, ό.π. (σημ. 3) 118 σημ. 468.
5. Εθνικό Μουσείο 238. R. Horn, *Stehende weibliche Gewandfiguren in der hellenistischen Plastik*, 2. Ergh. *RM* (1931) 88, πίν. 44,1. Linfert ό.π. (σημ. 3) 101 σημ. 356α και 117.
6. Εθνικό Μουσείο 2715. G. Libertini, *ASAtene* NS. 14–16, 1952–1954, 363 κ.ε. H. von Roques de Maumont, *Antike Reiterstandbilder* (1958) εικ. 49. B.G. Kallipolitis, *AAA* IV, 1971, 45–46, εικ. 1. Linfert ό.π. (σημ. 3) 118.
7. Εθνικό Μουσείο 237. Schäfer ό.π. (σημ. 3) 67.
8. Schäfer ό.π. (σημ. 3) 55.
9. D. Mackenzie, *JHS* 17, 1897, 122–123.
10. Είναι ενδιαφέρουσα η πορεία των ευρημάτων πρώτα στο εξωτερικό, αργότερα στο Εθνικό Αρχαιολογικό Μουσείο στην Αθήνα και τέλος στον τόπο τους.
11. Η βάση, όπως παραδίδει ο Πιττάκης (*ΑΕφημ* 1859, 51, αρ. 3507), βρέθηκε "άνωθεν του εκεί θεάτρου, εκατόν βήματα μακράν, προς το βόρειον μέρος αυτού". *IG* XII, 3, 1097. J. Marcadé, *Recueil des signatures* II (1957) 105.
12. Marcadé ό.π. (σημ. 11) 104. 105.
13. *IG* XII, 3, 1242.
14. C. Blümel, *Katalog der Sammlung antiker Skulpturen* V (1938) 23–24, K 237, πίν. 51 και 63. O. Rubensohn, *JdI* 50, 1935, 52–53. W.D. Heilmeyer – H. Heres, *JbBerlMus* 34, 1992, 15 κ.ε., εικ. 9 κ.ε.
15. Rubensohn ό.π. (σημ. 14) 53–54.
16. E. Löwy, *Inschriften griechischer Bildhauer* (1885) 466. Lippold, *Plastik*, 382. Rubensohn ό.π. (σημ. 14) 50 κ.ε.
17. Schäfer, ό.π. (σημ. 3) 65–66.
18. *IG* XII, 3, 1241.
19. A. Corso, *Xenia Antiqua* IV, 1995, 27–32.
20. *RE* 4,2, 2078–2079 (C. Robert). *EAA* II (1959) 999–1000 (D. Mustilli).
21. *Πρακτ* 1972, 136–137, εικ. 9.
22. Π. Θέμελης στο O. Palagia και W. Coulson (επιμ.), *Sculpture from Arcadia and Laconia* (1993) 100–102. Του ιδίου, "Damophon" στο O. Palagia και J.J. Pollitt (επιμ.), *Personal Styles in Greek Sculpture* (1996) 168.
23. Σωζ. ύψος 0, 45 μ.
24. Στο μέσο της επίπεδης επιφάνειας όπου γινόταν η ένωση υπάρχει ένας τετράπλευρος τόρμος. 'Ενας παρόμοιος θα υπήρχε στην επιφάνεια του κάτω κορμού. Στους δύο τόρμους θα έμπαινε ένας σύνδεσμος που ενίσχυε την ένωση των δύο βασικών κομματιών του σώματος˙ της γυναίκας.
25. Linfert ό.π. (σημ. 3) 49, εικ. 73.
26. Linfert ό.π. (σημ. 3) 160–163.
27. Linfert ό.π. (σημ. 3) 114 σημ. 453. J. Marcadé (επιμ.), *Sculptures Déliennes* (1996) 208, αρ. 94 (F. Queyrel).
28. R. Kabus-Preisshofen, *Der hellenistische Plastik der Insel Kos*, 14. Beih. *AM* (1989) 245, αρ. 56, πίν. 63–64.
29. Mackenzie ό.π. (σημ. 9) 129, εικ. 8. A. Lewerentz, *Stehende mänliche Gewandstatuen im Hellenismus* (1993) 89. 155–157. 200, Kat. III,5, εικ. 20.
30. 'Ενας τέτοιος κομός υπήρχε στο ύψος των μηρών και προκάλεσε τον αποχωρισμό των δύο κομματιών κατά τη μεταφορά του αγάλματος από την αποθήκη στο Μουσείο το Μάιο του 1984. 'Εναν παρόμοιο κομό παρατήρησα και στον πίσω δεξιό γλουτό του ιππέα.
31. Η επιφάνεια που το δεχόταν είναι επίπεδη, δουλεμένη με βελονάκι και ντεσιλίδικο και έχει στο μέσο

τετράπλευρο τόρμο αρκετά μεγάλο σε διαστάσεις 0,07 μ. x 0.07 μ. και βάθος 0,11 μ., όπου θα έμπαινε ο σύνδεσμος που ενίσχυε τη στήριξη. Η επιφάνεια αυτή σώζεται σε ένα μόνο τμήμα στην αριστερή πλευρά του αγάλματος, όπου πέφτουν οι συγκεντρωμένες πτυχές του άκρου του ιματίου.

32. Mackenzie ό.π. (σημ. 9) 126, εικ. 4. Linfert ό.π. (σημ. 3) 118. Lewerentz ό.π. (σημ. 29) 152. 155. 285–286, Kat. S5, εικ. 39–40.
33. Ύψος των συγκολλημένων σκέλους και άκρου ποδιού 1,10 μ.
34. J. Marcadé, *Au Musée de Délos* (1969) 332 σημ. 1.
35. Lewerentz ό.π. (σημ. 29) 156.
36. Η εγκοπή στο σκέλος έχει σ. βάθος 15 εκ. και πλάτος 4,8 εκ.
37. Mackenzie ό.π. (σημ. 9) 125, εικ. 2–5. S. Reinach, *RSt* II (1898) 819,4. Σωζ. ύψος 1,51 μ.
38. Η εγκοπή στον κορμό έχει σ. βάθος 10 εκ., πλάτος κάτω 4 εκ. και πάνω 4,5 εκ. Από τη σπασμένη έξω πλευρά του ιματίου το βάθος υπολογίζεται σε 20 εκ.
39. Στα. 379, P. Amandry, *ASAtene* 24–26, 1946–48, 181–198 και *Collection Hélène Stathatos. Les bijoux antiques* (1953) 91–96, πίν. 35. G. Becatti, *Le oreficerie antiche* (1955) 94–95, πίν. 123, αρ. 445. W. Fuchs, *Die Vorbilder der neuattischen Reliefs* (1959) 109, αρ. 3. F. Matz, *SarkRel* IV, 70 και *Gnomon* 41, 1969, 426–427. *LIMC* III (1986) s.v. Dionysos, αρ. 274 (C. Gasparri).
40. Pasquier ό.π. (σημ. 2) 66–78.
41. Linfert ό.π. (σημ. 3) 101 και 117.
42. Marcadé, *Au Musée de Delos*, 470–483.
43. Γ. Δοντάς, *ΑΔελτ* 21, 1966, Μελ. 85, πίν. 37. Linfert ό.π. (σημ. 3) 100 σημ. 349, εικ. 237–238.
44. Linfert ό.π. (σημ. 3) σημ. 349, εικ. 237–238.
45. G. Gualandi, *ASAtene*, NS 38, 1976, 187–188, αρ. 189, εικ. 236.
46. *LIMC* III, s.v. Dionysos, σελ. 415.
47. B. Schmidt-Dounas, *Εγνατία* 4, 1993–1994, 86.
48. Th. Reinach, *Mithridate Eupator, roi de Pont* (1890) 49 κ.ε. και *Trois royaumes de l'Asie Mineure* (1888) 185. B.C. McGing, *The Foreign Policy of Mithridates VI Eupator, King of Pontus* (1986) 90 κ.ε.
49. F. Chapoutier, *Délos* (1935) 13–43. O. Durrbach, *Choix d'inscriptions de Délos* (1921–22) και (1973)^2 214–215, αρ. 133–136 διατυπώνει την υπόθεση ότι ο Ηλιάναξ, ο ιερέας που αφιέρωσε το ναϊσκόμορφο κτίριο στον Μιθριδάτη, ήταν ροδιακής καταγωγής. Βλ. και McGing ό.π. (σημ. 48). Για το προσωνύμιο Διόνυσος του Μιθριδάτη και για τους λόγους που το πρόσεθεσε στο όνομά του μας πληροφορεί ο Αππιανός, *Μιθρ.* 10 και ο Πλούταρχος, *Quaest.conviv.* I.6.2. Βλ. επίσης Cicero, *Pro Flacco* XXV. Δίων Χρυσόστομος II.294.
50. Cicero, *In Verrem* II.65.159.

Neither School nor *Koine*: The Local Workshops of Delos and their Unfinished Sculpture

Philippe Jockey

Introduction

Delos may have failed not only to be the center of a specific regional school in the Hellenistic period, but also to become part of a *koine*.[1] To be the center of a specific regional school, a site or a region needs one or more of the following features (Fig. 1): local or regional quarries; local or regional sculptors; local or regional unfinished works; a local or regional trade; a local or regional tradition of stoneworking; a success which is not only local or regional but also widely spread and also, of course, specific stylistic technical and typological features which, sometimes, do not allow innovation. The Attic school has its particular tradition of sculptors, stone quarrying and working, and trade;[2] for the Rhodian school, there are one or two great original creations, as the Colossus by Chares of Lindos or the Laocoon. Yet, in the case of Delos, most of the required features are lacking.

Delos, an International Sanctuary

It is well known that the status of *panhellenic* or *federal* sanctuaries do not make easy the emergence of local trends. In these sanctuaries, on Delos as elsewhere, all external styles or schools tend *a priori* to remain pure, without any contamination. To quote de la Coste Messelière, "in a panhellenic sanctuary, each city aims at offering the most complete expression of its proper genius."[3] We shall see that what is for sure true for the archaic period cannot without restriction be said of the Hellenistic period, where a *koine* could have appeared on Delos. In neither case was it easy for local trends to become a school.

Local Quarries

If local quarries are known on Delos, though from time to time their reality has been denied, Fraisse and Kozel

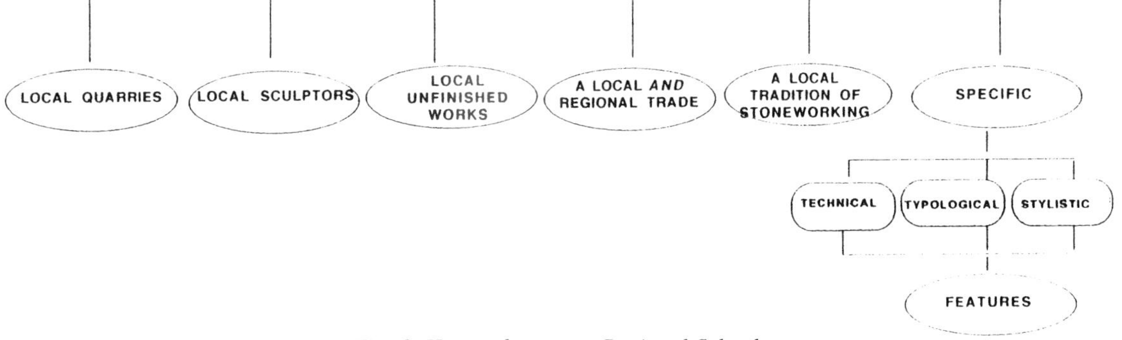

Fig. 1. How to become a Regional School.

have shown recently, by studying and publishing one example, that their use was confined to some architectural works. This is so because the marble of these small quarries is of bad quality, with characteristics which do not allow its use in sculptural works.[4] Because of its formation process, the Delian marble is subject to faults, and its coloring is not unified, but varies from white to blue-grey, with yellowish streaks. The quarries of Delos have never provided material supplies for sculptural purposes, and from the very beginning of votive sculpture on Delos, marble was imported from neighboring areas, such as Naxos or Paros, or from further afield, as Attica.[5]

Local Tradition of Working Marble Before the Hellenistic Period

Delos was known in antiquity to have been one of the greatest centers of production of bronze statuary, if not the greatest one, as Pliny the Elder tells us in his *Natural History*.[6] But we have no evidence for these Delian *officinae* on Delos itself, with the exception of moulds for the production of pieces of furniture, despite the strong local tradition.[7]

The textual tradition, however, of marble workshops on Delos is entirely lacking; no writer speaks of Delos as a great center of production of sculpture. Partly because of the lack of marble of good quality, we cannot observe on Delos any textual tradition nor evidence of stoneworking until the Hellenistic period.

During the archaic period sculptures are imported from Naxos or Paros, or from Attica. The discovery of an unfinished kouros on Delos, many years ago, does not supply evidence strong enough to indicate any local tradition of stoneworking.[8]

For the classical period, Hermary has shown that none of the preclassical or classical sculptures found on Delos was part of a local tradition. This is in contrast with the following period, to which belong not only most of the unfinished sculptures which excavations have brought to light since the late nineteenth century, but also the signatures of sculptors who were living on Delos.[9]

Local Sculptors

Marcadé has shown in his publication of the epigraphical testimonia of sculptors on Delos[10] that none of these sculptors, from the first year of the Independence[11] to the end of the second century B.C., was "Delian." Two main periods have been distinguished by him: the first was before 166 B.C., the year of the beginning of the second Athenian domination of the sanctuary; the second after 166 B.C. Between 314 and 166 B.C., 24 signatures of sculptors have been registered by Marcadé, from which 15 sculptors were known from elsewhere. For most of them, we have only one signature from Delos. These sculptors did not live on Delos, but stayed only for a short time. This is not true for the second period, which covers the period of the second Athenian domination (166–69 B.C.). A total of 26 names out of 67 signatures are known from other contexts. Thus, for some 80% of the names on Delos, we have no signatures outside Delos, a fact which suggests that the sculptors were living and working on the island. It also suggests that Delian sculpture was local and not exported widely. These sculptors were probably making bronze items, now lost, and not marble sculpture.

Only seven sculptors are known in this period to have also made marble statues (Fig. 2): Agasias, son of Menophilos, of Ephesos, who appears to have supervised the iconographic program of the Agora of the Italians;[12] Aristandros, son of Skopas, of Paros, who was hired to restore some of the damaged sculptures of Agasias, at the beginning of the first century B.C., just after the first sack of the island;[13] Dionysios, son of Timarchides, and Timarchides, son of Polykles, of Athens[14] (the father and son are the sculptors of the statue of Caius Ofellius Ferus in the Agora of the Italians;[15] this family is well-known not only in Attica but in Italy itself, as Queyrel has recently pointed out);[16] Glaukos, son of Epidauros,[17] who

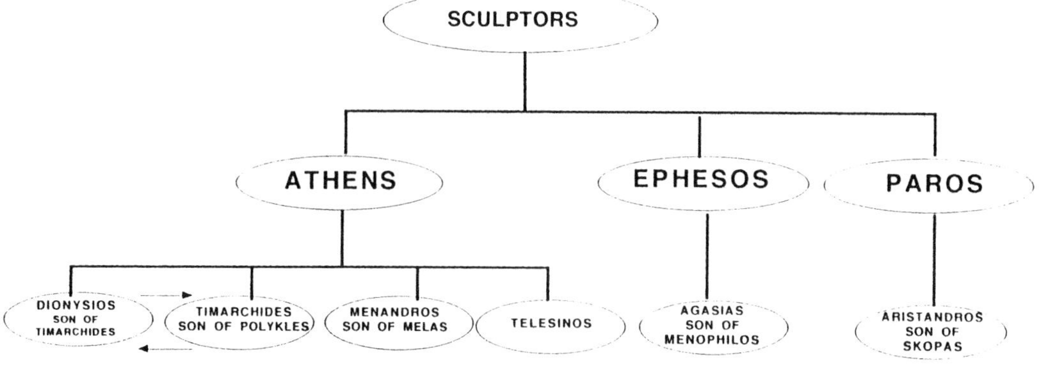

Fig. 2. Marble sculpture carved on Delos after 166 B.C.: epigraphical testimonia.

worked at the very end of the second century B.C.; Menandros, son of Melas, of Athens;[18] and, Telesinos, of Athens.[19] But we have evidence for more than one signature only in one instance.[20]

Local Unfinished Works

In contrast with the lack of evidence for bronze statuary, except for one well-known masterpiece,[21] the excavations on Delos have brought to light more than 160 unfinished sculptures or fragments of unfinished sculptures, such as pieces of statues of colossal size and statuettes, which provide evidence for the activity of local workshops between 166 and the sack of the island in 88 B.C. by Mithridates VI and again in 69 B.C. by pirates.[22] Unfortunately, among this high number of unfinished items, only few have a definite origin. They nevertheless testify to a strong local activity. Most of them have been found in the sanctuary, but a large number have also been found in the living quarters.

Stylistic and Typological Features

Some twenty years ago, Linfert pointed out,[23] after Marcadé, the extent to which Delian sculpture was influenced by workshops from Attica and Western Asia Minor; such influence may have taken the place of a Delian School. Marcadé had previously laid out the conditions required for Delos to have a school.[24] These conditions were, first, that sculptors stay for a long time or even live on Delos, and second, that enough time is allowed for sculptors to create a technical and stylistic tradition.

There are four areas on Delos which could be identified as containing the physical remains of a workshop or school;[25] yet neither flourished because of the sack of the island at the beginning of the first century B.C.

The House of the Diadoumenos (GD 61):[26] a "Club" with Workshop Activity (Fig. 3)

Situated in the north quarter of the island and named after the copy of the famous Polykleitan work (Athens, National Museum 1826), this house was excavated at the end of the last century[27] and published in the first quarter of the present one.[28] Judging by its size (36 x 36 m), scholars agree that it might be the headquarters of an organization as, for example, the establishment of the Poseidoniasts of Berytos, rather than a private house. Besides the Diadoumenos, which is finished, three unfinished works were found at the time of the excavations:[29] the so-called Pseudo-Athlete;[30] a head (A 4189) of a portrait statue[31] and the so-called round altar.[32]

The Pseudo-Athlete is unfinished, as seen by the tool marks (probably a point) left on the tree-trunk. A head "with Neanderthal features" was connected with the idealistically represented body, providing one of the first examples of a practice which became common in Roman sculpture.[33] The head is also unfinished, as shown by its socket and tenon joint, as well as by work on the back where tool marks (a point) can be seen. It should be noted that, whereas the carving of the features is finished, the head itself is not. This may suggest the beginning of a new practice, in opposition to the general tendency on Delos, to assemble pieced statuary in an early stage of carving. On the so-called round altar are carved in low relief two archaistic female figures which are part of a feminine triad.

Beyond this apparent thematic diversity, these finished and unfinished works appear to have been commonly inspired by classical examples and mixed with new features, such as that of attaching portrait heads on ideal bodies.[34] The Pseudo-Athlete is, in fact, one of the very first examples of this new practice.

Was the House of the Diadoumenos a workshop? There is no evidence for tools, installations, or marble dust and chips. More likely, at the very time of its destruction, the House welcomed sculptors who were working on the same sculptural program; this might have been a commission from the landlords of the place, perhaps a "club," as the Establishment of the Poseidoniasts. Because of their size and for security reasons, the statues were carved on the spot. As the sculptures are unfinished, so is also the attempt to create a *new tradition* by piecing together an ideal body and a realistic head, a formula later common in Roman sculpture.

The Workshops of the Agora of the Italians (GD 52)

At the southwest corner of the Agora built by the Italian community around 120 B.C., stood two sculptors' workshops, Rooms 103 and 106 (Fig. 3).[35] Their identification as workshops has been proved by a network of evidence; besides the 30 unfinished works, the excavators described a thick layer of marble chips and dust, a fact which recalls the famous description of Sculpture by Lucian of Samosata with the words: τιτάνου καταγέμουσα.[36]

The activity of these workshops is of great interest since it can be precisely dated; according to the dates of construction (last quarter of the second century) and destruction (88 B.C.), it took place in the first twenty years of the first century B.C.[37] In sharp contrast with the workshop of the House of the Diadoumenos, the products of both these workshops do not seem to show any kind of thematic unity. Among the unfinished works found in the rooms are pieces of furniture such as table supports, statuettes, a funerary stele of Isis Pelagia, and a miniature copy of the Herakles Farnese.[38] There was also the bottom part of a pieced statue of Artemis (Fig. 4). In sum, there is no difference between the finds of Delian houses and those of the two workshops (or their area), whose activity was focused on the production of "garden sculpture."[39]

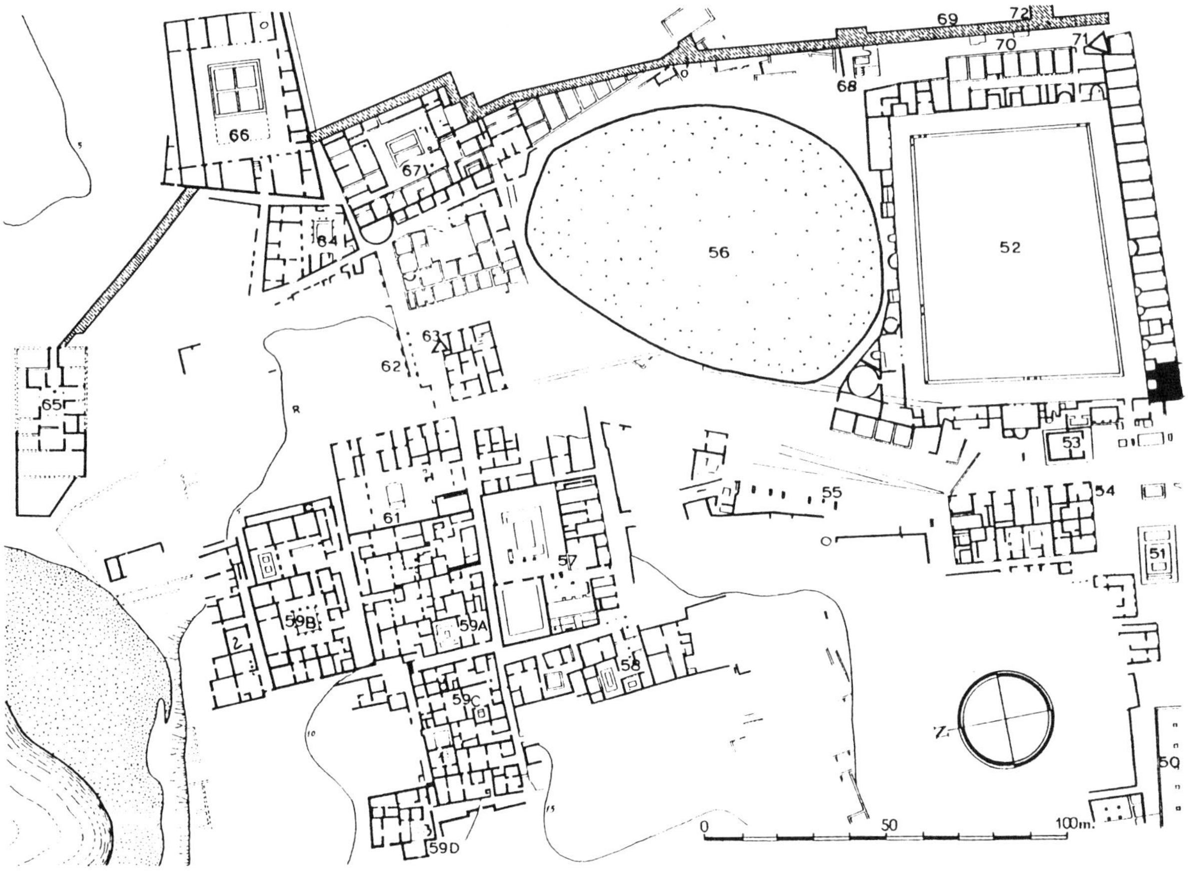

Fig. 3. Delos, detail of the Quarter situated at the north of the sanctuary: the House of the Diadoumenos is number GD *61; the workshops 103 & 106 of the Agora of the Italians* (GD *52) are in black (After* Guide de Délos *[1983] pl. II).*

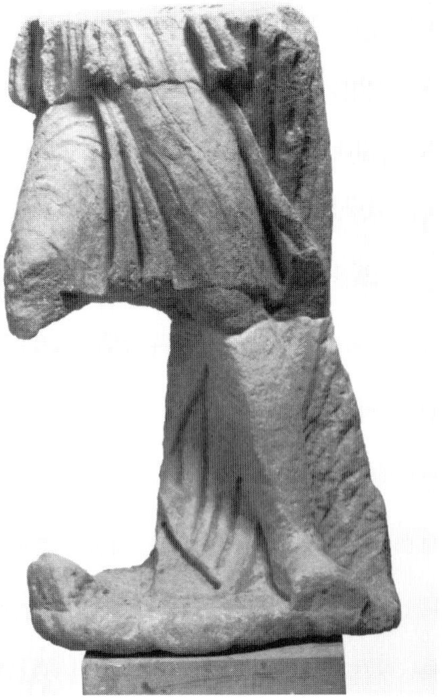

Fig. 4. Lower part of an unfinished Artemis, carved by piecing together the two main parts of the body. Found at the southwest corner of the Agora of the Italians. Delos Museum A 5182. H. = 0.39 m. (E.F.A./Ph. Collet).

The Workshop of the Stoa of Philip (Fig. 5)

In contrast to the two previous workshops, the precise location of the workshop of the Stoa of Philip is not known, and it is only through its production that its importance can be appreciated. The excavations have brought to light a series of unfinished statuettes, which were found in the area of the Stoa set up by Philip V of Macedon at the end of the third century B.C.[40] There is no trace of the workshop itself. Nevertheless, the statuettes form a homogeneous set; the same types are recurrent; they are all close in size and exhibit a great similarity of style and technique.

The first series consists of two types of Aphrodite, one derived from Praxiteles' Knidian and the other from the Pudica type. The second series involves a third type, Aphrodite untying her sandal. There are, in fact, a large number of examples of the third type. Because they exhibit various stages of incompleteness, the statuettes enable one to follow each step of the sculptor's work, from the first strokes of the point to rasp levelling. At the beginning, the general form is roughed out with a *point* (Fig. 6). In the next stage a new tool is introduced, the *flat chisel*. The modelling of the limbs is achieved through the specific technique of "faceting."[41] It is applied to the different types of the Aphrodite from the Stoa of Philip (Fig. 7).

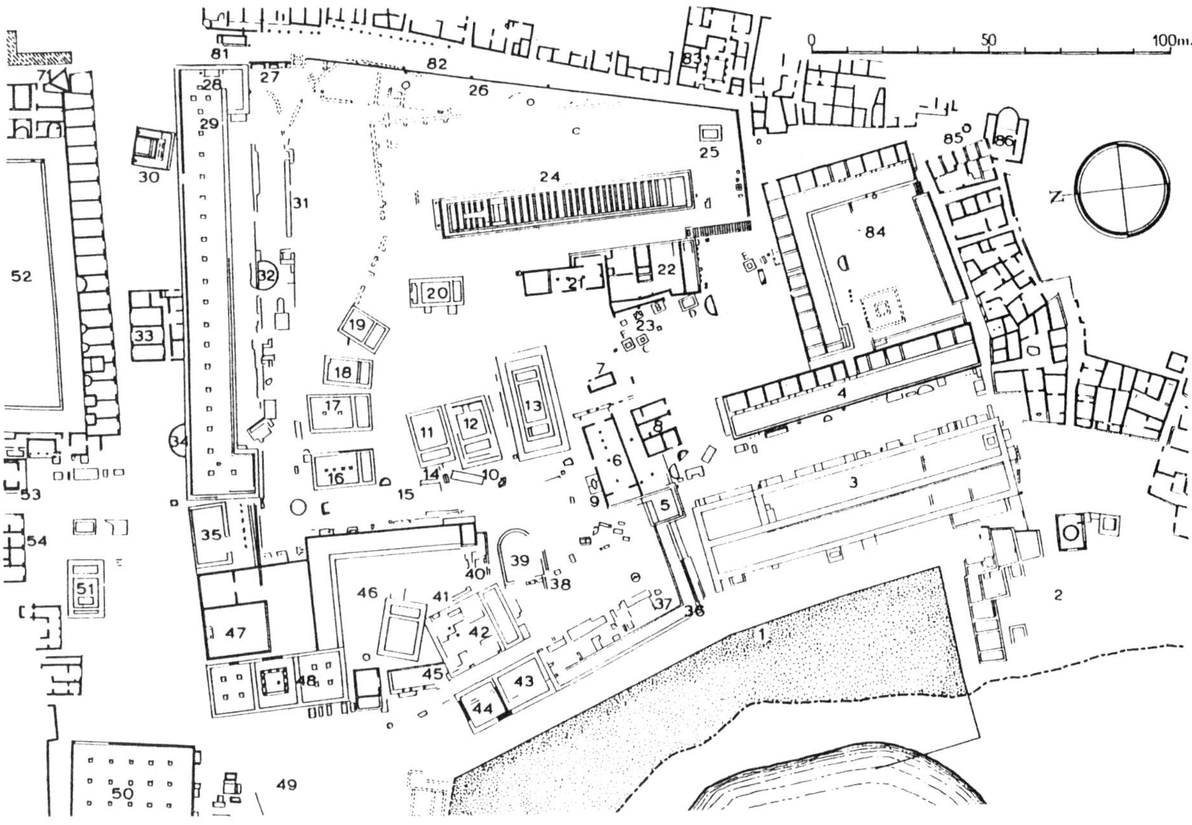

Fig. 5. Delos, area of the sanctuary of Apollo. The Stoa of Philip is number 3 (After Guide de Délos *[1983] pl. I).*

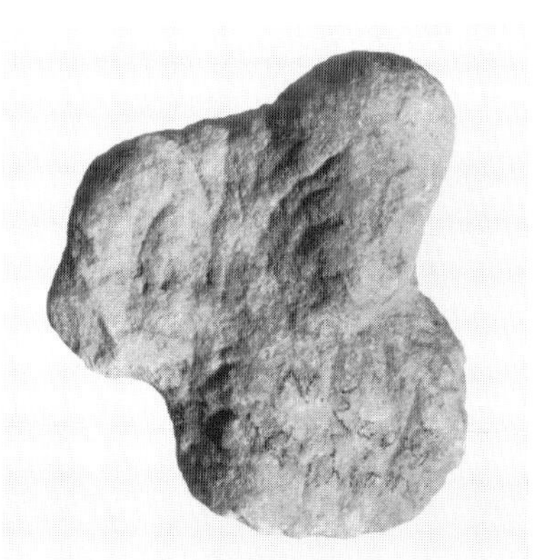

Fig. 6. Upper part of an Aphrodite arranging her hair. This unfinished work was found in the south side of the Stoa of Philip. Delos Museum A 5636. H. = 0.091 m. (E.F.A./ Ph. Collet).

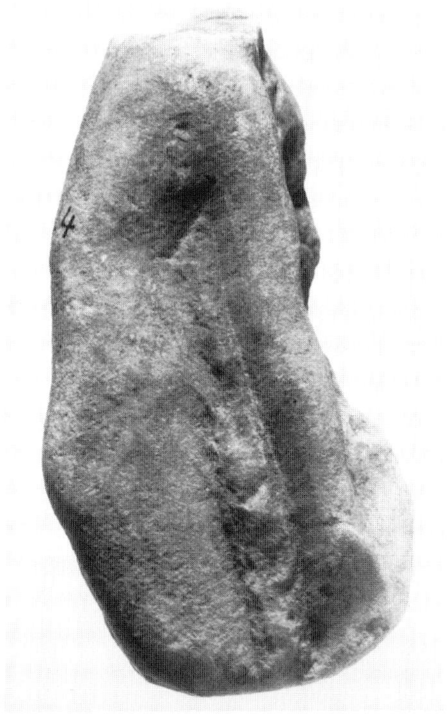

Fig. 7. Right profile of an unfinished statuette of Aphrodite untying her sandal. Found in the north side of the Stoa of Philip (Phase II,1). Delos Museum A 5124. H. = 0.122 m. (E.F.A./Ph. Collet).

Still during the modelling process, but in a second phase, limbs receive their final shapes and are partially detached from the body with a third tool, the *drill*, by the joint application of two well-known methods, the honeycombing method and the running drill.[42] This technique, applied to limbs, is very specific to this workshop's production (Figs. 8 and 9). Once this stage has been completed, it becomes easy for the remaining thin membrane of marble to be cut with the drill. There only remains to erase the marks left by the drill, to smooth away the edges left by

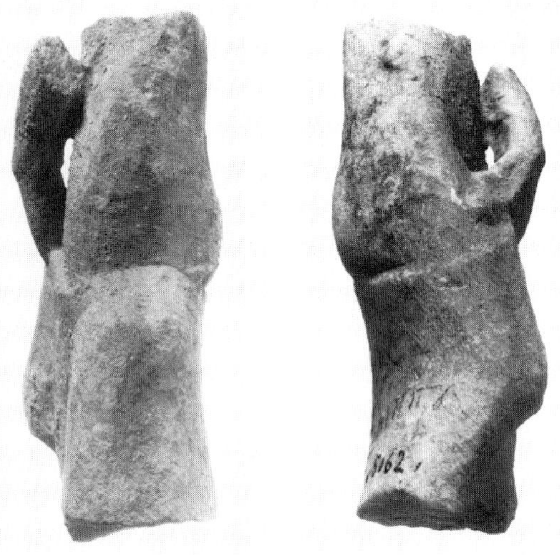

8 9

Figs. 8 & 9. Left and right profile of an Aphrodite lifting her drapery. Found in the Stoa of Philip (Phases II,2 & III,1). Delos Museum A 5062. H. = 0.125 m. (E.F.A./Ph. Collet).

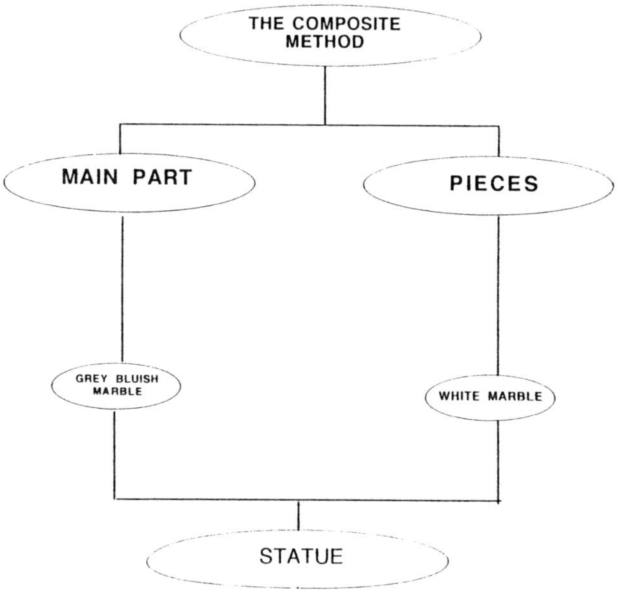

Fig. 11. General features of the composite method of carving on Delos.

STAGE	TOOL	OPERATION
Roughing out	point	pitting (piquage) striking long furrows (griffage)
Shaping (1)	flat chisel	to chisel in long, harsh strokes
Shaping (2)	drill	honeycombing method running drill
modelling	rasp	rasping
Finishing	rasp abrasives	rasping smoothing away

= Stage 1 = Stage 2 = Stage 3

Fig. 10. Stages of workmanship of the Aphrodites of the Stoa of Philip.

faceting, and to complete the last details of the work.

The main characteristics of the products from the Stoa of Philip are as follows: types are confined to a few representations of Aphrodite; these types are reproduced in a large number of copies and made in a single cycle; this series is itself characterized by its summary approach,[43] its simplicity, and its lack of precision (Fig. 10).[44]

This method of production belongs "par excellence" to a *koine* because of its standardization, its vagueness and its depressing uniformity.[45] Yet, by the application of a new method of carving, this workshop could have become a school.

The Composite Method of Carving (Fig. 11)

Among sculptures produced on Delos, a few can be grouped on the basis of a specific feature: they are all carved by the composite method, that is, piecing together two pieces of marble with different physical characteristics, as color, grain, and texture.[46]

On Delos we find the combination of two marbles; one is a white and fine grained marble; the other is blue-grey, also fine grained, whose workability is almost identical to the white one. Eight pieces show that this specific method of carving was in use during the Hellenistic period on Delos.[47] Two of these are discussed below.

1. The Artemis from the House of Five Statues (Fig. 12)

Found during the excavations of the House,[48] this small statue of Artemis,[49] as identified by her clothes and other attributes, about 1.39 m. high, was carved in six pieces. The torso is in blue-grey marble; the two arms, left foot, and part of the back of the head, including the *chignon*, were, on the contrary, carved in white, translucent marble. The piecing method appears to be uncommon; instead of keeping the difference between the nude and the draped parts and of playing on the contrast between the two marbles, a common practice in Roman statues,[50] the joins are concealed by a singular practice, here called "strad-ling". This is a specific way of carving drapery details on the naked part. At the end of the carving process, the entire sculpture is painted so that the contrast between the two different marbles is not at all apparent.

2. The Portrait of the House of Dionysos (Fig. 13)

The head was found in the House of Dionysos, the body in the House of Five Statues.[51] The figure is about the same size as the Artemis, 1.23 m. high. The head, right

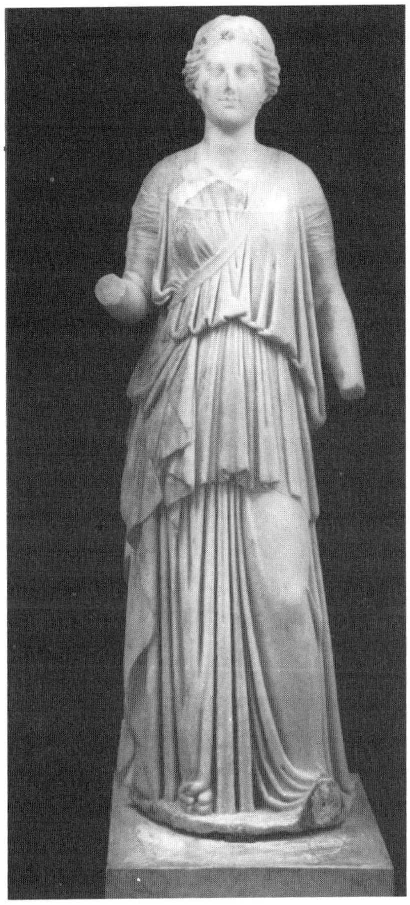

Fig. 12. Small statue of Artemis found in the House of Five Statues and carved by the composite method. Delos Museum A 4126. H. = 1.31 m. (E.F.A./Ph. Collet).

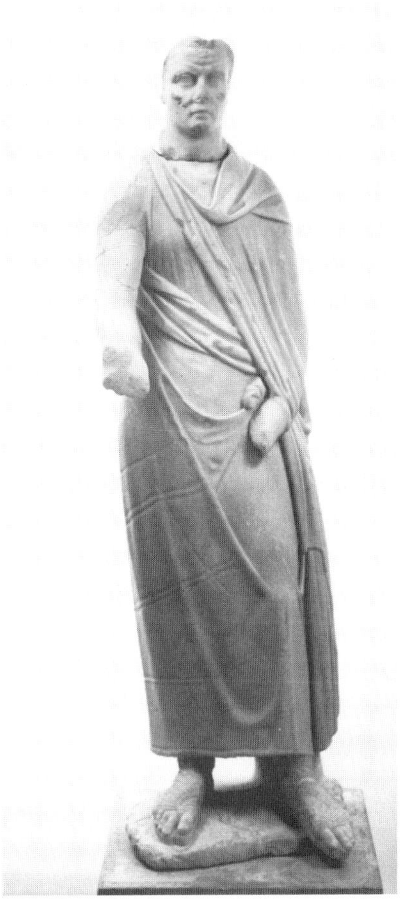

Fig. 13. Small statue of a male figure found in the House of Dionysos and carved by the composite method. Delos Museum A 4142. H. = 1.23 m. (E.F.A./Ph. Collet).

arm, left hand, and left foot were carved separately in the same white, translucent marble, in contrast with the torso in blue-grey marble of poorer quality. Again, the joints were concealed with care by "straddling" and by painting the whole statue.

On Delos, this rather unusual practice is applied to the same type of sculpture, classicizing but mixed with realistic features. The closest parallels appear to come from Kos, especially from the Odeion of Kos, where four statues were carved by the same method.[52] Kabus-Preisshofen has suggested that three of these were carved around the middle of the first century A.D.[53] If so, we have again on Delos the beginning of what could have become a school, i.e. a local tradition with specific methods, types, and trends, but which was transferred to Kos after the second sack of 69 B.C.

Stewart concludes that "in contrast to the obsession with the past, late Hellenistic Delos announces the future."[54] By the creation of new types and new carving methods, it could have done so, but evidently did not. As Marcadé says, "L'histoire de la sculpture hellénistique de Délos est un peu celle d'une école manquée."[55]

Abbreviations

Signatures II	J. Marcadé, *Recueil des signatures de sculpteurs grecs* II (1957).
MD	J. Marcadé, *Au Musée de Délos*, *BEFAR* 215 (1969).
Sculptures déliennes	J. Marcadé (ed.), *Sculptures déliennes* (1996)
Jockey	Ph. Jockey, "Unfinished sculpture and its workshops on Delos in the Hellenistic period," in Y. Maniatis, N. Herz, Y. Basiakos (edd.), *The Study of Marble and Other Stones Used in Antiquity* (1995) 87–93.

Notes

1. About the history, use and meaning of *school*, see *MD* 249 ff., and now D. Viviers, *Recherches sur les ateliers de sculpteurs et la cité d'Athènes à l'époque archaïque* (1992) 21–33.
2. For the archaic period, however, Viviers (supra n. 1) 31 has shown that, instead of speaking of an Attic School as a single and homogeneous unit, it would be better to use the term "workshops" (ateliers).

3. P. de La Coste Messelière, *Delphes* (1943) 32–35. See also id., *Au Musée de Delphes*, *BEFAR* 138 (1936) 444: "A peine en effet serait-il paradoxal de soutenir que, pour les *véritables* oeuvres d'art, les "écoles" se révéleraient mieux qu'ailleurs dans un centre "panhellénique" comme Delphes, où les cités envoient leurs propres produits (jusqu'aux pierres de leurs carrières, quand c'est possible, ce qui doit les représenter *elles-mêmes* sous les aspects les plus accusés."
4. Ph. Fraisse, T. Kozel, *BCH* 115, 1991, 283–296.
5. See, for instance, *Sculptures déliennes*, nos. 1–19.
6. Pliny, *NH* 34.4, "Antiquissima aeris gloria Deliaco fuit, mercatus in Delo celebrante toto orbe et ideo cura officinis. Tricliniorum pedibus fulcrisque ibi prima aeris nobilitas, pervenit deinde et ad deum simulacra effigiemque hominum et aliorum animalium."
7. G. Siebert, *Études déliennes*, *BCH* Suppl. I (1973) 583–585, figs. 31 & 33.
8. Delos Museum A 4083: W. Deonna, *Les Apollons archaïques* (1909) no. 87, figs. 106–108; G.M.A. Richter, *Kouroi, Archaic Greek Youths*[3] (1970) 105, no. 111, figs. 342; 345.
9. A. Hermary, *La Sculpture classique*, *Délos* 34 (1984).
10. *Signatures* II.
11. I.e., between 314 and 166 B.C.
12. *Signatures* II, 4.
13. *Signatures* II, 23.
14. *Signatures* II, 41.
15. F. Queyrel, *BCH* 115, 1991, 389–464.
16. (Supra n. 15) 448–464.
17. *Signatures* II, 56.
18. *Signatures* II, 67.
19. *Signatures* II, 124.
20. Agasias, son of Menophilos, of Ephesos, is known on Delos by a large number of signatures: *ID* 1657; 1699; 1725; 1967a; 2001; 2489; 2491; 2492; 2493; 2495.
21. Athens, National Museum 14612, "Tête de la Vieille Palestre;" *Sculptures déliennes* no. 100.
22. All of them will be published by the author in *Délos*, forthcoming.
23. A. Linfert, *Kunstzentren hellenistischer Zeit* (1976) 112–116.
24. *MD* 249–259.
25. For more information about the first three, see Jockey 87–93.
26. The monuments are here named after their number in *Guide de Délos* (1983).
27. L. Couve, *BCH* 19, 1895, 509; 515–516, pl. IV.
28. J. Chamonard, *Le Quartier du théâtre*, *Délos* VIII, 2 (1922–1924) 426–431, pl. XXX.
29. For more details about these works, see Jockey 88–89, figs. 1–3.
30. Athens, National Museum 1828: bibliography in *Sculptures déliennes*, 192, no. 86.
31. Delos Museum A 4189: C. Michalowski, *Les Portraits hellénistiques et romains*, *Délos* XIII (1932) 14–16, fig. 9, pl. XII–XIII; *MD* 104 n. 2.
32. Delos, *in situ*: C. Blümel, *Griechische Bildhauerarbeit*, 11. Ergh. *JdI* (1927) 58, no. 18, pl. 25 C; *MD* 103; 105; Jockey 87, fig. 3.
33. A. Stewart, *Greek Sculpture. An Exploration* (1990) 228.
34. R.R.R. Smith has expressed in his book *Hellenistic Sculpture. A Handbook* (1991) the significance of one or two masterpieces like the portrait of a woman, Delos Museum A 4196, "probably the first objective-looking portrait of a woman from the ancient world" (p. 257) or like the Pseudo-Athlete, which undoubtedly appears now to be of "great importance in the history of portrait statues" (p. 258).
35. E. Lapalus, *L'Agora des Italiens*, *Délos* XIX (1939).
36. Lucian, *Somnium, sive vita Luciani*, 6.
37. Jockey 89–90, figs. 4–7.
38. *Sculptures déliennes*, 164, no. 72.
39. Stewart (supra n. 33) 226.
40. R. Vallois, *Le Portique de Philippe*, *Délos* VII, 1 (1923).
41. Though very well attested on Delos, this technique is not described in handbooks. For a description of it, see Jockey 91, fig. 8.
42. For a definition of these methods, see, for instance, S. Adam, *The Technique of Greek Sculpture in the Archaic and Classical Periods*, *BSA* Suppl. 3 (1966) 40–73.
43. The operating line is shortened and restricted in gesture.
44. The choice of direct carving, without model, or *proplasma*, precludes the exact copy of an original; a general look is enough.
45. Marcadé has expressed this "habileté moyenne des fabricants de statues et de statuettes (qui) suffit trop souvent à une clientèle commerciale qui va s'élargissant (...) L'on peut bien parler, en ce sens, d'une *vulgarisation* de l'art" (*MD* 254).
46. D. Mustilli, in *EAA*, s.v. "acrolito": "Del resto, vengono comunemente designate con il nome di pseudo-a. sculture nelle quali le estremità sono di marmo o altro materiale diverso e, generalmente, di maggior pregio di quello del corpo" (p. 49). This technical feature, somewhat original, is generally neglected by scholars.
47. Delos Museum A 4142; A 4126; A 4129; A 4124; A 4134; A 4126; A 1006 & A 4144.
48. F. Mayence, G. Leroux, *BCH* 31, 1907, 398 ff.
49. Delos Museum A 4126: *Sculptures déliennes*, 114, no. 47. H. = 1,31 m.
50. See, for instance, in the Naples Museum, the Ephesian Artemis, inv. 6278, or the seated Apollo, inv. 6281 (*Le collezioni del Museo Nazionale di Napoli* I, 2 [1989] nos. 115 & 118).
51. Delos Museum A 4142: *Sculptures déliennes*, 206, no. 93 H. = 1.23 m.
52. R. Kabus-Preisshofen, *Die hellenistische Plastik der Insel Kos* (1989) nos. 36–37; 42 & 56.
53. Nos. 36–37 & 42.
54. Stewart (supra n. 33) 226.
55. *MD* 253.

Some Observations Concerning Late Hellenistic Bronze Production on Delos

Beryl Barr-Sharrar

A speculation raised by several of the authors contributing to the recent two-volume publication of the Mahdia shipwreck, *Das Wrack: der antike Schiffsfund von Mahdia*, is the possibility that some or all of the bronzes found in the cargo and now in the Bardo Museum in Tunis were produced in a late Hellenistic foundry on Delos. According to Pliny the Elder (*NH* 34.9), Delos was famous in antiquity for its bronzes, which were sought there, he says, by the whole world.

In a complex article on the sculptors Boethoi, the late Andreas Linfert implied that all the Mahdia bronzes were produced by a family of sculptors including and descended from the Boethos of Chalcedon who signed the bronze archaizing herm (Fig. 1).[1] Linfert identified the artist of the herm with Boethos, son of Athanaeon, who signed the base of a portrait of Antiochos IV on Delos which dates the artist's activity there to around 166–163 B.C. Linfert believed that the same Boethos signed the statue base found in the Athena sanctuary in Lindos dated to around 184 B.C. (as son of Athanaeon of Chalcedon) and that Pliny (*NH* 33.355) referred to the same artist, implying that he worked in silver as well as bronze. Devising a fictive family tree, Linfert suggested that it was a nephew or grandson of this artist, also named Boethos, who signed, together with the sculptor Theodosios, the Delian statue base of Epigenes, son of Dios from Miletos, about 124 B.C., and that just before Mithridates VI's destruction of the island in 88 B.C., another member of this family of sculptors moved the ancestral bronze workshop from Delos to Athens.

Thus it was, according to Linfert, that the Mahdia klinai and other bronzes as well as the marbles retrieved from the shipwreck, most of which are Pentelic, were put on board the doomed ship in Athens. That Athens was the port of embarkation was an opinion proposed in 1963 by Werner Fuchs.[2] Fuchs, who dated the Madhia material to the second half of the second century B.C., believed a workshop in Athens belonging to the same Boethos of Chalcedon who signed the bronze archaizing herm was responsible for the bronzes, as well as the Pentelic marble neo-Attic kraters and candelabra on the ship. Linfert connected the neo-Attic marble kraters with the Athenian workshop set up after 88 B.C. by the progeny of his proposed line of distinguished sculptors (whose work in toreutic could be presumed traditional), with the appropriate reminder that their Dionysiac relief designs were probably first conceived for execution on metal vessels.[3] Linfert concluded the family tree with a putative Boethos active in Athens.

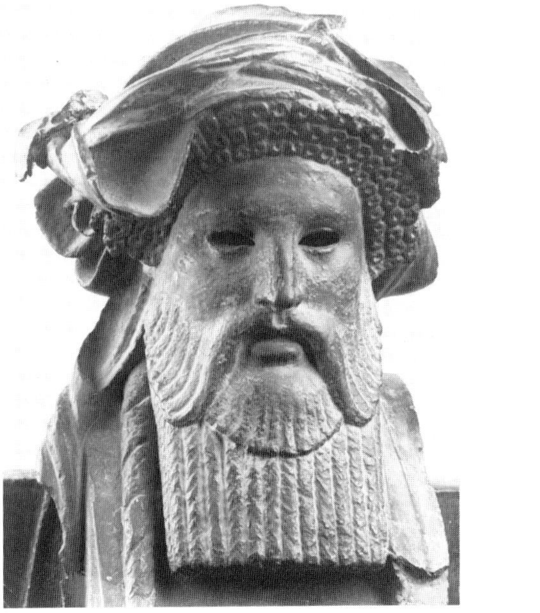

Fig. 1. Head of the bronze herm from the Mahdia shipwreck. Photo Rheinisches Landesmuseum, Bonn.

Most recent commentators have concurred with Linfert and Fuchs to the extent that, whatever the workshop origin(s), most of the material on board the Mahdia ship was commissioned merchandise being sent to Roman buyers for use and display in their villas on the west coast of central Italy, the assumed destination of the ship.[4] This theory is complicated, however, by indications that some of the bronzes, as well as a few of the marbles, represent plunder. The two largest bronzes, the somewhat

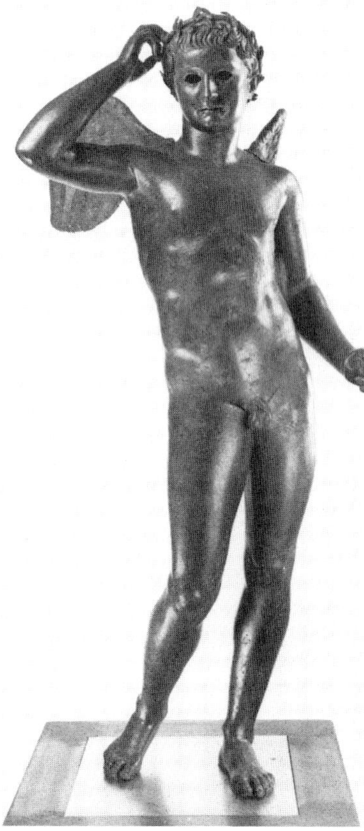

Fig. 2. Bronze Eros crowning himself in victory from the Mahdia shipwreck. Photo Rheinisches Landesmuseum, Bonn.

under life-size winged youth crowning himself in victory (Fig. 2) and the archaizing herm with Boethos' signature (Fig. 1), now known to have been independent from the winged youth,[5] reveal signs of installation on statue bases. The winged youth has a lead dowel on the bottom of his left foot for insertion into a stone base.[6] While it is possible that the lead dowel was affixed in the workshop and never melted to actually secure the statue on a base, its presence together with the additional lead inserted into the figure's left foot as well as his left hand and arm, counterbalancing the wings that were applied separately to his shoulders and holding in place the attributes once held in his hand, suggest previous upright placement.[7] The circumstances of the archaizing herm are even more explicit. Still in place in the bottom of the hollow cast shaft of the herm is a lead filling incorporating a fragment of marble that can only be part of a former base to which the lead once connected it. The bronze shaft itself was damaged towards the bottom in a manner indicating it had been pried off the base with some force.[8]

A third sculptural example, the pair of bronze fixtures with corresponding Dionysos and Ariadne busts equipped with nail holes for attachment, must have been produced as accoutrements for a commemorative statue base or monument in the well-known shape of a ship's prow,[9] whether or not they had actually been installed on one. Although they were undoubtedly of considerable value for secondary, decorative use in a Republican villa, it is highly unlikely that they were made for this purpose. Further, of the seventeen or eighteen individual bronze vessels represented by the fragments found in the Mahdia shipwreck, almost all may have been produced for, or have had originally sacral purposes and been stolen from religious contexts.[10] That some of the marbles retrieved from the shipwreck are believed to have been installed in a heroon strengthens the hypothesis of an illicit origin for the bronzes.[11]

The source of plunder most frequently cited is Sulla's sack in 86 B.C. of Athens and its port of Piraeus, not only because the largest number of marble objects on board the ship were the newly carved Pentelic products mentioned above, but also because of the presence of some typically Attic fourth-century B.C. marble grave markers and reliefs, as well as some inscribed marble stelai clearly taken from the Piraeus.[12] The secure Athenian origin of the fourth-century B.C. marbles and inscriptions and the probable Athenian origin of the neo-Attic kraters and marble candelabra, as well as the column shafts and some of the capitals, however, does not demand the production of the cast bronzes in Athens. Nor does it locate the origin of plundered bronzes in either Athens or the Piraeus even if the Mahdia ship set sail *only* from the Piraeus.

The name Boethos, recurring among members of Linfert's presumed (and plausible) lineage of sculptors, has been associated with *klinai* in the designation *lecti Boethiaci* found only in a commentary on one of the epistles of Horace (1.5.1) by the late antique writer Pomponius Porphyrio, and its meaning in that context is obscure.[13] Whatever the Boethos or Boethoi who worked on Delos may or may not have had to do with the production of klinai, Pliny tells us that Delian bronze was first prominent in the production of dining couches (*NH* 34.9). Elsewhere he speaks of beds of a *Deliaca specie* (*NH* 33.144). And, indeed, in a series of excavations on Delos by the École Française d'Athènes between 1961 and 1968, not only were various bronze parts of actual Hellenistic beds uncovered,[14] but so were numerous fragments of plaster molds for casting the elements of their elegantly silhouetted tubular legs, a clear indication of kline production.[15]

The French excavations which yielded this material were in the Skardhana quarter of Delos, which had a burned level providing a *terminus ante quem* of the second quarter of the first century B.C., that is, some years after the destruction of the city by Mithridates in 88 B.C. Gérard Siebert, who published most of these finds, suggested that the klinai industry was still flourishing on Delos at or just before the time of the burned level, which he related to the island's second devastation, at the hands of Cilician pirates, in 69 B.C.[16] This just accommodates the lowest of the most narrow approximate limits recently proposed for the last voyage of the Mahdia ship, between 80 and 70 B.C., based on the ceramic finds with an emphasis on the amphora shapes by Susan Rotroff.[17]

From sometime in the late second century to 67 B.C., when the Romans, under Pompey, finally, and rather quickly, put an end to it, the coasts and islands of the Mediterranean were subject to relentless invasions by Cilician pirates that brought terrible destruction and pillaging.[18] Seeking protection from the Romans after a law was passed suggesting their initial period of toleration had, at least officially, ended,[19] the pirates had allied themselves with Mithridates VI well before his attack on Delos in 88 B.C. Pausanias reports that the pirates affiliated with Mithridates in his sack of Delos looted much of the merchandise and all the votive offerings (3.23.3). Appian says that to ally the Athenians to Mithridates, his general Archelaos sent the island's sacred treasure, under heavy guard, to Athens (*Mithr.* 28).[20] The destination of the pirates' Delian spoils was very likely Athens, as well, but not for political reasons. Both in 88 and perhaps to an even greater extent in 69 B.C. when the pirates, having once tasted large gains (*Mithr.* 92), sacked Delos again, this time of their own accord, Athens was very likely the most profitable clearing-house for stolen goods. Agents in the city, principally, perhaps, Romans with good connections like the twenty-year-long resident Atticus, who moved there sometime after the autumn of 86 B.C.,[21] must have represented the most secure and profitable market. Wealthy Roman citizens with country estates, like Atticus' friend Cicero, were increasingly willing to pay high prices for original Greek art and artifacts. These Romans comprised the principal market for the works of art looted by the Cilician pirates just as they comprised the principal market for the slaves for which the pirates, through Delos, were the primary purveyors (Strabo 14.5.2).[22]

It is within reasonable possibility that the winged youth crowning himself, the archaizing herm, the sacral bronze vessels, the Dionysos and Ariadne fixtures, and others, perhaps *all*, of the bronzes (as well as the Parian marble tondo busts from the shipwreck)[23] were plundered from Delos by the Cilician pirates during one of their assaults on the island and taken to Athens for sale before being loaded on board the Mahdia ship. If so, given the reputation of Delos as a world-renowned provider of bronzes, it is logical to suppose they were produced there. Further, rather than Roman commissions, the twenty-two klinai represented by the bronze elements discovered in the shipwreck, perhaps implicating Delos more emphatically than any of the other bronzes, may themselves represent plunder. While they could have been stolen from a *hestiatorium*,[24] since they are believed to be from the same workshop[25] and appear to be new, without repairs,[26] the klinai could well have been taken from a bronze foundry or related workshop targeted by the pirates for theft. Familiar with the island, indeed, through their trade in slaves an integral part of its economy (tens of thousands of slaves changed owners in a day there according to Strabo [14.5.2]), the pirates would know well where to find the most valuable goods, not only in sanctuaries, but in the business establishments on Delos. It is conceivable that all the bronzes from the Mahdia shipwreck that do not bear conclusive signs of former installation or use, and perhaps even some that do, were taken from a single foundry and its related workshop on Delos and sent to Athens for sale.

A bilingual consular law of 58 B.C. that decrees the restoration of temples and shrines, also grants *libertas* and immunity from Roman taxation to the Delians (administration was local under an Athenian *epimeletes*). Indicative of the very considerable private material losses resulting from the pirates' two invasions of the island, the inscription suggests that, as Athens was *parti-pris* during the wars, only a Roman tribunal could determine restitution.[27] Given the fact that the pillaged property had changed hands, there was little hope of its return. One of the speeches given in 70 B.C. by Cicero during his prosecution of Verres, whom he accuses, among other odious charges, of conniving with pirates for his own benefit, suggests both the richness of the plunder that found its way to Roman villas, and the futility of its recovery. "...the country houses of the men to whom I refer are furnished to overflowing with countless beautiful things which they have stolen from our most loyal allies. What do you suppose has become of the wealth of these foreign nations which are now so poor when you see (the treasures of) Athens, Pergamon, Kyzikos, Miletos, Chios, Samos, nay, all Asia and Achaia, all Greece and Sicily, concentrated in a few country houses? Yet I repeat, gentlemen, that today your allies are not attempting, and not caring, to recover any of these treasures..." (*Verr.* 2.5.48).[28]

While the surviving bronze components of the twenty-two klinai found in the cargo are considered to have been recently produced when they were put on board the Mahdia ship, therefore to be dated to the first quarter of the first century century B.C., a number of the other bronzes have been dated on the basis of their style to around 100 B.C. or a little later, and a few are dated stylistically as early as the last quarter of the second B.C.[29] The proposed robbery in 88 B.C. of a workshop or factory in which some bronzes may have been stored during the destabilization of commerce that must have accompanied the piracy on the Mediterranean during the previous decades might accommodate dates at least as high as around 100 B.C. but perhaps not higher. Supposing more of the ship's goods to have consisted of pillaged goods installed for some time before in sanctuaries and civic areas, and conceivably even homes, on Delos, the proposal of a theft either in 88 or in 69 B.C. can easily be sustained.[30]

Further, the marked absence of stylistic homogeneity presented by the bronzes from the Mahdia shipwreck may not necessarily be only a matter of a few years or decades between their dates of manufacture. It may well be, more essentially, a function of their production at the end of the Hellenistic period, a time when the number of formal prototypes was more extensive than at any other time in

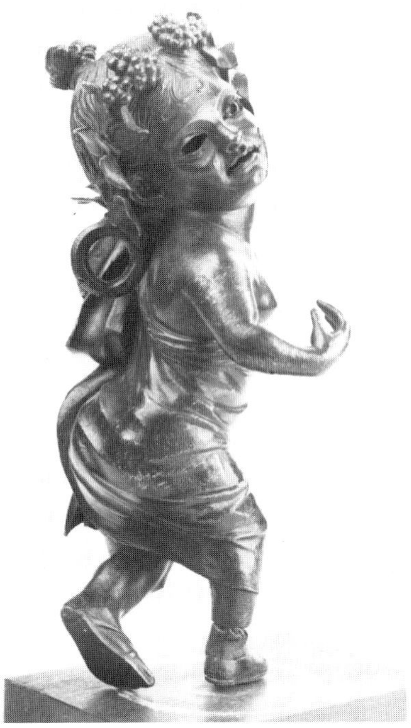

Fig. 3. Bronze dancing dwarf with ivy leaf garland from the Mahdia shipwreck. Photo Rheinisches Landesmuseum, Bonn.

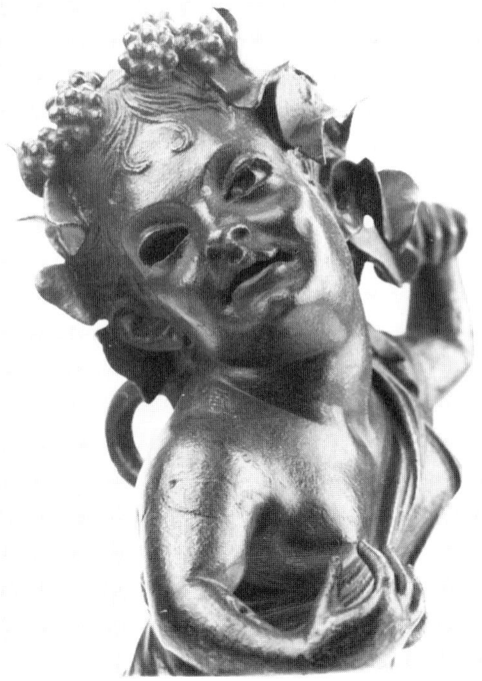

Fig. 4. Head of the bronze dancing dwarf with ivy leaf garland from the Mahdia shipwreck. Photo Rheinisches Landesmuseum, Bonn.

the history of Greek sculpture. Not only did the availability of prototypes reach back into the past for centuries (the ultimate prototypes of the winged youth and some of the bronze vessels is fourth-century), but it extended to areas throughout the Mediterranean world. The bronze female dwarf wearing an ivy wreath (Figs. 3–4) may have been made on Delos or in Athens or elsewhere, but the prototype – the original conception behind the image – is almost surely Alexandrian, with or without the ring on the back for suspension and, almost certainly without what has been called its classicizing aspect. The moderation of the raw vigor of its probable prototype is the effect of the artist's appraisal and use of the Alexandrian grotesque, a working attitude that sought and achieved in the figure, however mannered it looks to us today, greater aesthetic appeal. Given the *terminus ante quem* of the shipwreck, and considering the accessibility of prototypes during the first quarter of the first century B.C., should we perhaps divorce what we think is temporal taste or stylistic development from the best-known types? Should the Mahdia bronzes be dated in a somewhat more narrow range than might at first appear appropriate?[31] Despite this diversity of prototypes, can any of the Mahdia bronzes be grouped among themselves, or with other bronzes?

There seems to be little question that the klinai elements from the Mahdia shipwreck and those from the Fourmigue C shipwreck off the coast of France near Golfe Juan, dated to about 70 B.C. by its amphora shapes, are from the same workshop. Both Sabine Faust, who published the Mahdia klinai[32] and the archaeologists who published the finds from Fourmigue C[33] are in agreement, suggesting the workshop of origin was on Delos. Comparison of the horse protome decorating a fulcrum attachment from Fourmigue[34] reveals striking similarity in mass and characterization to a larger one from Mahdia (Fig. 5), especially in the detailing of the formation of the double and triple strands of spiraling locks with tapering ends in the horses' manes. The Artemis bust from the same fulcrum attachment from Fourmigue[35] is clearly based on the same prototype as its corresponding larger counterpart from Mahdia (Fig. 6), but more telling are the mannerisms of modeling which the two busts share.

Although it is damaged, one of the four Athena busts from the Mahdia shipwreck (Fig. 7),[36] larger than the Mahdia Artemis bust, and not an appropriate subject for a kline decoration, bears it (and the Fourmigue C Artemis) more than passing resemblance in both formal conception and details. The set of the oval-shaped head, high on a long and massive neck in a pseudo-heroic pose, more theatrical than dramatic, are features of the Artemis bust (Fig. 6). The delineation of the two double-strand hair locks with tapering ends on the shoulder of the Athena resembles in its modeling those forms on the horse protome (Fig. 5).[37]

The Nike bust from the Mahdia shipwreck (Fig. 8)[38] is similar in size and scale to the Athena (Fig. 7) and shares with it an artificially proportioned relationship of head, elongated neck, and large chest, which, in the Nike, is emphasized by the low placement of the breast. Through the worn surface of the Athena bust can be seen the angular facial features of the Nike, and the eyes of both have deeply pierced pupils. The Nike's sloping, fleshy shoulder

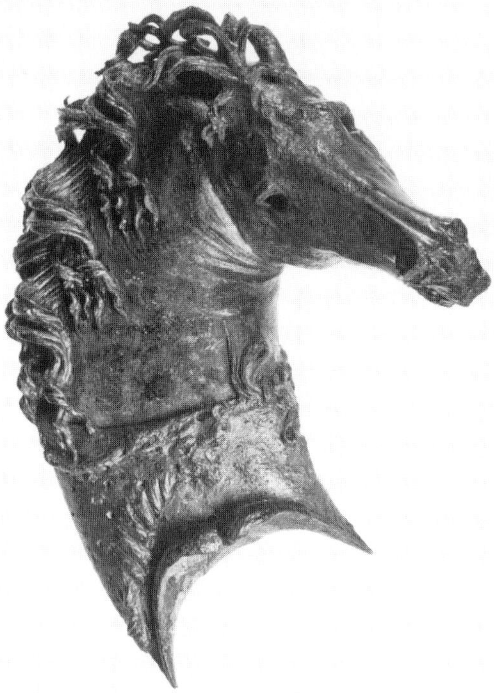

Fig. 5. Bronze horse protome on a fulcrum attachment from the Mahdia shipwreck. Photo Rheinisches Landesmuseum, Bonn.

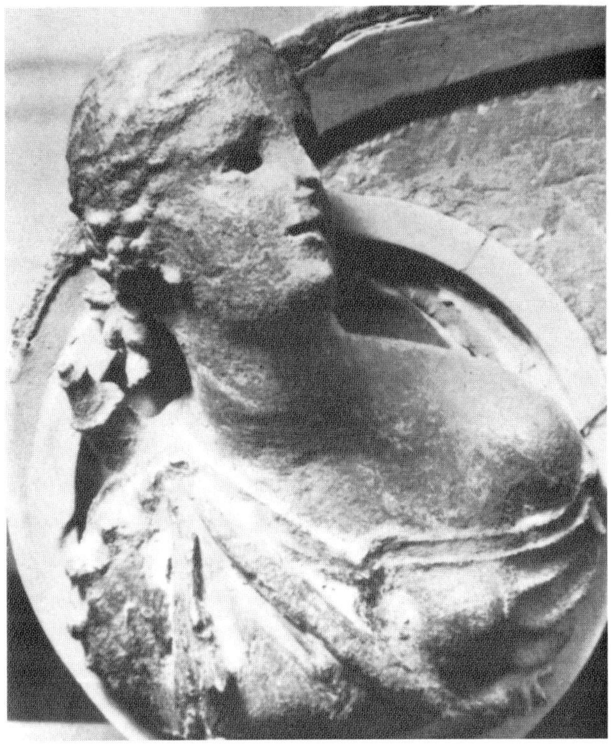

Fig. 6. Bronze bust of Artemis on a fulcrum attachment from the Mahdia shipwreck. Photo Rheinisches Landesmuseum, Bonn.

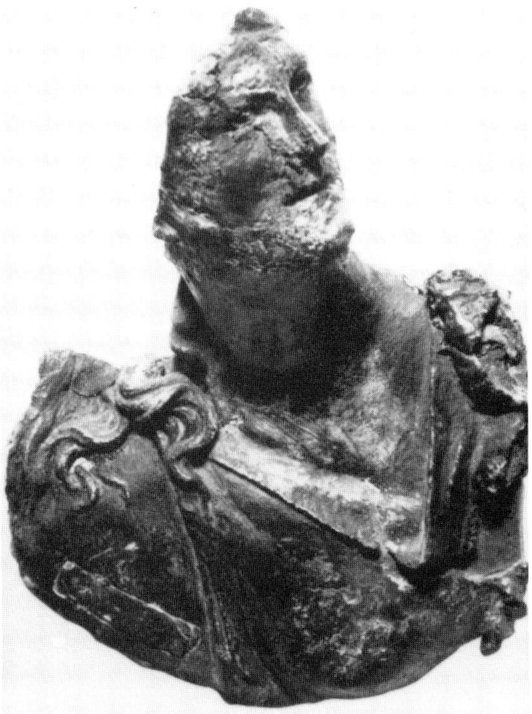

Fig. 7. Bronze bust of Athena from the Mahdia shipwreck. Photo Rheinisches Landesmuseum, Bonn.

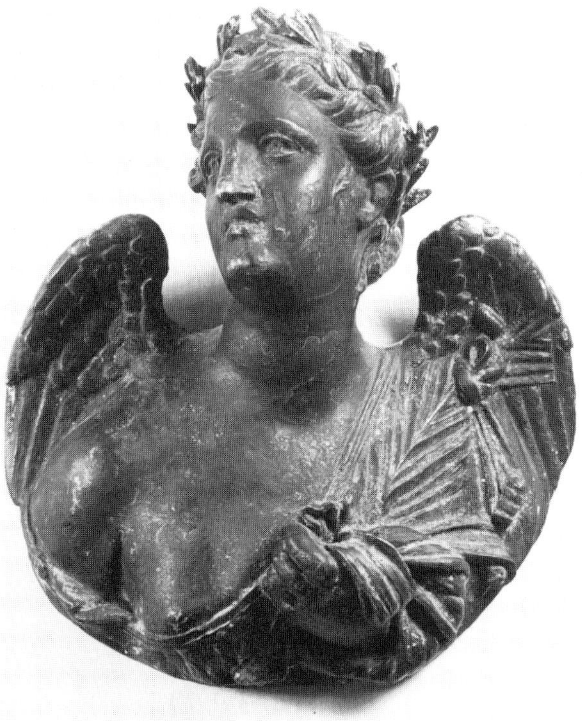

Fig. 8. Bronze bust of Nike from the Mahdia shipwreck. Photo Rheinisches Landesmuseum, Bonn.

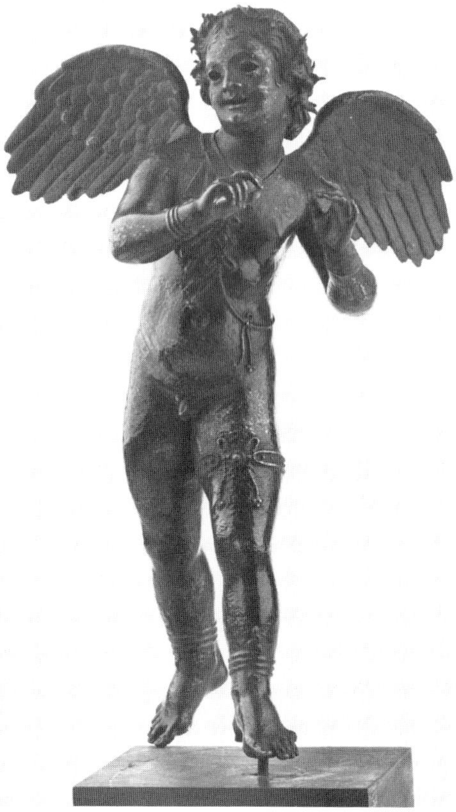

Fig. 9. Bronze Eros with a lyre from the Mahdia shipwreck. Photo Rheinisches Landesmuseum, Bonn.

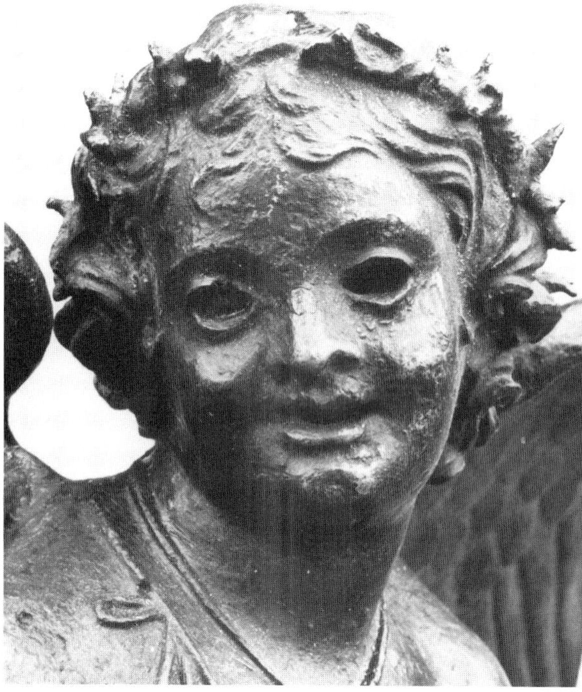

Fig. 10. Head of Eros with a lyre from the Mahdia shipwreck. Photo Rheinisches Landesmuseum, Bonn.

is a feature found on the Mahdia Artemis (Fig. 6).[39] These three busts can thus perhaps be loosely grouped more or less in accordance with standard methods of stylistic analysis. But what of bronzes from the Mahdia shipwreck whose prototypes differ more radically?

Clearly the bronze dwarf with ivy wreath made for suspension (Figs. 3–4) and the flat-backed Nike bust (Fig. 8), a high-relief plaque, are based on widely divergent conceptions and were designed for two very different uses. Their prototype origins may have been different both geographically and temporally. It is worth considering some details of modeling, however, which suggest an affinity. Both have soft, fleshy body modeling and notably (and surprisingly) similar, small conical breasts. Further, the simpler and less distorted bearing of the Nike bust is as mannered as the more complex pose of the full-figured dwarf, and, in its way, the face of the bust is as idiosyncratic as that of the dwarf. Are these particular methods of modeling a figure, achieved in the wax prior to casting and lending what seems to be common expression to bronzes of very different stylistic origins and purposes, clues to the characterization of a workshop identity?[40]

While they certainly do not belong together as a pair, the little female dwarf with an ivy wreath (Figs. 3–4), who probably had a male dwarf pendant, and the Eros with the lyre from the Mahdia shipwreck, also made for suspension (Figs. 9–10), were considered entirely compatible in style by the venerable Karl Anton Neugebauer.[41] Although Stephanie Böhm, most recent commentator on the Eros with the lyre,[42] rejects any similarity in technique or style between it and any other bronze from the Mahdia shipwreck, she does not rule out "eine gemeinsame werkstattliche Herkunft" between these two bronzes, which she does not define. While elusive in the extreme, it is just such a workshop origin that is under discussion here.

In both the female dwarf with an ivy wreath (Figs. 3–4) and the Eros with the lyre (Figs. 9–10), the modeling of the body is soft, de-emphasizing muscles and bones (except in the fingers of the Eros, to whose characterization as a lyre-player they are an important area of focus), with rounded, fleshy shoulders. Interestingly, the neck to shoulder proportion of the Eros with the lyre is comparable to that of the Nike bust (Fig. 8); both wear their wings on exaggeratedly long, sloping shoulders. While the hairstyles of the two figures made for suspension (Figs. 4 and 10) are different from each other, the individualization of each is achieved by the same *means*, perhaps a defining mark of workshop practice. The hair is modeled above the face in string-like, low-relief locks with ornamental wisps artfully placed on the narrow forehead below. There is also a correspondence in both the placement and disposition of the facial features of the two figures. The open (singing) mouths of both (pierced in the dwarf) have a bow-shaped upper lip with distinct philtrum, a wide nose bridge and flared nostrils (the tip of the dwarf's nose turns up), bulging cheek pads, and a small dimpled chin.

Neugebauer proceeded to group with these two the largest bronze from the Mahdia shipwreck, the slightly under life-size winged youth crowning himself in victory (Fig. 2).[43] While the underlying structure of the youth's compact, less soft and fleshy body is more pronounced than those of the smaller bronzes (he is an ephebe; the Eros with the lyre is a child), the surface modeling is basically smooth. There is almost no depression between the pectoral muscles, while other tendinous intersections of the trunk are indicated with shallow modeling only. When compared to the faces of the female dwarf (Fig. 4) and the Eros with the lyre (Fig. 10), the face of the youth (Fig. 11) reveals a corresponding breadth and fullness, with a comparably narrow horizontal forehead area delineated by the lower edge of a decorative row of flat, stringy hair locks (here brushed forward), a similarly shaped (but closed) mouth with wide philtrum, but a longer nose with smaller nostrils. In profile, the pointed noses of the winged youth and lyre-playing Eros figures are similar, as is the construction and shape of the eyes, hollow for inlay, although those of the smaller figure are placed somewhat further apart. The eyes of the dwarf are almond-shaped, but the eyebrow formation is the same as that of the Eros with the lyre. (Only the youth has the hairs of the brows indicated.) What is said to be identical residual core material in the female dwarf and in the winged youth may support the notion of a common origin between them.

What is the material evidence from the Skardhana quarter on Delos other than the klinai leg molds which might lend support to the hypothesis of a Delian origin sometime before 69 B.C. for the bronzes from the Mahdia shipwreck?

None of the few bronzes surviving from the Skardhana quarter allows at first examination the striking comparison to Mahdia material afforded by the Fourmigue C shipwreck fulcrum attachment with horse protome and Artemis bust discussed above. Hilde Hille found a correspondence in the faces of the two bronze figure-lamps, *lychnouchoi*, from the shipwreck (whose bodies have the same smooth modeling as bronzes discussed above) to a Delian bust of Hermes[44] and Ursula Höckmann compared the Mahdia Hermes statuette to the same bust, appropriately emphasizing the similarity of the hair.[45] The method of modeling the hair on both Mahdia and Delian Hermes images, into thick, slightly curving locks arranged in distinct rows, is found on other bronzes from the Skardhana area. Justifiably, Gerard Siebert found the hair modeling sufficiently distinctive to publish photographic details of this feature as it appears on three Delian bronzes: the top of the head of the Hermes, the back of a dog, and the top of a lion's mane.[46] It may not be a coincidence that the same stylization of hair appears on the panther-skin harness worn by a mule protome from the Fourmigue C shipwreck.[47]

As for other bronzes from the Skardhana area of Delos: the bust of a laughing satyr boy from a fulcrum attachment is closely related but not identical in type to a slightly larger bust of the same subject from the Mahdia shipwreck (related in pose to the Mahdia Artemis). The two are clearly roughly contemporary, but their different prototypes and the damage to the surfaces of both make comparison difficult. While the volumes of their faces are differently arranged, a similar modeling of the hair, in tufts, may be significant. A small, scowling Silenus bust from Delos is manifestly different in type from the Silenus bust on the fulcrum attachment with the mule protome mentioned above from the Fourmigue C shipwreck, but, given the treatment of panther-skin hair on the mule's harness, this may not necessitate different origins for these fixtures.[48]

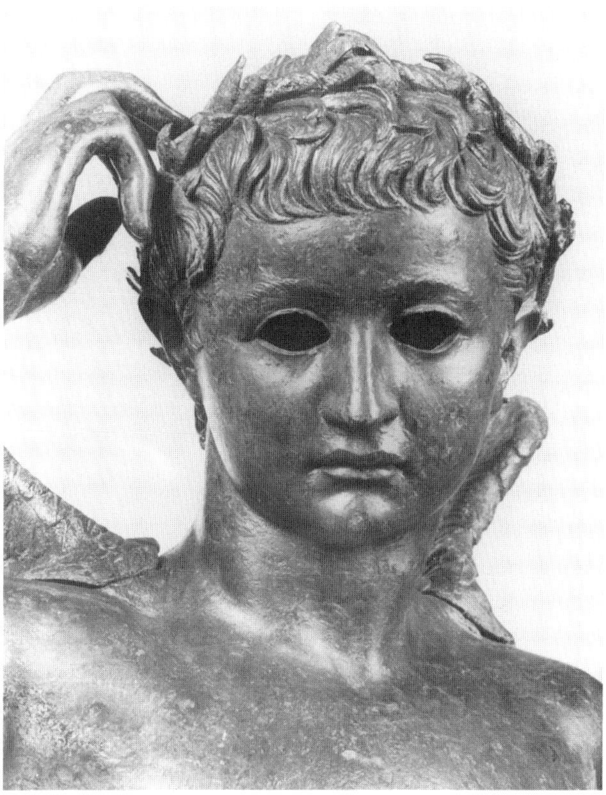

Fig. 11. Head of Eros crowning himself in victory from the Mahdia shipwreck. Photo Rheinisches Landesmuseum, Bonn.

A small bronze theater mask found in the ruins of a house in the Skardhana area of Delos, very similar to the one from Mahdia from a three-nozzled lamp, and almost certainly from a lamp of the same type, helps support the 80–70 B.C. date of the shipwreck, but, however tantalizing, cannot secure the origin of its Mahdia counterpart. Curved on the back for application, the mask is a female New Comedy character with two ribbons in her hair,[49] probably the character Pollux calls the little courtesan (*Onomasticon* 4.153). It is the same size as the mask of the New Comedy character who is probably "the oldest, most excellent youth," the rolled fillet on his head askew as he comes home from a banquet (Pollux, *Onomasticon* 4.146), from the three-nozzled lamp with relief garland found in the Mahdia shipwreck.[50] The Delian mask was probably one of three, together with masks of the youth and a slave, decorating the sides of a lamp of the same three-nozzled type, which has not survived. Only a side-by-side comparison of the masks from Delos and Mahdia might lead to an identification of common workmanship, but they have a greater affinity than either of the two has to the three New Comedy masks on a triple nozzled lamp with garland from Pompeii.[51] The affinity of several small bronze lamps from the Skardhana quarter to the considerably larger single- and double-nozzled lamps found in the Mahdia shipwreck is noteworthy.[52]

Whether or not Linfert has correctly identified the origin of the archaizing bronze herm with the signature of Boethos of Chalcedon (Fig. 1), there is probably no Hellenistic site so identified with herms as Delos. Delian inventories confirm the ancient presence in the *Prytaneion*, its vestibule, and its courtyard of a large series of similar marble herms dating from as early as 314 B.C., and there are many later examples of a great diversity of types elsewhere on the island.[53] Herm types executed in different sizes in both bronze and marble have been found on Delos.[54]

As early as 1953, Jean Marcadé pointed to the correspondence in head type between the archaizing Mahdia herm (Fig. 1) and a small marble herm from Delos (Fig. 12) which seems to copy it.[55] The Delian marble herm wears the same rather unusual tri-partite beard with long corkscrew curls as the Mahdia herm, and the same triple row of snail-shell curls over the forehead (which is not

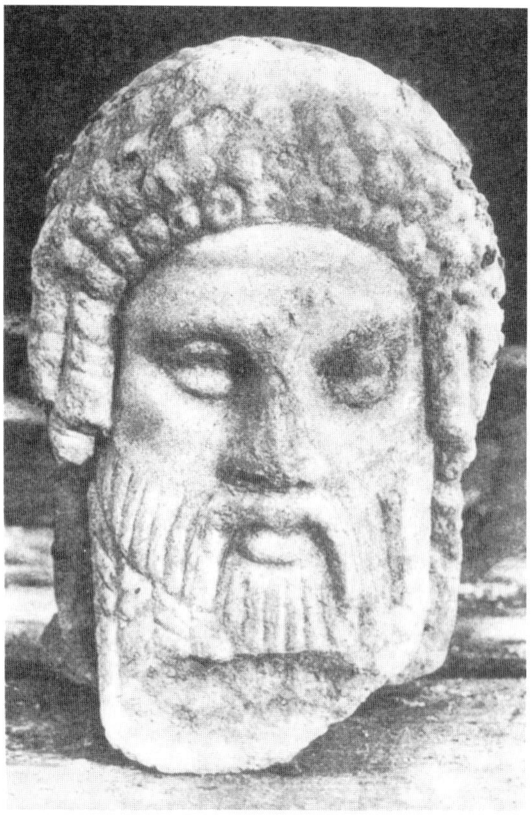

Fig. 12. Marble head of a herm from Delos. Photo after Marcadé, Au Musée de Délos, *pl. 13.*

unusual). It does not have fillets draped into the elaborate (and improbable) headdress that crowns the head of the Mahdia herm, but such a complicated *tour-de-force* of improvised illusionism is more at home in bronze, duplicating its prototype wax original (the wide ribbons look like manipulated strips of soft wax). While versions of related headdresses exist in marble,[56] it is unlikely that the highly artificial draped fillet adornment, further elaborated with a garland of grape leaves,[57] originated in that medium. If the signatory artist, Boethos of Chalcedon, whatever his date, invented this elegant, theatrically sartorial version of the archaizing herm, it was well worth signing.

By the correction of an early restoration that rendered his left leg longer than his right, the winged youth crowning himself (Fig. 2) has been released from his long accepted posture of stepping up with his shorter leg on a modern base added to the archaizing herm. The correction has effected the entire appearance of the figure. He now stands evenly balanced in an uncomplicated, typically Hellenistic resting pose.

Removed from the herm, the winged figure, who has the traditional hairstyle of an Erös, with a braid on the back of his head, has been identified as Eros by Magdalene Söldner, as it was by Fuchs, rather than Agon, as it was previously called.[58] Instead of the palm branch that Fuchs and others thought the figure once held in his left hand, Söldner has suggested a bow. In the Eros' left hand, near the fingers, a small, worn circular knob lies close behind the equally worn remains of a triangular shaft (Fig. 13), of which a short length extrudes from the hand below (Fig. 14). X-rays of the remnants within the hand reveal that the attributes they supported, made separately of cast bronze, were held in place by the lead that completely fills the hand. A small bow, triangular in cross-section, and a round bowstring were suggested, and a bow was placed in the left hand of the winged youth in the plaster cast of the figure constructed during its restoration.[59] It was adjusted to conform to the diagonal thrust forward from the hand as suggested by the angle of what survived.

The bronze figure is already clearly identified by his wings and hairstyle as an Eros, and as he is making a gesture unequivocally indicating a victory, a large palm branch in his left hand might well be considered a more appropriate attribute. A palm branch, of which the stem is triangular in cross-section, would have been at least as aesthetically pleasing as the bow, and, burdened with leaves, its weight would have tipped it forward from the hand, the stem satisfactorily corresponding to the diagonal inclination indicated by the remnants.[60] It seems likely that the hand would grasp the branch along its length, thus engaging leaves with stem. The round element close behind the triangular element, in circumference almost one-third its size (too large for a bow-string?), could have held one or several leaves which emerged from the hand near the stem as the branch was grasped. As for the technical problems of producing a realistic bronze palm

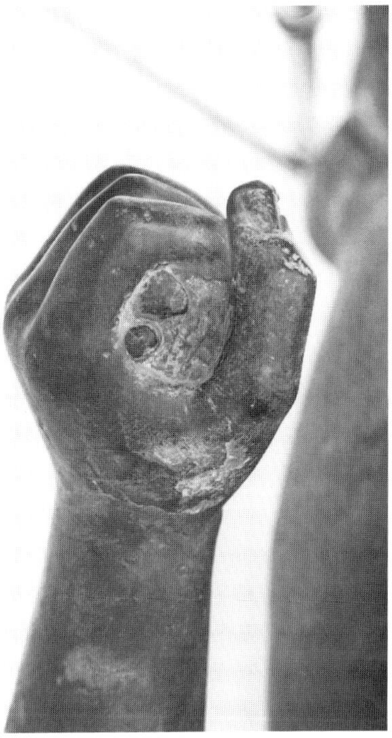

Fig. 13. Top of the left hand of Eros crowning himself in victory from the Mahdia shipwreck. Photo Rheinisches Landesmuseum, Bonn.

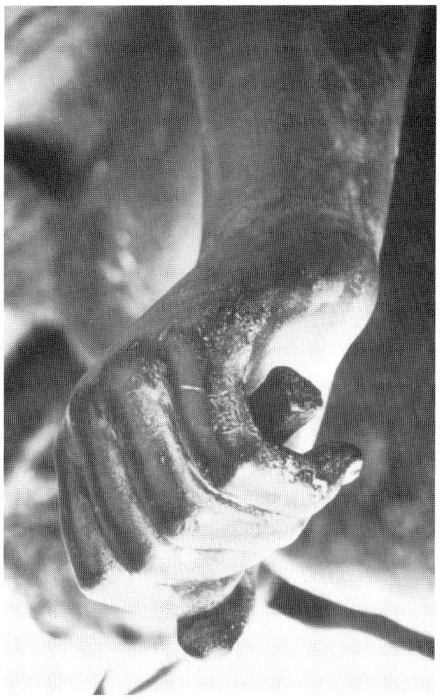

Fig. 14. Bottom of the left hand of Eros crowning himself in victory from the Mahdia shipwreck. Photo Rheinisches Landesmuseum, Bonn.

branch, the most cursory study of the elaborate bronze floral crowns and motifs on the feet of the Mahdia bronze candelabra[61] indicates a competence in casting and piecing leaves and stems in the late Hellenistic period fully equal to the task.[62]

Representations of a winged youth crowning himself are not common. There are two relief examples precisely relevant in date; in both, the youth holds a palm branch in his left hand. One is dated to 96/95 B.C., a few years before the assault on Delos of Mithridates VI and his pirate allies in 88 B.C., and a decade or so before the highest limit of the Mahdia shipwreck (80–70 B.C.). There can be little question as to its relationship to the island of Delos. The second was found in the Skardhana area of Delos with its *terminus ante quem* of 69 B.C.

The first is the obverse of a silver tetradrachm of the so-called Athenian New Style (Fig. 15).[63] An owl, symbol of Athens, which had administered Delos as a colony since 166 B.C. when Delos was returned by Rome to Athens for that purpose, perches on an amphora turned on its side. To the right of the owl is a small image of a winged youth crowning himself with his right hand while holding a large palm branch along its length in his left.

Symbols or devices of this nature were selected by the first monetary official or mint magistrate, in this case Aropos, whose name can be seen on the coin along with that of his associate, Mnesagoras. According to an inscription, Aropos, son of Leon, was *epimeletes* and also *agonothetes* on Delos, thus associated with the athletic competitions there in 96/95 B.C. It is very likely that he was

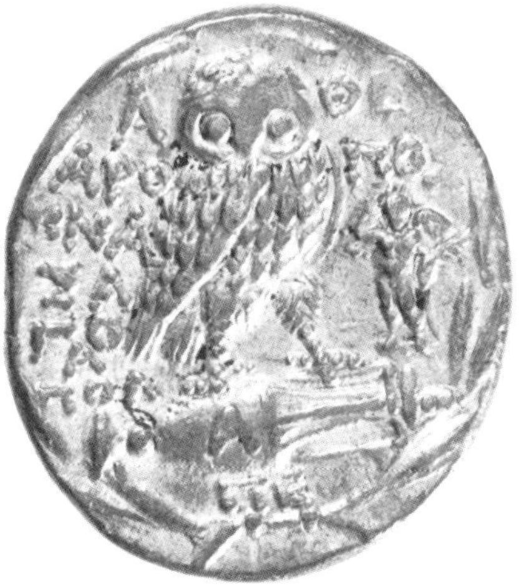

Fig. 15. Athenian New Style tetradrachm minted in 96/95 B.C. Photo courtesy of the American Numismatic Society, New York.

the same Aropos who, as first monetary magistrate, minted this coin in 96/95 B.C.[64]

The amphora on the coin, representing the prize, suggests the athletic nature of the victory being celebrated, but does not concomitantly identity the figure as Agon. Pausanias describes an altar to Eros in the gymnasium in Elis (6.23.3) and a relief in a palaestra there of an Eros holding a palm branch which a second Eros tries to take away from him (6.23.5). These descriptions suggest the appropriateness of Eros both to athletics and to com-

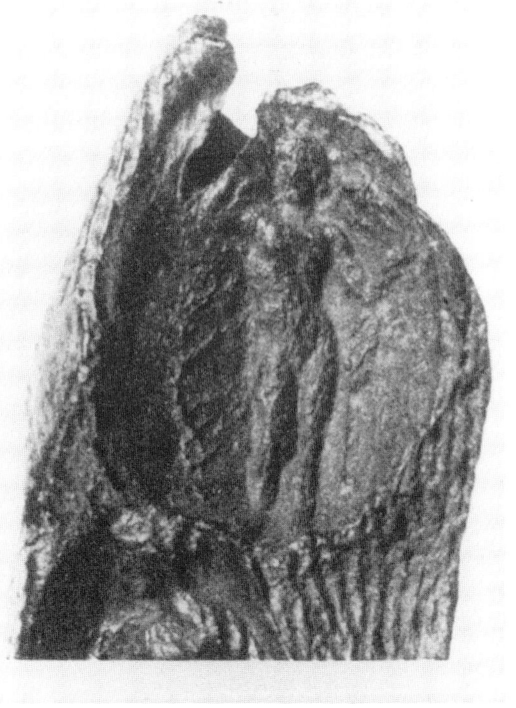

Fig. 16. Clay sealing from the Skardana quarter of Delos. Photo after Stambolides, Les sceaux de Délos, *pl. 38,8.*

petitive triumph.[65] The choice of an Eros *Enagonios* as the magistrate's symbol, when the magistrate is identified as Aropos, son of Leon, signifies his service as *agonothetes* on Delos. The figure could refer to a bronze statue on Delos (conceivably the magistrate's own dedication), perhaps installed in the gymnasium, a building in which images of Eros were traditional.

An image of Eros *Stephanoumenos* on a clay sealing (Fig. 16) similar to that on the coin, was recently published by Nikos Stambolides with other clay sealings from the Skardhana area of Delos.[66] In his left hand, held up somewhat higher than in the coin or the Mahdia figure, the Eros holds a palm branch, clasping it along its length near the top. This image, too, could refer to a bronze statue on the island of Delos. Although the two little images could be as far apart in date as twenty years and are not duplicates, they could just conceivably refer to the same statue.

The figures on both coin (Fig. 15) and sealing (Fig. 16) have the same stance, wings of the same proportion to the body, and gestures identical to those of the Mahdia youth. The body of the Eros figure on the coin is squatter than that of the Mahdia youth, while the Eros *Stephanoumenos* on the sealing has a body identically proportioned. The Eros on the coin holds his palm branch in a way that suggests its flexibility (and movement forward), while the sealing figure grasps his palm near the top and it falls vertically beneath his hand. Just how accurately such images copied their models is open to question, of course, if a single or two models were in fact copied.

Taking into consideration the compressed space alloted to it, the Eros *Enagonios* image (designating it by its context on the coin) is the closer of the two to the Mahdia winged youth. Considered at the most conservative level, these images at least indicate the familiarity of this Eros type on Delos, and it seems very likely that the type existed there.

Statues of Eros were plentiful in the Delian gymnasium. In an inventory made on Delos under the archon Kallistratos (156–155 B.C.), several statues of Eros are mentioned as dedications in the gymnasium. One is described as wearing the attributes of Herakles, another carried a small vessel, presumably a competition prize. The type of a third is not specified. Graffiti scratched on stone benches from the gymnasium and on a stele found in the palaestra which is probably from the gymnasium, include four images of Eros which are believed to be drawings of still other statues dedicated there. Three are childlike Eros figures, the fourth is a winged ephebe. One of the three has a wreath in his hand, indicating victory, another holds a torch in each hand, the third steps forward holding a bow with both hands as if to shoot. The drawing of the winged ephebe is too indistinct for the pose to be determined. Futher evidence exists in inscribed statue bases surviving from the gymnasium. One of these bore a figure of Eros beside a hydria (possibly an Eros *Enagonios*), apparently a double dedication.[67]

Thus, there existed on Delos a credible ambience for the winged youth crowning himself from the Mahdia shipwreck. Proof exists that the type was known there by at least 96/95 B.C. and was still familiar sometime before 69 B.C. Further, whether installed on a base in the gymnasium or elsewhere on the island, the bronze figure could well have been the casualty of looting during one of the two pirate attacks on Delos. Its tenuous, but defendable, relationship to other bronzes from the Mahdia shipwreck, which, by extension, may well include the klinai, strengthens the hypothesis of a Delian origin for many, conceivably all, the figurative bronzes.

Can these bronzes from the Mahdia shipwreck be characterized as the plunder from a single Delian manufacturer of klinai and bronze sculpture produced from many prototypes and for many purposes? Were the single dwarf with ivy wreath, the Eros with the lyre, and others of the figurative bronzes produced for votive dedication, as the winged youth must have been? Were they stolen from a sanctuary on Delos, or conceivably a civic building, or were they taken from a workshop, having been produced as "decorative" sculpture for the Roman trade?

As for the archaizing bronze herm, nothing except the Boethos of Chalcedon signature suggests it could have been produced as early as 164 B.C., as Linfert suggested. If relating it to other bronzes from the Mahdia shipwreck is an elusive task, this is mostly so because the archaizing of the herm at first glance renders the image somewhat neutral. However, whatever the bronze herm's relationship to the little marble one on Delos that imitates its beard and face, it is the unusual headdress of draped fillets that distinguishes it in a way that must have been distinctive to the artist and workshop that produced it.

In its artificiality and pleasing elegance (with baroque loops and folds), the herm's headdress is as *mannered* in its realization as the figure of the little dwarf with ivy wreath or the Nike bust. This synthetic quality, evasive of description, is what seems to group many of the Mahdia bronzes together. Because of the fillets looped on his head, the herm may be added to this group. Linfert's identification of a later Boethos of Chalcedon, then, would indeed be correct, but the artist's foundry and related workshop would have remained on Delos, home of the long lineage of illustrious sculptors which Linfert so ingeniously surmised. It seems incontrovertible that the herm was ripped from a marble base. If it was not installed in a sanctuary, the gymnasium, or elsewhere on the island, despite the fact that the grape leaf garland originally garnishing the headdress has Dionysiac overtones, it is conceivable that the herm was placed at the door of the family workshop.

If Delos was, in fact, the source of many, if not all, of the Mahdia bronzes, the Cilician pirates' second raid on Delos, in 69 B.C., may be the more likely of the two they perpetrated there to have been responsible for the theft. Elements from the Skardhana quarter of Delos are suggestive. The proportions of the kline leg elements silhouetted in the molds from the Skardhana quarter are identical to those from the shipwreck (cast in sections including groups of contiguous elements which were then cut apart, finished, and assembled over wooden and iron supportive cores). Evasive, but visible workshop characteristics seem to exist on bronzes from the Skardhana quarter and bronzes from both the Mahdia and Fourmigue C shipwrecks. Further, *if* the New Style Athenian coin and the sealing from the Skardhana quarter represent the same Eros statue, and there is any possibility that this statue, dated by the coin to, or somewhat before, 96/95 B.C., is the Mahdia Eros, the *terminus ante quem* of the sealing may suggest it was still on Delos in 69 B.C.

But perhaps the most persuasive argument in favor of the 69 B.C. date is historical. After Mithridates withdrew his forces sometime after his sack of Athens in 86 B.C., Cilician pirates had almost unlimited power over the Mediterranean Sea (Appian, *Mithr.* 92–96). For the next two decades, until Pompey began his war against them in 67 B.C., the pirates' transport to Athens of goods looted from Delos and elsewhere, and the subsequent dispersal of these spoils to the estates of wealthy Romans in Italy, Sicily, and France could be achieved without anticipated impediment. The cargo of other shipwrecks dated to this period, Fourmigue and Anticythera most notably, may well consist, in part, of pirate loot.

Abbreviations

Das Wrack	G. Hellenkemper Salies, H.-H. von Prittwitz und Gaffron and G. Bauchhenss (edd.), *Das Wrack: die antike Schiffsfund von Mahdia* (1994)
Decorative Bust	B. Barr-Sharrar, *The Hellenistic and Early Imperial Decorative Bust* (1987)
Die Klinen	S. Faust, "Die Klinen," *Das Wrack*, 573–606
Études déliennes	*Études deliennes*, *BCH* Suppl. 1 (1973)
Fourmigue C	C. Baudoin, B. Liou, L. Long, *Une cargaison de bronzes hellénistiques. L'épave Fourmigue C à Golfe-Juan* (1994)
Fuchs	W. Fuchs, *Der Schiffsfund von Mahdia* (1963)
Fulcra	S. Faust, *Fulcra* (1987)
Marcadé	J. Marcadé, *Au Musée de Delos* (1969)

Notes

1. A. Linfert in *Das Wrack*, 831–848. See also here p. 153, Fig. 7.
2. *Fuchs*, *passim*. While opinions about the origin(s) of the bronzes and the non-Pentelic marble objects vary, Athens is generally now considered the principal if not the only port of departure of the ship.
3. *Fuchs* 44–46 saw some stylistic correspondence between the marble kraters and some of the bronzes.
4. The ship is presumed to have been blown miles off course by powerful winds from the northeast similar to those which Saint Paul encountered on his voyage from Lycia to Rome around A.D. 60. Paul's ship was forced to sail for many days before the wind, finally running aground on the island of Malta (*Acts of the Apostles* 27): H. Hellenkemper in *Das Wrack*, 153–164.
5. M. Söldner in *Das Wrack*, 399–429.
6. F. Willer *Bjb* 196, 1996, 337–346, figs. 1–6.
7. F. Willer (supra n. 6) 971–984.
8. The damage to the shaft is difficult to explain otherwise: Willer in *Das Wrack*, 953–958, color pl. 34.
9. H.G. Horn in *Das Wrack*, 451–467 dates them to the last quarter of the second century B.C. and believes they were on a monument in Athens or the Piraeus.
10. Some of the sacral vessels show signs of use. R. Petrovszky in *Das Wrack*, 663–700 dates the vessels to 90–60 B.C.
11. H.-H. von Prittwitz und Gaffron in *Das Wrack*, 303–328, where they are dated to about 120 B.C. See also the same author, here pp. 69–73.
12. G. Bauchhenss in *Das Wrack*, 375–380; G. Petzl ibid., 381–397, with older bibliography.
13. See comments in *Die Klinen*, 577 with n. 15. To the author's bibliography on the subject, add *Marcadé* 78 and 83 n. 3.
14. G. Siebert in *Études déliennes*, *passim*; id., *BCH* 100, 1976, 799–821, figs. 24–25.
15. For one of the plaster molds (and a modern positive from it), Siebert, *Études déliennes*, 584, fig. 31 (both published upside-down). Claude Rolley has suggested that the Madhia kline legs could not have been made on Delos

because they are constructed of many separate elements, whereas the molds from the Skardhana Quarter of Delos include several contiguous elements (the one published by Siebert, above, has four). (Conversation with C. Rolley, October, 1996; also now in *RA* 1996, 285). Upon reflection, and after having examined the molds, the following observations might be made in response. The appearance of the plaster mold fragments from Delos suggest that molds for casting the round, hollow bronze kline legs were taken in two halves from wooden lathe-turned "model" legs divided into vertical sections (each including several elements of the elaborate silhouette) representing those sections of the leg in between which horizontal elements of the bed would eventually be fitted, and, in the case of the lowest section, one end of which would be inserted into the foot. It is both easier and less time-consuming, when it can be done, to cast pieces in bronze which must be fitted together exactly by casting them in one length. After casting, the pieces would then have been cut apart where necessary, and finished to facilitate the insertion of the wooden and iron, and perhaps plaster, filling material which was added to strengthen the hollow legs sufficiently to support weight. This procedure would have been expedited by making molds of lathe-turned wooden models of reasonable length (the sections into which the legs fell naturally) rather than separate molds of as many as thirteen small elements, each of which would have required a separate mold and casting procedure.

For the reconstruction of the Mahdia klinai and discussion of the filling material, U. Sobottka-Braun in *Das Wrack*, 999–1006. The two hollow tubes with the appearance of bronze kline legs found with their clay molds and published by W. Deonna in *Délos* 18, 1–2, pl. 5, 50–51, are only 9.5 cm high and may have been intended for a toy or votive bed. They are differently proportioned from the Skardhana molds and the Mahdia kline legs, which correspond in silhouette.

As yet no remains of a foundry have been identified on Delos. See *Marcadé* 83–84 with n. 2.

I am grateful to the Ephoreia of the Cyclades and to the École Française d' Athènes for the privilege of examining the molds as well as the bronzes from the Skardhana quarter, and would like to thank all concerned.

16. Siebert, *BCH* 93, 1969, 1036–1039.
17. S.I. Rotroff in *Das Wrack*, 133–152.
18. Plutarch, *Pompey* 24–29; Appian, *Mithr.* 92–96. Plutarch says the pirates from Cilicia, in Asia Minor, captured 400 cities, mentioning assaults on the cities and sanctuaries at claros, Didyma, Samothrace, Hermione, the Asklepios sanctuary at Epidauros, the temples of Poseidon at the Isthmus of Corinth, at Tainaron, and at Kalauria, the temples of Apollo at Aktion and Leukas, and those of Hera at Samos, Argos and Lacinium; Appian describes the 88 B.C. assault on Delos, and adds Iasos and Klazomenai to the list. Appian says that from Samothrace (where Sulla was staying at the time of the attack [about 83 B.C.]), the pirates stole temple ornaments valued at 1000 talents. The pirates' control of the Mediterranean might well have prevented Linfert's notional transfer of a Boethos family workshop from Delos to Athens prior to 88 B.C.
19. In 100 B.C. Rome passed a law stating its intention of dealing with piracy (Roman statute, no. 12) : M. Crawford, *The Roman Republic* (1993) 133.
20. Appian says that the sacred treasure of Delos was sent to Athens with an Athenian citizen, Aristion, and 2000 soldiers to guard it. Pausanias says it was Aristion who "persuaded the Athenians to prefer Mithridates to the Romans" (1.20.5). Plutarch has the same view, but calls Aristion "the tyrant" (*Sulla* 12.1).
21. Atticus probably moved to Athens just a few years after Mithridates' sack of Delos. He is believed to have left Italy for Athens after his father's death in 88 B.C., but not before the autumn of 86 B.C. See D.R. Shackleton Bailey (ed.), *Cicero's Letters to Atticus* (1965) 3–4.
22. Even taking into consideration the exaggeration of the rhetoric, Cicero's speeches during his prosecution of Verres suggest he may not knowingly have bought plundered goods, or, at least, did not wish to *appear* to have done so. See infra n. 28. But a letter written to Atticus in 54 B.C. (4.16.7) suggests no such compunctions with regard to Caesar's second expedition to Britain, which had discovered no silver on the island and, writes Cicero, from which there was "no hope for booty other than captives." It is notable that Rome tolerated the Cilician pirates long after its stated intention in 100 B.C. to stop their marauding activities. Only in 67 B.C., when the city's corn supply was threatened and Romans were themselves subject to attack, did they take action against them. See M.I. Finley, *The Ancient Economy* (1973) 156, with reference to Strabo (14.5.2). Strabo says plainly that heretofore the Romans had not hindered the pirates' increasing power.
23. Supra n. 11. For another suggested provenance of the Parian marble busts see H. von Prittwitz, here pp. 69–73.
24. For possible *hestiatoria* on Delos, see G. Roux in *Études déliennes*, 525–554. Roux suggests that each of the two rooms of the pseudo-Thesmophorion could have accommodated at least twenty-three klinai, with others placed in the courtyard between the rooms.
25. *Die Klinen*, 831–848.
26. Like candelabra, beds from *hestiatoria* were often repaired: supra n. 24.
27. Published and discussed by É.Cuq, *BCH* 46, 1922, 198–215. The inscription, on a marble stele from Delos found on Mykonos, is at least reassurance of Roman interest.
28. *...at istorum villae sociorum fidelissimorum plurimis et pulcherrimis spoliis ornatae refertaeque sunt. Ubi pecunias exterarum nationum esse arbitramini, quae nunc omnes egent, cum Athenas, Pergamum, Cyzicum, Miletum, Chium, Samum, totam denique Asiam, Achaiam, Graeciam, Siciliam tam in paucis villis inclusas esse videatis? Sed haec, ut dico, omnia iam socii vestri relinquunt et neglegunt, iudices.*
29. Dated to the last quarter of the second century are the winged youth (Söldner, supra n. 5), the Dionysos and Ariadne fixtures (Horn, supra n. 9), the larger statuette of a satyr (C. Klages in *Das Wrack*, 531–538) and, by implication, the dancing dwarves (Pfisterer-Haas, infra n. 31) and the bronze candelabra (Baratte, infra n. 61). Most of the other bronzes are dated to around 100 B.C. or a little later; the three-nozzled garland lamp can be

dated to the first quarter of the first century B.C. Barr-Sharrar in *Das Wrack*, 639–644.

30. The pair of statuettes of grotesque dancing dwarves were affixed to their round stone bases when they were put on board the ship. What this might mean in terms of prior use or placement is difficult to say. The bases were at first believed to be weights: D. Baatz in *Das Wrack*, 105–107. For their attachment to their bases see Willer (supra n. 7) 356–360, figs. 17–22. The bronze base on the statuette of Hermes (U. Höckmann in *Das Wrack*, 469–481) was probably fabricated in the same workshop as the statuette and affixed there.

31. S. Pfisterer-Haas in *Das Wrack*, 486–490, dates the Alexandrian prototype of this dancing dwarf with ivy wreath to the middle of the second century B.C., the bronze itself somewhat later, suggesting Athens as an origin because of its classicising aspect. How much later than its prototype this bronze was made is perhaps an open question, the shipwreck affording a *terminus ante quem*.

 The tentative suggestions of provenance for some of the Mahdia bronzes made by this writer in *Decorative Bust*, 23–26, I no longer hold valid after having had the opportunity to study them. (The lack of autopsy was an explicit *caveat* to the earlier suggestions). However, in the above case, and possibly others, they may well indicate prototype origin. Such prototypes may have been of different size, fabric, and even medium.

32. *Die Klinen*.

33. *Fourmigue C*, 31–60.

34. *Fourmigue C*, 47, fig. 25 (after cleaning).

35. *Fourmigue*, 48, fig. 27 (after cleaning). Side-by-side comparisons of the Fourmigue and Mahdia fulcrum attachment horse protomes and Artemis busts, 57, fig. 35. See also *Die Fulcra*, nos. 196–200. The Mahdia Artemis bust is 12.7 cm in height; the Fourmigue bust is 10.35 cm. (*Die Klinen*, 604 n. 37) The difference in size between these two Artemis busts (as that between the two horse's heads: 20.4 cm to 17.05 cm in length) is worthy of special note in view of their obvious dependence on the same model or prototype.

 Among the Mahdia kline busts and protomes there is no evidence of serial casting, i.e., indirect casting of more than one decorative bust or horse or mule protome from the same mold or molds, or from a mold or molds taken from the same prototype, a technique that would result in duplicate objects of the same size. In fact, as far as this writer knows, their are no examples at all of exact duplication in cast bronze kline sculpture from antiquity, which is perhaps surprising. Faust has published two mule protomes that, like the Mahdia and Fourmigue Artemis fulcrum attachments, appear to be from the same workshop (*Die Fulcra*, nos. 82 and 324), but one is 7.4 cm larger than the other. Neither plaster nor terracotta molds shrink to this extent upon drying; certainly not 15% as Rolley has suggested (supra n. 15, 281). Shrinkage of such molds is usually less than 1%. This suggests that with the possible exception of the elements of the cylindrical legs, *every kline was a unique product.*

 A duplication process was used for more simple bronze products of similar date, however. Among the small decorative bronze appliqués from the Mahdia shipwreck are several series produced by a duplication process. The two bronze masks of the New Comedy figure of the angry old man were probably cast from the same mold. See Barr-Sharrar in *Das Wrack*, 559, figs. 1–2. This is true also of the bronze plaques with two griffins flanking a krater, ibid., 560–562, figs. 3–5, and possibly others of the appliqués, *passim*.

36. Barr-Sharrar in *Das Wrack*, 551–558.

37. It is worth considering the fact that the three bronzes from Mahdia have similar alloy contents, or percentages of copper to tin to lead (with 1 to 1.5% lead) and do not share the higher percentage of tin found in the tubular kline leg elements. This tin, which in some of the leg elements is as high as 15.4%, was no doubt added to strengthen the hollow legs, into which were placed wooden cores. (See supra n. 15.) It would also lighten the color of the bronze which, when highly polished, would appear golden. Since all the klinai elements must have been produced in the same workshop, to be united in the final construction of the beds, it is apparent that different alloy mixtures were available in the same foundry to be used at least to some extent in accordance with the purposes for which the bronzes were intended.

 For the bronze analyses, E. Pernicka and G. Eggert in *Das Wrack*, 1041–1061. For the reconstruction of the klinai, U. Sobottka-Braun in *Das Wrack*, 999–1006.

38. Barr-Sharrar (supra n. 36).

39. The alloy content, like that of the Athena, is similar : supra n. 37.

40. The assumption of the nature of a Hellenistic bronze workshop where the original wax model was created prior to casting (whether directly or indirectly) is one dominated by a single artist who imposed his working method on everything that was produced, informing it with a distinctive manner or look. This perhaps should not be called style, given the variety of prototypes and their "styles."

 The dwarf, who had castanets in both hands, has a very different ratio of copper to tin to lead than the Nike bust, with tin at levels common to all the klinai legs and decorative elements on the frame of the beds, but, unlike them, a high percentage of lead: 15.8%. This high lead content is found in the other small bronze figures from the Mahdia shipwreck: the pair of dancing dwarves (10–15%), the two lamp bearers (31% and 22%), and the satyr who held a tray or bowl in his hands (23%) (supra n. 37).

41. Neugebauer believed all the Mahdia bronzes to be contemporary and from the same workshop. Neugebauer in *VI. internationaler Kongress für Archäologie. Berlin 1939* (1940) 416–425. The dancing dwarf with ivy wreath and the Eros with the lyre have a similar alloy pattern (supra n. 37).

42. S. Böhm in *Das Wrack*, 505–509.

43. Neugebauer (supra n. 41). Böhm mentions the similarity of the wreaths worn by the two figures (supra n. 42).

44. H. Hiller in *Das Wrack*, 524–525, fig. 24. The Hermes face is badly corroded.

45. U. Höckmann in *Das Wrack*, 473.

46. *Études déliennes*, 560, fig. 8 (herm), 572, fig. 20 (bust, dog, and lion). The locks are comma-shaped, sometimes with a single depression in the middle. On the top of the

Hermes head, the top of the lion's mane, and at the highest point of the dog's back, locks pile up into a luxurious assembly, full, rich and highly decorative. The relationship of these bronzes is clear from this detail alone. It is an individual or workshop mannerism and, as such, is akin to those details by which vase painting experts recognize the hands of vase painters. See, for example, D.Williams, *RA* (1992) 227–252.

47. For the Fourmigue mule protome, *Fourmigue C*, 50, fig 30. While it is characteristic of the panther-skin harnesses on mule protomes from the first quarter of the first century B.C. to have thickly modeled hair, the regularity of the lines of locks is as particular to the Fourmigue protome (see *Fulcra*, plates *passim*) as it is to the Delos bronzes named and to the Mahdia Hermes statuette.

48. For both satyr boy busts, see *Decorative Bust*, 57, C96 and C97, pls. 31–32. For the Delos example also Siebert in *Études déliennes*, 562, figs. 9 and 11; 556, fig. 1, no. 5. For the Silenus bust from Delos, see *Decorative Bust*, 33–34, C3, pl. 1; Siebert in *Études déliennes*, 560, fig. 7; 556, fig. 1, no. 1; 558, fig. 4. For the Silenus from Fourmigue C, see *Fourmigue C*, 107, pl. 1,b ; 50, fig. 31. No analysis of the alloys of the Delian bronzes has been made to date.

49. *Études déliennes*, 579, no. 23, fig. 21; 556, fig. 1,23.

50. See Barr-Sharrar in *Das Wrack*, 639–644. The dimensions of the Delos mask are H. 3.8 cm, W. 4 cm as preserved (the proper left hair locks are missing); of the Mahdia mask, H. 3 cm, W. 4.8 cm. The courtesan is somewhat greater in height because of the bow on her head.

51. The lamp from Pompeii is identical in type and only a few centimeters smaller than the one from the Mahdia shipwreck, but is probably not from the same workshop. All three of its masks survive. The masks are the youth, the courtesan and a slave with a semi-circular trumpet mouth. A lamp of the same type which has lost its masks survives from the Spargi shipwreck off the coast of Sardinia, dated from the mid-80s to about 75 B.C. by its amphora shapes (supra n. 50).

52. Siebert published a small two-nozzled lamp from the Skardhana quarter in *Études déliennes*, 578, no. 22, fig. 26 on p. 577. Two other lamps, one a small replica of the single-nozzled Mahdia lamp with a shell lid, from the Archegesion, are published in W. Deonna, *Délos* 18, pl. 35 (4780 and 4781). The shape of the little so-called Delian-type lamps of clay, of which so many were found on Delos, are not so different from the Mahdia single spout lamp.

53. *Marcadé* 146–152. In the so-called House of the herm, excavators found eight marble herms and the bases of many others. See M. Kreeb, *Untersuchungen zur figürlichen Ausstattung Delischer Privathäuser* (1988) 64. Höckmann discusses herms on Delos (supra n. 45) 475–476.

54. Herakles hip herms of similar type exist in both bronze and marble versions of varying size from Delos. For a fine, small bronze Herakles hip herm from a house in the Skardhana quarter of Delos, see Siebert, *BCH* 99, 1975, 76; 720, fig. 7 (before cleaning). Siebert believed it reinforced the hypothesis of the permanence of a local industry in bronze in the late Hellenistic period. For marble versions of similar type, see *Marcadé* pls. 19–20. These are the precursors of the Roman Imperial Herakles hip herm pilasters from Sparta and elsewhere. See O. Palagia in S. Walker and A. Cameron (edd.), *The Greek Renaissance in the Roman Empire*, *BICS* Suppl. 55 (1989) 122–129.

55. J. Marcadé, *BCH* 77, 1953, 506, figs. 9–10. Also *Marcadé* 153, pl. 13, A 1866 (11 cm high).

56. C.C. Mattusch in *Das Wrack*, 43 n. 19, fig. 14. They also exist in terracotta, ibid., figs. 11–12.

57. Mattusch (supra n. 56) 444. A leaf protrudes on the proper right side of the folded fillets.

58. Söldner (supra n. 5). *Fuchs* 12–14 suggested that the figure be identified as Eros *Enagonios*. The iconography of Agon is not a settled one. He is not always depicted or described in ancient literature as winged. In vase painting he is frequently a youth shown running or with instruments of sporting events. See *LIMC* I (1981) s.v. Agon, 303–305 and figs. 16–17 on p. 225.

59. Söldner (supra n. 5) 406–407, figs. 11–14.

60. A helpful observation made by Frank Willers, the restorer, when I suggested to him the alternative of a palm branch. Letter to the writer, April 19, 1996.

61. F. Baratte in *Das Wrack*, 607–628.

62. The bronze palm tree dedicated on Delos in 417 B.C. by Nikias is believed to have been realistic in appearance. See P. Courbin in *Études déliennes*, 157–172. For a bronze palm branch from Samos, ibid., 168, fig. 7. Also U. Jantzen, *Samos* 8, 32ff., pl. 36. For the palm tree of Eurymedon in Delphi that supported a statue, P. Amandry, *BCH* 78, 1954, 295–315.

63. The chronology of the Athenian New Style coinage was first established by M. Thompson, *The New Style Silver Coinage of Athens* (1961). Her published date at that time for this tetradrachm was 128/127 B.C. Subsequently, her chronology was corrected and considerably lowered (apparently with her approval), and the coin is now dated 96/95 B.C. For the widely accepted new chronology, see O. Mørkholm, *NNM* 29, 1984, 29–42; M.J. Price in G. Le Rider, K. Jenkins, N. Waggoner, and U. Westermark (edd.), *Kraay-Mørkholm Essays*. Numismatic Studies in Memory of C.M. Kraay and O. Mørkholm (1989) 233–243; H.B. Mattingly, *NumChron* 150, 1990, 67–78. I am grateful to Carmen Arnold-Biucchi for these references.

64. Discussed by Thompson (supra n. 63) 555. But as her high dating of the coin did not coincide with the date of Aropos, son of Leon, but was 32 years too early, she somewhat reluctantly gave up an attempt to identify the two as the same man. For the dating of Aropos, son of Leon, to 96/95, see C. Habicht, *Chiron* 21, 1991, 1–23.

65. See also *LIMC* III (1986) s.v Eros, no. 712.

66. N. Stambolides, *Les sceaux de Délos* 2 (1992) 173, no. 4.8, M1 (696), pl. 38,8. Söldner mentions both this sealing and the Athenian New Style tetradrachm as images identified as Eros, strengthening her designation of the Mahdia bronze as Eros, but does not relate them directly to the bronze (supra n. 5): the sealing, 428 n. 118; the coin, 421, dating it to 128/127 B.C. A.

67. A. Jacquemin, *BCH* 105, 1981, 155–169, especially 157–163 with related illustrations. Also H. von Hesberg in M. Wörrle and P. Zanker (edd.), *Stadtbild und Bürgerbild im Hellenismus*. Colloquium, Munich, 24–26 June, 1993 (1995) 13–27, fig. 18.

Problems in Provenance and Patronage: A Group of Late Hellenistic Statuettes from Paestum

John Pedley

Fieldwork at Paestum, both recent and not so recent, has uncovered much of the city inside the walls, while sanctuaries and cemeteries outside but within the area of the city's territory have also been explored.[1] Among suburban and rural sanctuaries recently investigated, a suburban sanctuary in the zone called Santa Venera has yielded the statuettes which are the subject of this paper.[2]

Santa Venera

The zone consists of a tract of land reaching from the city wall some 800 meters southward. Cemeteries of the fifth and fourth centuries B.C. cover much of the area, while only a little further to the south is the cemetery in which was found the Tomb of the Diver.[3] Almost adjacent to the city wall, and therefore in a significant location between the wall and cemeteries, a sanctuary of Aphrodite came into being in the sixth century B.C., and continued until the eruption of Vesuvius in A.D. 79.

The sanctuary offers rare architectural forms both of the fifth century B.C. and of the first century A.D. The early fifth century saw the construction of a Rectangular Hall (for dining), and of an Oikos temple, paralleled in the unusual plan of its cella by the contemporary building outside the west wall of the Altis at Olympia; and in its lateral entrance-way by the shrine of Aphrodite recently uncovered at Locri by Marcella Barra Bagnasco and her team. A portico was later added to the south side of the Hall, and the Oikos underwent repairs in the second century. In the years ca. 50 B.C. the Oikos was more substantially fixed up and extensive work of rehabilitation was begun in the west wing. The interior of the Hall was wholly reworked ca. 20 A.D., and several horseshoe-shaped niches for which no exact parallels have yet been found were installed. A piscina was built to the south of the Hall at the same time.[4] There is much other information on the history and practice of the cult, derived largely from pottery, inscriptions and figurines.[5]

In the early 1930s the area saw the construction of an industrial establishment directly east of the modern road and atop part of the sanctuary. Some 20 years after the building of this factory, the area to the east (but only to the east) was explored by the then Superintendent of Antiquities, Pellegrino Sestieri. He identified the area investigated by him as part of a sanctuary, but did not publish anything more than a couple of paragraphs in the *Fasti*.[6] In spite of the fact that the industrial complex, a tomato paste factory no less, was obviously sited on archaeologically rich ground, the factory was authorised, in late 1956, to extend itself southward.

In the course of the archaeological survey of the designated area, prior to the construction of the extension, a number of antiquities was found among which were fragments of inscriptions and statuettes. According to the report filed in the offices of the Superintendency in Salerno, the sculptural fragments included parts of nine marble statuettes – one seated male figure, the others standing females; six marble heads were also reported to have been found. Seven of the nine figures were found lying inside a ruined fountain of Roman date. The land where these discoveries were made was then occupied by the new wing of the Cirio factory; it is accordingly archaeologically inaccessible and will remain so until this commercial eye-sore, no longer in use, is destroyed.

Another female figure had been found in Sestieri's excavations in 1953; and it is on the basis of this figure that Sestieri identified Aphrodite as the major deity in the sanctuary. He found, and I quote from his paragraph in the *Fasti*, "un torsetto marmoreo femminile con himation che copriva la sola parte inferiore del corpo." She was evidently a half-draped Aphrodite.

There are in the Paestum Museum today eight marble statuettes from the site – a seated male, and seven draped or half-draped females, all headless. The state of preservation varies. Preserved height also varies from ca. 0.34 m to 0.59 m.

Identification

The Male Figure (Fig. 1)

The male figure is seated on a rocky outcrop. The hole at the foot of the rock shows that he served as an ornamental fountain head; it seems sure, then, that he originally decorated the fountain, and was one of the figures found lying inside it. He leans sharply backward turning to his left; he holds the left leg drawn back, only the toes resting on a rocky shelf; the right leg is extended to the front and right presenting an open posture. The torso and legs are worked fully in the round; the abdomen too is carefully modelled with realistic creases of flesh above the navel. Modelling around the waist is also effective with hip muscle and roll of flesh clearly articulated.

The youth and softness of the flesh allow the suggestion that this may be a representation of a seated Eros. The seated Eros appears in fourth-century B.C. vase painting in a posture similar to that of the Santa Venera figure.[7] Moreover, several examples of Erotes as fountain figures exist, often accompanied by animals or dolphins; unpublished examples in the Ostia Museum also show Eros seated on rocks, again accompanied by beasts.[8] Yet the Paestum figure has no companions, and no parallel for a solitary Eros seated on a rock seems to exist. The backward leaning attitude of the figure finds analogies in some representations of a seated, naked Apollo . Only a single example of Apollo as a fountain figure was known to Kapossy, however, so that this identification seems improbable.[9]

The posture is reminiscent of the bronze Hermes from Herculaneum.[10] Though the Paestum figure leans backwards, does not wear sandals, and the positioning of the right arm is puzzling, he seems to be a variant of the famous Lysippan type. Other variants may be cited, whether leaning backward, or without sandals. In particular, a number of small bronzes which evidently echo the Lysippan prototype seem to prefigure our Paestum type. Other comparable figures of the seated Hermes as fountain head are to be found in St. Petersburg, Florence, and Athens, with perhaps yet another in Cyrene.[11]

The Three Half-draped Aphrodites

Of the females, three are recognisable examples of half-draped Aphrodite/Venus types. The largest is an adaptation of the Venus Anadyomene. The other two had museum tags showing that they entered the Museum on February 27, 1957. The Anadyomene however did not, which may suggest that she was the figure found by Sestieri.

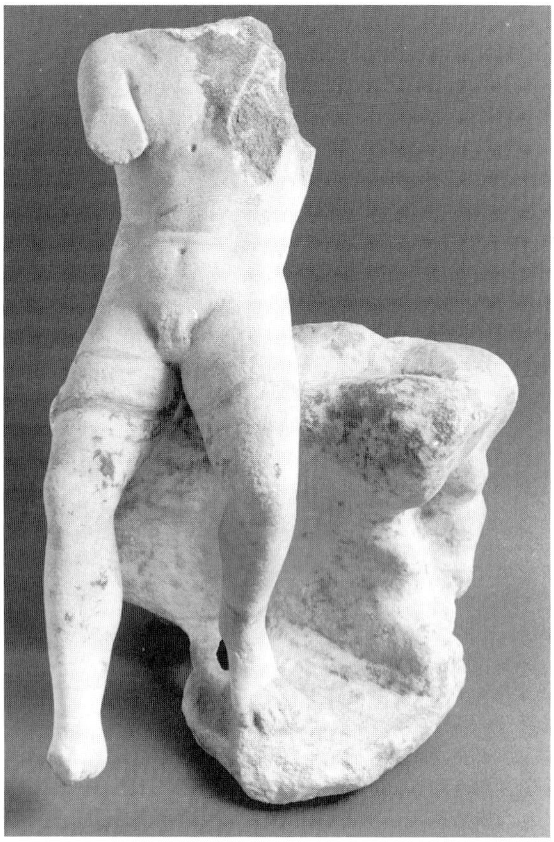

Fig. 1. Seated Hermes as ornamental fountain head. Note hole, for fountain spout, in rock behind left ankle. H. (as preserved) = 0.34 m.

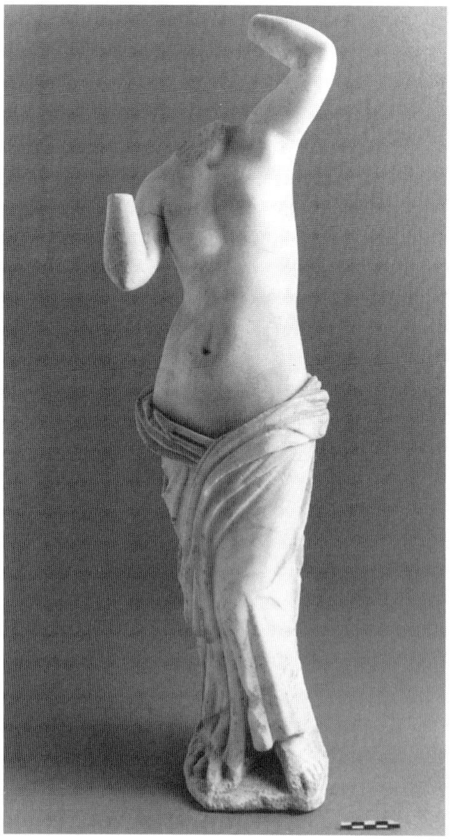

Fig. 2. Variant of the Venus Anadyomene type. H. (as preserved) = 0.58 m.

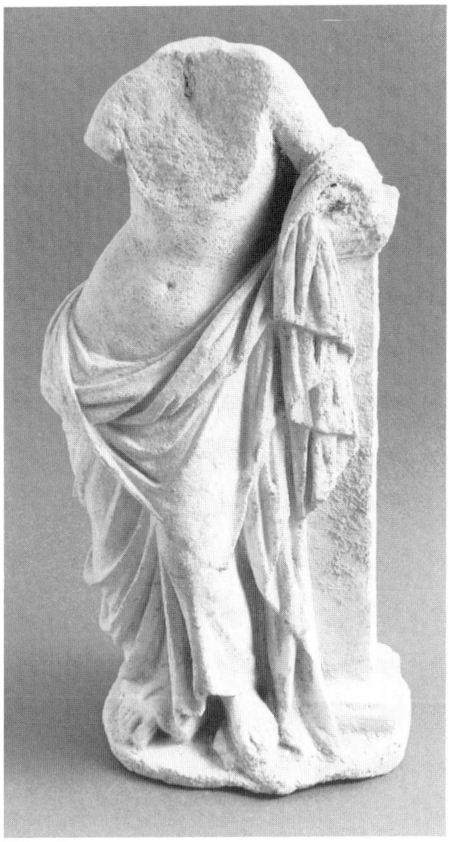

Fig. 3. Variant of the Leaning Aphrodite type. H. (as preserved) = 0.35 m.

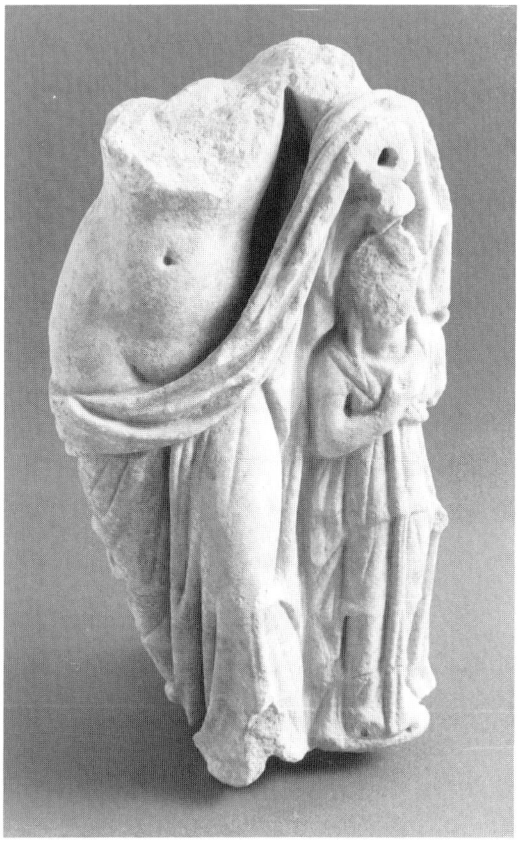

Fig. 4. Variant of the Aphrodite of Miletus type. H. (as preserved) = 0.32 m.

The *Anadyomene* type normally presents the drapery – since she holds her hands aloft – securely knotted in front.[12] The Paestum example (Fig. 2), however, does not. Yet she does offer posture, gesture and torso in customary manner – though reversed. The arrangement of her drapery comes close to that of the Aphrodite of Melos (here p. 173, Figs. 12–13), who similarly offers a precarious garment, though she cannot match the complexity of folds the Melian Aphrodite displays. She is also like the Melian Aphrodite in her complex and reversed movement; the left knee angles sharply to the right and downward while the upper torso twists upward and to the left. Proportions are elongated, an effect arrived at by narrowing the upper part of the torso by comparison with the hips. Such attenuation introduces a level of instability and is characteristic of works of the first century B.C.

Of the other two half-draped Aphrodites, one (Fig. 3) is a variant of the *Leaning Aphrodite* type, on which the sculptor has grafted passages more usually associated with the type known as the Venus Marina. She is linked to the Venus Marina by the triangle of drapery falling over the left knee. But posture is more supple; the weight is on the right leg, not the left; and the drapery does not cover the left upper arm. In terms of posture, and the leftward leaning against a rectangular pier at elbow height, the Paestum figure is much closer to the Leaning Aphrodite; closer, too, in terms of drapery since the Leaning Aphrodite type has the great swag of drapery looping across in front of the figure, winding around the advanced left forearm, and falling in stylised zigzags in front. Terracottas of the Leaning Aphrodite type appear in the fourth century B.C. and continue into the second half of the first. Slim proportions of the Santa Venera statuette suggest the later date.[13]

The third (Fig. 4) is an example of the *Aphrodite of Miletus* type. Noteworthy is the wide-ranging popularity of this type (Athens, Pompeii, Cyrene, Skepsis) and the ample evidence of piecing. The prototype is thought to have been of the second century B.C., with a terracotta figurine from Myrrhina signed by Aglaophon ca. 150 B.C. being the oldest example of a copy or adaptation which has survived.[14]

The Two Draped Aphrodites

Three other fully draped figures also represent divinities of which two again are images of Venus. One (Figs. 5–7), the largest of the whole ensemble, is a variant of the *Aphrodite Tiepolo* type; she leans casually on a cylindrical pillar, and has an Eros or Pothos perched on her right shoulder. Her drapery includes chiton, peplos and mantle.

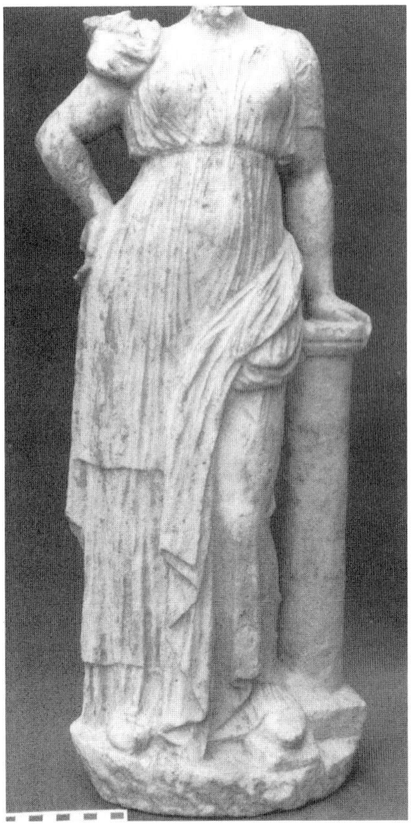

Fig. 5. Variant of the Aphrodite Tiepolo (Aphrodite Hegemone ?) type (= Venus Genetrix ?). H. (as preserved) 0.59 m. Frontal view.

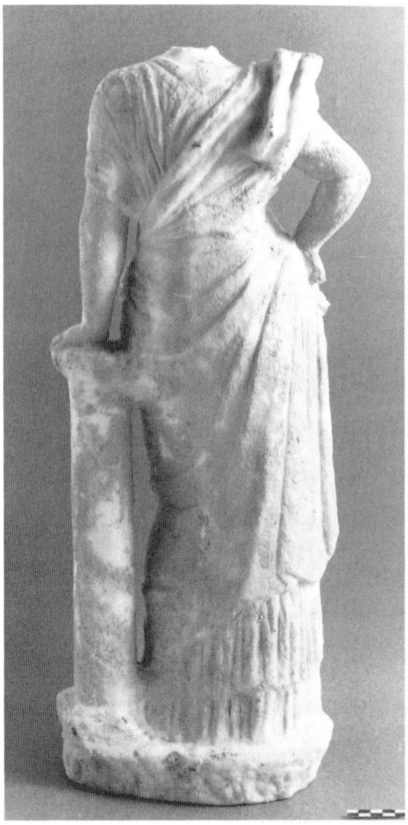

Fig. 6. Rear view of Fig. 5 showing legs of Eros or Pothos on shoulder.

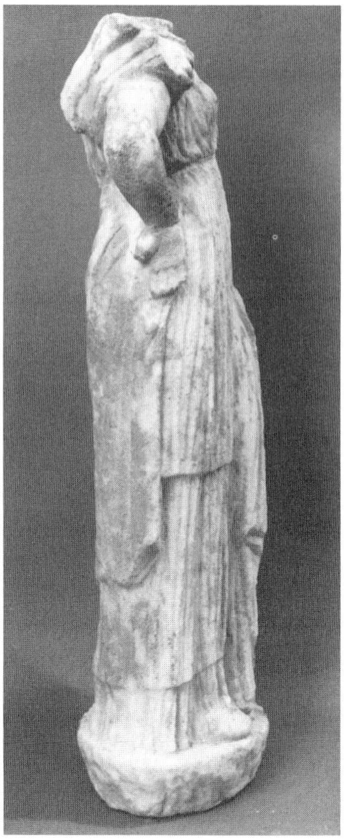

Fig. 7. Profile (right) view of Fig 5.

The chiton appears at the bottom of the figure and displays a buttoned sleeve along the left arm; the peplos is worn short and belted high, with a very long overfold which accounts for the two hem lines; the mantle, bunched up on the shoulder as a pad for the Eros figure, covers the back and swings forward over the left hip to the zigzag folds stacked in front.

The draping of the mantle to display the left leg brings to mind the *Aphrodite Hypolympidia* from the Isis sanctuary at Dion; with the difference that the north Greek Aphrodite is larger (though under life-size), deploys different gestures, and enjoys richer, more deeply carved drapery. The extra layers of clothing of the Santa Venera statuette, beyond those normally worn by examples of the type, may suggest a special stipulation or local variation. The type is represented in the Athenian Agora by an over life-size Hellenistic statue which may signal the origin of the type, and may have been an image of Aphrodite Hegemone of the Demos.

Connection between the Paestum version and the cult statue of Venus Genetrix has not gone unnoticed. Of special interest is the appearance of the Eros on Venus' shoulder as shown in *denarii* minted in 46 B.C., the very year of the dedication of the Forum of Caesar and the temple of Venus Genetrix in Rome.[15]

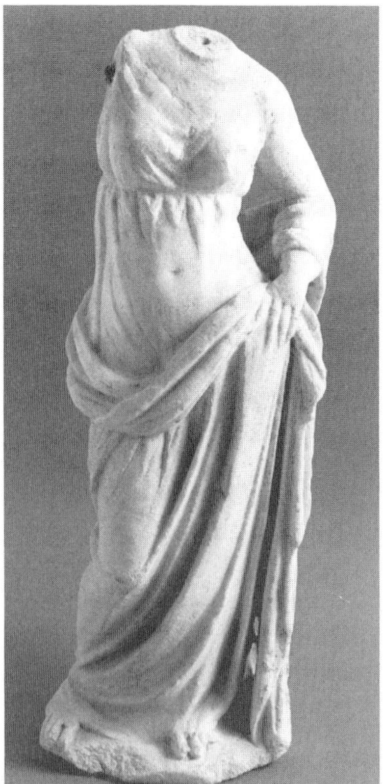

Fig. 8. Variant of standing draped Aphrodite (Tiepolo type ?). H. (as preserved) 0.46 m.

As to the other draped *Aphrodite* (Fig. 8), the angled movement of the upper part of the body contrasts both with the hipshot lateral displacement and the forward motion of the right knee, in typical Hellenistic juxtapositions. The motion so palpable in frontal view is imperceptible from the back. The structure, with narrow upper torso and broad hips, offers elongated proportions characteristically Late Hellenistic in date. Simplified from the chiaroscuro of second-century work, the drapery too seems typical of the first century. Fingers of the hand spread on the hip with index finger pointing are another Hellenistic trait, popular on Rhodes. Posture and gesture are again reminiscent of the *Aphrodite Hypolympidia* from Dion, though the principal incident of the drapery, the broad swathe of cloth from left hand to right ankle is obviously different.[16]

THE ARTEMIS (Fig. 9)

The final divinity is an Artemis identified by the peplos and baldric she wears. The composition is motionless with rigid limbs and still drapery. Treatment of folds is summary. At the back the surface is rough picked as if unfinished or meant to be invisible. At the front grooves and ridges of the overfold of the peplos seem mechanical, while in the lower part of the figure the presence of folds is only hinted at, the surface rough hewn, again as if unfinished. This is a schematic work the banality of which is typified by the right hand equipped with its four fingers but without a thumb.[17]

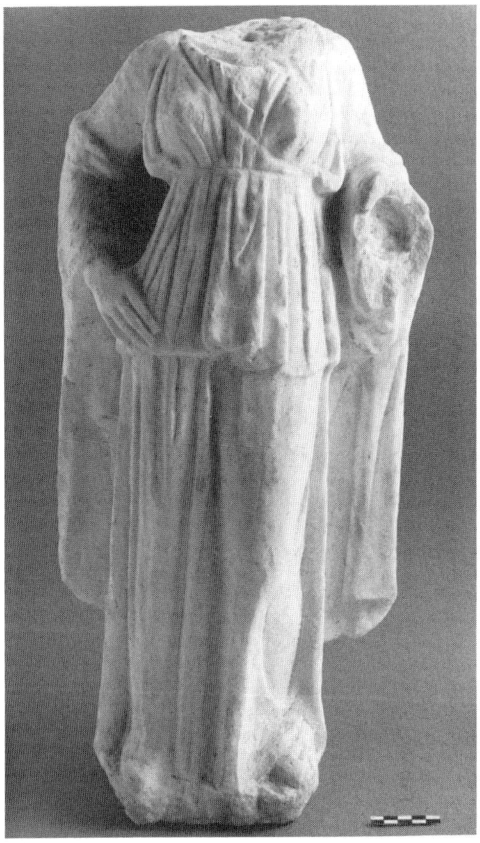

Fig. 9. Frontal Artemis. H. (as preserved) 0.53 m.

THE MORTAL (Fig. 10)

The seventh female statuette is of a heavily draped type, reminiscent of the women of Herculaneum. She holds an unidentified object in her left hand and wears a ring prominently on the second finger. This makes her a mortal, speaks to her high social standing, and allows us to think of her as a priestess or patroness. A similar female figure, under life-size and marble, wearing a ring and identified as a priestess, has come to light at Messene.[18]

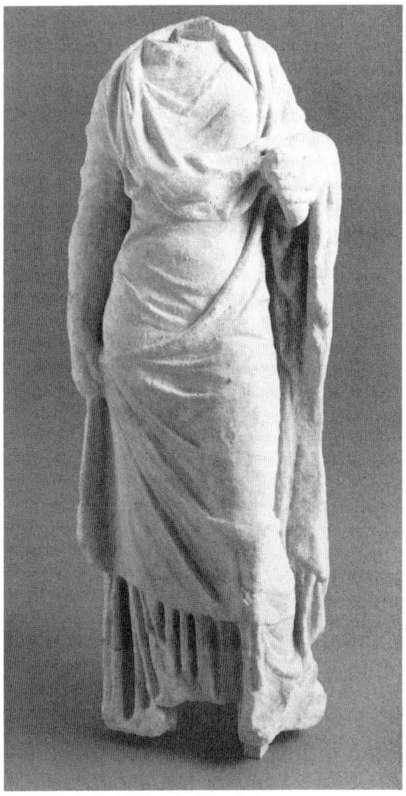

Fig. 10. Standing draped female figure (a priestess ?). H. (as preserved) 0.39 m.

The Group as a Whole

This group of statuettes bears witness to an impressive interest in classicism in certain circles in Paestum in the first century B.C. All the types represented evoke Greek prototypes; the subject matter is in origin Greek. Yet all are modified by Hellenistic variation of posture, gesture, composition, scale, or drapery. It is the altered poses in particular which suggest fresh characterisation and fresh aesthetic appeal.[19] Typological diversification and Hellenistic proportions work on Greek models with the result that the new versions are both retrospective and contemporary. How then were these statuettes displayed? Where were they made? And who paid for them?

Display

Since most, if not all, the figures were found in the ruined remains of a fountain, and since Venus figures and Hermes are at home in the context of nymphaea (and a draped non divine female also finds parallels among figures decorating fountains) it is logical to suppose that many of the figures were part of the sculptural ornament of the fountain.[20] It is probably useless to speculate on the precise arrangement beyond remarking that three of the figures were finished all the way round (the Hermes, the Anadyomene, and the Venus with Eros), and that they were therefore likely to have been visible from all sides. It is conceivable then that the Anadyomene and the Venus with Eros (the Genetrix) were more votive in character, though it is sure that the Hermes was ornamental. Others display varying degrees of completion, and will likely have stood in niches decorating the façade of the fountain.[21]

The choice of images will have been dictated partly by the cult, and by suitability to the architecture. Indeed, the appropriateness of Venus figures to a fountain may have influenced the choice of a fountain as a construction project in the first place. The choice will also have been influenced by the wishes of donors seeking prestige and popularity among those who visited the sanctuary and gazed at the fountain. Visitors will have appreciated the utility and amenity of the fountain and its symbolic meanings, and they will have known who the benefactors were. Shared visual experience of expressions of religious piety might have been thought to work towards social cohesion; and that might have been one motive. But it would be as well to bear in mind that one of the statuettes represents a non divine figure, and that whether she makes allusion to an actual person or not, all sculptural images can act as emblems of wealth, power, social distinction and ideology.[22] The juxtaposition of Greek sculptural types and Roman architectural form provides another example of that cultural schizophrenia – to use Coarelli's apt phrase[23] – which Cicero typifies when he rails publicly at Greeks in his speeches, but in the privacy of his home seems rather delighted by Greek things.

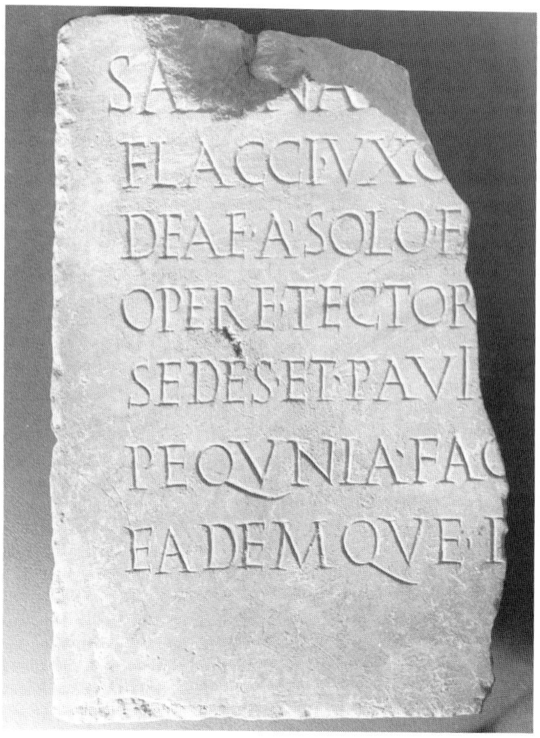

Fig. 11. Preserved left half of inscription detailing the contributions of Sabina (line 1) to the repair of the Oikos in the first century B.C. H. (as preserved) 0.387 m.

The Donors

Epigraphic evidence from the site tells of two major donors, both women, to the sanctuary. First, a certain Sabina who paid for the refurbishment of the Oikos (Fig. 11), and whose matrimonial career and chronology have been mapped for us by Mario Torelli.[24] A priestess in the sanctuary, and well-connected socially, she was active in the period ca. 50–10 B.C. A second benefactor, Valeria, grand-daughter of Sabina, paid for the reorganisation of the interior of the Hall, improvements to the West Wing, the installation of a kitchen, and the construction of the fish pond in the years ca. 10 B.C. – ca. A.D. 30.[25]

Cultural affiliation to events in Rome is evident. The interest of Julius Caesar and of Augustus in re-emphasising details of the foundation of Rome, Rome's mythological past, and Venus' role in it, is echoed here. As is the dictatorial and imperial zest for religious renewal, and for classical images as emblems of cultural unity and continuity. Enthusiasm for connection with a Greek past is clear not only in the use of Greek sculptural types in the fountain, but also in the use in Latin inscriptions from the site of Greek words such as "strongyla" and "mnamon".[26] Such verbal and visual reverence, and reference, allows the self concept of the sanctuary's religious and social élite to be seen both as an echo of Greek culture and as a synthesis of Greece and Rome.

In Rome, the forum of Caesar and the temple of Venus Genetrix were dedicated in 46 B.C. After Caesar's assassination, they were completed by Augustus; continuity of the ideological program was thus ensured.[27] Denarii struck in 46 B.C. depict the statue of the goddess. The goddess who founded the gens Julia was thus exalted. In Paestum, members of the local élite were quick to follow with the repair and elaboration of the ancient sanctuary of Aphrodite/Venus. Nothing could serve their aspirations, social and religious, more comprehensively than assimilation into the hierarchy of the cult of Venus, and thereby the achievement of a level of identification with the imperial family and the fate of Rome herself. The Oikos temple underwent repair from top to bottom at this time, as the archaeology tells us. It seems probable that the fountain was built at this time also since style, scale, and type of all the statuettes associated with it are at home in the first century B.C. But where were the statuettes made?

Workshops

Numerous statuettes of the many types of Venus, Artemis and Hermes have been recovered from all kinds of sites across the Roman world; they have been found in courtyards of houses, in gardens, shrines, small temples, and in fountain houses.[28] Not a few have come from Pompeii. Robert Cohon has shown, from the evidence of stone table supports, that marble carvers were active in Paestum ca. 20 B.C. – A.D. 70. Such craftsmen ae unlikely to have restricted their work to table supports and would probably also have produced oscilla and statuettes. So, it seems possible that the Santa Venera statuettes were produced locally. But Cohon's dates for the ateliers in Paestum seem too late for the Santa Venera pieces.[29] Other aspects which require attention, then, are (a) the marble itself, (b) where parallels are most frequently to be found, and (c) the social climate which called for the creation of the figures.

The Marble

The isotopic analysis of the Santa Venera statuettes, conducted by Professor Norman Herz and his team at the University of Georgia, suggests that four of the Paestum pieces are made of Parian, and four of Pentelic marble. Cohon identifies the marble of the table supports from Paestum as Pentelic or Carrara. He excludes Parian, and cites Martin Fredericksen on the sudden and wide ranging use of Carrara in Pompeii from the time of Augustus onward. This suggests that – merely on the basis of the origin of the marble – the Paestum statuettes made of Parian may not be dated to the first century A.D. Had they been made then, and in Italy, they would likely have been made of Carrara.

It is well-known that marble architectural elements, furnishings, statuettes and statues were exported from Greece in the first century, and more than 30 late Republican shipwrecks are known. The Mahdia shipwreck provides evidence for the earliest datable export of such materials, dated ca. 70 B.C. on the basis of the pottery used by the crew. The pristine surfaces of the architectural members show that these items had been recently finished, even if some were found broken. They had not been pillaged, but had been prepared specifically for export. The statues and statuettes on board were of Parian marble, but the architectural marbles – no fewer than 70 columns, capitals and bases – were of Pentelic. This quantity of Pentelic architectural members together with craters made of Pentelic marble and a number of Attic inscriptions show that most of the cargo came from Athens.[30]

The several (over a dozen) large scale statues retrieved from the other famous wreck, the Antikythera wreck, dated to ca. 80–50 B.C. by utilitarian pottery and stamped amphora handles, are all made of Parian marble. Both the Mahdia and the Antikythera vessels are thought to have been bound for Italy.[31] Moreover, the work of E. Rawson, M. Torelli and F. Coarelli, among others, has amply documented the involvement of rich Romans in the antiquities trade from Greece to Rome in the first century B.C.[32] Cicero himself (e.g. *Ad Fam.*7.23; *Ad Att.*1.8.2) of course was involved in this. So, the Paestum figures might have been imported from the East. If so, where from?

The Parallels

The figures made of Parian marble are the Hermes, the Leaning Aphrodite, the Miletus type and the index-finger pointing Venus. Where are parallels to be found? The sculpture of Hellenistic Paros remains largely unknown, and Samos' few Hellenistic statuettes provide no parallels. On Melos, production favoured large-scale figures (see here pp. 167–175). On Kos, only eight of 58 figures recently discussed by Renate Kabus-Preisshofen are statuettes; but earlier work had shown that statuettes were produced in some quantity. Statuettes are particularly plentiful on Delos (see here pp. 177–184), where literally hundreds have come to light, and Rhodes (see here pp. 137–148), both of which favoured Parian marble.[33]

Rhodes

There is much overlap of type and style between these two islands.[34] In terms of technique, both use much piecing; in terms of proportions of the female types, both prefer elongated torsos with narrow shoulders and broad hips; and both enjoy varied drapery arrangements. Three of the four Paestan figures made of Parian marble find parallels on both islands; the exception is the seated Hermes who only seems to appear on Rhodes. The index-finger pointing Venus seems to have enjoyed particular popularity there too, so that it would be logical to associate these two pieces – and maybe all four – with that island.[35] Other evidence for the import of statuettes from Rhodes into Italy is to be found in the material from the sanctuary of Artemis Mephitis at Rossano di Vaglio in Lucania. There, the statuettes, which include figures of Artemis, a head of Aphrodite, an Eros and the torso of a Hermaphrodite, are thought to have been made on Rhodes (or nearby) and brought to Rossano di Vaglio some time in the second century B.C., some pieces as late as ca. 100 B.C.[36] Female statuettes from Palestrina, of the last years of the second century, have also been associated with Rhodes, and provide more evidence for the reception of Greek figural products in Italy in the years following the conquest of Greece.[37] But, on the basis solely of typological parallels and marble quality, the Paestan examples of the Miletus type and the Leaning Aphrodite may equally well have come from Delos.

Delos

Marcadé proposed the existence on Delos of at least seven workshops, and pointed to the large quantities of unfinished sculpture found in the Agora of the Italians.[38] The quantity of production suggested to him that the commercial activities of Roman agents included a brisk trade in sculptures. Mithridates sacked the island in 88 B.C., but sculptural production continued until another ransacking of the island by pirates in 69.[39] Thereafter, the production of portraits ceased, but epigraphic evidence tells of Roman entrepreneurs on the island until ca. 50 B.C. Accordingly, Bruneau suggested a slow deterioration of conditions on Delos with neither Mithridates nor the pirates doing irreparable damage.[40] So it might be possible to conclude that marble statuettes, if not portraits, continued as items of commercial activity until the inscriptions stop at mid century. It would then be arguable that the Miletus type and the Leaning Aphrodite, both of Parian marble, come from Delos. This seems rather far-fetched, and it is easier to suppose that they were made on Rhodes, where parallels exist, than to imagine that statuettes continued to be made on Delos when portraits did not.

Athens

The statuettes made of Pentelic marble are the Venus Anadyomene, the Artemis, the decorous Roman matron and the Venus with Eros. The Anadyomene finds parallels everywhere. The surface has a rather waxy look, which might be described as marzipan-like and associated with Delos.[41] Yet, the use of Pentelic on Delos is so rare that the figure was more probably an Athenian product. The Venus with Eros on her shoulder is found in Athens and Corinth, but is unknown (so far) to me on Rhodes or Delos.[42] She wears the filmy clinging drapery with folds and creases more engraved than modelled which is characteristic of the city in Late Hellenistic times. The Artemis finds parallels on Rhodes and Delos, but of island, not Pentelic marble. The Roman matron is paralleled on the Greek mainland, but not, to my knowledge so far, elsewhere. So, these four figures may have come from Athens. Sulla sacked the city in 86 B.C., to be sure, and many artists probably perished or fled.[43] But revitalisation is evident by the middle years of the century, stimulated by lavish gifts to the city first by Pompey and then by Julius Caesar. And there is plenty of evidence to show that rich Romans seeking Greek things with which to bedeck their gardens, libraries and their villas looked to Athens.

The Social Climate

Social and religious conditions in Paestum in the middle years of the first century emphasise the appeal which association with a gift of Greek marble statuettes to a sanctuary would have had for a member of the upwardly mobile local élite like Sabina, wife (probably though not certainly) of the Caesarian senator, C. Cocceius Flaccus. It seems likely then that the fountain and its decorative sculpture were a part of the sanctuary's renovation begun by her. The persistence of the use of Greek sculptural types, however modified by novelty of posture, gesture, scale, drapery and placement for use in Roman contexts, speaks eloquently to the strength of the conservative strain in Roman life. It reminds us both that most practitioners of sculpture in Italy itself in the first century B.C. were of Greek origin, and that large numbers of Greek statues and statuettes were imported from Greece. It reminds us too that the Roman manipulators of this cultural heritage were adept at the use of religious revival and the visualisation of the mythological past for political ends.

In terms of provenance and the identification of specific characteristics of particular schools, it is hard to know whether to give more weight to typological parallels or to technical observation of surface treatment or to historical conditions or to scientific analysis of the marble. Certainly the Paestum statuettes have resisted any attempt to group them on these bases as the products of a single shop; and it may be that their presence as a group contributes to the theory that no distinctions may be drawn between shops, and that all workshops used many styles and types, at the discretion of the patron. It is always possible that Arkesilaos or one of his colleagues made the whole lot somewhere in Italy before the use of Cararra became the rage. The discussion is, perhaps inevitably, indecisive. But I risk the conjecture that four were made in Athens (the Anadyomene, the Venus with Eros, the priestess and the Artemis), on the basis of typological parallels and the marble used; and that the other four were made on Rhodes (the Hermes, the Index-finger pointer, the Miletus type and the Leaning Aphrodite) on the same grounds. It looks as if they formed a job lot put together by an agent in Athens in answer to an order placed from Paestum for "*statues suitable for a fountain in a sanctuary of Venus*" along the lines of Cicero's requests to Atticus.[44]

Acknowledgements

I am grateful to many colleagues for advice in the preparation of this paper. I wish to acknowledge a special debt to Olga Palagia who made many helpful suggestions, and to Mario Torelli whose insights are a constant source of pleasure and satisfaction.

Notes

1. On the walls see H.Schlager, *RM* 69, 1962, 21ff.; id., *RM* 76, 1969, 355ff. On the temples, F.Krauss, *Paestum, die griechischen Tempel* (1941); id., *Die Tempel von Paestum*, I,1. *Der Athenatempel* (1959); D. Mertens, *Der Alte Heratempel in Paestum und die archaische Baukunst in Unteritalien* (1993). On other structures and topography within the walls, E. Greco & D. Theodorescu, *Poseidonia-Paestum* I (1980), II (1983), III (1985). On extramural sanctuaries, various authors, *I Santuari* in *Atti di CMGr* (1988); A. Ardovino, *I culti di Paestum*

antica e del suo territorio (1986); M. Cipriani, *San Nicola di Albanella, scavo di un santuario campestre nel territorio di Poseidonia-Paestum* (1989).

2. Much of the area south of the city has been surveyed and reported on by colleagues and students of E. Greco (documents in the offices of the Soprintendenza), while the area northeast of the city and astride the route of the Salso stream has been surveyed by M. Skele, *A Chorography of Poseidonia* (diss. Washington University, 1994). See also E. Greco, *DialA* 1, 1979, 51ff. On the sanctuary at Santa Venera see J.G. Pedley, *Greeks and Romans in Southern Italy* (1990) 129ff.; J.G. Pedley, M. Torelli (et al.), *The Sanctuary of Santa Venera at Paestum* (1993) *passim.*
3. On cemeteries : various authors, *Il Museo di Paestum* (1986) 101ff.; A. Greco Pontrandolfo & A. Rouveret in *La mort, les morts dans les sociétés anciennes* (1982) 229ff.; M. Cipriani, *DialA* 7, 1989, 71ff.; on the Tomb of the Diver, M. Napoli, *La Tomba del Tuffatore* (1970), rev. R. Bianchi Bandinelli, *DialA* 4–5, 1970–1971, 135ff.
4. On the architecture of the sanctuary see J.G. Pedley – J. Higginbotham in Pedley – Torelli (supra n. 2) 55ff.; for the Olympia building, A. Mallwitz, *Olympia und seine Bauten* (1972) 266ff.; for the late archaic shrine of Aphrodite at Locri, see M. Barra Bagnasco (ed.), *Locri Epizefiri* IV: *Lo scavo di Marasà Sud, Il sacello tardo arcaico e la "casa dei leoni"* (1992).
5. On a group of terracotta figurines which testify to the use of the sanctuary as an open air shrine in the sixth century and to connections with oriental prototypes see R. Miller Ammerman, *AJA* 95, 1991, 203ff.
6. P. Sestieri, *FA* 1953, 131, no. 1710, fig. 39.
7. *LIMC* III (1986) s.v. Eros, no. 482 (H. Cassimatis).
8. B. Kapossy, *Brunnenfiguren der hellenistischen und römischen Zeit* (1969) 38–40.
9. *LIMC* II (1984) s.v. Apollon, no. 165 (O. Palagia); Kapossy (supra n. 8) 21.
10. Most conveniently in M. Bieber, *The Sculpture of the Hellenistic Age*[2] (1961) 41–42, figs. 106–108.
11. *LIMC* V (1990) s.v. Hermes, nos. 961-962,"Hermès en repos" (G. Siebert); M. Bieber, *AM* 37,1912, 174ff.; B.S. Ridgway, *Fifth Century Styles in Greek Sculpture* (1981) 242.
12. The type is widespread: *LIMC* II (1984) s.v. Aphrodite, nos. 667–677 (A. Delivorrias); M. Bieber, *Ancient Copies* (1977) 68; D. Brinkerhoff, *Hellenistic Statues of Aphrodite* (1978) 56ff.; W. Neumer-Pfau, *Studien zur Ikonographie und Gesellschaftlichen Funktion hellenistischer Aphrodite-Statuen* (1982) 157ff., 242f; H.H. von Prittwitz und Gaffron, *Der Wandel der Aphrodite: archäologische studien zu weiblichen halbbekleideten Statuetten des späten Hellenismus* (1988); C.M. Havelock, *The Aphrodite of Knidos and her Successors* (1995) 86ff.
13. *LIMC* II, s.v. Aphrodite, nos. 554–555; 570–576; G. Becatti, *Ninfe e divinità marine. Ricerche mitologiche, iconografiche e stilistiche* (1971) 17–23; 50–57; R. Calza – M. Squarciapino, *Museo Ostiense* (1962) 31; E. Paribeni, *Catalogo delle sculture di Cirene* (1959) no. 243.
14. *LIMC* II, s.v. Aphrodite, nos. 551–553; Bieber (supra n. 12) 95f.
15. *LIMC* II, s.v. Aphrodite, nos. 293–306. Eros appears with the standing Aphrodite in numerous arrangements: seated on a pillar (*LIMC* II, s.v. Aphrodite, nos. 582–583, fourth century B.C.), standing on a pillar (*LIMC* II, s.v. Aphrodite, no. 586, second century B.C.), clinging onto Aphrodite's upper right arm (*LIMC* II, s.v. Aphrodite, no. 268, third century B.C.), standing on the left hand and leaning against the left shoulder of Venus Genetrix (= Antonia Minor). He appears seated on the shoulder of the statuette found at Chaironeia in Boeotia and now in Athens (Athens, National Museum 680), and poised on the shoulder, as with the Santa Venera figure, of the statuettes from the Athenian Agora and from Corinth (*LIMC* II, s.v. Aphrodite, nos. 300 and 303). On the over life-size Hellenistic representative of the type (though without the Eros) see E.B.Harrison, in *Akten des XIII internationalen Kongresses für klassische Archäologie. Berlin 1988* (1990) 346. On the coins, see M. Crawford, *Roman Republican Coinage* (1974) 473 and 92. On the appearance of the image elsewhere see M. Torelli, *Typology and Structure of Roman Historical Reliefs* (1982) 73ff., with which cf. D. Kleiner, *Roman Sculpture* (1992) 100; 146; R. Cappelli, *Ostraka* II.1, 1993, 57ff., esp. 63. On the pair as a statuary group see V. Machaira, *Les groupes statuaires d'Aphrodite et d'Eros* (1993) 101–111.
16. *LIMC* II, s.v Aphrodite, nos. 293–296, for posture and gesture. G. Merker, *SIMA* 40, *The Hellenistic Sculpture of Rhodes* (1973) no. 20, figs. 20–21; no. 21, figs. 22–23; no. 22, figs. 24–25. R. Horn, *Stehende weibliche Gewandstatuen in der hellenistischen Plastik* (1931) 89f. *Aphrodite Hypolympidia*: D. Pandermalis, *Δίον. Αρχαιολογικός χώρος και Μουσείο.* (Athens 1997) 26–27; 74.
17. *LIMC* II, s.v. Artemis, no. 521 (L. Kahil – N. Icard); Bieber (supra n. 12) 72; M. Fullerton, *AM* 102, 1987, 259ff.; id., *The Archaistic Style in Roman Statuary, Mnemosyne* Suppl. 110 (1990) 13ff.
18. Bieber (supra n. 10) figs. 524–525; 744–745 (Pudicitia types); 748; 751 (women of Herculaneum); A. Linfert, *Kunstzentren hellenistischer Zeit* (1976) 58–60; 147–156; 160–163. For such a figure in a nymphaeum context see G. Bendinelli, *ASAtene* 1, 1914, 139, fig. 3; and E. Herkenrath in T. Wiegand (ed.), *Milet* I, Heft 5, *Das Nymphaeum* (1919) 58, fig. 5. For a fragment of a similar female figure, under life-size and marble, wearing a ring, holding a figurine and identified as a priestess, see N. Kaltsas, *Αρχαία Μεσσήνη* (1989) 38, no. 16, fig. 25; G. Despinis, *Χαριστήριον εις Ά. Όρλάνδον* II (1966) 233–235; P. Themelis in R. Hägg (ed.), *Ancient Greek Cult Practice from the Epigraphical Evidence* (1994) 115–116, fig. 19 (references I owe to the kindness of Olga Palagia).
19. On Roman versions of Greek prototypes see P.Zanker, *Klassizistische Statuen* (1974) *passim*; V.W. Strocka, *JdI* 94, 1979, 143ff.; B.S. Ridgway in E. MacDougall and W.F. Jashemski (edd.), *Ancient Roman Gardens* (1981) 7–28; on Aphrodite, D. Brinkerhoff in D.G. Mitten, J.G. Pedley and J. Scott (edd.), *Studies Presented to G.M.A. Hanfmann* (1971) 9ff.; P. Karanastassis, *AM* 101, 1986, 207ff.; M. Brinke, *Kopienkritische und typologische Untersuchungen zur statuarischen Überlieferung der Aphrodite Typus Louvre-Neapel* (1991) *passim*; other aspects, see Fullerton, *The Archaistic Style in Roman Statuary*, 190–206; E. Bartman, *Ancient Sculptural Copies in Miniature* (1992) 1–48.

20. On Roman fountains and their decoration see N. Neuerburg, *L'Architettura delle fontane e dei ninfei dell'Italia antica*, Memorie dell'Accademia di Archeologia Lettere e Belle Arti di Napoli 5 (1965); G. Hornbostel-Huttner, *Studien zur römischer Nischenarchitektur* (1979); F. Gläser, *Antike Brunnenbauten (KPANAI) in Griechenland*, Österreichische Akademie, Phil.Hist.Klasse Denkschriften 161 (1983); W. Letzner, *Römische Brunnen und Nymphaea in der westlichen Reichshalfte* (1990). On the nymphaeum of Pollio at Ephesos see F. Miltner, *ÖJh* 43, 1956–1958, Beibl. 48; 45, 1960, Beibl. 28–41; A. Bammer, *ÖJh* 51, 1976–1977, Beibl. 76–91, and B. Andreae in *Festschrift F. Brommer* (1977) 1–13. See also B. Andreae et al., *Baia: Il ninfeo imperiale sommerso di Punta Epitaffio* (1983); R. Bol, *Das Statuenprogram des Herodes-Atticus Nymphaeum, OF* XV (1984); G. Bendinelli, *ASAtene* 1,1914, 139ff.
21. For other sanctuary groups of marble statuettes see R. Kabus-Jahn, *AntPl* XI (1972) 7ff., and R. Kabus-Preishofen, *AntPl* XV (1975) 31ff.
22. E. Gruen, *Culture and National Identity in Republican Rome* (1992) 131–182.
23. F. Coarelli, *DialA* 3 series, 1, 1983–1984, 45–53.
24. M. Torelli, *Annali della Facoltà di Lettere e Filosofia*, Università degli Studi di Perugia 18:1, 1980–1981, 103ff.; id. in Pedley – Torelli (supra n. 2) 204ff.
25. Torelli in Pedley – Torelli (supra n. 2) 195ff.
26. Torelli (supra n. 25) 200–203.
27. On ideology and idealism in Rome at this time see P. Zanker, in *Le Classicisme à Rome*, Entretients Fondation Hardt 25 (1978) 283ff.; J.J. Pollitt, *TAPA* 108, 1978, 155ff.; R. Neudecker, *Die Skulpturen Ausstattung römischer Viller in Italien* (1988); P. Zanker, *The Power of Images in the Age of Augustus* (1988); B.A. Kellum in K. Raaflaub and M. Toher (edd.), *Between Republic and Empire: Interpretations of Augustus and his Principate* (1990) 276ff.; M. Torelli in M. Pani (ed.), *Continuità e trasformazioni fra reppublica e principato* (1991) 47ff. On the geography of the cult of Venus Genetrix see J. Rives, *Phoenix* 48, 1994, 294–306.
28. For the contexts in which such statuettes were placed see: P. Grimal, *Les Jardins romains* (1943) *passim*; Kapossy (supra n. 8) 12–18; 27; C.C. Vermeule, *Greek Sculpture and Roman Taste* (1977) 11ff.; E. Dwyer, *Pompeian Domestic Sculpture* (1982) 246ff.; B.S. Ridgway, *Roman Copies of Greek Sculpture: the Problem of the Originals* (1984) 72ff.; E. Gazda and A. Haeckl (edd.), *Roman Art in the Private Sphere* (1991) 73ff. For a contrast between more opulent, varied decor and more modest see S. de Caro, in *Ancient Roman Villa Gardens* (1987) 77ff. Such examples in marble had their yet more numerous counterparts in terracotta, for which, for example, see D. Kassab, *Statuettes en terre cuite de Myrina* (1988) 32ff.; 46ff.; 53ff., where countless Aphrodite types are listed.
29. R. Cohon, *Stone Table Supports* (diss. New York University, 1988) 100ff.; 152ff.
30. For shipwrecks in the later first century B.C. see P. Gianfrotta and P. Pomey, *Archeologia subacquea* (1981) 190ff. On the Mahdia shipwreck see W. Fuchs, *Der Schiffsfund von Mahdia* (1963); for a convenient summary of the marbles on board see A. Stewart, *Greek Sculpture: An Exploration* (1990) 229; for an overview of some aspects see B. Barr-Sharrar, *The Hellenistic and Early Imperial Decorative Bust* (1987) 23ff. Most importantly, see G.H. Salies, H.H. von Prittwitz und Gaffron, G. Bauchhens (edd.), *Das Wrack. Der Antike Schiffsfund von Mahdia* (1994) in which, see, for the date of the wreck on the basis of the pottery, S. Rotroff, 143, and for the marble from which the sculptures were made, N. Overtani, 297. Most recently, W. Geominy, *Archeo* 10, 1995, 48ff, and B.S. Ridgway, *JRA* 8, 1995, 340ff.
31. On the Antikythera wreck see G.D. Weinberg, V.G. Grace, G.R. Edwards, H.S. Robinson, P. Throckmorton, E.K. Ralph, *TAPS* n.s. 55.3, 1965; P.C. Bol, *Die Skulpturen des Schiffsfundes von Antikythera* (1972); for the date of this wreck on the basis of the utilitarian pottery on board and stamped amphora handles, see Rotroff in *Das Wrack* (supra n. 30) 139, and for the destination of this vessel and the Mahdia ship, see H.-U. Cain, O. Drager in *Das Wrack* (supra n. 30) 257.
32. For this commerce see E. Rawson, *BSR* 43, 1975, 36ff.; M. Torelli, *MemAmAc* 36 (1980) 313–323; F. Coarelli, *DialA* 3 series, 1, 1983–1984, 45–53.
33. For Samos see R. Horn, *Hellenistische Bildwerke auf Samos, Samos* XII (1972); for Kos see L. Laurenzi, *ASAtene* 17–18, 1955–56, 59ff. R. Kabus-Preisshofen, *Die hellenistische Plastik der Insel Kos,* 14. Ergh. *AM* (1989); for Rhodes see Merker (supra n. 16); G. Gualandi, *ASAthene* 54, 1976, 7ff.; here pp. 137–148; for Delos see J. Marcadé, *Au Musée de Délos* (1969); M. Kreeb, *Untersuchungen zur figürlichen Ausstattung Delischer Privathauser* (1988); here pp. 177–184.
34. Marcadé (supra n. 33) 484ff.
35. For a parallel to the Hermes, see Gualandi (supra n. 33) 143; for the Index finger pointer see Merker (supra n. 16) figs. 20–23.
36. On the sanctuary at Rossano di Vaglio see D. Adamesteanu & H. Dilthey, *Macchia di Rossano: il santuario della Mefitis* (1992) and M. Denti *La Statuaria in marmo del santuario di Rossano di Vaglio* (1992). In this context see also F. Coarelli, in *Storia di Roma. 2. L'Impero mediterraneo.* I. *La republica imperiale* (1990); P. Bilde, I. Nielsen, M. Nielsen (edd.), *Aspects of Hellenism in Italy: Towards a Cultural Unity? Acta Hyperborea* 5, *Danish Studies in Classical Archaeology* (1993).
37. On the Palestrina analogies, and others see Denti (supra n. 36) 30. For Sicilian comparisons see N. Bonacasa and E. Joly, in *Sikanie. Storia e civiltà della Sicilia greca* (1985) 277ff., figs. 321–322.
38. Marcadé (supra n. 3) 102ff.; restated by F. Coarelli in *DialA* 3 series, 1, 1983–1984, 48–50; see also C.F. Moss, *Roman Marble Tables* (diss. Princeton, 1989) 120ff.
39. Coarelli (supra n. 38) 48.
40. P. Bruneau, *BCH* 92, 1968, 671ff.
41. Stewart (supra n. 30) 226; id., *Attika: Studies in Athenian Sculpture of the Hellenistic Age, JHS* Suppl. 14 (1979) 90.
42. E.g. *LIMC* II, s.v. Aphrodite, no. 300.
43. Plutarch, *Sulla* 14; Appian, *Mithr.* 38.
44. Cicero's correspondence with Atticus on this topic is conveniently compiled by M. Marvin, in *Retaining the Original: Multiple Originals, Copies, and Reproductions, Studies in the History of Art* 20, National Gallery of Art, Washington, D.C. (1989) 29–45.

Τα ανάγλυφα φατνώματα του Ιερού της Σαμοθράκης

Αλέξανδρος Μάντης

Η επιστροφή μου σε ένα θέμα που με απασχόλησε πριν από μερικά χρόνια,[1] υπαγορεύθηκε από νέα ευρήματα και διαπιστώσεις, που εντάσσουν τα έργα, τα οποία θα σχολιάσουμε σε έναν χώρο, που αποτελεί αντικείμενο πολυετών αρχαιολογικών ερευνών της διοργανώτριας αυτού του συνεδρίου Αμερικανικής Σχολής Κλασικών Σπουδών.

Το αποσπασματικά σωζόμενο ανάγλυφο του Μουσείου Θάσου Λ 3255 (εικ. 1–4), τυχαίο και αστρωματογράφητο εύρημα του 1973 από την θέση Νυστέρνι της Θάσου, έμελλε στα χρόνια που ακολούθησαν από την εύρεσή του να μας αποκαλύψει, όχι ανώδυνα, την αρχική του προέλευση και να μας διαφωτίσει για μια κατηγορία αρχιτεκτονικών αναγλύφων εξαιρετικά σπάνιων στον ελλαδικό χώρο.

Το ανάγλυφο από χονδρόκοκκο θασίτικο μάρμαρο, που κοσμείται με παρασταση κενταύρου στραμμένου προς τα δεξιά έχει ύψος 40, μήκος 54,5 και πάχος 16,5 εκ. Η λεπτή πλάκα, πάνω στην οποία προβαλλόταν, πάχους από 2,8 έως 4 εκ., είναι σπασμένη σύριζα σχεδόν στο περίγραμμα του σωζομένου κορμού. Το έργο στις πρώτες συνοπτικές αναφορές του χαρακτηρίσθηκε ως μετόπη, τόσο από την Χ. Κουκούλη,[2] όσο και από τον ερευνητή της θασιακής πλαστικής B. Holtzmann,[3] ο οποίος μάλιστα διέκρινε τότε και στυλιστική σχέση του με τα γλυπτά του Παρθενώνα.

Οι εκτιμήσεις αυτές για τον χαρακτηρισμό του αναγλύφου δεν άφησαν προφανώς ανεπηρέαστο τον συνάδελφο Ζ. Μπόνια,[4] που ασχολήθηκε διεξοδικά με το ανάγλυφο καταλήγοντας και αυτός στο ίδιο συμπέρασμα, όχι μόνο από το θέμα του αλλά και από ορισμένα τεχνικά χαρακτηριστικά, όπως κάποιες ανεπεξέργαστες γλυπτές επιφάνειες και το πάχος της πλάκας, ασυμβίβαστα κατά την άποψή του με την μορφή ενός ελέυθερου αναγλύφου.

Το ανάγλυφο αποκαταστάθηκε σχεδιαστικά ως μετόπη, παρά την επισήμανσή του, ότι "ανάγλυφη μετόπη με θέμα την κενταυρομαχία είναι πρωτόφαντο εύρημα για την Θάσο" και οι αρχικές διαστάσεις του υπολογίσθηκαν περίπου σε 80x75 εκ. Στην παράσταση αναγνωρίσθηκε ένας τοξευμένος κένταυρος, τη στιγμή που προσπαθεί να αποσπάσει με το δεξί του χέρι το βέλος από το σώμα του και υποτέθηκε ότι στην επόμενη προς τα δεξιά μετόπη θα πρέπει να εικονιζόταν ο Ηρακλής κατά το πρότυπο του αναγλύφου της ομώνυμης πύλης της Θάσου, στο τόξο του οποίου οφείλεται ο τραυματισμός του κενταύρου.

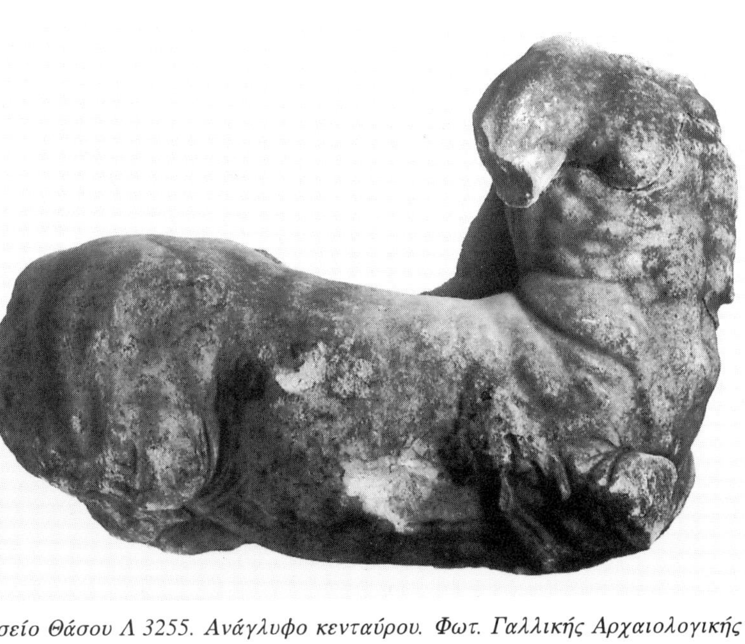

Εικ. 1. Μουσείο Θάσου Λ 3255. Ανάγλυφο κενταύρου. Φωτ. Γαλλικής Αρχαιολογικής Σχολής.

Το ανάγλυφο χρονολογήθηκε στην κλασική εποχή, γύρω στα 430 π. Χ. και ο συγγραφέας υπαινίχθηκε κάποια πιθανή σχέση του με το Ηράκλειο της Θάσου.

Το ανάγλυφο όμως δεν προσφέρει στοιχεία για μια χρονολόγηση στα κλασικά χρόνια, όπως υποστηρίχθηκε. Η απόδοση των ανατομικών λεπτομερειών με τις σφικτοδεμένες φόρμες και την έντονη διακύμανση των όγκων, μαρτυρούν μιαν άλλη πλαστική αντίληψη και προσεγγίζουν το έργο περισσότερο σε ελληνιστικές δημιουργίες. Το θέμα του κενταύρου άλλωστε, με εξαιρετικά φτωχή εικονογραφική παράδοση στον βορειοελλαδίτικο χώρο (υπολείμματα ψηφιδωτών στην Πέλλα[5] και στην Ολυνθο[6]) όπως έδειξε η Schiffler,[7] απουσιάζει τελείως από την αρχιτεκτονική πλαστική αυτής της περιοχής με εξαίρεση μόνον την Σαμοθράκη.

Στη Σαμοθράκη, όπου εμπλέκονται από τον προηγούμενο ήδη αιώνα οι δραστηριότητες τεσσάρων ξένων αρχαιολογικών αποστολών, των Γάλλων, των Αυστριακών, των Τσεχοσλοβάκων και των Αμερικανών, η σκαπάνη του Conze το 1873 αποκάλυψε θραύσματα από έξεργα ανάγλυφα κενταύρων από θασίτικο μάρμαρο,[8] τα περισσότερα από τα οποία αξιοποιήθηκαν από τον γλύπτη K. von Zumbusch στη Βιέννη, προκειμένου να αποκατασταθεί

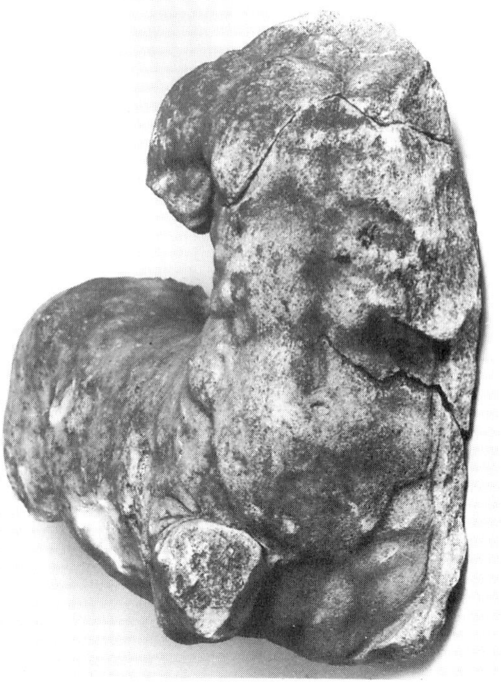

Εικ. 2. Μουσείο Θάσου Λ 3255. Ανάγλυφο κενταύρου. Φωτ. Γαλλικής Αρχαιολογικής Σχολής.

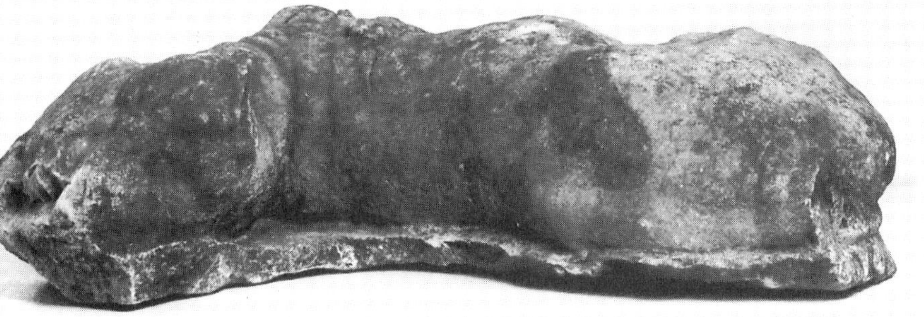

Εικ. 3. Μουσείο Θάσου Λ 3255. Ανάγλυφο κενταύρου. Φωτ. Γαλλικής Αρχαιολογικής Σχολής.

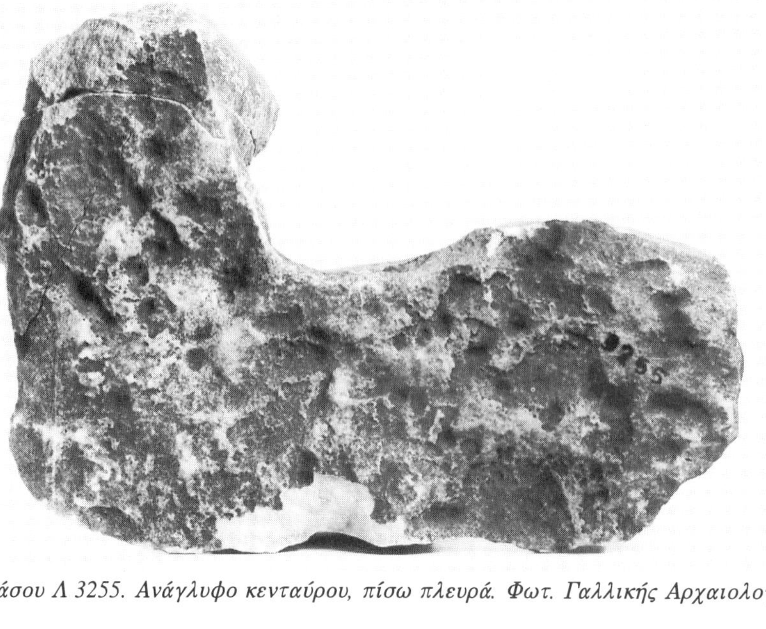

Εικ. 4. Μουσείο Θάσου Λ 3255. Ανάγλυφο κενταύρου, πίσω πλευρά. Φωτ. Γαλλικής Αρχαιολογικής Σχολής.

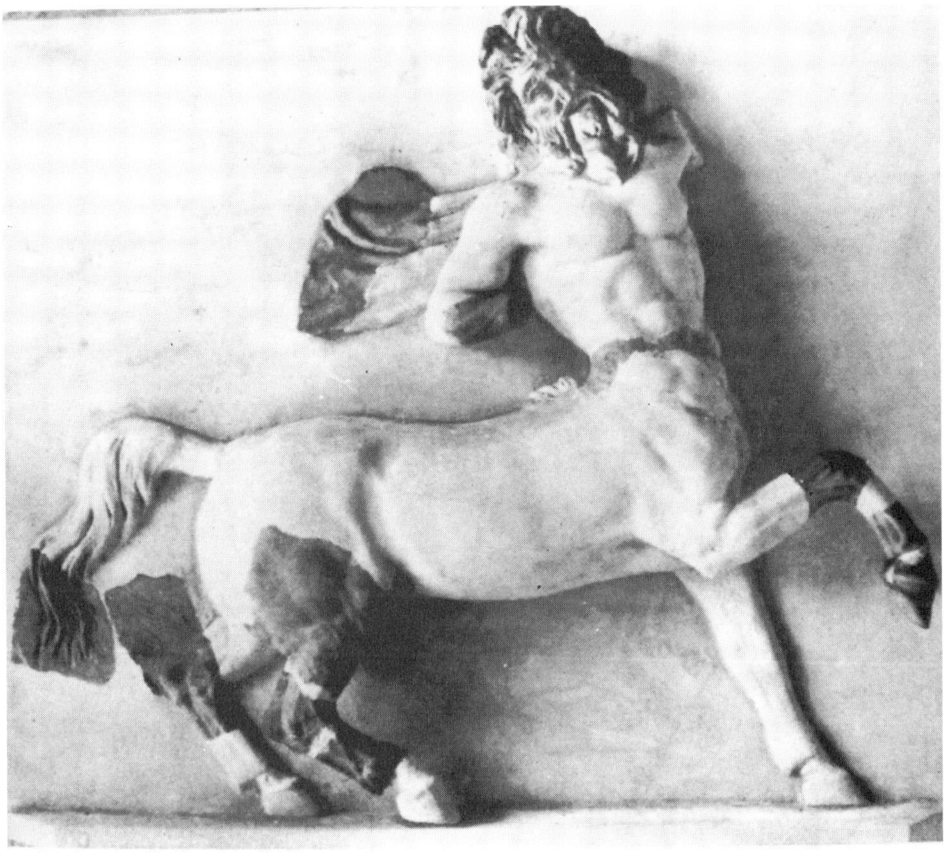

Εικ. 5. Βιέννη, Kunsthistorisches Museum. Αποκατάσταση αναγλύφου με παράσταση κενταύρου. Αναπαραγωγή από Samothrace 3, 1, εικ. 187.

μια ανάγλυφη πλάκα με παράσταση καλπάζοντος και στραμένου προς τα δεξιά κενταύρου (εικ. 5), άγνωστου όμως προορισμού.[9] Στα θραύσματα της Βιέννης προστέθηκαν αργότερα και άλλα, που αποκάλυψαν οι Αμερικανικές ανασκαφές υπό τον K. Lehmann στο χώρο του Ιερού.[10] Τα νέα θραύσματα, που προέρχονταν και αυτά από δεξιόστροφους κενταύρους, επιβεβαίωναν σε γενικές γραμμές την αποκατάσταση στο Kunsthistorisches Museum της Βιέννης και μαρτυρούσαν ότι πρέπει να υπήρχαν περισσότερες παρόμοιες πλάκες. Στο μεταξύ, η μελέτη της μαρμάρινης οροφής του προνάου του Ιερού από τον M. Jones, οδηγούσε στην διαπίστωση ότι αυτή περιελάμβανε διαφόρων μεγεθών φατνώματα, που δέχονταν ξεχωριστά δουλεμένα καλύμματα, τα μεγαλύτερα από τα οποία συνέπιπταν στις διαστάσεις τους με τα ανάγλυφα των κενταύρων, εφόσον αυτά τοποθετούνταν στο εσωτερικό επίπεδο των φατνωμάτων, που έχει διαστάσεις 81,6 x 81,6 εκ.[11] Η απόδοση των αναγλύφων με τους κενταύρους στα μεγάλα φατνώματα του προνάου ήταν πλέον φανερή. Καθοριστικό ρόλο σε αυτή τη σκέψη έπαιξαν τα μικρά καλύμματα φατνωμάτων με τις προτομές, που βεβαιωμένα προέρχονται από την οροφή του προπύλου του Τεμένους,[12] όπως και άλλα γνωστά παραδείγματα από τον μικρασιατικό χώρο (π.χ.Μαυσωλεία Αλικαρνασσού[13] και Belevi[14] κ. ά.).

Οι ερευνητές του Ιερού της Σαμοθράκης δέχονται σήμερα ότι πέντε τέτοιες ανάγλυφες πλάκες με παράσταση καλπάζοντος κενταύρου, κάλυπταν ισάριθμα μεγάλα φατνώματα του προνάου του Ιερού.[15] Από την παράθεση των στοιχείων και την αντιπαραβολή των εικόνων γίνεται φανερό ότι ο κένταυρος της Θάσου προέρχεται από ένα παρόμοιο αναγλυφο. Τα φατνωματικά ανάγλυφα της Σαμοθράκης, όπως άλλωστε και τα υπόλοιπα γλυπτά και τα αρχιτεκτονικά μέλη είναι κατασκευασμένα από το ίδιο χονδρόκοκκο θασίτικο μάρμαρο, στοιχείο καθοριστικό για μερικούς μελετητές για την απόδοσή τους σε θασίτικο εργαστήριο.[16]

Από την εξέταση των θραυσμάτων στα Μουσεία της Βιέννης και της Σαμοθράκης, προκύπτει ότι ορισμένα θα μπορούσαν να σχετίζονται με τον κένταυρο της Θάσου. Τις περισσότερες πιθανότητες συγκεντρώνει το κεφάλι του κενταύρου στην Βιέννη (εικ. 6), που σώζει τμήμα της αριστερής ωμοπλάτης και μέρος της πλάκας του αναγλύφου πίσω από το δεξί αυτί. Αποφασιστικά όμως για την συσχέτιση είναι δύο θραύσματα του Μουσείου της Σαμοθράκης, το πάχος της πλάκας τών οποίων και η τραχειά επεξεργασία της πίσω πλευράς, ανταποκρίνονται απόλυτα προς την πλάκα του αναγλύφου της Θάσου.[17]

Τέλος θα πρέπει ακόμα να σημειωθεί ότι οι τεχνικές λεπτομέρειες σε δύο άκρα δεξιά χέρια στα Μουσεία της Βιέννης[18] και της Σαμοθράκης (εικ. 7–8),[19] που αφορούν στην στερέωση ένθετων αντικειμένων, ανταποκρίνονται απόλυτα στις τεχνικές λεπτομέρειες που σώζουν τα υπολείμματα του δεξιού χεριού του κενταύρου της Θάσου. Οι αντιστοιχίες αυτές δεν αφήνουν, νομίζω, αμφιβολίες για την προέλευση του αναγλύφου της Θάσου από τα φατνωματικά ανάγλυφα του προνάου του Ιερού της Σαμοθράκης.

Η βέβαιη πλέον απόδοση του κενταύρου της Θάσου στα φατνωματικά ανάγλυφα της οροφής του προνάου της Σαμοθράκης επαναφέρει στο προσκήνιο το πρόβλημα της χρονολόγησης όλου του γλυπτού διάκοσμου του προνάου, που από τους Αμερικανούς ανασκαφείς χρονολογήθηκε με στυλιστικά κυρίως κριτήρια μετά τα μέσα του 2ου π.Χ. αιώνα, ταυτόχρονα με την αποπεράτωση του κτιρίου. Αλλοι όμως ερευνητές, όπως ο Linfert και η Ridgway,[20] εξακολουθούν να υποστηρίζουν την παλαιότερη χρονολόγηση στον 3ο π.Χ. αι. αξιολογώντας διαφορετικά από στυλιστική άποψη τόσο τα εναέτια γλυπτά του προνάου, όσο και το κεφάλι του κενταύρου στην Βιέννη. Οι υποστηρικτές της πρωιμότερης χρονολόγησης επιμένουν στην στυλιστική σχέση του κεφαλιού της Βιέννης με κεφάλια κενταύρων από τα φατνωματικά ανάγλυφα του Μαυσωλείου του Belevi, σε ένα από τα οποία παρατηρείται πράγματι μια κοινή διάθεση στην αναλυτική διευθέτηση των βοστρύχων της κόμης και στην απόδοση των αυτιών.[21] Παρόλα αυτά έχει υποστηριχθεί ότι το κεφάλι της Βιέννης στερείται της εσωτερικής πνοής του παραλήλλου του από την Εφεσο και χαρακτηρίζεται από μια ηρεμότερη έκφραση και μαλακότερες φόρμες στην απόδοση των μαλλιών και των ματιών.[22] Σε αυτή την συνάρτηση η συνεισφορά του θασίτικου αναγλύφου στην στυλιστική εκτίμηση των αναγλύφων των κενταύρων είναι διδακτική. Ο κένταυρος της Θάσου σε έξεργο ανάγλυφο βάθους (13,5 εκ.) διπλάσιου σχεδόν από τα φατνώματα του Μαυσωλείου του Belevi (7 εκ.) απελευθερώνεται με μια περίοπτη διάθεση από τον κάμπο του αναγλύφου. Αυτό το στοιχείο είναι που υποχρεώνει και τον Holtzmann να θεωρεί ότι οι κένταυροι των αναγλύφων Σαμοθράκης – Θάσου διαπνέονται με τις τεχνητές υπερβολές στην απόδοση των ανατομικών λεπτομερειών τους από την γραφική συμβατικότητα του μεταπεργαμηνού στυλ. Βέβαιο πάντως είναι ότι οι κένταυροί μας βρίσκουν τα πλησιέστερα παράλληλά τους, όπως άλλωστε και το

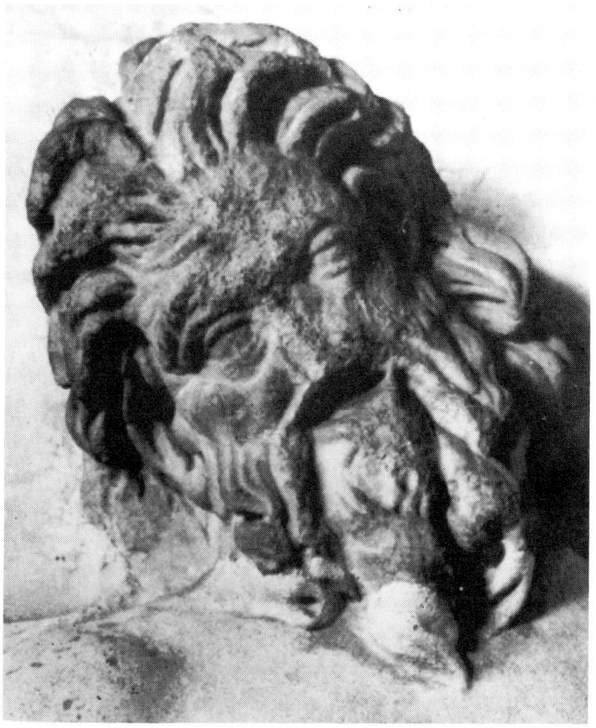

Εικ. 6. Λεπτομέρεια της εικόνας 5. Αναπαραγωγή από Samothrace 3, 1, εικ. 204.

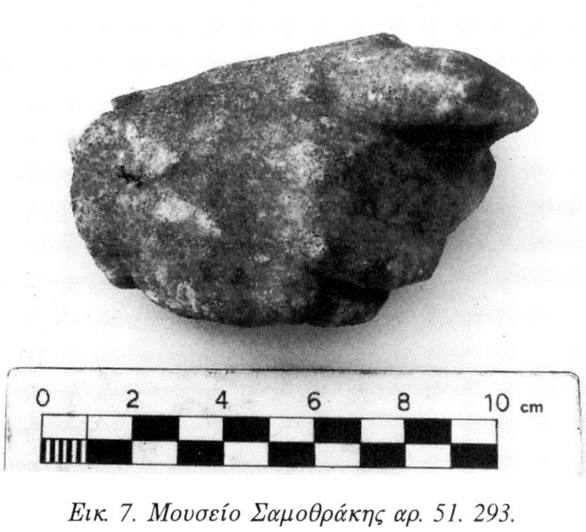

Εικ. 7. Μουσείο Σαμοθράκης αρ. 51. 293. Ακρο δεξί χέρι. Φωτ. Εφορείας Προϊστορικών και Κλασικών Αρχαιοτήτων Κομοτηνής.

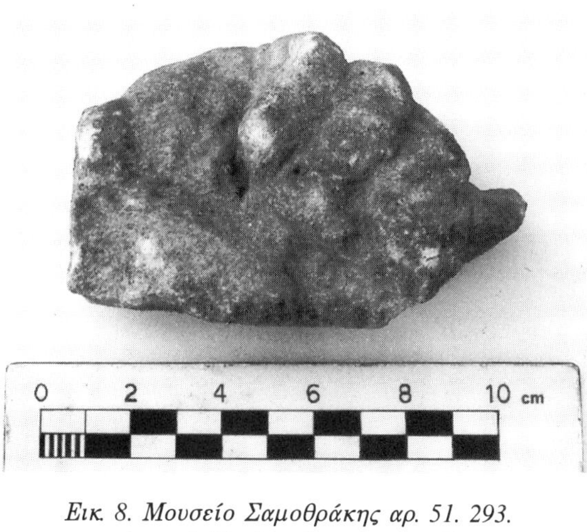

Εικ. 8. Μουσείο Σαμοθράκης αρ. 51. 293. Ακρο δεξί χέρι. Φωτ. ως εικ. 7.

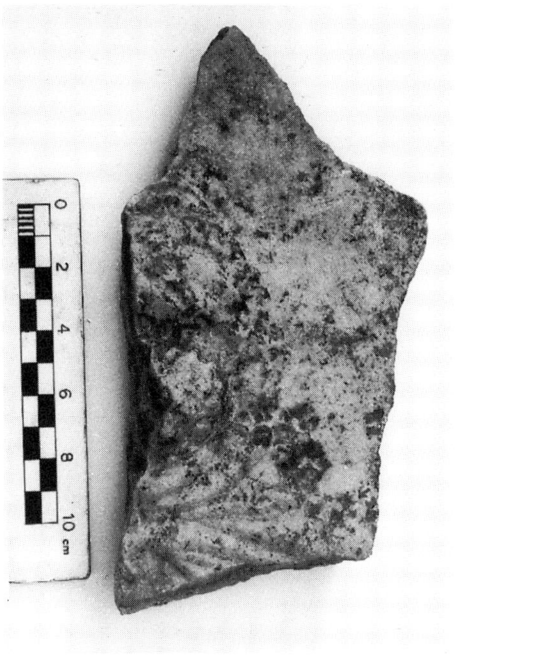

Εικ. 9. Μουσείο Σαμοθράκης αρ. 48. 579. Ανάγλυφο. Φωτ. ως εικ. 7.

είδος της αρχιτεκτονικής πλαστικής από την οποία προέρχονται, στον μικρασιατικό χώρο. Στην περίοπτη πλαστική ενδιαφέρουσες είναι οι συγκρίσεις με τους ελληνιστικούς κενταύρους του Ασκληπιείου της Περγάμου[23] καθώς επίσης και με τους κενταύρους των μικρασιατών καλλιτεχνών από την Αφροδισιάδα Αριστέα και Παππία, που ανάγονται σε πρότυπα του πρώτου μισού του 2ου π.Χ. αιώνα.[24] Με τους κενταύρους των Αριστέα και Παππία οι κένταυροι των αναγλύφων της Σαμοθράκης έχουν κοινή όχι μόνον τη στροφή προς τα δεξιά, αλλά και το μοτίβο της απόδοσης του ανθρώπινου κορμού σε τρία τέταρτα προς τα δεξιά. Και στις δύο περιπτώσεις οι κένταυροι στηρίζονται στα τρία από τα τέσσερα σκέλη τους, ενώ το μπροστινό δεξί σκέλος είναι ανασηκωμένο και λυγισμένο στο γόνατο.

Τα παραδείγματα από τον μικρασιατικό χώρο που αναφέραμε, οριοθετούν και προσδιορίζουν την πλαστική αντίληψη από την οποία διαπνέεται και ο κένταυρος της Θάσου, αλλά είναι αμφίβολο αν ενισχύουν την χρονολόγηση των ανάγλυφων φατνωμάτων του προνάου του Ιερού της Σαμοθράκης μετά τα μέσα του 2ου αι. π.Χ. που πρότειναν οι Lehmann.

Η διάταξη και η σημασία των κενταύρων στην οροφή του προνάου του Ιερού

Οι Αμερικανοί ανασκαφείς κατένειμαν τα θραύσματα της Σαμοθράκης και της Βιέννης σε πέντε συνολικά ανάγλυφα κενταύρων, όσα δηλαδή ήταν και τα μεγάλα τετράγωνα φατνώματα της οροφής του προνάου. Οι τέσσερις από αυτούς, που κοσμούσαν τα γωνιακά φατνώματα, βρίσκονταν σε καλπασμό προς τα δεξιά, ενώ ο πέμπτος, που κοσμούσε το κεντρικό φάτνωμα, υποτέθηκε ότι ήταν ανορθωμένος απέναντι ακριβώς στον εισερχόμενο υποψήφιο μύστη.[25] Η κάλυψη του κεντρικού φατνώματος με έναν ανορθωμένο και διαφοροποιημένο από τους υπόλοιπους κένταυρο, ενίσχυε η μάλλον εξυπηρετούσε την άποψη του Lehmann,[26] ότι ο κεντρικός κένταυρος ήταν αυτός στον οποίο αναφέρεται ο Καλλίστρατος κατά την είσοδό του στον πρόναο ενός ιερού.[27] Η αποδοχή όμως ενός πέμπτου, ανορθωμένου και διαφοροποιημένου ως προς το μοτίβο κενταύρου, γύρω από τον οποίο κινούνταν πάντα προς τα δεξιά οι άλλοι τέσσερις, δεν ενισχύεται μέχρι σήμερα από κανένα αποφασιστικό θραύσμα. Παρά το γεγονός ότι τα σωζόμενα σπαράγματα κενταύρων αξιολογούνται από τους Αμερικανούς ανασκαφείς ως προερχόμενα από πέντε (τουλάχιστον) ανάγλυφα κενταύρων, το κεντρικό θέμα εξακολουθεί να παραμένει άγνωστο και σκοτεινό και είναι ενδεικτικός ο πρόσφατος προβληματισμός του B.Holtzmann, ο οποίος αμφιταλαντεύεται να αποφασίσει αν στο κεντρικό φάτνωμα εικονιζόταν ο Φόλος ή ο Ηρακλής.[28] Σίγουρο όμως πρέπει να θεωρείται ότι οι τέσσερις γωνιακοί κένταυροι κινούνταν σε πορεία προς τα δεξιά, διαγράφοντας μια κυκλική τροχιά πάνω από τον εισερχόμενο επισκέπτη.

Η αποκρυπτογράφηση πάντως της ερμηνείας των κενταύρων στην οροφή του προνάου του Ιερού συναρτάται με την θρησκευτική σημασία του οικοδομήματος που εχρησιμοποιείτο για την μύηση στον υψηλότερο βαθμό (εποπτεία) των μυστηρίων της Σαμοθράκης.[29] Μολονότι είναι γνωστή η συμμετοχή των κενταύρων στον διονυσιακό θίασο στην πλαστική του 2ου π.Χ. αιώνα[30] και δεδομένη η υιοθεσία διονυσιακών στοιχείων, όπως η μουσική και η άμπελος στην λατρεία των Καβείρων,[31] δεν είναι καθόλου βέβαιο ότι οι κένταυροι στην οροφή του προνάου αποτελούν θίασο, όπως παλαιότερα τους είχαν αποκαλέσει οι Αμερικανοί, ενώ είναι μάλλον απίθανη η γνώμη του Holtzmann, ό οποίος θεωρεί ότι οι κένταυροι σε αυτή την εποχή πλέον καταντούν να είναι διακοσμητικά περισσότερο μοτίβα. Αλλωστε μια συνολική αποτίμηση του ανάγλυφου διακόσμου της οροφής του προνάου είναι επί του παρόντος αδύνατη εφόσον δεν είναι γνωστοί οι άλλοι τύποι φατνωματικών αναγλύφων που κάλυπταν τα μικροτέρου μεγέθους φατνώματα της οροφής. Πιστεύω, όμως, ότι στην περίπτωση του προνάου του Ιερού, υπάρχουν κάποια στοιχεία για μια πιο συγκεκριμένη ερμηνεία τους. Σε ένα από τα θραύσματα αναγλύφων, που βρέθηκε κατά τις αμερικανικές ανασκαφές στο χώρο του Ιερού, διαστάσεων 18,5 x 10 εκ. (εικ. 9) σώζονται τμήματα δύο φύλλων αμπέλου και ένα τσαμπί σταφύλια. Το θραύσμα, που δεν σώζει στοιχεία εικονιστικού θέματος, αποδόθηκε από τους ανασκαφείς στα μικρά τετράγωνα φατνώματα της οροφής του προνάου, οι διαστάσεις των οποίων προσφέρονταν για την απόδοση του θραύσματος. Η εναλλαγή αυτή έντονων εικονιστικών θεμάτων, με ήρεμα φυτικά κοσμήματα, θεωρήθηκε ως η πλέον ενδεδειγμένη και αποδεκτή για την οροφή. Το πάχος όμως του θραύσματος, που είναι 2,8 εκ. και η τραχειά επεξεργασία της πίσω πλευράς, που συμπίπτουν απόλυτα με το σωζόμενο τμήμα της πλάκας του αναγλύφου της Θάσου, δεν αφήνουν και σε αυτή την περίπτωση αμφιβολίες, όπως υποστήριξα και παλαιότερα,[32] ότι το θραύσμα με το σταφύλι προέρχεται από κάποιο ανάγλυφο κενταύρου, άποψη με την οποία φαίνεται τώρα να συμφωνεί και ο Holtzmann.[33]

Η απόδοση αυτή σε συνδυασμό με το γεγονός ότι δύο από τα σωζόμενα άκρα δεξιά χέρια κενταύρων κρατούσαν επιμήκη αντικείμενα (attributes), μας οδηγεί στο συμπέρασμα ότι οι κένταυροι χαρακτηρίζονταν από φυτικά στοιχεία, κλαδιά κ. ά. και όχι από μουσικά όργανα, όπως είχαν υποθέσει παλαιότερα οι Αμερικανοί. Δεν αποκλείεται, λοιπόν, οι τέσσερις κένταυροι στις γωνίες του προνάου, να συμβόλιζαν τις τέσσερις εποχές, όπως βάσιμα μας επιτρέπει να υποθέσουμε το θραύσμα με το σταφύλι. Η άποψη αυτή είχε υποστηριχθεί με αφορμή τους κενταύρους του Ασκληπιείου του Περγάμου για μια πιθανή παραλλαγή του συντάγματος στο Βέλγιο.[34]

Τα ανάγλυφα φατνώματα του προπύλου του Τεμένους της Σαμοθράκης

Η ερμηνεία των μικρών τετράγωνων αναγλύφων, πλευράς 21 εκ., που κοσμούνται με προτομές, ως καλυπτήριων φατνωματικών πλακών κάποιου κτιρίου της Σαμοθράκης, δεν ήταν από την αρχή αυτονόητη. Με αφορμή τα τρία πρώτα θραύσματα, που προέκυψαν από τις αυστριακές έρευνες στο χώρο, έγιναν διάφορες υποθέσεις για την προέλευση των αναγλύφων, μέχρι να γίνει τελικά αντιληπτό ότι τα τετράγωνα ανάγλυφα, με την διπλή πλαισίωση στην όψη, τον βυθισμένο κάμπο του αναγλύφου, τα ίχνη οπών στις πλαϊνές πλευρές και την χαρακτηριστικά ανώμαλη, αδρή, σαμαρωτή διαμόρφωση της πίσω πλευράς, συνιστούν καλυπτήριες φατνωματικές πλάκες. Αλλά και μετά από αυτή την διαπίστωση δεν ήταν απόλυτα βέβαιο, την οροφή ποίου κτιρίου κοσμούσαν αυτά τα ανάγλυφα καλύμματα φατνωμάτων. Οι αμερικανικές ανασκαφές στη Σαμοθράκη, που διπλασίασαν το διαθέσιμο υλικό των αναγλύφων φατνωμάτων και η συστηματικότερη διερεύνηση των αρχιτεκτονικών στοιχείων των οροφών των κτιρίων, διαφώτισαν οριστικά πλέον την προέλευση των ιδιόρυθμων αυτών αρχιτεκτονικών αναγλύφων.[35]

Η αύξηση του υλικού, με τα νέα παραδείγματα που εντοπίσθηκαν στην Θάσο, και δημοσιεύθηκαν πρόσφατα από τον B. Holtzmann,[36] επιβάλλει την επανεξέταση όλου πλέον του υλικού, από την οποία προκύπτουν ενδιαφέροντα στοιχεία.

1. Βιέννη, Kunsthistorisches Museum I 676

Αποσπασματικά σωζόμενο κάλυμμα φατνώματος σπασμένο από όλες τις πλευρές. Μικρά τμήματα της πλαισίωσης σώζονται στην επάνω και κάτω πλευρά. Εικονίζεται σχεδόν κατενώπιον κεφαλή γενειοφόρου, με ελαφρά κλίση προς τα αριστερά. Τα μαλλιά χωρίζονται στο κέντρο και πέφτουν κυματιστά σε κάθε πλευρά του κεφαλιού, μέχρι που ενώνονται με την πυκνή γενειάδα. Το κρεμαστό μουστάκι καλύπτει το στόμα αλλά αφήνει να διακρίνεται το σαρκώδες κάτω χείλος. Τα μάτια βαθειά τοποθετημένα με φαρδειά χαμηλωμένα βλέφαρα. Κατεστραμμένη αλλά τριγωνική μύτη και σαρκώδη μάγουλα. Κοντός και παχύς λαιμός.

Ο κάμπος πλαισιώνεται από δύο τετράγωνα στοιχεία πλαισίωσης, τα οποία σώζονται στο υψηλότερο δεξί τμήμα του αναγλύφου.

Ύψος εσωτερικού πλαισίου 1,5 εκ. Εξωτερικού 2 εκ. Μέγ. πλάτος 16,5 εκ. Μέγ. ύψος 20,5 εκ. Ύψος κάμπου 13,5 εκ. Η πίσω πλευρά αδρά δουλεμένη με το βελόνι και αποστρογγυλωμένη στις πλευρές.

Βρέθηκε "on the "Platform" east or northeast of the Hieron, i.e. the Temenos."

Βιβλ. S I, 11. 28, πίν. 51 (δεξιά). S II, 68, αρ. 1. H. Heydemann, 13. *HallWPr* (1988) 12. O. Kern, *Hermes* 25, 1890, 13 σημ. 2. A. Schober, *ÖJh* 29, 1935, 14. F. Chapouthier, *Les Dioscures au service d' une déesse* (1935) 177 κε., εικ. 180. K. Lehmann, *Hesperia* 20, 1951, 16. *Samothrace* 5, 151 κε., εικ. 125, πίν. 40,1. H. Ehrhardt, *Samothrake* (1985) 155 κε., εικ. 46. Tancke 23 κε. 232, αρ. 4,1, πίν. XX 1–2.

2. Βιέννη, Kunsthistorisches Museum I 675

Θραύσμα ενός καλύμματος φατνώματος. Η αριστερή, επάνω και κάτω γωνία σπασμένες. Τα εξωτερικά πλαίσια και στις τρεις πλευρές είναι καταπονημένα. Η πίσω πλευρά αδρά χονδροδουλεμένη και επίπεδη. Στο επάνω και κάτω πλαίσιο υπολείμματα από κυκλικούς τορμίσκους. Η επιφάνεια είναι διαβρωμένη και ο κάμπος του αναγλύφου πατιναρισμένος.

Εικονίζεται αγένεια ανδρική κεφαλή σε προφίλ προς τα δεξιά. Τα πυκνά κυματιστά μαλλιά διευθετημένα λοξά προς τα εμπρός καλύπτουν τα αυτιά. Τα μάτια είναι βυθισμένα με χαμηλά βλέφαρα.

Μέγιστο πλάτος περίπου 20 εκ. Μέγιστο ύψος περίπου 21 εκ. Κάμπος αναγλύφου 14,4 x 14,4 εκ.

Βρέθηκε το 1873 ανατολικά ή ΒΑ του Ιερού.

Βιβλ. S I, 11. 28, πίν. 51 (αριστερά). S II, 14. 68, αρ. 1. Heydemann, ό.π. (αρ. 1) 3, 12 κε. και σημ. 45. O. Kern, *Hermes* 25, 1890, 13 σημ. 2. R. Pettazzoni, *Ausonia* 3, 1908, 87. Schober ό.π. (αρ. 1). Chapouthier ό.π. (αρ. 1) 177 κε., εικ. 18. K. Lehmann ό. π. (αρ. 1). Ph. W. Lehmann, *Skopas in Samothrace* (1973) 9 σημ. 56, 14 σημ. 96–98, εικ. 51. A. F. Stewart, *Skopas of Paros* (1977) 107 κε. 171 σημ. 44. *Funde aus Ephesos and Samothrake* (1978) αρ. 218. Ph. W. Lehmann στο: *Μέγας Αλέξανδρος, 2300 χρόνια από τον θάνατό του* (1980) 184 κε., πίν. 3. *Samothrace* 5, 152 κε., εικ. 126, πίν. 40,3. H. Ehrhardt, *Samothrake* (1985) 155 κε., εικ. 44. R. Fleischer, *Gnomon* 56, 1984, 261 κε. Tancke 24 σημ. 179–189. 232 πίν. XX 3–4. Holtzmann 93.

3. Βιέννη, Kunsthistorisches Museum I 1702

Θραύσμα από την κάτω αριστερή γωνία ενός αναγλύφου καλύμματος φατνώματος, Λαιμός ανθρώπινης κεφαλής, που στρέφει προς τα αριστερά. Ισχυρά διαβρωμένο.

Ύψος εσωτερικού πλαισίου 0,8 εκ. Εξωτερικού 2,6 εκ. Σωζόμενο ύψος θραύσματος 7,6 εκ. Σωζόμενο πλάτος 10,8 εκ. Σωζόμενο ύψος λαιμού 4,5 εκ.

Βρέθηκε το 1875 στη Σαμοθράκη, χωρίς ακριβή προέλευση, αλλά υποθετικά όπου τα δύο προηγούμενα.

Βιβλ. S II, 14, εικ. 3. Heydemann ό.π. (αρ. 1) 12. Kern ό.π. (αρ. 1). Pettazzoni ό.π. (αρ. 2) 88. Schober ό.π. (αρ. 1). Chapouthier ό.π. (αρ. 1) 178 κε. K. Lehmann, *Hesperia* 20, 1951, 16. Lehmann, *Skopas in Samothrace*, 28 σημ. 56. Stewart ό.π. (αρ. 2) 107. 171, σημ. 38. *Samothrace* 5, 153 κε., εικ. 127. Tancke 233, αρ. 4,3.

4. Μουσείο Σαμοθράκης αρ. 66.611

Θραύσμα ενός καλύμματος φατνώματος με πλαίσιο επάνω. Η πίσω πλευρά αδρά δουλεμένη. Τα εξωτερικά πλαίσια ισχυρά κατεστραμένα και η επιφάνεια διαβρωμένη.

Σώζεται τμήμα μιας ανδρικής κεφαλής σε τρία τέταρτα προς τα δεξιά. Η μύτη, το στόμα και η περιοχή του σαγονιού είναι αποκρουσμένα. Κοντά σγουρά μαλλιά, που αφήνουν ελεύθερο το αριστερό αυτί. Βαθειά τοποθετημένα μάτια με χαμηλά βλέφαρα.

Μέγιστο πλάτος 13,5 εκ. Μέγιστο ύψος 14,2 εκ.

Βρέθηκε το 1966 στη Σαμοθράκη, στην επίχωση πάνω στον ανατολικό λόφο.

Βιβλ. G. Daux, *BCH* 91, 1967, 740, εικ. 6. J. R. McCredie, *ΑΔελτ* 22, 1967 Β 2 Χρονικά 433, πίν. 330c. Ph. W. Lehmann στο: *Μέγας Αλέξανδρος, 2300 χρόνια από τον θάνατό του* (1980) 183 κε., 187, πίν. 2α. *Samothrace* 5, 156 κε., εικ. 130, πίν. 40,4. Tancke 233, αρ. 4,4, πίν. XXI 1–2.

5. Μουσείο Σαμοθράκης αρ. 55. 149 (εικ. 10)

Αποσπασματικά σωζόμενο κάλυμμα φατνώματος. Λείπει η κάτω αριστερή γωνία. Ιχνη από οπές προσήλωσης στα εξωτερικά πλαίσια δεξιά και επάνω.

Εικονίζεται νεανική γυναικεία μορφή, στραμένη προς τα δεξιά. Η επιφάνεια είναι διαβρωμένη, αλλά τα ίχνη της πεπονοειδούς κόμμωσης ορατά. Μάτια αρχικά βαθειά τοποθετημένα με χαμηλές βλεφαρίδες. Διπλό περίγραμμα στο επάνω βλέφαρο. Σαρκώδη χείλη και στρογγυλεμένο (σπασμένο σήμερα) πηγούνι. Ιχνη από ένα μικρό αυτί.

Ύψος: εσωτ. πλαισίου 1,5 εκ. Εξωτ. πλαισίου 2 εκ. Ύψος του κάμπου 14,3 εκ. Πλάτος του κάμπου 15,2 εκ. Μέγ. πλάτος 22 εκ. Μέγ. ύψος 19,5 εκ.

Αγνωστες οι συνθήκες εύρεσης. Αγοράσθηκε από τον Chapouthier, από κάποιον χωρικό. Πιθανόν ήταν ο Chapouthier, που το μετέφερε στο Εθν. Μουσείο, όπου καταγράφηκε με τον αριθμό 3632. Επεστράφη στο Μουσείο της Σαμοθράκης το 1955. Ο Chapouthier, 178 κε. υπέδειξε ότι το θραύσμα της Βιέννης Ι 1702 θα μπορούσε να είναι η ελλείπουσα κάτω αριστερή γωνία αυτού του φατνώματος. Οι διαστάσεις των πλαισίων και η θέση του λαιμού φανερώνουν όμως ότι τα δύο θραύσματα δεν συνανήκουν.

Βιβλ. Chapouthier ό.π. (αρ. 1) 178–179 σημ. 1, εικ. 18. K. Lehmann, *Hesperia* 20, 1951, 16 αρ. 52. Του ίδιου, *AJA* 61, 1957, 123, πίν. 37,5. *Samothrace* 3, 1, 323 κε., εικ. 185. Lehmann, *Skopas in Samothrace*, 28 κε. σημ. 56. 60, εικ. 33. Stewart ό.π. (αρ. 2) 107. 171 σημ. 38. *Samothrace* 5, 154, εικ. 128, πίν. 40,2. Tancke 233 κε., πίν. XXI 5–6.

6. Μουσείο Σαμοθράκης αρ. 70.848.

Θραύσμα ενός καλύμματος φατνώματος με μικρό υπόλοιπο του επάνω πλαισίου. Η πίσω πλευρά αδρά δουλεμένη. Οι πλάγιες πλευρές αποστρογγυλωμένες. Πολυάριθμες αποκρούσεις. Ισχυρά ίχνη διάβρωσης.

Εικονίζεται γυναικείο κεφάλι σε όψη τριών τετάρτων προς τα αριστερά. Το πίσω μέρος της κεφαλής και ο λαιμός έχουν αποσπασθεί. Πεπονοειδής κόμμωση. Βαθειά τοποθετημένα μάτια με χαμηλά βλέφαρα. Γεμάτο πηγούνι και στόμα με σαρκώδη χείλη.

Μέγιστο πλάτος 14,8 εκ. Μέγιστο ύψος 15,5 εκ.

Βρέθηκε το 1970 στη Σαμοθράκη.

Βιβλ. J. McCredie, *ΑΔελτ* 26, 1971, 443, πίν. 438a. Ph. Lehmann, *Skopas in Samothrace* (1973) 9. 26, αρ. 56, εικ. 36. Stewart ό.π. (αρ. 2) 107. 171 σημ. 38. *Samothrace* 5, 157 κε., εικ. 131, πίν. 40,5. Tancke 233, πίν. XXI 3–4.

Μουσείο Σαμοθράκης αρ. 49. 355

Αποσπασματικά σωζόμενο κάλυμμα φατνώματος. Μόνον ένα τμήμα του κάτω μέρους και το χαμηλότερο αριστερό μέρος του αναγλύφου έχει σωθεί. Ανώμαλα σπασμένο επάνω και στις πλευρές. Εικονίζεται ανδρικό κεφάλι στραμμένο προς τα δεξιά. Εχει σωθεί ο λαιμός και η αρχή του ώμου. Μάζα μαλλιών, τυλιγμένη σε σπείρα πέφτει στον αυχένα πάνω από τον ώμο. Απλός, κιονωτός λαιμός που είναι συγγενικός με αυτον του καλύμματος αρ. 55.149 στο στυλ και στην κλίμακα.

Ύψος εσωτ. πλαισίου 1,5 εκ. Εξωτ. πλαισίου 2,4 εκ. Σωζ. ύψος του κάμπου 11,7 εκ. Σωζ. πλάτος του κάμπου 16,5 εκ.

Βρέθηκε βόρεια του αναλημματικού τοίχου, στο χαμηλότερο επίπεδο του Τεμένους.

Βιβλ. K. Lehmann, *Hesperia* 20, 1951 16, πίν. 6d. Lehmann, *Skopas in Samothrace*, 28, αρ. 56. *Samothrace* 5, 155 κε., εικ. 129. Tancke 234, αρ. 4,7.

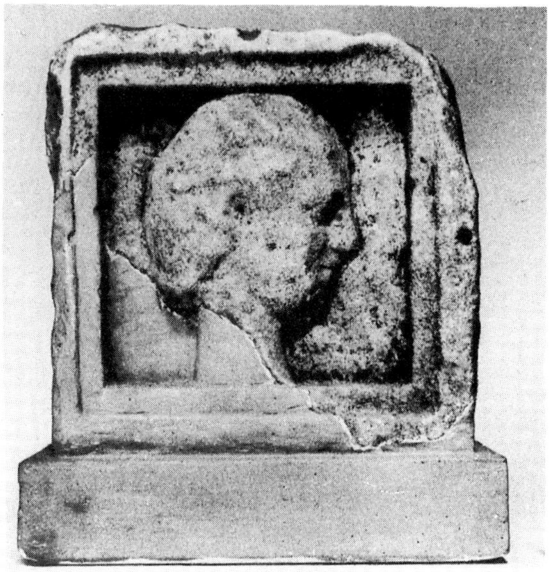

Εικ. 10. Μουσείο Σαμοθράκης αρ. 55. 149. Ανάγλυφο κάλυμμα φατνώματος. Φωτ. ως εικ. 7.

8. Μουσείο Θάσου αρ. 3256 (εικ. 11)

Αποσπασματικά σωζόμενο κάλυμμα φατνώματος. Λείπει η επάνω δεξιά γωνία και η δεξιά πλαισίωση. Στο κέντρο των εξωτερικών πλαισίων των τριών διατηρημένων πλευρών, υπάρχουν οπές για την προσήλωση καρφίδων. Το είχε δεί πλήρες ο Charles Picard το 1911 και ξαναβρέθηκε

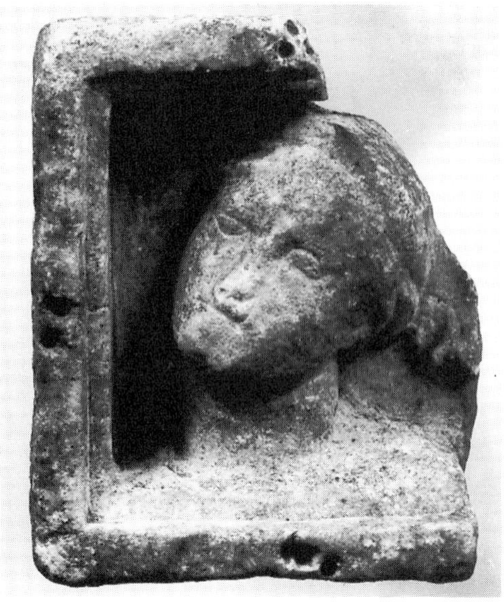

Εικ. 11. Μουσείο Θάσου αρ. 3256. Φωτ. Γαλλικής Αρχαιολογικής Σχολής.

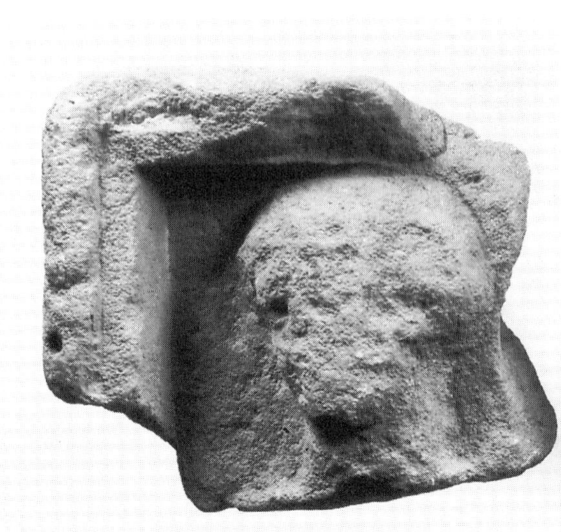

Εικ. 12. Μουσείο Θάσου αρ. 1539. Φωτ. Γαλλικής Αρχαιολογικής Σχολής.

το 1973. 21,5 εκ. x 18 εκ. x 8 εκ. Βάθος αναγλύφου 1,5 εκ. Ύψος εσωτ. πλαισίου 0,9 εκ. Εξωτ. 2 εκ. Η πίσω πλευρά και οι πλάγιες όψεις, που έχουν λεπτυνθεί, σχηματίζουν μία επιφάνεια σχεδόν κυρτή.

Στο πεδίο, που είναι σχεδόν τετραγωνισμένο, εικονίζεται μια γυναικεία κεφαλή με ελαφρά στροφή προς τα αριστερά, αλλά ισχυρή κλίση προς τα δεξιά. Στο ύψος του στήθους διακρίνεται η παρυφή του ενδύματος στην μία και στην άλλη πλευρά του λαιμού.

Holtzmann 87, αρ.18, πίν. XXVa.

9. Μουσείο Θάσου αρ. 1539 (εικ. 12)

Αποσπασματικά σωζόμενο κάλυμμα φατνώματος. Βρέθηκε το χειμώνα του 1958–59 στην περιοχή της βόρειας συνοικίας, στην πύλη του Ερμού. 17,5 x 19 x 10 εκ. Βάθος αναγλύφου 4,5 εκ. Επιφάνεια πολύ διαβρωμένη σε χρώμα ώχρας. Εικονίζεται γυναικεία κεφαλή αρκετά φθαρμένη.

Το ίδιο πλαίσιο, όπως και στο προηγούμενο κομμάτι, με πολύ ελαφρές διαφοροποιήσεις στο πάχος και το μήκος των δύο στοιχείων του πλαισίου. Στα αριστερά, επάνω στο εξωτερικό πλαίσιο μία οπή προσαρμογής, παρόμοια με εκείνη που υπάρχει στο προηγούμενο κομμάτι, υποδεικνύει το κέντρο της πλευράς η οποία επομένως πρέπει να ήταν γύρω στα 21 εκ.

Το γυναικείο κεφάλι εικονίζεται σε όψη 3/4, ελαφρά σκυμένο και γυρισμένο προς τα αριστερά. Από το πρόσωπο δεν διακρίνεται παρά μόνον τμήμα του δεξιού περιγράμματος και ένα τμήμα του αυτιού, το οποίο είναι διαβρωμένο. Τα μαλλιά φαίνεται να είναι διευθετημένα ανάμεσα σε δύο ταινίες, που θα μπορούσαν στο πίσω μέρος του κεφαλιού να συγκρατούν ένα σάκκο. Επάνω δεξιά μια αμφίκοιλη αύλακα απομονώνει το βάθος.

Holtzmann 89, αρ. 19, πίν. XXVb.

10. Μουσείο Θάσου αρ. 3734 (εικ. 13)

Η κάτω αριστερή γωνία από κάλυμμα φατνώματος. Βρέθηκε στην ανασκαφή της περιοχής Ψαθερής το 1975. Διαστ. 15,5 x 13,5 x 9 εκ. Βάθος αναγλύφου 4 εκ. Μάρμαρο, όπως το προηγούμενο. Επιφάνεια καλοδιατηρημένη σε μπεζ χρώμα.

Η εσωτερική γωνία έχει ένα βάθος πλαισίου παρόμοιο με τα προηγούμενα. Εν τούτοις το εξωτερικό τμήμα του πλαισίου μοιάζει να είναι μεγαλύτερο (2,5 εκ.) σε σύγκριση με τα δύο προηγούμενα κομμάτια. Η πίσω και η πλάγια όψη έχουν λεπτυνθεί.

Από το κεφάλι, που εικονίζεται κατενώπιον και κατελάμβανε το κέντρο του πεδίου σώζεται τμήμα του λαιμού. Η απουσία παρυφής ενδύματος θα μπορούσε να υποδεικνύει ότι πρόκειται για ανδρικό κεφάλι.

Holtzmann 89, αρ. 20, πίν. XXVc.

11. Μουσείο Θάσου αρ. 3735 (εικ. 14)

Θραύσμα από το κάτω μέρος του καλύμματος. Βρέθηκε το 1983 κατά την διάρκεια της ανασκαφής στην περιοχή Βαλμά σε επιφανειακό στρώμμα κάτω από το δυτικό τμήμα του κυκλικού πηγαδιού. Διαστ. 10 7. x 11,5 x 5,5 εκ. Βάθος αναγλύφου 2,3 εκ. Επιφάνεια καλα διατηρημένη

Πρόκειται για θραύσμα πλαισίου του ιδίου τύπου με τα προηγούμενα με την αρχή ενός λαιμού που αποδίδεται κατενώπιον. Το εξωτερικό πλαίσιο, πλάτους μόνον 2 εκ. δεν αρκεί για μια οπή προσαρμογής. Η πίσω πλευρά είναι διαβρωμένη.

Holtzmann 89, αρ. 21, πίν. XXVd.

12. Λιμένας Θάσου (εικ. 15)

Κάλυμμα φατνώματος εντειχισμένο πάνω από μία είσοδο οικίας, που βρίσκεται στην βόρεια γωνία της πλατείας του Λιμένα. Εντοπίσθηκε από τον Charles Picard το 1910 στο σπίτι του Δ. Σταυρόπουλου.

21 x 22,5 εκ. πεδίο 15 x 15 εκ. (κατά τον Picard). Επειδή η επιφάνειά του έχει ασβεστωθεί πολές φορές, είναι αδύνατο να λάβει κανείς τις ακριβείς διαστάσεις του αναγλύφου. Εικονίζεται γενειοφόρος στραμένος προς τα αριστερά, του οποίου τα μαλλιά σχηματίζουν ένα χονδρό δακτύλιο γύρω από το κρανίο. Το γένι είναι πλούσιο και μακρύ. Τα μάτια είναι βυθισμένα στις οφθαλμικές κοιλότητες. Η άκρη ενός ενδύματος ανεβαίνει αρκετά ψηλά στον αυχένα.

Holtzmann 89, αρ. 22, πίν. XXVe

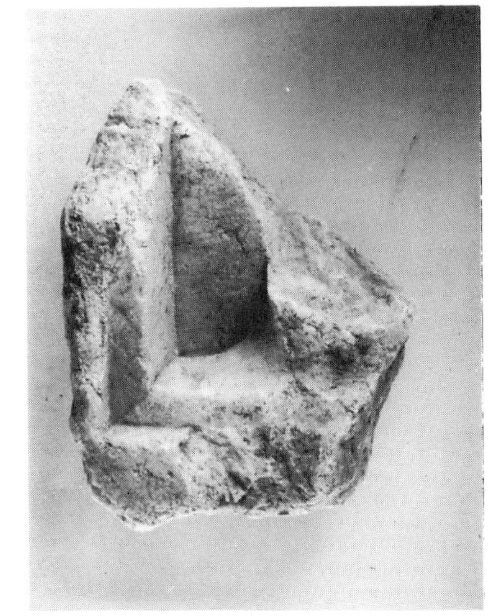

Εικ. 13. Μουσείο Θάσου αρ. 3734. Φωτ. Γαλλικής Αρχαιολογικής Σχολής.

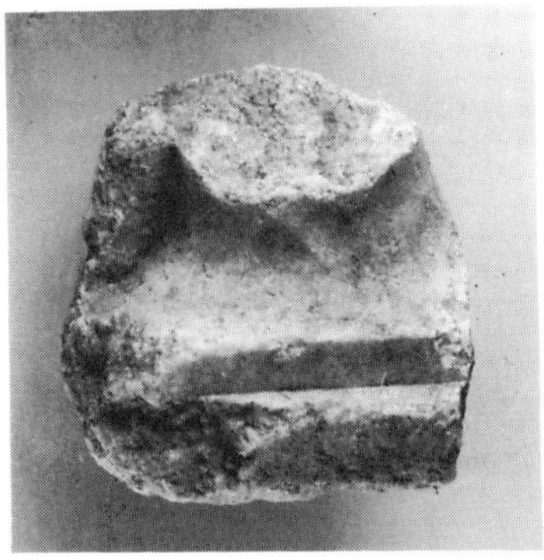

Εικ. 14. Μουσείο Θάσου αρ. 3735. Φωτ. Γαλλικής Αρχαιολογικής Σχολής.

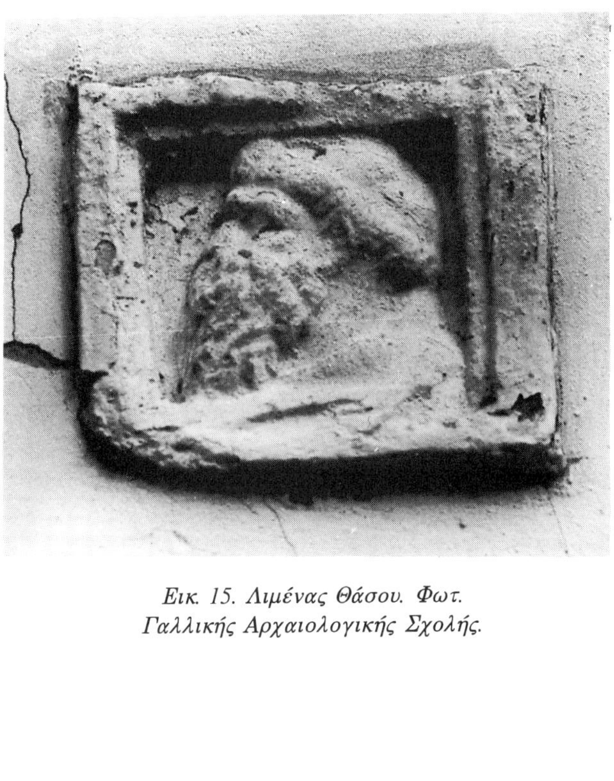

Εικ. 15. Λιμένας Θάσου. Φωτ. Γαλλικής Αρχαιολογικής Σχολής.

Τα πέντε παραδείγματα της Θάσου, που διπλασιάζουν σχεδόν το διαθέσιμο έως πρόσφατα υλικό των μικρών φατνωμάτων, συντείνουν στην κατανόηση της διάταξης της ανάγλυφης διακόσμησης της οροφής του προπύλου του Τεμένους. Με τα παραδείγματα της Θάσου επιβεβαιώνονται και άλλες, διαφορετικές στροφές αλλά και κλίσεις των κεφαλών, που δεν είχαν υποτεθεί από τους Αμερικανούς μελετητές με βάση το διαθέσιμο από αυτούς υλικό. Χαρακτηριστικό παράδειγμα αποτελεί το φάτνωμα αρ. 8 (εικ. 11), που μας παραδίδει μια άλλη παραλλαγη της στροφής της κεφαλής σε τρία τέταρτα προς τα αριστερά.

Στην δωδεκάδα των σωζομένων μικρών φατνωμάτων ή σπαραγμάτων, που αντιπροσωπεύουν το 50% του αρχικού υλικού διαπιστώνονται τα εξής:

α) Τέσσερα έως (ίσως) πέντε παραδείγματα εικονίζουν βεβαιωμένα ανδρικές κεφαλές.
β) Τέσσερα παραδείγματα εικονίζουν βεβαιωμένα γυναικείες κεφαλές.
γ) Σε τρία παραδείγματα από το κάτω μέρος των φατνωμάτων, που σώζουν τμήματα των λαιμών, δεν είναι σαφής ο προσδιορισμός του φύλου της μορφής.
δ) Τρία τουλάχιστον παραδείγματα βεβαιώνουν στροφή της κεφαλής σε προφίλ προς τα δεξιά.
ε) Ενα τουλάχιστον παράδειγμα βεβαιώνει στροφή κεφαλής σε προφίλ προς τα αριστερά.
στ) Τρία τουλάχιστον παραδείγματα βεβαιώνουν στροφή κεφαλής σε 3/4 προς τα αριστερά ή τα δεξιά.
ζ) Ενα τουλάχιστον παράδειγμα βεβαιώνει στροφή κεφαλής σε 2/3 προς τα αριστερά.
θ) Ενα έως τρία παραδείγματα βεβαιώνουν απόδοση κεφαλής σχεδόν κατενώπιον.

Από τα παραπάνω στοιχεία μπορεί, νομίζω, να συμπεράνει κανείς ότι μορφές και των δύο φύλων φαίνεται να εκπροσωπούνται ισόποσα, ενώ φαίνεται να εναλλάσσονται οκτώ διαφορετικοί τρόποι απόδοσης των στροφών και των κλίσεων των κεφαλών. Μετά την αποκάλυψη και των θασίτικων παραδειγμάτων είναι βέβαιο πλέον ότι η προταθείσα διάταξη των φατνωματικών αναγλύφων της οροφής του προπύλου από την Ph. Lehmann, δεν ευσταθεί. Η Lehmann συμπεραίνει μόνον πέντε τρόπους απεικόνισης των κεφαλών, των οποίων η εκπροσώπηση δεν είναι ισόποση, εφόσον τα μισά (12) φατνώματα καλύπτονται από κεφαλές κατενώπιον, ενώ τέσσερα μόνον από κεφαλές με στροφές 3/4.[37] Η διάταξη, τέλος, των αντωπών προτομών δεν είναι καθόλου πειστική, γιατί δεν προϋποθέτει μια συμμετρική και προοδευτική θέαση των μορφών από τον εισερχόμενο μύστη.

Αλλά και η διάταξη που αντιπροτείνεται από τον Holtzmann[38], με το παρακάτω σχήμα

"3 profils droits	_	3 faces	3 3/4 droits	_	3 faces	3 faces	_	3 3/4 gauches	3 faces	_ 3 profils gauches"

μολονότι φαίνεται να κινείται σε πιο σωστή κατεύθυνση από την άποψη της κατανομής, εν τούτοις πρέπει να θεωρηθεί εσφαλμένη ως προς την επανάλειψη των δύο τριάδων με τις κατενώπιον κεφαλές αμέσως μετά τις δύο τριάδες των κεφαλών σε προφίλ αριστερά και δεξιά.

Πιθανότερη, λοιπόν, φαίνεται η κατανομή με βάση τις οκτώ τριάδες που σχηματίζουν τα μικρά φατνώματα στην οροφή του προπύλου ως εξής: Από αριστερά προς τα δεξιά, σε σχέση με τον εισερχόμενο στο πρόπυλο, εικονίζονταν στην πρώτη τριάδα των μικρών φατνωμάτων τρεις κεφαλές σε προφίλ προς τα δεξιά. Στην δεύτερη τριάδα φατνωμάτων τρεις κεφαλές σε τρία τέταρτα προς τα δεξιά, στην τρίτη τριάδα τρεις κεφαλές με στροφή και κλίση προς τα δεξιά αντίστοιχη με αυτή του φατνώματος αρ. 8 και στην τέταρτη τριάδα τρεις κεφαλές κατενώπιον με ελαφρά κλίση προς τα δεξιά. Τις αντίθετες στροφές και κλίσεις απέδιδαν οι κεφαλές που εικονίζονταν στις άλλες τέσσερις τριάδες φατνωμάτων, όπως ενδεικτικά και σχηματικά δηλώνεται παρακάτω.

3 προφίλ> 3 3/4> 3 2/3> 3 κατενώπιον> 3 <κατενώπιον 3 <2/3 3 <3/4 3 <προφίλ

Το συμπέρασμα αυτό βοηθά, νομίζω, την κατανόηση της διάταξης των μικρών φατνωμάτων στην οροφή του προπύλου. Δεν αποκλείεται μάλιστα με την διάταξη αυτή να συναρτάται και η ερμηνεία των μορφών. Η διάταξη δηλαδή πιθανόν να μην εξυπηρετούσε μόνον μια προοπτική διαφοροποίηση, που εξασφάλιζε ικανοποιητικότερη θέαση στους εισερχομένους, αλλά ίσως μια σημασιολογική και θρησκευτική διαβάθμιση. Με αυτό το ενδεχόμενο θα πρέπει κανείς να επανεξετάσει το ζήτημα της ερμηνείας των μορφών, στις οποίες έχουν κατά καιρούς αναγνωρισθεί οι Μεγάλοι Θεοί της Σαμοθράκης μαζί με άλλες θεϊκές και μυθολογικές μορφές αλλά και ιστορικά πρόσωπα.[39]

Η αποκάλυψη μικρών φατνωμάτων από το πρόπυλο της Σαμοθράκης στη Θάσο, επιβεβαιώνει πλέον με κατηγορηματικό τρόπο την προέλευση του κενταύρου της Θάσου από τα μεγάλα φατνώματα του προνάου του Ιερού της Σαμοθράκης. Η στατιστική αποτίμηση της διασποράς του υλικού, ανοίγει βάσιμα πλέον αισιόδοξες προοπτικές για τον εντοπισμό και την ταύτιση νέου υλικού από τα φατνώματα σε περιοχές εκτός Σαμοθράκης.

Οι τύποι των ανάγλυφων καλυμμάτων φατνωμάτων των κτιρίων της Σαμοθράκης

Δεδομένο πάντως παραμένει το γεγονός ότι μέχρι σήμερα βεβαιώθηκαν δύο μόνον τύποι ανάγλυφων φατνωμάτων στη Σαμοθράκη, τα μεγάλα δηλαδή ανάγλυφα φατνώματα των κενταύρων στην οροφή του προνάου του Ιερού και τα μικρά φατνώματα με τις κεφαλές στην οροφή του προπύλου του Τεμένους. Και στις δύο όμως περιπτώσεις η μελέτη του αρχιτεκτονικού υλικού της οροφής βεβαίωσε την παρουσία φατνωμάτων διαφόρων μεγεθών, τα οποία συνδυάζονταν μεταξύ τους, όπως φαίνεται στις αποκαταστάσεις, με συμμετρικό και αρμονικό τρόπο. Υποστηρίχθηκε μάλιστα από τους μελετητές, ότι ενώ στην περίπτωση του προπύλου κοσμούνταν τα μικροτέρου μεγέθους φατνώματα με εικονιστικά θέματα, τις ανάγλυφες δηλαδή προτομές, στην περίπτωση του προνάου του Ιερού, εικονιστικά θέματα, οι κένταυροι δηλαδή, κοσμούσαν τα μεγαλυτέρου μεγέθους φατνώματα. Οι υπόλοιποι τύποι των φατνωμάτων, που συνδυάζονταν στις οροφές των δύο κτιρίων που προαναφέραμε, οι οποίοι επίσης έφεραν ξεχωριστά δουλεμένα καλύμματα, υποστηρίχθηκε ότι δεν κοσμούνταν με εικονιστικά, αλλά μάλλον με φυτικά και εν γένει διακοσμητικά θέματα, ανάγλυφα ή ζωγραφιστά. Το θραύσμα αναγλύφου του Μουσείου Σαμοθράκης αρ. 48.579,[40] σπασμένο από όλες τις πλευρές, που σώζει τμήματα δύο φύλλων και ανάμεσά τους ένα τσαμπί σταφύλια (εικ. 9) φάνηκε να ενισχύει αυτή την άποψη. Οι Αμερικανοί ανασκαφείς νόμισαν ότι το θραύσμα, διαστάσεων 18,5 x 10 εκ., θα μπορούσε να συνιστά έναν άλλο τύπο φατνώματος με φυτικό κόσμημα, που θα μπορούσε να αποδοθεί στα μικροτέρου μεγέθους φατνώματα της οροφής του προνάου του Ιερού. Το θέμα όμως του αναγλύφου, αλλά κυρίως το λείο φόντο, το πάχος της πλάκας (2,8 εκ.) και η τραχειά επεξεργασία της πίσω πλευράς, δεν αφήνουν καμμιά αμφιβολία, όπως ανέφερα παραπάνω, ότι και σε αυτή την περίπτωση έχουμε να κάνουμε με ένα σπάραγμα των αναγλύφων των κενταύρων. Τα δύο τρίτα, λοιπόν, της επιφάνειας των οροφών, που προαναφέραμε, παρέμεναν, ως προς τους τύπους των φατνωμάτων τους αρχαιολογικά άγνωστα.

Το ανάγλυφο του Μουσείου Καβάλας Λ 41 (εικ. 16)

Ενα ανάγλυφο του Μουσείου Καβάλας, το οποίο δεν έχει προσεχθεί ως σήμερα, ανοίγει νέες, όπως πιστεύω, διαστάσεις στην έρευνα του ανάγλυφου διακόσμου των φατνωματικών οροφών των κτιρίων της Σαμοθράκης. Το ανάγλυφο από θασίτικο χονδρόκοκκο μάρμαρο, είναι τετράγωνο, εξωτερικής πλευράς 39,5 εκ. και πάχους στο όριο της πλαισίωσης 5 εκ. Πλαισιώνεται από όλες τις πλευρές από πλατειά, σχεδόν ισόπαχη, επίπεδη αλλά όχι λεία ταινία, που οριοθετεί το έγκοιλο τετράγωνο, πλευράς 25 εκ. περίπου, με παράσταση κεφαλής σε τρία τέταρτα προς τα αριστερά. Η προέλευσή του είναι άγνωστη αλλά το ευρετήριο του Μουσείου Καβάλας μας παραδίδει μια σημαντική λεπτομέρεια, που πιστοποιεί την παλαιότητα του ευρήματος. Το ανάγλυφο βρέθηκε σε τάφρο της αυλής του παλαιού Μουσείου το 1954, όταν ένα συνεργείο εργατών, σύμφωνα με τον Δ. Λαζαρίδη έσκαψε και βρήκε λίγα γλυπτά και άλλα αρχαία, που είχαν χρησιμοποιήσει οι Βούλγαροι στην κατασκευή πολυβολείου η καταφυγίου.[41] Θα πρέπει, λοιπόν, να ήταν προπολεμικό έκθεμα στο Μουσείο της Καβάλας.

Το ανάγλυφο, που παρουσιάζεται εδώ για πρώτη φορά, όσο γνωρίζω, μετά από ευγενική παραχώρηση της κ. Χ.Κουκούλη, θεωρήθηκε παλαιότερα

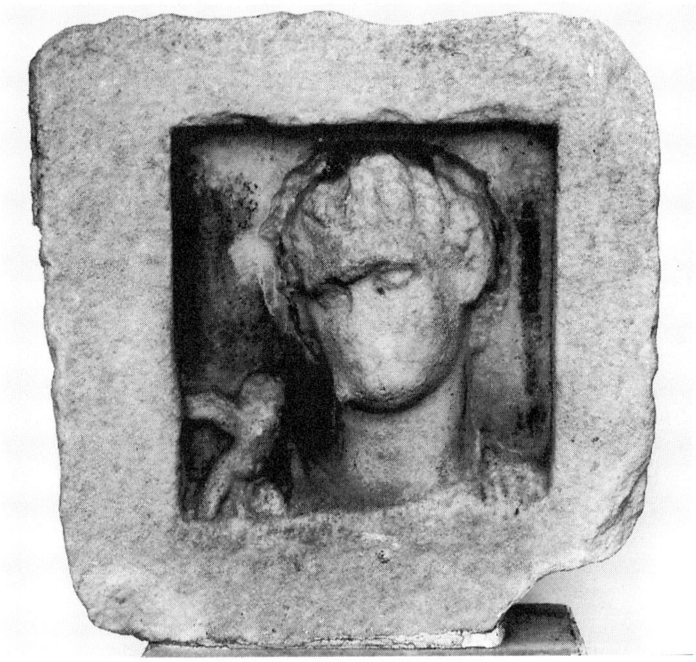

Εικ. 16. Μουσείο Καβάλας Λ 41. Φωτ. Εφορείας Προϊστορικών και Κλασικών Αρχαιοτήτων Καβάλας.

επιτύμβιο,[42] στην παράστασή του αναγνωρίσθηκε μια ανδρική μορφή και χρονολογήθηκε στον 2ο μ.Χ. αι. Οι εκτιμήσεις όμως αυτές δεν ισχύουν. Ο αρχιτεκτονικός τύπος του αναγλύφου δεν έχει ως προς την μορφή του, καμμιά σχέση με όσα ξέρουμε από τα επιτύμβια και τα αναθηματικά ανάγλυφα των ελληνικών και ρωμαϊκών χρόνων. Η κεφαλή άλλωστε, παρά την φθορά του προσώπου ανήκει, όπως προκύπτει από την κόμμωση (μια παραλλαγή της Melonenfrisur) σε γυναικεία και όχι σε ανδρική μορφή. Η απόδοση των μαλλιών δείχνει διευθετημένες προς τα επάνω πλεξίδες και όχι απολήξεις βοστρύχων. Τα μαλλιά είναι διευθετημένα σε χαλαρές συστάδες, που ξεκινούν από το μέτωπο προς το πάνω και πίσω μέρος της κεφαλής, όπως περίπου στην κεφαλή της Αφροδίτης Υπολυμπιδίας από το Δίον.[43] Δεν αποκλείεται μάλιστα στο κέντρο της κεφαλής να σχηματιζόταν λαμπάδιο. Η παρυφή του ενδύματος διακρίνεται στην ρίζα του λαιμού, ενώ στον αριστερό ώμο μια μάζα πτυχών υποδηλώνει ίσως τμήμα του ιματίου, που κάλυπτε τον αριστερό ώμο. Η παράσταση, τέλος, του γονυπετούς έρωτα στον δεξιό ώμο της, ενισχύει ακόμα περισσότερο την αναγνώριση μιας γυναικείας μορφής. Αλλά ούτε στοιχεία, που να συνηγορούν για μια όψιμη χρονολόγηση στα ρωμαϊκά χρόνια ανιχνεύονται στο ανάγλυφό μας. Αντίθετα, στις καλλίτερα σωζόμενες επιφάνειες του προσώπου, διαπιστώνεται καλής ποιότητας εργασία, που θα μπορούσε να ανάγεται στα ελληνιστικά χρόνια, όπως υποδηλώνει άλλωστε και ο τρόπος απόδοσης του Ερωτα.

Αντίθετα, τα τεχνικά χαρακτηριστικά του αναγλύφου, αλλά και το θέμα του υπαγορεύουν, νομίζω, μια άλλη ερμηνεία του. Η κανονικότητα του σχήματος με το αυστηρά τετραγωνισμένο περίγραμμα, το πάχος του αναγλύφου, που κυμαίνεται από 5 εκ. στην πλαισίωση έως 10 εκ. στο μέσο περίπου της πίσω πλευράς, η πλατειά ταινία που το πλαισιώνει, αλλά κυρίως η επεξεργασία της πίσω πλευράς, με την ελαφρά κυρτή, σαμαρωτή, κολουροπιραμιδική διαμόρφωση (εικ. 17), είναι στοιχεία αποφασιστικά για την ερμηνεία του ως αναγλύφου καλύμματος φατνώματος. Το ανάγλυφο δεν εξασφαλίζει έδραση με καμμιά άλλη πλευρά πλην της μπροστινής. Μια παρόμοια εξέχουσα μορφή πλαισίωσης φέρουν και τα ανάγλυφα καλύμματα φατνωμάτων του Μαυσωλείου της Αλικαρνασσού,[44] που κοσμούνται, όπως τα αντίστοιχα από τον ναό της Αθηνάς στην Πριήνη,[45] με μυθολογικά θέματα και μας έχουν σωθεί μόνο σε σπαράγματα. Η ταινία πλαισίωσης στα ανάγλυφα του Μαυσωλείου είναι παρόμοια αδροδουλεμένη και απέχει από τον κάμπο του αναγλύφου 5 εκ., ενώ η αντίστοιχη απόσταση στο φάτνωμα της Καβάλας είναι 3,5 εκ.

Από την στιγμή, που δεχθούμε την ερμηνεία του ως φατνώματος, το ανάγλυφο του Μουσείου Καβάλας μας παραδίδει ένα τύπο φατνώματος γνωστό και πολλαπλά μαρτυρημένο. Ζωγραφιστά φατνώματα διακοσμημένα με προτομές, μας είναι ήδη γνωστά από το μνημείο των Νηρηίδων στην Ξάνθο,[46] ενώ έχει υποτεθεί ότι τα "καλύνματα προσώπων", που αναφέρει η οικοδομική επιγραφή της Επιδαύρου,[47] αφορούσαν στην διακόσμηση των φατνωμάτων της οροφής του ναού με εικονιστικά θέματα. Στην ανάγλυφη πλαστική όμως το αντιπροσωπευτικότερο παράδειγμα του είδους προέρχεται από την Σαμοθράκη. Πρόκειται, όπως είδαμε ήδη, για τα μικρά ανάγλυφα καλύμματα φατνωμάτων με προτομές, που κοσμούσαν ένα μεγάλο μέρος της οροφής του προπύλου του Τεμένους. Ο τύπος μας είναι γνωστός και από μεταγενέστερα παραδείγματα, όπως στο ναό του Απόλλωνα στα Δίδυμα[48] η στο Σεραπείο της Μιλήτου.[49]

Πιστεύω ότι το φάτνωμα του Μουσείου Καβάλας μόνο μια περιοχή του βορειοελλαδίτικου χώρου μπορεί να το διεκδικήσει: το είδος του μαρμάρου, η παράσταση του αναγλύφου, οι διαστάσεις και η τεχνική της κατασκευής του, παραπέμπουν μονοσήμαντα και σε αυτή την περίπτωση στα ανάγλυφα καλύμματα φατνωμάτων των κτιρίων της Σαμοθράκης. Οι περιπέτειες των οικοδομικών λειψάνων των κτιρίων της Σαμοθράκης, όπως διαφαίνεται αρχικά από τις αφηγήσεις των περιηγητών[50] και αργότερα από τις δημοσιεύσεις των ανασκαφέων,[51] συνιστούν μια πρωτοφανή περίπτωση διαρπαγής και διασποράς του υλικού, που εκτείνεται στις απέναντι θρακικές και μικρασιατικές ακτές, στην Αίνο, την Καλλίπολη αλλά και στην Θάσο, όπως είδαμε, μη υπολογίζοντας τα σύνολα που κατέληξαν στα Μουσεία του Λούβρου, της Κων/πολης και της Βιέννης.

Η πιθανότητα μάλιστα να προέρχεται το ανάγλυφό μας από την Θάσο, όπου έχουν εντοπισθεί θραύσματα των δύο άλλων κατηγοριών φατνωμάτων, είναι πολύ μεγάλη. Από τις αρχές του αιώνα είναι μαρτυρημένες εκτεταμένες μεταφορές αρχαίων από την Θάσο στην Καβάλα, όπως πιστοποιεί όχι μόνον η περίπτωση της στήλης Θάσου-Καβάλας, που αποκάλυψε ο Γ. Μπακαλάκης,[52] αλλά και η συλλεκτική δραστηριότητα που παρατηρείται στην πόλη της Καβάλας γύρω στα 1900, με αντιπροσωπευτικότερο παράδειγμα τη συλλογή Wix,[53] που αργότερα κατέληξε στην Βιέννη.

Για την απόδοση του φατνώματος της Καβάλας στην Σαμοθράκη, θα μπορούσε να κάνει κανείς δύο σκέψεις. Η πρώτη σκέψη είναι να το αποδόσει στην οροφή του προπύλου του Τεμένους, τα μικρότερα φατνώματα της οποίας, βεβαιωμένα γνωρίζουμε ότι κοσμούνταν με προτομές στις οποίες τυπολογικά, εικονογραφικά και κατασκευαστικά παραπέμπει το φάτνωμα της Καβάλας. Εξαιτίας των διαστάσεών του (39,5 x 39,5 εκ.), που είναι διπλάσιες περίπου από τις διαστάσεις των μικρών φατνωμάτων (21 x 21εκ.), θα μπορούσε καταρχήν να σκεφθεί κανείς ως υποψήφια τα αμέσως μεγαλύτερα τετράγωνα φατνώματα, με ορατή ελεύθερη επιφάνεια πλευράς 33 εκ., γιατί τα αμέσως μεγαλύτερα ορθογώνια με μικρή διάσταση 39 εκ. εκ των πραγμάτων αποκλείονται.[54] Σ, αυτή την περίπτωση θα πρέπει να φαντασθούμε ότι μεγάλο τμήμα της πλαισίωσης παρέμενε ορατό και το φάτνωμα εδραζόταν σε ζώνη πλάτους μόλις 3 εκ. Η πιθανότητα όμως απόδοσής του αποδυναμώνεται ακόμα περισσότερο από την επισήμανση των Αμερικανών ότι και τα μεγαλύτερα τετράγωνα καλύμματα φατνωμάτων του προπύλου προσηλώνονταν στο φάτνωμα όπως τα μικρά.[55] Ιχνη όμως οπών στο φάτνωμα της Καβάλας δεν εντοπίζονται.

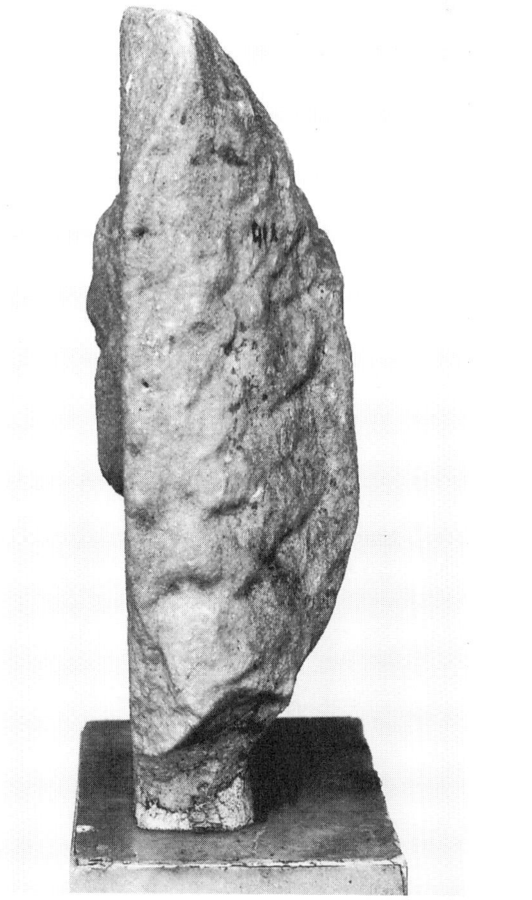

Εικ. 17. Μουσείο Καβάλας Λ 41. Φωτ. ως εικ.16.

Ως μόνη, λοιπόν, δυνατότητα φαίνεται να διαγράφεται πλέον η απόδοση του φατνώματος στα μικρά τετράγωνα φατνώματα του προνάου του Ιερού, που είναι μικρότερα από τα αντίστοιχα του προπύλου, και η ελεύθερη ορατή επιφάνειά τους (πλευράς 28 εκ. περίπου) ταιριάζει περισσότερο με τις διαστάσεις του έγκοιλου τετραγώνου του φατνώματος της Καβάλας, που είναι 25 x 25 εκ. Για την απόδοση αυτή συνηγορούν και ορισμένες τεχνικές λεπτομέρειες των αρχιτεκτονικών πλαισίων των φατνωμάτων αυτής της κατηγορίας, που σχηματίζουν μια επιφάνεια έδρασης πλάτους 10 εκ. στην επάνω επιφάνειά τους.[56] Η πατούρα του φατνώματος της Καβάλας είναι κατά δύο περίπου εκατοστά στενότερη.

Αλλά και η στυλιστική προσέγγιση της κεφαλής του φατνώματος με άλλα γλυπτά του προνάου, όπως η κεφαλή μιας εναέτιας μορφής,[57] υποστηρίζει αυτή την απόδοση. Κοινά στοιχεία είναι το γεμάτο σαρκώδες πρόσωπο, το αποστρογγυλωμένο πηγούνι και τα βυθισμένα μάτια.

Η απόδοση αυτή αλλάζει πλέον δραστικά την εικόνα της ανάγλυφης διακόσμησης της οροφής του προνάου του Ιερού. Μαζί με τα φατνώματα των κενταύρων φαίνεται ότι εναλλάσσονταν στην οροφή και φατνώματα με προτομές, κατά το πρότυπο της

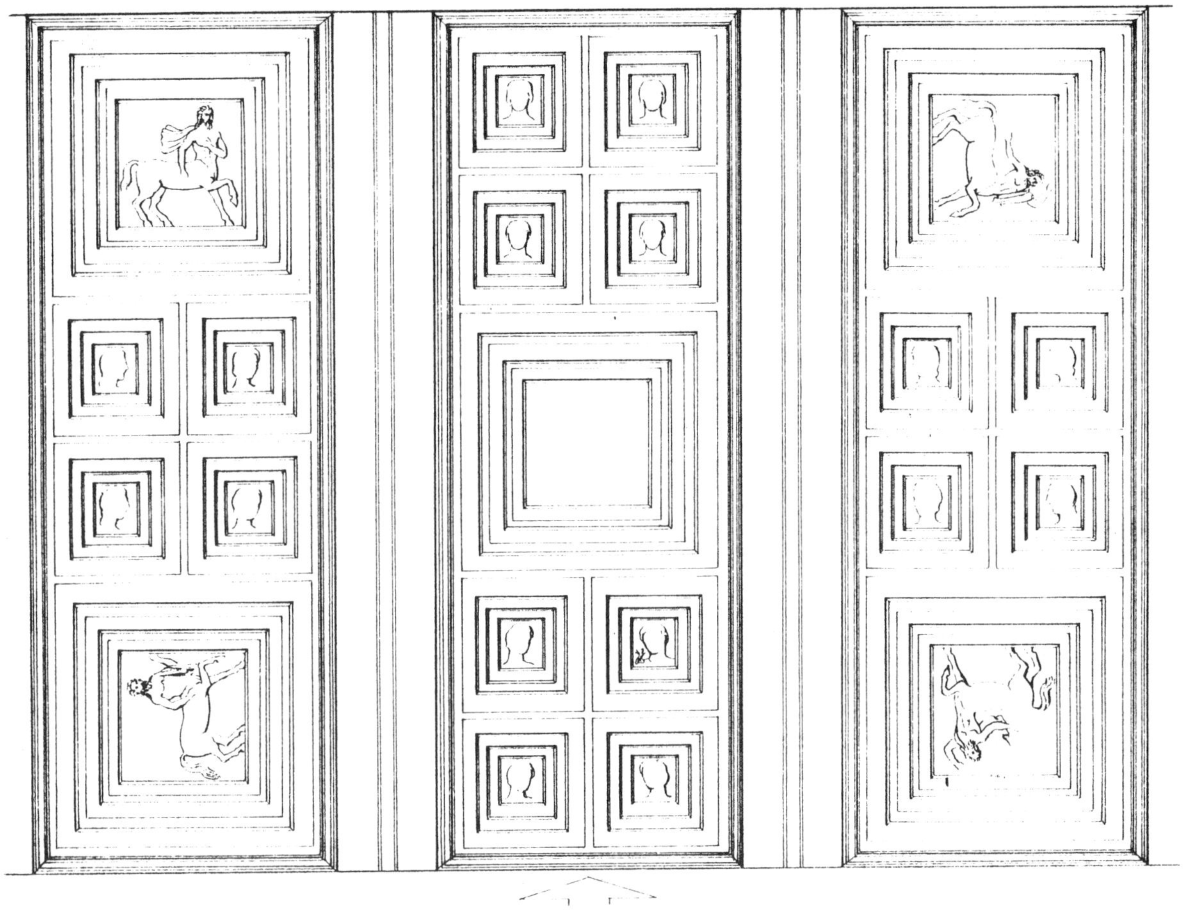

Εικ. 18. Σχεδιαστική αποκατάσταση της οροφής του προνάου του Ιερού της Σαμοθράκης. Κ. Ηλιάκης.

οροφής του προπύλου του Τεμένους. Κάτι τέτοιο μάλιστα είχε υποτεθεί από τους Αμερικανούς ότι είχε προβλεφθεί για τον πρόναο του Ιερού, στην αρχική φάση της σχεδίασής του. Ποια ήταν όμως ακριβώς η διάταξη, η σχέση και η σημασία μεγαλυτέρων και μικροτέρων φατνωμάτων στην οροφή του προνάου, θα παραμείνει ίσως για αρκετό ακόμα διάστημα άγνωστο. Πολύ πιθανό όμως είναι να σκεφθεί κανείς ότι στα φατνώματα με τις προτομές συνδυάζονταν οι στροφές και οι κλίσεις των κεφαλών, που παρατηρούνται και στα μικρά φατνώματα του προπύλου, με κύριο πάντα κριτήριο το οπτικό πεδίο που προσέφερε η οροφή στον εισερχόμενο μύστη. Μια λογικοφανής διάταξη μεγαλυτέρων και μικροτέρων φατνωμάτων προτείνεται στην αναπαράσταση της οροφής που φιλοτέχνησε ο ζωγράφος Κ. Ηλιάκης (εικ. 18).

Το φάτνωμα του Μουσείου Καβάλας (εικ. 16) προσφέρει αποφασιστικά στοιχεία για την ερμηνεία της μορφής. Η μορφή του μικρού φτερωτού ερωτιδέα στον δεξιό ώμο της, σε γονατιστή στάση, με στηριγμένο τον αριστερό της βραχίονα στον ώμο της μορφής, τείνει το δεξί χέρι, σπασμένο σήμερα, και εγγίζει την δεξιά παρειά και το πηγούνι της μορφής, όπως δείχνουν τα υπολλείμματα ενός πουντέλου σε αυτό το σημείο. Αποτελεί δηλαδή, προσδιοριστικό στοιχείο της (attribute). Δεν απομένει, λοιπόν, παρά να αναγνωρίσουμε στην γυναικεία κεφαλή την Αφροδίτη, ή μια γυναικεία μορφή, που εικονίζονταν όπως η Αφροδίτη. Με ένα παρόμοιο τρόπο προσδιορίζονται οι προτομές θεϊκών μορφών και Μουσών σε ανάγλυφα φατνώματα ρωμαϊκών χρόνων όπως στο ναό του Διδυμαίου Απόλλωνα και στο Σεραπείο της Μιλήτου. Σε αυτή την περίπτωση ο Ερμής χαρακτηρίζεται από το κηρύκειο, η Αρτεμις από την φαρέτρα και ο Ποσειδών από την τρίαινα, ενώ ο Απόλλων αποδίδει τον τύπο του λατρευτικού αγάλματος.

Η ερμηνεία αυτή καθιστά το φάτνωμα του Μουσείου Καβάλας ιδιαίτερα ενδιαφέρον, σε συνάρτηση μάλιστα με τις ερμηνείες που έχουν προταθεί για τις μικρές προτομές της οροφής του προπύλου, στις οποίες πιστεύεται ότι εικονίζονται οι Μεγάλοι Θεοί της Σαμοθράκης Αξίερος, Αξιοκέρσα και Αξιόκερσος μαζί με άλλες θεϊκές μορφές και μυθικά πρόσωπα, που σχετίζονται περισσότερο ή λιγότερο με τον Κόσμο των Μυστηρίων, μολονότι δεν υπάρχει πάντοτε απόλυτη ομοφωνία στις επιμέρους ερμηνείες.

Στην περίπτωση πάντως του φατνώματος της Καβάλας η ερμηνεία της μορφής δεν επιδέχεται αντιρρήσεις. Η λατρεία της Αφροδίτης στη Σαμοθράκη ανιχνεύεται από πολύ πρώιμη εποχή και αποκτά κυρίαρχη θέση στο πλευρό της μεγάλης μητέρας αργότερα. Από τους Αμερικανούς ερευνητές έχει επισημανθεί ότι η Αφροδίτη είναι η συχνότερα αναφερόμενη θεότητα στις φιλολογικές πηγές μετά τους Μεγάλους Θεούς[58] και η παρουσία της έχει υποτεθεί, χωρίς όμως σαφείς ενδείξεις στα μικρά φατνώματα του προπύλου. Η πληροφορία, τέλος, του Πλίνιου (36.25) για το σύμπλεγμα Αφροδίτης και Πόθου έργο του Σκόπα στην Σαμοθράκη,[59] επιβεβαιώνει την σημασία της λατρείας της στο νησί.

Η προτομή του φατνώματος της Καβάλας δεν αποκλείεται να εξαρτάται από έναν αγαλματικό τύπο Αφροδίτης, όπως έχει υποτεθεί άλλωστε και για ορισμένες από τις προτομές που κοσμούσαν την οροφή του προπύλου. Το ότι υποδηλώνεται κάποια σχέση προς το χαμένο έργο του Σκόπα, είναι πολύ τολμηρό να το σκεφθούμε. Τον αγαλματικό πάντως τύπο θα μπορούσαμε κατά προσέγγιση να τον φαντασθούμε στον τύπο του αγάλματος της ακέφαλης Αφροδίτης της Αρχαίας Αγοράς S 473,[60] όπου ο ποσπασματικά σωζόμενος Ερωτας κάθεται σε ένα παρόμοιο μοτίβο στον αριστερό ώμο της μορφής (εικ. 19).

Επίμετρο: Το ανάγλυφο του Μουσείου Θάσου Λ 2811 (εικ. 20)

Παρόλα όσα εκτέθηκαν παραπάνω, το ανάγλυφο του Μουσείου Καβάλας δεν θα αρκούσε ως μοναδικό παράδειγμα να πιστοποιήσει ένα τύπο αναγλύφου καλύμματος φατνώματος, μέχρι τώρα αμάρτυρο και άγνωστο και μάλιστα από κτίριο της Σαμοθράκης. Ζητούμενο, λοιπόν, ήταν η επισήμανση και ο εντοπισμός και άλλων παραδειγμάτων, που θα επιβεβαίωναν τις σκέψεις που διατυπώθηκαν και θα πιστοποιούσαν τον τύπο του φατνώματος που προσδιορίσαμε παραπάνω. Ενα απροσδόκητο εύρημα στο νέο Μουσείο της Θάσου[61] είναι αρκετά διαφωτιστικό για το θέμα μας.

Το θραύσμα αναγλύφου του Μουσείου Θάσου Λ 2811 προέρχεται από ένα παρόμοιο ανάγλυφο με αυτό του Μουσείου Καβάλας Λ 41. Σώζεται μόνο το επάνω αριστερό τμήμα του, αλλά οι ομοιότητες των λεπτομερειών των επί μέρους στοιχείων προς το φάτνωμα του Μουσείου Καβάλας δεν αφήνουν την παραμικρή αμφιβολία για την αποκατάσταση της μορφής του. Το θραύσμα Λ 2811 είναι επίσης από χονδρόκοκκο θασίτικο μάρμαρο, εξαιρετικά όμως φθαρμένο σε σχέση με το προηγούμενο. Σώζει το μεγαλύτερο τμήμα της αριστερής και άνω πλαισίωσης του, που ελέγχεται ως ισοπαχής περίπου προς το φάτνωμα της Καβάλας, και ικανό τμήμα της πίσω επιφάνειάς του, που βεβαιώνει την ίδια σαμαρωτή, κολουροπυραμιδική διαμόρφωση. Από την παράσταση σώζεται το μεγαλύτερο τμήμα αρκετά φθαρμένης κεφαλής σε τρία τέταρτα προς τα δεξιά.

Το ανάγλυφο βρέθηκε, σύμφωνα με το ευρετήριο

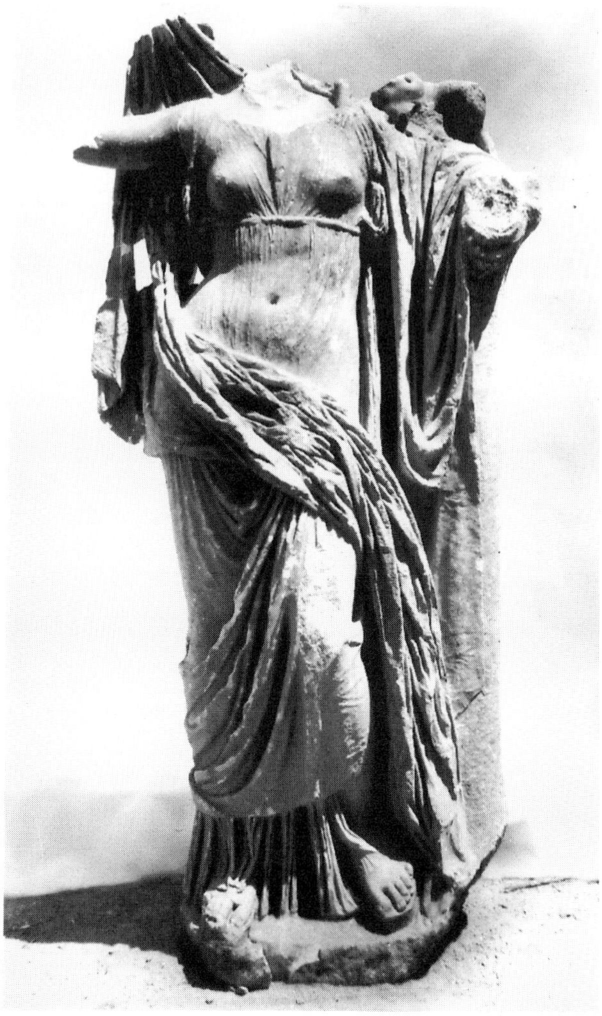

Εικ. 19. Αθήνα, Μουσείο Αρχαίας Αγοράς S 473. Φωτ. Ανασκαφών Αεχαίας Αγοράς

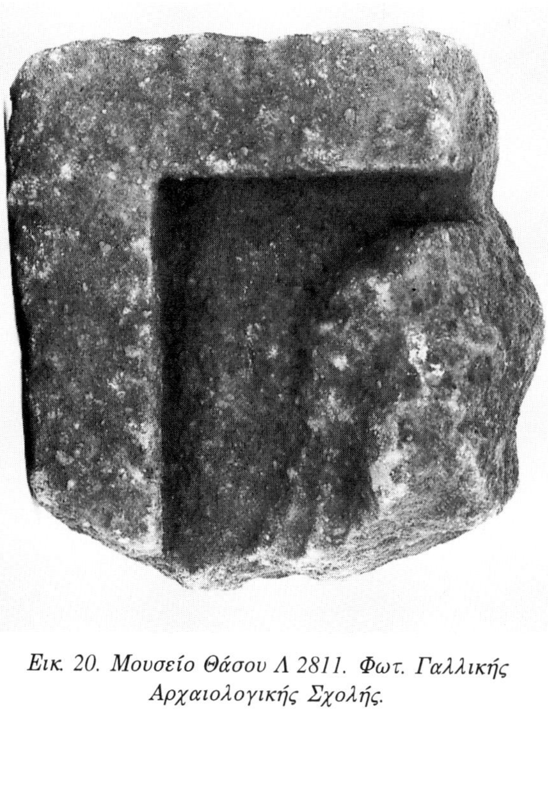

Εικ. 20. Μουσείο Θάσου Λ 2811. Φωτ. Γαλλικής Αρχαιολογικής Σχολής.

του Μουσείου Θάσου, σε ανασκαφή της Γαλλικής Αρχαιολογικής Σχολής στον αγρό Δητριάδη, στη βόρεια συνοικία[62] και είναι προφανώς επιφανειακό και αστρωματογράφητο εύρημα, όπως άλλωστε και τα περισσότερα από τα μικρά φατνώματα του προπύλου, που βρέθηκαν στη Θάσο.[63] Εχει μέγιστο σωζόμενο ύψος 27 εκ. και μέγιστο σωζόμενο πλάτος 24 εκ. Η ταινία που το περιβάλλει δεν είναι λεία και απέχει από τον κάμπο του αναγλύφου 3,5 εκ. όπως συμβαίνει και στο φάτνωμα της Καβάλας Λ 41.

Η αρκετά φθαρμένη κεφαλή αποδίδεται με την αντίθετη στροφή και κλίση από αυτή του φατνώματος της Καβάλας. Στο ευρετήριο του Μουσείου Θάσου,[64] η μορφή αναφέρεται ως γυναικεία αλλά μια προσεκτικότερη εξέταση της κεφαλής δεν αφήνει αμφιβολίες ότι πρόκειται για ανδρική γενειοφόρα μορφή. Παρά την φθορά του προσώπου, μπορεί ακόμα να διακρίνει κανείς ό, τι απέμεινε από τους έντονα βυθισμένους οφθαλμούς, το τριγωνικό μέτωπο, τη μάζα των μαλλιών και κυρίως τον όγκο της πυκνής γενειάδας, που πιστοποιεί και το φύλο της μορφής.

Στα δεξιά του κάτω μέρους της κεφαλής, στον κάμπο του αναγλύφου εικονίζονται ίχνη αναγλυφικών εξαρμάτων από ευθύγραμμα στελέχη, τα οποία φαίνεται να συγκλίνουν προς τα πάνω και τα οποία θα μπορούσε να εκλάβει κανείς ως τμήματα πλοκάμων η πτυχών ενός ενδύματος, που πέφτει από το κεφάλι της μορφής. Κατά την εξέταση όμως του αναγλύφου, η φθορά της επιφάνειας δεν επέτρεψε να διαφανεί με ακρίβεια η συνάρτηση των λεπτομερειών που περιγράψαμε με την μάζα των μαλλιών στο άνω και δεξί τμήμα της κεφαλής. Δεν αποκλείεται, λοιπόν, τα αναγλυφικά εξάρματα που περιγράψαμε να αποτελούν μέρος ενός αυτοτελούς αντικειμένου, το οποίο πιθανότατα στηρίζεται στον δεξιό ώμο της μορφής. Ενα τέτοιο ενδεχόμενο παραπέμπει, κατά το πρότυπο πάντα του φατνώματος του Μουσείου Καβάλας, σε ένα attribute, σε ένα "λαλούν σύμβολο" δηλαδή, που προσδιόριζε την μορφή που εικονίζεται στο ανάγλυφο. Τα υπολείμματα αυτών των αναγλυφικών εξαρμάτων θα μπορούσαν, κατά μία υπόθεση, να αποτελούν τις αιχμές μιας τρίαινας. Σύμφωνα με αυτή την ερμηνεία το ευθύγραμμο τμήμα θα μπορούσε να αποτελεί το μεσαίο στέλεχος, ενώ τα ίχνη δεξιά και αριστερά, τα ακραία στελέχη της τρίαινας.[65] Μια τέτοια ερμηνεία του αντικειμένου παραπέμπει στον Ποσειδώνα, με την υπόσταση του οποίου εναρμονίζεται και ο εικονογραφικός τύπος της κεφαλής. Αυτός ο τρόπος χαρακτηρισμού των προτομών του Ποσειδώνα, με συντετμημένο το προσδιοριστικό του στοιχείο, την τρίαινα, είναι ήδη γνωστός όχι μόνον από νομίσματα,[66] αλλά και από παραδείγματα ρωμαϊκών φατνωματικών αναγλύφων. Πρόκειται κυρίως για το πήλινο φατνωματικό ανάγλυφο από την οροφή μιας ρωμαϊκής βίλλας στο Porcigliano, που κοσμείται με προτομή Ποσειδώνα που χαρακτηρίζεται από την τρίαινα και βρισκόταν προπολεμικά στην Γλυπτοθήκη του Μονάχου,[67] καθώς επίσης και για ένα απότμημα μαρμάρινου φατνωματικού αναγλύφου από το Σεραπείο της Μιλήτου, το οποίο σώζει μόνο την τρίαινα, και έχει υποτεθεί ότι εικόνιζε τον Ποσειδώνα.[68]

Το φάτνωμα του Μουσείου Θάσου Λ 2811 επιβεβαιώνει τις σκέψεις που διατυπώθηκαν παραπάνω, με αφορμή το φάτνωμα του Μουσείου Καβάλας Λ 41 και αποκαθιστά ένα ακόμα χαμένο κρίκο στην μακρά αλυσίδα της αναζήτησης της προέλευσης αλλά και της κατανόησης αυτών των αρχιτεκτονικών αναγλύφων. Η προέλευσή τους από την Σαμοθράκη, υστερα από την πολλαπλή διαπίστωση στη Θάσο φατνωμάτων των δύο άλλων κατηγοριών, πρέπει να θεωρείται βέβαιη. Τα δύο παραδείγματα Καβάλας-Θάσου δεν πιστοποιούν μόνον έναν άγνωστο ως τώρα τύπο φατνωματικού αναγλύφου από τον πρόναο του Ιερού της Σαμοθράκης, αλλά διαφωτίζουν ταυτόχρονα την ερμηνεία και την κατανόηση της ανάγλυφης διακόσμησης της οροφής του προνάου. Μολονότι αντιπροσωπεύουν μόνο το 12,5% του αρχικού υλικού, εφόσον από τα 16 συνολικά φατνωματικά ανάγλυφα αυτής κατηγορίας, σύμφωνα με την σχεδιαστική αποκατάσταση της οροφής του προνάου (εικ. 18), έχουν σωθεί μόνον τα δύο, εν τούτοις αρκούν για να βεβαιώσουν ότι στην οροφή του προνάου, μαζί με τα ανάγλυφα των κενταύρων εναλάσσονταν και προτομές θεϊκών μορφών, με προσδιοριστικά μάλιστα της ονομασίας τους στοιχεία. Τα δύο παραδείγματα, που ενδεικτικά παραπεμπουν στην παράσταση ενός δωδεκαθέου στην οροφή του προνάου ανακαλούν τα αινιγματικά "καλύνματα προσώπων", που αναφέρει η οικοδομική επιγραφή της Επιδαύρου και ίσως έμεσα συντείνουν στην ερμηνεία των μικρών φατνωματικών προτομών του προπύλου του Τεμένους.

Για την παροχή φωτογραφιών ευχαριστώ την Γαλλική Αρχαιολογική Σχολή, την Διεύθυνση των ανασκαφών της Αρχαίας Αγοράς και τις Διευθύνσεις των Εφορειών Προϊστορικών και Κλασικών Αρχαιοτήτων Καβάλας και Κομοτηνής. Ευχαριστώ θερμά τον καθηγητή Γ. Δεσπίνη για την συζήτηση γύρω από το ανάγλυφο του Μουσείου Καβάλας Λ 41 και την θερμή αποδοχή εκ μέρους του της ερμηνείας του ως καλύμματος φατνώματος, την συνάδελφο Β. Μαχαίρα για διάφορες διευκολύνσεις και πληροφορίες, την καθηγήτρια Ο. Παλαγγιά για την υπομονή της στη βελτίωση και συμμόρφωση των υποσημειώσεων και τις επισημάνσεις της σχετικά με το πρόβλημα χρονολόγησης των γλυπτών του προνάου του Ιερού της Σαμοθράκης, και τον φίλο ζωγράφο Κ. Ηλιάκη για την συζήτηση του θέματος και την σχεδιαστική αποκατάσταση της οροφής του προνάου της εικ. 18.

Συντομογραφίες

SI: A.Conze – A.Houser – G.Niemann, *Archäologische Untersuchungen auf Samothrake* (1875)

S II: A.Conze – A.Houser – O.Benndorf, *Neue Archäologishe Untersuchungen auf Samothrake* (1880)

Samothrace 3: Ph.W.Lehmann, *Samothrace* 3, *The Hieron* I.II (1969)

Samothrace 5: Ph.W.Lehmann κ.ά., *Samothrace* 5, *The Temenos* (1982)

Holtzmann: *Études Thassienes* XV, *Corpus des reliefs* 1 (1994)

Tancke: K.Tancke, *Figuralkassetten griechischer und römischer Steindecken* (1989)

Σημειώσεις

1. Α. Μάντης, *Θρακική Επετηρίς* VII, 1987–1990 (αφιερωμένος στην 80ή επέτειο των γενεθλίων του καθηγητού Γεωργίου Μπακαλάκη) 159–170.
2. Χ. Κουκούλη-Χρυσανθάκη, *ΑΔελτ* 29, 1973/74, Χρονικά 778.
3. B. Holtzmann, *Thasiaca*, *BCH* Suppl. 5, 1979, 9 σημ. 31. Πρβλ. Holtzmann 90 σημ. 35.
4. Ζ. Μπόνιας στο H. Kyrieleis (επιμ.), *Archaische und klassische griechische Plastik* II (1986) 35–44, πίν. 91–92.
5. Χ. Μακαρόνας – Ε. Γιούρη, *Οι οικίες αρπαγής της Ελένης και Διονύσου της Πέλλας* (1989) 140, πίν. 25.
6. D.M. Robinson, *Olynthus* V (1933), 13, πίν. 17, A- B.
7. B. Schiffler, *Die Typologie des Kentauren in der antiken Kunst vom 10. bis zum Ende des 4. Jhs. v. Chr.* (1976) 107–109. Πρβλ. *LIMC* VIII (1997), λ. Kentauren (Hellenistisch, Kommmentar) (S. Drougou).
8. S I, 12. 23. 27–28. πίν. LII.
9. Βιέννη, Kunsthistorisches Museum, αρ. 238. Conze ό.π. (σημ. 8). *Samothrace* 3,1, εικ. 187. *Kunsthistorisches Museum Wien. Katalog der Antikensammlung* II, *Funde aus Ephesos und Samothrake* (1978) 133–134, εικ. 116–118. Tancke 41, Kat. 7, 1, πίν. XXXI 1–2. Της ίδιας, *AW* 1989,4, 34, εικ. 18.
10. K. Lehmann, *Hesperia* 21, 1952, 42. Του ίδιου, *Hesperia* 22, 1953, 12. Του ίδιου, *Samothrace* (1955) 87. *Samothrace* 3, 1, 237–253. Tancke 41. 263–64, 7,7–15. Μάντης ό.π. (σημ. 1) 163–165.
11. K. Lehmann, *AJA* 61, 1957, 123 κε.
12. *Samothrace* 5, 148 κε.
13. A.H. Smith, *Catalogue of Greek Sculpture in the Department of Greek and Roman Antiquities* II (1900) 1038–1042. Tancke 18–22. 229–232, 3,1–10, πίν. X-XIX.
14. C. Praschniker στο *Das Mausoleum von Belevi. FiE* VI (1979) 73 κε. Πρβλ. Tancke 25–30. 234–242, 15,1–21, πίν. XXII-XXV.
15. *Samothrace* 3, 1, 110–116 (αρχιτεκτονική), 237–253 (γλυπτική), πίν. LXXXI. LXXXIV-LXXXV.
16. A. Linfert, *Kunstzentren hellenistischer Zeit* (1976) 126–128. O Holtzmann 91, προσγράφει τα ανάγλυφα των κενταύρων, πιθανόν και την σύλληψη του σχεδιασμού τους, σε θασίτικο εργαστήριο.
17. Πρόκειται για το θραύσμα αναγλύφου αρ. 51.368, που σώζει το μεγαλύτερο τμήμα, από το γόνατο και κάτω ενός μπροστινού αριστερού σκέλους αλόγου και έχει πάχος πλάκας 0,04 μ. [K. Lehmann, *AJA* 61, 1957, 123 κε., εικ. 3. *Samothrace* 3, 1, 241, C(S)4, εικ. 195. Tancke 263, αρ. 7,10. Μάντης ό.π. (σημ.1) 165, αρ. 10, 166. Holtzmann 91, σημ.40] και το θραύσμα αναγλύφου αρ. 48.579, που σώζει φύλλα και ένα τσαμπί σταφύλια και έχει πάχος πλάκας 0,028 μ. [*Samothrace* 3, 1, 243 κε., C(S)10, εικ. 202. Μάντης ό.π. (σημ.1) 165, αρ. 16, 166. Holtzmann 91, σημ. 40].
18. Πρόκειται για το θραύσμα I 1717 στην αποθήκη της Antiken-Sammlung (*Samothrace* 3,1, 240, C(V)6, εικ. 192. Μάντης ό.π. (σημ. 1) 164, αρ.6, 166 σημ. 18. Tancke 262, αρ. 7,6. Holtzmann 91 σημ.43) από ένα ελεύθερα δουλεμένο δεξί άκρο χέρι, που κρατά ένα κωνικό αντικείμενο και είναι σπασμένο πάνω και κάτω. Το χέρι κρατούσε ανάμεσα στον αντίχειρα, που δεν σώζεται και στον δείκτη ένα αντικείμενο, όπως δείχνει μια αύλακα 1,2 εκ. βαθειά και 0,6 εκ. πλατειά.
19. Αρ. 51.293. Πρόκειται για ένα ελεύθερα δουλεμένο, δεξί ανδρικό άκρο χέρι, σπασμένο στον καρπό. Το χέρι κρατούσε ένα κυλινδρικό αντικείμενο ανάμεσα στην παλάμη και στα λυγισμένα δάκτυλα. Μια αβαθής κοιλότητα στην παλάμη, περίπου 1,5 εκ. εξυπηρετούσε την ένθεση του αντικειμένου. K. Lehmann, *AJA* 61, 1957, 123 κε., εικ. 2. *Samothrace* 3,1, 243, C(S)9, εικ. 199–201. Tancke 264, αρ. 7,15. Μάντης ό.π. (σημ. 1) 165 κε., αρ. 15. Holtzmann 91 σημ. 43.
20. Linfert ό.π. (σημ. 16). B.S. Ridgway, *Hellenistic Sculpture* I (1990) 158–161. Και οι δύο χρησιμοποιούν το επιχείρημα ότι η κεραμεική στην περιοχή θεμελίωσης του προθαλάμου δεν χρονολογείται μετά τα μέσα του 3ου π. Χ. αιώνα. Πρβλ. I.C. Love στο *Samothrace* 3, 2, 173 κε. Τελευταία η P.A. Webb (*Hellenistic Architectural Sculpture* [1996] 144–147) υποστήριξε μία επίσης υψηλή χρονολόγηση στις αρχές του 3ου αιώα π.Χ.
21. R. Fleischer στο *Das Mausoleum von Belevi. FiE* VI (1979) 136, εικ. 108. 137, εικ. 110. Η σύγκριση και η χρονολόγηση στα μέσα του 3ου π. Χ. αιώνα έχει γίνει ήδη από τον H. Kaehler, *Der grosse Fries von Pergamon* (1948) 172 σημ. 57. Πρβλ. K. Lehmann, *AJA* 61, 1957, 124 σημ. 12.
22. P.C. Bol, *AntPl* X (1970) 81–90, εικ. 18. Η κεφαλή του κενταύρου της Βιέννης επανειλημένα αποτιμήθηκε στυλιστικά μέσα από τον απόηχο των μορφών της ζωφόρου του Περγάμου, ενώ επισημάνθηκε ιδιαίτερα η ομοιότητά της με τον αντίπαλο της Μοίρας στη ζωφόρο του βωμού. Συγκρίσιμα θεωρήθηκαν ακόμα και μερικά κεφάλια από την ζωφόρο του Εκατείου στην Λάγινα: Tancke 43. Η κεφαλή συγκρίθηκε από τους K. και Ph. Lehmann με τον "Ποσειδώνα Jameson" του Λούβρου και την κεφαλή του Χείρωνα στο Palazzo Conservatori (*Samothrace* 3, 1, 247–251).
23. J. Schäfer στο *Pergamenische Forschungen* I.*Pergamon gessammelte Aufsätze* (1972) 164 κε., εικ. 1–11.
24. Helbig[4] II, αρ. 1398 (H. v. Steuben). G.M.A. Richter, *The Sculpture and Sculptors of the Greeks* (1970) 240. 247, εικ. 844–845. K. Kell, *Formuntersuchungen zu spät- und nachhellenistischen Gruppen* (1988) 37 κε. R.R.R. Smith, *Hellenistic Sculpture* (1991) 132, εικ. 161–163.
25. *Samothrace* 3, 1, 115: "All five of the centaurs moved toward the right, four prancing, the fifth rearing. Surely the rearing centaur occupied the central field of the ceiling and faced the initiates as they entered the pronaos."
26. Ο.π. (σημ. 11) 123–127. Σύμφωνος και ο H. Ehrhardt, *Samothrake* (1985) 339 κε.
27. Καλλίστρατος, "εἰς τὸ κενταύρου ἄγαλμα". Κατά την Tancke 42 σημ. 332, η περιγραφή του Καλλίστρατου είναι πολύ γενικόλογη, ενώ με τη λέξη "ἄγαλμα"

νοείται, ως συνήθως, ένα περίοπτο έργο και όχι ένα ανάγλυφο. Για τον Καλλίστρατο βλ. *RE* VII Suppl. (1940) 317 κε., λ. Kallistratos (Bernet).
28. Holtzmann 91.
29. Για την σημασία του "Ιερού" της Σαμοθράκης, βλ. K. Lehmann στο *Samothrace* 3,2, 3 κε. ιδιαίτερα 20.
30. Roscher, *ML* II 1 (1890–1894) 1050 κε. Kell ο.π. (σημ. 24). Smith ό.π. (σημ. 24) 127 κε. Πρβλ. *LIMC* VIII Suppl. (1997) λ. Kentauren (Hellenistisch- Kommentar. S. Drougou).
31. Lehmann ό.π. (σημ. 11) 124. *Samothrace* 3, 1 252 κε. και σημ. 25. Πρβλ. Tancke 42.
32. Μάντης ό.π. (σημ. 1) 165, αρ. 16, 166. Βλ. και σημ. 17.
33. Holtzmann 91 σημ. 41.
34. Schäfer ό.π. (σημ. 23) 186 κε., 188 σημ. 24.
35. Για την αποκατάσταση των φατνωμάτων της οροφής του προπύλου, βλ. D. Spittle στο *Samothrace* 5, 74 κε. *Samothrace* 5, 139 κε., 148 κε., εικ. 139, πίν. 34–40, 44,2, 46, 47, 50. Πρβλ. Tancke 22–25, 232–234.
36. Holtzmann 87–89 και 92–94.
37. *Samothrace* 5, 165.
38. Holtzmann 93.
39. Για τα ερμηνευτικά ζητήματα αλλά και την χρονολόγηση των μικρών φατνωμάτων, βλ. αναλυτικά Tancke 23–25. Πρβλ. Holtzmann 93 κε.
40. *Samothrace* 3, 1, 115–116.
41. Δ. Λαζαρίδης, *Νεάπολις, Χριστούπολις, Καβάλα* (1969) 76–78. Στις προσωπικές του σημειώσεις, όπως με πληροφόρησε η συνάδελφος Κ. Λαζαρίδη, το θεωρεί παλαιό εύρημα άγνωστης προέλευσης.
42. Λαζαρίδης ό.π. (σημ. 41) 84, Λ. 41. Το ανάγλυφο εικονίζεται στον πίνακα 23.
43. D. Pandermalis, *Dion. Die Heilige Stadt der Makedonen* (1987) 12.
44. Tancke 18–22. 229–232 (Κατ. 3,1- 3,10), πίν X-XIX.
45. J. C. Carter, *The Sculpture of the Sanctuary of Athena at Priene* (1983). Πρβλ. Tancke 30–41. 243–261 (Κατ. 6,1–65), πίν. XXV-XXIX.
46. P. Coupel – P. Demargne, *Le monument des Néréides. FdX* III 1 (1969) 94 κε., εικ. 1. Tancke 12–14, πίν. IX 1.
47. *IG* IV^2 102. G. Roux, *L'architecture de l'Argolide* (1961) 84 κε. Tancke 14–17.
48. Tancke 103–105.
49. Tancke 105–108.
50. Βλ. σχετικά Σ. Ν. Παπαγεωργίου, *Σαμοθράκη* (Αθήνα 1982).
51. Για τους βανδαλισμούς στο χώρο του ιερού κατά τον προηγούμενο αιώνα, βλ. G. Deville – E. Coquart, *Archives des missions scientifiques et litéraires*, 2d ser., 4, 1867, 259 κε. 268. 275 κε. Πρβλ. S II, 9 κε.
52. Γ. Μπακαλάκης, *Ανάγλυφα* (1969) 21 κε.
53. H. Sitte, *ÖJh* 11, 1908, 142–164. Πρβλ. Holtzmann 156, αρ. 96.
54. Για τους τρεις διαφορετικούς τύπους φατνωμάτων της οροφής του προπύλου, βλ. *Samothrace* 5, 75 κε., (πίν. XLVII B) και 148, όπου η Ph. Lehmann θεωρεί απίθανο ότι οι δύο άλλες κατηγορίες φατνωμάτων εκτός των μικρών κοσμούνταν με εικονιστικά θέματα.
55. Samothrace 5, 75 πίν. XXXIX,1 (+44).
56. Για τους τρεις διαφορετικούς τύπους φατνωμάτων, που συνδυάζονταν στην οροφή του προνάου, βλ. *Samothrace* 3, 1, 112 κε. Τα πλαίσια των φατνωμάτων,που υποδέχονταν ως καλυπτήριες πλάκες τα ανάγλυφα των κενταύρων, είχαν στο επάνω μέρος τους πατούρα πλάτους 8 εκ. (σ. 114 σημ. 196). Στην περίπτωση πάντως του προνάου τα καλύμματα των φατνωμάτων δεν στερεώνονταν με καρφίδες, όπως συνέβαινε στο πρόπυλο.
57. *Samothrace* 3, 1, 266 εικ. 229, 308 εικ. 257.
58. N. Lewis, *Samothrace. The Ancient Literary Sources*, 137 (indexes).
59. Το πολυσυζητημένο, χαμένο και άγνωστο από αντίγραφα σύμπλεγμα, είναι πιθανότερο ότι εικόνιζε δύο μόνον μορφές, όπως διατείνεται και η Ph. Lehmann, *Samothrace* 5, 276 κε. σημ. 38 κε.), με την οποία συμφωνεί και ο R. Fleischer (*Gnomon* 1985, 263) και όχι τρεις μορφές, όπως το αποκατέστησε σχεδιαστικά ο A.F. Stewart (*Skopas of Paros* [1977] 109 κε., εικ. 7) ακολουθώντας μια παλαιότερη υπόθεση του K. Kerenyi (*SOslo* 31, 1955, 141 κε.).
60. V. Machaira, *Les groupes statuaires d' Aphrodite et d' Eros* (1993) 44–45, αρ. 4, πίν. 8–9.
61. Για την διευκόλυνση της έρευνας στις αποθήκες των Μουσείων Καβάλας και Θάσου, στις 29 και 30. 4. 96, ευχαριστώ θερμά την Εφορο Αρχ/των κ. Χ. Κουκούλη και τον συνάδελφο Ζ. Μπόνια.
62. Στην δημοσίευση της ανασκαφής (υπεύθυνος F. Salviat), G. Daux, *BCH* 86, 1962, 935, το εύρημα δεν αναφέρεται.
63. Holtzmann 87–89. 92. Στην βόρεια συνοικία, στην πύλη του Ερμού, είχε βρεθεί και το μικρό ανάγλυφο φάτνωμα του Μουσείου Θάσου αρ. 1539. Holtzmann 88, αρ. 19, πίν. XXVb.
64. "Ανω αριστερόν τμήμα αναγλύφου σώζον δεξιόν μέρος γυναικείας κεφαλής".
65. Εξεταστέο πάντως παραμένει και το ενδεχόμενο τα στελέχη που περιγράψαμε να αποτελούν τις ακτίνες ενός κεραυνού, μια ερμηνεία που θα μας υποχρέωνε να αναγνωρίσουμε στην ανδρική μορφή τον Δία. Θα πρέπει όμως να επισημανθεί ότι λείπει η σχετική εικονογραφική τεκμηρίωση, που δείχνει το θεό να κρατά τον κεραυνό στο ύψος του ώμου ("κατωμαδίαν"), ενώ παραμένει αδιευκρίνιστο το αντικείμενο που χαρακτήριζε τον Δία σε ένα ρωμαϊκό φατνωματικό ανάγλυφο από τον ναό του Διδυμαίου Απόλλωνα: H. Knackfuß, *Didyma* I. *Die Baubeschreibung* (1941) 96, πίν.171 F.459. K. Tuchelt, *Vorarbeiten zu einer Topographie von Didyma*. 9. Beih. *IstMitt* (1973) 38. 86. 109 σημ. 73, πίν. 32,1. S. Pülz, *Untersuchungen zur kaiserzeitlichen Bauornamentik von Didyma* (διατριβή Mainz 1984, αδημ.) 62 κε. Κατ. 107 KsD 1, πίν. 45,2. Tancke 104. 295, αρ. 43,1, πίν. LXVI 3.
66. *BMC* Macedonia 16, 67–68. *SNG* Cop. 1244. *LIMC* VII (1995) λ. Poseidon αρ. 55 (E. Simon).
67. Το ανάγλυφο που είχε αριθμό Γλυπτοθήκης 185 καταστράφηκε στον πόλεμο. Χ. Καρούζος, *ΑΔελτ* 13, 1930/31, 95 κε., εικ. 38. B. S. Ridgway, *The Severe Style in Greek Sculpture* (1970) 111–112, εικ. 144. *LIMC* VII, λ. Poseidon, αρ. 28a.
68. H. Knackfuß, *Milet* I 7. *Der Südmarkt und die benachbarten Bauten* (1924) 202, εικ. 212. Tancke 107 σημ. 790.

Ο πώρινος Άτλας από την αρχαία Αγορά της Θεσσαλονίκης

Θεοδοσία Στεφανίδου-Τιβερίου

Ο Άτλας[1] που βρέθηκε το 1966 στην αρχαία Αγορά της Θεσσαλονίκης είναι από τα πιο αξιοπρόσεκτα γλυπτά του Αρχαιολογικού Μουσείου της πόλης (εικ. 1–4).[2] Παρόλο που δεν είναι λαξευμένος σε μάρμαρο, αλλά σε καστανό πωρόλιθο, η ρωμαλέα πλαστική διατύπωση των όγκων του τραβά αμέσως την προσοχή. Δεν γνωρίζουμε δυστυχώς ποιά ήταν η αρχική θέση του έργου, αφού βρέθηκε εντοιχισμένο σε "λείψανα αρχαιοτέρων κατασκευών ... κάτω από το πλακόστρωτο της Αγοράς".[3] Παρά ταύτα δεν υπάρχει αμφιβολία ότι πρόκειται για ένα σημαντικό λείψανο της ελληνιστικής Θεσσαλονίκης, πιθανότατα από ένα μνημείο με επίσημο χαρακτήρα, όπως θα δούμε στη συνέχεια.

Σώζεται το επάνω μέρος της μορφής, ύψους 99 εκ., που ήταν χωριστά λαξευμένο έως την ηβική χώρα. Ένα μέρος του, δηλαδή η ισχιακή χώρα με τα γεννητικά όργανα, είναι συγκολλημένο από περισσότερα κομμάτια. Λείπουν τα δύο χέρια από τη γένεση των βραχιόνων, καθώς και μικρά τμήματα από το πάνω μέρος των γλουτών και τη δεξιά ωμοπλάτη. Αποκρούσεις υπάρχουν στο πρόσωπο, στα γένεια, στα γεννητικά όργανα, και μικρότερα χτυπήματα σε όλη σχεδόν την επιφάνεια του γλυπτού, ενώ τρύπες από διάβρωση παρατηρούνται στην πίσω όψη.

Το κάτω μέρος του σωζόμενου τμήματος (πλ. 46,5 εκ.) είναι οριζόντια κομμένο και στην επιφάνεια αυτή είναι ανοιγμένος προς τα πίσω ένας σχετικά ακανόνιστος τόρμος (διάμ. 10 εκ. περίπου, βάθ. 5,5 εκ.) για τη σύνδεση με τα σκέλη, που ήταν κατασκευασμένα από ξεχωριστό κομμάτι. Ο δεξιός

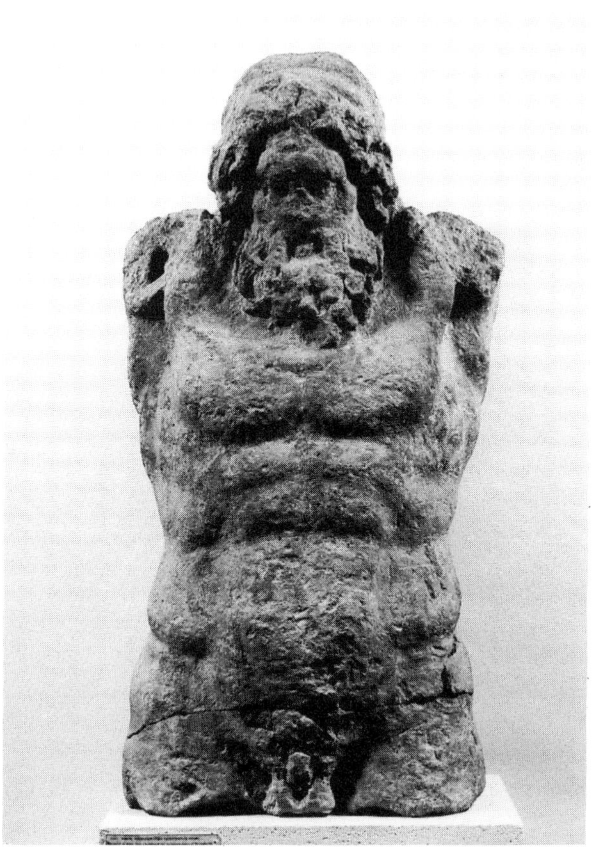

Εικ. 1. Θεσσαλονίκη, Αρχ. Μουσείο αρ. 10301. Πώρινος Άτλας.

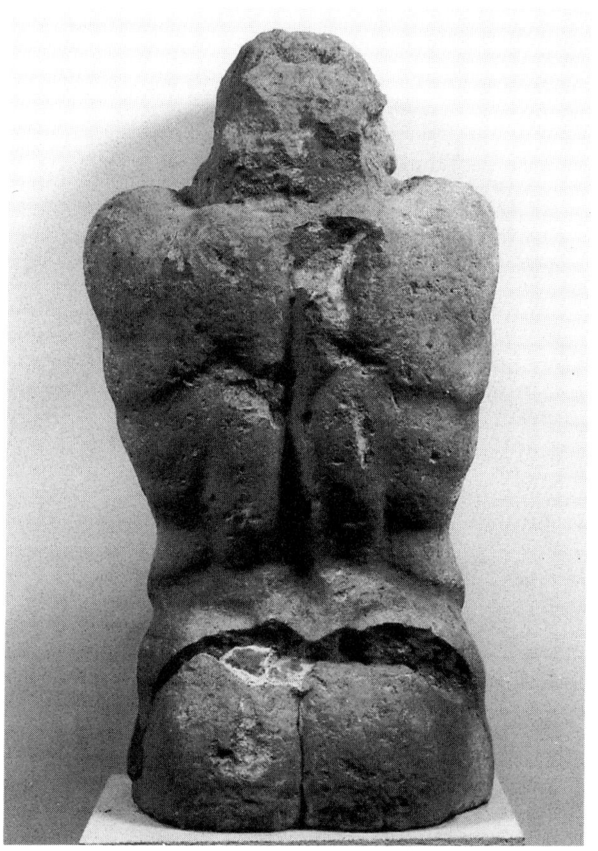

Εικ. 2. Πίσω όψη του Άτλαντα της εικ. 1.

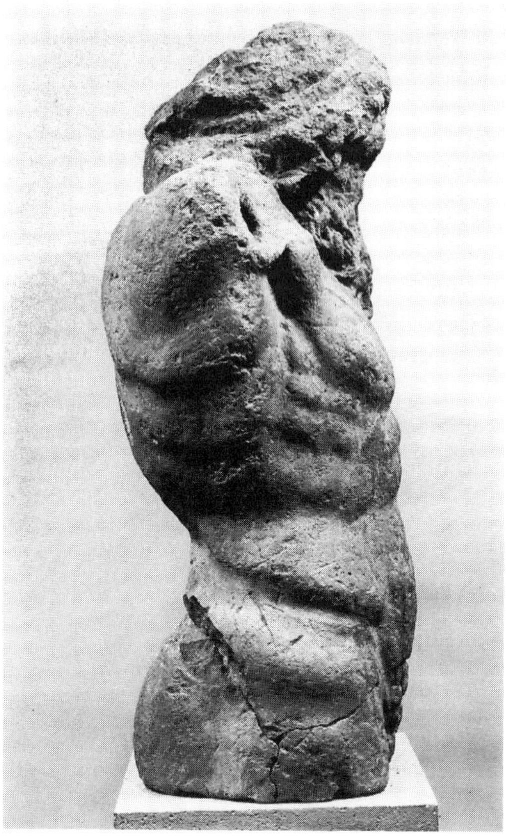

Εικ. 3. Πλάγια δεξιά όψη του Άτλαντα της εικ. 1.

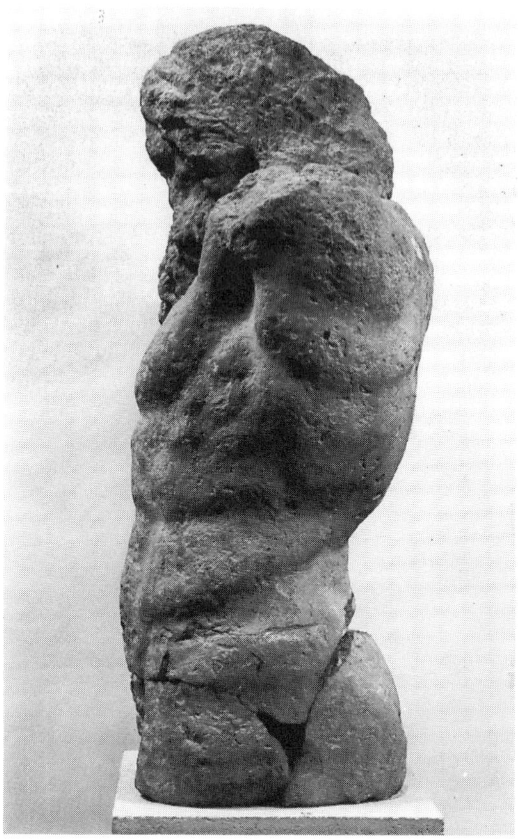

Εικ. 4. Πλάγια αριστερή όψη του Άτλαντα της εικ. 1.

βραχίονας της μορφής συγκολλήθηκε με τη βοήθεια ενός ορθογώνιου τόρμου (4 x 2 εκ., βάθ. 9,5 εκ. περίπου) (εικ. 1. 3). Το πέος είναι ένθετο και κάτω από αυτό υπάρχει κυκλικός τόρμος μολυβδοχόησης. Γύρω από τον αυχένα και στο πίσω μέρος του κρανίου υπάρχει άπεργος όγκος, αποκρουσμένος εν μέρει, που στο μέσο χωρίζεται καθέτως από μια αδρή αυλακιά. Το πάνω μέρος του κρανίου και ένα τμήμα των πλάγιων πλευρών του παρουσιάζουν αδρή επεξεργασία και γύρω από τη δεξιά και επάνω πλευρά του κρανίου δημιουργείται ένα είδος πρόχειρα λαξευμένης ταινίας. Στο σημείο που ο θόλος του κρανίου γυρίζει προς τα πίσω υπάρχει ορθογώνιος τόρμος (2,5 x 4 εκ., μέγ. σωζ. βάθ. 4 εκ.) (εικ. 2. 4).

Ένας γυμνός γενειοφόρος, ώριμος άνδρας με έντονη σωματική διάπλαση εικονίζεται κατενώπιον. Η οριζόντια θέση των βουβώνων και των ισχίων, όπως και η θέση των γλουτών του, που βρίσκονται στο ίδιο επίπεδο, δείχνουν ότι το βάρος του κορμού μοιραζόταν εξίσου στα δύο σκέλη, τα οποία πρέπει να αναπαρασταθούν τεντωμένα και τοποθετημένα παράλληλα το ένα δίπλα στο άλλο. Ο κορμός παρουσιάζει πάνω από τη μέση μια μικρή στροφή προς τα δεξιά του και η δεξιά ωμοπλάτη ανυψώνεται προβάλλοντας ελαφρά προς τα εμπρός (εικ. 2). Οι μύες είναι έξεργοι αλλά και οργανικά συνδεδεμένοι μεταξύ τους, τόσο στη μπροστινή όσο και στις πλάγιες πλευρές, ιδιαίτερα τονισμένοι είναι όμως στην πίσω όψη, την οποία διατρέχει η βαθιά αυλακιά της σπονδυλικής στήλης. Την κίνηση του κορμού ακολουθεί και το κεφάλι, που στρέφεται ελαφρά προς τα δεξιά και σκύβει συγχρόνως λίγο προς τα εμπρός. Παρά τη μέτρια διατήρηση του προσώπου, διακρίνεται η έξαρση των όγκων του στις παρειές και το μέτωπο, που σκιάζει τα μάτια. Γύρω από το πρόσωπο η κόμη αποδίδεται με μια μόνον σειρά βοστρύχων, που ορθώνονται πάνω από το μέτωπο και πέφτουν στο πλάι σκιάζοντας τους κροτάφους και τις παρειές. Πίσω από τους βοστρύχους αυτούς αρχίζει η αδρή εργασία που προαναφέρθηκε. Τα γένεια αποτελούνται από ομάδες κοντών βοστρύχων με διαφορετική κατεύθυνση, που δημιουργούν ένα ασύμμετρο σχήμα, καθώς στην αριστερή πλευρά πέφτουν χαμηλότερα σε τρεις σειρές, ενώ στη δεξιά μόνον σε δύο. Οι δύο βραχίονες της μορφής, όπως φαίνεται κυρίως στις πλάγιες όψεις (εικ. 3–4), υψώνονταν λοξά προς τα εμπρός, χωρίς να ακουμπούν στους κροτάφους. Οι αγκώνες θα πρέπει επομένως να αναπαρασταθούν έντονα λυγισμένοι και οι πήχεις σε οριζόντια θέση, με κατεύθυνση προς τα πίσω. Μπορούμε να δεχτούμε ότι αρχικά οι πήχεις κολλούσαν στα πλάγια του κρανίου, δηλαδή στα τμήματα που σήμερα παρουσιάζονται ως άπεργο και χωρίζονται μεταξύ τους από την αδρή αυλακιά. Στο ζήτημα όμως αυτό θα επανέλθω παρακάτω.

Η μορφή εικονιζόταν λοιπόν κατά πάσα

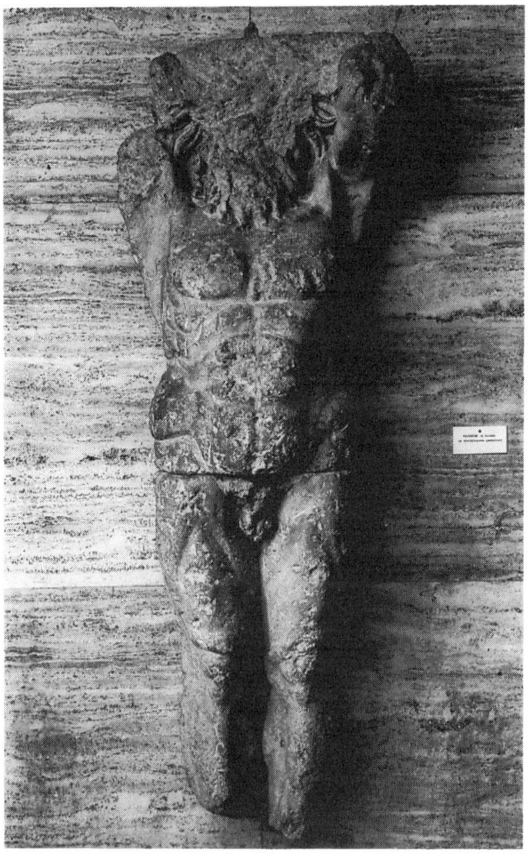

Εικ. 5. Reggio Calabria, Εθνικό Μουσείο. Άτλας. (DAI Ρώμης 84.5886).

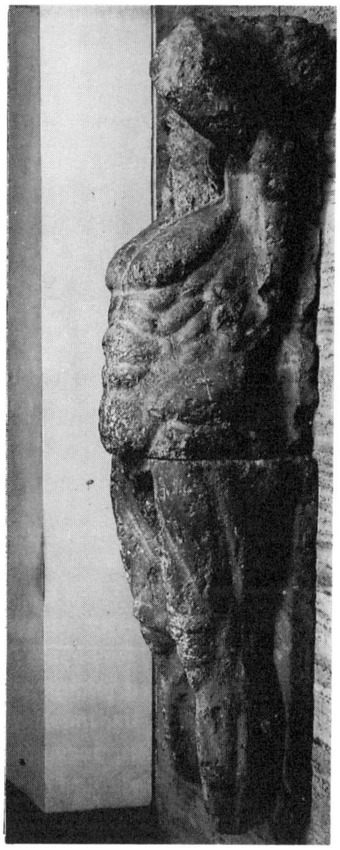

Εικ. 6. Όψη τριών τετάρτων από αριστερά του Άτλαντα της εικ. 5. (DAI Ρώμης 84.5888).

πιθανότητα σε ένα μοτίβο γνωστό από φέρουσες μορφές ενταγμένες σε αρχιτεκτονήματα, δηλαδή από Άτλαντες (ή Τελαμώνες) με την έννοια που δίνει στον όρο ο Βιτρούβιος (6.7.6),[4] αλλά και με την ειδικότερη έννοια που δίνει σε αυτόν η σύγχρονη έρευνα: το βάρος φέρεται όχι μόνον με το κεφάλι ή τον αυχένα αλλά και με τα δύο υψωμένα χέρια.[5] Η περίπτωση να πρόκειται για το μοτίβο του κρεμασμένου ή δεμένου Μαρσύα θα πρέπει να αποκλειστεί για πολλούς λόγους. Η καμπύλωση που παρουσιάζουν προς τα εμπρός οι ωμοπλάτες (εικ. 3–4) και κυρίως η απόδοση των μυών του κορμού δείχνουν ότι πρόκειται για μορφή που φέρει βάρος και όχι για μορφή με κρεμασμένο ή τεντωμένο σώμα.[6] Ούτε όμως και τα εικονογραφικά χαρακτηριστικά της συνηγορούν για μια τέτοια υπόθεση. Η εξαιρετικά μυώδης και στιβαρή κατασκευή του κορμού, η ήπια έκφραση του προσώπου και η έλλειψη οποιωνδήποτε γνωρισμάτων της ζωώδους φύσης του Σιληνού, αποκλείουν, θα έλεγα, την αναγνώριση του Μαρσύα.

Η κατενώπιον παράσταση και η συμμετρική δομή της ανδρικής μορφής, η κατασκευή του κορμού της με την έντονη μυική διάπλαση, ο τύπος του γενειοφόρου κεφαλιού που σκύβει ελαφρά, και βέβαια το μοτίβο των χεριών, μας πείθουν ότι πρόκειται για Άτλαντα, και μάλιστα του τύπου που μας είναι γνωστός από τη Σικελία και την Κάτω Ιταλία.[7] Όπως είναι αποδεκτό γενικά, ο σικελικός τύπος ή, όπως χαρακτηρίζεται ειδικότερα, ο "τύπος των Συρακουσών"[8] κατάγεται άμεσα από τους κολοσσικούς Άτλαντες του ναού του Διός στον Ακράγαντα, ο οποίος χρονολογείται μετά τη νίκη του τυράννου των Συρακουσών Θήρωνα εναντίον των Καρχηδονίων (480 π.Χ.).[9] Στη μνημειακή αρχιτεκτονική ο τύπος επανεμφανίζεται, με τα σημερινά δεδομένα, μόλις στην πρώιμη ελληνιστική περίοδο και γνωρίζει μεγάλη διάδοση καταρχήν στη Σικελία (εικ. 5–6) και κατόπιν στην Κάτω Ιταλία, κυρίως έως την εποχή του Αυγούστου.[10] Η αρχιτεκτονική του χρήση βεβαιώνεται από ευρήματα σε θέατρα, αλλά και σε διάφορα άλλα κτίσματα με δημόσιο ή ιδιωτικό χαρακτήρα, ακόμη σε ταφικά οικοδομήματα.[11] Μαρτυρείται μάλιστα και σε επίσημα αρχιτεκτονήματα του 3ου αι. π.Χ. Έτσι, από τον γιγαντιαίο βωμό του Ιέρωνα Β′ στις Συρακούσες είχαν διασωθεί τμήματα – σήμερα χαμένα – δύο γυμνών ανδρικών μορφών στο μοτίβο αυτό, που πλαισίωναν την είσοδο στην πρόθυση.[12] Επιπλέον, το πολυτελές πλοίο του Ιέρωνα, ένα πλωτό παλάτι,[13] που έφερε το όνομα Συρακοσία και που κατασκεύασε ο ίδιος με επόπτη τον Αρχιμήδη και δώρησε στον Πτολεμαίο Γ′, ήταν διακοσμημένο με σειρά από Άτλαντες. Οι μορφές είχαν ύψος έξι πήχεις (2,60 μ. περίπου) και περιέτρεχαν εξωτερικά το πλοίο τοποθετημένοι σε κανονικές αποστάσεις: "ἄτλαντές

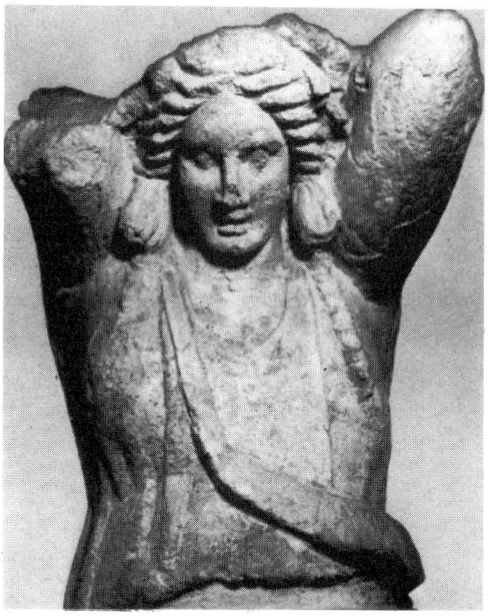

Εικ. 7. Συρακούσες, Εθνικό Μουσείο αρ. 37379. Μαινάδα στο μοτίβο του Άτλαντα. (Isler-Kerényi, πίν. 22,1).

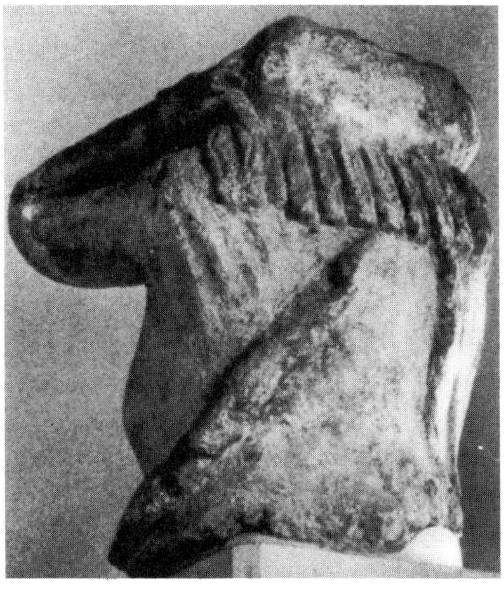

Εικ. 8. Πίσω όψη της Μαινάδας της εικ. 7. (Isler-Kerényi, πίν. 23,1).

τε περιέτρεχον τὴν ναῦν ἐκτὸς ἐξαπήχεις, οἵ τοὺς ὄγκους ὑπειλήφασιν τοὺς ἀνωτάτω καὶ τὸ τρίγλυφον, πάντες ἐν διαστήματι συμμέτρῳ βεβῶτες" (Αθήναιος 5.208b).[14]

Οι στιβαρές ανδρικές μορφές που εικονίζονται στον τύπο αυτό συχνά δεν παρουσιάζουν άλλα ιδιαίτερα εικονογραφικά χαρακτηριστικά, πράγμα που συμβαίνει και στη δική μας περίπτωση. Επομένως η αναγνώρισή τους χωρίς επιπλέον ενδείξεις για τον χαρακτήρα των κτιρίων που διακοσμούσαν είναι δύσκολη. Εξάλλου ο πολλαπλασιασμός των Ατλάντων συνεπάγεται την αποβολή του μυθολογικού περιεχομένου της μορφής.[15] Ορισμένες φορές όμως, λ.χ. όταν χρησιμοποιούνται σε θέατρα ή και άλλα οικοδομήματα, οι μορφές χαρακτηρίζονται ως μέλη του διονυσιακού θιάσου, δηλαδή ως Σιληνοί, έτσι ο τύπος υιοθετείται και για τα γυναικεία μέλη του θιάσου, δηλαδή τις Μαινάδες (εικ. 7–8).[16] Οι λίθινοι αυτοί Άτλαντες της Δύσης, που είναι συχνά κατασκευασμένοι από περισσότερα κομμάτια με οριζόντιους αρμούς, δεν αποτελούν – εκτός ορισμένων εξαιρέσεων – ελεύθερα στηρίγματα, αλλά είναι μορφές έξεργα λαξευμένες και ενσωματωμένες στην όψη ενός τοίχου ή σε πεσσόμορφες προβολές του (εικ. 5–6).[17]

Με τον Άτλαντα της Θεσσαλονίκης βεβαιώνεται για πρώτη φορά η παρουσία του τύπου στη μεγάλη τέχνη του ελληνικού χώρου και διαπιστώνεται η άμεση εξάρτησή του από τα δυτικά πρότυπα. Από αυτά διαφέρουν τυπολογικά τα παραδείγματα Ατλάντων-Σιληνών που γνωρίζουμε από τον ελληνικό χώρο, την Αθήνα ή τη Δήλο, όπου έχουμε είτε μορφές γονατιστές είτε όρθιες αλλά με δομή που βασίζεται στο contrapposto και είναι επομένως ασύμμετρη.[18] Έτσι λοιπόν θα πρέπει να δεχτούμε ότι και ο δικός μας Άτλας, όπως και τα δυτικά του παράλληλα, είχε αρχιτεκτονικό προορισμό, παρόλο που είναι περίοπτα λαξευμένος. Τον συνδέουν με τα έργα εκείνα όχι μόνον ο τύπος, αλλά και το υλικό και η τεχνική της κατασκευής. Ένας Άτλας του τύπου αυτού δύσκολα θα μπορούσε άλλωστε να νοηθεί στημένος ελεύθερα στον χώρο. Ο περίοπτος χαρακτήρας του γλυπτού δεν αποτελεί πρόβλημα. Μορφές περίοπτες ως ελεύθερα αρχιτεκτονικά στηρίγματα, που φέρουν το βάρος του θριγκού μέσω ενός επικράνου ή πόλου στο κεφάλι, είναι γνωστές στην ελληνική αρχιτεκτονική από την αρχαϊκή εποχή. Πρόκειται για τον τύπο της Καρυάτιδας, που για πολλούς αιώνες χρησιμοποιείται χωρίς σημαντικές αλλαγές.[19] Κατ' αναλογία προς αυτόν απέκτησαν, όπως φαίνεται, περίοπτο χαρακτήρα και μορφές στον τύπο του Άτλαντα. Έτσι λ.χ. η Μαινάδα-Ατλας από το θέατρο των Συρακουσών (σωζ. ύψ. 72 εκ.) αποτελούσε περίοπτο στήριγμα και βάσταζε το βάρος με τη βοήθεια ενός προσκεφαλαίου, που είναι λαξευμένο επάνω στον αυχένα και το κεφάλι, ανάμεσα στους αναδιπλωμένους πήχεις της (εικ. 7–8).[20] Και στον Άτλαντα της Θεσσαλονίκης ο άπεργος όγκος του λίθου που περιβάλλει τον αυχένα και το πίσω μέρος του κρανίου, δείχνει ότι αρχικά θα διαμορφωνόταν ένα επίθημα συμφυές με το κρανίο, που είναι πιθανό να έφτανε έως το σημείο που δημιουργείται η αδρή "ταινία". Θα υπήρχε δηλαδή και εδώ ένα είδος προσκεφαλαίου που θα λειτουργούσε ως άβακας.

Με την αρχιτεκτονική λειτουργία της μορφής δεν είναι αντίθετη η κίνηση που παρουσιάζουν ο κορμός και το κεφάλι του Άτλαντα. Αντίθετα μάλιστα αυτή μπορεί να ερμηνευτεί με την ύπαρξη μιας πάρισης μορφής (pendant), αν υποθέσουμε ότι δύο τουλάχιστον όμοιες θα αποτελούσαν την αρχιτεκτονική πρόσοψη.

Στην περίπτωση μιας μεγαλύτερης πρόσοψης, μπορούμε να υποθέσουμε ότι η στροφή των μορφών προς δύο αντίθετες κατευθύνσεις θα έδινε στο σύνολο μια ρυθμική κίνηση που θα οδηγούσε προς τον άξονα της κατασκευής. Οπωσδήποτε η κλίμακα του αρχιτεκτονήματος δεν πρέπει να ήταν μεγάλη, αφού και το ύψος του σωζόμενου Άτλαντα μαζί με το βάθρο και το επίκρανο δεν θα ξεπερνούσε ίσως τα τρία μέτρα. Την ύπαρξη περίοπτων Ατλάντων ως ελεύθερων στηριγμάτων μαρτυρούν εξάλλου και νομίσματα της Σίρτης επί Ιόβα Α' της Μαυριτανίας (60–46 π.Χ.). Στη μια όψη τους (εικ. 9) παριστάνεται μια διώροφη αρχιτεκτονική πρόσοψη, που ερμηνεύτηκε ως ναός, ως ανάκτορο ή ως πρόπυλο ιερού.[21] Τρεις Άτλαντες επάνω σε υψηλά βάθρα εναλλάσσονται με δύο κίονες και βαστάζουν τον οριζόντιο θριγκό.

Ωστόσο ορισμένα από τα τεχνικά χαρακτηριστικά του γλυπτού δεν ερμηνεύονται από τη χρήση που δεχτήκαμε και οδηγούν στην υπόθεση ότι ο σωζόμενος σήμερα Άτλας επισκευάστηκε και χρησιμοποιήθηκε για δεύτερη φορά μετά από μια καταστροφή που θα υπέστη το αρχιτεκτόνημα. 'Οτι έτσι συνέβη πράγματι το δείχνει ο τρόπος με τον οποίο έγινε η συγκόλληση του δεξιού βραχίονα (εικ. 1. 3). Ο τόρμος που ανοίχτηκε για τον σκοπό αυτό βρίσκεται σε σπασμένη επιφάνεια και όχι σε επίπεδη, όπως αντίθετα συμβαίνει με αυτόν της κάτω πλευράς του κορμού· δεν πρόκειται λοιπόν για αρχική εργασία αλλά για επισκευή. Κατά την επισκευή αυτή απολαξεύτηκαν, όπως φαίνεται, και τα τμήματα των πήχεων που κολλούσαν στον αυχένα μαζί με τα εναπομείναντα τμήματα του προσκεφαλαίου, όπως δείχνουν οι βελονιές που διακρίνονται στον άπεργο όγκο, στην αριστερή (εικ. 4) και εν μέρει στην πίσω πλευρά (εικ. 2). Είναι πολύ πιθανό ότι επισκευάστηκε και το αριστερό χέρι, σε χαμηλότερο όμως από το σωζόμενο σημείο. Τέλος, και ο τόρμος στο πίσω μέρος του κρανίου (εικ. 2. 4) δεν δικαιολογείται από την αρχική λειτουργία του Άτλαντα, αφού δεν είναι δυνατόν να σχετιστεί με τη στήριξη κάποιου φερόμενου αρχιτεκτονικού μέλους.[22] Η νέα χρήση του γλυπτού δεν είναι δυνατόν να προσδιοριστεί, φαίνεται πάντως πολύ δύσκολο να ήταν αρχιτεκτονική.

Για τη χρονολόγηση του Άτλαντα τα τυπολογικά παράλληλα της Δύσης δεν βοηθούν, αφού είναι δημιουργίες μιας διαφορετικής καλλιτεχνικής παράδοσης. Η σύγκρισή του με τους Άτλαντες από το Monte Iato[23] ή από το Monte Scaglioso (εικ. 5–6)[24] κάνει φανερή την ποιοτική του υπεροχή, αφού ο Άτλας της Θεσσαλονίκης συνδυάζει την αίσθηση για οργανική δομή με την έντονη πλαστικότητα των όγκων. Το δικό μας έργο εντάσσεται στυλιστικά στην ανατολική καλλιτεχνική παράδοση. Οι εύχυμοι και δυνατοί όγκοι του θα πρέπει να κατανοηθούν στη συνέχεια των γλυπτών του περγαμηνού βωμού, από τα οποία ο Άτλας της Θεσσαλονίκης δεν μπορεί να απέχει πολύ. Στο κεφάλι, όπως και στο κορμί, έχει μετριαστεί η διαφοροποίηση και η μεγάλη ένταση των όγκων που χαρακτηρίζουν τις μορφές στη μεγάλη ζωφόρο του βωμού.[25] Ο Άτλας βρίσκεται έτσι πιο κοντά σε λίγο νεότερες δημιουργίες, όπως ο Τεύθρας της μικρής περγαμηνής ζωφόρου ή ο "Ήρωας" του Βερολίνου, και οπωσδήποτε προηγείται από τον Ποσειδώνα της Μήλου, στον οποίο η συνολική όψη παρουσιάζεται πιο ήρεμη.[26] Μπορούμε λοιπόν να προτείνουμε για τον Άτλαντα μια χρονολόγηση στο δεύτερο μισό του 2ου αι. π.Χ., και μάλλον πιο κοντά προς τα μέσα παρά προς το τέλος του.

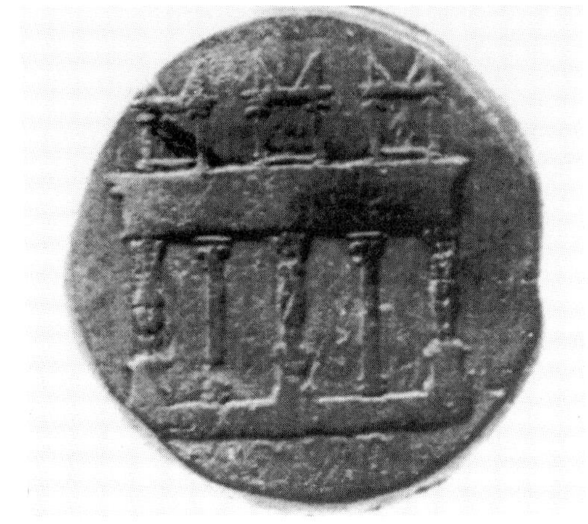

Εικ. 9. Παρίσι, Cabinet des Médailles. Νόμισμα της Σίρτης, επί Ιόβα Α' της Μαυριτανίας (60–46 π.Χ.). (Lloyd-Morgan, 147, εικ. 10,8).

Η χρονολόγηση μιας αξιόλογης αρχιτεκτονικής κατασκευής στη Θεσσαλονίκη την περίοδο μετά το 150 π.Χ. φαίνεται προβληματική. Ο τόπος εύρεσης του Άτλαντα κάτω από το πλακόστρωτο της ρωμαϊκής Αγοράς κάνει πιθανή τη σκέψη η αρχική του θέση να ήταν στην προγενέστερη, ελληνιστική Αγορά της πόλης, πράγμα που αυξάνει τη σημασία του μνημείου.[27] Είναι εύλογο να υποθέσουμε ότι προέρχεται από την πρόσοψη ενός σημαντικού κτιρίου στον δημόσιο αυτό χώρο, για τη μορφή και τη λειτουργία του οποίου δεν γνωρίζουμε τίποτε. Αν όμως η χρονολόγηση που προτείναμε για τον Άτλαντα είναι σωστή, τότε και το μνημείο από το οποίο προήλθε ανήκει στην περίοδο μετά την κατάλυση της μακεδονικής βασιλείας και μάλιστα μετά τη δημιουργία της ρωμαϊκής επαρχίας της Μακεδονίας (148 π.Χ.). Η Θεσσαλονίκη ως πρωτεύουσα της επαρχίας αυτής ήταν έδρα του Ρωμαίου διοικητή. Πρώτος διοικητής (στρατηγός ανθύπατος) διετέλεσε ο νικητής του Ανδρίσκου Κόιντος Καικίλιος Μέτελλος, που έμεινε στη Μακεδονία έως το 146 π.Χ.[28] και για τον οποίο στήθηκε στη Θεσσαλονίκη τιμητικός ανδριάντας.[29] Δεν αποκλείεται λοιπόν ο Άτλας που έφτασε ως εμάς να προέρχεται από ένα μνημείο της ρωμαϊκής νίκης.

Σειρά από Άτλαντες διακοσμούσε, όπως αναφέρθηκε, το περίφημο πλοίο του Ιέρωνα Β'. Το πλοίο αυτό, που ήταν ένα επίτευγμα τεχνικής, ξεχώριζε για την πολυτέλεια της κατασκευής και της διακόσμησης, που σκοπό είχαν να καταδείξουν τον πλούτο του βασιλιά και να τον εξισώσουν με τους μεγάλους ελληνιστικούς μονάρχες.[30] Είχε όμως επιπλέον και πολεμικό χαρακτήρα, αφού ήταν εφοδιασμένο με πύργους και όλον τον απαραίτητο στρατιωτικό εξοπλισμό.[31] Δεν θα ήταν λοιπόν αστήρικτη η πρόταση να συνδέσουμε την παρουσία των Ατλάντων στην περιφέρεια του πλοίου με τη στρατιωτική ισχύ του Ιέρωνα και να υιοθετήσουμε την άποψη που διατυπώθηκε στην έρευνα ότι αποτελούσαν σύμβολο εξουσίας και δύναμης.[32] Ο εικονογραφικός αυτός τύπος ήταν ασφαλώς οικείος στους Ρωμαίους, πιθανότατα και ο συμβολισμός του, όταν μάλιστα ο Ιέρων υπήρξε, ως γνωστόν, για πενήντα σχεδόν χρόνια φίλος και σύμμαχός τους, "ὁ πάντα 'Ρωμαΐοις φίλος" (Αθήναιος 5.206e).[33] Είναι λοιπόν εύλογο να υποθέσουμε ότι οι Ρωμαίοι μετέφεραν από τον ιταλικό χώρο στη Μακεδονία τον τύπο του Άτλαντα, για να δηλώσουν με συμβολικό τρόπο την εξουσία τους στην πρωτεύουσα της νεοϊδρυμένης επαρχίας.[34]

Σημειώσεις

1. Για την άδεια μελέτης και δημοσίευσης του γλυπτού – στο πλαίσιο της ετοιμασίας του επιστημονικού καταλόγου των γλυπτών του Μουσείου Θεσσαλονίκης – θερμά ευχαριστώ τον Διευθυντή του Μουσείου κ. Δ. Γραμμένο. Για χρήσιμη συζήτηση σχετικά με τα προβλήματα του γλυπτού θα ήθελα να ευχαριστήσω τους Εμ. Βουτυρά και Μ. Τιβέριο, και κυρίως τον Γ. Δεσπίνη. Οι φωτογραφίες των εικ. 1–4 είναι του Μ. Σκιαδαρέση.
2. Βλ. αρ. ευρ. 10301, όπου σημειώνεται: "Αρχαία αγορά Θεσσαλονίκης. 1966". Για περισσότερες πληροφορίες σχετικά με την προέλευση βλ. σημ. 3.
3. Φ. Πέτσας, *Μακεδονικά* 9, 1969, 150, πίν. 47. Βλ. επίσης Φ. Πέτσας, *ΑΔελτ* 22, 1967, Χρον. Β2, 386· ο ίδιος, *ΑΔελτ* 23, 1968, Χρον. Β2, 325, αρ. 2. 330, πίν. 280α· ο ίδιος, *ΑΔελτ* 24, 1969, Χρον. Β2, 291 με σημ. 19· ο ίδιος, *Μακεδονικά* 14, 1974, 305 και ο ίδιος, *Αρχαία Μακεδονία* I, 1970, 224. Βλ. και P.M. Fraser, *ARepLond* (1968–69) 23. J.-P. Michaud, *BCH* 94, 1970, 1062. 1066, εικ. 383. M. Vickers, *JHS* 92, 1972, 163 με σημ. 46. Στο γλυπτό αυτό αναφέρονται ακόμη: C. Isler-Kerényi στο H. Bloesch – H.P. Isler, *Studia Ietina* I (1976) 47 σημ. 56. A. Schmidt-Colinet, *Antike Stützfiguren* (1977) 180 σημ. 221. M.C. Sturgeon, *AJA* 81, 1977, 49 σημ. 90. E. Schmidt, *Geschichte der Karyatide* (1982) 212 σημ. 732. *Θεσσαλονίκη. Από τα προϊστορικά μέχρι τα χριστιανικά χρόνια* (1986) 27. 147, εικ. 10 (Ι. Βοκοτοπούλου). S.A. Muscettola στο *La romanisation du Samnium aux IIe et Ier siècles av. J.-C., Actes du colloque, Naples 1988* (1991) 207 σημ. 7.
4. "Item si qua virili figura signa mutulos aut coronas sustinent, nostri telamones appellant, cuius rationes, quid ita aut quare dicantur, ex historiis non inveniuntur, Graeci vero eos atlantes vocitant". Βλ. W.H. Plommer, *JHS* 99, 1979, 101 κε. *EAA* VII (1966) 668 στο λ. Telamone (Red.).
5. Schmidt-Colinet ό.π. (σημ. 3) 44. 47. Schmidt ό.π. (σημ. 3) 112. Πρβλ. *LIMC* III (1986) λ. Atlas, σ. 16 (J. Arce – L.J. Balmaseda).
6. Για τα μεγάλα αντίγραφα του γνωστού αγαλματικού τύπου του Μαρσύα, όπου τα χέρια είναι τεντωμένα, βλ. H. Meyer, *Der weisse und der rote Marsyas* (1987) και A. Weis, *The Hanging Marsyas and its Copies* (1992). Σε μικρότερα έργα, όπως τραπεζοφόρα, τα χέρια είναι λυγισμένα και δεμένα πίσω στον αυχένα, βλ. Θ. Στεφανίδου-Τιβερίου, *Τραπεζοφόρα με πλαστική διακόσμηση. Η αττική ομάδα* (1993) 141, πίν. 80.
7. Βλ. F. Schaller, *Stützfiguren in der griechischen Kunst* (1973) 149 κε. L. Castiglione στο B. Andreae – H. Kyrieleis, *Neue Forschungen in Pompeji* (1975) 212 κε. Isler-Kerényi ό.π. (σημ. 3) 36 κε. Schmidt-Colinet ό.π. (σημ. 3) 47 κε. Schmidt ό.π. (σημ. 3) 113 κε. R.J.A. Wilson στο M. Henig, *Architecture and Architectural Sculpture in the Roman Empire* (1990) 70 κε. P. Pensabene στο M. Tagliente, *Italici in Magna Grecia. Lingua, insediamenti e strutture* (1990) 292 κε. Για τον τύπο βλ. ακόμη M. Denti στο *Da Leucania a Lucania. La Lucania centro-orientale fra Pirro e i Giulio-Claudii, Venosa 1992–1993* (1992) 76 κε. *LIMC* III λ. Atlas, σ. 11. 16. Για άλλα παραδείγματα του τύπου βλ. R. Belli Pasqua, *Catalogo del Museo Nazionale Archeologico di Taranto* IV, 1 (1995) 99 κε. (IV.20). Για ορισμένα τραπεζοφόρα με τον τύπο βλ. ό.π. 173 κε. (V.41 και 42) και D. Adamesteanu – H. Dilthey, *Macchia di Rossano. Il Santuario della Mefitis* (1992) 77, πίν. LIII.
8. Castiglione ό.π. (σημ. 7) 215.
9. Για τα κολοσσικά αυτά έργα βλ. *LIMC* III λ. Atlas, αρ. 53. Βλ. επίσης G. Pugliese Carratelli – G. Fiorentini, *Agrigento. Museo archeologico* (1992) 92 κε. Βλ. και παρακάτω σημ. 32. Σχετικά με το πρόβλημα της αναπαράστασης των μορφών, που σύμφωνα με ορισμένους μελετητές εικονίζονταν με ανοιχτά σκέλη, βλ. J. de Waele, *AA*, 1980, 204 κε., εικ. 12. P. Griffo στο *Απαρχαί. Nuove ricerche e studi sulla Magna Grecia antica in onore di Paolo Enrico Arias* I (1982) 253 κε., εικ. 3. P. Griffo, *Il Museo Archeologico regionale di Agrigento* (1987) 153 κε.
10. Για τη διάδοση και χρονολόγηση των μνημείων που παραδίδουν τον τύπο βλ. Schmidt-Colinet ό.π. (σημ. 3) 47 κε. Schmidt ό.π. (σημ. 3) 114 κε. Για τα ανάλογα μνημεία στην Ετρουρία βλ. J.-R. Jannot, *MEFRA* 96, 1984.2, 579 κε. *LIMC* III λ. Atlas, σ. 11 κε.
11. Castiglione ό.π. (σημ. 7) 214 κε. Schmidt ό.π. (σημ. 3) 114 κε. Jannot ό.π. (σημ. 10) 580.
12. R. Koldewey – O. Puchstein, *Die griechischen Tempel in Unteritalien und Sicilien* (1899) 72, εικ. 54. 74. Schaller ό.π. (σημ. 7) 157. Schmidt-Colinet ό.π. (σημ. 3) 48 με σημ. 215. 91. 243 M5. *LIMC* III λ. Atlas, αρ. 55.
13. Βλ. K. Schefold, *Römische Kunst als religiöses Phänomen* (1964) 98 κε. Για το πλοίο, την περιγραφή του οποίου από τον Μοσχίωνα διέσωσε ο Αθήναιος, 5. 206d-209, βλ. και H. Berve, *König Hieron II* (1959) 72 κε.
14. Schmidt-Colinet ό.π. (σημ. 3) 48. 132. 243 M6 (το πλοίο δωρήθηκε στον Πτολεμαίο Γ' και όχι τον Δ'). Jannot ό.π. (σημ. 10) 594 κε. *LIMC* III λ. Atlas, αρ. 58. Βλ. και παρακάτω σ.234 με σημ. 32.
15. Schaller ό.π. (σημ. 7) 146 κε. 150 κε. *LIMC* III λ. Atlas, σ. 16.

16. Schaller ό.π. (σημ. 7) 155 κε. Schmidt-Colinet ό.π. (σημ. 3) 47. Schmidt ό.π. (σημ. 3) 114 κε. Castiglione ό.π. (σημ. 7) 215. Χαρακτηριστικό παράδειγμα αποτελούν οι Σιληνοί και οι Μαινάδες από το θέατρο στο Monte Iato, Isler-Kerényi ό.π. (σημ. 3) 13 κε. Στο ίδιο μοτίβο παριστάνονται και οι γυμνόστηθες γυναικείες μορφές στο "Υπόγειο των Καρυατίδων" στο Vaste, A.D'Amicis κ.ά., *Vecchi scavi, nuovi restauri. Museo Archeologico Nazionale-Taranto. Dal 14 marzo 1991* (1991) 149 κε. και κυρίως G.L'Arab, *Taras* XI, 1, 1991, 19 κε.
17. Schaller ό.π. (σημ. 7) 150. Schmidt ό.π. (σημ. 3) 112 κε. 114. 116. Για ορισμένες εξαιρέσεις βλ. παρακάτω σημ. 20.
18. Για τις μορφές του διονυσιακού θεάτρου βλ. R. Herbig, *Das Dionysos-Theater in Athen* II. *Die Skulpturen vom Bühnenhaus* (1935) 9 κε. 14 κε. 34 κε., πίν. 1 και 5. Castiglione ό.π. (σημ. 7) 215, εικ. 224. Isler-Kerényi ό.π. (σημ. 3) 39 κε. και M. Fuchs, *Untersuchungen zur Ausstattung römischer Theater* (1987) 128. Για τους Άτλαντες της Δήλου βλ. J. Marcadé, *Au Musée de Délos* (1969) 198 κε. 448 κε., πίν. 22. 24. Castiglione ό.π. (σημ. 7) 215, εικ. 223.
19. Schmidt ό.π. (σημ. 3) 72 κε. 89 κε.
20. G.E. Rizzo, *Il teatro greco di Siracusa* (1923) 97 κε., εικ. 42, πίν. VI. E. Langlotz, *Die Kunst der Westgriechen* (1963) 99, αρ. 156. Schaller ό.π. (σημ. 7) 157 (αρ. 183). Isler-Kerényi ό.π. (σημ. 3) 39, πίν. 22,1–2. 23,1. H. Schmidt ό.π. (σημ. 3) 115 με σημ. 701 θεωρεί τη Μαινάδα ως ελεύθερο στήριγμα αλλά τοποθετημένο κοντά σε τοίχο. Επίπεδη αλλά χωρίς στήριγμα είναι η μορφή ενός Άτλαντα από τον Τάραντα, Belli Pasqua ό.π. (σημ. 7) 100.
21. J. Mazard, *Corpus Numorum Numidiae Mavritaniaeque* (1955) 51, αρ. 91. *SNG Nat.Mus. Kopenhagen* 42: *Africa, Syrtica-Mauretania* (1969) αρ. 534–535. Schmidt-Colinet ό.π. (σημ. 3) 50. 134. 247 M21. M.J. Price – B.L. Trell, *Coins and their Cities. Architecture on the Ancient Coins of Greece, Rome, and Palestine* (1977) 33. 244, αρ. 18, εικ. 38. G. Lloyd-Morgan στο Henig ό.π (σημ. 7) 147, εικ. 10.8. *LIMC* III λ. Atlas, αρ. 64.
22. 'Ισως να σχετίζεται με τη στερέωση του γλυπτού σε κάποιο τοίχο.
23. Isler-Kerényi ό.π. (σημ. 3) 36 κε., πίν. 8.10.18. Schmidt ό.π. (σημ. 3) 114 κε.
24. Schmidt ό.π. (σημ. 3) 116 με σημ. 704, πίν. 28 (ύψ. 2,01 μ.). *LIMC* III λ. Atlas, αρ. 57 (ύψ. 2,50 μ.).
25. Βλ. G. Krahmer, *GöttNachr* 1936, 229 κε. και εικ. 12–14. Για το στυλ της μεγάλης ζωφόρου βλ. και H. Kähler, *Der grosse Fries von Pergamon* (1948) 80 κε.
26. Βλ. J. Schäfer, *AntPl* VIII (1968) 62, εικ. 5–7. 16–17. Έως τώρα ο Άτλας της Θεσσαλονίκης αναφέρεται στη βιβλιογραφία απλώς ως υστεροελληνιστικό έργο, βλ. Πέτσας, *Μακεδονικά*, 1969, ό.π. (σημ. 3). Vickers ό.π. (σημ. 3). Isler-Kerényi ό.π. (σημ. 3). Schmidt-Colinet ό.π. (σημ. 3). Schmidt ό.π. (σημ. 3). Θεσσαλονίκη ό.π. (σημ. 3). Muscettola ό.π. (σημ. 3).
27. Δεν έχει ακόμη επιβεβαιωθεί η εύλογη υπόθεση ότι η ελληνιστική Αγορά βρισκόταν στη θέση της ρωμαϊκής, πάντως ένα τιμητικό ψήφισμα του 60 π.Χ., *IG* X II 1, αρ. 5, που προοριζόταν να στηθεί στην Αγορά, βρέθηκε σε οικοδομή της οδού Ολύμπου, δηλαδή ακριβώς πάνω από τη βόρεια πλευρά της Αγοράς. Οι νεότερες έρευνες που διεξάγονται στον χώρο αυτό θα φωτίσουν πιθανότατα το ζήτημα. Για τις νεότερες έρευνες στην Αγορά βλ. Γ. Βελένη – Ι. Βοκοτοπούλου – Δ. Κυριακού – Ζ.Αλ Σααγιάχ, *Αρχαιολογικό Έργο στη Μακεδονία και Θράκη* 5 (1991) 247 κε. Επίσης σε νεότερους, υπό εκτύπωση τόμους της ίδιας αρχαιολογικής συνάντησης.
28. Θ.Χ. Σαρικάκης, *Ρωμαίοι άρχοντες της επαρχίας Μακεδονίας* 1 (1971) 27 κε. F. Papazoglou, *ANRW* II 7.1 (1979) 306 κε. 310.
29. Βλ. *IG* X II 1, αρ. 134. Papazoglou ό.π. (σημ. 28) 306 με σημ. 11.
30. Berve ό.π. (σημ. 13) 74.
31. Ό.π. 73.
32. Schaller ό.π. (σημ. 7) 157 κε. Castiglione ό.π. (σημ. 7) 214. Schmidt-Colinet ό.π. (σημ. 3) 132 κε. O Jannot ό.π. (σημ. 10) 594 κε., θεωρεί ότι πρόκειται για μια συνειδητή εκ μέρους του Ιέρωνα υιοθέτηση του τύπου του Άτλαντα. Με τον τρόπο αυτό εμφανίζεται ως κληρονόμος του μεγαλείου της Σικελίας μετά τη νίκη της Ιμέρας και συνδέεται με το ένδοξο παρελθόν της. Εξάλλου και το πρότυπό του, δηλαδή ο ναός του Ακράγαντα, όπου για πρώτη φορά χρησιμοποιήθηκαν Άτλαντες (βλ. παραπάνω σ.232 με σημ. 9) ερμηνεύτηκε ως μνημείο της νίκης εναντίον των Καρχηδονίων, βλ. H.H. Büsing, *Die griechische Halbsäule* (1970) 69. Πρβλ. Schmidt ό.π. (σημ. 3) 113. Για την ερμηνεία των ίδιων των μορφών βλ. Schaller ό.π. (σημ. 7) 150 κε.
33. Για τις σχέσεις του Ιέρωνα Β′ με τη Ρώμη βλ. A.M. Eckstein, *Chiron* 10, 1980, 183 κε.
34. Για μια συντομότερη μορφή του κειμένου αυτού στα αγγλικά βλ. G. Despinis – Th.Stefanidou-Tiveriou – Em. Voutiras, *Catalogue of Sculpture in the Archaeological Museum of Thessaloniki* I (1997) no. 39 (Th. Setfanidou-Tiveriou).

The Lion from the Lion Tomb at Cnidus

G. B. Waywell

The reclining lion from the summit of the Lion Tomb at Cnidus, now in the British Museum (BM 1350), is one of the largest and finest Greek lion sculptures to survive.[1] Yet its date remains controversial, as does that of the Doric pyramidal tomb-building on which it rested, suggestions ranging over a period of more than two hundred years between Newton's 394 B.C., in a hopeful association with the Athenian admiral Conon's sea-victory off Cnidus in that year, and Krischen's 175 B.C., by analogy with the architecture of the Bouleuterion at Miletus.[2] The purpose of this paper is to re-examine the detail of the sculpture, to consider comparisons both for the lion statue and its monument, and to attempt to come to a clearer conclusion as to whether this famous ensemble is late Classical, early Hellenistic or middle Hellenistic; and further whether its stylistic links lie with Athens, with Caria, with Rhodes, or some alternative east Greek locality.

As is well known, the Lion Tomb and its crowning sculpture were discovered by Sir Charles Newton during his campaign of excavations at Cnidus in 1859.[3] The tomb building lay some 5 km outside the city of Cnidus, to the east, and was placed in a spectacular position, south-facing, overlooking a headland that fell 200 feet sheer to the sea (Figs. 1–2). The lion statue was excavated from where it had fallen from the building, and its lifting and transfer on board ship represented a challenge and triumph for Lieutenant Robert Murdoch-Smith and his team of Royal Engineers, one of whom is seen with Newton, posing in front of the lion as it was slung on the lifting gear.

The lion is of impressively large scale (Figs. 3–8). According to my recent measurements taken at its present location at the British Museum in the Wolfson Basement (north), it is 3.01 m, or 10 feet, in length as preserved. Allowing for its missing forelegs, its original length would have been at least 30 cm more. Its height is 1.80 m., or 6 feet, and its thickness, 1.17 m., or about 4 feet. It is carved out of a single block of marble which, although it has not yet been scientifically analysed, has all the appearance of being Pentelic, judging from its colour, its fine crystals, its marked micaceous grain which causes it to

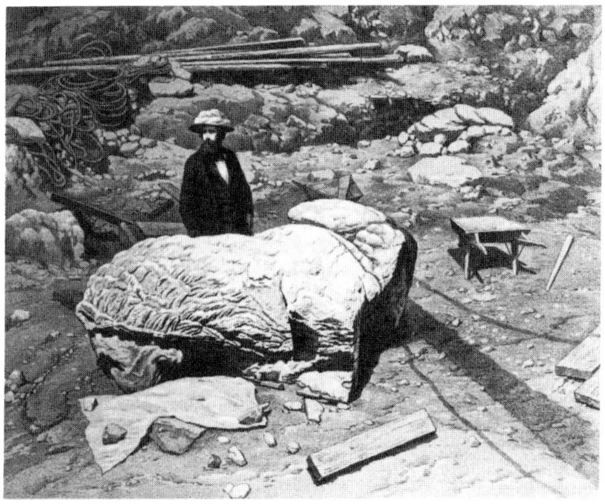

Fig. 1. The Cnidus lion, as excavated, with C.T. Newton in the background (After Newton, HD, *pl. 61,1).*

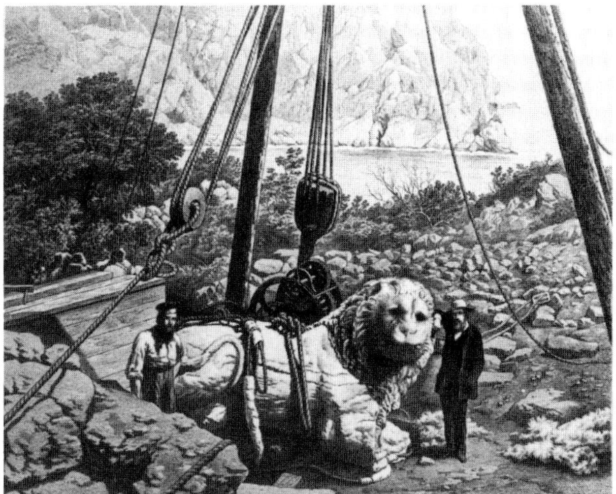

Fig. 2. The Cnidus lion, ready for winching on to ship (after Newton, HD, *pl. 61,2).*

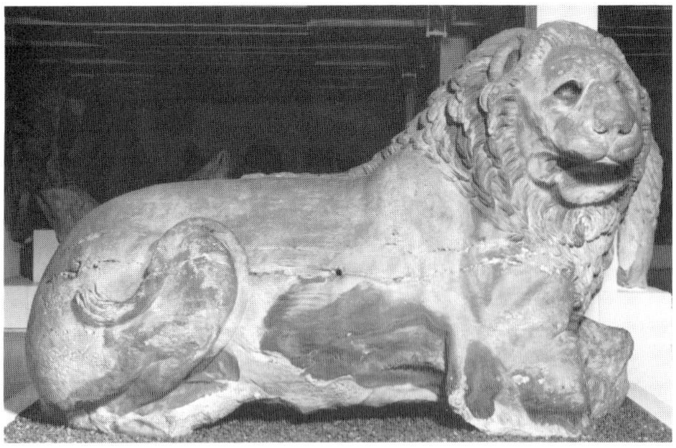

Fig. 3. The Cnidus lion, front view. Photo: British Museum.

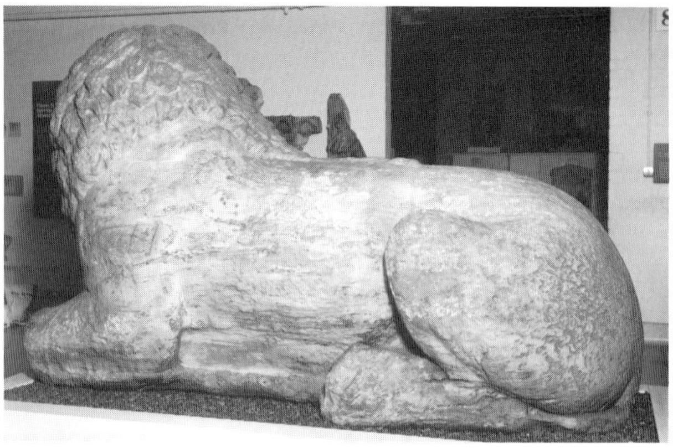

Fig. 4. The Cnidus lion, back view. Photo: British Museum 303520.

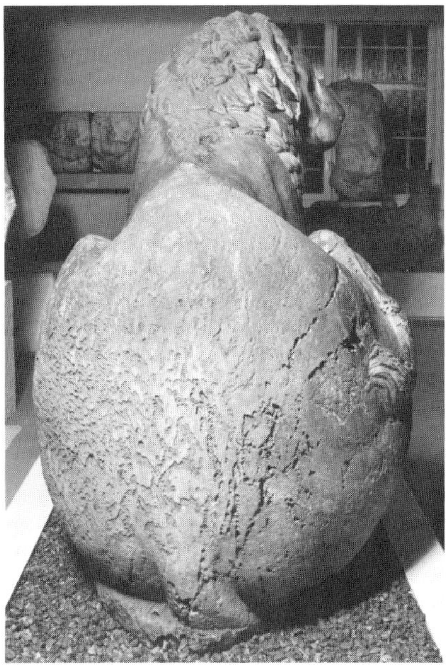

Fig. 5. The Cnidus lion, rear end view. Photo: British Museum 303518.

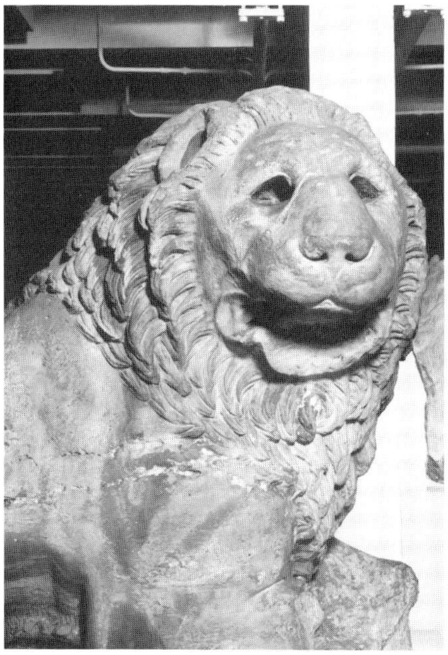

Fig. 6. The Cnidus lion, detail of forepart. Photo: British Museum 303519.

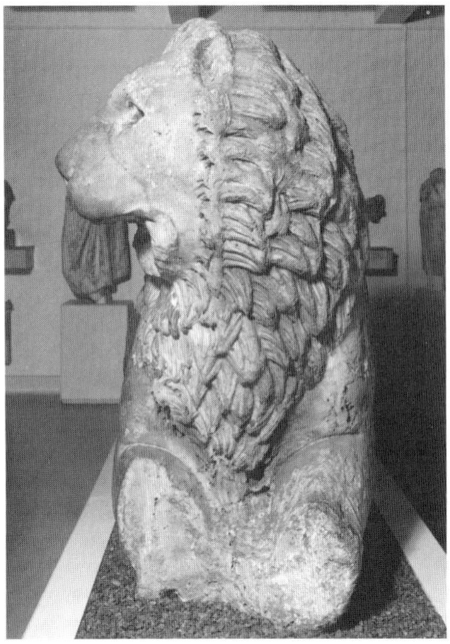

Fig. 7. The Cnidus lion, front end view. Photo: British Museum 303522.

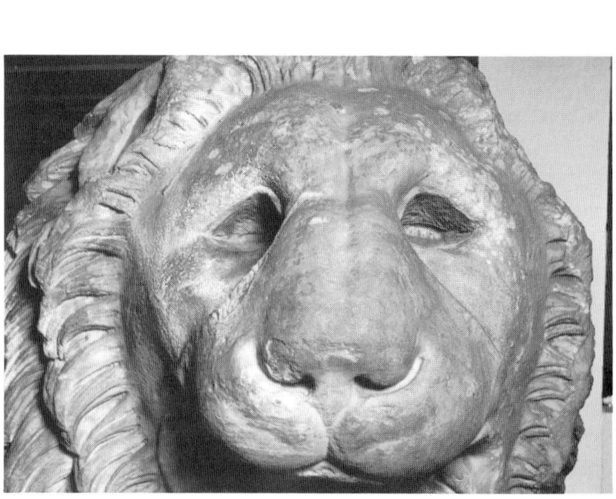

Fig. 8. The Cnidus lion, detail of face. Photo: British Museum 303521.

weather into holes, and from its characteristic patina colour on the right flank, which ranges from rusty yellow to deep brown.[4] It is tolerably complete, the missing parts being the front of the left leg and paw, most of the right foreleg and the plinth below, the right rear leg and paw, the lower jaw, and the tips of both ears. But the surface is severely weathered, resulting from exposure over the centuries to the elements, particularly on the animal's left side, or back view, which was upturned when the statue fell from the building (Figs. 1; 4–5).

Certain technical details are worthy of note. The underside of the lion is hollowed out with the point along its entire length to a depth of c. 20 cm, in an attempt to reduce the weight of the sculpture, leaving walls at front, back and sides of about 20 cm thickness.[5] At the same time the plinth on which the lion rests is much understated, following closely the line of the body at the back and sides, and projecting only at the front, where it broke at its point of weakness. Then again, in the carving of the surface details of the lion, much use has been made of the running drill, the grooves of which are visible in the nostrils, in the flews at the corners of the mouth, at the join between the front legs and the body, and dividing up the locks of hair in the lion's mane (Figs. 6–7). Another interesting feature is the treatment of the eye sockets, which have been hollowed out to a depth of 10 cm (compared with their width of 12.5 cm) to receive separate eyes, presumably of reflecting quartz or semi-precious stone (Fig. 8). As Newton first noted, this recalls the reference in Pliny (*NH* 37. 66) to the stone lion on the tomb of a certain king Hermias on Cyprus (date unknown), which had inserted eyes of smaragdus (?emerald), which reflected the light so brightly that they frightened away the fish in the sea.[6]

In its pose the Cnidus lion is reclining, or couchant, one of the varieties that was favoured for large-scale guardian statues, with the belly and legs lying flat on the ground, and the head turned to the animal's right at somewhat less than 90 degrees (about 70). The tail comes forward under the body and curves around and over the right rear haunch, on the side of the main viewpoint. The mane is richly carved particularly on the right side, and is arranged in a series of ruffs either side of the face, the locks of which then extend down the chest nearly to the forelegs, and along the spine of the back for a distance of some 70 cm. This arrangement finds close parallels in the manes of the standing lions from the Mausoleum at Halicarnassus.[7]

As the researches of Willemsen and others have shown into the typology of Greek lions, the Cnidus lion is matched for pose and scale by a number of other lion statues of Classical and Hellenistic date.[8] The earliest of these is likely to be the reclining lion of colossal proportions on the right of the entrance to the Arsenal in Venice, one of two brought by Morosini from Greece in the late seventeenth century, and probably originating from the Piraeus (Fig. 9).[9] In scale and composition this

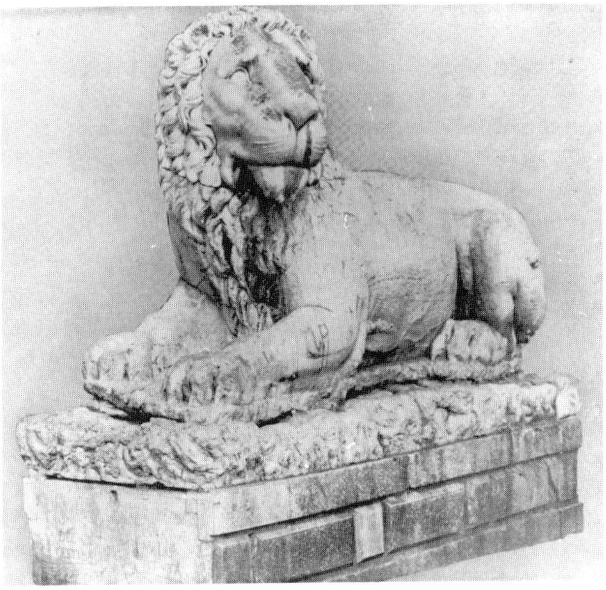

Fig. 9. Reclining lion in Venice, Arsenal. After ArchCl *4, 1952, pl. 4.*

lion is quite close to the Cnidus lion, although it faces in the other direction (unusually for this type of lion), has somewhat slimmer proportions, and a more elevated neck (on which most of the head has been restored). Notice how the tail curves round the hind leg in similar fashion. Stylistically the lion is of Attic workmanship, it has close links with the colossal reclining mastiff from the Kerameikos, and in all probability it dates to the second half of the fourth century B.C.

Two colossal reclining lions were found close to the north harbour at Miletus, where they are believed to have guarded its entrance, one placed on each mole.[10] If this were so, it is perhaps surprising that they were not posed symmetrically in opposite directions. As it is, both face to the right, like the Cnidus lion, and have their heads turned at a right angle to the front. The east lion, which is much better preserved, has a length of 4.01 m., which makes it even larger than the Cnidus lion (Fig. 10). Its date is uncertain, but it would seem to be Hellenistic. Von Gerkan in his publication, ventures a date of sometime after c. 300 B.C., and sometime before an inscription was cut into the flank in the first century B.C. Willemsen tentatively suggests a third century B.C. origin. Unlike the Cnidus lion, the eyes are solid and not inserted, and the head of a bull is placed beneath the slightly raised left foreleg, as if the lion has raised his head to look at the spectator in the midst of feeding.[11]

This detail of composition is found also on the fine lion in Rhodes Museum, no. 221, reclining to the right, where a bull's head rests under the left paw (Fig. 11).[12] Here the eyes are hollowed, for separate insertion, as on the Cnidus lion, but the overall scale of the animal is much smaller, with a length of 1.55 m , which is only about half that of the Cnidus lion. The proportions and

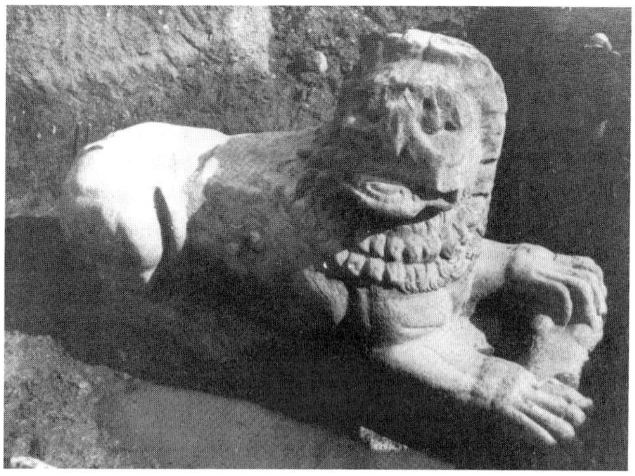

Fig. 10. Reclining lion from Miletus, east harbour mole. After Milet II. 3 (1935) fig. 82.

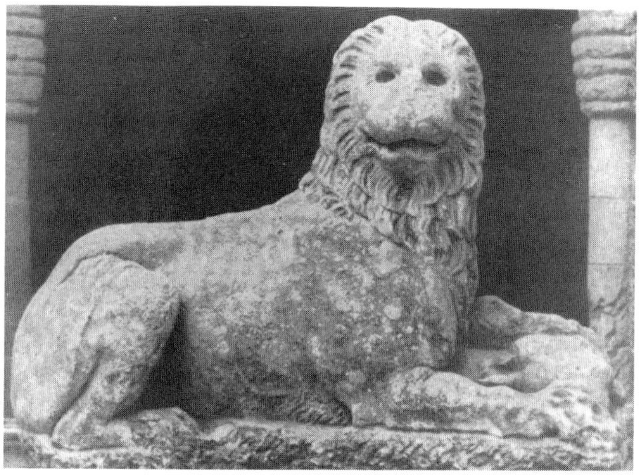

Fig. 11. Reclining lion in Rhodes Museum, no. 221. After Willemsen, pl. 65 below.

attitude also differ, and there is some doubt about the date. Maiuri, in his *Clara Rhodos* publication, considered it to be "decorative work of the Roman period". Willemsen, on the other hand, assigns a Hellenistic date in the third century B.C., which illustrates an all-too-common divergence of opinion in attempts to date lion sculptures.[13]

Where does the Cnidus lion fit stylistically in this sequence of reclining lions? To me it seems earlier than the Miletus and Rhodian lions, and much closer to the lion now in Venice. As already noted above, the arrangement of the lion's mane, and also the proportions of the head, find close parallels in the Mausoleum lions, as illustrated by the head and forepart BM 1083 (Fig. 12),[14] and the Cnidus lion has been assigned to the fourth century by several scholars for this reason (including Willemsen, Vermeule, Fedak).[15] There is, however, a significant difference in the technique of carving, in that the running drill is widely used on the Cnidus lion, whereas it is not employed on the manes of the Mausoleum lions, although it does occur elsewhere on the Mausoleum sculptures.[16] This technical consideration should be sufficient to exclude the date of 394 B.C. proposed by Newton for the Cnidus tomb monument and its lion, in an association with Conon's victory at the sea-battle off Cnidus in that year, for there is little evidence for the use of the running drill so early in the fourth century, at any rate on lion sculptures.[17] A dating in the later fourth century after the Mausoleum sculptures, but not too far removed from them, perhaps in the early Hellenistic period, does seem a distinct possibility from the style of the sculpture. This would bring the reclining Cnidus lion into close comparison with its related type, the upright squatting lion, colossal examples of which decorated the summit of several monumental tomb or victory monuments in the period c. 340–300 B.C.[18] Another comparable colossal lion, this time of springing type, is the lion from Kantzas in Attica (2.60 m long and of Pentelic marble), considered by Knigge to be close in style and date to the lion of Chaironeia, for which she argued a dating of after 316 B.C.[19] Although we do not know how long the sculptural characteristics of late Classical lions lasted on into the Hellenistic period, the exaggerated anatomies of the standing lions from the so-called heroon at Limyra in Lycia, associated with Ptolemy II, suggest that by the middle of the third century a different style of representation was being applied to a figure type that was manifestly derived from the Mausoleum lions.[20] It is not clear whether or not the hollowed-out eyes of the Cnidus lion should be regarded as a Hellenistic feature, rather than a patron's idiosyncracy.

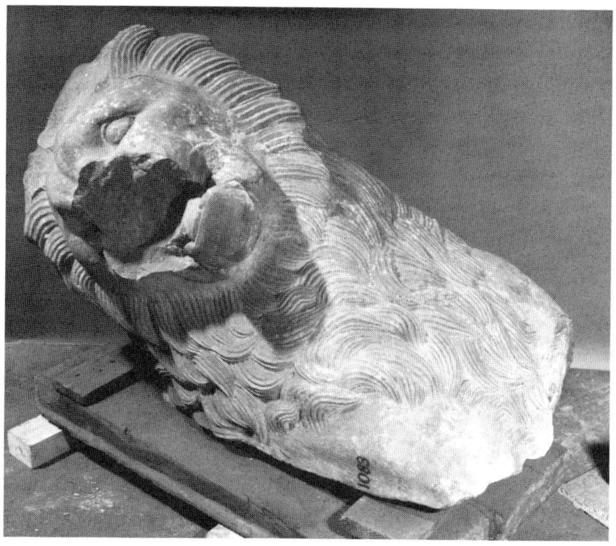

Fig. 12. Forepart of lion from the Mausoleum at Halicarnassus, BM 1083. Waywell, FSM *no. 402. Photo: British Museum 3173.*

The date of the lion statue carries with it that of the tomb monument.[21] Can a late Classical or early Hellenistic dating for the lion be reconciled with the architectural form of the Lion Tomb? This is square in plan, with a low podium of drafted masonry, engaged Doric columns with a shield emblem in the intercolumniation, a pyramid roof seemingly influenced by that of the Mausoleum

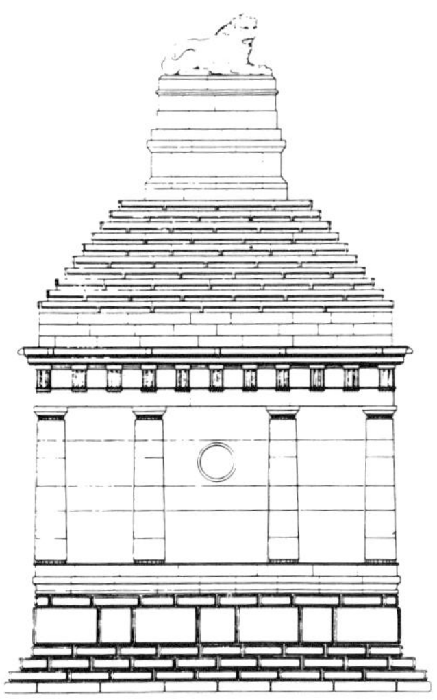

Fig. 13. Newton and Pullan's reconstruction of the Lion Tomb at Cnidus (after Newton, HD, *pl. 63).*

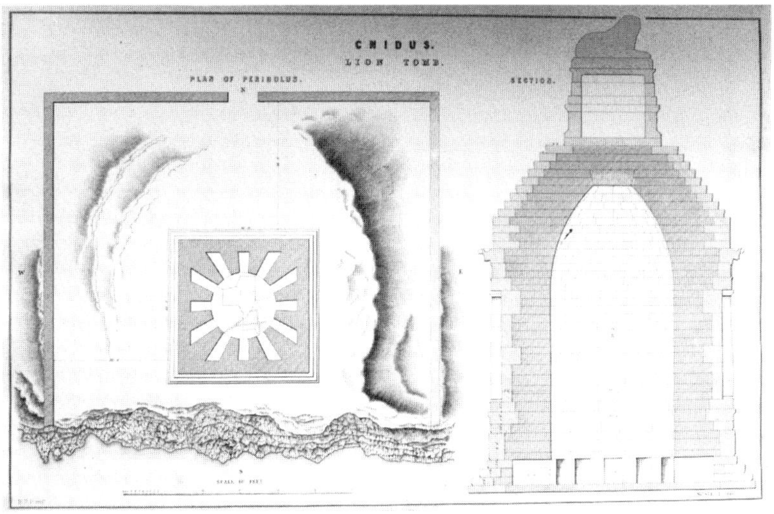

Fig. 14. Ground plan and section of reconstruction of the Lion Tomb at Cnidus (after Newton, HD, *pl. 62).*

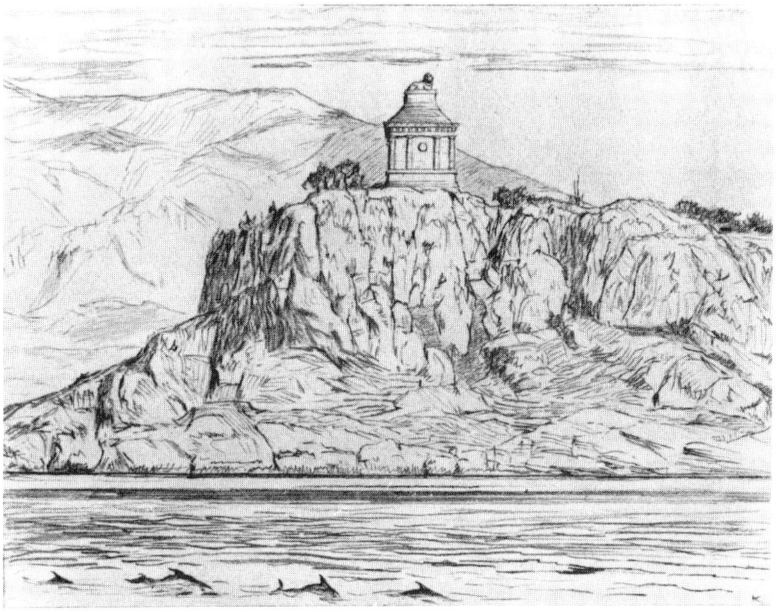

Fig. 15. Krischen's reconstruction of the Lion Tomb at Cnidus (after RM *59, 1944, pl. 29).*

at Halicarnassus, and an internal circular corbelled room with multiple burial places (Figs. 13–14). The date of 394 B.C., suggested by Newton and his architect Pullan, was rejected by Krischen who proposed instead a dating in the early second century B.C. by analogy with the Doric engaged architecture of the Bouleuterion at Miletus (175–164 B.C.).[22] Krischen made some valid criticisms of Pullan's reconstruction of the Lion Tomb, eliminating his low attic of three courses between the cornice and the pyramid roof, extending the pyramid upwards by two steps to make twelve in all, and removing the lower of his two bases for the lion statue.[23] But his emendation was only ever published in a distant sketch (Fig. 15), and his arguments on dating have not been wholly convincing.[24] While there is undoubtedly a group of second century B.C. structures, including bouleuteria, which employ Doric engaged orders and shield decoration in intercolumniations, there is equally no doubt that such features occur in the late Classical and early Hellenistic periods.[25]

More valid comparisons for the Cnidus Lion Tomb might be drawn with the architecture of other monuments crowned by lion sculptures, notably those at Chaironeia and Amphipolis, which are usually dated to the late fourth or early third centuries B.C.[26] In the case of the Amphipolis monument, at least, there is good reason for supposing the existence of an engaged Doric order and a shield decoration in relief.[27]

As the researches of several scholars have recently shown, there are few features of the Doric order of the Lion Tomb which could not be accommodated to the late Classical or early Hellenistic periods. The small perforated rings, or ears, at the upper outer sides of the triglyphs can be paralleled on the Doric friezes of the Hecatomnid dining rooms (*andrones*) at Labraunda, dating before 344 B.C.[28] The Doric order was frequently used in Macedonian tomb architecture, and square Doric podia also occurred on the Belevi tomb and the so-called Ptolemaeum from Limyra, both of which are probably to be dated to the first half of the third century B.C.[29] In these two monuments also, it is noteworthy that the style of the sculptures seems further removed from the Mausoleum sculptures, than does that of the Cnidus lion. A further Doric tomb monument was constructed at Bargylia, surmounted by a sculptured Scylla, which from the development of her iconography would seem to be datable to the first half of the second century B.C.[30] This monument, with its change of crowning sculpture, has the appearance of being a variation on earlier lion monuments like that of Cnidus.

In conclusion: there are no architectural features of the Lion Tomb at Cnidus that need necessarily be dated later than c. 300–250 B.C., and it could be earlier than this, belonging to the second half of the fourth century B.C. Given the stylistic closeness of the Cnidus lion to the Mausoleum sculptures and to other colossal lions from the later fourth century, and bearing in mind the use of Pentelic marble, one may reasonably conclude that the sculpture lies within the sphere of mixed Ionian-Athenian influence that characterises the sculptures of the Mausoleum at Halicarnassus, and which continues through the later fourth century into the early Hellenistic period.[31] Its position on the summit of a Doric pyramidal monument reflects the changes that had been brought to such structures in the generation or two after the Mausoleum at Halicarnassus under Macedonian influence.

Abbreviations

Fedak	J. Fedak, *Monumental Tombs of the Hellenistic Age* (1990)
Krischen	F. Krischen, *RM* 59, 1944, 173–181
Newton, *HD*	C.T. Newton, *A History of Discoveries at Halicarnassus, Cnidus, and Branchidae* (1862).
Rumscheid	F. Rumscheid, *Untersuchungen zur kleinasiatischen Bauornamentik des Hellenismus* (1994)
Waywell, *FSM*	G.B. Waywell, *The Free-Standing Sculptures of the Mausoleum at Halicarnassus* (1978)
F. Willemsen	Willemsen, *Die Löwenkopf-Wasserspeier vom Dach des Zeustempels, OF* 4 (1959)

Notes

1. Newton, *HD* 480–511; Newton, *Travels and Discoveries in the Levant* II (1865) 214; Newton, *Essays on Art and Archaeology* (1880) 82; A.H. Smith, *British Museum, A Catalogue of Greek Sculpture* II (1900) no. 1350, pp. 214–6; M. Collignon, *Les statues funéraires dans l'art grec* (1911) 232, fig. 151; Brunn-Bruckmann, Text to nos. 641–45; G.M.A. Richter, *Animals in Greek Art* (1930) 8, fig. 26; G. Lippold, *Die griechische Plastik* (Munich, 1950) 231 n. 11; Willemsen 51; 59; C.C. Vermeule and P. von Kersburg, *AJA* 72, 1968, 100; Vermeule, *AJA* 76, 1972, 54 n. 2; Fedak 76–79, figs. 85–89.
2. Newton, *HD* 493–4; Krischen 173. Dates suggested by other scholars have tended to polarise between the two extremes. Those who have supported Newton's early fourth century date (after 394 B.C.) include F. Matz, *Die Antike* 4, 1928, 270, fig. 2; H. Büsing, *Die griechische Halbsäule* (1970) 21 n. 2, figs. 1a; 29; and C. Bruns-Özgan, *Lykische Grabreliefs des 5. u. 4. Jhs. v. Chr.* (1987) 20 n. 22. Adherents to Krischen's second century B.C. date include K. Jeppesen, *Paradeigmata* (1958) 65–66, fig. 54. Intermediate datings, in the mid- to later fourth century, are proposed by Vermeule (supra n. 1), Willemsen (supra n. 1); G.B. Waywell, *Yayla* 3, 1980, 5–7, fig. 3; and Fedak (supra n. 1). Cautious circumspection is offered by Rumscheid, I 20; 282; II 28, no. 92, pls. 59,5 – 60,3, who reviews the evidence for the architectural style and comparanda.
3. Newton, *HD* (supra n. 1); W.K. Dickson, *The Life of Major-General Sir Robert Murdoch Smith* (1901) 119–133; I.D. Jenkins, *Archaeologists and Aesthetes in the Sculpture Galleries of the British Museum* (1992) 187–188.
4. Newton, *HD* 482, was firmly of the opinion that the marble was Pentelic.
5. Compare the similar, but rougher, hollowing out of the front joining surface of the hind-part of the Mausoleum chariot horse, BM 1003: Waywell, *FSM* no. 2, p. 87, fig. 10.
6. Newton, *HD* 482–3.
7. Waywell, *FSM* 26–34, nos. 401–649 (pp. 180–209).
8. Willemsen 51–59. For other detailed studies on the typology of Greek lions, see: D. Woysch-Méautis, *La représentation des animaux et des êtres fabuleux sur les monuments funéraires grecs de l'époque archaïque à la fin du IVe siècle av. J.-C.* Cahiers d'archéologie romande de la bibliothèque vaudoise 21 (1982); M. Mertens-Horn, *RM* 93, 1986, 1–61; ead., *Die Löwenkopf-Wasserspeier des griechischen Westens in 6. u. 5. Jht. v. Chr. im Vergleich mit den Löwen des griechischen Mutterlandes*, 28. Ergh. *RM* (1988); B.M. Scarfi, *The Lion of Venice* (1990); cf. L. Polacco, *Quaderni Ticinesi di Numismatica e Antichità Classiche* 24, 1995, 97–111; F. Queyrel in E. Will and F. Larché, *Iraq al Amir. Le Château du Tobiade Hyrcan*, Institut Français du Proche-Orient (1992) 219–241.
9. G.Q. Giglioli, *ArchCl* 4, 1952, 8, pl. 4; Vermeule, *AJA* 76, 1972, 53 n. 14; Mertens-Horn, *RM* 93, 1986, 51 n. 304. Newton, *HD* 498, considered it to be virtually the twin of the Cnidus lion.

10. A. von Gerkan, *Milet* I. 6 (1922) 84; 90; 104; *Milet* II. 3 (1935) 112, figs. 82–84; Willemsen 55.
11. According to Vermeule (supra n. 9) 52, the motif of the animal's head under the paw, which becomes common in the Hellenistic and Roman periods, begins in Attica c. 325 B.C.
12. A. Maiuri, *ClRh* II (1932) 75, fig. 40.
13. Willemsen 55.
14. Waywell, *FSM* no. 402.
15. Supra n. 2.
16. Waywell, *FSM* 66 n. 182.
17. S. Adam, *The Technique of Greek Sculpture* (1966) 51; 66. Although A. F. Stewart, *BSA* 70, 1975, 199–200, and *Greek Sculpture* (1990) 39, has argued for an experimental introduction of the running-drill from c. 400 B.C. onwards, it does not seem to me to come into widespread use until after c. 370 B.C., as Adam maintained, and as Stewart agreed (more firmly in 1975 than 1990). There is one instance of the use of the running drill on the Parthenon sculptures (west pediment Athena): O. Palagia, *The Pediments of the Parthenon* (1993) 46.
18. The Lion of Chaironeia: Willemsen 52, pls. 58–59; Mertens-Horn, *RM* 93, 1986, 51 n. 300; 52–55, pl. 18, 2.
    The Lion of Amphipolis: J. Roger, *BCH* 63, 1939, 4–42; O. Broneer, *The Lion Monument at Amphipolis* (1941); Mertens-Horn, loc.cit., pl. 18, 1.
    The Lion of Ecbatana, 3.25 m long, of sandstone: H. Luschey, *ArchMittIran* n.s. 1 (1968) 115–122, pls. 45–50, who interprets it as belonging to a cenotaph for Hephaistion who died in 324 B.C.
19. U. Knigge, *AM* 91, 1976, 166–173. She places the lion of Kantzas just before the anti-luxury decree of Demetrius of Phaleron in 317 B.C., and speculatively associates it with a tomb of Demosthenes who died in 322 B.C. Her date of after 316 B.C. for the Lion of Chaironeia is rejected by Mertens-Horn (supra n. 18) 52 n. 307, who prefers the usual dating of c. 338–335 B.C.
20. G. Stanzl in J. Borchhardt and others, *ÖJh* 61, 1991–2, Beibl. 151–160; J. Borchhardt, *RA* 1991, 309–322, esp. figs. 9–11 for the lions; id., in G. Dobesch and G. Rehrenböck (edd.), *Hundert Jahre Kleinasiatische Kommission der Österreichischen Akademie der Wissenschaften, Akten des Symposiums vom 23. bis 25. Oktober 1990*, Denkschriften 236 = *ETAM* 14 (1993) 71–84, pls. 3–8; Rumscheid I 24; 92–98; II, cat. no. 130, pp. 35–36. A date of c. 280–270, or at any rate within the reign of Ptolemy II (289–246 B.C.), has been proposed by Borchhardt. For a suggestion that this should be lowered to 250–225 B.C., see M. Pfrommer, *IstMitt* 37, 1987, 151 n. 38.
21. Lippold's curious assertion (supra n. 1), that the Cnidus lion tomb may be a Hellenistic renewal of an earlier monument seems to arise from an attempt to reconcile conflicting theories over the date of the structure and its crowning sculpture, rather than to be based on any evidence from the site of the monument.
22. Supra n. 2.
23. Krischen 173–174; id., *Weltwunder der Baukunst in Babylonien und Ionien* (1956) 82, pl. 30.
24. A more fully drawn out elevation of the Lion tomb, based on Krischen's arguments, was published by Büsing (supra n. 2).
25. Rumscheid I 282.
26. Supra n. 18.
27. The architectural remains are published in detail by S.G. Miller and S.G. Miller, *ADelt* 27A, 1972, 140–169. See especially p. 156 for a reconstruction of the columns with a shield in between, and pp. 157–158 for the problems of reconstructing the Lion Tomb.
28. P. Hellström and T. Thieme, *MedMusB* 16, 1981, 58–74; P. Hellström in J. Isager (ed.), *Hekatomnid Caria and the Ionian Renaissance, Halikarnassian Studies* I (1994) 41; Rumscheid I 313 n. 432; II nos. 116–117.
29. Belevi: C. Praschniker and M. Theuer, *FiE* VI (1979); B. S. Ridgway, *Hellenistic Sculpture* I (1990) 187–196, with n. 39 on p. 206; W. Hoepfner, *AA* 1993, 111–123; Rumscheid I 70–76; II no. 28.
    Limyra: supra n. 20.
30. G.B. Waywell, *Akten des XIII. internationalen Kongresses für klassische Archäologie, Berlin 1988* (1990) 386–388, pl. 58,3. A full publication of the architecture and sculpture of the monument by G.B. Waywell is in *AntPl* 25 (1996) 75–119, pls. 59–66..
31. Waywell, in Isager (supra n. 28) 58–72.

After the Mausoleum: Hellenistic Sculptures from Bodrum in the British Museum

Peter Higgs

The excavations and explorations of the city of Bodrum in the nineteenth century uncovered a variety of sculptures that were not part of the Mausoleum's architectural programme. Both Charles Newton in 1856–8 and Alfred Biliotti in 1865 concentrated on discovering and investigating the site of the famous tomb of Maussollos, but they also found other interesting, if fragmentary, pieces of sculpture that were later in date. These were mostly acquired by the British Museum, but are generally unpublished and unknown. In the light of the recent revival of interest in the sculptural production of Karia and the Dodecanese, which has generated conferences, individual studies of specific works and published old and new evidence simultaneously, it seemed timely to re-examine the miscellaneous pieces in the British Museum.[1] Three of these merit particular interest because of their large scale and their unique characteristics. Unfortunately, practically all of the non-Mausoleum sculptures found on the site were discovered re-used as building material or in marble dumps. A few others were stray finds in the town and their exact findspots are not given in the notebooks and diaries of Newton or Biliotti.[2] The three sculptures in question represent draped female figures and date to the Hellenistic period. One is about life-size, the other two larger than life.

1 Torso of a standing woman. GR 1870.3–15.1 (Figs. 1–5).
Dimensions: Height – 0.84 m; width – 0.42 m; depth – 0.28 m. (The full figure would have been approximately 1.60 m, or about life-size).
Marble: Medium crystal, white marble with grey streaks. According to isotopic analysis the marble is Proconnesian and is almost identical with that used for the Amazon frieze and certain architectural elements of the Mausoleum.[3]
Provenance: It was found in Hussein Aga's house near the Mausoleum but exactly where this property was located is not clear. This sculpture is probably the one mentioned in a letter sent in 1870 from Biliotti to Newton as the "Body of a female from Bodrum. It is a headless and footless statue which you (Newton) had tried to get."[4] It is clear from this that the figure was known to Newton and that he had probably been unable to procure it during his own excavations in the city.

The condition of the torso is fair, but it has lost much of its extremities including the lower legs, the right knee, the left shoulder and arm, the right breast, arm and shoulder and the head. Many of the loose folds of the himation that hung by the woman's left side have also broken away. The surface is in fine condition with few obvious signs of weathering, except for where the edges of the folds that form the coil of material beneath her

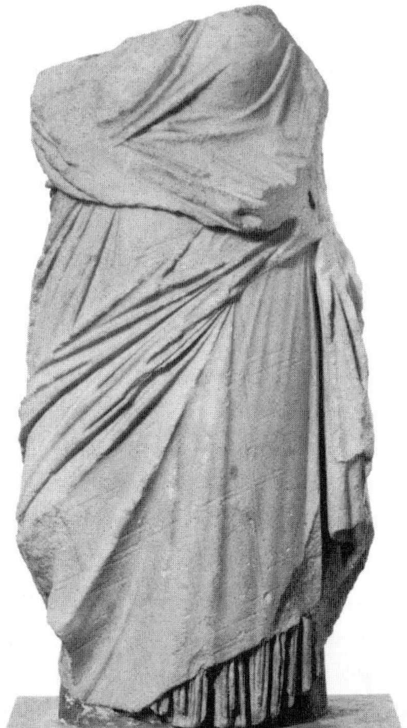

Fig. 1. London, British Museum GR 1870.3–15.1 (Sculpture 1102). Torso of a woman from Bodrum.

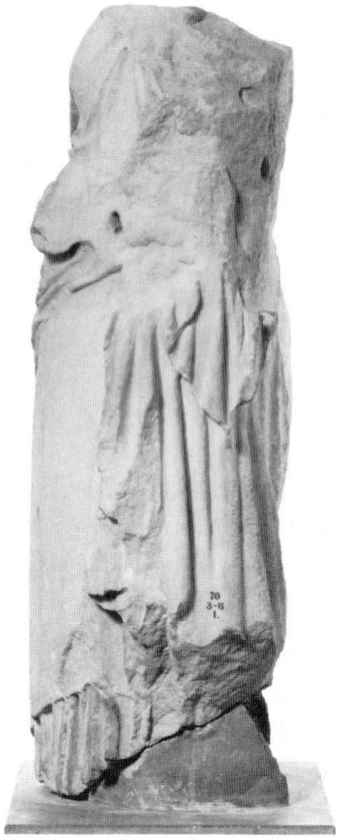

Fig. 2. London, British Museum GR 1870.3–15.1 (Sculpture 1102). Left side of statue.

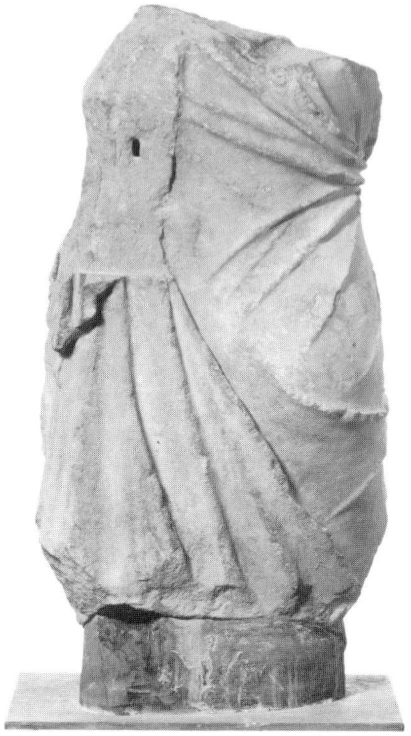

Fig. 3. London, British Museum GR 1870.3–15.1 (Sculpture 1102). Rear view.

breasts have been worn smooth. The back of the figure is slightly more weathered than the front. The front and sides of the sculpture have been carefully finished, but there are still signs of the flat chisel at the back of her right thigh. When first discovered the torso was covered in plaster, much of which has since been removed: an indication that it was re-used at a later date as a building block. Some of the missing elements of the statue were originally carved from separate pieces of marble and attached. There are two rectangular dowel holes, one on the left side (24 mm x 11 mm) and one at the back (30 mm x 12 mm) (Figs. 2 and 3). The separate piece attached at the back probably formed a large overhang of surplus material from the himation. At the left side the worked surface and dowel hole were for the attachment of the separately made arm. Much of the surface of the join has broken away, but a flat area smoothed with the claw chisel survives at the front. It seems likely that the head was carved in one piece with the body as, in the damaged upper surface of the torso, there is no trace of the deep cavity required to insert a tenon.

This sculpture was catalogued by Smith in 1904; he briefly describes the piece, but does not suggest a date or illustrate the torso.[5] It has not been published since, and does not appear in Linfert's study of the regional schools of sculpture during the Hellenistic period.[6] What survives is a remnant of a standing female figure wearing a himation that is firmly but not tightly coiled around her body. Underneath this she wears a chiton, now only visible

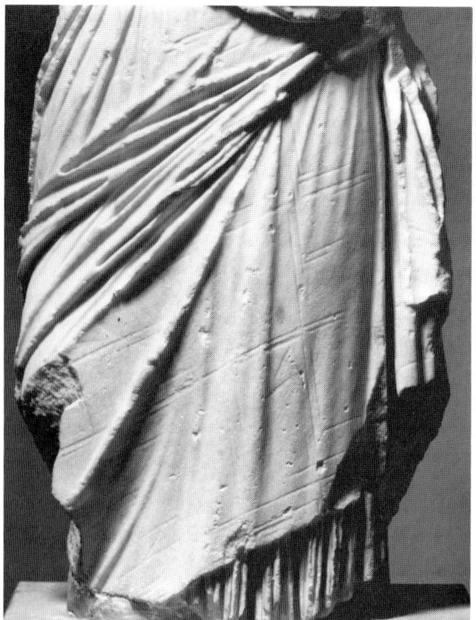

Fig. 4. London, British Museum GR 1870.3–15.1 (Sculpture 1102). Detail of drapery showing so-called "press-folds" or pattern indicators.

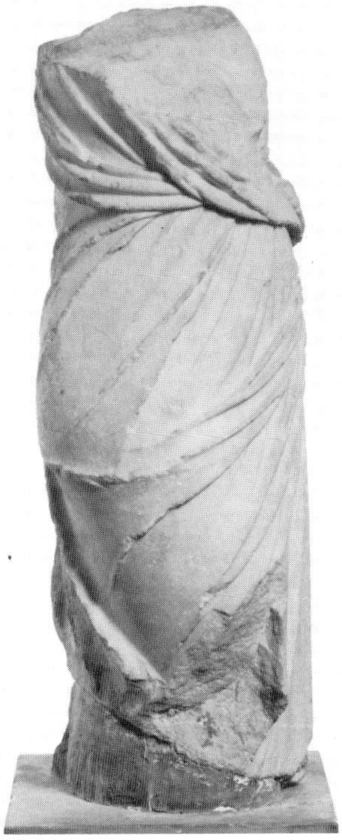

Fig. 5. London, British Museum GR 1870.3–15.1 (Sculpture 1102). Right side.

around her lower legs. The drapery arrangement is simple but effective, with a variety of patterns and shadows caused by the varying textures of the material. Just below the breasts the material of the himation forms a roll that is then slung over the left arm, which may have been outstretched. Around the middle of the torso the material of this garment is pulled into a series of oblique creases that run diagonally from the bent right knee to the left hip. This area contrasts effectively with the tautly stretched material over the weight-bearing leg. Here the sculptor has created a large expanse of material, and decorated it with a series of so-called press-folds that form a chequered pattern over much of her himation.[7] These parallel grooves create loosely formed squares, and may in fact be indicators for painted patterns (Fig. 4). If this is the case, the whole effect would have been chequered, almost like tartan.

The irregularly spaced folds of the chiton have been carefully carved and the grooves between them cut deeply using the so-called running drill technique. The chiton is mostly hidden beneath the himation, but its heavy folds are hinted at through the thinner material of the cloak above, particularly around the stomach. Further differentiation in texture is achieved in the broad and naturalistically carved, loose folds of the himation that hang down the left side of the statue. At the rear, the workmanship is less meticulous, with the material forming broader, flatter folds. The visual impact of the drapery folds is quite stunning, not least because it produces a variety of patterns and textures that give life to an otherwise statically posed figure. Furthermore, the garments effectively highlight the rounded forms of the woman, particularly the right hip, buttock and leg, the stomach and the left breast (Fig. 5). Yet at the same time, the folds running at an angle across her lower body serve to obscure the forms beneath.

Given the variety of the statue's distinctive features, it should be possible to find parallels that may suggest a date for the sculpture. On first sight, were it not for the presence of so many of the so-called press-folds, we could be forgiven for thinking that the statue might be a late Classical original.[8] It bears some resemblance to the so-called Artemisia from the Mausoleum, especially as regards the finely carved, deep channelled folds of the lower chiton, and to some extent the arrangement of the himation around the right leg and thigh.[9] The similarities, however, cannot be pushed too far, and at any rate, the Bodrum fragment is both too small and carved from the wrong type of marble to be a surviving remnant of one of the heroic-scale female figures from the Mausoleum itself.[10] Moreover, it shows none of the severe signs of weathering that most of the Mausoleum sculptures exhibit.[11] It is, however, reasonable to suggest that this figure may have been inspired by a similar, but larger, figure from the Mausoleum.

Close parallels are rare, but the general design of the figure can be compared with some late Classical originals, few of which are securely dated. Related to both the Mausoleum sculptures and the Bodrum torso are the Muses on the base from Mantineia.[12] Compare in particular the Muse holding the double pipes whose loosely draped himation extends just below the knees, like that of the Bodrum torso.[13] Of a similar style are the female figures on the reliefs on the so-called Tribune found in the sanctuary of Echmoun in Sidon. The figure identified as Artemis by Stucky, in his analysis of the monument, wears a himation arranged like that of the Bodrum piece, although lacking press-folds.[14] Also from Sidon is the Sarcophagus of the Mourning Women, on which the female figures again bear a passing resemblance to the Bodrum torso, although they are closer in design to the women on the Tribune. The stylistic connection with the sculptures from the Mausoleum is obvious and has been used to date the sarcophagus. One of the figures on the sarcophagus, similar to the "Artemis" from the Echmoun monument, provides a general parallel for the Bodrum torso, but again it lacks the elaborate press-folds.[15] Proposed dates for these three comparable monuments range from around 375–325 B.C.[16] None of them provide us with specific stylistic parallels for the torso from Bodrum, and in any case it is difficult to compare a statue in the round with figures carved in relief on a small scale.

Essentially, the Bodrum torso shows vague stylistic affinities with many sculptures that have been dated from the mid fourth to the early third centuries B.C. Three figures found together at Delphi, that probably come from the same group, and include the so-called philosopher (here p. 62, Fig. 2) a standing man and a woman (here p. 63, Figs. 4 and 3), are similar to this torso in their general form, and their drapery arrangements also echo those from the Mausoleum. They have been dated to about 300 B.C., just slightly earlier than the statue of Kore from Kallipolis (here p. 52, Fig. 10) who also resembles the Bodrum torso.[17] The upper halves of the aforementioned figures differ greatly from that of the Bodrum torso, but the treatment of the drapery over the legs is similar, and it is possible that the left arm of the Bodrum statue may have been positioned at a similar angle to that of the Kallipolis statue. Many of these comparative figures have been considered to derive from Attic workshops, and it is possible that the sculptor of the Bodrum piece was also an Athenian, or at least trained in Athens.

The region of the Dodecanese and Karia was the focus of some important and famous sculptures during the late Classical and early Hellenistic periods, including of course both of Praxiteles' statues of Aphrodite; the draped one on Kos, the nude figure at Knidos. The excellent quality of the Bodrum torso suggests that it too was carved by a major sculptor, perhaps an Athenian. The torso in question seems too late in date to be by Praxiteles, but his sons Kephisodotos and Timarchos were working on the altar at the Asklepieion on Kos in the first decade of the third century B.C., and may well have worked in Halikarnassos too.[18]

Some of the surviving sculptures from Kos have been associated by Kabus-Preisshofen amongst others, both with the sculptures from the Mausoleum, and with the style of Praxiteles and his sons. One of these is a female figure dated to the late fourth century B.C. that compares well with the Bodrum piece.[19] Firstly in the manner in which the loosely draped himation reveals only sporadic hints of the garment beneath, and secondly in the deeply cut folds of the chiton that emerge beneath the himation. The statue from Kos is an inferior work in terms of quality and her garments lack the variations in texture seen on the Bodrum torso, but the figure does at least demonstrate another possible restoration for the missing arms of the Bodrum piece. The Koan woman raises her right arm and crosses it over her body and the other hand is concealed in the material of the heavy himation. Whether the Bodrum torso is to be restored with the right arm free of the drapery and crossing her body, or alternatively, with the arm concealed within the himation is impossible to determine. Another female statue from Kos demonstrates the latter arrangement, with a similar overfold of material as seen on the Bodrum torso over her left shoulder.[20] Apart from this possible restoration, this statue from Kos bears little resemblance to the Bodrum piece; its thin, revealing himation and conical shape seem to exhibit later Hellenistic characteristics, and the figure is dated by Kabus-Preisshofen to the end of the second century B.C.

That this type of drapery arrangement carries on well into the third century is demonstrated by one further parallel with the Bodrum statue, on the figure of a Muse from the Altar of Athena at Priene, now in Berlin.[21] Carter, who dates the altar to the last decade of the third century, generates an interesting discussion about the date of this piece, and many of the issues that he raises about the drapery scheme and the shape of the figure apply equally well to the Bodrum torso. Both wear himatia that reveal only a hint of the garment beneath, which is unlike the later, second-century female figures that are examples of the so-called drapery through drapery technique. A second comparison between the two sculptures is that the material of their himatia bunches up into a roll of folds beneath the breasts, although this runs slightly lower down on the Bodrum statue. The end of the third century, if this is the correct date for the Priene altar, would then perhaps be the lowest date that we could apply to the Bodrum torso.

Most of the works discussed above, while similar in style, derive from a wide geographical area spreading from Delphi to Sidon. The general period 350–200 B.C. is one when sculptors were travelling eastward into western Asia Minor and beyond and working on grand buildings. There is, however, a notable lack of free-standing sculpture dating to the early Hellenistic period from sites in western Asia Minor, so the Bodrum piece, perhaps best dated to the period from 325–225 B.C., is an important addition in this respect. It is also interesting to observe that there now seem to be more female figures of early Hellenistic date than was once thought.[22] Whatever the exact date of this work, it is a remnant of a superbly carved sculpture of the early Hellenistic period, the identification of which is rendered almost impossible by its lack of any distinctive characteristics. Its type served equally well for a representation of a goddess or a portrait statue. Its context is even more difficult to determine, but it could have been a later dedication on the Mausoleum site, a reasonable suggestion supported by the possible use of a Mausoleum marble block in its production. It may have stood in the as yet unexcavated Agora, or in the nearby sanctuary of Demeter and Kore.[23]

2 Fragment of a female statue. GR 1972.8–4.2 (Figs. 6–9).
Dimensions (as preserved) height (waist to hips) – O.43 m; width – 0.55 m; depth – 0.31 m. (An approximate height for the entire figure is about 2.50 m).
Marble: medium crystal, probably local in origin. The surface has weathered to a yellow-brown colour. Isotopic analysis of the marble demonstrates that the stone used is practically identical with that used in the peribolos wall of the Mausoleum.[24] The marble, therefore appears to be of local origin.
Provenance: This sculpture can be identified with a fragment found on the site of the Mausoleum by Biliotti and referred to in his diary on Friday 12th May 1865. He describes it as follows, "The only thing discovered is a fragment from a colossal draped statue – it seems to be

part of the breast – this piece is cut at one end and was joined, very likely at the waist, to another piece of marble forming the lower part of the statue. There is here as well as on one side a hole for an iron pin".[25] On first reading, this description does not seem to be appropriate for the Bodrum piece, comprising the waist and hips of a female figure, but it appears that Biliotti was looking at the sculpture the wrong way up. When found, the sculpture was found covered in plaster, as it was until recently cleaned, so this mistake is certainly forgivable. What little survives of this monumental piece is chiefly of interest for its piecing technique.

The top section has been worked to receive the upper body, and carved with a raised wedge-shaped block that would have fitted into a cutting in the upper body part (Fig. 7). Technically known as an inverted socket and tenon join, this dowel roughly measures 24 mm x 22 mm, but on the left and front face the surface is damaged.[26] To keep the two pieces in place a metal dowel was originally secured within a square dowel hole cut in the centre of the "wedge" (30 mm x 30 mm and 12 mm deep). To secure the two sections further, another cutting was made at the right side (37 mm x 28 mm x 70 mm deep). A roughly cut hole on the right hip of the statue, buried beneath the coil of folds that run around the hips may have been intended to secure either the right hand, if it was placed on the hip, or perhaps an object held in that hand (Fig. 8).

This entire method of piecing was designed to ensure a snug fit between the separate pieces, but this technique is not easy to parallel in other sculptures mainly because publications rarely show the surfaces of joins. Those Hellenistic female statues that were pieced were usually joined just below the breasts, more often than not with a girdle marking the point of contact, as in this case. This can be seen in many sculptures, for instance the so-called Amphitrite from Melos and on a statue from Pergamon now in Berlin, and thought to represent an Attalid queen.[27] Unfortunately there are no published photographs of the joining surfaces of these two sculptures or records of the methods used in their construction. Of more help is a fragment of the upper body of the cult statue of Amphitrite from Isthmia which has anathyrosis on its under surface. It is not quite the same technique as that used on the Bodrum fragment, but at least it demonstrates a similar method of a shallow wedge and socket joint.[28] Further detailed publications are required to really understand the different processes involved in the piecing of ancient sculpture.

Despite the battered nature of the Bodrum fragment, the surface is not particularly weathered. Over the left hip, only a few drapery folds survive, but the original carved surface is relatively well preserved on the right hip, and at the front. The back of the fragment has been completely smashed away. There is a large area on the upper left side that is damaged, and most of the coil of folds forming the upper part of the himation, that was

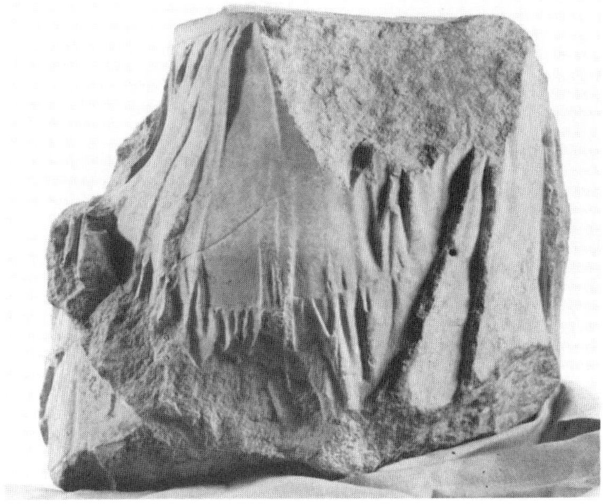

Fig. 6. London, British Museum GR 1972.8–4.2. Fragment of waist and hips of female figure from Bodrum.

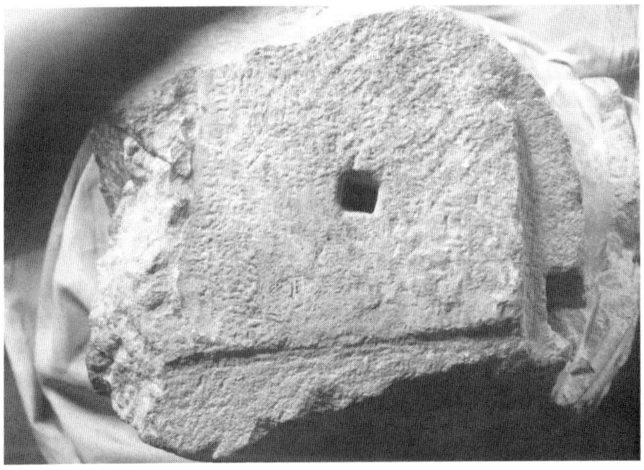

Fig. 7. London, British Museum GR 1972.8–4.2. Detail of the inverted socket and tenon join and the cutting on the right hip.

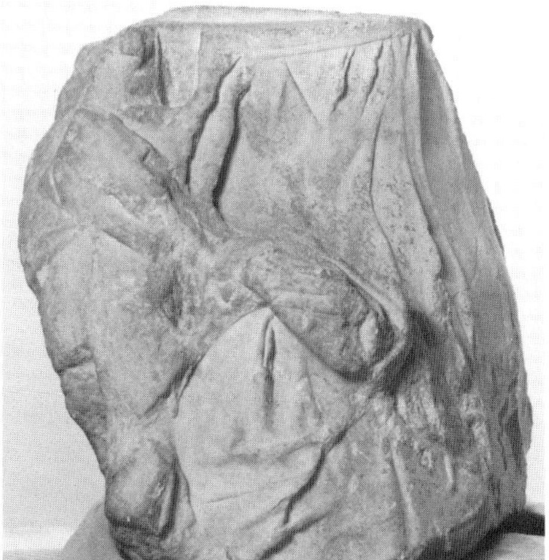

Fig. 8. London, British Museum GR 1972.8–4.2. Right side of fragment showing cutting beneath the coiled folds of the himation.

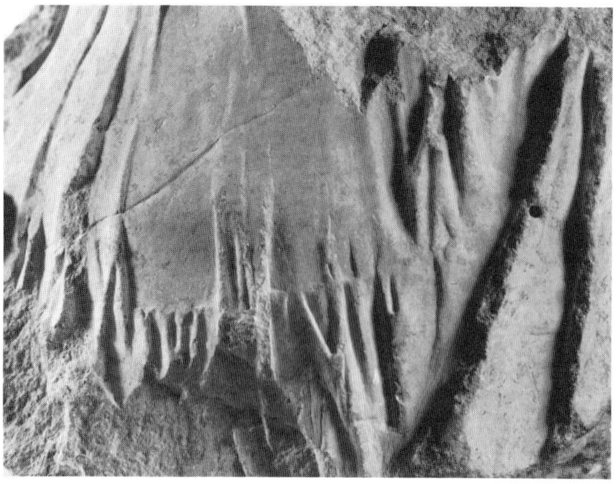

Fig. 9. London, British Museum GR 1972.8–4.2. Detail of stomach of figure showing "undergarment" and associated drill hole.

originally wrapped around her abdomen and thighs, is missing. What survives shows that the woman wears a close-fitting, lightly wrinkled chiton that is girded around the waist, but some of the pleats in this garment that lie over the stomach have flat tops and are not easily explained (see Fig. 9 for a detail). If a mistake had been made by the sculptor here, it would have been easy for him to rectify this and extend the folds further upwards. Just above this pleated line the marble has been sharply cut at an angle that deviates from the rounded contours of the rest of the stomach. This flatter surface and the presence of peculiar folds are, so far as I know, unparalleled. This strange carving technique may have been done for effect, although it is possible that it was intended to show the use of a cord pulling the material, almost like a draw-string. This cord could be connected with the small drill-hole on the left side of the stomach that perhaps originally secured a metal button. Just above this line of flat-topped folds, on the right side of the stomach, the chiton also folds into one very small pleat that runs across the stomach, and beneath this the tool marks have not been smoothed away (Fig. 9). This is also a rare feature in material, but can be seen on the so-called Maussollos, just over his left thigh and below the knees.[29] These rather unusual patterns provide additional textures and show that the sculpture was the work of an imaginative and technically competent sculptor.

The material of the himation over the right hip contrasts effectively not just with the clinging chiton and the small pleats of the under-garment, but also with the folds of the himation at the front (Fig. 8). Here the material has a plastic quality; in some places producing sharp folds, and over the right thigh becoming taut and revealing the contours of the body. The material here looks soft and retains a polish that perhaps, along with colour, marked the distinction between the different garments. Over the front left side the folds of the chiton are broader, flatter and triangular in shape, and originally had sharp edges, now broken away (Fig. 6). These textural contrasts in the garment are probably caused by the marked contrapposto of the figure. She may have originally leaned towards the left where the garment hangs more loosely than where it clings to her body on the right. A similar posture, although in reverse, can be seen on the colossal Aphrodite from the Athenian Agora.[30] Another closer parallel, but of Roman date, is a statue said to be a Muse in the National Museum, Rome.[31] This figure stands with her weight on her right leg, and the resulting stance thrusts the hip out sharply on that side. The himation slips away from her right hip, but is pulled up to her left side where it is secured. The workmanship is harsh when compared to the Bodrum piece, but the pose is similar. This posture also finds counterparts in several terracotta sculptures, most notably one found at Priene in a house that was destroyed by fire about 150 B.C. This monumental terracotta, 52.5 cm in height, is the best parallel for the Bodrum fragment in terms of its exaggerated contrapposto and in its drapery arrangement.[32] Its pose is elegant despite its thrust-out hip, and the Bodrum fragment could easily be reconstructed standing in a similar posture, perhaps with the right hand placed firmly on that hip.

Such a reconstruction does not, however, help to resolve questions about an identification for the marble figure from Bodrum. It may represent a goddess (the sumptuous treatment of the drapery, and the way in which it clings to the voluptuous forms suggest an Aphrodite). Alternatively it could be the remains of a portrait statue or cult image. The large scale of the piece certainly suggests that it was a major dedication, but whether it was originally part of a later monument in the temenos of the Mausoleum, or brought in as building material from elsewhere is impossible to ascertain. A suitable date for the fragment is suggested by the above parallels, that all tend to be stylistically dated to the second century B.C., and judging from its similarity to the Priene terracotta, more specifically to around 150 B.C.

3 Lower portion of a standing female figure. British Museum 1103 (Figs. 10–12).

Dimensions (as preserved) height – 0.63 m; width – 0.55 m; depth – 0.50 m (an approximate height for the whole figure would be about 2.50 m).
Marble: large grained, grey marble of local origin. Isotopic analysis has again shown a match between the marble used for this sculpture and that used for the peribolos wall and the Amazon frieze of the Mausoleum.

The final fragment is from a statue of a similar scale to the last piece, and consists of the lower part of a heavily draped standing woman. Exactly where the fragment was discovered is uncertain, but in the British Museum's guide to the Mausoleum room published in 1886 it is mentioned

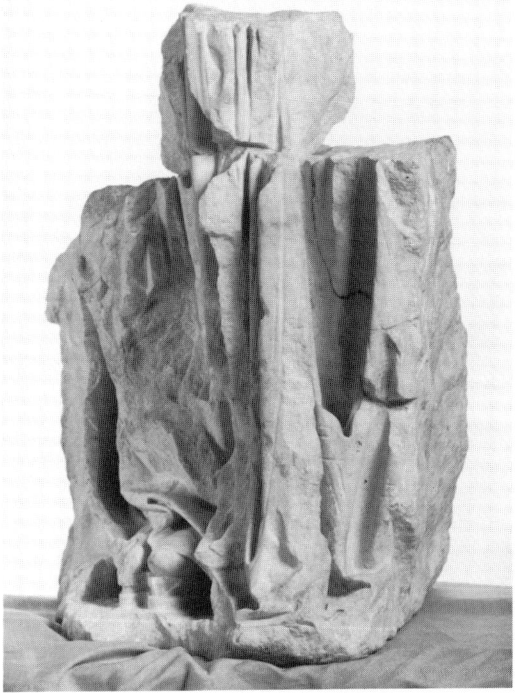

Fig. 10. London, British Museum (Sculpture 1103). Lower right portion of standing woman from Bodrum.

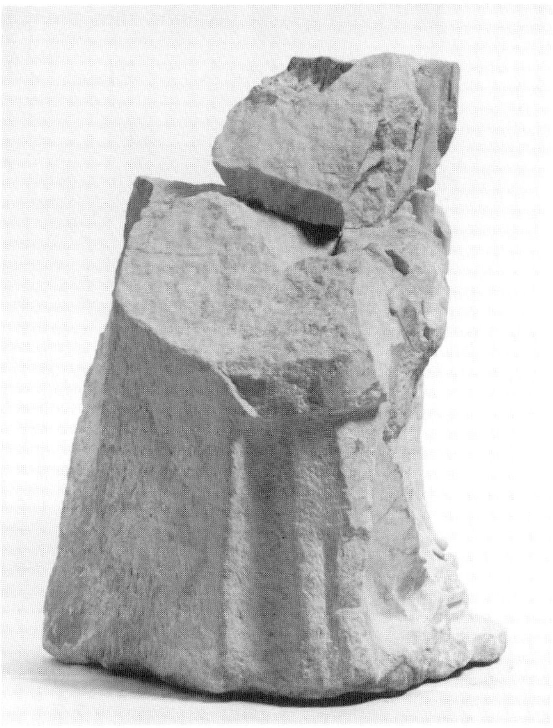

Fig. 11. London, British Museum (Sculpture 1103). Rear view of fragment showing the flat area at the back, part of the cutting in the top and the overhanging himation at the right.

alongside miscellaneous pieces from Bodrum, and catalogued by Smith as such.[33] The fragment has been reconstructed from three pieces, constituting a very small proportion of what was once a large and superbly carved statue. Only the lower folds of a chiton are preserved, covering most of the right foot. All of the left side that would have included the left leg and foot is missing. The surface is in a fair condition, but there are areas of damage to the ridges of folds, and to the drapery hanging over the right leg. Most of the plinth on which it stood has broken away. Several other fragments of drapery found during the excavations of the Mausoleum may belong with this figure, and help to secure this site as the sculpture's findspot. These fragments of drapery are carved in a similar plastic and vibrant manner. A feature unique to these drapery fragments and the larger piece are small diagonal and horizontal parallel grooves cut into the folds (not easy to see in the photographs). These are not exactly press-folds, but perhaps small creases instead. None of the small pieces, however, can be joined to the larger fragment.

The Bodrum figure was pieced together at about knee level where there is a rectangular cutting to receive the upper part.[34] This is an unusual place for a join and the only parallel I can find is a recently discovered statue of a woman from Cyrene, that was apparently carved from re-used architectural blocks.[35] A trace of another garment on the Bodrum fragment, probably a himation, can be seen projecting over the chiton on the right side. The himation may then have crossed over the chiton diagonally up to the left hip (Fig. 11).

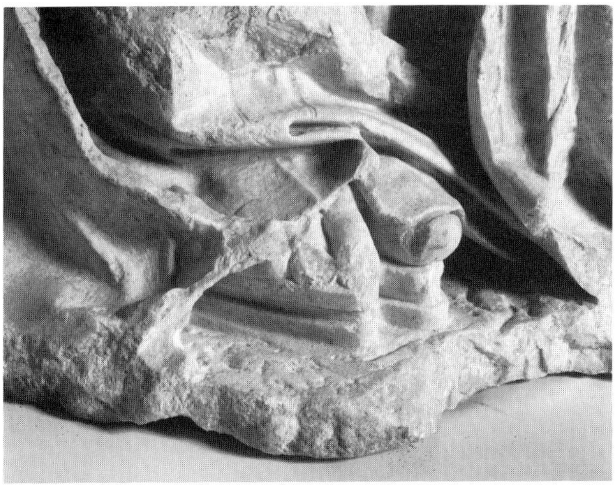

Fig. 12. London, British Museum (Sculpture 1103). Detail of the right foot.

The foot is the best preserved feature, but only the tips of the toes are exposed resting on a high, triple-soled sandal (Fig. 12). The deep undercutting of the himation reveals more of the sandal behind, and this is as carefully carved and finished as the uncovered part of the foot. The sandal has a deep indentation between the large and second toe, similar to that found on the sandals of some of the female figures found at Pergamon and Kos.[36] The sandal on the Bodrum piece, however, has no visible thong. The tips of all but the big toe have been broken away, but what is left of this toe-nail shows careful workmanship. Most of what survives is heavy drapery, carved in deeply wrought folds, that hang around the right foot and in the space between this and the other, now missing, leg. The drapery is arranged in an animated manner, and there is a great variety in the direction of the lavish folds; vertical and deeply undercut between the legs, horizontal and softly spreading over the preserved foot. Towards the back of the right side, the folds of the himation are only roughly blocked out, and behind this the surface is flat, having been worked first with a punch and then with the claw chisel. This type of working can be seen on several statues dating to the second and first centuries B.C., for example on the statue of Saufeia from Magnesia on the Maeander.[37] These statues may have been left deliberately unworked at the lower back because they were placed in niches; alternatively they may have been cut down to fit it into an architectural setting.

Stylistic parallels for the Bodrum piece can be found amongst the female figures from Kos, Pergamon, Magnesia on the Maeander, Erythrai and from Samos.[38] Most of these statues are dated stylistically from the second century to the first quarter of the first century B.C., so that a similar date for the Bodrum fragment is most likely. The style and design of this piece do not differ greatly from all the above parallels, the subjects of which cannot now be identified. The Bodrum piece is an example of a standard type used for images of both immortal and mortal women, and like many of its type it is superbly carved. It is unfortunate that the original context is not known, but it would seem that there were still wealthy enough patrons in Halikarnassos during the second century B.C. to commission large sculptures, which were carved by highly qualified sculptors.

To conclude this analysis of three diverse, yet technically accomplished fragments of sculpture, it would be desirable to assess the motives for their production. Unfortunately, like so many of the other monumental draped female figures of the Hellenistic period, these three Bodrum examples have lost their original context. The lack of inscribed bases or architectural settings allows us only to hypothesise about their original meaning. Hellenistic Halikarnassos has not been the subject of a thorough study, and a useful research project would be one like that undertaken by Kirsten Höghammar, who analysed the inscribed statue bases from nearby Kos, and that of Virginia C.Goodlett who analysed the sculpture workshops on Rhodes.[39]

A study of similar statue bases from ancient Halikarnassos would perhaps identify some of the subjects provided with honorary or cult statues during the Hellenistic period. Apart from the three sculptures discussed in this paper, there are other Hellenistic pieces from Bodrum in the British Museum, that show a diversity in style, scale and technique.[40] The piecing technique of many of these resembles the three main fragments in this paper, but they are probably parts of different statues. There are other sculptures in the Bodrum Museum as well as a late Classical peplophoros statue in the Louvre, said to have been found on the Mausoleum site.[41] It is possible that many of these statues were originally set up as dedications within the temenos wall of the Mausoleum itself, along with small terracotta figures, fragments of which were found during the nineteenth-century excavations.[42] What is important is that all of these sculptures show a continuation of a fine sculptural tradition in ancient Halikarnassos. The sculpture from the Mausoleum itself may have inspired postures and drapery styles, but the Hellenistic sculptors created a variety of different images which find parallels all over the Hellenistic world. The three main fragments from Bodrum show a great affinity with sculptures from the nearby island of Kos, but do not really present any stylistic traits that can be regarded as exclusive to that region: they are examples of a general Hellenistic type used for female figures.

Acknowledgements

I would like to thank Susan Bird, Lucilla Burn, Ian Jenkins, Susan Walker, Dyfri Williams and Ken Evans of the Greek and Roman Department and Keith Matthews of the Department of Scientific Research in the British Museum. Further thanks go to Geoffrey Waywell for giving me useful advice. Photographs reproduced by Courtesy of the Trustees of the British Museum, taken by Nick Nicholls.

Notes

1. See in particular J. Isager (ed.), *Hekatomnid Caria and the Ionian Renaissance: Halicarnassian Studies* I, *Acts of the International Symposium at the Department of Greek and Roman Studies, Odense University, 28–29 November 1991* (1994); I. Jenkins and G.B. Waywell (edd.), *Sculptors and Sculpture of Caria and the Dodecanese* (1997).
2. See C.T. Newton, *Papers respecting the excavations at Budrum* (1858). Biliotti's diary is kept in the library of the Department of Greek and Roman Antiquities in the British Museum. It was published by P. Pedersen, *The Maussolleion at Halikarnassos* 3.1, *Text and Appendices. The Maussolleion Terrace and Accessory Structures* (1991) 117–171.
3. I am indebted to Keith Matthews of the Department of Scientific Research in the British Museum for analysing the marble, and to Susan Walker for assisting me in interpreting the results. The block used for this piece may either have been cut for, but then rejected from, the Mausoleum, or alternatively, quarried from the same marble source.
4. Extracted from an unpublished letter in the Department of Greek and Roman Antiquities in the British Museum, dated 15th January 1870. I thank Don Bailey for recog-

nising the association between the statue and the description in the letter.

5. A.H. Smith, *A Catalogue of Sculpture in the Department of Greek and Roman Antiquities* II (1900) 136, no. 1102.
6. *A. Linfert, Kunstzentren hellenistischer Zeit* (1976). See pp. 207–208 for a list of the sculptures from the British Museum that are discussed in the text.
7. For an analysis of "press-folds" see H. Granger-Taylor, *Bulletin of the Cleveland Museum of Art* 74.3 (1987) 114–123.
8. I know of no late Classical sculptures that have such an abundance of "press-folds". In fact, a male statue from Kos, dated by Kabus-Preisshofen to the first century B.C., is perhaps the best parallel in terms of the amount of these creases rendered on the garment. See R. Kabus-Preisshofen, *Die hellenistische Plastik der Insel Kos* (1989) cat. 38, pl. 53,2–3.
9. British Museum 1001. For a detailed discussion of the "Artemisia" and other fragments of both the colossal and heroic scale female figures from the Mausoleum see G.B. Waywell, *The Free-Standing Sculptures of the Mausoleum at Halicarnassus in the British Museum* (1978) especially 103–105.
10. Waywell (supra n. 9). A few fragments of women of the heroic-scale survive from the Mausoleum, see Waywell cat. 91; 93; 98.
11. See Waywell (supra n. 9) 14.
12. Athens, National Museum 215–217. W. Amelung, *Die Basis des Praxiteles aus Mantinea* (1895). For more recent discussions and better photographs see B.S. Ridgway, *Hellenistic Sculpture* I*: The Styles of ca. 331–200 BC* (1990) 253–254, pls. 132a–c; A. Ajootian in O. Palagia and J.J. Pollitt (edd.), *Personal Styles in Greek Sculpture* (1996) 122–124, fig. 68.
13. Ridgway (supra n. 12) pl. 132b, the Muse on the left of the slab.
14. See R.A. Stucky, *Tribune d'Echmoun* (1984) particularly pl. 9,1, the figure on the right.
15. Istanbul Archaeological Museum 368. R. Fleischer, *Der Klagefrauensarcophag aus Sidon* (1983) particularly female figure A1, pl. 18. The upper half of the figure is not similar to the Bodrum torso, and the workmanship is much slighter and less detailed, but the general design of the lower half is similar.
16. The Mantineia base has been dated to the later years of Praxiteles, and identified as a product of his workshop. Ridgway (supra n. 12) 14, dates it to the third quarter of the fourth century B.C. A. Stewart, *Greek Sculpture: An Exploration* (1990) 177 and J. Boardman, *Greek Sculpture:The Late Classical Period* (1995) caption to fig. 28, both date the base to about 330 B.C. The monument in the Echmoun sanctuary has been dated by Stucky to the middle of the fourth century B.C., Stucky (supra n. 14) 29, and dated stylistically more recently by the same author to the third quarter of the fourth century B.C., based on a comparison with dated funerary and record reliefs. R.A. Stucky, *Die Skulpturen aus dem Eschmun-Heiligtum bei Sidon* (1993) cat. 247, 109–110, pls. 58–61. Ridgway also agrees with this mid fourth-century date. The Sarcophagus of the Mourning Women is generally dated to the reign of Straton I (374–358 BC) and so contemporary with the Mausoleum at Halikarnassos but earlier than the so-called Tribune from Sidon and the Mantineia base. Stewart agrees with Fleischer that the sarcophagus could belong to Straton I.
17. For other illustrations of the Delphi group M. Flashar and R. von den Hoff, *BCH* 110, 1993, 407–433. For the Kallipolis Kore see also ibid., fig. 18.
18. It is now almost universally agreed that Vitruvius was incorrect in associating Praxiteles with the Mausoleum, and that he did not actually work in Karia but, as in the case of the Knidia and the Aphrodite on Kos, sold his works to clients in this region. Andrew Stewart, however, makes an interesting point, claiming that it is feasible that the elderly Timotheos may have actually died during his work on the tomb, and his work was continued by Praxiteles. Stewart (supra n. 16) 181.
19. Kos Museum. Kabus-Preisshofen (supra n. 8) cat. 51; 233–236, pls. 19,1–2 and 20,1.
20. Kos Museum. Kabus-Preisshofen (supra n. 8) 245–248, cat. 56, pls. 63–64.
21. See J.C. Carter, *The Sculpture of the Sanctuary of Athena Polias at Priene* (1983) especially 199–201. For the Muse in Berlin see 204–207, cat. 69, pls. 31–32.
22. See present conference proceedings for several recently found and published sculptures of this type.
23. Little is known about the sanctuary of Demeter and Kore other than the information derived from Charles Newton's excavations. Terracottas found on the site do not seem to date beyond the fourth century B.C. If the sanctuary went out of use shortly after this time, its sculptural dedications may have been moved elsewhere in the city, perhaps within the sacred Mausoleum temenos.
24. The source of this marble may either be from Mylasa or Herakleia. See Pedersen (supra n. 2) 189–192. The marble used for the peribolos wall of the Mausoleum is similar to that used for architectural blocks from the theatre and from the Temple of Ares (Mars) in Bodrum.
25. See Pedersen (supra n. 2) 135. The sculpture was found in Mehmeda's propery on the south side of the Mausoleum site.
26. See A. Claridge, in *Marble: Art Historical and Scientific Perspectives on Ancient Sculpture* (1990) 135–162, particularly 146. The illustration, fig.12, shows a fragment preserving the top half of a male figure in the Museo Nazionale in Rome, where the method of joining the lower half of the statue has been reconstructed using the cutting in the upper part. The cutting is much deeper than that needed for the Bodrum fragment, which is only 1 cm high at the back.
27. "Amphitrite" from Melos, Athens, National Museum 236: Linfert (supra n. 6) 117–118, pl. 53, no. 279. "Queen" from Pergamon, Berlin, Pergamon Museum P 87: R.R.R. Smith, *Hellenistic Royal Portraits* (1988) 81; 160–161, cat. 29, pl. 23,2.
28. Isthmia Museum IS 1. For an illustration see M.C. Sturgeon, *Isthmia* IV. *Sculpture* 1*: 1952–1967* (1987) pl. 37b.
29. British Museum 1000. Waywell (supra n. 9) pls. 13 and 15.
30. Agora S 378. E.B. Harrison, in *Akten des XIII internationalen Kongresses für klassische Archäologie, Berlin 1988* (1990) pl. 50,1.
31. Terme 114896. A. Giuliano (ed.), *Museo Nazionale*

Romano: Le sculture I,1 (1979) 118–121, cat. 87, ill. on p. 120.

32. For the most recent publication of the terracottas from Priene in Berlin see J.Raeder, *Priene:Funde aus einer grieschischen Stadt* (1984) especially 34, cat. 4, fig.12. This terracotta comes from House 29. See also J.P. Uhlenbrock, in *The Coroplast's Art: Greek Terracottas of the Hellenistic World* (1990) 78–79.
33. C.T. Newton, *Synopsis of the contents of the British Museum. Department of Greek and Roman Antiquities: Mausoleum Room* (1886) 62, no. 155. Smith (supra n. 5) 136, cat. 1103. The sculpture is referred to as a work similar to those of the Pergamene school.
34. The cutting is now damaged on two sides, but what remains is 7.8 cm in length. The interior has been worked roughly with the punch.
35. I am grateful to Susan Walker for this information, and see her article in J. Reynolds (ed.), *Cyrenaican Archaeology: An international Colloquium, Libyan Studies* 25 (1994) 172, figs. 12–13.
36. See K.D. Morrow, *Greek Footwear and the Dating of Sculpture* (1985) fig. 67, and Kabus-Preisshofen (supra n.8) cat. 53, pl. 56. For the Pergamon figure see F. Winter, AvP vii: *Die Skulpturen* (1908) cat. 54, pl. XXI. The lower part of this colossal woman is similar to the Bodrum fragment, particularly the way in which it helps us to restore the latter figure's left, relaxed leg.
37. Istanbul Archaeological Museum 822. D. Pinkwart, *AntPl* XII, 1973, pl. 53a.
38. For a selection of similar pieces see R. Horn, *Stehende weibliche Gewandstatuen in der hellenistische Plastik* (1931) pls. 21; 38. The large marble statue of a woman from Erythrai in the British Museum (Sculpture 1684) is another parallel piece that shows the same posture but in reverse. For an illustration see Linfert (supra n. 6) pl. 20, figs. 101–103.
39. K. Höghammar, *Sculpture and Society* (1993); V.C. Goodlett, *AJA* 95, 1991, 669–681.
40. See Waywell (supra n. 9) cat. 775–794 for a list of pieces rejected from the Mausoleum sculptures. The fragments of sculpture in the British Museum are mostly unpublished.
41. Louvre Ma 2838. M. Hamiaux, *Les sculptures greques* I. *Des origines à la fin du IV siècle avant J.C.* (1992) cat. 299.
42. See L. Burn, in Jenkins and Waywel (supra n. 1) 84–90.

Hellenistic Sculpture under the Roman Empire: Fishermen and Satyrs at Aphrodisias

R. R. R. Smith

This paper is concerned with one area of continuity in Hellenistic sculpture under the empire – statues of fishermen and satyrs – and presents the results of recent research carried out at Aphrodisias in Caria on the sculpture found at the site.[1] First, the wider setting of this material and its relevance in this context.

The theme of the conference ('Regional Schools in Hellenistic Sculpture') is a challenging one – in both its geographical and chronological dimensions. Regional studies and catalogues are clearly the best way to gather much of the material, but without external information it is usually difficult to attribute pieces securely to particular regions. In the central areas of the Greek world where interchange was constant and statuary was as much an expression of common cultural identity as of local preference, we may ask what *kind* of regional styles should we expect?[2]

The chronological axis is also difficult to control. Without more externally dated monuments, it is difficult to divide the material between the later Hellenistic period and the early empire. Some aspects of sculpture production in the Greek East were strongly affected by the Augustan new order at Rome – some male portrait heads, for example. But there were clearly categories of statues, for example, female figures, that were purposefully unaffected by political change in Rome. Indeed we should recognise that our late Hellenistic material probably flows over the firm-looking boundary of 31 B.C. into the first century A.D. and later.[3]

Aphrodisias has a particularly well documented Hellenistic afterlife in a wide range of products: honorific statuary, architectural sculpture, decorative relief, as well as copies and versions after well-known figures from the Hellenistic repertoire. The reliefs of the Sebasteion include mythological compositions of direct Hellenistic inspiration.[4] And there are precise replicas of famous works, such as the Epikouros portrait and the Achilles and Penthesileia group,[5] as well as free statuary essays after familiar Hellenistic themes and subjects, especially Dionysian figures from the world of the Hellenistic genre countryside – centaurs, satyrs, fishermen. These were clearly a speciality of Aphrodisian sculptors, and their works in this vein are found both at home and abroad, for example at Tivoli, Rome, and Constantinople.[6]

This paper seeks to isolate the products of one Aphrodisian workshop, and to take them as a test case of how one can identify a single point of production on grounds of technique, theme and repeated mannerism, as opposed to the identification of broader regional trends that would theoretically unite different workshops in one locale. This is a more limited but more precise inquiry – the demonstration of technical workshop connections as opposed to purely stylistic connections.

The material to be discussed comes principally from two areas: the Hadrianic Baths and a Sculptor's Workshop behind the Council House. Now whether this second context, the sculptural facility, was, or was not, the place of production for these statues is not my concern. The archaeology of this complex is a separate and interesting question that bears directly on questions of chronology, but which I will leave aside for the moment.[7] The workshop I would like to isolate is a more abstract phenomenon – a group of statues united by common technique and Hellenistic style and subject.

Fishermen

My starting point is some new material. In 1989 a fine head was excavated at the west end of a large pool in the S. Agora at Aphrodisias – a bearded, slightly frowning head finished with a high polish (Fig. 1).[8] At first sight, it has a strikingly portrait-like effect, and indeed the drilled eyes and some of the sophisticated physiognomical modulations are clear borrowings from the language of portrait sculpture. Prof. Erim recognised immediately, however, that the new head should join a torso of the type of the Hellenistic Old Fisherman found in the Hadrianic Baths in 1904 and now in Berlin.[9] In 1991, a cast of the Berlin torso was tested against the new head in Aphrodisias. The two were found to join perfectly, break to break. A cast of the head was then

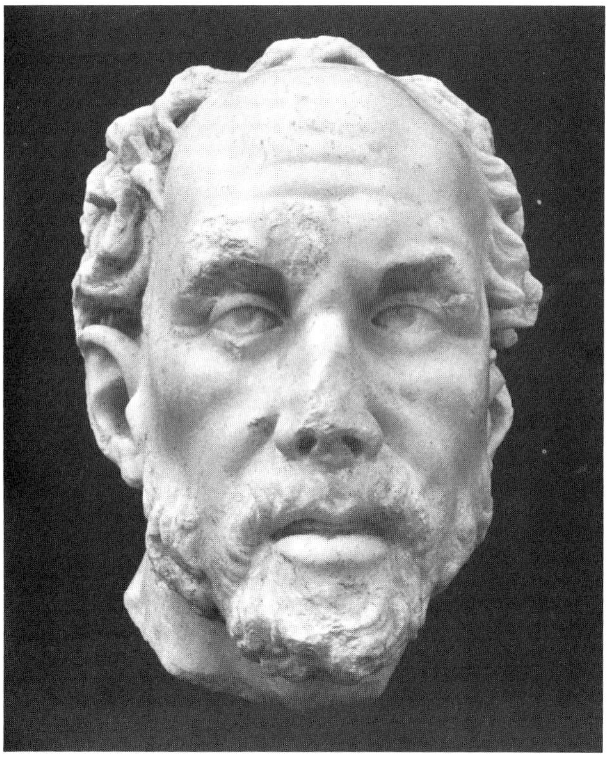

Fig. 1. Old Fisherman, head from S. Agora. Aphrodisias (89–3).

attached to the torso in a preliminary plaster reconstruction (Figs. 2–3). The figure of the Old Fisherman was a famous Hellenistic statue reproduced in about 20 Roman marbles.[10] The Aphrodisias example is not only the finest version technically, it is also a very striking re-interpretation. Other copies show the original had a rather crass, rustic physiognomy and a sagging, withered body. The Aphrodisias Fisherman, however, has a re-styled body of some power and a lean, sensitive expression. This is a refined, philosophical-looking fisherman, re-interpreted to serve as tasteful decoration in a bath complex.

Further parts of this Fisherman statue have also been identified in fragments in the storerooms at Aphrodisias: the base and feet, parts of the legs, a very sensitively worked right hand, and part of the right forearm at the elbow – all easily recognised by scale, workmanship, and anatomical style as belonging to the Fisherman, even though they do not join. A full reconstruction of the figure – head, torso, and legs – may in the future be possible.

The body not only has a distinctive treatment of the thin, wiry legs and the curiously ideal muscle development on the flanks, it also has a very distinctive finish – a high

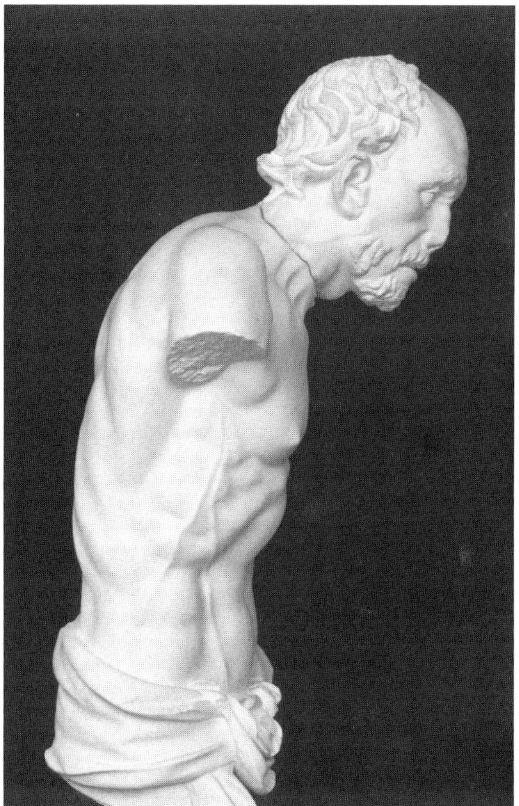

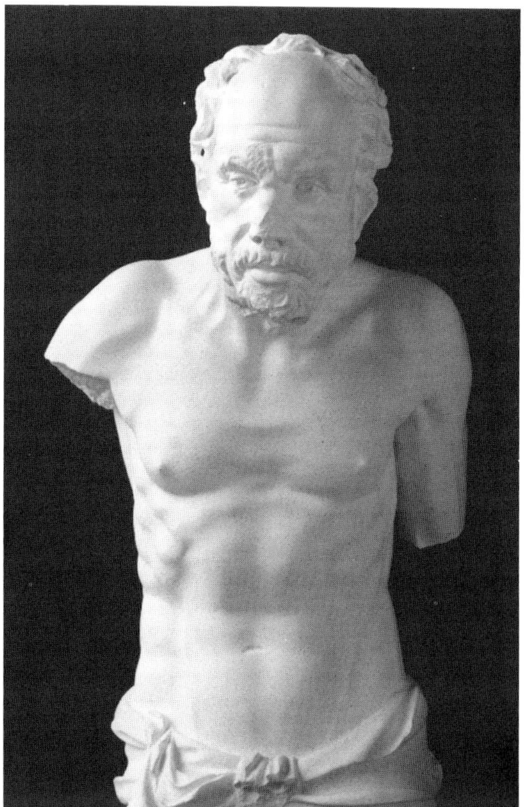

Fig. 2–3. Old Fisherman, cast reconstruction combining head (Aphrodisias 89–3) and torso from Hadrianic Baths (Berlin 1630). Aphrodisias.

polish under which the pronounced veins and muscles blend smoothly into the surface. (The veins and muscles stand out much more in the plain, matt finish of the cast than they do in the glossy, translucent surface of the original). We may note especially the veins on the flanks (Fig. 2). The refined surface treatment has the added characteristic of being confined to the front of the upper body. On the lower legs and on the sides and back of the figure, the polish falls away quickly to a rasped surface bearing a lot of tool traces.

During a recent visit to Berlin, I was able to study both this torso and the torso of a smaller Fisherman statue of the same type (about half-lifesize), bought in Smyrna in 1904 by T. Wiegand, who says he found it there in a garden at Bornova (Fig. 4).[11] Its body forms and surface treatment (where preserved on sides and back) show quite clearly, however, that it is from the same workshop as the larger torso. The muscle pattern on the flanks, the form of the chest, and the same quick 'fading' of the refined surface finish of the front to a rasp finish on the sides and back are identical in terms of technical finish. The small Berlin Fisherman, therefore, surely also came from Aphrodisias and was probably another unrecorded find from the excavations of 1904.

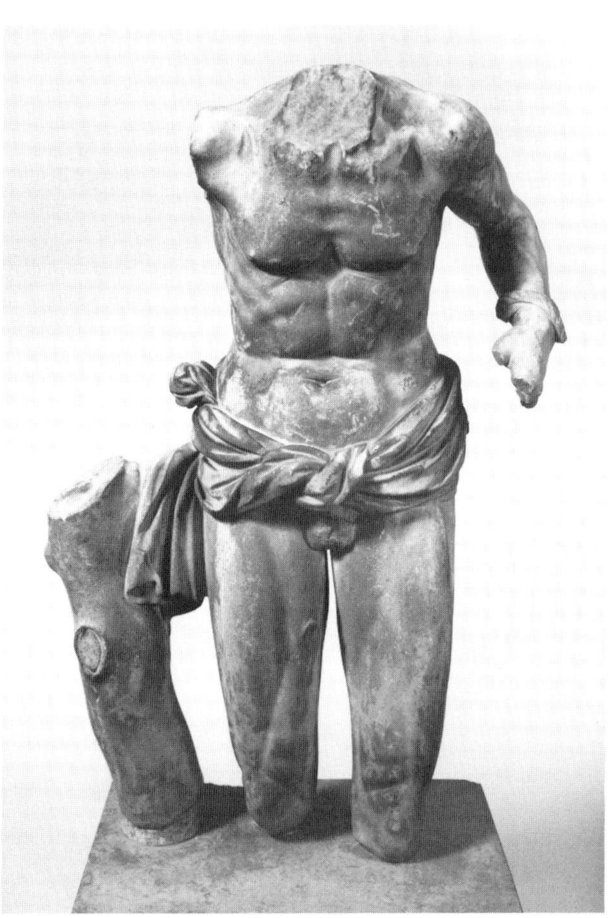

Fig. 4. Small Fisherman, torso bought in Smyrna. Berlin (1742).

Satyrs

Large and small statues of the same Hellenistic type and from the same workshop bring to mind another pair of statues from Aphrodisias: the large and small versions of the Satyr carrying the Baby Dionysos (Figs. 6–7).[12] They were found in the 1960's in the excavation of the area behind the Bouleuterion together with the complex of material thought to come from the Sculptor's Workshop. Technically and formally, the two satyrs, with their lithe, sinewy legs, short torsos, and knobbly preternatural muscle patterns, are clearly of one manufacture. The details of the marble technique for the hair, eyes, skin surfaces, and veins also suggest quite clearly that they are from the same workshop as the two Fishermen.

Particularly telling in connecting the large Fisherman and the large Satyr are several details: (1) the anatomical style of the feet and knobbly toes; (2) the same veins on the right side of the torsos which form in each case an inverted 'V' starting high on the upper flank (Figs. 2 and 5) (this pattern of veins is found on both the Fishermen and both the Satyrs); and (3) the following detail at the backs of the heads (Figs. 8–9). In the hair at the back of the neck the Fisherman had two large curls of hair worked free from the nape (Fig. 8, also visible in profile in Fig. 2) which were not part of the Hellenistic model – the hair of the Fisherman type should here be cut plain and short. Precisely the same two curls are found on the nape of the large Satyr (Figs. 9 and 11), and they seem to constitute a mannerism of the local sculptor. He has deployed these curls on his imaginatively re-styled Old Fisherman contrary to the authorised form of the

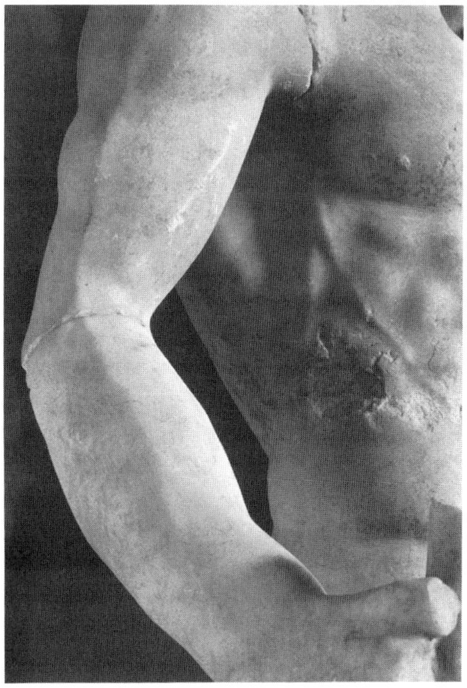

Fig. 5. Large Satyr with Baby Dionysos, detail of right flank. Aphrodisias.

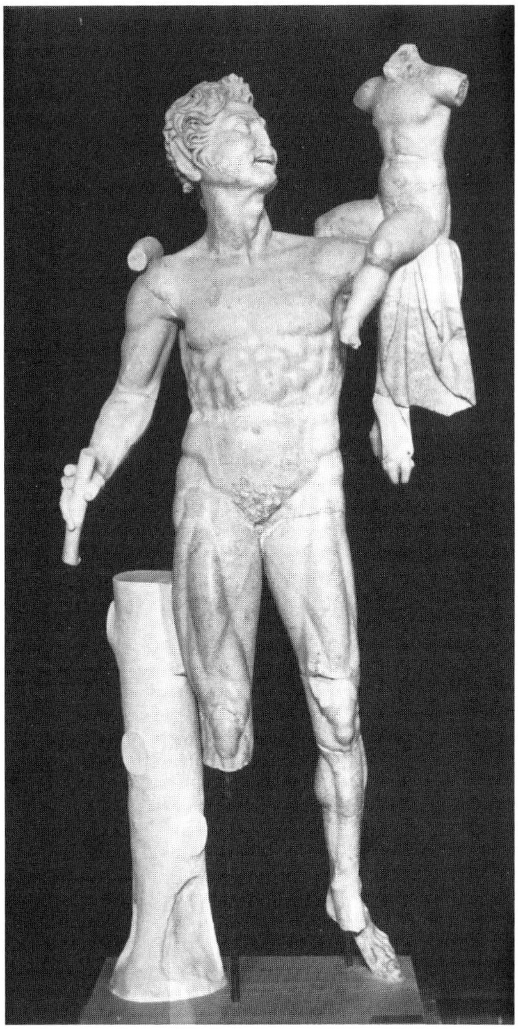

Fig. 6. Large Satyr with Baby Dionysos, from behind Bouleuterion. Aphrodisias (67–557 and 588 ff). Tree support is modern.

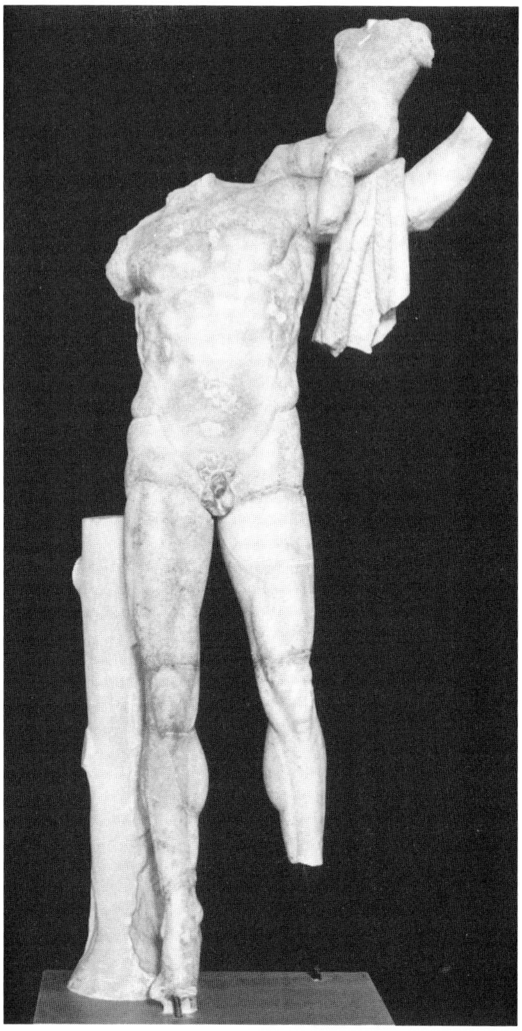

Fig. 7. Small Satyr with Baby Dionysos, from behind Bouleuterion. Aphrodisias (67–577 ff). Tree support is modern.

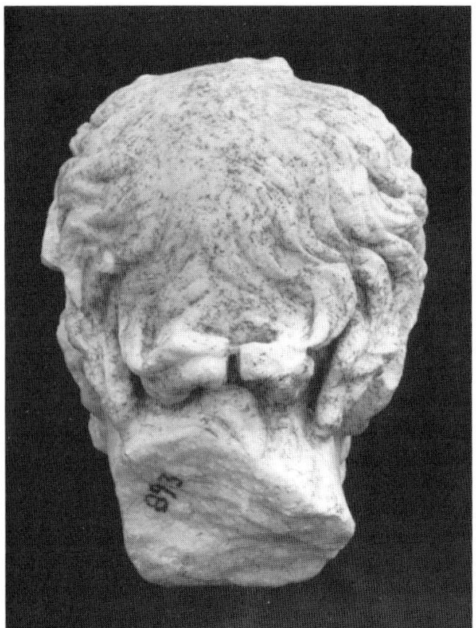

Fig. 8. Old Fisherman, back of head. Aphrodisias (89–3).

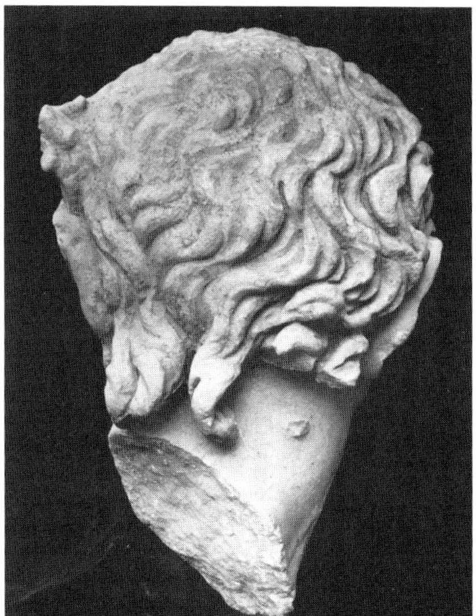

Fig. 9. Large Satyr, back of head. Aphrodisias (67–575).

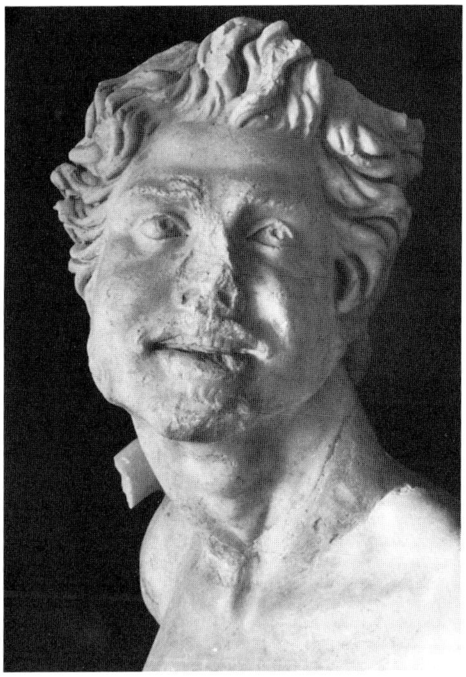
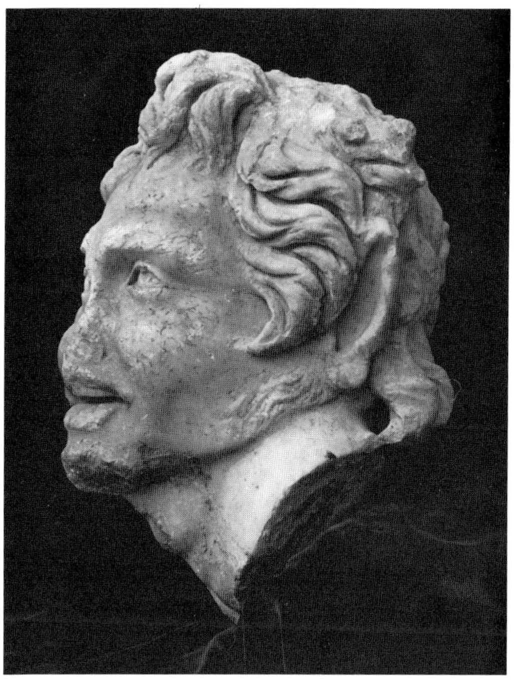

Fig. 10–11. Large Satyr, head. Aphrodisias (67–575).

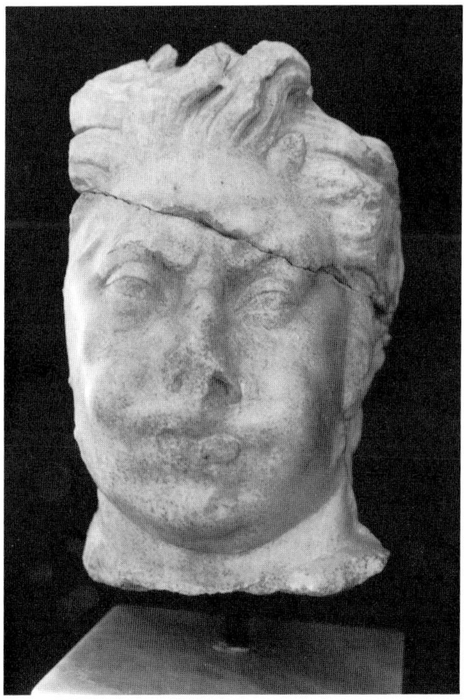
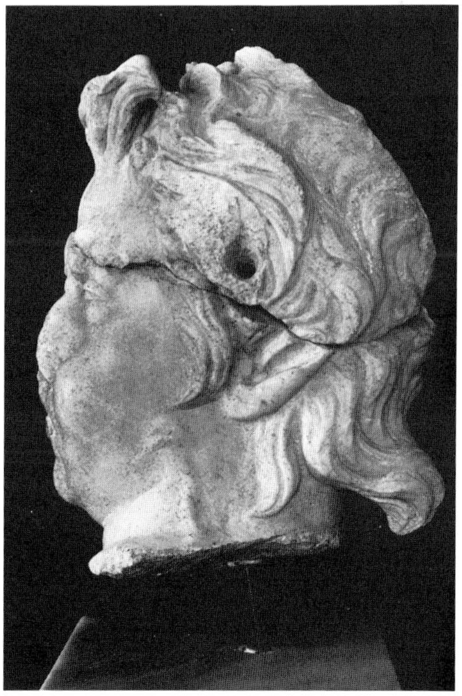

Fig. 12–13. Head of Satyr blowing double flutes, from Hadrianic Baths. Aphrodisias (65–236).

Hellenistic model, giving the figure thicker, longer hair borrowed from the hair vocabulary of his Satyrs. One sees clearly in this detail how the local sculptor was interpreting his Hellenistic model from memory – using the model as a recognisable iconographic type, but around which he worked his own sculptural essay.

Another piece with the same technique is a fine head, also from the Hadrianic Baths, of a Satyr blowing the double flutes (Figs. 12–13).[13] It has the same surface finish, same eye technique, and same prominent veins on the forehead as those of both the large Fisherman and the large Satyr. The hair is brushed back from the forehead in the same three or four thick strands, separated by wide drill channels (Figs. 10–13). There are also clear remains of the same two mannered curling locks at the back of the head (Fig. 13).

Some much smaller pieces may be also connected with the same workshop, by theme and context, but at such a small scale, hardly by technique. There are, for example, a third, very small version of the Fisherman type and a small Spinario group of Pan removing a thorn from a young Satyr's foot.[14]

'Herakles'. There is one further well-preserved major piece, with a different subject: a lithe Hellenistic-style male figure clearly of the same technical and stylistic manner (Fig. 14).[15] The lean, stripped muscle style of the legs and details of the veins and anatomical formulations connect it closely to both the Large and Small Satyrs. Such details are, for example, (1) the short upper arms, sharply squared in section, with prominent, 'leading-edge' veins and (2) a distinctive diamond-shaped area of empty or 'dead' space at the small of the back.

The upper body has the tight narrow chest and sloping shoulders of the professional Hellenistic athletic build, and the ideal young head wears a wreath with large leaves and short hair. The figure was identified by Erim as a youthful Herakles, probably because of the hair and athletic build and because the pose loosely recalls a known Hellenistic Herakles type (Herakles Lenbach). But neither the lithe body forms nor the head type recalls Herakles. Another possible identification, that would suit the short hair, small beardless features, and the runner anatomy, might be Hermes – perhaps, if a thematic link to the other sculptures of this workshop were needed, Hermes in some connection with a child Dionysos.

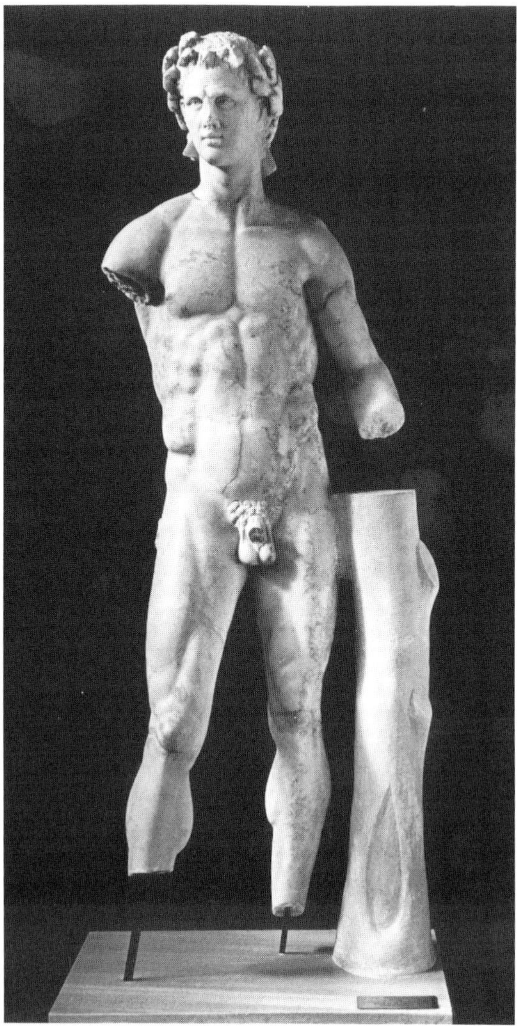

Fig. 14. 'Herakles', from behind Bouleuterion. Aphrodisias (67–556). Tree support is modern.

Chronology

We have been able to identify on the basis of technique, sculptural and stylistic mannerism, and Hellenistic theme about seven or eight important sculptures as the products of one workshop. They all employ a distinctive technical finish and a common local sculptural vocabulary. This distinctive local workshop style was a reformulation of the high Hellenistic sculptural language devised for figures of the Dionysian landscape, such as satyrs and centaurs, peasants and fishermen.

When was this workshop active? The date of the sculptures discussed above will be controversial, because they will surely enter the current debate about dates in the middle or late empire for similar decorative statuary – such as the Esquiline statues from Rome now in Copenhagen: second or fourth century? Erim came to favour late dates for much of the newer material from Aphrodisias, and current opinion is leaning strongly in favour of late dates for this and related material elsewhere.[16] I do not want to go into this question here, and offer two very simply contrasted arguments that the new material from Aphrodisias itself might suggest.

One argument is the context of the Sculptor's Workshop behind the Bouleuterion. The sculptural activity here, according to both the phasing of the building and the latest datable find (an unfinished portrait statue of the mid-later fourth century A.D.) was clearly mainly late, and taken at face value might argue for a fourth-century date for the main production of the finds from this area – the Satyrs included.[17]

However the archaeology of the complex and the preservation and find-situation of the relevant pieces is not so straightforward. Some of the large Dionysian pieces were clearly not in this context because they had just been carved. The main parts of the Large Satyr were found not *in* the Sculptor's Workshop but built into a later wall located between the back of the Bouleuterion and the row of chambers in which the workshop room was situated. The statue had been broken up, and a crude, secondary groove had been cut around its waist. And other pieces, such as a reclining Satyr of familiar type, that look at first glance unfinished and so evidence of late manufacture of such statues, are in fact not unfinished at all. Rather they were completed older pieces on which fourth-century sculptors (trainees?) were practising or working – that is, the rough tooling is secondary work into a finished statuary surface (there are several examples).[18] So, while the find-situation in a late sculptor's yard may be suggestive of a late date, it is hardly conclusive.

A contrasting argument would compare technical details of datable statues. Here the obvious comparanda in terms of eye drilling, hair technique, and especially highly polished, highly modulated surface treatment are statues of the mid-later second century – the same period, for example, as the virtuoso Centaurs from Hadrian's Villa.[19] The proximity of the technical handling of the polished surfaces and of the hair and eye techniques of the large Fisherman (Fig. 1) to that of some datable high-imperial works, such as the head of the statue of a priest from the Bouleuterion of the mid-second century,[20] are as suggestive as the find-context of the Satyrs. The value of comparing an ideal head and a portrait head might be contested, and normally it is not a helpful procedure. However since the sculptor of the Fisherman's head (Fig. 1) was clearly borrowing from contemporary portrait vocabulary to render his fisherman more immediate, human, and accessible, such a comparison may here be legitimate. The purely technical similarities of eye-drilling and type of surface polish between the Fisherman and the Priest from the Bouleuterion are anyway strikingly close.

Whatever their exact date, these statues of Fishermen and Satyrs show how one can, when the material is available, isolate a technical workshop style within a broader local preference. They give us an unusually detailed view of the inventory of a specialist Hellenistic workshop of the Roman period, and show the strong continuity of traditional techniques, styles, and subjects under the empire. The most natural or primary categorisation of such material is surely under 'Hellenistic Sculpture'. In this, as in other areas of cultural life in the Greek East, Hellenistic forms long outlived the Hellenistic period.

Acknowledgements

The photographs for Figs. 1–3 and 5–14 were taken by M.Ali Döğenci. The photograph Fig. 4 was taken by G. Stenzer and is reproduced by kind permission of the Staatliche Museen, Berlin.

Abbreviations

Aph.Papers 1	C. Roueché, K.T. Erim (edd.), *Aphrodisias Papers* 1 (1990)
Aph.Papers 2	R.R.R. Smith, K.T. Erim (edd.), *Aphrodisias Papers* 2 (1991)
Aph.Papers 3	C. Roueché, R.R.R. Smith (edd.), *Aphrodisias Papers* 3 (1996)
Erim, *Aphrodisias*	K.T. Erim, *Aphrodisias: City of Venus Aphrodite* (1986)
Erim, *Guide*	K.T. Erim, *Aphrodisias: A Guide to the Site and its Museum* (1989)
Smith, *Hell.Sc.*	R.R.R. Smith, *Hellenistic Sculpture* (1991)

Notes

1. This work is part of a new program of archaeological research at Aphrodisias undertaken by the Institute of Fine Arts and the Faculty of Arts and Science of New York University under the author's direction since 1991. One of this program's principal aims is to document the excavations and finds made by the late Professor Kenan Erim at the site between 1961 and 1990. On the program of sculpture documentation, see: R.R.R. Smith, *Aph.Papers3*, 11–72, at 52–65; R.R.R. Smith & C. Ratté, *AJA* 99, 1995, 33–58, at 53–55, and *AJA* 100, 1996, 5–33, at 25–30.
2. On problems of regional style and chronological development, cf. Smith, *Hell.Sc.*, 17–18; 269–271.
3. The material from Cos, for example, offers plenty of such cases: R. Kabus-Preisshofen, *Die hellenistische Plastik der Insel Kos* (1989). There is a good example with a documented context at Aphrodisias – a draped, Hellenistic-looking female statue from the Agora Gate, signed by one Menodotos, son of [Niko?]machos, grandson of Menodotos, to be dated probably after the mid-first century A.D.: Erim, *Aphrodisias*, fig. 136; Smith, *Hell.Sc.*, 272, fig. 236; K.T. Erim, J. Reynolds, *Festschrift für Jale Inan* (1989) 517–538, at 524, no. 7, pl. 201.
4. For which, see provisionally Smith, *Aph.Papers* 1, 89–100.
5. Epikouros portrait: inv. 76–161. Achilles and Penthesileia: Erim, *Aphrodisias*, fig. 98a and *Guide*, 98, fig. 133.
6. Tivoli, two signed Centaurs, now in Capitoline: M.F. Squarciapino, *La scuola di Afrodisia* (1941) 32–34; Helbig[4] II, 1398 (H. von Steuben); Smith, *Hell.Sc.*, 132, figs. 162–163. Rome, signed statue of Satyr with Baby Dionysos from the Esquiline, now in Copenhagen: M. Moltesen, *Aph.Papers* 1, 133–146, at 139, figs. 9–10. Constantinople, gods and giants in black and white marble from Silahtarağa, in the Istanbul Archaeological Museum: N. de Chaisemartin, E. Örgen, *Les documents sculptés de Silahtarağa* (1984). The gigantomachy sculptures from this complex at least are now proved to be from Aphrodisias by the discovery of a very similar giant's anguiped leg in black marble at the site in 1993: Smith & Ratté, *AJA* 99, 1995, 54, fig. 30.
7. The archaeology of this complex and the sculpture from it are being studied for publication by Julie Van Voorhis. For preliminary observations: P. Rockwell, *Aph.Papers* 2, 127–143. For more recent archaeological investigation of the complex carried out in 1994: Smith & Ratté, *AJA* 100, 1996, 5–7 and 9–13.
8. Inv. 89–3. Smith, 'Aphrodisias 1991', *XIV. Kazı Sonuçları Toplantısı* (1993) II, 382–383, fig. 6–7; Smith, *Aph.Papers* 3, 20 and 58–63, figs. 54–58.
9. Berlin, Staatliche Museen, inv. 1630: T. Wiegand, 'Torso eines Fischers aus Aphrodisias', *Jhb.Preuss.Kunst Sammlungen* 37, 1916, 1–13.
10. Recent replica list: H.P. Laubscher, *Fischer und Landleute: Studien zur hellenistischen Genreplastik* (1982) 99–103.
11. Berlin, Staatliche Museen, inv. 1742 (H: 78.5 cm): Wiegand (supra n. 9) 8–10, fig. 5 – '... den ich vor wenigen Jahren in einem Garten zu Burnabat bei Smyrna fand.'
12. K.T. Erim, in *Mélanges A.M. Mansel* (1974) 767–775;

Erim, *Aphrodisias*, fig. 105b and *Guide* 96–98, figs. 131–132; Rockwell (supra n. 7) 131, figs. 4–5; Smith, *Hell.Sc.*, 129, fig. 156.

13. Inv. 65–236. Smith, *Aph.Papers* 3, 61–63, fig. 63.
14. Miniature Fisherman torso, from the house to the north of the Sebasteion: inv. 81–106; Smith, *Aph.Papers* 3, 61–63, fig. 60 (there are also fragments of a small-scale version of the Hanging Marsyas from the same context). Small Spinario group, from Sculptor's Workshop behind Bouleuterion: inv. 67–559.
15. Inv. 67–556. Erim, *Aphrodisias*, fig. 66; Smith, *Hell.Sc.*, 272, fig. 335.
16. Esquiline statues: Moltesen (supra n. 6). On the date of their signatures: K.T. Erim, C. Roueché, *PBSR* 50, 1982, 102–115. Recent firm opinions on this subject may be premature: N. Hannestad, *Tradition in Late Antique Sculpture* (1994); B. Kiilerich, H. Torp, *IstMitt* 44, 1994, 307–316.
17. On the phasing of the complex: Smith & Ratté (supra n. 7) 9–13. Unfinished togate portrait statue: K.T. Erim, in J. Inan, E. Alföldi-Rosenbaum, *Römische und frühbyzantinische Porträtplastik aus der Türkei* (1979) no. 195.
18. Reclining satyr: Rockwell (supra n. 7) 136, fig. 14. Several other pieces fall in the same category – a statue of Poseidon, the lower part of a seated male figure, as well as the obvious case of a philosopher bust: Rockwell (supra n. 7) figs. 8–10 and 17–18.
19. Tivoli Centaurs: supra n. 6.
20. J. Inan, E. Rosenbaum, *Roman and early Byzantine portrait sculpture in Asia Minor* (1966) no. 239; Erim, *Guide*, 99; 102, fig. 136 (not Constantinian, as there said, but, as most would probably now agree, mid-second century).

Votive Reliefs to Apollo Kitharoidos from Asia Minor: External and Regional Influence

Linda Jones Roccos

Votive reliefs are rarely considered in works on Greek sculpture, and admittedly, they are for the most part not of great artistic quality. It is right, however, that they be considered along with major sculptural commissions. The votive reliefs present the relationship between ordinary individuals and their deities in a visually forthright manner and in a form and style typical of their era. The Hellenistic votive reliefs dedicated to Apollo from Mysia in northern Asia Minor, especially around Cyzicus, are good examples of the variety and individuality that can be obtained from a purposefully limited repertoire of motifs: divinity and altar, worshipper and animal. Scenes on these extremely classicizing reliefs depict a distinctive type of Apollo, standing frontally, holding kithara and phiale, and wearing a long chiton and back-mantle. The repetitive *and* memorable Apollo Kitharoidos image in the votive reliefs from the Cyzicus area seems to recall a highly recognizable figure. It was probably not meant to be a faithful copy of a particular statue, however, but an archetypal image of the god.

Cyzicus was one of the earliest colonies founded by Miletus in the first half of the seventh century B.C.[1] Strategically situated on the southeast part of the peninsula of Arctonnesus along the southern shore of the Propontis, or Sea of Marmora, it became an extremely wealthy and important trading city in the Hellenistic and Roman periods (Fig. 1).[2] The monumental ruins of the Temple of Hadrian evoke its past grandeur even today.

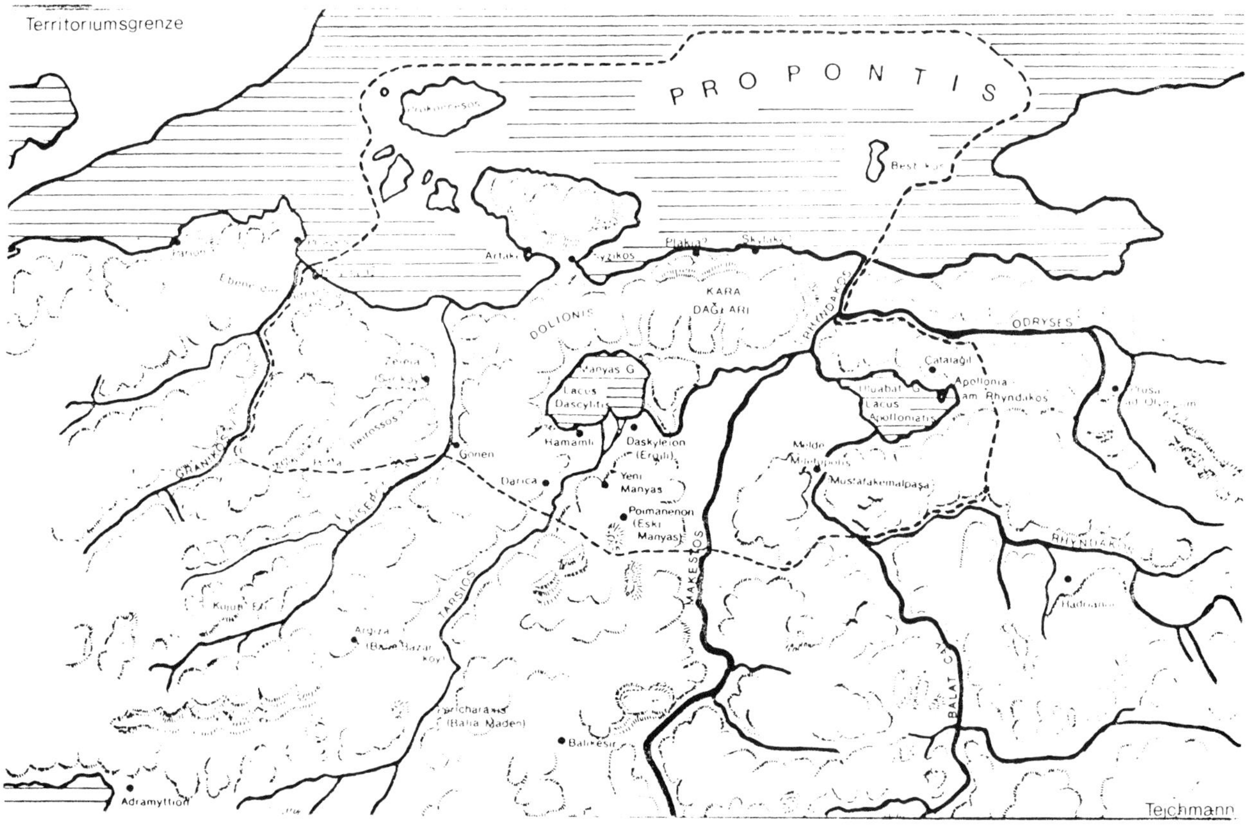

Fig. 1. Map of Mysia. After Studien zum antiken Kleinasien. F. K. Dörner zum 80 Geburtstag gewidmet *(1991) 150, fig. 1.*

According to Strabo (12.8.11),[3]

> "The city rivals the foremost cities of Asia in size and beauty and in its excellent system of government for peace and war. Its adornment appears to be of a type similar to that of Rhodes, Massalia, and ancient Carthage."

Cyzicus was at its height in the Hellenistic period, remaining allied with Pergamon throughout. Cyzicus controlled the area north of Pergamon and east of the Troad, from the Granicus River in the west to the Rhyndacus River in the east, from the island of Proconnesus with its marble quarries north of Cyzicus, to the inland area of Eski Manyas in the south. This southern region is the findspot of scores of votive reliefs and inscriptions, mostly built into Byzantine and modern walls, and the area has been proposed as the site of the ancient city of Poimanenon known from coins and from the *Tabula Peutingeriana*.[4]

Nearly all of what we know about legendary Cyzicus comes from the *Argonautica* of Apollonius Rhodius (1.956–1153), who got his information from other third-century sources, particularly Neanthes of Cyzicus. According to legend, a Pelasgian king named Cyzicus fled to this peninsula (once an island) from Thessaly, having been ousted from there by the Aetolians.[5] Jason and his men landed at the western port of Artaki (now Erdek) and sacrificed to Apollo Ecbasius. The Argonauts then sailed around the peninsula and became engaged in battle with the Cyzicenes at the opposite port near the mainland city of Panormus (now Panderma or Bandirma), where King Cyzicus was killed. Herakles participated in this adventure and was left at Cyzicus to battle some island Giants. A third-century votive relief from Cyzicus may depict this scene with Herakles, which is a thinly veiled reflection of real third-century battles with the Gauls.[6]

Inscriptions and ancient sources frequently connect Cyzicus with Pergamon. A Cyzicene maiden named Apollonis married Attalus I of Pergamon, and became Queen of Pergamon.[7] Two of her four sons, Eumenes II and Attalus II, built a temple in her honor at Cyzicus, probably before 159 B.C. Relief images in that temple, known from the Palatine Anthology, represented mythological examples of filial devotion such as Cleobis and Biton.[8] By the second century B.C., Antiochus IV was on friendly terms with Cyzicus and gave numerous presents to its Prytaneion. The Cyzicenes fended off Mithridates in 74 B.C., earning Rome's gratitude with free city status.

Excavations and explorations in the area have occurred in three stages. First, in the early years of this century Wiegand and Hasluck investigated the area, and Hasluck published many of the inscriptions first in *JHS*, then in an informative book on Cyzicus, still useful for its legendary, historical, and epigraphical sources.[9] In the 1950's Akurgal explored the area northeast of Eski Manyas and the village of Ergili, which he proposed for ancient Dascyleum, site of a Persian palace.[10] At present German archaeologists from the Westfalian University in Münster are re-exploring the entire area including Cyzicus itself, and Turkish archaeologists are re-examining Akurgal's work at Dascyleum.[11] Cyzicus was continuously occupied throughout antiquity, until an earthquake under Justinian and a final one in A.D. 1063 left the once great city abandoned. Few books on Asia Minor give Cyzicus more than a passing mention, and the Propontis coastal areas of Asia Minor remain largely forgotten.

Most of the votive reliefs with Apollo Kitharoidos from Asia Minor have turned up in the villages around Cyzicus and Eski Manyas. None have been excavated. Several locations other than the former have been suggested for an Apolline cult center: Zeleia, slightly north of Eski Manyas, and the hot springs at Gönen, site of later baths of Artemis.[12] None have so far yielded any material evidence.

Louis Robert collected the votive reliefs from the Cyzicus area and published additional reliefs in the Ankara Museum storerooms in 1955.[13] Robert, like Hasluck, was most interested in the stelai for their inscriptions, not for their sculptural decoration. Deubner listed many in his 1934 work on the Hellenistic Apollo types.[14] Palagia classified the Apollo votive reliefs by groupings for the *LIMC* in 1984: Apollo alone, Apollo with worshippers, or Apollo with other gods.[15] I have included many of these reliefs in my study of figures who wear the shoulder-pinned back-mantle in Greek and Roman sculpture.[16] Most recently Flashar included the votive reliefs with Apollo in his book on Apollo Kitharodos, in a list of the Hellenistic sculptures depicting the "long-robed standing kitharodes."[17] The Hellenistic votive reliefs from Mysia show essentially the same image of Apollo, the frontal standing kitharode type with phiale.

From this repetitive image of static frontal pose with kithara and phiale, it may first appear that the Apollo on these votive reliefs *reflects* a statue, but, as noted earlier, there is no intent to copy a specific statue. Slight differences of pose, for instance a left or right supporting leg, or a hand raised slightly higher or lower, do not suggest several different images. Most mainland Greek kitharodes stand on the left leg, the natural position to support the heavy kithara, consistently held in the left hand.[18] A change in weight leg on many reliefs also suggests that the sculptors were referring only to a general type of Apollo, a remembered image, or possibly a drawing. The Apollo Kitharoidos on these votive reliefs is a *generic* image of the god. There are many of these relief images, at least twenty-five with essentially the same kithara and phiale-holding Apollo. They all date from the Late Hellenistic period, appearing suddenly and apparently without precedent. Although the reliefs show the same frontal image of Apollo wearing a high-belted and long-sleeved chiton with back-mantle, the inscriptions with several different epithets indicate that this same image of Apollo served for a variety of local cults, none of which are attested elsewhere. It seems unlikely that so many obscure cults all had the same statue of Apollo. It seems more likely that these local cults all refer back to an archetypal image of the god from elsewhere.

The largest group of eight relief images and two known only from inscriptions are dedicated to Apollo Crateanus.[19] Most of the dedications to Apollo Crateanus are said to have come from the area south of Lake Manyas, known as Eski Manyas. Despite many explorations in the area for over a century, no cult site has yet turned up. The cult place may have been a sacred grove with little architecture, since a tree is prominent in many of these relief scenes. Dedications to Apollo Crateanus include an altar, usually a sacrificial lamb with a boy leading it, one or more worshippers, and often a tree. **Louvre 2864 (Appendix 5)** dedicated by Menander is particularly representative of the series, displaying all salient features of the Apollo Crateanus dedications (Fig. 2). Apollo stands frontally at right, holding the kithara in his left arm and a phiale in his outstretched right hand over the altar. The family of worshippers arrives from the left, here a woman and a man, along with a boy leading the sacrificial lamb. A large tree with spreading branches fills the background space.

A tree behind the altar is a distinguishing feature in several of the Apollo Crateanus dedications, as well as in four additional stelai in Ankara without provenience and without complete inscriptions. The tree is, of course, not common to Apollo alone, but does occur in other votive reliefs from the area. A stele from near Panormus in the vicinity of Cyzicus, now in Istanbul, has a frontal image of Zeus with scepter and phiale at right, a worshipper at left, an altar in center, and a tree in the background.[20] In addition to **Louvre 2854 (5)** from Eski Manyas, **Istanbul 4258 (3)**, also from Eski Manyas and dedicated by Andromachus, includes the tree behind the altar as well as two worshippers, again a male and a female, and the boy with a lamb (Fig. 3). A relief in **Vienna (8)**, probably from Eski Manyas, has the same features of tree, altar, and boy with two lambs, perhaps

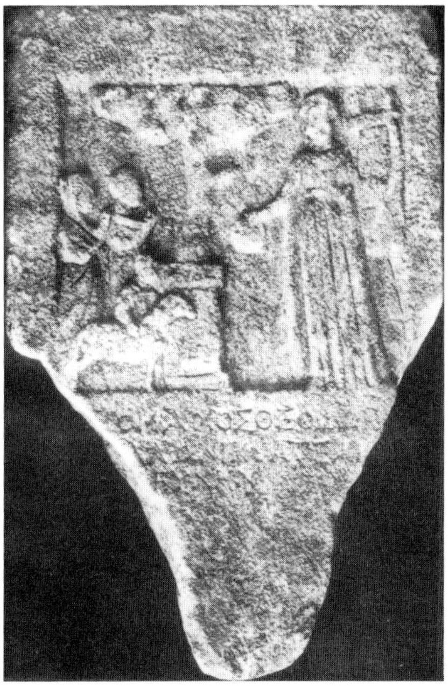

Fig. 3. Istanbul, AM 4258. From Eski Manyas? To Apollo Crateanus. (Appendix no. 3). After Robert pl. 25.

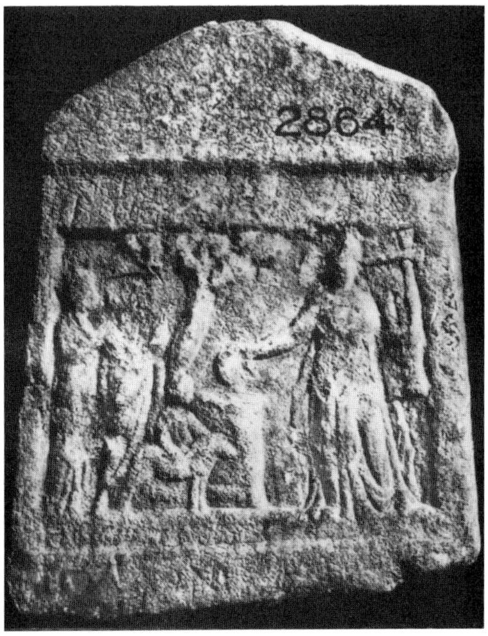

Fig. 2. Paris, Louvre 2864. From Eski Manyas. To Apollo Crateanus. (Appendix no. 5). Museum photograph.

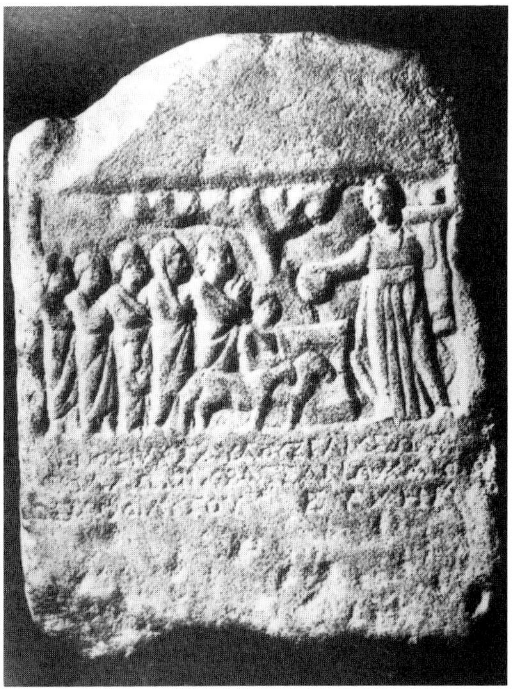

Fig. 4. Vienna, Kunsthist. Mus. From Eski Manyas. To Apollo Crateanus. (Appendix no. 8). After Robert pl. 15.2.

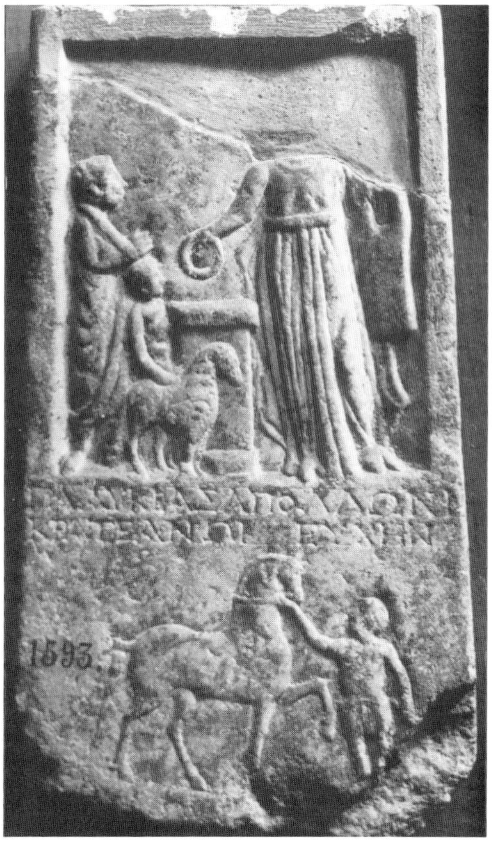

Fig. 5. Istanbul, AM 1593. From Eski Manyas. To Apollo Crateanus. (Appendix no. 2). After Flashar fig. 46.

Two stelai with dedications to Apollo Bathylimenites (of the deep harbor) published by Robert (**11–12**) come from the Cyzicus area and suggest a local cult, although they have the same image of Apollo Kitharoidos as the Apollo Crateanus dedications. **Istanbul 4737 (12)** dedicated by Diocles has the most minimal features similar to some of the Crateanus dedications: Apollo at right, one worshipper at left, and an altar in the center.

Istanbul 4407 (11), dedicated to Apollo Bathylimenites, Zeus Megistos, and Artemis, no doubt by Romans inscribing their names in Greek (Quintus Fabius, son of Lucius and Quintus Fabius Eutychus), has a relief scene as unusual as the inscription (Fig. 6). Apollo Kitharoidos stands to the right of a nude archaistic kouros type of Apollo, with an omphalos between them. The two Apollos are flanked by Artemis at left and Zeus at right. All four figures stand frontally and hold phialai in their lowered right hands. The separate relief zone below the inscription depicts the worshipping scene, a large group of five from the left, a boy with bull from the right.[21] This unusual stele with its distinctive names indicates how recognizable the image of Apollo Kitharoidos was to the Romans as well as to the Greeks in the Cyzicus area.

Artemis is included with Apollo Kitharoidos in some reliefs, which have dedications to Artemis or to Zeus, but Apollo remains the same frontal figure with kithara and phiale.[22] On a fragmentary relief from the **Cyzicus area (14)**, Apollo Kitharoidoș is flanked by Artemis

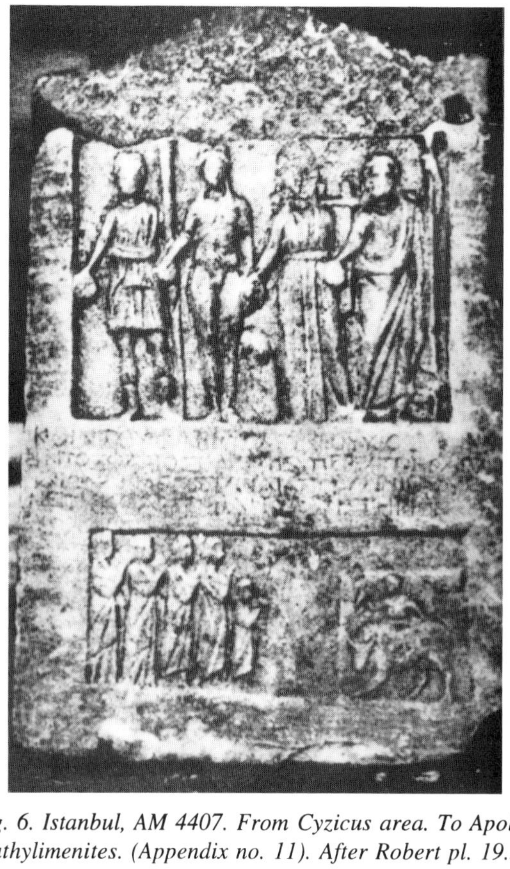

Fig. 6. Istanbul, AM 4407. From Cyzicus area. To Apollo Bathylimenites. (Appendix no. 11). After Robert pl. 19.3.

for the large group of five worshippers (Fig. 4). Robert published several fragmentary stelai in Ankara, which may have come from the Eski Manyas area. All have the same frontal standing image of Apollo Kitharoidos with phiale, worshippers, and altar. Four depict a tree in the background, **Ankara 19?** and **Ankara 29**, **Ankara 199**, and an unnumbered stele in **Ankara (23)**. Like the stele in Vienna, the latter stele (**23**) has five worshippers. Since few other reliefs with Apollo Kitharoidos have the tree in the background – only two from Bithynia, **Athens NM 1485 (17)** and **Bursa Museum (18)** – these fragmentary reliefs in Ankara may also have been dedicated to Apollo Crateanus.

Istanbul 1593 (2), dedicated by Glaucias, is an abbreviated version of the scene, without the tree and with only four features: Apollo at right, a male worshipper at left, and a boy leading a lamb to the altar (Fig. 5). There could have been a tree painted in the background area. **Louvre 2865 (6)** dedicated by Menodotus to Apollo Crateanus shows an even more abbreviated version with Apollo at right, a male worshipper at left, and only a lamb at the altar. Other dedications to Apollo Crateanus from the Cyzicus area portray Apollo in this minimal setting, such as yet another stele in the **Louvre MND 742 (7)** from Panormus and dedicated by Apollodorus Asclepidou, which has one worshipper, unusually a bull before an altar, and Apollo at right.

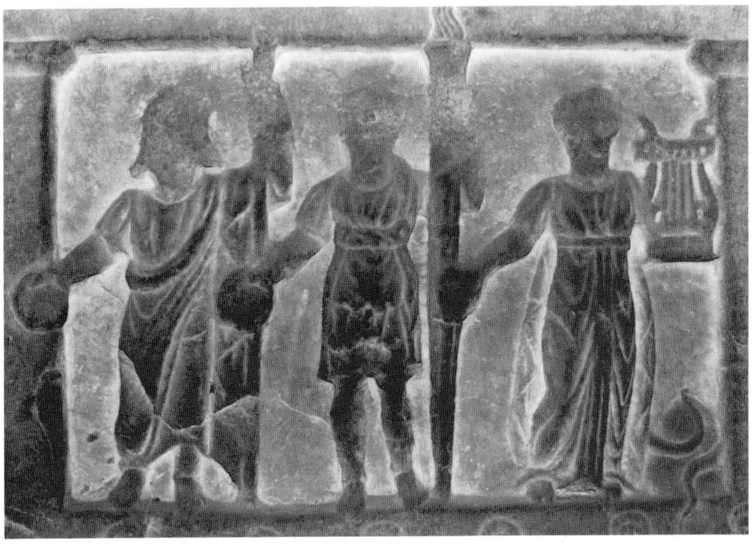

Fig. 7. London, BM 817. From Panormus. (Appendix no. 16).
After LIMC *II (1984) s.v. Apollon, no. 795, pl. 254.*

and Zeus, in frontal poses similar to the Istanbul relief. On **Istanbul 264 (15)**, dedicated by Dionysius, only Artemis stands with Apollo. A votive relief in **Baljik (9)** depicts the frontal standing Apollo Kitharoidos with another deity, perhaps Zeus, on the right, and a worshipper before an altar at left. Artemis is flanked by Zeus and Apollo Kitharoidos on **London 817 (16)** from Panormus, dedicated to Zeus Hypsistus (Fig. 7). The three divinities here all stand frontally and hold phialai, like those on the relief from the Cyzicus area. Zeus and Artemis, like the Apollos, are very similar figures on **Istanbul 4407 (11)** and **London 817 (16)**.

As we noted earlier, two stelai from Bithynia depict the same frontal standing Apollo Kitharoidos, together with elements similar to the Mysian stelai, particularly a tree in the background. **Athens NM 1485 (17)** from Nicaea or Apamea, dedicated by a guild of men and women to Apollo and Cybele, is similar to the Crateanus reliefs, with worshipper from the left, a boy bringing a ram to an altar, and a tree in the background (Fig. 8).[23] This stele, like **London 817 (16)**, has a banqueting scene in the zone below.[24] In the **Bursa Museum (18)** is a stele dedicated by Demetrius Dionysiou to Apollo Libotenus, with the frontal standing Apollo Kitharoidos at right, three worshippers from the left, a boy with sheep before an altar, and a tree in the background, much like the Apollo Crateanus votive reliefs (Fig. 9).

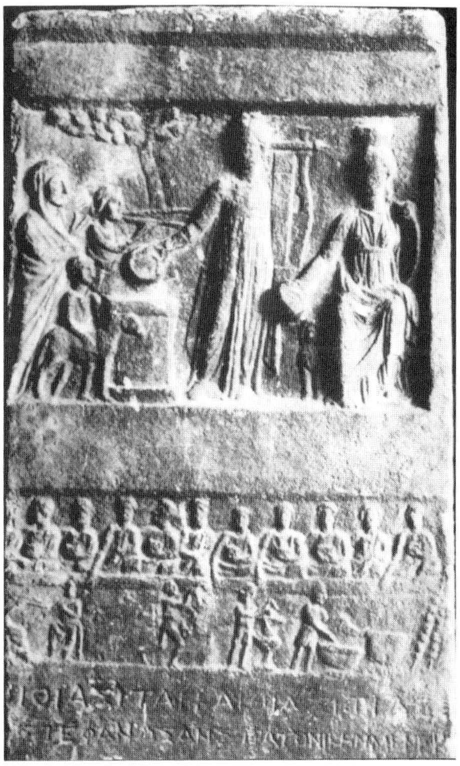

Fig. 8. Athens NM 1485. From Nicaea. (Appendix no. 17).
After LIMC *II (1984) s.v. Apollon, no. 964, pl. 267.*

According to Robert, the earliest of these votive reliefs are mid second century B.C. They are all dedicated by Greeks, except for the unusual stele **Istanbul 4407 (11)**. The dedicants were probably local citizens since no ethnic is given. The names are common ones, usually male, and similar to Greek names elsewhere: Apollodorus, Aristomachus, Glaucias, Menander, Menophanes, etc.[25] By the mid second century B.C., Rome controlled most of Asia Minor, and many of the centuries-old Anatolian conflicts had abated.[26] Cyzicene sculptors would then have been freer to move around and work in Bithynia, or Bithynian sculptors to work in Cyzicus. Cyzicus in the Hellenistic age kept to traditional Greek cult practices, and from the appearance of its sculpture, it kept its traditional artistic views as well.

With zigzag mantle folds and a stiffly frontal stance, Apollo appears to be an archaizing image in many of

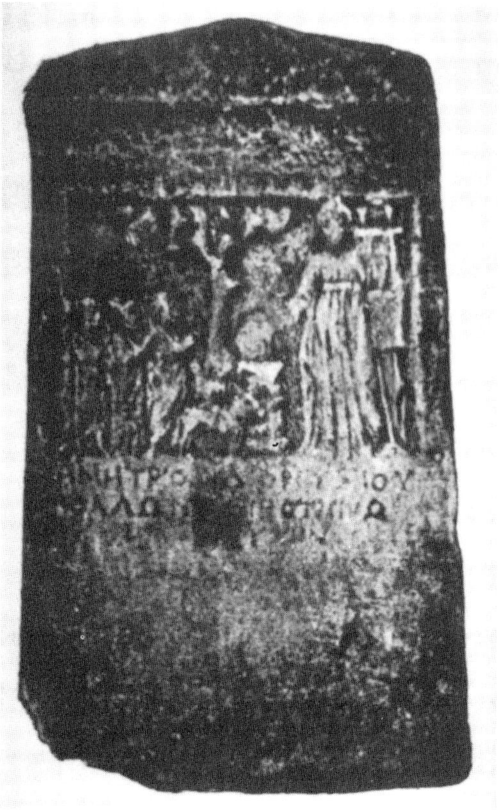

Fig. 9. Bursa Museum. From Bursa. To Apollo Libotenus. (Appendix no. 18). After Mendel, BCH *33, 1909, 277, fig. 15.*

the relief scenes, particularly **Istanbul 1210 (10)** and **Louvre MND 742 (7)**. This type of Apollo Kitharoidos was, however, unknown before the fourth century B.C., so that its archaizing is an invented element to convey antiquity. On many of the reliefs, Apollo's back-mantle is shown in a distinctive manner. The hanging edge on both sides swings out nearly to a sharp corner, clearly visible on **Istanbul 1593 (2)**, **Louvre 2864 (5)**, and the stele in **Vienna (8)** (Figs. 2; 4–5).

The worshippers evoke the fourth-century Athenian votive reliefs with rows of standing worshippers, and in this respect the Hellenistic scenes with Apollo Kitharoidos are strongly classicizing. In the fourth-century votive reliefs, however, divinity and worshipper are connected through a casual confrontation of three-quarter views; human and divine alike stand relaxed in the same visual space and differ only in size.[27] Furthermore, the stark contrast of profile worshippers and frontal deity is strikingly unclassical. Late Hellenistic votive reliefs more often emphasize the difference between divinity and worshipper, with the necessary altar as a clear separator. The god appears now more remote, distancing himself from humanity by clear distinctions of pose, scale, and style.

The landscape setting suggested from the tree in **Louvre 2864 (5)** and **Istanbul 4258 (3)** is a telling feature of these votive reliefs, which have no architectural elements other than the ubiquitous altar, no walls, no columns or pillars (Figs. 2–3). Trees in these Hellenistic votive reliefs are wide and leafy, spreading over the worshippers like an umbrella, and differ markedly from the stumps or branchless background trees of the Classical votive reliefs.[28] No evidence of a temple or physical remains of a sanctuary to Apollo has been found in the area from Cyzicus to the south around Eski Manyas, and the inclusion of a tree rather than any architectural elements suggests that Apollo's cult places were sacred groves. Birge points out that Apollo had the most sacred groves of any Greek divinity, many attested in Asia Minor, at Didyma, Colophon, Clarus, Troy and on Mt. Ida.[29] Without a temple or cult statue, the image of Apollo presented on the reliefs must have been adapted from an image elsewhere. Apollo Kitharoidos on the votive reliefs from Mysia appears not as a statue in a temple, but as the god himself.

The same image of Apollo Kitharoidos in chiton and back-mantle appears on Hellenistic coins from Asia Minor, from Colophon, Harpasa, and Lampsacus.[30] On Hellenistic coins of Antiochus IV Epiphanes of ca. 166 B.C., Apollo again appears as the same image as in the votive reliefs, although standing in profile (Fig. 10).[31] The image of Apollo Kitharoidos in chiton and back-mantle remains strong into the Imperial period, for the god stands within his temple on a series of Hadrianic and Antonine cistophoroi.[32]

It may be that it is Apollo as Founder, Archegetes or Patroos, who is shown in this way: with long garment, back-mantle, and kithara. The Apollo Patroos of Euphranor from the Agora in Athens wears the back-mantle with peplos and carries the kithara.[33] Apollo Patroos is, however, a slightly swaying, almost moving figure. A late fourth-century statue of Apollo at Delphi wears a chiton with back-mantle and moreover is a rather stiffly posed frontal figure, very like the image of Apollo on the votive

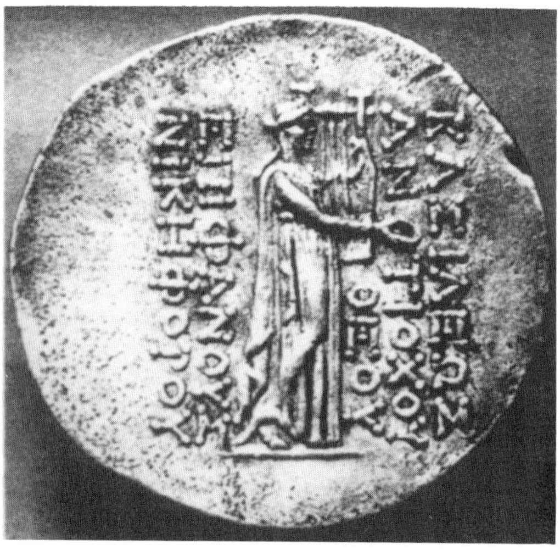

Fig. 10. Coin of Antiochus IV Epiphanes. After LIMC *II (1984) s.v. Apollon, no. 411, pl. 215.*

reliefs.[34] This statue may be from the pediment of the fourth-century temple or even from the cella, and while it specifically may not be the source of the Apollo image in the votive reliefs, something very much like it must have been. Delphi was important to Cyzicus; a decree concerning games at Cyzicus was set up at Delphi and on Delos in the early second century B.C.[35] A similar statue of Apollo Kitharoidos in chiton and back-mantle was found on Delos, along with Artemis, Leto, and two Muses.[36] We cannot rule out a statue of Apollo Kitharoidos at Cyzicus or even Poimanenon (Eski Manyas), but only future excavations may lend support to such possibilities. What is important here in Mysia is that Apollo wearing a chiton, a traditional Ionian garment, was the chosen image.

It is not a particular statue of Apollo, however, which appears on the Mysian votive reliefs, but a remembered image of Apollo from various sources such as the statues in Delphi and on Delos.[37] A type similar to these Apollos may be behind all the later images of Apollo Kitharoidos known from the votive reliefs and the coins. It represents an archetypal image of Apollo to the Hellenistic cities of Asia Minor, perhaps the founding father image for so many local cults, which adopted the same figure: Apollo Crateanus (**1–8**), Apollo Bathylimenites (**11–12**), Apollo Tadocomites (**13**), and Apollo Libotenus (**18**).

The mid second century B.C. is right for a renewal of a Late Classical image of Apollo, and the extraordinary surge in the production of so many votive reliefs with that figure suggests that a widely known image is purposely being recalled. In a similar manner, Antiochus IV isssued coins with a seated Zeus imitative of the Olympian Zeus.[38] The interest in foundation myths observed on the Telephus frieze at Pergamon may suggest that a similar interest in foundation myths at Cyzicus led to the reemergence of Apollo at the same time, perhaps to support their Milesian connections with the Didymaean Apollo.

A combination of classicizing worshippers in strict profile view and an archaizing-classicizing divinity in full frontal view yields a scene that may seem awkward to our modern eyes, but it was a scene that the Cyzicene dedicator would find comforting, even necessary. The scene retained the traditional elements of figure placement in a classicizing format, but added Hellenistic conceptions of space and landscape. One can see in the juxtapositions of figure style and pose almost a precursor to Roman aesthetic concerns. During this time of Roman domination after 133 B.C., the value of keeping the Greek past alive may have been all important, more important than dedicating something contemporary or innovative. Zanker says very much the same thing about the grave reliefs from Smyrna, "But the more beautiful these cities became, the more their civic life tended to harden into ritual. . . . the Greek cities tried to preserve their identity by looking back to past glory."[39] Cyzicenes may have visited Athens or Delphi and observed votive reliefs with similar elements of worshippers, boy with animal, altar, and divinity. The simplistic statement of the locally produced votive reliefs, both in iconography and in style, leaves us with a clear message. They depict the memory of a famous and powerful image of Apollo Kitharoidos, surely a generic Apollo known from many sources. The image is one that stands for the god himself in these dedications, aloof and remote from the mass of all too human worshippers.

Acknowledgements

I would like to thank Olga Palagia and William Coulson for the opportunity to present this paper at the conference. The comments made by Carol Lawton and Olga Palagia, who kindly read a draft of this work, are greatly appreciated.

Abbreviations

Deubner	O. Deubner, *Hellenistische Apollogestalten* (1934)
Flashar	M. Flashar, *Apollon Kitharodos* (1992)
Hasluck	F.W. Hasluck, *Cyzicus* (1910)
Robert	L. Robert, *Hellenica* X, 1955, 134–153

Notes

1. For Cyzicus see Hasluck; R. Stillwell (ed.), *The Princeton Encyclopedia of Classical Sites* (1976) 473–474, s.v. Kyzikos (E. Akurgal); M.R. Alföldi, in *Studien zum antiken Kleinasien. F.K. Dörner zum 80 Geburtstag gewidmet* (1991) 131–138. For Mysia, B. Umar, *Mysia* (1984); for Bithynia, B. Umar, *Bithynia* (1988).
2. Map from J. Teichmann in *Studien zum antiken Kleinasien* (supra n. 1) 139–150, fig. 1. For earlier plans, see R. de Rustafjaell, *JHS* 22, 1902, 174–189, pl. 11; F.W. Hasluck & A.E. Henderson, *JHS* 24, 1904, 135–143, pl. 6.
3. Translation from M. Rostovtzeff, *The Social and Economic History of the Hellenistic World* (1941) 588.
4. W. Hamilton in 1837 was the first to identify Eski Manyas as Poimanenon from a Latin inscription built into a water tower. Hasluck 115. F.-M. Kauffmann and J. Stauber, in *Studien zum antiken Kleinasien* II (1992) 43–86.
5. The Parian Chronicle gives the supposed date of the foundation of Cyzicus as 34 years after Ilium. N. Ehrhardt, in *Studien zum antiken Kleinasien* III. *Asia Minor Studien* 16 (1995) 23–46. For King Cyzicus, who appears on coins of Cyzicus, see *LIMC* VI (1992) s.v. Kyzikos I (R. Vollkommer). The personification of the city also appears on coins, see *LIMC* VI, s.v. Kyzikos II (R.Volkommer). See also *ML* II.1 (1890–1894) s.v. Kyzikos (W. Drexler, H. W. Stoll); *RE* XII.1 (1924) s.v. Kyzikos (W. Ruge).
6. Istanbul, AM: *LIMC* V (1990) s.v. Herakles, no. 2813, pl. 110 (J. Boardman et al.); B.S. Ridgway, *Hellenistic Sculpture* I (1990) 357; R.R.R. Smith, *Hellenistic Sculpture* (1991) fig. 211.
7. E.V. Hansen, *The Attalids of Pergamon* (1971).

8. H.van Looy and K. Demoen, *EpigAnat* 8, 1986, 133–144; R. Stupperich, in *Mysische Studien. Asia Minor Studien* 1 (1990) 33–82.
9. T. Wiegand, *AM* 29, 1904, 254–330. F.W. Hasluck, *JHS* 22–27, 1902–1907. For sculptures other than the votive reliefs, see Hasluck, *BSA* 8, 1901, 190–196.
10. E. Akurgal, *Anatolia* 1, 1956, 15–24. See also M. Mellink, *AJA* 59, 1955, 235–236; 60, 1956, 383; 62, 1958, 101; 63, 1958, 85; 64, 1968, 662.
11. *Mysien Studien. Asia Minor Studien* 1 (1990); *Studien zum antiken Kleinasien* II, *Asia Minor Studien* 8 (1992); and *Studien zum antiken Kleinasien* III, *Asia Minor Studien* 16 (1995). Inscriptions from Asia Minor are extensively published recently in the series *IK (Inschriften griechischer Städte aus Kleinasien)*, although those from Cyzicus have not yet appeared. See now the Turkish reports in *KST* 14:2, 1993, 223–245 for 1991 work; 25:2 for 1992 work; M. Mellink, *AJA* 94, 1990, 149–150; 95, 1991, 151–152; 96, 1992, 147–148; 97, 1993, 132; M.-H. Gates, *AJA* 98, 1993, 276; 99, 1995, 246.
12. For Zeleia and Gönen, see the map Fig. 1, and Hasluck 101–104.
13. Robert 134–153. E. Michon had collected several of the votive reliefs, including inscriptions without relief scenes in *REG* 19, 1906, 305–307 (a–l). Robert pl. 24, shows the three main types of long-robed kitharode Apollo on the votive reliefs: pl. 24,1 is a kithara-playing figure and pl. 24,3 is the plektron-holding figure with free right leg swung to the side, both appearing rarely in Asia Minor; pls. 24,2 and 24,4 show the phiale-holding type common to Asia Minor and discussed here.
14. Deubner. Robert does not seem to have known of this work.
15. *LIMC* II (1984) s.v. Apollon, nos. 200–202; 298–299 (O. Palagia).
16. L.J. Roccos, *The Shoulder-pinned Back-mantle in Greek and Roman Sculpture* (diss. New York 1986).
17. We consider here Flashar nos. 1–23, pp. 79–80.
18. M. Maass and J.M. Snyder, *Stringed Instruments of Ancient Greece* (1989) 53–78. For a good example of the need to support a heavy object, see the statue of Eirene who supports the child Ploutos on her standing left hip and leg: A. Stewart, *Greek Sculpture. An Exploration* (1990) (hereafter Stewart) 173, figs. 485–486; J. Boardman, *Greek Sculpture. The Late Classical Period* (1995) fig. 24.
19. Hasluck 273, nos. 41–50; Robert 134–150; Flashar 80, nos. 8–14. The theory that this Apollo came from Cratea in Bithynia is unfounded, see also *RE* 11 (1922) s.v. Krateia (Ruge); Roscher, *ML* 2.1 (1890) s.v Krateanos (Höfer) and Krateia (Roscher).
20. Istanbul AM: Hasluck 224, fig. 21.
21. F. van Straten, in A. Bulloch et al. (edd.), *Images and Ideologies. Self-definition in the Hellenistic World* (1993) 248–264, esp. 254–255, notes the increasing distancing of men and gods with this separation device.
22. For the Classical votive reliefs with Apollo and Artemis, see G. Güntner, *Göttervereine und Götterversammlungen auf attischen Weihreliefs* (1994) 61–66. For gods with phialai, see E. Simon, *Opfernde Götter* (1953). For the Delian twins (mostly on vases), see also *LIMC* II, s.v. Apollon, nos. 265–268 (Lambrinudakis), and s.v. Artemis, nos. 1060–1103 (Kahil).
23. A similar stele from Nicaea, Athens NM 1486, also shows a frontal standing Apollo, but not the kitharode type: J.N. Svoronos, *Das Athener Nationalmuseum* (1908–37) pl. 112; van Straten (supra n. 21) 254, fig. 13.
24. J.-M. Dentzer, *Le motif du banquet couché dans le proche-orient et le monde grec du VIIe au IVe siècles avant J.-C.* (1982) 626, nos. R508–R509, pl. 118.
25. M.J. Osborne and S.G. Byrne (edd.), *A Lexicon of Greek Personal Names* I. *Aegean, Cyprus, Cyrenaica* (1987) and II. *Attica* (1994).
26. R. Magie, *Roman Rule in Asia Minor* (1950); A.N. Sherwin-White, *Roman Foreign Policy in the East 168 B.C. to A.D. 1* (1983).
27. Typical is a votive relief to Demeter in the Louvre: Stewart 49, fig. 521; or the relief from Brauron with an Artemis similar in type to the statue of Artemis Vatican 2834: G. Neumann, *Probleme des griechischen Weihreliefs* (1979) pls. 40b; 41a; and van Straten (supra n. 21) fig. 1.
28. M. Carroll-Spillecke, *Landscape Depictions in Greek Relief Sculpture* (1985) 41–56; 108. For a possible painted tree in the background of a fourth-century votive relief, see Ṡ. Karouzou, in *Studies in Classical Art and Archaeology. A Tribute to Peter Heinrich von Blanckenhagen* (1979) 111–116.
29. D.E. Birge, *Sacred Groves in the Ancient Greek World* (diss. Berkeley 1982) 23–27. D. Birge, in J. Solomon (ed.), *Apollo. Origins and Influences* (1994) 9–19. Comparable may be the early sacred grove of Apollo Cyparissius on Cos, site of the later Asklepieion. See also F. Graf, in *Les bois sacrés* (1993) 23–29.
30. Colophon: *BMC* 16 *Ionia*, 40, no. 38; 41, no. 42, pls. 8,8 and 8,10; *LIMC* II, s.v. Apollon, no. 409 (Palagia). Harpasa: *BMC* 18 *Caria*, 113, no. 1, pl. 19,5. Lampsacus: *BMC* 14 *Mysia*, 86, no. 68, pl. 20,6; *LIMC* II, s.v. Apollon, no. 144 (Palagia).
31. O. Mørkholm, *Studies in the Coinage of Antiochus IV of Syria* (1963) 30, nos. A54–A55, pl. 10. *LIMC* II, s.v. Apollon, no. 411, pl. 215 (Palagia); Flashar figs. 44–45.
32. L. Weber, *NumChron* 1913, 1–30; W.M. Metcalf, *The Cistophoroi of Hadrian. Numismatic Studies* 15 (1980). Apollo serves also as the image of the city in the alliance coins, see *BMC* 25 *Phrygia*, 256–264, pl. 51.
33. H.A. Thompson, *AEphem* 1953/54 III [1961] 30–44; O. Palagia, *Euphranor* (1980) 13–20, figs. 6–17; *LIMC* II, s.v. Apollon, no. 145, pl. 195 (Palagia); Stewart 191, fig. 512; Boardman (supra n. 18) fig. 30; Flashar 50–60, figs. 37–39.
34. Delphi Museum 1344 and 2380: J. Marcadé, in *BCH* Suppl. 4, 1977, 389–408, figs. 1–4; A.F. Stewart (who identifies the figure as Dionysus) in *Macedonia and Greece in Late Classical and Early Hellenistic Times. Studies in the History of Art* 10, National Gallery of Art, Washington D.C. (1982) 205–227; Stewart 196, fig. 599; *LIMC* II, s.v. Apollon, no. 101 (Palagia, who prefers the head as Dionysus, the torso Apollo); Flashar 60–70, figs. 30–31; 36.
35. Hasluck 300; L. Robert, *BCH* 102, 1978, 460–477.

36. Delos A 4125: Deubner 58, no. 8; J. Marcadé, *Au Musée de Délos* (1969) pl. 29; *LIMC* II, s.v. Apollon, no. 104, pl. 192 (Palagia); Flashar 81, no. 39.
37. B.S. Ridgway, *Roman Copies of Greek Sculpture: The Problem of the Originals* (1984) 37–43, suggests that strict copying from the pan-Hellenic sanctuaries at Delphi and Olympia was prohibited. For a list of Hellenistic statuettes of Apollo Kitharoidos, see Flashar 80–82, nos. 24–26; 39–42; 46–48; 52–56.
38. Antiochus IV coins with Zeus: Mørkholm (supra n. 30) 14–24, pl. 4; Stewart 221.
39. P. Zanker, in *Images and Ideologies* (supra n. 21) 212–230, esp. 212.

APPENDIX

A. Votive Reliefs to Apollo Crateanus from Cyzicus Area

1. Ankara. Mus. 217 frg. From Cyzicus. Altar, lamb, Apollo.
Robert 137, no. 6, pl. 30,4b; Flashar 80, no. 11.
2. Istanbul, AM 1593. From Eski Manyas. Dedicated by Glaucias. One worshipper, boy with lamb, altar, Apollo. Below: man leads horse right. (Fig. 5).
Hasluck 231, fig. 23; 273, no. 43; Mendel III, 62–64, no. 852; Deubner 59, no. 18c; Robert 139 n. 4; *LIMC* II (1984) s.v. Apollon, no. 961 (Palagia); Flashar 80, no. 8, fig. 46.
3. Istanbul, AM 4258. From Eski Manyas? Dedicated by Aristomachus Theodorou. Two worshippers, boy with lamb, altar, tree, Apollo. (Fig. 3).
Hasluck 273, no. 41; Deubner 59, no. 18c; M. Mansel, *AA* 1933, 139, no. 2; Robert 140 n. 1, pl. 25; Flashar 80, no. 14.
4. Istanbul, AM 4259 frg. From Eski Manyas? Dedicated by Metrophanes Apolloniou. One? worshipper, boy with lamb, altar, Apollo (feet only).
Hasluck 273, no. 45; Mansel, *AA* 1933, 138, fig. 22; 139, no. 3; Deubner 59, no. 18c; Robert 139 n. 8.
5. Paris, Louvre 2864. From Eski Manyas. Dedicated by Menodotus. Two worshippers, boy with lamb, altar, tree, Apollo. (Fig. 2).
Hasluck 273, no. 47; Robert 138 n. 3, pl. 26; Flashar 80, no. 10.
6. Paris, Louvre 2865. From Eski Manyas. Dedicated by Menander. One worshipper, lamb, altar, Apollo.
Hasluck 273, no. 48; Robert 138 n. 4, pl. 27,1; Flashar 80, no. 12.
7. Paris, Louvre MND 742. From Panormus. Dedicated by Apollodorus Asclepidou. One worshipper, bull, altar, Apollo.
Hasluck 273, no. 49; Robert 138 n. 5, pl. 42; *LIMC* II, s.v. Apollon, no. 962, pl. 267 (Palagia); Flashar 80, no. 13.
8. Vienna, Kunsthist. Mus. From Eski Manyas. Dedicated by Menophilus Aulouzelmeos. Five worshippers, boy with two lambs, altar, tree, Apollo. (Fig. 4).
Hasluck 273, no. 44; Deubner 59, no. 18c; Robert 138 n. 2, pl. 15,2; Flashar 80, no. 9.

B. Votice Reliefs with Apollo Kitharoidos from Cyzicus Area

9. Balcik Museum. Worshipper, altar, Apollo.
T. Wiegand, *AM* 29, 1904, 307ff., fig. 33; Deubner 59, no. 18b; Flashar 79, no. 2.
10. Istanbul, AM 1210 (ex-Robert College). From Aidinjik. Apollo alone.
Hasluck 229, fig. 22; Mendel III 61–62, no. 851; Deubner 59, no. 17; Robert, 136 n. 1, pl. 24,2; *LIMC* II (1984) s.v. Apollon, no. 414, pl. 216 (Palagia); Flashar 80, no. 17.
11. Istanbul, AM 4407. From Cyzicus area. Dedicated by Quintus Fabius, son of Lucius, and Quintus Fabius Eutychus to Apollo Bathylimenites, Zeus Megistos, and Artemis. Artemis, nude Apollo, omphalos, Apollo Kitharoidos, Zeus. Below: Five worshippers, altar, boy with bull (Fig. 6).
Robert 125–127, pl. 19,3; Flashar 80, no. 4.
12. Istanbul, AM 4737. From Cyzicus area. Dedicated by Diocles to Apollo Bathylimenites. One worshipper, altar, Apollo.
Robert 127–128, pl. 19,2; Flashar 79, no. 3.
13. London, BM 777. From Cyzicus. Dedicated by Asclepiodotus to Apollo Tadocomites. Worshipper, boy with ram, altar, tree, Apollo Kitharoidos from knees down.
Hasluck 273, no. 52; Deubner 60, no. 18d.

C. Votive Reliefs with Apollo Kitharoidos & Artemis from Cyzicus Area

14. Cyzicus area. Artemis, Apollo, Zeus.
Robert 296, pl. 30,2; Flashar 80, no. 5.
15. Istanbul, AM 264. From Cyzicus. Dedicated by Dionysius. Artemis, Apollo.
Mendel III 64–65, no. 853.
16. London, BM 817. From Panormus. Zeus, Artemis, Apollo. Below: Banquet scene. (Fig. 7)
Hasluck 271, no. 13; Deubner 59, no. 17; *LIMC* II, s.v. Apollon, no. 795, pl. 254 (Kokkorou-Alewras); Flashar 80, no. 20.

D. Votive Reliefs with Apollo Kitharoidos from Bithynia

17. Athens NM 1485. From Nicaea, Bithynia. Worshipper, flutist, boy with animal, altar, tree, Apollo, Cybele. Below: Banquet scene (Fig. 8).
    Hasluck 269, no. 38A; Deubner 59, no. 14; *LIMC* II, s.v. Apollon, no. 964, pl. 267 (Palagia); T. Corsten, *IK* 32, 1987, 53ff., no. 35; Flashar 80, no. 19.
18. Bursa, Museum. Dedicated by Demetrius Dionysiou to Apollo Libotenus (Fig. 9).
    G. Mendel, *BCH* 33, 1909, 277, no. 35, fig. 15; Deubner 59, no. 18a; *LIMC* II, s.v. Apollon, no. 963 (Palagia); Flashar 79, no. 1.
19. Istanbul, AM 5499. From Yalova. Dedicated to Apollo. Apollo alone.
    Sahin, *IK* 7, 1987, 39ff., no. II.5, pl. 7; Corsten, *IK* 32, 1987, 123–124, no. 117; Flashar 80, no. 18.

E. Votive Reliefs with Apollo Kitharoidos from Asia Minor

20. Ankara, Mus. 19? frg. Two worshippers, boy with lamb, altar, tree?, Apollo.
    Robert 136, no. 3, pl. 23,6; Flashar 80, no. 22.
21. Ankara, Mus. 29. frg. Worshipper?, tree, Apollo.
    Robert 137, no. 5, pl. 23,1; Flashar 80, no. 23.
22. Ankara, Mus. 199. frg. Dedicated by Asclepias. Two worshippers, boy with lamb, altar, tree, Apollo.
    Robert 134–136, pl. 30,4a; Flashar 80, no. 21.
23. Ankara, Mus. (nn.). frg. Five? worshippers, tree, Apollo.
    Robert 136, no. 4, pl. 23,4b; Flashar 80, no. 7.
24. Berlin, Staatl. Mus. frg. From Pergamon. Apollo alone.
    Winter, *AvP* VII,2 (1908) no. 336; Deubner 59, no. 15; *LIMC* II, s.v. Apollon, no. 415 (Palagia); Flashar 80, no. 16.
25. Izmir, Mus. 379 frg. Apollo.
    Robert 151, no. 7, pl. 24,4; Flashar 80, no. 6.

Dangerous is Beautiful. The Elemental Quality of a Hellenistic Scylla

Elena Walter-Karydi

For Giorgos Despinis

A bronze bust of considerable size from the Black Sea coast of northern Asia Minor (Figs. 1–2), has an unusual theme: the ferocious female is not a Tritoness, as she has been called, but the deadly Scylla.[1] Tritonesses are mild mermaids, counterparts and mates of the Tritons; we may compare one cradling an infant Eros, on a later third century B.C. gold armband from Macedonia (Fig. 3);[2] on the second armband of the pair a bearded Triton, also holding Eros, turns to face her. The hair of the Tritonesses is not wildly tousled, like that of the female Figs. 1–2. They may even have their hair neatly tied up in a head-cloth, like one on a mosaic of the later second century B.C. on Delos, who likewise had a Triton as partner in another panel; Eros, hovering above, suggests a flirtatious mood.[3]

In order to consider the particular character of the female Figs. 1–2, let us look at earlier Scylla images in Greek art. There is a discrepancy between Homer's description of the hideous monster with twelve feet waving in the air and six overlong necks ending in horrible heads with two triple rows of teeth (*Od.* 12. 85–97) and Scylla in art.[4] Morover there are no archaic Scylla images. She first appears in the late second quarter of the fifth century, and then only in the minor arts: 'Melian' reliefs, gems, vase paintings etc.[5] The dog foreparts alone distinguish her from the other so-called mermaids, as she has likewise a human torso combined with a sea snake ending in a fish tail.

The Scylla on a 'Melian' relief of about 470–460 B.C. contemplates neither murder nor loot.[6] The difference

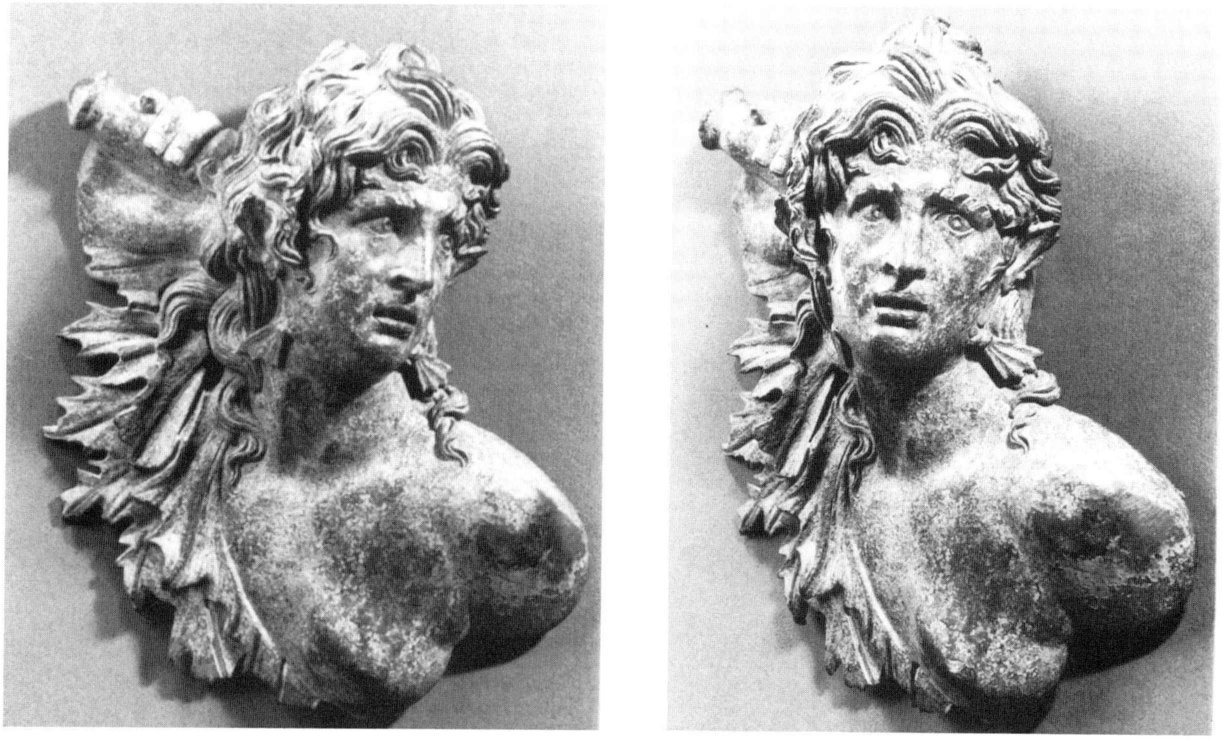

Figs. 1, 2. Scylla. Bronze bust. Cleveland Museum of Art. Photo Museum.

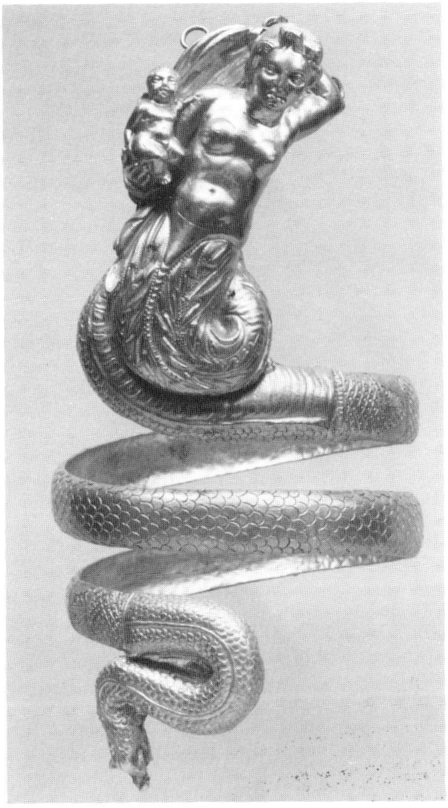

Fig. 3. Tritoness from a pair of gold armbands. New York, Metropolitan Museum of Art. Photo Museum.

to the figure Figs. 1–2 is significant. The fact that she is dressed indicates her nobility; the head is slightly bent, the hair neatly tied up, the face serious; the hand raised to her chin underlines her thoughtful mood. This is only to be found in Early Classical Scylla figures. In the late fifth century Scylla is, as a rule, a wild sea demon; on the coins of Acragas (420–415 B.C.) she appears naked, with windblown hair, one hand raised looking out for quarry.[7] Incidentally, the nudity of Scylla was not invented by South Italian artists; we should be wary of crediting them with every new trait in Scylla images.[8]

Nudity is henceforth a regular feature of Scylla but, strangely enough, ferocity is not. On the contrary, around 400 B.C. a new Scylla image emerges, characteristic of fourth-century art: she is not aggressive and even gives up sometimes her 'splendid isolation' to join other sea creatures, like the Nereids carrying Achilles' weapons. On an Attic krater of the beginning of the fourth century (Fig. 4) Scylla carries Thetis, who, holding the shield for her son, sits on the monster having evidently nothing to fear from it.[9] On an Apulian vase painting of the thirties of the century with the same subject Scylla even turns amiably to the Nereid she is carrying.[10] Incidentally, the skirt of fins marking the join between the human part and the sea snake is a new trait, appearing on the Tritons as well, and will henceforth be canonical.

In several fourth-century mythological scenes Scylla joins other sea creatures simply as spectator of a deed

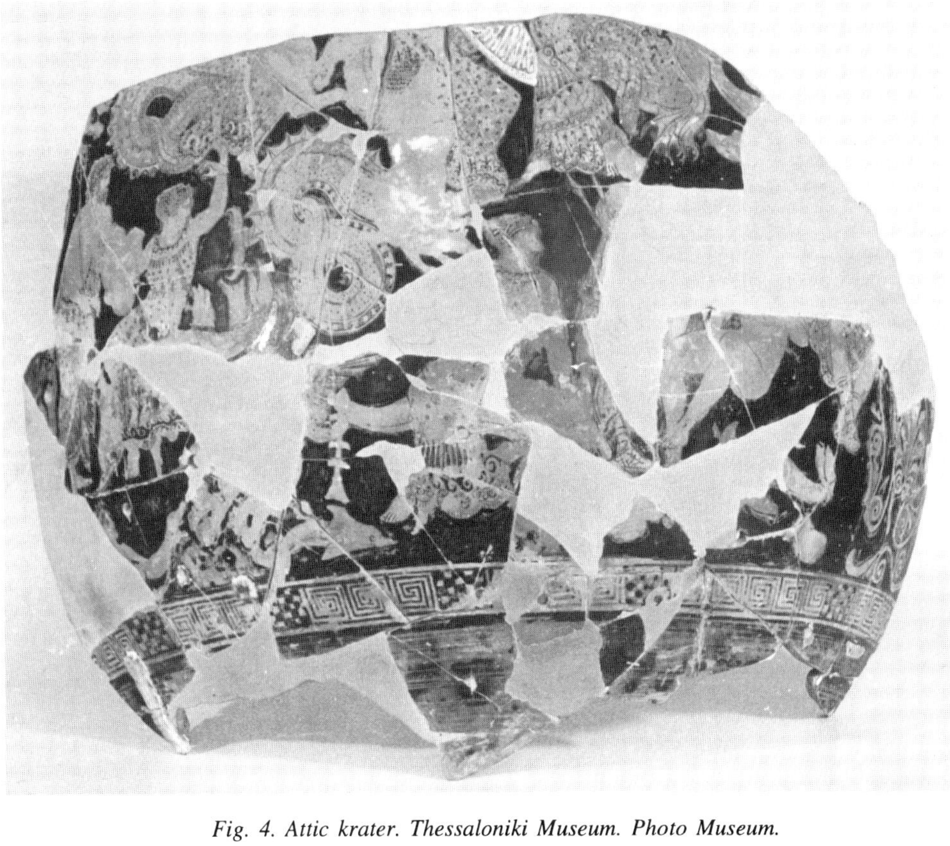

Fig. 4. Attic krater. Thessaloniki Museum. Photo Museum.

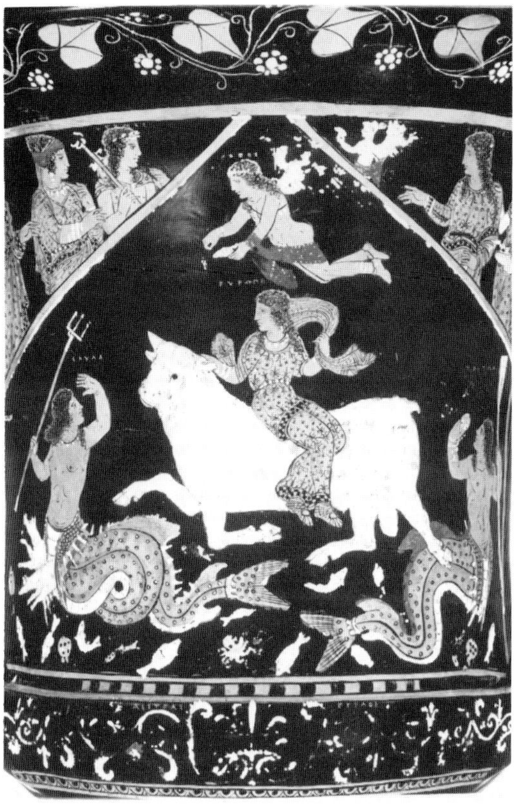

Fig. 5. Paestan calyx krater by Asteas. Malibu, J.P. Getty Museum. Photo Museum.

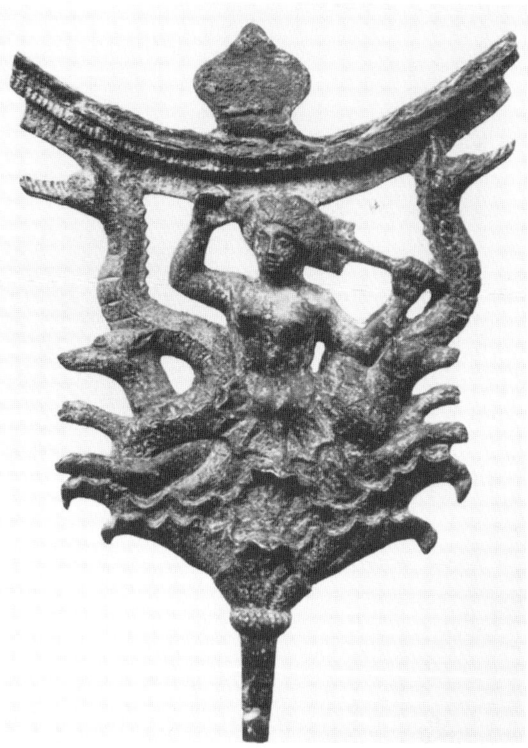

Fig. 6. Scylla. Bronze mirror handle. Paris, Louvre. Photo Museum.

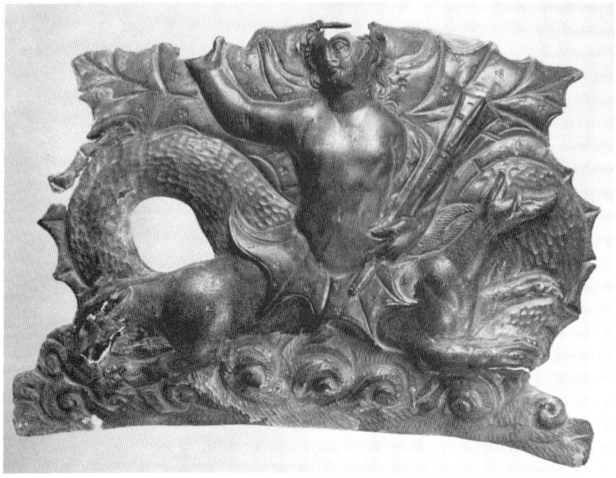

Fig. 7. Scylla. Bronze appliqué. Athens, National Museum. Photo Museum.

she has nothing to do with, for instance the rape of Europa. On a krater by Asteas of about 350–340 B.C. (Fig. 5) Scylla and Triton, as creatures of the waves, greet the godly pair flying over them.[11] The presence of Pothos, god of erotic desire, hovering above, is appropriate to this love scene, while Scylla, in order to appear here, has certainly to forgo her murderous identity.

The same applies to vase paintings where Scylla, together with other sea creatures, looks on Phrixos and Helle riding the ram over the waves,[12] or even watches Perseus vanquishing the ketos and she a sea monster herself![13] This image of an amiable Scylla, standing out only by her quaint looks among other mermaids, found its way even into major painting – as in one by Androcydes of Cyzicus (early fourth century) mentioned in literary sources[14] –, in mosaics,[15] as well as in sculpture, at least of small size, such as a Locrian mirror handle in the Louvre of about 330 B.C. (Fig. 6).[16] The maidenly face is crowned by luxuriant but not windblown hair and the rudder is simply the attribute of a sea creature, like the octopus in the hand of another Scylla on an Apulian rhyton.[17] Both raise a hand in friendly greeting, as does a Scylla peacefully holding a trident on a gilt silver disk from Epidamnus (Dyrrachium), a North Greek piece of the late fourth century.[18] The symmetrical sea snake bodies of the Scylla Fig. 6 do not end in fish tails as usual, but in ketos heads, while those of the Epidamnus figure end in crayfish claws. Obviously, there is no fixed type of Hellenistic Scylla. Thus an amiably greeting one on a bronze vase-appliqué from Dodona of about 330–320 B.C. (Fig. 7), not only has the usual fin skirt but also fin wings.[19] It must be stressed that such fantastic traits, appearing in the later fourth century, are not accidental but meant to illustrate her marine nature. Such elemental traits now appear in other sea demons as well, Triton first of all (who is often multiplied at this time) and are indeed characteristic of Hellenistic art.

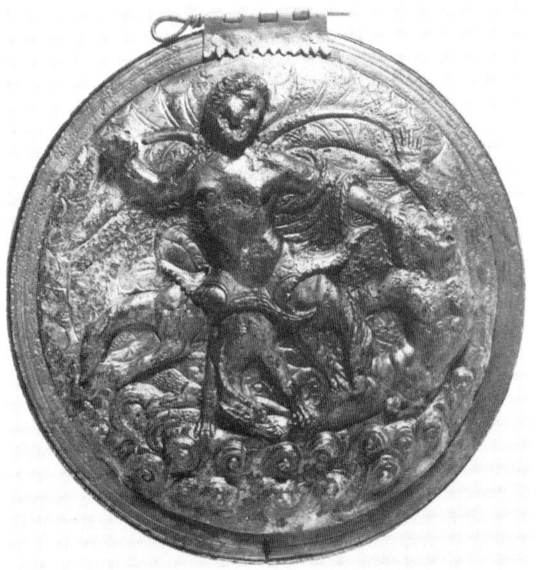

Fig. 8. Scylla. Bronze mirror relief. Berlin, Staatliche Museen. Photo Museum.

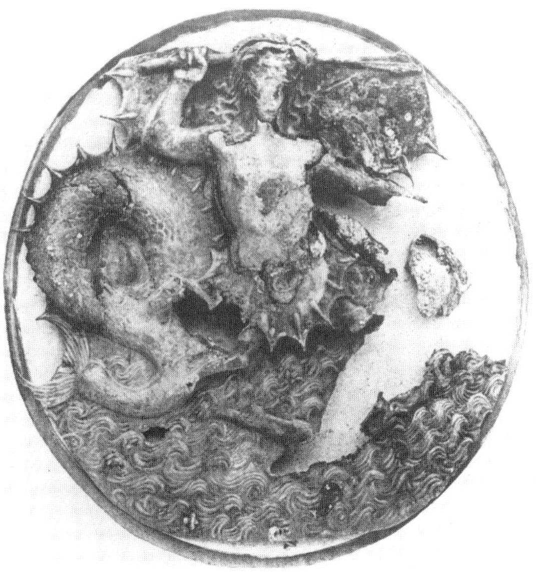

Fig. 9. Scylla. Bronze mirror relief. St. Petersburg, Hermitage. Photo Museum.

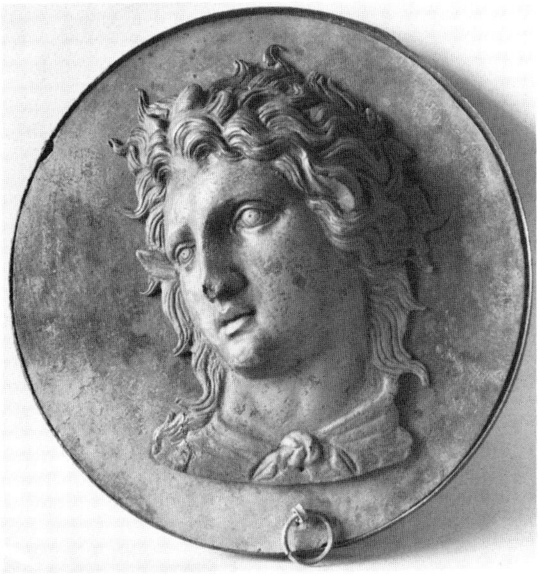

Fig. 10. Head of Pan. Bronze mirror relief. New York, Metropolitan Museum of Art. Photo Museum.

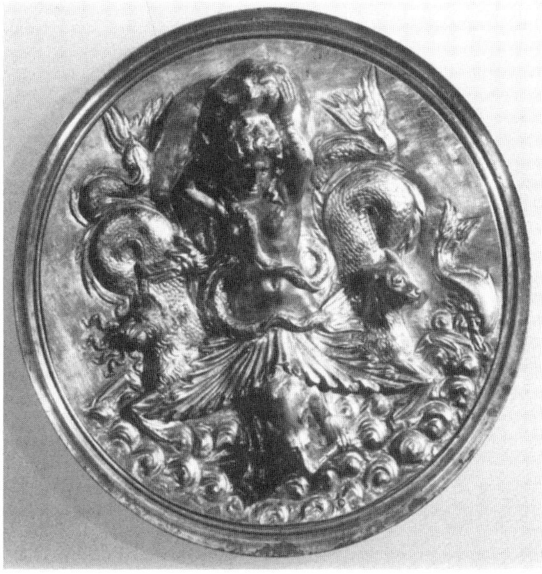

Fig. 11. Scylla. Bronze disc, partly gilt. New York, Metropolitan Museum of Art. Photo Museum.

A new Scylla image is the deadly female with a human victim. The earliest known are two mirror-cover reliefs of about 330–320 B.C. (Figs. 8–9).[20] On Fig. 8 Scylla, hurling a stone, seizes a youth by the hair and her dogs bite him savagely. This raging monster and the amiable mermaid Fig. 7 appear on pieces that are not only contemporary but also belong to the Epirotan School of sculpture.[21] A satyr head appliqué from Dodona,[22] as well as the head of a young Pan on a box mirror of unknown provenance (Fig. 10)[23] may serve as examples of roughly contemporary Epirotan pieces that are stylistically akin to the Scylla reliefs (Figs. 8–9). Incidentally, the Scylla Fig. 8, apart from the traits shared with Fig. 7, wears a fish skin over the left arm, and her dogs have ketos heads; the elemental quality is more emphasized. On the mirror relief Fig. 9, from Taman in South Russia, Scylla looks like the one on Fig. 8 clutching her victim in the same way, but swings a rudder which will henceforth be her usual weapon, occurring too on the Cleveland bust (Figs. 1–2).

The stone that Scylla is hurling on the relief Fig. 8 is a rare motif,[24] as rare as the rock she is flinging with both hands on a South Italian emblem of the early third century B.C. (Fig. 11).[25] The victims here are indeed not human beings but a fish and an octopus that two of the dogs are devouring, while the third dog is aiming at a dolphin. Scylla as a deadly foe of sea creatures is an old notion, occurring in Homer as well as in fourth-century vase paintings,[26] but is less frequently represented than the man-devouring monster. This theme is highlighted by a pebble mosaic, probably of the second half of the fourth century, from a house in Eretria, representing Scylla fighting against Triton.[27] Her weapon is the usual rudder, his a trident; however, he also has a panther skin over the outstretched left arm, not unlike Scylla's fish skin (Fig. 8), and this decidedly Dionysiac attribute is indeed unusual for a sea creature. It is only to be explained by the fourth-century diffusion of Dionysiac motifs which intrude even in scenes having nothing to do with Dionysus. Triton is of course not Scylla's victim like the fish and other sea dwellers (Fig. 11); he appears here as an equal opponent, and it is indeed him who faces right as victors usually do in Greek art. No myth is represented here but, as it were, the mightiest sea creature against the deadly foe who destroys so many of its companions. It is a long way from this fight to the images where the amiable Scylla and Triton side by side greet Zeus and Europa (Fig. 6); thus two distinct aspects of Scylla in the fourth century are reflected in art.

The elemental traits of Scylla Fig. 11 are again slightly different from those we have already seen: she has namely no fin wings, but instead a wolf-headed ketos encircles her upper body and two of her dogs have fins for feet.

The Scylla images with a human victim do *not* represent the Homeric episode but simply Σκύλλα ὀλοόφρονα (= murderous Scylla), as Apollonius Rhodius (third century B.C.) calls her in his *Argonautica* (IV.828). Hera charges Thetis to warn the Argonauts off the mighty rock and the hideous lair of the deadly Scylla, so that she does not swoop with her horrible jaws upon them and destroy the best of them. Incidentally, the image Apollonius evokes recalls the Homeric one and remains equally distant from Scylla's representations in art.

In the second century, or rather the second half of the third, there appear for the first time certain representations of Odysseus' ghastly encounter with Scylla, and then only in the minor arts, such as relief vases. On a relief bowl from Rhodes Scylla snatches a companion of Odysseus from the ship, while her dogs are already devouring others.[28] On a bowl from Thebes a warrior with shield and spear (Odysseus) is standing on the ship, poised to attack Scylla (named), who threatens swinging the rudder.[29] Small-scale images like these certainly do not testify to the existence of corresponding monumental groups; they may be, and indeed mostly are, independent creations.[30] There is greater variety of themes in the minor arts, compared with monumental sculpture – and this applies not only to Classical but also to Hellenistic art. The significant question is, in fact, *when* does a theme become so important for the current mentality that it is given the eminence of monumentality. At what time then did Scylla appear in monumental sculpture?

The earliest known is a colossal group on a funerary monument in Bargylia (Caria), dated by G.B. Waywell about 200–150 B.C.[31] The group consists of Scylla and *one* victim, as on the reliefs Figs. 8–9, as well as in a pedimental group of an Aetolian funerary stele which is roughly contemporary or slightly earlier: Scylla raises the rudder against a victim lying to her right, not to her left as in Figs. 8–9.[32] The composition of this small-size and modest pedimental group cannot of course be compelling for the reconstruction of the colossal, high-quality one from Bargylia. Anyway, these funerary sculptures certainly do not represent a mythological story but the deadly Scylla.[33] Another Scylla as a silver rhyton dedicated on Delos in the late second century B.C. is mentioned in a Delian inscription and expressly designated as the deadly destroyer of men and ships.[34] It seems indeed that, on the whole, Scylla herself became an important theme in Hellenistic art, rather than the stories about her – which are, by the way, strikingly few.[35] The Bargylia group need not be the earliest monumental Scylla in Greek sculpture. The Scylla theme may have been taken up in monumental sculpture in the later fourth century but this is not the place to go into that.

The Cleveland bust Figs. 1–2 must be about contemporary with the Bargylia group or slightly earlier; it must have been created at the turn to the second century, in the years before the so-called pathos in sculpture explodes, as in the figures of the great frieze of the Pergamon Altar.

Since the theme of this conference concerns 'Regional Schools,' it is time to consider the question of the affiliation of the Cleveland bust. Its provenance from the

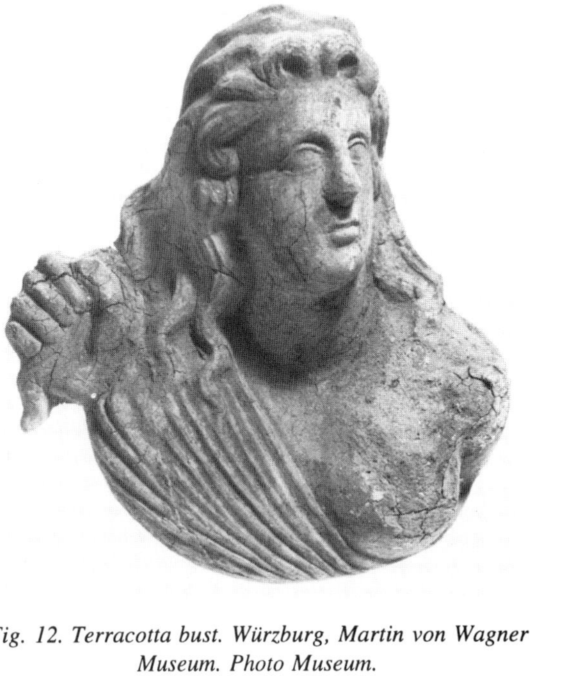

Fig. 12. Terracotta bust. Würzburg, Martin von Wagner Museum. Photo Museum.

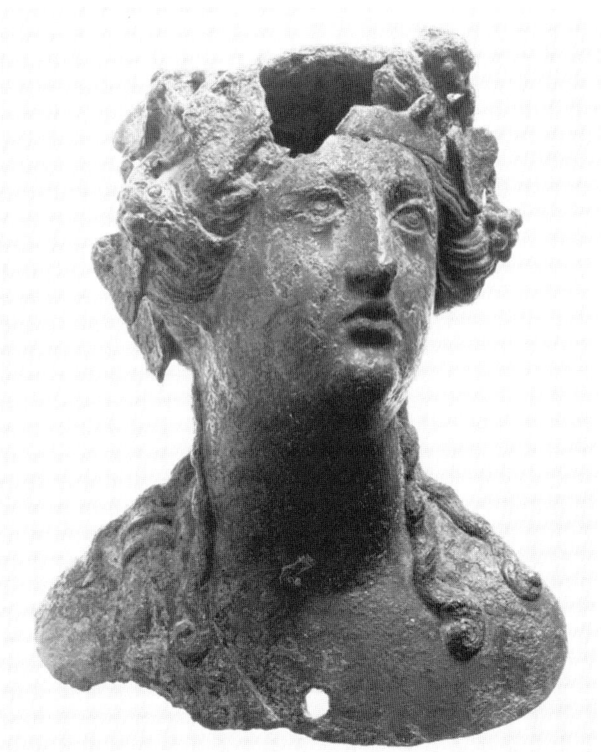

Fig. 13. Dionysus. Bronze bust. Bonn, Akademisches Kunstmuseum. Photo Museum.

Black Sea coast tallies with its similarity to a series of terracotta busts made in Amisus, where a great number of such pieces has been found. The example in Würzburg (Fig. 12)[36] is 15.7 cm high: the terracotta busts are usually about this size, that is, considerably smaller than the Cleveland bust. They represent females wearing a chiton that leaves one breast bare and holding a lock of their long hair; some are turned to the right, others to the left. They have been called female mourners, presumably attached to wooden sarcophagi, and this may well be the case. On the Scylla bust Figs. 1–2 the hand grasping the rudder is a little oversized and awkward and as such recurs in the modest terracotta busts.

In addition to the difference in quality, the bust Fig. 12 also looks much later than the Cleveland Scylla and indeed akin to and about contemporary with a small bronze bust of Dionysus from Amisus in Bonn (Fig. 13).[37] In both pieces the forms of the fleshy face are, as it were, toned down; this is characteristic of one of the tendencies in Late Hellenistic sculpture; both busts may belong to the beginning of the first century B.C. It is a long way indeed from the energy and intensity that distinguish the High Hellenistic bust Figs. 1–2.

This Scylla seems to be a masterpiece by a bronze worker of northern Asia Minor. A second such masterpiece is a bronze Pan pouring wine, said to be from Cyzicus (Fig. 14).[38] This high-quality statuette that has a strong facial kinship to the Cleveland Scylla suggests an important artistic activity in northern Asia Minor already in the Early Hellenistic period.

The Cleveland bust represents the deadly Scylla swinging the rudder as her lethal weapon; she is easily recognizable even without the ferocious dogs and the helpless victim. Striking is her *elemental* quality. The eyebrows are seaweed, the ears are fins; add to this the jutting fins on the neck. In addition, she wears a diagonal fin himation. This garment does not mean of course a return to the dressed Scylla of Early Classical art; it is indeed another elemental trait, like Scylla's fish skin in Fig. 8. The same applies to Hellenistic Tritons who, being naked as a rule, sometimes wear a fish skin; for instance in a marble copy of a High Pergamene original in the Vatican: a young Triton wears it over both shoulders tied into a knot in front, just like the panther skin of Hellenistic satyrs.[39] Scylla's fish skin likewise corresponds to the fawn skin of Maenads, as for example in an early Augustan bust from Asia Minor.[40] The meaning of these garments is in fact not so different: the animal skin denotes a creature of the wilderness, the fish skin a creature of the sea.

The Cleveland bust shows the only preserved Scylla head of High Hellenistic date, and one of excellent

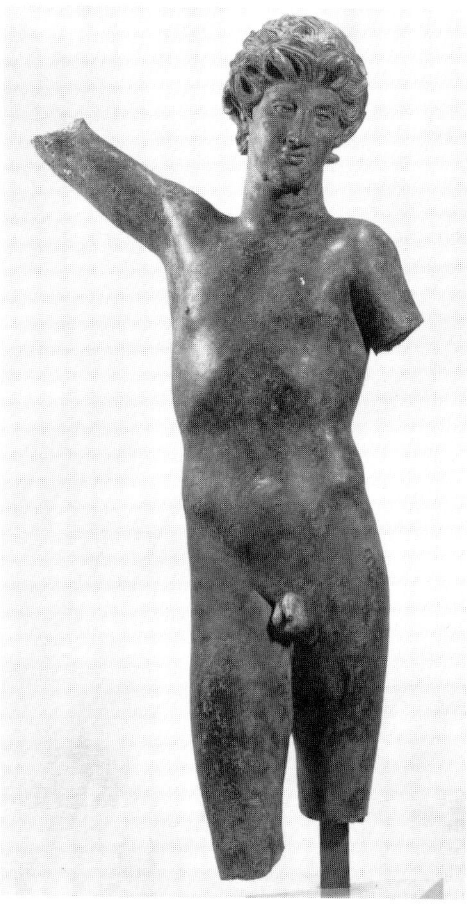

Fig. 14. Pan. Bronze statuette. Paris, Louvre. Photo Chuzeville.

quality at that. It bears witness to the explicit way of expressing elemental quality in this art. Even if the lost head of the Bargylia group was different in detail – as already stressed, there exists no fixed type of the monster – the elemental quality was there too; it is significant that the neck (as described in the British Museum Catalogue) is "terminating in seaweed"; moreover, the Bargylia dogs have ketos heads.[41]

Scylla is not the only creature distinguished by its elemental quality in Hellenistic art. For the Greeks of that period nature is enlarged to a cosmic whole and the sea creatures – as well as the earth creatures like the giants – illustrate this change through their new features. In the great frieze of the Pergamon Altar the fight of the gods against the giants is for the first time a battle of the elements. Only the Olympian gods are free of elemental traits, because, even to the Hellenistic mind, the Olympians stand above the elements. Thus, the frieze sea gods, except for Poseidon, show elemental traits not unlike those we have considered.[42]

Triton on the west side of the north Altar wing is an individual god; he occurs as such in Hellenistic art alongside the generic Tritons that people the sea thiasos. Triton, like Scylla, has no fixed iconographic type; only the fin skirt and sea snake bodies (singly or in pairs) are canonical. Thus, the winged Triton with snakes springing out of his head on a mosaic of the early third century B.C. in Rhodes has an elemental wildness although he holds the oar peacefully,[43] while another, without wings and snakes, on a mosaic of the later third century B.C. in Sparta, uses his oar as a weapon.[44] A similar young Triton with oar and trident on an excellent gem of the later third century B.C. is indeed not fighting, but the energy of his twisting movement characteristic of figures created in these years makes him look as if he is going to use the trident as a weapon.[45] His intensity recurs in Scylla Figs. 1–2.

In the Pergamon frieze Triton is also naked, with wet, windblown hair; his animal part is enhanced with the forepart of a horse, like the sea Centaurs, moreover he has fin wings, as well as fins in many parts of his body. The quaint, mighty god fights not only with the sword but also with the sea snake bodies, so that he vanquishes three giants at once. In the narrow space near the steps, the dignified figure of old Nereus wears a fish skin over head and shoulders. Next to him his wife Doris, grasping the hair of a giant with long snake legs, wears sandals of fish skin and fin; fins spread even to her opponent – and him an earth creature![46] Poseidon on the north side of the Altar wing fights surrounded by sea creatures as his followers and war companions.[47] Poseidon's chariot is drawn by hippocamps; rich patterns of fins, masterly rendered, give these fantastic creatures a reality that is identical with their elemental quality. The sea creatures that fought beside Poseidon are preserved only in fragments. Scylla was surely not among them; in this period she fights only her own fights, for loot and murder; it is only the amiable Scylla of the fourth century that joins the other sea creatures.

We may conclude that the elemental quality, so evident in the Cleveland bust, is an essential feature of Hellenistic Scylla figures, a feature they share with the other sea creatures in Hellenistic art. The great number of sea thiasos images, with new monsters created expressly to enrich it, the sea thiasos theme taken up in monumental sculpture – all this suggests that the elemental as such appealed strongly to the Greeks of the Hellenistic period. In the rich diversity of this imagery Scylla, representing the most appalling sea dangers, adopts the elements that suit her and finds a dangerous beauty of her own.

Notes

1. Cleveland Museum of Art 85.184 (Leonard C. Hanna Jr. bequest). A. Kozloff, *Classical Art. A Brief Guide to the Collections* (1989) 12. Height 22.4 cm. The eyes and lips are copper inlaid. For the photos and permission to publish them I thank A. Kozloff.
2. Metropolitan Museum of Art 16158 (Rogers Fund, 1956). A. Oliver Jr., *BMetrMus* 24, 1965/66, 279; *PropKunstgesch* I (1967) 208, colour pl. VIII (A. Greifenhagen); M. Pfrommer, *Untersuchungen zur Chronologie früh- und hochhellenistischen Goldschmucks* (*IstForsch* 37, 1990) 134, SR 65.66; D. Williams – J. Ogden, *Greek Gold* (1994) no. 37.
3. Ph. Bruneau – C. Vatin, *BCH* 87, 1964, 252ff., figs. 1–5, colour pl. XI; Ph. Bruneau, *Délos* XXIX (1972) 174 ff., no. 75, figs. 88–91.
4. Cf. Roscher, *ML* IV (1909–15) 1024ff., s.v. Scylla (O. Waser); *RE* III A1 (1927) 647ff., s.v. Scylla (J. Schmidt); K. Tuchelt, *IstMitt* 17, 1967, 173–194; P. Themelis, *AEphem* 1979, 118–153, pls. 24–32; B. Andreae, *Odysseus* (1982) 50ff; G.B. Waywell in *Ulisse. Il mito e la memoria* (Exhibition Rome, 1996) 108ff.
5. P. Jacobsthal, *Die melischen Reliefs* (1934) nos. 71–74. Gems: Paris, Bibliothèque Nationale, de Luynes 264 (J. Boardman, *Greek Gems and Finger Rings* [1970] pl. 453); Berlin F301 (E. Zwierlein-Diehl, *AGDS* II, no. 154) etc. Cf. also an Attic lekythos (K. Schauenburg, *RM* 87, 1980, 40, pl. 24,2), a bronze disc from Eretria (Themelis [supra n. 4] 138ff., fig. 6, pl. 30b–c).
6. Jacobsthal (supra n. 5) no. 71.
7. P. Franke – M. Hirmer, *Die griechische Münze*² (1972) pl. 60 below r. Cf. Tuchelt (supra n. 4) 190 with other examples; Waywell (supra n. 4) 110, fig. 1.
8. Schauenburg (supra n. 5) 41 has already refuted the assumption that the new Scylla image was a South Italian creation. Two Boeotian vase paintings are marginal: on the krater, about 430 B.C., appears a fighting male Scylla with a sword as her weapon (*CVA* Louvre 17, pls. 44,3; 45,1); on the pyxis, of the late 5th c. B.C., a dressed Scylla, hurling a stone (E. Langlotz, *Griechische Vasen. Martin-von-Wagner Museum* [1932] no. 821, pl. 238).
9. From Olynthus. D.M. Robinson, *Olynthus* V (1933) 109ff., no. 131, fig. 13 (on fig. 13 a fragment on the right does not belong there, as was established in the

Thessaloniki Museum). Cf. S.G. Miller, *AJA* 90, 1986, 160ff., no. 1, pl. 12, fig. 1,2); S. Karusu, *AEphem* 1974, 32f., pls. 13–15. There is perhaps another Attic vase painting of Scylla among the Nereids (from Chersonesus: *AJA* 97, 1993, 543, fig. 12 frg. on the left; this vase must be a little earlier than the krater from Olynthus).

10. H. Sichtermann, *Griechische Vasen in Unteritalien* (1966) K74, pls. 128–131; Trendall, *RVAp* I, 403f., 43, pl. 142,5.

11. *CVA* J.P. Getty Mus. 4, pls. 231–234.

12. Calyx krater by Asteas in Naples: A.D. Trendall, *The Red-figured Vases of Paestum* (1987) 84, no. 126, pl. 45; *LIMC* VI (1992) s.v. Nephele II, no. 1, pl. 453 (M. Pipili).

13. Apulian pelike: K. Schauenburg, *Perseus* (1960) 59, pl. 23; id. (supra n. 5) 37 n. 66; Trendall, *RVAp* II, 536, 306; J. Barringer, *Divine Escorts. Nereids in Archaic and Classical Greek Art* (1995) 116, pl. 121.

14. Athen. VIII.341a (after Polemon); Plut. *Sympos.* IV.2.3.8. Androcydes must have been active in the early fourth century since a battle piece by him in Thebes belongs to the years around 380 B.C. (cf. T. Hölscher, *Griechische Historienbilder des 5. und 4. Jhs.* [1973] 114). The theme 'sea monster Scylla' is certain only for Androcydes' work because of the fish expressly mentioned, while the Scylla paintings by Nicomachus and Phalerion, likewise known through literary sources, may have represented the daughter of Nisus of Megara who appears in Roman wall paintings (cf. *LIMC* VII [1994] s.v. Skylla II [F. Canciani]), as H. Brunn (*Geschichte der griechischen Künstler* 2 [1889] 168) and O. Waser (in Roscher, *ML* IV, 1043) already pointed out.

15. E.g. one of the late fourth century B.C. from Nea Paphos in Cyprus (D. Salzmann, *Untersuchungen zu den antiken Kieselmosaiken* [1982] 126, no. S3, pl. 64,1; W.A. Daszewski, *BJb* 186, 1986, 754); Waywell (supra n. 4) 110, fig. 2.

16. Paris, Louvre. A. de Ridder, *Les bronzes antiques* II (1915) no. 1686, pl. 76; Tuchelt (supra n. 4) 191, no. 32. This piece has often been dated before 400 B.C., but its style as well as the fin skirt suggest a later date. There is still a production of such mirrors in the fourth century, cf. P. Oberländer, *Griechische Handspiegel* (diss. Hamburg 1967) 204, no. 299.

17. Sichtermann (supra n. 10) K128, pl. 168; Trendall, *RVAp* II, 614f., no. 76. Cf. also the Scylla of an Apulian rhyton in Matera (A. Bottini, *BdA* 1990, 5/6, 234, fig. 5; on the other side of the rhyton a Triton).

18. *Albanien. Schätze aus dem Land der Skipetaren* (Exhib. Hildesheim, 1988) no. 316; M. Treister, *OJA* 13, 1994, 86, fig. 3.

19. A. Neugebauer, *JdI* 49, 1934, 174, fig. 12: Tarentine; Tuchelt (supra n. 4) 192, no. 41; Themelis (supra n. 4) 130ff., fig. 4, pl. 28a–b.

20. Fig. 8: "from Eretria." Neugebauer (supra n. 19) 174, fig. 13: Tarentine; W. Züchner, *Griechische Klappspiegel*, 14. Ergh. *JdI* (1942) KS 78, figs. 66; 120: South Italian, about 275 B.C.; Tuchelt (supra n. 4) 192, no. 42: Tarentine, second half of the fourth century B.C.; Themelis (supra n. 4) 118ff., pl. 24a–b: end of the fourth century B.C.; Andreae (supra n. 4) 51: South Italian, about 275 B.C.; K. Schefold, *Die Sagen von den Argonauten, von Theben und Troia in der klassischen und hellenistischen Kunst* (1989) 345, fig. 307: about 320 B.C.; Waywell (supra n. 4) 111, cat. 2,61: about 300–275 B.C., perhaps Tarentine. Fig. 9: from Taman (South Russia). Züchner KS77: Ionian, about 275 B.C.; Tuchelt (supra n. 4) 192, no. 43: second half of the fourth century B.C.; Themelis (supra n. 4) 128ff., fig. 3, pl. 29a: about 340–320 B.C. Cf. also the small limestone pedimental groups from Tarentum, e.g.:
1.The Hague, Scheurleer Coll. 1599. H. Klumbach, *Tarentinische Grabkunst* (1937) no. 120, pl. 21; J.C. Carter, *The Sculpture of Taras* (1975) pl. 8,c28; Themelis (supra n. 4) pl. 29c; S.B.M. van d. Noordaa – D. van d. Bussche, *Allard Pierson Mus. Meded.* 50, 1991, 14ff., figs. 1–2.
2.Tarentum 166. Klumbach no. 8, pl. 1; Carter no. 191; Themelis (supra n. 4) 136, pl. 29b.
3.Vienna, Kunsthistorisches Museum I-780. Andreae (supra n. 4) 51f. with illustration.
4.New York, A. Herrmann Coll. D. Buitron – B. Cohen, *The Odyssey in Ancient Art and Literature* (Exhibition Annandale-on-Hudson, 1992) no. 49.

21. Neugebauer (supra n. 19) has already pointed out that the reliefs Figs. 8–9 belong to the same regional school of sculpture, but he localised them in Tarentum, as most scholars thereafter did. Themelis (supra n. 4) first rejected this attribution leaving the question open. Epirotan school of the fifth-fourth centuries: cf. E. Walter-Karydi, *JbBerlMus* 23, 1981, 11ff. The relief Fig. 8 was found in Dodona and the relief Fig. 9, if the provenance "Eretria" is true (it is only a dealer's statement: the piece was bought in Athens), was an Epirotan import to that city.

22. Louvre: de Ridder, *Les bronzes antiques* I (1913) no. 490; Neugebauer (supra n. 19) fig. 9; Walter-Karydi (supra n. 21) 48, fig. 58.

23. Metropolitan Museum of Art 25. 78. 44a–d (Fletcher Fund, 1925). Züchner (supra n. 20) 78, KS105, fig. 37; H. Walter, *Pans Wiederkehr* (1980) 101, fig. 81; J. Mertens, *Greek Bronzes in the Metropolitan Museum of Art* (1985) no. 29. The same subject occurs on a bronze cuirass plaque of unknown provenance which must be Epirotan as well (*A Passion for Antiquities. Ancient Art from the Collection of B. and L. Fleischman*, Exhibition J.P. Getty Museum – Cleveland Museum of Art, 1994, no. 28).

24. It occurs also on a mosaic of the third century B.C. from a house in Eretria (Salzmann [supra n. 15] no. 42, pls. 49,3; 50,2; 102,3; Themelis [supra n. 4] 144ff. fig. 7, pl. 30d).

25. Metropolitan Museum of Art 1981. 11. 21. D. v. Bothmer, *BMetrMus* 42, 1984, 55, no. 95; J.R. Mertens, *Metropolitan Museum of Art. Greece and Rome* (1987) 60f., no. 60; Waywell (supra n. 4) 110, fig. 3.

26. As on an Apulian krater of the second quarter of the century (H. Cahn Coll. 234. H.J. Bloesch, *Das Tier in der Antike* [Exhibition Zürich, 1974] no. 260); Trendall, *RVAp* I, 168, 27. no. 7/27.

27. Found in March 1996 and reported in *Ta Nea* 13.3.1996 with illustration, after which a tentative date is given here. The mosaic will be published by the excavator, E. Sakellaraki.

28. Berlin, Staatliche Museen. B. Andreae – B. Conticello,

Skylla und Charybdis (*AbhMainz* 14, 1987) fig. 46; B. Andreae, *Laokoon und die Gründung Roms* (1988) fig. 27. N. Himmelmann, *Sperlonga* (1995) 32, pl. 11a. The bowl: A. Greifenhagen, *Beiträge zur antiken Reliefkeramik*, 21. Ergh. *JdI* (1963) 52ff., figs. 46; 48; 50; 52.

29. Paris, Louvre. *CVA* Louvre 15 pl. 6,1–5. U. Sinn, *Die homerischen Becher*, 7. Beih. *AM* (1979) MB 19, fig. 4,1; Buitron - Cohen [supra n. 20] no. 51. Cf. also the Calenian bowls (Tuchelt [supra n. 4] nos. 50–55; K. Odegard, *ActaAArtHist* 8, 1992, 1ff.).
30. Cf. recently N. Himmelmann, *AntK* 34, 1991, 105ff.; id. *Gymnasium* 103, 1996, 37.
31. In *Akten XIII. internationalen Kongresses für klassische Archäologie, Berlin 1988* (1990) 386–388, fig. 1, pl. 58,3; id. (supra n. 4) 112, fig. 4; id., *AntPl* 25 (1996) 75–119, pls. 59–66. The fragments: A.H. Smith, *Catalogue Sculpture British Museum* III (1904) no. 1542.
32. Agrinion Museum (ex Athens, National Museum). H. Möbius, *Die Ornamente der griechischen Grabstelen* (1927; 1968^2) 68f., pls. 60c; 61a.
33. G. Waywell (supra n. 31) on the contrary sees in the Bargylia group the Odysseus episode.
34. *ID* 2549; B. Hebert, *Schriftquellen zur hellenistischen Kunst* (1989) 5f.
35. This was pointed out by Schefold (supra n. 20) 345.
36. E.M. Schmidt, *Katalog der antiken Terrakotten* I (1994) no. 309, pl. 56. Cf. the examples in the Louvre (S. Besques, *Catalogue terres cuites* III, D508, pl. 110 and D529ff., pls. 114e; 115a.b: mourning women, made in Amisus), Munich (J. Sieveking, *AA* 1912, 126, no. 17, from Madytus; id., *Slg. Loeb*, 1939, 19f., pl. 19,2, from Cerasus: maenad).
37. N. Himmelmann, *Drei hellenistische Bronzen in Bonn* (*AbhMainz* 1975,2) 20ff., pls. 10–11 (inv. C72; height 12 cm). For the photo and permission to publish it I thank W. Geominy.
38. Louvre br4359. J. Charbonneaux, *RArtMus* 4, 1954, 42; C. Rolley, *Die Bronzen* (*Mon. Gr. et Rom.* V1, 1967) no. 125; id., *Die griechischen Bronzen* (1984) 96, fig. 176. Height 55 cm; the statuette must have been about 70 cm. high.
39. *Helbig*^{4} I (1963) no. 118 (H. v. Steuben); S. Lattimore, *The Marine Thiasos in Greek Sculpture* (1976) 59, pl. 26, fig. 37.
40. Berlin, Staatliche Museen. A. Greifenhagen, *RA* 1968, 257ff.; B. Barr-Sharrar, *The Hellenistic and Early Imperial Decorative Bust* (1986) no. C142, pl. 43; *Die Antikensammlung Berlin* (1992) no. 152.
41. *Ulisse* (supra n. 4) 59, fig. 2,17.
42. H. Winnefeld, *AvP* III2 (1910) 84ff.; H. Kähler, *Der grosse Fries von Pergamon* (1948) pls. 1; 18–19; E. Rohde, *Pergamon. Burgberg und Altar* (1976) 63f., figs. 46–47.
43. Salzmann (supra n. 15) no. 112, pl. 47; E. Walter-Karydi, *JdI* 106, 1991, pl. 62,3.
44. Salzmann (supra n. 15) no. 169, pls. 82,1–3; 102,5–6.
45. G. Richter, *The Engraved Gems of the Greeks and the Etruscans* (1968) no. 525; E. Zwierlein-Diehl, *AGDS* Berlin II, no. 217.
46. Winnefeld (supra n. 42) 89, fig. 23.
47. Winnefeld (supra n. 42) 81f.; 142, pl. XX; Kähler (supra n. 42) 46; 114, pl. 23; Rohde (supra n. 42) 62f., pl. II; Walter-Karydi (supra n. 43) 253f., fig. 4.

The "Alexander Sarcophagus" of Abdalonymos: A Hellenistic Monument from Sidon

Caroline Houser

The "Alexander Sarcophagus" (Figs. 1–4) is one of the most celebrated works from Classical antiquity.[1] Its photograph – often in color – is almost a prerequisite for a book that treats art of the Hellenistic period. Even though a suggestion that the sarcophagus was made for Alexander the Great was dismissed nearly a century ago, the famous name remains attached to the sarcophagus because Alexander's portrait appears in at least one scene on the exterior.[2]

The sarcophagus is one of the few early Hellenistic works of art that can be tied to a precise location and a fairly secure date. Almost all scholars believe that it was made for Abdalonymos of Sidon, who became king of that Phoenician city-state by the grace of Alexander in 332 B.C., and they also agree that the sarcophagus was made during the last third of the fourth century B.C.[3] It must have been commissioned after 332 B.C., and it probably was completed by the end of the fourth century, although 311 B.C. can no longer be considered the latest date for the sarcophagus.[4]

I shall not argue here for or against iconographic or stylistic interpretations;[5] instead, I will consider the "Alexander Sarcophagus" in its Phoenician context, because its uncontested provenance and firm date, as well as its splendid quality, make it a crucial monument in the investigation of regionalism in Hellenistic art. Its find spot naturally played an important role in identifying the person for whom the coffin was created. Considering the sarcophagus in its Phoenician setting is equally important, I believe, for understanding its place in terms of Hellenistic art and culture.

Fortunately, the archaeological context of the "Alexander Sarcophagus" is well-documented. It is one of seventeen sarcophagi discovered in 1887 in a rock-cut necropolis in Aya'a on the eastern outskirts of Saïda in modern Lebanon, the ancient Phoenician Sidon, so famous for its fleet and strategic position in Hellenistic times.[6] The subterranean complex, divided into two hypogea, consisted of a series of rooms in use at least as early as the first part of the fifth century B.C., apparently as a royal necropolis that had undergone remodeling at several times to accommodate new entombments.[7] The room cut as the most recent addition to the larger hypogeum held the sarcophagus made for Abdalonymos.[8] The apartment complex that housed these tombs apparently went out of use when Sidon became a republic in or about 280 B.C.[9]

The "Alexander Sarcophagus" is a very large horizontal chest, rectangular in plan both outside and inside, made to hold a human body in extended position.[10] The box and lid are each carved from one piece of imported white marble, traditionally identified as Pentelic.[11] The bulky box weighs about fifteen tons and its lid about half that amount, so it was not designed for transport.[12] Crisp sculpted edges and unweathered surfaces indicate that it always stood in a protected location. Except for loss of color and the damage apparently inflicted by tomb robbers who pried the lid off, the sarcophagus remains in remarkably good condition.[13]

Its rectangular composition with gabled roof implies that the "Alexander Sarcophagus" served as a house or temple for its owner. Four recumbent lions guarded it, one glaring from each roof corner. Lavish decoration covers the chest with architectural elements cut precisely and carefully, most of which are prominent in the Greek Ionic vocabulary: meander, guilloch, Lesbian leaf, bead and reel, egg and dart, dentils, a tiled roof crowned with double flaming palmette above each peak, and figured relief panels. A band of rhythmically undulating vine leaves carved in low relief runs around the bottom of the lid in the position of a cornice frieze.

The six sculptural relief panels decorate the vertical sides of the box: one on each long wall, one on each short wall, and one on each pediment. All six scenes depict human figures in action. The long side that faced the center of the burial chamber shows the scene that gives the sarcophagus its romantic name (Figs. 1 and 3): Alexander rides in from the left end of a battle scene between men whose clothing (or in some cases, their nudity) identifies them as Greeks and Persians. On the other long side (Figs. 2 and 4), which faced toward the wall of the chamber, men and wild beasts fight for their lives in a hunt scene. Scenes of violent conflicts, men

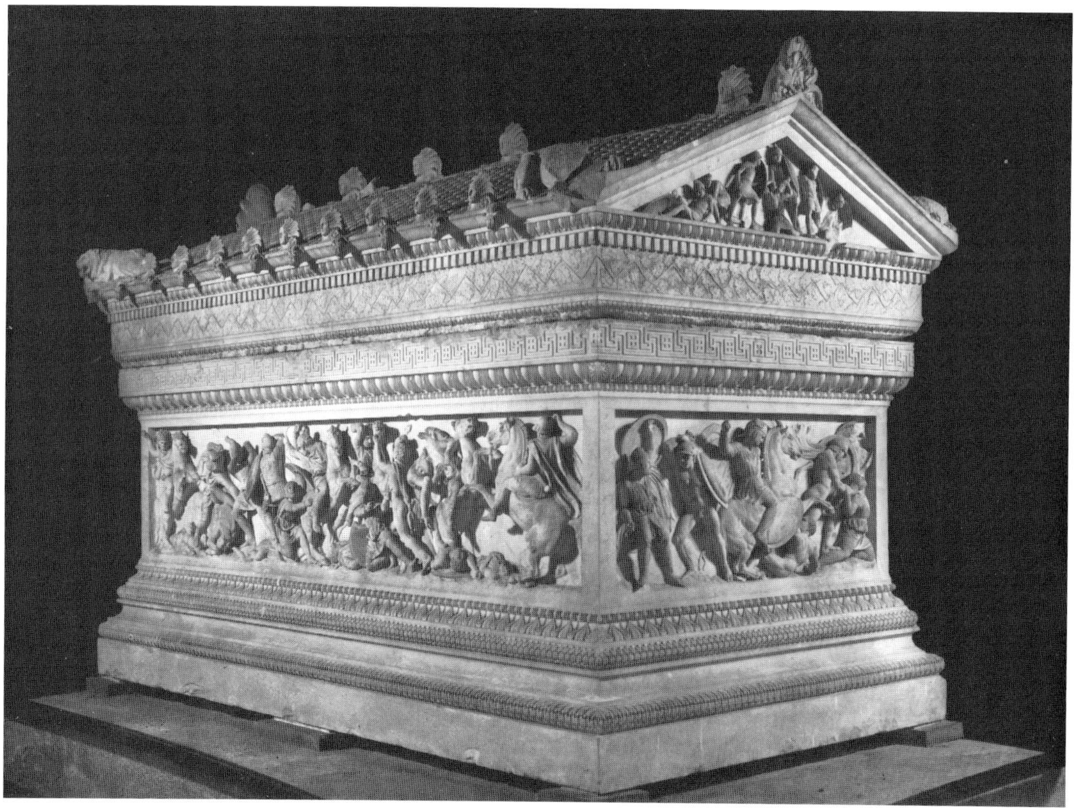

Fig. 1. The "Alexander Sarcophagus." Long and short sides with battle scenes. Istanbul, Archaeological Museum 370. Photo: German Archaeological Institute, Istanbul 8117.

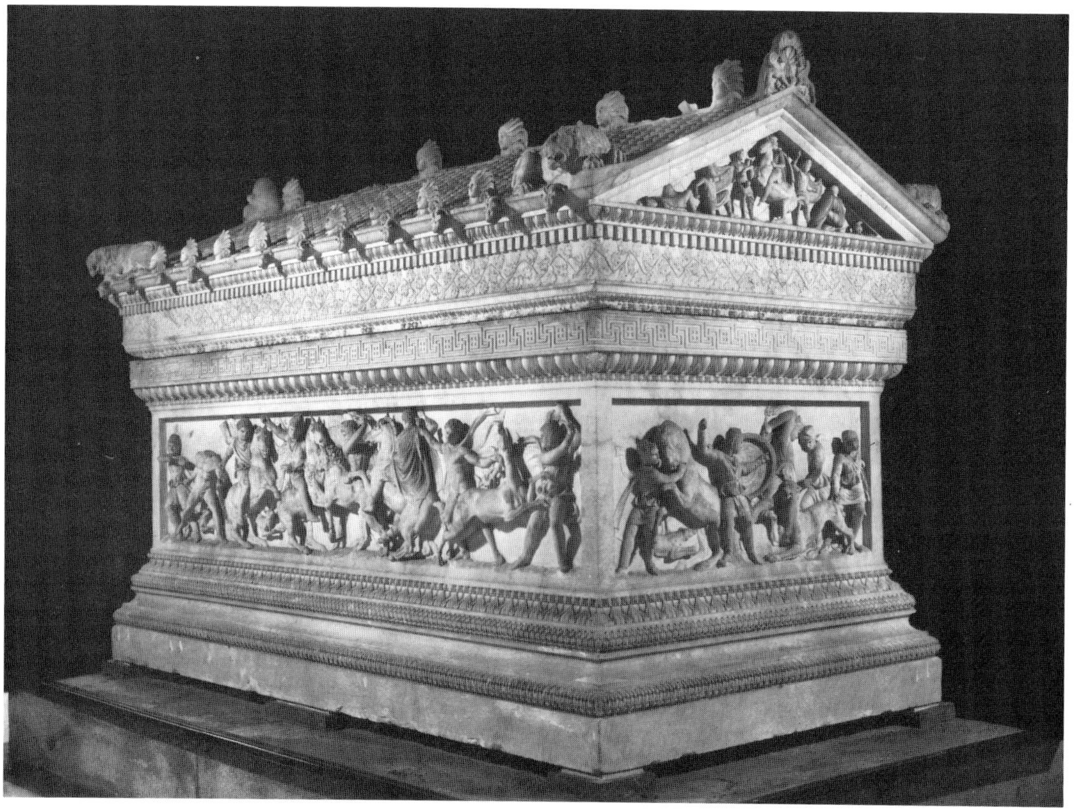

Fig. 2. The "Alexander Sarcophagus." Long and short sides with hunt scenes. Istanbul, Archaeological Museum 370. Photo: German Archaeological Institute, Istanbul 8111.

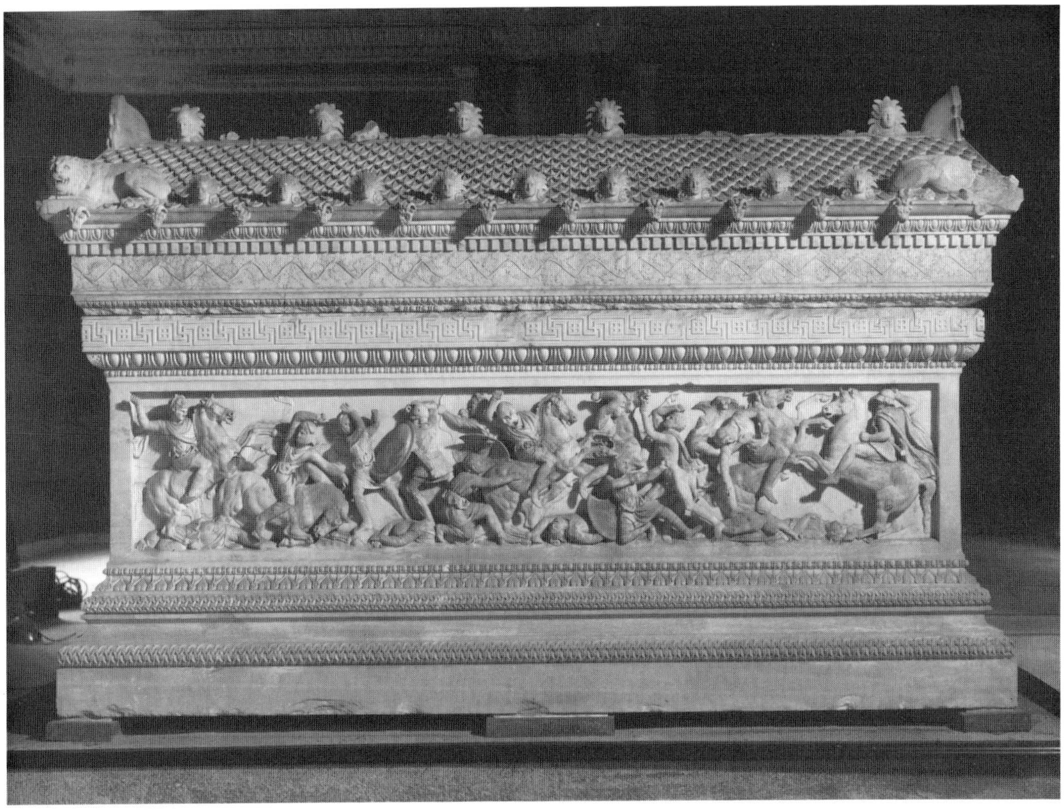

Fig. 3. The "Alexander Sarcophagus." Long side with battle scene. Istanbul, Archaeological Museum 370. Photo: German Archaeological Institute, Istanbul 8122.

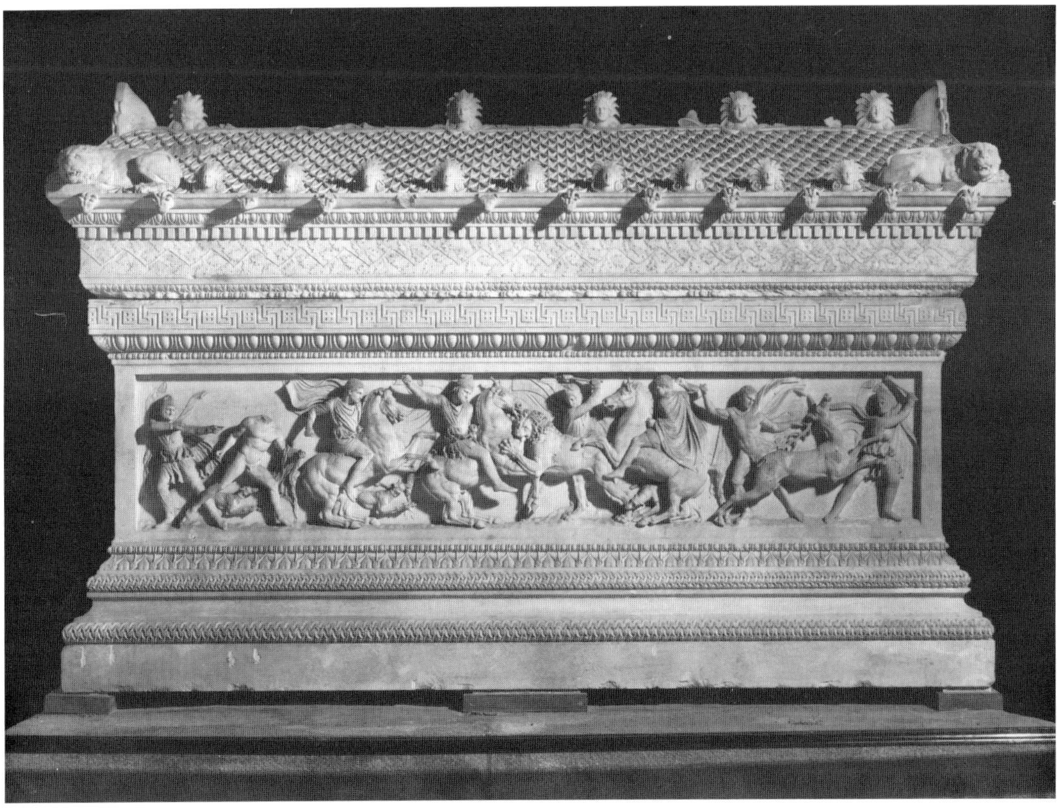

Fig. 4. "The Alexander Sarcophagus." Long side with hunt scene. Istanbul, Archaeological Museum 370. Photo: German Archaeological Institute, Istanbul 8120.

against men and men against wild beasts, fill the walls and pediments of the short sides (Figs. 1 and 2): the end wall panels complement the long frieze pictures with one hunt and one battle scene, while both pediments show soldiers fighting.

Bright colors painted on almost every surface remained visible when the sarcophagus came to light in 1887. The earliest description of the sarcophagus says that the background of the vine frieze was painted and reports "blue eyes, scarlet cloaks, blue tunics, [and shields painted] to represent the circle of the heavens with stars...and figures of animals... Mounted warriors have under them flat, padded saddle-cloths richly worked and painted with bright colors."[14] Descriptions of scarlets, reds, lavenders, purples, violets, blues, and yellows fill the early records.[15] Even though the hues quickly faded when exposed to air and light, faint colors remain, indicating the yellow lion-skin helmet Alexander wears, crimson blood spurting from wounded men and beasts, scarlet cloaks swirling around blue-eyed and brown-eyed men who wear tunics in various shades of reds, blues, and yellows and hold shields with red or gold rims.[16] Swords, spears, and axes made of silver (and perhaps of bronze and gold, too) gave added color and texture to the sculptures.[17] Originally the sarcophagus must have been ablaze with color, obliterating the line between sculpture and painting and giving the scenes an intensity that neither painting nor sculpture could do alone.

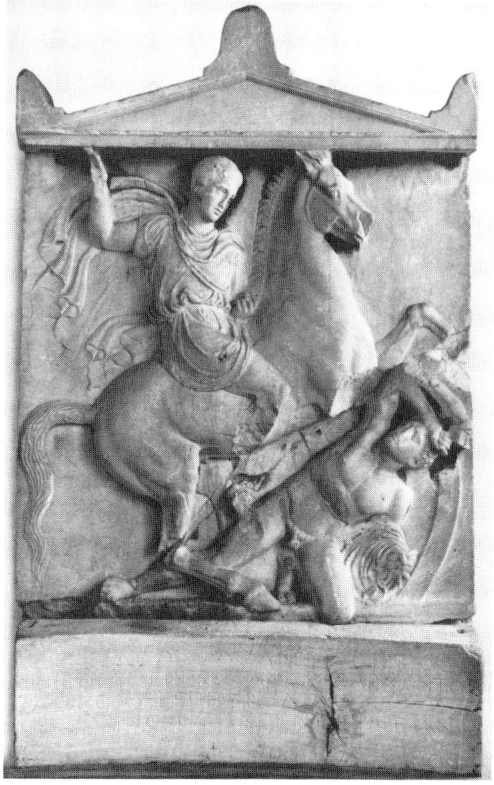

Fig. 5. Stele of Dexileos. Athens, Kerameikos Museum. Photo after R. Lullies and M. Hirmer, Greek Sculpture *(1960) pl. 192.*

So comfortably do the sculptural elements appear to fit within the tradition of mainstream Greek art, that the sarcophagus appears in almost every survey of the subject as a prime example of Greek sculpture in the fourth century B.C. Most of the architectural ornament is Greek, part of the vocabulary that flourished in the Greek east and was established in Athens by the second half of the fifth century B.C. The sculpted figures are closely related to late classical and early Hellenistic art in Athens and other places where patronage beckoned, such as Halikarnassos. For example, the Dexileos stele in Athens (Fig. 5) appears to be the forerunner of several riders on the sarcophagus, especially the image of Alexander in battle (Figs. 1 and 3) and those of the two Greeks or Macedonians who, in the lion hunt on the other long side (Figs. 2 and 4), frame the lion flanked by men in Persian dress. The action in the battle and hunt scenes parallels those from the temple of Apollo at Bassae, the Mausoleum at Halikarnassos, and the "Alexander Mosaic" of the House of the Faun in Pompeii, although the intensity of the compact composition on the "Alexander Sarcophagus," especially in the compositions on the two long sides, more closely resembles what is reflected in the "Alexander Mosaic" and approaches that of the later Gigantomachy frieze from the Pergamon Altar.[18] In comparison, the massing of combatants in a dense carpet on many battle scenes shown on Roman sarcophagi makes the design of the battle and hunt scenes on the casket of Abdalonymos seem relatively spacious.[19] In addition, the very material of the sarcophagus, if the marble is indeed from Mt. Pentelikon in Attica, links the sarcophagus to Athens.

On the other hand, some aspects of Abdalonymos' casket relate more closely to art found outside the confines of the Greek world – art from the Levant, western Asia, the western Mediterranean, and Egypt – than they do to mainstream Greek art. The guardian lions on each corner of the roof come from a long line of Asian sentries, icons firmly established by Hittite Lion Gates at Bogazköy made in the 14th century B.C.[20] The form, the placement, and undoubtedly the purpose of the lions on Abdalonymos' tomb find precedents on two Cypriot sarcophagi from the first half of the fifth century B.C.[21] As another element outside the Greek world, one notes the strange heads on the base of the sarcophagus lid; although they project from the sima in the position occupied by lion-head spouts in canonical Greek architecture, the heads on the "Alexander Sarcophagus" are images of fantastic animals that appear to have three ram horns growing on feline heads, strangers to basic Hellenic zoography.[22] To find parallels in classical or Hellenistic times for the human-headed antefixes perched on the sima and the roof ridge that may represent a Phoenician goddess in a head-dress of radiating leaves,[23] we would look to architectural decorations found in Italy.[24]

While the relief panels have antecedents in Athens, they also are related to Lycian sculptures,[25] which owe artistic debts to the palace reliefs at Persepolis.[26] So close are the figures representing Amazons battling Greeks on a sarcophagus from the eastern Mediterranean and now in Vienna to those on the "Alexander Sarcophagus" in terms of figural style and composition, that the two might have been designed and sculpted by the same master at different stages in his career or by the same workshop.[27] While depictions of frenzied battle and hunt demand greater agitation than depiction of a dance, even one by maenads, flying drapery on the coffin of Abdalonymos sways and billows in idealized graceful movements similar to those on the figures in the lower register of the "Tribune," a fourth century B.C. monument excavated in Sidon at the sanctuary of Eshmun.[28]

Despite those disparate stylistic affinities, however, the comparanda closest to the "Alexander Sarcophagus" are the other coffins found in the same tomb complex at Sidon. Three sarcophagi (Figs. 6–8) that shared the room of Abdalonymos' tomb in the hypogeum follow its architectural format and, with subtle variation, its Ionic decorative scheme, set in a similar configuration.[29] All carry an elegant, calligraphic vine-leaf frieze, executed in low relief similar to the distinctive one on the Abdalonymos sarcophagus. They, too, show similar superb standards of excellence in design and carving, and they were also made from Pentelic marble and painted.[30] Except for being smaller[31] and bearing no figural decoration, they are almost identical to the tomb of Abdalonymos.

In terms of figural sculptural relief and its placement, the best parallels for the "Alexander Sarcophagus" and the closely-related Amazon Sarcophagus now in Vienna are three other coffins excavated in the same necropolis at Sidon: the Satrap Sarcophagus (Fig. 9),[32] the Lycian Sarcophagus (Fig. 10),[33] and the Weeping Women Sarcophagus (Fig. 11).[34] Created for kings who preceded Abdalonymos, they must have been made between the mid-fifth and the mid-fourth centuries B.C. They carry a framed picture executed in relief on each of their four vertical sides, and the pediments of the Lycian and Weeping Women coffins also bore relief sculptures. This second group of three close parallels also matches the "Alexander Sarcophagus" in terms of format, material, color, purpose, and placement. The Lycian Sarcophagus adopts the design of a house tomb of Lycia, while the Satrap and Weeping Women Sarcophagi assume the canonical Greek architectural model followed by the "Alexander Sarcophagus" and the three from the same room. Like the "Alexander Sarcophagus" and the simpler versions of it, this second group of three appears to be made from Greek marble; the stone of the Weeping Women Sarcophagus is also described as Pentelic, while the Satrap and Lycian Sarcophagi are identified as marble from Paros.[35] Vivid naturalistic hues appeared on all.[36] The most obvious difference between these sarcophagi and that of Abdalonymos is scale: as is true of the three sarcophagi with vine-leaf friezes from the same room as the tomb of Abdalonymos, the lengths of the Satrap, the Lycian, and the Weeping Women Sarcophagi fall about a meter short of the length of the "Alexander Sarcophagus."[37]

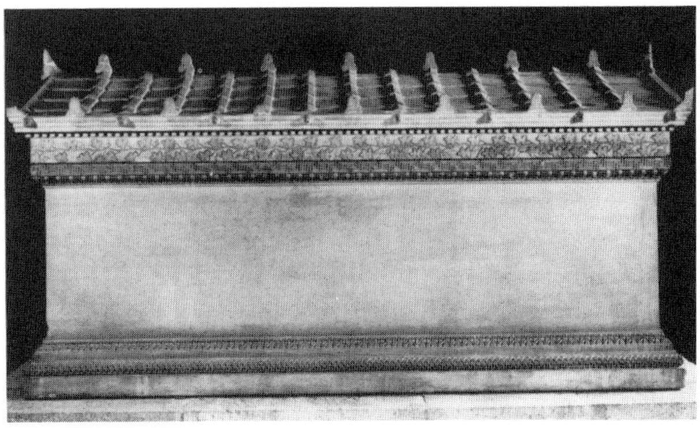

Fig. 6. Architectural Sarcophagus. From Sidon. Istanbul, Archaeological Museum. Photo after von Graeve, Alexandersarkophag *pl. 20.*

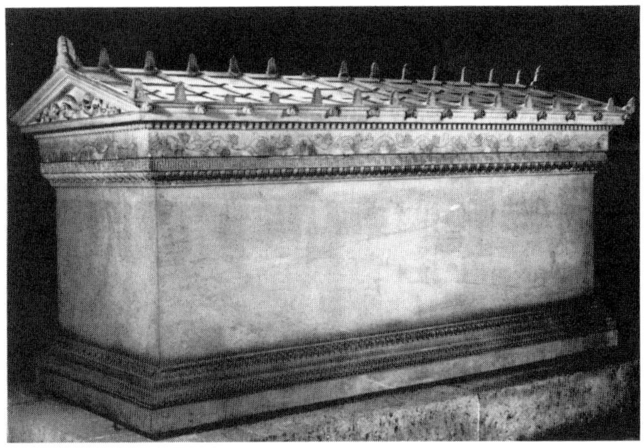

Fig. 7. Architectural Sarcophagus. From Sidon. Istanbul, Archaeological Museum. Photo after von Graeve, Alexandersarkophag *pl. 21.*

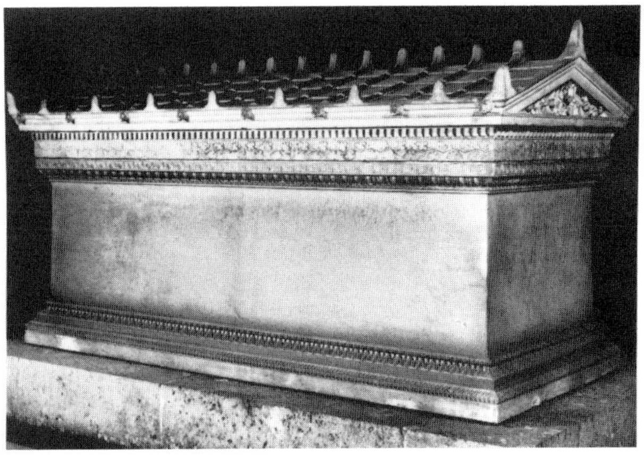

Fig. 8. Architectural Sarcophagus. From Sidon. Istanbul, Archaeological Museum. Photo after von Graeve, Alexandersarkophag *pl. 19.*

From the same necropolis as the "Alexander Sarcophagus" also came four sarcophagi of the category called anthropoid that underscore the strong connection between Sidon and sarcophagi. Anthropoid coffins represent the

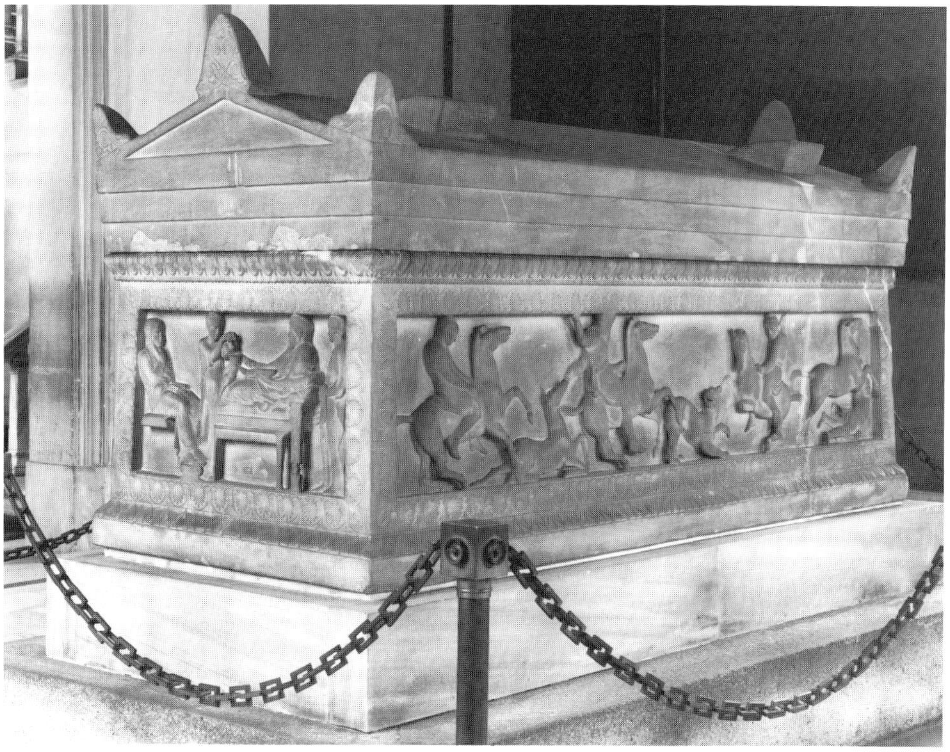

Fig. 9. Satrap Sarcophagus. From Sidon. Istanbul, Archaeological Museum 367. Photo: German Archaeological Institute, Istanbul 70/46.

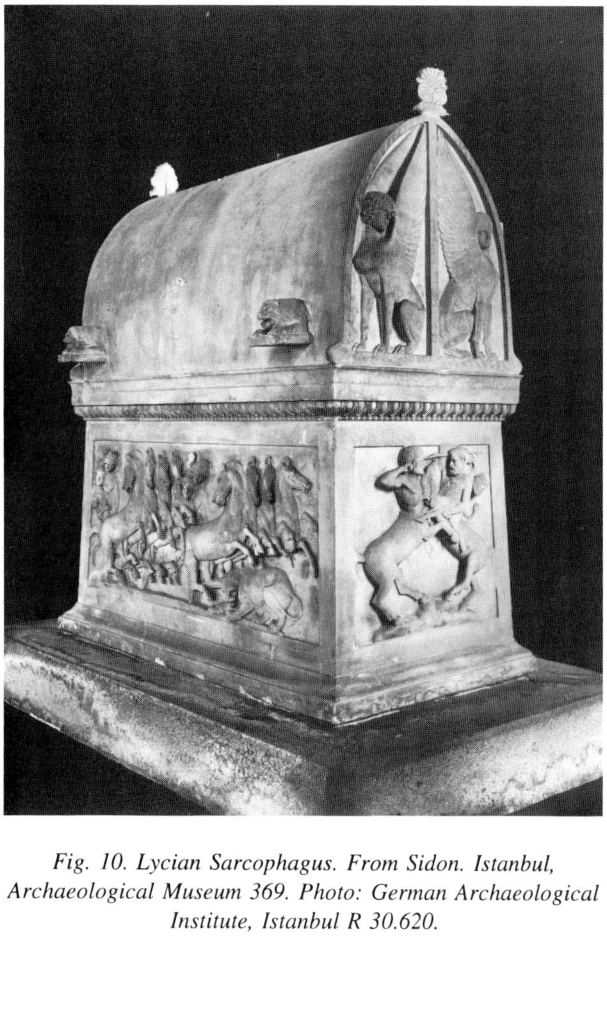

Fig. 10. Lycian Sarcophagus. From Sidon. Istanbul, Archaeological Museum 369. Photo: German Archaeological Institute, Istanbul R 30.620.

body as though it were wrapped as a mummy while portraying a precisely articulated face, so the form appears to be a mummy with a mask. Two of the anthropoid coffins found with the coffin of Abdalonymos are carved from black basalt or diorite and are Egyptian in style: one held Tabnit, who was king of Sidon in the late sixth or early fifth century B.C., and the other held a woman whose identity is lost.[38] They are very similar to a casket found about a mile away from them that held Eshmunazar, Tabnit's son who followed him as king of Sidon.[39] Tabnit's coffin carries a hieroglyphic inscription saying that it was designed for Pen-Ptah, an Egyptian general, but a later inscription in Phoenician characters proclaims Tabnit as the occupant. Eshmunazar's coffin is inscribed in Phoenician letters,[40] but neither it nor the unfinished Egyptian sarcophagus used for the unidentified woman carry hieroglyphs. Iconography, except for the Phoenician lettering, on both decorated coffins is Egyptian. All three probably were made in Egypt and appropriated by the Sidonians.[41]

Those Egyptian anthropoid coffins appear to be the inspiration for the creation of a new category of stone caskets, known as "Sidonian Sarcophagi," that further links the Phoenicians with sarcophagi. The type is represented by the other two anthropoid coffins excavated by Hamdy Bey with the casket of Abdalonymos, one representing a man[42] and the other a woman.[43] As is true of the Egyptian anthropoid coffin, the "Sidonian Sarcophagi" combine an articulated face with a mummiform

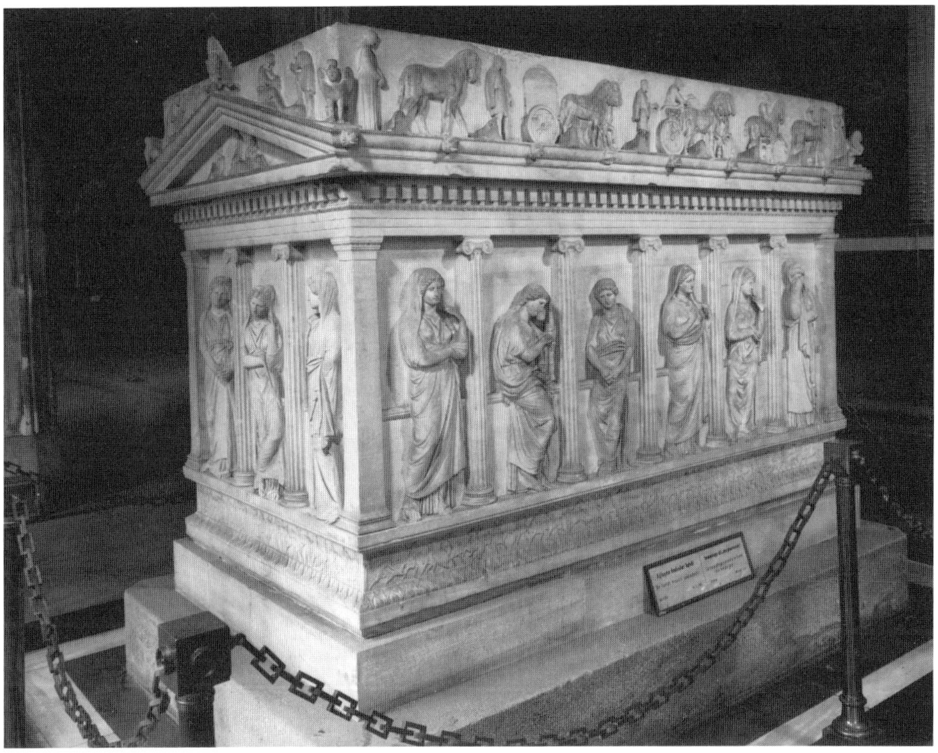

Fig. 11. The Weeping Women Sarcophagus. From Sidon. Istanbul, Archaeological Museum 368. Photo: German Archaeological Institute, Istanbul 64/236.

body, but the differences between the black Egyptian and the white Phoenician types are clear from the beginning by their forms as well as by the color of their materials. Although the face on a "Sidonian Sarcophagus" is idealized (and often called "Greek"), the distinctive individualized features appear naturalistic in comparison with those on the mask of its Egyptian counterpart, which are carved in lower relief. On the other hand, the mummiform body on a typical "Sidonian Sarcophagus" indicates body contours only summarily, making the contrast between face and body more disparate than is true of Egyptian anthropoid coffins. Even though examples appear throughout modern Lebanon as well as in most places around the Mediterranean where ancient Phoenicians settled, the type is so firmly connected with Sidon that it takes its generic name today from that city.[44] Unlike their Egyptian counterparts, which usually are carpeted with hieroglyphs and religious icons carved in sunken relief, the Sidonian sarcophagi seldom carry inscriptions or any decoration that would give us easy clues for understanding more about them than the obvious expense and effort they represent for preservation of the body.

Human remains and textile fragments in coffins of all shapes found in Sidon show that Phoenicians mummified and wrapped in linen strips the bodies of those buried in the sarcophagi, a practice that reflects a desire to preserve the body that is similar to the goal evident in the material used to construct the caskets: stone, a non-perishable material. Both inscriptions on sarcophagi discovered in Sidon, those of Tabnit and of Eshmunazar, give similar evidence for the reason that the Sidonians wanted to protect the body, which seems unrelated to any Egyptian religious beliefs: the Phoenician inscriptions state clearly that their burial boxes are to provide a final resting place for their occupants.[45] The two most terrible fates that the curses call upon any would-be violator of their tombs is that the offender have neither heirs nor a final resting place himself.[46] They indicate that the power for enforcing their curses will come from Astarte, the Phoenician supreme goddess, whom they testify to having served well.[47] All the coffins found in Sidon, therefore, should be understood as sarcophagi defined as large stone caskets made to safeguard the occupant's corpse; this definition is quite different from the meaning of the Greek word coined later to refer to coffins built of "flesh-eating" limestone that gives us the word sarcophagos (σαρκο + φάγος, flesh + eater), a word not used by the Phoenicians or Egyptians.[48]

The impressive series of sarcophagi carved from stone is not surprising to find in one of the Phoenician city-states, where that tradition can be traced for at least half a millennium before Alexander arrived there. For example, the big sarcophagus constructed of stone and covered with painted relief for King Ahiram of Byblos (Fig. 12),[49] was made sometime between the 13th and the ninth century B.C.[50] While many Phoenician sarcophagi are challenging to date, the necropolis that held the "Alexander Sarcophagus" provides solid evidence that kings of Sidon (and apparently their closest family members) were interred in large stone coffins for generations that spanned about

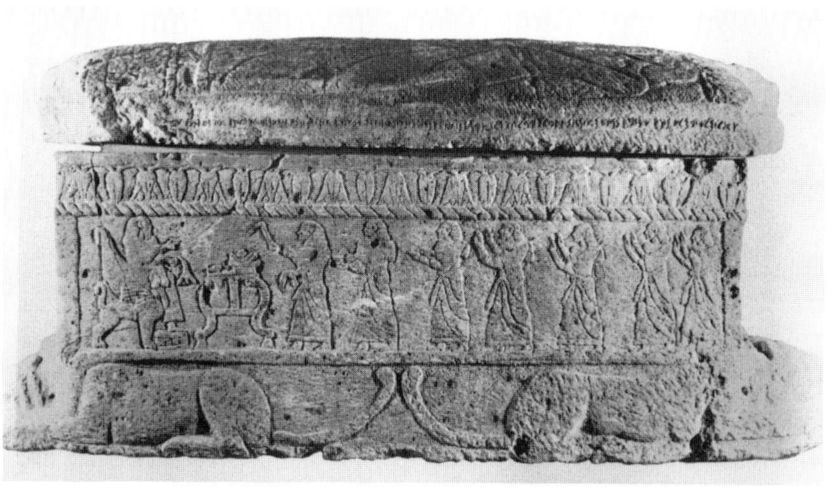

Fig. 12. Sarcophagus of king Ahiram of Byblos. Beirut, National Museum. Photo after N. Jidedjan, Byblos Through the Ages *(1968) frontispiece.*

two centuries before the "Alexander Sarcophagus" was made. While the Phoenicians undoubtedly picked up the idea for making large stone coffins and for mummifying the dead from the Egyptians, the Phoenicians developed their own style of sarcophagi and maintained their own religion.[51] Phoenician burials, unlike the Egyptian ones, show no interest in providing goods or guides for the afterlife.

The abundance of extant Roman and Early Christian stone sarcophagi obfuscates their scarcity in the earlier ancient world; the form is especially foreign to the Greek world before the Hellenistic period. Egyptians produced large stone burial boxes in an architectural mode, carved and painted to imitate a palace, in the Old Kingdom as early as the 26th century B.C.,[52] but in the Greek world sarcophagi appear relatively late. Painted clay larnakes or wooden chests, so small they could only hold a body folded in a fetal position, satisfied Minoans and Mycenaeans.[53] In the sixth century B.C. Ionian Greeks in Clazomenae made full-sized painted clay coffins, which they sent throughout the Mediterranean; and a few Greeks made a small number of pre-fabricated containers for cist tombs that sometimes are called sarcophagi.[54]

Marble sarcophagi made before the mid-fourth century B.C. are rare. We know of only eleven, all found in or near a Phoenician or Greek seaport: three came from Sidon, four from Agrigento, and one each from Athens, Cumae, Samos, and Parion.[55] Only nine other similar burial boxes in other kinds of stone (limestone, sandstone, or tufa) made before the mid-fourth century B.C. have come to light. They, too, stood in or near sites with a sizable number of Greek and/or Phoenician residents: four were found in the eastern edge of the Mediterranean and five came from sites in Sicily or southern Italy.[56] Traces of paint survive on most of these stone sarcophagi, indicating that vegetal or architectural forms decorated them when they were new. On the coffins with covers in the shape of a pitched roof, free-standing palmettes usually crown each end of the peaks as well as the four corners of the roof. Other relief, however, is rare. Two of the marble boxes carry architectural forms: representations of Ionic columns are carved in low relief on the exterior of the one from Samos, and a Doric triglyph and metope frieze runs around one at Agrigento.[57] Ionic pilasters also appear in low relief on a tub-shaped limestone sarcophagus at Agrigento.[58] Figures carved in relief appear on only seven of the stone sarcophagi dated before the mid-fourth century B.C.: all stood in the far eastern edge of the Mediterranean – three in Sidon (Satrap, Lycian, and Weeping Women), three in Cyprus,[59] and the one newly discovered near ancient Parion, where the Hellespont opens into the Sea of Marmara.[60]

The number of stone sarcophagi that can be assigned to the second half of the fourth century, the time that the "Alexander Sarcophagus" was made, jumps dramatically to 31. Of those 19 are from Phoenician cities, five come from Sicily and South Italy, four from mainland Greece, one from the Black Sea, one from Cyprus, and one is said to be from either Cyprus or Ephesos. Figural sculpture appears on eleven of these early Hellenistic sarcophagi: ten out of the eleven are from the Phoenician cities of Sidon or Carthage; the eleventh is the Amazon Sarcophagus in Vienna that has the undocumented provenance of Cyprus or Ephesos.

The large stone coffin of King Ahiram and others like it, especially those found in the house of the dead where Abdalonymos had room, offered a wide selection of models for the person or people responsible for the composition of the Abdalonymos Sarcophagus to consider. What he or they selected is the architectural and figural narrative mode, the form followed by the more Hellenic of the earlier sarcophagi created in Sidon. We might be tempted to explain that choice simply as a reflection of the new political ties Sidon had with Greeks, but the choice should also be understood as part of the adoption of classical Greek artistic ideas that had been going on for at least a century in this Phoenician port; examples can be seen not only in the Satrap and the Weeping Women Sarcophagi, but also in sculptures excavated at the temple of Eshmun.[61] Exchanges of cultural and artistic ideas between Phoenicians and Greeks in the fourth century B.C. simply continued what had been going on between the two sea-faring societies at least as early as the ninth and eighth centuries B.C. The introduction of alphabetic writing by the Phoenicians to the Greeks, arguably the most dramatic manifestation of that exchange in Greece, is one of numerous examples.[62]

Art historians traditionally describe the "Alexander Sarcophagus" as an example of Greek art, but it is not simply Greek art produced in Hellenistic times for a site in Asia Minor. Seeing the "Alexander Sarcophagus" in its original context and recognizing its Sidonian heritage marks the "Alexander Sarcophagus" as a blending of Phoenician and Greek ideas and practices with debts to forms and concepts from the Levant, western Asia, the eastern Mediterranean, and Egypt. The result is a sophisticated re-ordering of ideas and forms from many regions, especially places closely connected with Phoenicia. The idea and popularity of stone coffins decorated with naturalistic figures carved in raised relief was quickly integrated into the Hellenistic repertoire and continued in countless Roman and Early Christian sarcophagi that followed. The "Alexander Sarcophagus" stands as a symbol of that Phoenician contribution to Hellenistic art.

Abbreviations

Besides the abbreviations in *AA* 1992, 743 ff. and in *ArchBibl* the following have been used:

Buhl	M.-L. Buhl, *The Late Egyptian Anthropoid Stone Sarcophagi* (1959)
Charbonneaux	J. Charbonneaux, R. Martin, F. Villard, *Hellenistic Art* (1973)
Eddy	W.K. Eddy, "Letter from Sidon, Phoenicia," *AJA* 3, Series 1, 1887, 97–101
Fenici	S. Moscati (ed.), *I Fenici, catalogue of an exhibition at the Palazzo Grassi, Venice* (1988)
von Graeve	V. von Graeve, *Der Alexandersarkophag und seine Werkstatt, IstForsch* 28 (1970)
Grainger	J. Grainger, *Hellenistic Phoenicia* (1991)
Hamdy – Reinach	O. Hamdy Bey and T. Reinach, *Une Nécropole Royale à Sidon* (1892/1896)
Hitzl	I. Hitzl, *Die griechischen Sarkophage der archaischen und klassichen Zeit* (1991)
JANES	*Journal of the Ancient Near Eastern Society of Columbia University*
Jidejian	N. Jidejian, *Sidon through the Ages* (1971)
Kukahn	E. Kukahn, *Anthropoide Sarkophage in Beyrouth* (1955)
Mendel	G. Mendel, *Musées Impériaux Ottomans: Catalogue des sculptures grecques, romaines et byzantines* I (1912)
Millar	F. Millar, "Phoenician Cities," *Proc CambrPhilSoc* 1983, 55–71
Moreno	P. Moreno, *Scultura ellenistica* (1994)
Pasinli	A. Pasinli, *Istanbul Archaeological Museums* (1989)
Pollitt	J.J. Pollitt, *Art in the Hellenistic Age* (1986)
Ridgway	B.S. Ridgway, *Hellenistic Sculpture* I: *The Styles of ca. 331–200 B.C.* (1990)
Robertson	M. Robertson, *A History of Greek Art* (1975)
Rosenthal	F. Rosenthal, "Canaanite and Aramaic Inscriptions," in J.B. Pritchard (ed.), *The Ancient Near East: Supplementary Texts and Pictures Relating to the Old Testament*[2] (1969)
Schefold	K. Schefold, *Der Alexander-Sarkophag* (1968)
Smith	R.R.R. Smith, *Hellenistic Sculpture* (1991)
Stewart	A. Stewart, *Faces of Power* (1993)
Studniczka	F. Studniczka, "Sidonischen Sarkophage," *JdI* 9, 1894, 204 ff.
Winter	F. Winter, *Der Alexandersarkophag von Sidon* (1912)

Notes

1. Istanbul, Archaeological Museum 370. Mendel no. 68, pp. 171 ff.; Pasinli 5.
2. For the first suggestion that it was designed to hold Alexander: Hamdy - Reinach 77 ff.
3. The sarcophagus was connected to Abdalonymos in 1894: Studniczka 226 ff. and 243 ff. Information now available, which I will discuss elsewhere, further strengthens recognition of Abdalonymos as the person for whom the sarcophagus was made.
4. Alexander would not have been portrayed on a sarcophagus in Sidon before he took control of the city from the Persians in 332 B.C. See Curtius, *History of Alexander* IV i, 15–26, for an account of Alexander in Sidon. In a tradition typical of many ancient monarchs, Abdalonymos probably commissioned the sarcophagus himself, so it could have been made at any time between his rise to power and his death. For Abdalonymos' death date and, therefore, the reason the coffin could be later than 311 B.C.: Grainger 34–35; 61–62.
5. The literature is vast. For early discussions: Mendel 197 ff. For more recent literature: Charbonneaux 237; Pollitt 38; Ridgway 37; 40 ff.; Smith 190 ff.; Stewart 53; Moreno 16 ff.
6. Eddy; Hamdy - Reinach; Mendel 171 ff. For rapid damage to the site: "Archaeological News: Saïda," *AJA* 6, 1st series, 1890, 186.
7. Studies of the royal tombs and sarcophagi assigned to the fifth and fourth centuries B.C.: J. Assmann, *AA* 78, 1963, cols. 690 ff.; modified by H. Gabelmann, *AA* 94, 1979, 163 ff., and *AA* 97, 1982, 493 ff. These investigations combine historical evidence with stylistic analyses but are limited by uncertainties about which tombs belong to which kings as well as by lack of information about the kings themselves; despite identification lacunae, the proposals are well worth consideration. Neither Assmann nor Gabelmann attempts to straighten out the murky chronology later than Abdalonymos.

8. Identified by Hamdy as Room III; for its position: Hamdy - Reinach 5 ff. and pl. III.
9. For analysis of the chronology of rulers in Sidon after Abdalonymos, including the question of whether Philokles was king or only a Ptolemaic pretender, see Grainger 61–65. Considering that the Phoenicians are credited with the invention of alphabetic writing, it is remarkable how little written information we have about them. Chronology of the kings has yet to be sorted out to everyone's satisfaction, although several scholars have given thoughtful attention to the question. For example, J. Elayi, *Sidon: cité autonome de l'empire perse* (1989) is useful while emphasizing the imprecision of our knowledge about the history of Sidon; older histories (e.g., F. C. Eiselen, *Sidon* [1907, reprinted 1966]) must be used only with caution.
10. From Hamdy - Reinach 178: length 3.18 m. (10′6″); width 1.67 m. (5′6″); height from base to the top of acroteria 1.95 m. (6′5″). For the ground plan and cross-section: ibid., pl. 23.
11. Hamdy - Reinach 64; Mendel 172.
12. Estimation of the weight: Hamdy - Reinach 13 n. 1. Discussion of the excavators' difficulties in moving it from the necropolis: ibid., 23 ff.
13. Eddy 98 ff. Illustrations of the casket made at the time of excavation show that the worst damage was to the northeast corner of the lid, the corner closest to the entrance: Hamdy - Reinach 68 ff. For a thorough report of condition in 1912: Mendel 172 ff.
14. Eddy 100.
15. Early colored illustrations provide a valuable record: Hamdy - Reinach pls. 34–37; Winter, all plates; paintings made in 1900 by J.L. Smith, published in *Tombs, Temples, and Ancient Art* (1956). For a careful description of both architectural and figural color: Mendel 173 ff.
16. For color photographs: Pasinli, and M. Seidel in Schefold. Even black and white photographs indicate color differences; for example, see *ibid.*, pl. 26.
17. Part of one silver axe from the north frieze remained for the excavators to recover: Hamdy - Reinach 72 ff.
18. Robertson pls. 119c; 142a–d; 155; 170d.
19. For examples, see representations on sarcophagi in the Museo Nazionale Romano, S. Aurigemma, *The Baths of Diocletian and the Museo Nazionale Romano* (1958): a battle between Romans and Germans, 31, no. 52 (inv. no. 112327), pl. 14, or of a battle between Romans and barbarians, *ibid.*, 88, no. 221 (inv. no. 8574), pl. 33.
20. E. Akurgal, *The Art of the Hittites* (1962) 113 ff., pl. XVI.
21. One, now lost, is known through publication and a line drawing: Hitzl 62–63; 67; 69 ff.; 126; 130; 221 with earlier literature and ill. 57. The second, New York Metropolitan Museum of Art 74.51.2451: Cesnola, *Cyprus* (1877) 110 ff.; Hitzl 61; 62 ff.; 70 ff.; 111 n. 8; 113; 117; 119 ff.; 126; 200 ff. with earlier literature and ills. 49–52. While Greeks did represent lions, theirs look less naturalistic than those on the Cypriot and "Alexander" sarcophagi; see H. Gabelmann, *Studien zum frühgriechischen Löwenbild* (1965).
22. The heads seem to have three horns or at least three protrusions. Perhaps they are related to griffins, which originated in Asia minor, or to heads found on Luristan horse-bits: R. Ghirshamn, *Iran* (1962) fig. 12; A. Pope, *Persian Art* (1945) 25, pl. 9b.
23. "Die grosse Göttin:" von Graeve 42 ff. For a connection of the heads with Isis: Schefold 11 and n. 7. Comparable human-headed antefixes in Italy may represent the protectress of family life: N. Winter, *RM* 85, 1978, 27 ff.
24. For example, an Etruscan "maenad" antefix from Cerveteri, M. Moretti, *Museo Nazionale di Villa Giulia* (1962) 78–81, fig. 54. Human-headed antefixes fell out of favor in Greece after the archaic period, but in Italy they continued to appear on temples and in necropoleis: N. Winter, *Terracotta Representations of Human Heads* (1978) 151 ff.
25. The Merehi Sarcophagus and the Nereid Monument found at Xanthos, the Heroon at Trysa, and the City Sarcophagus at Telmessos provide strong parallels. For these and other Lycian relief sculptures: S. Haynes, *Land of the Chimaera* (1974); W.A.P. Childs, *The City-Reliefs of Lycia* (1979); C. Deltour-Levie, *Les piliers funéraires de Lycie* (1982); and B. Jacobs, *Griechische und persische Elemente in der Grabkunst Lykiens zur Zeit der Achämenidenherrschaft* (1987). For carved reliefs specifically on Lycian tombs, see J. Zahle, *Arkaeologiske studier i lykiske klippegrave og deres relieffer* (1983) and *JdI* 94, 1979, 245 ff. I thank R. Bridges for discussions about Lycian tombs and for references to Zahle's studies.
26. For the Persepolis reliefs: R. Ghirshman, *Perse* (1963) 147 ff. For relationship between reliefs at Persepolis and reliefs in Lycia and Sidon, ibid., 349 ff.
27. Vienna, Kunsthistorisches Museum 169. According to one version of the provenance, the Amazon Sarcophagus came from Cyprus but another version places its discovery in Ephesos: Hitzl 100; 122–123 and 219 with earlier literature; Ridgway 45–46; 68 n.32 and pls. 18–21; Moreno 83 n. 156, fig. 92.
28. R.A. Stucky, *Die Skulpturen aus dem Eschmun-Heiligtum bei Sidon*, 17. Beih. *AntK* (1993) 109 ff. with previous literature, and pls. 58–61.
29. Istanbul Archaeological Museum nos. 372, 373, and 374. Hamdy - Reinach nos. 4, 5, and 6 and pls. 38–40; Mendel 201 ff., nos. 72–74; von Graeve 9 ff.; Hitzl 182–183, nos. 20–22, with previous literature.
30. Mendel 201 ff.
31. Heights and lengths (from Mendel 178 and 202): the "Alexander Sarcophagus" – 1.95 m., 3.81 m.; Inv. no. 72 – 0.915 m., 2.620 m.; Inv. no. 73 – 0.987 m., 2.635 m.; Inv. no. 74 – 0.892 m. 2.600 m. Drawings in von Graeve figs. 1–3, show the relative scales clearly.
32. Istanbul, Archaeological Museum 367. I.Kleemann, *Der Satrapen-Sarkophag aus Sidon* (1958); Hitzl 76 ff.; 100; 110 n. 7; 117; 119 ff.; 126; 177, no. 16 with previous literature.
33. Istanbul, Archaeological Museums 369. B. Schmidt-Dounas, *Die lykische Sarkophag aus Sidon*, 30. Ergh. *IstMitt* (1985). Also see Pasinli 35 ff.; Hitzl 75 ff.; 100; 110; 113 ff.; 117; 121; 128; 178.
34. Hitzl 67; 77 ff.; 101; 117; 119; 123 ff.; 126; 179 ff.; R. Fleischer, *Der Klagefrauensarkophag aus Sidon*, 34 *Ist Forsch* (1983); M.E. Weller, *CalifStClAnt* 3, 1970, 219 ff.
35. Mendel 33; 48; 158.
36. Mendel 34; 49; 159.

37. Length of the Satrap Sarcophagus, 2.863 m.; the Lycian, 2.535 m.; and the Weeping Women, 2.653 m. (Mendel 34; 51; 160.) Supra n. 31 for comparisons.
38. Istanbul Archaeological Museum nos. 800 and 793. Hamdy - Reinach 6 ff.; 81 ff.; 86 ff.; 127 ff.; 129 ff.; 375 ff. and pls. 41–44; Mendel 210 ff., nos. 78 and 79. Buhl 32 ff., no. C, a 3; 142, no. K IV; 181 ff.; 213; 215.
39. Paris, Louvre A O 4806. Hamdy - Reinach 127 ff., ill. 52; Buhl 32, no. C, a 5; 213.
40. Rosenthal; Jidejian 56 ff.; Buhl 34.
41. Buhl 181 ff.
42. Istanbul Archaeological Museum 799. Hamdy - Reinach 145 ff., no. 3, pl. 42; Mendel 225 ff., no. 81.
43. Istanbul Archaeological Museum. Hamdy - Reinach 145 ff., no. 11, pl. 42; Mendel 222 ff., no. 80.
44. Kukahn; M.-L. Buhl in *Atti del II Congresso Internazionale di Studi Fenici e Punici* 2 (1991) 675–681.
45. Rosenthal 662; Jidejian 56 f. For Phoenician deities: J. Teixidor, *The Pagan God* (1977) 19–60.
46. Rosenthal 662.
47. Rosenthal 662. For Astarte: Teixidor (supra n. 45) 34–39. As the goddess of generation and fertility, Astarte shares many characteristics with Aphrodite / Venus (especially Aphrodite Urania), Artemis, and Ceres, so she sometimes is equated with them; she was prominently worshipped at Kition in Cyprus, Eryx in Sicily, on Malta, and at Carthage, as well as in Sidon, Byblos, and Ascalon.
48. In a discussion of remarkable stones, Pliny (*NH* 36.27.131) reports that the bodies buried in the sarcophagus stone ("sarcophagus lapis") found at Assos will be consumed except for teeth within forty days.
49. Beirut, National Museum. Hitzl 170 ff., figs. 3–5; N. Jidejian, *Byblos through the Ages* (1968) 29 ff.; *Fenici* 292 ff.
50. Some theories about the time Ahiram lived are based on archaeological material in his tomb, but most are founded on the date of the inscription carved on his sarcophagus. Formerly, epigraphers assigned the inscription a date in the 13th century B.C., as P. Montet explained in *Byblos et l'Egypte* (1928) 215 ff., but E. Porada, *JANES* 5 (1973) 354 ff., lowered the date to about 1000 B.C. and more recently, R. Wallenfels, *JANES* 15 (1983) 79 ff. proposed an even later date, one not earlier than the mid-ninth century B.C.
51. E.O. James, *The Ancient Gods* (1960) 8 and 297 suggests a fusion of Astarte and Isis by the third century B.C. If an earlier fusion of the two goddesses were discovered, it might explain a religious reason for the development of the Sidonian type of sarcophagus.
52. For example, see the sarcophagus of a high official, found at Giza, published with illustration in M. Saleh - H. Sourouzian, *Official Catalogue, The Egyptian Museum, Cairo*, trans. by P. Der Manuelian - H. Jacquet-Gordon (1987) no. 34.
53. C. Davaras, *Guide to Cretan Antiquities* (1976) 174 ff., s.v. "larnakes." Even in the case of the unique limestone chest found at Hagia Triada, the dimensions stayed under life size and the decorations remain in paint: *ibid.*, 275, s.v. "Hagia Triada." For excellent illustrations of Mycenaean clay larnakes made during the Bronze Age: K. Demakopoulou and D. Konsola, *Archaeological Museum of Thebes* (1981) 82–85; 93, pls. 42–44.
54. For the Clazomenae coffins: R.M. Cook, *Clazomenian Sarcophagi* (1981). For cist tombs: H. Palmer, *The North Cemetery, Corinth* 13 (1964) 71 ff.; D.C. Kurtz - J. Boardman, *Greek Burial Customs* (1971) 267.
55. Four are from Agrigento (Hitzl cat. nos. 4–6 and 70), three from Sidon (Hitzl cat. nos. 6; 17–18); one from Athens (Hitzl cat. no. 8); one from Cumae (Hitzl cat. no. 14), and one from Samos (Hitzl cat. no. 43). For the sarcophagus found in the area of Parion, north of Troy (Kızöldün Tumulus), see I. Özgen and J. Öztürk, *The Lydian Treasure* (1996) 56, figs. 123–124; N. Sevinç, *Studia Troica* 6 (1996) 251–264. The primary narrative portrayed on this recently discovered sarcophagus that is now in the Çanakkale Archaeological Museum courtyard, has been identified as a representation of the sacrifice of Polyxena executed in late archaic or early classical style. I thank John Camp for telling me about it.
56. Hitzl cat. nos. 2 (Agrigento); 10 (Byblos); 42 (Camarina); 37–38 and 54 (Cyprus); 57 (Megara Hyblea); 48 (Syracuse); 50 (Taranto).
57. For the Samos Ionic sarcophagus: I. Kleemann in N. Himmelmann (ed.), *Festschrift für Friedrich Matz* (1962) 44 ff., pls. 12–15; Hitzl 27; 30 ff.; 37 ff.; 43 ff.; 113; 123; 125; 209 with previous literature, figs. 17–20. For the Agrigento Doric sarcophagus: Hitzl 43; 52 ff.; 106; 117; 124; 151; 164 with previous literature and fig. 33.
58. Hitzl cat. no. 2, ills. 36–37.
59. One (Inv. no. 74.51.2451) from the necropolis at Golgoi: see V. Tatton-Brown, *RDAC* 1984, 169–179 ("ca. 475–460 B.C."), pl. 32; and Hitzl 61; 62 ff.; 70 ff.; 111 n. 8; 113; 117; 119 ff.; 200–201 ("500–470 B.C.") with previous literature; 126, pls. 49–52. The other (Inv. no. 74.51.2453) is from Amathus: see V. Tatton-Brown in A. Hermary, *Amathonte* II (1981) 74 ff., no. 80, pls. 15–18; Hitzl 61; 63; 66 ff.; 70 ff.; 97; 110 n. 7; 113; 117; 119 ff.; 126; 202 ff. with previous literature, pls. 53–56. The present location of the third, which came from Athienu, is unknown: Hitzl 62–63; 67; 69 ff.; 126; 130; 221 with earlier literature.
60. Çanakkale Archaeological Museum courtyard. Supra n. 55.
61. For sculpture of the temple: Stucky (supra n. 28); E. Will, *BCH* 100, 1976, 565 ff.
62. Herodotus (5.58) states that Phoenicians brought the Greeks the alphabet and other kinds of learning, and he indicates that Phoenicians resident in Thebes deserve special credit for teaching Greeks to make alphabetic letters; however, the time, place, and name of the person actually responsible for introducing "Phoenicians letters" to the Greeks is a complicated issue. See J.D. Muhly, *Berytus* 19, 1970, 19 ff.; L.H. Jeffery in W.C. Brice (ed.), *Europa: Festschrift für Ernst Grumach* (1967) 152 ff.; R. Pfeiffer, *History of Classical Scholarship* (1968) 21 ff.; R. Edwards, *Kadmos the Phoenician* (1979). Visual evidence found at Eretria, Lefkandi, Chalcis, and Thebes show extensive contact between Greeks in those sites and Phoenicians during the ninth and eighth centuries B.C.; see J.N. Coldstream in H. G. Niemeyer (ed.), *Phönizier im Westen, MB* 8, 1982, 261 ff.; S. Morris, *Daidalos and the Origins of Greek Art* (1993). For the influence of Greek art on the art of the Phoenicians during the fifth and fourth centuries B.C., see J. Boardman, *The Diffusion of Classical Art in Antiquity* (1994) 53 ff.